PHILOSOPHY OF HISTORY

Philosophy of History is an essential introduction to a vast body of writing about history, from classical Greece and Rome to the contemporary world. M.C. Lemon maps out key debates and central concepts of philosophy of history, placing principal thinkers in the context of their times and schools of thought.

Lemon explains the crucial differences between *speculative* philosophy as an enquiry into the course and meaning of history, and *analytic* philosophy of history as relating to the nature and methods of history as a discipline. Part I offers a guide to the principal thinkers from pre-historical times to the present, covering thinkers such as Vico, Hegel, and Marx. Part II is a critical summary of the leading issues raised by critical theorists of history, incorporating topics such as objectivity, ideology, historical explanation and narrative. Part III revisits the two branches in the light of contemporary contributions to the discipline.

This guide provides a comprehensive survey of historical thought since ancient times. Its clear terminology and lucid argument will make it an invaluable source for students and teachers of history alike.

M.C. Lemon is a lecturer in the history of political thought and political theory at the University of Ulster. His past publications include *The Discipline of History and the History of Thought* (1995).

PHILOSOPHY OF HISTORY

A Guide for Students

M.C. Lemon

Routledge
Taylor & Francis Group

LONDON AND NEW YORK

First published 2003
by Routledge
11 New Fetter Lane, London EC4P 4EE

Simultaneously published in the USA and Canada
by Routledge
29 West 35th Street, New York, NY 10001

Routledge is an imprint of the Taylor & Francis Group

Typeset in Goudy by
Keystroke, Jacaranda Lodge, Wolverhampton
Printed and bound in Great Britain by
Antony Rowe Ltd, Chippenham, Wiltshire

British Library Cataloguing in Publication Data
A catalogue record for this book is available from the British Library

Library of Congress Cataloging in Publication Data
Lemon, M. C. (Michael C.), 1945–
Philosophy of history : a guide for students / M.C. Lemon.
p. cm.
Includes bibliographical references and index.
1. History—Philosophy.   2. History—Historiography.
3. Historiography.   4. History, Ancient—Historiography.
5. History, Modern—Historiography.   I. Title.
D16.8 .L375 2003
2002014645

ISBN 0–415–16204–1 (hbk)
ISBN 0–415–16205–x (pbk)

BRIEF CONTENTS

FULL CONTENTS

CONTENTS

CONTENTS

ACKNOWLEDGEMENTS

In some chapters I have leaned heavily on the enviable knowledge displayed in other academics' writings, namely, H. Frankfort *et al.*, R. Nisbet, S. Jaki, and G. Trompf in chapters 2 to 4, and B. Mazlish, and F. Manuel in chapter 8. I have also benefited from encouragement and advice from my former editor, Heather McCallum, my present editor, Victoria Peters, and from Professor Donald Sassoon of Queen Mary College, University of London, and from the technical help of Ruth Jeavons, Laila Friese, and Jane Horton. Whatever deficiencies this book displays are of course entirely my responsibility.

INTRODUCTION

This book has a dual purpose. Primarily I hope to introduce the subject 'philosophy of history' to those history students, academics, and teachers who may to varying degrees be unfamiliar with an extensive branch of writings relating to their discipline. Nowadays such relative unfamiliarity is commonplace amongst historians. There are at least two (related) reasons for this – first, a claustrophobic compartmentalisation of disciplines, certainly in the Anglo-American world, where professional pressures tend towards narrow discipline bases – and second, specifically in historians, an air of indifference towards 'philosophy of history', either as an example of such compartmentalisation, or as a more deliberate stance emanating from some unfortunate encounter with philosophy, best forgotten. Such diffidence *may* be justified, but only on the basis of some familiarity with 'philosophy of history' – and a principal purpose of this 'guide' is to furnish precisely that.

This book, then, is offered as an *historians'* guide, but not because the ideas of our philosophers of history are, patronisingly, to be simplified because of 'fear' of philosophy – rather, because within the extensive literature of 'philosophy of history' it concentrates more on what might interest historians than philosophers. And as for being a *guide*, again the intention is not to condescend, but rather to map out what, with respect to even one of its two branches, has rightly been called 'a boundless land' of 'semi-monstrous' proportions.[1]

A secondary purpose of this 'guide' relates more urgently to the contemporary nature of historical study, for it is under attacks sourced precisely from the two branches of philosophy of history, namely, 'speculative' and 'analytic'. First, from recent signs of a revival in 'speculative' philosophy of history which, as we shall see, tries to construct some kind of 'universal history' of the world (the rise and decline of great states, empires, and cultures), complaints have arisen that modern historians have lost that sense of the grand sweep of time – that their writings are narrowly focused specialist studies, more akin to the mentality of 'antiquarians' or 'laboratory workers'[2] than efforts to make sense of the unfolding of human history. Some even go so far as to suggest that 'history' proper is disappearing from schools and universities, replaced by a mish-mash of controversial contemporary 'social' studies ranging over ethnic, gender, and other ideological concerns, leaving

1

students bereft of any sense of an accepted past from which they can appreciate their present as emerging and thus achieve a salutary perspective.[3]

Another attack arises from the other branch of philosophy of history, namely, 'analytic' (or 'critical')[4] philosophy of history which, as we shall see, attempts to bring to the surface and examine the validity of those presuppositions which underly the thinking and writings of historians. For example: what is a fact, can one be objective about the past, do historians explain things in a special way? Stemming from more general 'philosophical' positions, the answers given to such questions vary and are by no means necessarily subversive of historians' work. Yet some are, and perhaps no more so than those critiques inspired by many so-called 'post-modern' philosophers which amount to a thorough-going refutation of the very possibility of the discipline of history having any validity. Why? Because they claim that *any* discourse has an inbuilt subjectivism due to the reference-systems and value-orientations embedded in perceptions of 'reality' and the language expressing them. From this viewpoint, historians are talking rubbish – or at least, one historian's rubbish is as good or as worthless as any other's.

It is in the light of all these considerations that this 'historians' guide to philosophy of history' is offered – to help familiarise historians with the principal outlines of an extensive, multi-faceted literature so they can better assess its relevance for them; also, as a by-product, to provide historians with relevant food for thought where they are subject to attack on the nature of their practice – i.e., studying, writing, and teaching history. Each reader will doubtless sort out the dross from the gold within 'philosophy of history' in his or her own way despite any critical edge offered in this exposition. For my own part, I have elsewhere argued for a 'productive marriage' between the discipline of history and philosophy of history, but one based only on the 'right' foundations!

Finally, some might argue a further rationale for this 'guide' – namely, the arrival of the new millennium. For them, this 'event' cannot but stimulate reflection upon 'the meaning of history'. Be this an artificial stimulus or not, less dubious is the fact that we now have another century of history to survey, which by any standards has included momentous changes for most of the world, and raises issues for the future perhaps more palpably than any previous century. Churlish indeed would be the historian who took exception at being the first everyone else asks for insight, interpretation, and divination of meaning! Yet does his discipline so equip him? Should it? Grappling with a moral problem, I once asked a distinguished moral philosopher for advice. He replied that the last person to ask what one *ought* to do is the *moral* philosopher! Appearances notwithstanding, then, is the historian the *last* rather than the first person to ask about 'history'? Should we turn instead to *philosophers* of history, leaving the *actual* historians mute? Perhaps this 'guide' may be of some service to those historians sensitive to the issue.

Part I begins by distinguishing between 'speculative' and 'analytic' philosophy of history, concentrating on the former, offering reasons why it might invite study by historians, and then offering a guide to its principal areas and noted individual contributions. Part II begins by explaining in general terms what 'analytic' philosophy of history is, again offering reasons why it might invite historians' attention, and then offers a guide to the principal issues it revolves around. Part III revisits both branches of philosophy of history, but brings matters up-to-date by exploring contemporary contributions from both its speculative and analytic angles which, it happens, differently announce 'the end of history'.

For ease of reading I have as far as possible restricted notes to references only, although for academic purposes these are necessarily extensive in those chapters where, in interpreting them, I have laboured to allow thinkers to speak for themselves.

Part I

SPECULATIVE PHILOSOPHY OF HISTORY

1

SPECULATIVE PHILOSOPHY OF HISTORY

What is it and why study it?

Introduction: the two branches of philosophy of history: speculative and analytic

When the famously 'enlightened' Frenchman, Voltaire, coined the term 'philosophy of history', he meant something akin to what we might now call 'critical cultural history'. In his 1769 *Essay on the Customs and the Spirit of Nations* he surveyed ancient and classical cultures (primarily in terms of their customs and religions), including China and India, as well as feudal times in Europe up to the reign of Louis XIV (1643–1715). Rather than present this huge historical vista as some kind of inherently meaningful pattern or story, his intention was to extract morally useful lessons from such 'history' (for example, to downplay sentimental or overawed respect for tradition and authority, and to highlight moral short-comings and absurdities in his own society, thereby raising not only the present but also the future, 'in the light of history'). In short, he was interested in this approach to 'history' because of the new *perspective* it offered regarding human progress. His own views on the latter could be pretty gloomy, and how much hope his 'philosophical history' gave him for the better future he desired is a doubtful matter. But one thing is clear – he meant his readers to *think about* history, not simply to read and research it 'for its own sake' as a residue of interesting facts and events.

A second aspect to Voltaire's 'philosophy of history' was closely related to the above, namely, his awareness that the *method of study* required for such a 'history' at least needed to be rational – that is, able to sidestep superstition and religious orthodoxy and to examine long-held beliefs. Therefore he recognised the need to attend to how the historian *works* on his material and how he thinks about what he is doing – that is, an aspect of his 'philosophy of history' concerned history as a discipline or method, in addition to 'history' as 'what happened'. In the event, however, his own views on the discipline of history were not especially innovative.[1]

Embryonic as Voltaire's coining of the phrase was, the essentials are already there to explain what 'philosophy of history' is. Leaving aside temporarily the term 'philosophy', we see that philosophy of history is concerned with the two different meanings of the term 'history'. On the one hand it treats of it as meaning past events, circumstances, and facts – in other words, 'history' as the material or 'object' to be studied; and on the other hand it treats it as the academic *discipline* which studies the former. In short, the meaning of the term 'history' is twofold, and can be expressed by saying that history as object is what the subject of history studies. Philosophy of history is concerned with *both* versions of 'history', thus consisting of two branches. Where it treats of history as 'object', it is usually called *speculative* (or *substantive*) philosophy of history, and where it treats it as a 'discipline' it is best called *analytic* philosophy of history.

'Philosophy'

The other term involved in our subject-matter is 'philosophy'. This is a term which has become more precise than in Voltaire's time, when it simply meant something like 'thoughtful knowledge' – and it is perhaps partly because of this that the term is intimidating to some. For example, doubtless some scientists are neglectful of philosophy of *science* because they are nervous of 'philosophy', just as some historians are de-motivated regarding 'philosophy of history'. But here we can return to our glimpse at Voltaire, for a third aspect to his philosophy is that he meant his readers to *think rationally* about both the material and the discipline of history – and there is a reassuring sense in which that is *almost* 'all' what we call 'philosophy' is, namely, to think rationally about something. All we need add is that such thinking only becomes 'philosophical' when there is not already a recognised 'method' for finding answers to questions – in other words, where the matter under scrutiny does not fall under existing academic disciplines or other accepted 'rules' of thought. For example, we now have scientific disciplines to approach such questions as 'what is illness?', 'what are stars?', and 'where did mankind come from?', (respectively, medicine, astronomy, and biology). Likewise, other disciplines such as social sciences, languages, and indeed history provide accepted approaches to different questions. Also, apart from academic disciplines, we have familiar ways of tackling questions such as 'when is the next flight to New York?', 'why did you spend so much money?', and 'where are my gloves?'. In all these cases we do not 'philosophise'. What this shows is that philosophy approaches those issues for which, in the absence of existing 'rules', we simply have to rely on our capacity to 'think out' a problem as best ('rationally') as we can. Thus it is that over the millennia 'philosophers' have pondered about justice, happiness, dreams, art, motion, the State, and much more. It is true the emergence of modern science and social studies has diminished the area of philosophical enquiry, but plenty of 'inaccessible' questions remain for philosophy to flourish (for example, perennial *moral* issues), as well as new ones emerging. Not least among them are whether there is such a thing as 'world-history' in any meaningful sense, (thus, 'speculative philosophy of history') and whether the practice of the subject, 'history' – i.e., the discipline of history – is fully valid, (thus, 'analytic philosophy of history').

In short, (and contrary to many philosophers who 'philosophise' precisely about 'what is philosophy?' – the answer is provided by the history of thought), there is no mystery enveloping 'philosophy' making it an esoteric subject which, for example, scientists and historians should respectfully leave to 'the experts'. It has no special *subject-matter* of its own (unlike all other viable academic disciplines), neither any special *method* (again, unlike all other viable disciplines). Rather, it simply means seeking knowledge or understanding, through the exercise of reason, of those matters otherwise inaccessible via known paths or rules of enquiry – and in the sense that this means trying to think something through 'on our own', it is a uniquely 'democratic' activity, open to everyone.

All this, however, is not to say philosophy is easy. Many brilliant thinkers adorn its history, and we tread respectfully in their wake to avoid thinking and saying silly things. Also, their reflections and arguments amongst each other over time have generated a special vocabulary better to denote certain recurring complex and/or abstract ideas, and not only is it as well to become familiar with some of this vocabulary in order to understand *their* writings, but its persistence shows its usefulness to our *own* efforts to 'think things through in a rational way'.

Speculative philosophy of history

If, then, 'philosophy' is more to be embraced than feared, let us look further into that branch of philosophy of history called *speculative* philosophy of history. As already intimated, this consists of thinking about the actual 'content' of (human) history to see in what sense 'it as a whole' is explicable or meaningful. It is hence not surprising that some who have attempted this employed the term 'universal history', and that one recent scholar described it as 'the central aspiration to afford a total explanatory account of the past'.[2] Although not all speculative philosophy of history is so overtly ambitious, those who engage in it are variously attempting to reach conclusions about the following kinds of questions: does history demonstrate a single giant unfolding story? If so, does the 'story' have an ending? And is that ending utopian, cataclysmic, or simply mundane? Or does history go round in circles ('cycles')? Can history be divided up into distinct periods such as 'the Dark Ages', and if so, what are they? And what does this tell us about the course of history? Is the history of the world necessarily a history of *progress* of humanity; if so, why? If not, why not? Do 'laws' govern historical development, or is it already begging the question to see history as 'developing'? Is the course of history *determined* by forces outside human control, or can individuals' actions make a difference? Can we learn anything from the flow of history, or is every situation unique?

In their turn, these large questions have generated a recognisable body of subsidiary issues. Is there such a thing as 'Fate'? Or 'Providence'? Has 'human nature' remained the same throughout history? Can we talk of different mentalities over the ages, such as an early 'mythical consciousness' as distinct from the modern 'scientific' outlook? Can the history of humanity be seen as analogous to the growth of the individual from infanthood, through childhood and youth, to maturity, and then old age? Why is it that great cultures have invariably declined? Is it inevitable?

9

Speculative philosophy of history, then, stems from the impulse to make sense of history, to find meaning in it, or at least some intelligible pattern. And it should not surprise us that at the heart of this impulse is a desire to predict the *future* (and in many cases to shape it). By any standards, then, this branch of philosophy of history is audacious, and there is a sense in which the term 'speculative' is not only appropriate but also carries derogatory implications for those historians and others who insist on a solely *empirical* approach to the past, i.e., on 'sticking to the facts'. In short, to some, the very project of speculative philosophy of history can appear misguided on the grounds that it is 'theoretical' in the bad sense of the term – factually unfounded, impossible of proof, prey to imaginative flights of fancy, and premised on an unrealistically encyclopaedic knowledge of history throughout recorded time and over most of the globe. To others, however, it is a worthwhile undertaking because it is so natural to a reflective being. Just as at times one gets the urge to 'make sense' of one's own life, either out of simple curiosity about its 'meaning', or through suffering a particularly turbulent phase, or because weighty decisions about one's *future* are looming, so some are drawn to reflect, not on themselves, but on the history of their species – mankind.

The relevance of speculative philosophy of history

Whether speculative philosophy of history is worthwhile or, instead, a fundamentally flawed exercise, it is surely an understandable venture. Here I revert to the analogy of the individual's reflections on his or her life. Firstly, attempts to discover a theory or 'philosophy' of history are intrinsically interesting because they try to make sense of the overall flow of history – even in some cases to give it meaning. And there is a sense in which to do particularly the latter is to offer answers to the question, 'what is the point of life?' (not of yours or mine, but of human life in general). The importance of such a question is either self-explanatory or nil, depending on an individual's assumptions. Some see it as *the* ultimate question to be answered, whereas others see it as symptomatic of an arrogant anthropomorphism which demands that 'life, the universe, and all that' be reduced to the petty model of merely human dimensions, where intention and reason are seen as the governing principles. But that individuals differ in this way is exactly the point, in the sense that speculative philosophy of history raises the issue directly into the light of argument, allowing us to examine our initial assumptions regarding the value or futility of such 'ultimate' questions. For example, one might ask sceptics whether they at least accept the notion that, on the whole, 'history has delivered' progress in the arts, sciences, economics, government, and quality of life. If the answer is 'yes', how do they account for it? Is it chance (thus offering no guarantees for the future)? Or if there *is* a reason for it, what is this 'reason' which is 'going on in history'? Similarly, if the sceptics answer 'no', then why not? Again, is it chance? Or is there some 'mechanism' underlying the course of history which prevents overall continuous progress? If so, what is it, and can it be defeated? And as for those who do believe in a history which delivers progress, what do they have to say about the immense catalogue of horrors still to be found in the world?

Whatever answers are given, whether from the enthusiast's or the sceptic's viewpoint, they cannot but be interesting to us in their own right, for since we are beings conscious of the passing of time and of the varying of events and circumstances, we cannot but wish 'to make sense' of this aspect of our being-in-the-world. In short, to be 'conscious' of this or that is to 'make sense' of it, in the most basic sense that human-beings are of necessity perpetually, instinctively engaged in the practice of 'understanding', or contriving meaning in, what they experience. Thus it would be strange indeed if historians, whose object is the past, did not find speculative philosophy of history intrinsically interesting, whether impressed or not by particular examples of it.

To pursue our analogy, there is a second reason why an impulse towards speculative philosophy of history, worthwhile or not, is at least understandable – namely, there are certain periods in history when many who are part of them feel their times are especially turbulent or in some way remarkable (just as when an individual, for example, falls seriously ill, undergoes a severe loss, wins the lottery, or retires). At such times, interest in 'making sense of the past' has a practical point – namely, the felt need to come to terms with the present through gaining a perspective on how one has got there. Such reflections serve the function of restoring, or confirming, a meaning to the present otherwise lost or at least jeopardized by an unprecedented flow of events. Only too aware of the *particular* narrative of events leading to our present situation, we attempt to regain our bearings by seeking more reflective *generalised* explanations for the state we are in. This urge to 'take stock' of affairs in turbulent times is 'natural', I suggest, for either of two reasons – first, the need not only for individuals but also for communities (local, regional, national, and even international) to preserve their sense of identity; and second, the need to find excuses or deflect blame, where the unsteadiness of the present is unpleasant and perceived as resulting from failure. This latter is probably no more than a particular case of the general need to preserve a sense of identity, for in finding 'excuses' for the parlous state one might be in, one is meaning 'it wasn't *me*, sir'! As we will see, if by a 'theodicy' is meant 'a justification of the ways of God to man', many speculative philosophies of history contain elements of 'a justification of the ways of *man* to man', (for which we might coin the term 'histodicy').[3] For example, 'America is still the land of the free despite some of the things it has "had" to do . . .', just as 'I am still "me" despite some of the things I have done . . .'.

To complete our analogy, a third reason why speculative philosophy of history is understandable is that there are periods in history when many intuit the coming to an end of an epoch, and the possibility, even necessity, of fashioning a new future. Thus the range of their vision extends beyond the short or medium term, and they look at themselves (either as individuals or, by analogy, as 'cultures', or even as 'mankind') in terms of their 'historic' possibilities. This involves an attempt

11

to supersede the 'details' of the past in order to abstract overall 'trends' and general 'laws' from which to predict the future. A variety of positions can follow, most of which have been proposed at one time or another by different philosophers of history. The prediction may be one of gloom, which we can do nothing about; or of gloom, but one we can at least mitigate; or of a gloom which can be entirely averted. Alternatively the prediction may be one of endless 'progress' which only has to be nurtured, or of limited progress in limited areas. There is even the 'prediction' that 'history' has stopped – that, at least politically and economically, mankind has reached a culmination from which we can expect no further fundamental changes or developments either in terms of regress or progress.

Is speculative philosophy of history worthwhile?

From the above, then, I suggest speculative philosophy of history is an understandable intellectual exercise and, to that extent, defensible. Broadly, its project is interesting in its own right since it purports to 'make sense' of history, and to that extent suggest answers to 'the meaning of life'. The latter issue has naturally occupied human beings (and always will) insofar as they are 'self-conscious' – i.e., 'meaning-constructing' beings. And in an increasingly secular age where religion is less appealed to for answers to that question, speculative philosophy of history is all we have left. Also, as suggested, for those who dismiss the question of 'the meaning of life' on the a priori grounds that there simply isn't one, perhaps the burden of proof is on them to *show*, from history, its meaninglessness (i.e., demonstrate it a posteriori). But in doing so, they would be engaging precisely in that which their a priori stance would appear to denigrate, namely, speculative philosophy of history!

We also saw two broadly *practical* reasons for engaging in speculative philosophy of history – namely, the urge in rapidly changing times to restore a sense of continuity, or at least intelligibility, in defence of a society's identity; and secondly, the impulse to predict the future, and hopefully influence it, on the basis of identifying general forces governing history.

From all this it is not surprising that certain themes recur in the writings of many speculative philosophers of history – the search for meaning or design in the flow of history, various theories of progress, the notion of recurring cycles, the issue of individual agency, the discovery of 'laws' of development which 'determine' history, and the question of the changeability of 'human nature'; in their turn, these themes generate subsidiary notions regarding the role of chance, Fate, or Providence, different periodisations of history, theories of different 'national' or 'cultural' characteristics of peoples, variously coloured predictions for the future, and attempts to make sense of human suffering.

As suggested, this is all intrinsically interesting. But one further theme which cannot but press itself on historians in particular, is whether, not only this or that example of a 'theory' of history, but the general rationale underlying *all* speculative philosophy of history (understandable as the impulse is) is *worthwhile* in the first place. According to the philosopher Hegel, writing in the early nineteenth century, historians only 'skim the surface', (i.e., record and analyse 'the facts' without comprehending their part in the larger scheme of things) – and in the Introduction I mentioned similar concerns voiced *today* about the teaching and writing of history. What is the point of studying history, it might be asked, if not to emerge with something to say about its overall meaning, direction, and significance? In short, one could turn the issue on its head and ask whether the study of history is worthwhile if it is *not* pointed deliberately towards wider horizons of understanding. Fascinating as the minutiae of the Crimean War might be, or the task of inferring a satisfactory account of the social origins of Victorian prostitution, are such piecemeal historical studies worthwhile in themselves? The practice of many historians today suggests they think it is. Others will argue that they study and teach, for example, the history of the Crimean War in order to enhance under-standing of, and gain perspective on, aspects of European history both before and after that war. To that extent, then, they are moving towards finding a grander 'design' or 'significance' to history. Alternatively, some may value studying history not because of any such leanings towards 'theorising' or 'speculating' about its course but because of that 'civilising' effect the discipline is supposed to have in virtue of being one of the 'humanities' subjects revitalised in the Renaissance. There may be other justifications for studying history[4] – but the point is made. If some historians question the value of speculative philosophy of history, the shoe can be put on the other foot – but in a more charitable spirit, for no speculative philosopher of history would question the value of the study of history, only the value of how it is undertaken in any particular instance.

Although the following chapters of Part 1 are far from being a *history* of speculative philosophy of history, they are at least suggestive of the framework such a history might employ. This is because they are chronological in order, thereby offering the possibility of conveying the sense in which the same thing (in this case, speculative philosophy of history) has changed over time, and of suggesting explanations for how and why. However, as elaborated upon at the beginning of the next chapter, rather than adopting the stricter definition of 'speculative philosophy of history' which a proper history would probably require, for the more general purposes of a 'guide' I have adopted a looser notion in order to accommodate what may be proposed as 'dominant general attitudes' towards the meaning of history in addition to specific speculative philosophies of history crafted by individual thinkers. As for the latter, this guide draws attention mainly to the most celebrated examples. But sufficient guidelines emerge from their study, I hope, to enable those interested in the genre to pursue lesser known examples from an informed perspective.

2

PRE-CLASSICAL IDEAS ON 'HISTORY'

Introduction: principles of selection

Some scholars claim that speculative philosophy of history did not begin until the sixteenth or even seventeenth century AD. Others, without explanation, have embarked on accounts of it based on that assumption, resulting nonetheless in a number of excellent books. Because the arguments for that starting-point are neither always clear nor form a consensus, and because I begin with earlier periods, it is helpful to comment on this issue as a way of explaining the principles of selection in the following chapters on 'speculative philosophy of history'. Firstly, to reserve the beginnings of speculative philosophy of history to the later period *is* justifiable, but only on the basis of various suppositions. One is that we restrict it to systematic, full-blown examples of the effort to construct, or make sense of, some kind of 'universal' history (such as Hegel's *Philosophy of History*). For our purposes, however, such examples can best be seen merely as speculative philosophy of history at its more highly developed. This leaves room to explore 'lesser' types represented by substantial reflections on history, or important attitudes towards it, found within writings neither so explicitly nor exclusively focused as the former. As perhaps an extreme example of this, we will explore how the so-called 'pre-rational', allegedly 'mythical', mind-set in early societies made sense of the past.

A second supposition justifying such a late beginning for speculative philosophy of history is that we should restrict the meaning of 'philosophy' strictly to the exercise of reason unshackled from 'belief' and/or superstition. Thus theories about the course and meaning of history which in particular originate from *religious* beliefs, impervious to criticism because held as axiomatically true, do not amount to 'philosophy proper'. Sympathetic as we may be to this notion, there are difficulties in upholding it. In general the relation between faith ('belief') and reason has been as unclear to many philosophers as it has to many theologians. It is still 'philosophised' about. A difficulty arising more specifically from *philosophy* of history is that a number of its exponents, otherwise undoubtedly 'philosophers', have so clearly introduced religious ideas into their philosophies of history. The above-mentioned Hegel is one example. We will encounter others from our own times, particularly those who argue an implicit connection between 'the idea of progress' and the view of history they claim as unique to the Christian religion. Given this equivocal relation between religious and philosophical thinking, we can adopt a more accommodating approach to 'speculative philosophy of history' which includes an exploration of ideas about history inspired by *religious* views. In particular we shall outline an alleged specifically Judaeo-Christian set of ideas relating to the course and meaning of history, including those of Augustine.

A third supposition which might justify locating the origins of speculative philosophy of history in the sixteenth or seventeenth centuries AD is that only *since* then has there been a more or less uninterrupted succession of different, often conflicting, philosophies of history such that the subject can be treated *historically*. In other words, if we wish to treat speculative philosophy of history as a distinctive 'tradition' of philosophical thought, we must treat it as constituting a *continuing* line of argument contributed to over time by a variety of thinkers responding to each other. Only then does speculative philosophy of history become a 'real' phenomenon subject to historical reconstruction rather than being a term which denotes randomly selected, radically disconnected, examples of 'its' sporadic appearances.

There is much to be said for this argument. Indeed, in a different context I would regard it as irrefutable[1], and would not doubt the sixteenth/seventeenth century AD starting point. However, not only is it *not* clear that those who begin their account of speculative philosophy of history at that point do so on this reasoning, their writings often fall short of that kind of genuinely *historical* account it implies. Some, although scrupulously informative about and instructively critical of the writers they treat of, are nevertheless content to organise their accounts more as a chronicle of successive thinkers than as a properly connected narrative. But if many appearing to take an historical approach to speculative philosophy of history are thus wanting in their practice, this 'guide' does not purport to be a history in the first place. Again, then, we can therefore allow our approach to encompass a more generous time-span, and one within which we can explore incidences of a more loosely defined 'speculative philosophy of history'. Relevant ideas of the Renaissance, and Machiavelli in particular, are an example.

Thus although good reasons can be found for restricting the study of speculative philosophy of history to the sixteenth or seventeenth century onwards, they are not sufficient in the context of this 'guide' to persuade us to ignore earlier ideas and 'theories'. Although not always 'pure philosophy', nor exclusively focused on 'history', these earlier notions are nonetheless of relevance – and particularly so for historians, interested as they are in the past rather than in philosophy for its own sake. But more than this, we will find that when we *do* reach that later period when speculative philosophy of history matures into a definite 'tradition', then its philosophers, in *their* efforts to make sense of history, invariably incorporate their own ideas and explanations of how those earlier cultures understood it.

A 'pre-historic' mentality?

A mythical consciousness of the past?

Although few writings of direct relevance survive from the early civilisations of ancient Egypt, Greece, and other Near and Middle East regions, scholars have found sufficient evidence to construct accounts of, or at least generate suggestions about, how those cultures 'understood the past'. Three features stand out – a *mythical* view of space and time; a belief in the eternal recurrence of 'cycles' of events; and following from these beliefs, the absence of any notion of the historic capacity of man to fashion what we call 'progress'.

Calling to mind ancient myths we think of often detailed, lengthy narratives involving the dramatic actions and interactions of gods, and of men of semi-divine, heroic stature. And we recognise that not only were these stories told to entertain; they usually contained some moral, and (inevitably, as narrative) 'explained' how this or that came about. For example, numerous early, or 'primitive', cultures had their own version of 'the story of creation', the origins of mankind, the invention of agriculture, and the forming of societies – and within these stories or 'mythical' accounts the forces of good and evil play their part, as well as such of attributes as strength, cunning, perseverance, and fidelity. But we should not confuse such 'stories' with those we find in fables. Fables are works of the explicitly fantastic imagination – nobody is expected to believe them, (although any morals they preach are meant to be taken seriously). Ancient 'myths', on the contrary, were regarded as sacred or divine in the sense of voicing truths of ultimate relevance to their societies. Does this mean these early peoples believed in the factual truth of the narratives, or were they supposed to recognise them as mere *allegories*, however sacred in import? This is a natural question for us to ask – one of many which the phenomenon of 'myth' has provoked in a huge body of frequently disputatious, abstract literature. However, the very asking of this question takes us to the heart of the matter, for it is a question from *our* point of view, not (so far as the evidence suggests) from that of those early peoples. It would not have occurred to them, for they did not see the world as something distinct from them, about which they as 'subjects' could make 'objective' statements. In other words, *we* think in terms of an external world of nature and happenings (i.e., of space and time) whose 'otherness' we can try to know (through science and history) by the exercise of observation and rational thought.

'I' and 'Thou'

'Pre-historic' peoples did not experience their being in the world in this latter manner. Rather, they saw 'nature' not as 'other' but as animated, just like themselves. They knew themselves as alive; wilful, emotional, calculating, and capable of agency. This is also how they 'saw' what we call the 'objects and events in nature'. The land, sky, stars, trees, hills, winds, deserts, plants, water – all were 'seen as' animated, alive, just like themselves. And 'events' such as storms, plagues, dawn, dusk, floods, animal migrations, eclipses, the turning of the seasons – all were 'seen as' the actions, or results of actions, taken by this animated nature around them. Let us be clear here. It is not so much that they saw nature 'as' animated – this could invite the false notion that they made *allegories* of nature, that they anthropomorphised it 'in order to' make sense of it. Rather than 'seeing' ('interpreting') nature in this way, they directly *experienced* it in this way. Their experience was that of being *part* of a totally animated world, not that of being separated from it, only to be reconnected through the intellectual mediation of some 'process of knowing'. It is in this sense, then, that the question of whether these peoples believed their great 'myths' to be true is posed from a false perspective. Rather, irrespective of listening to classic 'mythical' sagas, they lived their daily lives *within* a 'mythical' consciousness in the first place. The grasses on the riverbank, for example, would be regarded as animated and be assigned as the property or work of a 'god'. For instance, if in picking reeds someone cut their hand, we have to imagine them regarding the offending reed as, for example, spiteful or malevolent. The god of plants must be offended, and consequently be propitiated via an appropriate ('ritual') offering – or the god may be trying to convey a message, such that the 'medicine-man', 'priest', or augurer needs to be consulted for its meaning.

We may summarise the above, and draw attention to a much fuller account of this 'ancient' mentality, by quoting from the editor's stimulating opening chapter in the book *Before Philosophy*. 'The fundamental difference between the attitudes of modern and ancient man as regards the surrounding world is this: for modern, scientific man the phenomenal world is primarily an "It"; for ancient – and also for primitive – man it is a "Thou"'.[2]

'Poetry'

We may also make two points commonly observed – first, this 'ancient' mentality is intrinsically highly *imaginative*, able to weave any number of 'fantastic' or 'poetic' accounts of a reality construed as consisting of a myriad of animated phenomena, each with their own individualistic 'characters' and subsumed under the powers of numerous 'gods' as idiosyncratic as the human personalities they were imagined from. This 'poetic' feature of the ancient mentality reaches its fullest expression in their great myths, then, but is not a 'special' vehicle reserved for these classic tales. Rather, the great myths are (one of) the major pieces of *evidence for* the kind of claims about the *generally pervasive* 'pre-classical' mentality sketched out above. In a later chapter we will see that Vico, one the first to make such claims, featured them prominently as the very foundation of his own speculative philosophy of history.

'Primitiveness'

The second observation is pre-figured where the passage quoted above refers to 'ancient' *and* '*primitive*' man, meaning contemporary 'primitives', suggesting the latter share this 'mythical', 'poetic' mentality. Indeed, if ancient myths are evidence for the latter, some anthropologists' studies of primitive tribes in modern times are another source of evidence. But for our purposes what is important is the *concept* of 'primitiveness', for it figures in subsequent efforts to 'make sense' of history, particularly in diverse attempts meaningfully to *periodise* history – also it is a concept of obvious significance to those who ponder over the question of 'human progress'. In other words, the notion of 'primitiveness' plays an important role in speculative philosophy of history, and thus the attempt to flesh out (at least) part of its meaning, by equating it to what is alleged above about the *'ancient'* mentality, should be of interest to us.

'Childhood'

One further observation, less common nowadays and doubtless controversial for psychologists, is related to this concept of 'primitiveness' – namely, the belief that certain analogies hold between 'the primitive' mind and early childhood. One of these, popularised by Rousseau in the mid-eighteenth century, was that 'primitive' or 'aboriginal' peoples share the *innocence* and naivety we like to associate with early childhood – and thus those speculative philosophers of history who equated their contemporary 'primitives' with peoples of *ancient* times used the notion to elaborate upon a metaphor of the 'history of mankind' as having started in 'childhood', and then passing through the equivalent stages of 'maturation' found in *individuals*. Another analogy between 'primitives' and children, again extended to (or derived from) ancient societies, returns us to those claims about a 'mythical', or even 'magical', mentality. Some argue there is a stage in early childhood when the child perceives the 'outside' world as 'animated' like his or her self – that it is only after a period of 'development' that children realise, for example, that the door cannot hurt them because, unlike them, it is only a (mindless, emotionless) *thing*. In other words, some claim we undergo an early phase of childhood surrounded, so to speak, by 'the gods' – that is, by powerful 'forces' and 'objects' which, like us, have a will of their own. Like ideas of an 'original innocence', this notion of a 'mythical' mentality, characteristic both of ancient cultures and of a natural stage of childhood psychology, has similarly been exploited by some speculative philosophers of history in their explorations of 'the history of humanity'. Indeed, one of these, the nineteenth-century thinker Auguste Comte, claimed that during a period of madness he had 'regressed' to just such a 'childlike' mentality, and then progressively 'grown out of it' – and that the illuminating experience informed his ambitious philosophy of history.

A *bizarre*, or *'workable'*, mentality?

This may lend weight to the notion that this ancient 'mythical' consciousness is *bizarre*, an impression hardly diminished when we are confronted by actual examples of ancient 'myths' abounding in the most 'extraordinary' accounts of a world peopled by gods, spirits, and demons. But as suggested, these classic myths are not special cases designed to entertain as fiction, but simply the highest expressions of a general consciousness about the world. As such, we have to accept that in an important sense these 'myths' – and more crucially, the general mentality they emerged from – *worked* in the sense that, 'bizarre' or not, it enabled early peoples not only to survive for thousands of years but also to build civilisations as impressive as the ancient Egyptian and Mesopotamian examples. The 'mythical' mentality of the ancients, then, cannot be dismissed as 'absurd' or 'fanciful', for if it were these things, they could not have managed the world around them. The task, then, is to see what they 'meant' in terms which must still be capable of being made sense of by us, for however much the world and/or 'human nature' has changed, neither can have changed so much as to imply that the ancients were as aliens in a different universe. One final word on this: for thousands of years, right up to the seventeenth century AD and beyond, people successfully farmed the land in the 'false' belief that the sun rises in the morning, and that it goes round the Earth. They were 'wrong' – these were 'fanciful' notions, but we can extract the 'sense' from them. Even more to the point, we may ask of a friend, 'how is the love-life treating you?', as if 'the love-life' were some whimsical individual power or force with its own agenda for our friend. Here, 'the love-life' is as a 'god'. And it is but a short step, rather than a giant imaginative leap, to say we might as well ask 'how do you stand with Aphrodite?' (the Greek goddess of love). No doubt if matters do not stand well, appropriate 'rituals' will be engaged in to propitiate her, such as a visit to the hair-stylist – or the augurs or oracles will be consulted, as in checking one's stars! Another example of this 'fetishising' mentality would be to complain, not that one was doing badly at work, but that 'work is not treating me very well at present', again implying a world peopled by animated 'forces' or 'gods' who unpredictably bestow their good or ill will upon one.

It is in this light, then, that we can treat the 'mythical' ideas of ancient cultures as not only meaningful but also 'practical', in the sense that they fulfilled their function of 'making sense' of peoples' experience. Whether their ideas were 'true' is hardly the point, just as a millennium from now our present 'scientific' mentality might be superseded by a different consciousness. Our present one 'works', and it would be up to future historians, anthropologists, philosophers, and psychologists to recover its 'sense'. *Our* task, however, is to recover the 'sense' of how, in particular, ancient cultures understood 'history', or the passing of time.

Ancient ideas of 'history'

Time

We may begin with their understanding of *time* itself. We now measure out time into discrete, equal, 'abstract' amounts such as hours, minutes, and seconds. These 'pieces' of time are not related to any events and, although abstractly identical, are each unique in the sense of being unrepeatable. It is true we also count time in terms of days, months, years, decades, and so on. But these are simply multiples of the smaller measures – a day is 24 hours. We give precise, unrepeatable dates to events.

However, there is another, more 'poetic', sense of time which we all appreciate – namely, when we refer to a certain time in more concrete, personal terms; 'that Monday morning feeling', 'the weekend', 'it was end of term'. This is more akin to how ancient peoples understood time – as distinct 'pieces' or 'regions' of time with recognised, similar content. But more than this, there seems a sense in which they regarded a 'piece of time' such as dawn, not as similar on each occasion, but essentially as identical recurrences of an original event. And because this archetypal event, such as the 'first morning', would of course be seen as resulting from the dramatic interactions of 'the gods' rather than in the impersonal terms of a scientifically governed nature, it would be truer to say that each dawn was seen not so much as a 'recurrence' but as a *re-enactment* of the original story. Thus, for example, in ancient Egyptian mythologies of creation, the sun-god emerged, self-created, on the solitary hillock surrounded by the primeval waters, and proceeded to bring order to the formless chaos such that the heavens, the sky, the earth, and the netherworld were ordered and fixed. Thus for the ancient Egyptians, each dawn (and New Year's Day) could be intuited as the re-enactment of the sun-god's emergence from the abysmal depths after a successful struggle with the forces of chaos and darkness. Consistent with their sense of active participation in this animated world, important rites and festivals marked the New Year, when sacrificial offerings were made, and praises sung, to the sun-god.

In this way ancient peoples 'mythologised' time and its passing. The succession of the seasons, the flooding of rivers, the changing of prevailing winds, the coming of harvest, the migrations of animals – all were seen as recurrences or re-enactments of archetypal stories, some going back to original creation myths which would see even the movements of the heavenly bodies in terms of a gigantic recurring cycle. Numerous early cultures shared the notion of 'the Great Year', a variously calculated (but always huge) 'time' in which key stars would return to their original places, signalling the re-beginning of an endless replication of all that had happened.

The passing of time

In the above we have only glimpsed the tip of an iceberg. Yet we can draw on this to make some further general observations on what sense these ancient peoples made of 'the past'. First, apart from the archetypal distant past in which things originated, there is a paradoxical sense in which the more immediate past did not seem important or interesting to them *as the past*. It is true they would chronicle centuries of time in terms of the reigns of different kings and the movements of the heavenly bodies, but the notion of a self-sustaining history of their own human past was not relevant. Clearly, if times had been particularly bad, good, or turbulent, they would be recorded – but no 'explanations' would be sought (as in modern history) other than celebrating or bemoaning their 'fate' at the hands of the gods.

Even more to the point, we have already intimated how the 'pastness' of past events was of no special relevance to their mentality, for 'the past' is ever-present in the re-enactment of events, and also beckons in the future. The important thing was to be alert to, and respect, what duties and 'rituals' the present (re-enactment of the) 'piece of time' required, so as to play one's proper part in the animated drama of existence, cooperating with the gods, however difficult they could be, to procure peace and prosperity. Is this that far, in practice, from our *own* sense of the past – at least, if we lead routinised lives? Or does life in today's 'advanced' societies preclude such disinterest in 'the passing of time'?

The archetypal past

Second, however, and as antidote to this disinterest in the 'pastness' of the past, we have already seen their intense interest in the *archetypal* past. Their 'creation myths' in particular, as well as myths relating to subsequent 'originating' events, explained the nature of the cosmos to them, described the character of the numerous forces or 'gods' they shared the world with, and served as a guide to how to conduct themselves in relation to their kings and lesser officials, their work, their home-life, and other aspects of their environment. What had 'happened' back in the origins of time had established the unalterable outlines of the drama of life. However, given that reality rarely lives up to propaganda, it is not surprising that these archetypal, original times were looked back to as *pristine*. Many ancient cultures clung to a belief in a 'golden age' long ago in their past – 'golden' in two (typically 'poetically' related) senses; an age in which gold was the only metal, and an age 'golden' for the primal freshness and splendour of its order.[3] Pessimism about the present is not a new phenomenon!

'Story-telling' and 'historical causality'

Another aspect of ancient peoples' ideas of the past, already noted, is worth elaborating on – namely, their use of 'story-telling' as the vehicle for explaining events. Seeing themselves as living in a totally animated environment, all happenings could not but be the result of the desires, impulses, and strategies of willful beings – either themselves or the gods, spirits, and demons around them. As Frankfort puts it: 'When the river does not rise, it has *refused* to rise. The river, or the gods, must be angry with the people who depend on [it]'.[4] All that happens does so through personal agency, and the only vehicle for explaining 'what happened' in this way is to tell it as a 'story' – that is, as a *narrative*. Now, what concerns us here is not whether, in telling a 'story', a particular narrative is fictional or factual, but that narrating a story is a *vehicle* or *form* of explanation – and what seems clear is that ancient peoples' view of the world necessitated their explaining what happened in it by putting events into the narrative structure. Now although there is more to say about 'narrative' later in this book, what we can already see is that narrative only works with personal agents who will this, decide that, and respond to circumstances. As a *form* of 'explanation' it does not appeal to abstract 'factors' or 'laws' governing events. Rather, each event is uniquely individual, precisely because the product of 'individuals', (in the case of the ancients, be these 'gods' or men – and even if events are 're-enactments', paradoxical as that might appear). What we can say, then, is that implicit in ancient cultures was a view of what we now call 'causality in history' – namely, that 'what happened and why' was always, and only, explicable in terms of the actions, responses, and interactions of beings (human and 'divine'), and thus only *communicable* in terms of narrating a story. The kind of modern historical analysis which introduces 'abstract' economic, sociological, and demographic factors into explaining 'what happened', or employs some general 'laws' of development, evolution, or political change, was absent in the 'historical' awareness of ancient peoples. Alternatively, we could say it would have been *irrelevant* to them. Indeed, we can see a sense in which the very notion of *causality* in history did not figure at all in their mentality, if by 'causality' we mean the operation of underlying impersonal 'laws' governing events. The river *refused* to rise – it was not '*caused*' not to rise.

A final comment is worth making here, particularly in the light of some contemporary complaints about 'narrative history'. If the earliest known way of 'explaining happenings' was to put them into 'stories', this does not necessarily mean that the story-*form* (or narrative *structure*) is therefore inherently naive, childish, or even non-explanatory altogether, as some modern critics would have us believe. On the contrary, one could turn this on its head by arguing that insofar as it has not been superseded either in ordinary speech or in much written history, the ancientness of the *narrative* approach to perceiving and explaining (past) events testifies to its intuitive appropriateness as the 'form' in which we apprehend succeeding events.[5]

'Progress'

The final observation to be drawn from our glimpse at the mentality common to ancient cultures is a negative one. They had no notion of 'historical progress', and consequently no belief in it. Because this may in fact challenge our modern imagination more than some other features of the ancient world-view, and because the theme of 'belief in progress' is of major (and controversial) importance for the remainder of this guide to speculative philosophy of history, it is worth elaborating upon. In the modern Western world the belief in 'human progress' is so deeply underlying that it is taken for granted. Brought to the surface, it is a fourfold belief – the notion that over the millennia, history has, despite dark periods, delivered 'progress', certainly in the arts and sciences, technology, economic welfare, the treatment of individuals, and political freedom; the notion that history is 'linear', in the sense that we do not go backwards, or round in some vast historical cycle; the notion that 'progress' will thus continue in the future; and the notion that an important task in our present is therefore to participate in planning and striving to bring about 'progress'. This general consciousness was, quite simply, absent in ancient cultures – as suggested, its absence may be one of the chief obstacles to our ability truly to empathise with so much of their outlook and behaviour. Nevertheless, to the extent we can *explain* this absence (although explaining a negative can be a dubious procedure), we can at least claim to understand ancient mentality that much better.

'Science'

One obvious explanation is that so much of what we call 'progress' results from science, and particularly its application in technology, and that ancient peoples were ignorant of it. But this raises more questions than it answers. Not all 'progress' results from science – in any event, the ancients were sophisticated in the kind of mathematics involved in their astronomical calculations. As for technology, they were superb craftsmen and builders. Alternatively, it might be suggested their lives were so bound up with physical survival in often harsh and unpredictable climates that they had no opportunity to 'develop'. Yet all ancient cultures had classes of (subsidised) priests and officials with time and resources to 'develop'. For these reasons the more relevant question is, why did they *not* develop science and technology? And the answer is that they had no concept of 'progress'. In short, the question should be turned on its head. It is not that their lack of 'science' precluded any idea of 'human progress'. Rather, their lack of any idea of 'human progress' caused, or at least significantly contributed to, their inability to develop science.

This certainly is the view of one scholar, worth quoting at some length, and it takes us back to those presuppositions underlying the ancients' mentality, particularly their 'mythical' view of nature and their cyclical view of time. Discussing the ancient Mesopotamians, Jaki tells us,

> [t]he promising creativity of Hammurabi's age was not followed up in later times either in literature, or in the arts, or in legislation, let alone in matters of scientific learning. The basic reason for this failure is neither geophysical nor socio-economic. . . . They remained trapped in the disabling sterility of a world view in which not reason ruled but hostile wilfulness. . . . Believing as they did that they were part of a huge, animistic, cosmic struggle between chaos and order . . . the animistic, cyclic world view made it . . . impossible for them to realise that to influence or to control nature one had to be able to predict accurately its future course. . . . As a result, the mastery of science could not become a proud feature of the culture of a land on which ziggurats cast their sombre omen.[6]

And the same author offers an essentially similar analysis of numerous other ancient cultures, from both East and West, which although stemming from his Christian inspired contempt for the ancients' cyclical view of time, is amply documented. For example, now referring to the ancient Hindus and Egyptians, he insists:

[t]heir common failure to reach the level of both scientific and historical thinking is not a coincidence. Science and historiography are but different types of a causal and rationally confident probing into the space-time matrix in which external events . . . run their irrevocable courses. To achieve science one has to recognise that these courses are not returning on themselves in a blind circularity.

As for the ancient Egyptians in particular,

[m]uch of their intellectual history had been a long stagnation in the morasses of an animistic and cyclic world view, which in turn rested on their conception of the Watery Abyss as the ultimate entity, . . . (one from which) there could not emerge an unambiguous and effective pointer suggesting the presence of clear, rational laws in the universe.[7]

The earthly life

To the extent, then, that belief in 'human progress' is related in different ways both to a 'scientific' and an 'historical' mentality, the world-view shared by so many ancient cultures did not accommodate such a belief because it precluded these two (apparently) necessary conditions. We may add another 'necessary' condition, absent in ancient cultures, of an outlook grounded on belief in 'progress' – namely, a perspective which affords genuine value and significance to life on this earth. In one version or another, ancient cultures looked to the afterlife, the defeat of death, or release from the eternal wheel of fate, as the only real value to be cherished. Nothing of ultimate worth could be expected from earthly life. Peace, order, and transient pleasures might be hoped for during it – but the impulse to make things better, to question and change things, to take control of circumstances (implying what to them would appear an absurdity, the 'conquest of nature'), was foreign to their mentality and thus absent from their psychology.

This apparently obvious connection between belief in 'progress' and the affording of genuine value and significance to actual earthly life is an issue which will heighten as we now move forward in time to map out the different ideas about 'history' which characterised the classical cultures of Greece and Rome, and which played an important role in early Christianity. All I will observe here is that, perhaps unlike other 'necessary conditions' whose absence contributed to the lack of any idea of 'human progress' in ancient cultures, the connection between the latter and the de-valuing of 'this earthly life' is more of a 'chicken–egg' relation. Did ancient peoples not believe in 'progress' because, as suggested, their underlying 'philosophy' afforded little significance to life on earth? Or is it the other way round – namely, they awarded such insignificance to this earthly life *because* they had no experience (and thus no concept) of 'progress'? The former explanation puts enormous weight on ideas, world-views, or 'philosophies' as determinants ('causes') of historical circumstances, whereas the latter gives scope for material

24

circumstances, *through* affecting peoples' mentalities, to play a much larger role in determining history. This is yet another issue within 'the philosophy of history' itself – namely, the clash between 'idealism' and 'materialism' – which we shall return to later.

Some reflections

Finally we may ask whether ancient cultures' ideas about 'the past' amount to much? In one sense the answer is no. Their ideas and thinking were not the product of 'reason', 'philosophy', 'science', or 'history' as we know it. Rather, they were the product of an intuitive anthropomorphic imagination, and as such might be dismissed as 'superstition', unworthy of serious consideration. At one level this is clearly so.

Yet in other senses they *do* amount to something of value for anyone inclined to think about the course and meaning of history. Insight into *their* 'mentality' puts *our* 'mentality' into perspective – first by making us that much more aware we *have* one in the first place, and second by perhaps humbling us with the possibility (I would say, certainty) that ours will not be the last. This would not mean some return to 'superstition'. (In any event, some argue that 'science' is simply one more 'superstition' – and many scientists, past and present, have held 'mystical' beliefs). But it might be a future mentality more in tune with a holistic perception of individual minds, societies, the natural world, and the fundamental 'laws' of the cosmos, such that (in a manner *akin* to ancient intuitions) the distinction between what we confidently call 'mind' and 'matter', so fundamental to *our* mentality, would be superseded in a new science and philosophy. Books would have to be written explaining how our present mentality centred on the belief or 'superstition' that individual 'minds' confronted something Other – namely, an 'It', or 'material reality'. And the implications of this 'extraordinary' view of existence would have to be drawn out.

Another reason why the ancients' world-view still amounts to something of interest is that some of their ideas are not as 'bizarre' or unfamiliar as we might think. I have already made passing, semi-jocular reference to a similarity between their notion of the 'gods' and our contemporary fetishistic attitudes and behaviour. But Karl Marx included an esteemed section in *Das Kapital* on 'the fetishism of commodities', by which he meant that the real attributes of people, and the actual social and power relations between them, are no longer transparent to us – we are, after all, all 'free and equal' members of our 'free and equal' 'democratic' societies. Rather, these real differences and powers are mapped out with precision by the *pricing* of '*commodities*', meaning not just material objects such as potatoes and gold necklaces, but also activities, particularly *work*. We feel powerless against a bustling, complex world functioning in terms of the exchange of 'commodities' (including our work-activity and our status) – they, the 'commodities', conduct busy, individual lives exchanging amongst themselves in infinite differentiations whilst we, the *real* source of wealth-production and of social and power relations, stand mutely passive, mutually captive to a world not recognised as of, but nonetheless of, our own making.

Some contemporary thinkers (e.g., Baudrillard) advance similar ideas, yet perhaps supersede them by focusing no longer on 'commodities' but on 'signs', suggesting that contemporary capitalism, particularly with the influence of advertising upon an affluent consumer society, functions more in terms of the manufacture and exploitation of 'logos', 'icons', or 'signs'. A world of meanings or 'significations' is abstracted whereby real qualities such as reliability, youthfulness, tastefulness, efficiency, and 'quality' itself, are represented by icons or signs. We buy a shirt with a logo announcing the appropriate attribute or status in ourselves, whether we have it or not, and whether the logo has anything to do with shirts. We are not yet confronted by a tin of baked beans with a Rolls-Royce or BMW logo, but when we are, some will buy them, entering a 'hyperreality' of 'significations' in which they submit themselves to a representation of their being in the world which has nothing to do with their real presence in it, (nor with baked beans!) – and over which they have no control other than the alluring deception of 'consumer choice'. In short, in fetishing real qualities they are communing with the 'gods' – no longer Osiris and Aphrodite, but corporate logos.[8]

Another sense in which ancient ideas still have resonance concerns their fascination in astronomy and astrology (interchangeable until the rise of modern science in the seventeenth century AD). Mindful partly of distant real or rumoured disasters such as 'the Flood', many ancient cultures devoted considerable resources to plotting and dating the movements of the moon, sun, planets, and stars. Believing that, as 'animated', the entire cosmos undergoes regular cycles of decay and renewal, they would for example seek the 'right time' to plant and harvest, to build, to instate kings, as well as 'prophesy' future cataclysmic events and changing epochs. Various calculations were made of the huge period in which the stars returned to their 'original' positions, permitting different accounts of the age of the universe and different astronomical calendars charting its future course. Today's recognition that some of their calculations regarding, for instance, eclipses and planetary phases were astonishingly accurate has encouraged a 'rogue' literature speculating upon what 'secrets' the ancients knew about the past and future of our planet – but one thing is clear, they spent much time surveying the night sky. So do we. There are hundreds of astronomical observatories around the world, expensively resourced. Costly 'state of the art' ones are being built at present, and more are planned. In addition, space telescopes have been developed. In short, today's world abounds with 'seers'. Why?

A final sense in which ancient cultures' ideas about time and history are still worth consideration is that awareness of them raises some of those larger issues which remain of relevance to any attempt to 'make sense' of the course of history, such as the idea of, and belief in, 'progress'; the influence or otherwise of the natural environment; the notion of changing 'mentalities' and 'human nature'; the appropriateness or otherwise of narrative logic in explaining history; and the general notion of 'cycles' of repetition in history. Additionally, where some of these issues had been explicit components of ancient cultures' ideas and were transmitted to subsequent times, then how those later cultures responded to them (either to challenge or accept them) helps explain and account for their own views on 'history'. As we shall now see, this was particularly and understandably the case in the Near East and Mediterranean basin with respect to the era immediately succeeding 'ancient', 'pre-historical' times – the classical world of the Greeks and Romans.

3

CLASSICAL GREEK AND ROMAN SPECULATIONS ON HISTORY

Introduction

The emergence from 'myth'

As we move forward in time, and geographically, into the period of Greek antiquity stretching from roughly 1200 BC to that flowering of Hellenic culture starting around 500 BC, we encounter a gradual emancipation of thought from that 'mythical' world-view described in the last chapter. As we will see, this shift in 'mentality' included changes in the way 'history' and the passing of time were understood. But let us first map out the general backcloth of the overcoming of the 'mythical' mind-set within which those changes occurred – namely, the transition to what is called the 'rational', or 'philosophical' consciousness which attempts to understand things purely through the exercise of 'reason' rather than from the imaginative, 'poetic' perspective of intimate involvement in an animated, anthropomorphised world.

Not surprisingly, this shift in outlook was not made all at once, but is traceable through the differing ideas of a number of thinkers who left writings (often fragments) or were reported on later. For example, in Hesiod (eighth century BC) we meet a poetic, mythical account of the origins of the gods and of men, sharing a number of beliefs with those ancient Near Eastern cultures in the previous chapter. But by the fifth century BC we are surrounded by philosophers, albeit of differing 'schools', who in their explanations of reality attained that level of rational intellectual abstraction epitomised by Plato and Aristotle. In addition, although not 'scientists', it is argued[1] that their mental approach centring on a belief in the ultimate intelligibility of the universe laid the foundations for that emergence of 'real' science which occurred in the Hellenistic period some two centuries later. As Frankfort puts it, '[t]his change of viewpoint is breathtaking',[2] and he attributes it primarily to the Ionian 'school' of philosophers originated by Thales (625–546 BC), contributed to by Anaximander (611–547 BC) and Anaximenes (570–500 BC), and which influenced the thinking of Heraclitus, (540–475 BC).

This school sought the 'origins' or explanation of things not in terms of the actions of gods but in terms of some ultimate 'principle' underlying all existence, be it in their case water, air, or fire. It is true that some also spoke of 'the gods', whereas logic might dictate their abandonment altogether (as it did to later 'materialists' such as Democritus (c. 460–370 BC), Epicurus (341–270 BC) and the Roman Lucretius (98–55 BC), who still spoke of 'the gods' but regarded them as irrelevant to explaining nature and human affairs). But logic is one thing and reality – in this case, social reality – another. Some were boldly 'atheistic' whilst others, including later and different 'schools' (even Plato, 428–347 BC), continued to pay lip-service to 'the gods', perhaps as much to assure their ideas a hearing as to avoid censure (a practice continued in subsequent Christian – and other – societies into our own times).

The point is, however, that such philosophers adopted a viewpoint or 'mentality' which *detached* them, as subjects, from the 'objective' world outside them, held that world to be intelligible, and therefore posed them the challenge of exposing its 'workings' or 'logic' through reasoned argument. Some, as above, sought to explain everything in material terms (e.g., the 'atomic' theory of Democritus), others exploited the notion of the interplay of opposites such as 'Being' and 'Becoming' (e.g., Heraclitus' theory of 'universal flux'), whilst others such as Parmenides (515–? BC) abandoned the search for some ultimate *material* 'principle' underlying reality. He proposed instead that the universe is a changeless, infinite unity beyond the senses, governed or 'made up' by *thought* – that insofar as material or 'phenomenal' reality is ultimately explicable in terms of 'the thought of it', then its explanation is to be sought within the world of ideas, which we can enter through our capacity to 'reason' or be 'logical'. In short, since reality is 'thought', it can only be apprehended *through* the nature or 'laws' of 'thought' – the 'idealist' position famously elaborated upon by Plato – rather than by perception of material things or through imagination.

Reasons for the shift

This dawning and triumph of 'philosophy' in classical Greece has understandably been the object of enormous interest amongst philosophers and historians of thought. Its importance in laying the foundations for Western culture is monolithic. Yet for all the studies of early Greek philosophy, quite *why* this shift from a 'mythical' consciousness occurred, why in Greece, and why at the time it did, remain historical questions perhaps impossible to supply answers to, since it is doubtful we have enough information and evidence from which to infer them. It is noticeable that even those who do focus on the *shift* from 'myth' to 'philosophy' do so by explaining its character and significance, but only hint at explanations of *why* it occurred (or offer none).[3] One observation common to some scholars, suggestive of an explanation, takes us back to Hesiod. Although he presented a 'mythopoeic' account of the origins of the gods and men, two things mark out his ideas as different from the ancient cultures of the Near East. First, he does not have a particularly reverent attitude towards the 'gods' – there is much intermarriage between 'gods' and men in his epic *Theogony* (Genealogy of the Gods) and this is taken as early evidence of a more familiar, less respectful attitude in Greek thought towards many of the gods. Second, a number of Greek thinkers, as Hesiod himself, were laymen. Not part of an official 'priesthood' obliged to guard the sanctity of traditional beliefs and 'mysteries', the freedom of thought enjoyed by individuals such as Hesiod, Thales, and Anaximander was naturally accompanied by *independence* of thought.[4] Apart from its other features, in his *Works and Days* Hesiod's frequent excursions into moral and political problems of the day, and practical advice on matters of farming and business, demonstrate the independence of mind of a secular thinker. Thus, despite the fate of Socrates (399 BC), the comparative freedom of thought enjoyed by the Greeks could be one explanatory factor in the shift from 'myth' to 'philosophy'.

Another factor sometimes suggested is the city life enjoyed by many Greeks. Perhaps thinking of the effects of urbanisation in the nineteenth century AD, a reasonable supposition might be that 'city-life' put a new distance environmentally and culturally between people and nature, diminishing the hold of the old 'animistic' mythological world-view. Yet we have to assume that Frankfort, for one, would find this unconvincing since he notes that urban life thrived in ancient Egypt and Mesopotamia, but that this 'in no way diminished man's awareness of his essential involvement in nature'.[5]

A further suggestion to explain this 'shift' could be the *geo-physical* environment experienced by the Greeks – a factor often appealed to in later philosophies of history to explain different 'mentalities' between peoples (although not as dramatically different as the 'shift' we are considering here). Wilson, Frankfort, and Jacobsen are not the only scholars to make much of the geo-physical environment in their explanations of, respectively, ancient Egyptian and Mesopotamian 'mythopoeic' world-views. Yet they refer to it more to explain the *differences in* the mythologies between these two civilisations, given the markedly different geographical and climatic features between the Nile delta and hinterland and those of the Tigris and Euphrates, than to explain the commonality of their basic mythical mind-set. In this connection it is perhaps significant that when the Frankforts turn to Greece and 'the emancipation of thought from myth', they make no reference to the geo-physical environment either as an aid to explaining this 'emancipation' or in accounting for the differences between ancient Near Eastern poetic mythology and its Greek counterpart *prior* to that 'emancipation'.[6] As we will see, a different writer *does* exploit features of the natural environment of the Greeks to explain a fundamental aspect of their early philosophy – the abundance of *growth* – but not to explain its emergence from myth in the first place.[7] Perhaps there is nevertheless a connection – namely, that the climate and geography of Greece was far more benign than its harsher, more unpredictable counterparts in Mesopotamia, and thus less likely to inspire fear and therefore 'superstition'; and that it was not dependent upon such a striking and singular feature as the flooding of the Nile in ancient Egypt, an obvious stimulant to 'myth-making'.

The above suggestions remain, however, purely speculative. Perhaps all we can say, ultimately, is that this fascinating and momentous period of the emergence from a 'mythical' mentality was 'bound to' happen somewhere, sooner or later, as mankind began to leave behind its 'childhood' and start to 'grow up' – in short, we might find *ourselves* employing that analogy of the 'natural' development *individuals* undergo in the process of maturation which we have already encountered as a common theme in 'speculative philosophy of history'! This may not be a particularly convincing explanation (and certainly not of the *particulars* – i.e., why Greece, and why then?) – but at least it directly introduces *us* to the challenges addressed by philosophers of history.

Classical Greek and Roman ideas on 'history'

If increasingly explicit *philosophical* writings are the most direct evidence of the shift from a 'mythopoeic' view of the world amongst the Greeks, the emergence of *historians* is almost as powerful a pointer. Of these, some of the most famous are: the widely travelled, so-called 'father of history', Herodotus (c. 484–425 BC), who wrote extensively of the customs and histories of numerous Middle Eastern cultures and, in the latter parts of his *History*, traced the great conflict between Greece and Persia in the early fifth century BC; the militarily experienced Thucydides (c. 460–400 BC), whose *History of the Peloponnesian War* covered the confrontations between Athens and Sparta which, beginning in 431 BC, lasted for some twenty-seven years; and Polybius (c.203–120 BC), the widely informed and thoughtful Graeco-Roman who, amongst other things in his *Histories*, analysed the history of Rome up to the point when, having defeated the Carthaginians by the mid-second century BC, it became ruler of most of the Romans' then 'known' world.

Just as no historian today thinks and writes in a vacuum, neither did the classic Greek and Roman historians. To differing degrees and with varying deliberateness they reflected broader, more 'speculative' attitudes abundant in other philosophical and literary works towards the past and the course of events. Our interest is in these broad presuppositions rather than in the more exact historiography of classical Greek and Roman historians (although we shall return to Polybius in particular as a masterful exploiter of prevailing, sometimes contrary, 'theories' of history). It should not surprise us that some, and the most important, of these broad 'presuppositions' about history were inherited from that ancient 'primitive' mentality, to be re-worked into more 'rational' ideas. Although intertwined in ancient mythologies, for the sake of exposition we can separate out three such 'ideas' which were inherited, adapted, and elaborated upon.

Historical cycles

First, there is the recurrent theme of 'cycles' – the notion that time, and the events it contains, goes round in a huge circle. To the 'pre-philosophical' mind this notion applied to the cosmos as a whole, and within that overall 'pattern' the cyclical regularities of nature on Earth were subsumed. Daily, monthly, yearly, and in larger movements, things would return to the point where they began. Thus the same natural events such as dawn, a new moon, the new year, and longer term cata-strophes such as flood, draught, and famine would return repetitively as inevitable 'effects' of the (endlessly) circular motion or 'logic' of time. Numerous Greeks and Romans not only retained this idea, but by Hellenistic times refined it into an elaborate and popular astrology. Others, however, were not so interested in pursuing its superstitious possibilities. Rather, they transferred the notion of *cosmic* cycles to actual *human* history – if 'nature' goes round in circles, so does man and society. For example, numerous passages in Plato's writings demonstrate his belief that history stretched back maybe hundreds of thousands of years, in which human societies were repeatedly devastated by natural catastrophes and had to begin anew the long and arduous path from primitive kinship groups to the eventual formation of city-states. These city-states themselves, as we shall see, were suggested by Plato to undergo their own (perhaps circular) course of development and decline. But in the larger picture all that might have been achieved in the way of civilisation was, and will be, swept away again as the inexorable cycle of time turns all around. 'Have not thousands upon thousands of city-states come into existence, and . . . have not just as many perished?'[8] In one of Plato's fables, indeed, it is suggested that because the Earth is a material thing, and thus imperfect, it cannot share the divine perfection of perpetual rotation but must periodically reverse its rotation, with catastrophic results – not only geographically (floods, eruptions) but, in the longer term, also *morally*. This is because in departing from the motion exemplified by 'God' or 'reason', the other 'force' governing the universe – chaos or disorder – gains the upper hand, and 'as this cosmic era draws to its close, this disorder comes to a head. The few good things it produces it corrupts with so gross a taint of evil that it hovers on the very brink of destruction, both of itself and of the creatures in it'.[9] Although Plato might not have believed this himself, it is a typical enough application of the doctrine of 'cyclical history' derived from the widely accepted notion of the causal potency of cosmic cycles.

Plato and others were thinking of broad-scale movements – the succession of aeons – and were not referring to the more intimate details of actual historical life. But in succeeding centuries the cyclical doctrine became increasingly entrenched, particularly amongst those Stoics who took it to the extreme of believing that

> as the planets retrace exactly the same route which they had already traversed, each being that had already been produced during the previous period will re-emerge once more in exactly the same manner. Socrates will exist again, and Plato as well, and also each man with his friends and fellow citizens; each of them will suffer the same trials, will manage the same affairs; each city, each village, each camp will be restored. This reconstitution of the Universe will occur not once, but in a great number of times; or rather the same things will reoccur indefinitely to no end.[10]

In like vein, it is clear (from a work wrongly attributed to Aristotle[11]) that this overall belief in the cyclical nature of history even engendered doubts as to the meaning of 'before' and 'after', since if the course of events has a beginning, and an end which heralds a re-beginning of the same course, are we 'after' the people of Troy, or, if nearer the beginning of the cycle, *before* them? Clearly these latter examples are extremes, perhaps matched by modern-day counterparts who seriously speculate upon, or believe in, 'parallel universes' – that is, who in doggedly following up the implications of an idea, irrespective of empirical evidence and the apparent claims of common-sense, do what the classical Greeks have been noted for by those who try to explain some of their ideas.

These extremes apart (although they tell their own story), there is ample evidence of a widespread general belief in *cosmological* cycles from at least the time of Heraclitus (540–475 BC), which many translated into a belief in an analogous repetitive cycle of not only natural but also human events. Such beliefs persisted for centuries, into the so-called 'Silver Age' of Latin literature exemplified by Seneca (4 BC–AD 65), later by the Emperor Marcus Aurelius (AD 121–180), and were clearly still widespread in St Augustine's times (AD 354–430) since, as we shall see later, he devoted considerable energy to combating them. Given such longevity and ubiquity of notions, however varied, about the world's cyclical history (human affairs included), we must therefore recognise overall general belief in the latter as an indispensable component of peoples' understanding of the past and the course events take – in other words, of how they saw 'history' and their place in it.

'Fate', 'Fortune', and 'the gods'

Another idea inherited from ancient times was that of 'fate' or 'fortune'. This is a notion as difficult to pin down then as it is in today's use. At one extreme it can mean 'blind chance', and at the other mean the 'force' which, sooner or later as 'fate' catches up with one, delivers the appropriate reward or punishment for the conduct of an individual or even of a nation. But even in the former guise as 'chance', the notion is used to refer to some force or 'agency' which determines affairs by overriding, and often confounding, human intentions and strivings – and it is probably unwise to go further in search of a formal definition. Rather, we have to look at how this 'umbrella' notion was *used* to see what 'fate' or 'fortune' meant for different individuals. We can draw a line, however, where 'fate' is not only equated with 'chance', but where 'chance' is construed as not in any sense a determining cause. In short, if one takes the view that 'things are simply as they are' (meaning there is no explanation for them), it adds nothing to that statement to attribute 'the way things are' to 'fate'. In that formula, 'fate' is literally meaningless. This may well have been the case for the 'materialist' thinkers, Epicurus (341–270 BC) and Lucretius (c. 98–55 BC), for although the former seemed to believe in 'the gods', he held that they are indifferent to human affairs; 'fate', where it does 'play a role' (sic), is in fact simply 'chance'. On the other hand, if in saying 'things are simply as they are' one *also* attributes them to 'fate', one means the latter to *add* something to the initial statement. In this case (apart from having contradicted oneself) one *does* mean something by 'fate'. One means there is a *reason* or *cause* for 'the way things are' or 'the way things turn out' – namely, 'fate'. It would appear that for centuries numerous Greeks and Romans at least subscribed to this somewhat indeterminate notion of 'fate' or 'fortune' governing events.

More than this, they would often personify 'fate' into the actions of 'the gods'. Here we are reminded of that 'primitive' mythopoeic mentality which no doubt persisted at various levels, but this could be misleading insofar as belief in the existence of gods (and/or 'God' – for example, Plato, and many Stoics, talked of both) need not equate with a fully mythopoeic world-view. For the latter to be dominant it would not be enough to regard an unexpected event as the *effect* of the actions of a god. Rather, the event itself would be understood as 'the god' acting. In short, 'fate' would not be a term used to indicate that something happened because the gods willed it – rather, 'fate' itself would *be* a god (that is, 'the river *refused* to rise'). And indeed, in both Greek and Roman *mythology*, so widely exploited and much beloved in classical literature, 'fate' *was* a god – namely, the Fates which determined one's character, destiny, and time of death.

Yet ubiquitous as was the classical Greek and Roman belief in 'gods', and difficult as it might be to judge quite what they meant to them and how seriously they took their presence, they did not play the same role in their consciousness as in the earlier 'mythopoeic' mentality. For the Greeks and Romans nature was nature. The gods might intervene in it, but nature itself was not animated. Similarly, it seems, for 'history'. For Greek and Roman historians, history was the enquiry into the course of human events – wars, treaties, law-giving, the founding of cities, invasions, conspiracies, constitution-building – a history 'made' in the immediate sense by human-beings. 'Underneath' this busy history, however, would be the governing force of 'fate', or (taken from cosmology) the impersonal Wheel of Fortune which would ensure a predictable circularity overall in human affairs. For Polybius, for example, 'Fortune' particularly favoured Rome, ensuring its unique stability and exceptional achievements – but even Rome would inevitably decline, (signs of which he claimed to detect in his own day). Or at a less impersonal level, 'the gods' may intervene in certain episodes – a way of 'explaining' the unexpected, or of highlighting a significant event, or of lending an air of inevitability to the outcome of a battle.

Finally, at an even less impersonal, more immediate level, 'Fortune' was personified into a *moral* force arbitrating on the deeds and character of individuals (and nations). Arrogance, insolence, impiety, the committing of shameful acts, and other moral failings, would sooner or later be punished by Fortune, just as virtue would be rewarded. From Herodotus onwards, many Greek and Roman historians, as well as dramatists and poets, made a point of extolling how, 'in the end', justice is inescapably dealt out to the wicked – the moral order is maintained inexorably, because if men do not see to it themselves, or are unable to restrain those bent on wickedness, Fortune will see to it that evil gets its just desserts. Here, fortune or fate is at its most tangible and 'interventionist' as a 'force', 'power', or 'factor' determining not only the overall course of history, but the histories of individuals.

Once again, how sincere this belief was is difficult to gauge. For some it might simply have been a device to preach good morals, whilst for others this belief in the moral intelligibility of life could simply have been the effect of wishful thinking. In any event, this brand of 'determinism' in history – the notion that some agency outside humankind operates to ensure justice and retribution – continued to exercise a powerful influence into Christian times, even if the day of reckoning is moved to *after* death and 'another place'. Even today there are those who, either from religious doctrine or from some notion akin to the classical notion of 'Fortune', believe for example that Hitler was *bound* to come to a sticky end 'sooner or later' because they cannot conceive of a history which is morally neutral, or even worse, 'corrupt'. Today's *historians*, on the other hand, are far too 'sensible' to entertain such an idea?

The principle of growth (the biological analogy)

The third idea of relevance to history which the Greeks inherited and adapted from the pre-philosophical, 'mythical' world-view of more ancient cultures was that of genesis, growth, and eventual decay. In the ancient mind this notion connected directly with that of an animated cosmos undergoing cycles of change. Surrounded by the natural world of plants and animals (including themselves) inexorably governed by the cycle of genesis, growth, decay, and rejuvenation, they transferred this overwhelming perception to the giant animal they conceived the universe to be. The Greeks rationalised and exploited this notion of 'growth' into an all-pervading principle which they applied now to 'physical science' and to history. (Nisbet suggests the Greek *climate*, in producing an abundance of plant life as well as a contrasting arid season, might have contributed to the pervasiveness of the concept of growth and decay in the Greek way of looking at things).[12] Aristotle (384–322 BC) is the best-known exponent of this principle. His extensive researches into biological and zoological life confirmed for him the overriding truth that all things come into being, grow to fulfil their 'end', and then decay. Observation of this process in a thing reveals its *nature*. For example, the acorn is a hard seed – but gradually it changes into a shoot, grows into a sapling, and 'finally' develops into the fully-fledged oak-tree, after which zenith it eventually decays. Here we have the notions of a *natural* process of *change*, through *growth*, towards a pre-programmed 'end' or 'purpose' (the mature oak), succeeded by gradual decay. This is the famous teleological principle (taken from *telos* – 'end' or 'final cause') whereby, barring accidents (e.g., seeds being eaten, saplings being trampled), things *necessarily* or 'by nature' come to be what they essentially 'are' through a process of *change, growth*, or *development*. They have an inbuilt 'end' or 'purpose' which is realised as the zenith of their being.

But this notion of organic growth towards a 'natural' end-fulfilment was not restricted to the realm of biology. Aristotle himself applied this way of understanding the *nature* of things to (amongst other things) geophysical and historical processes. 'If the earlier forms of society are natural, so is the state, for it is the end of them, and the completed nature is the end. For what each thing is when fully developed, we call its nature, whether we are speaking of a man, a horse, or a family'.[13] Indeed, so compelling did this method of understanding reality seem to many, that 'the realm of final causes stood . . . for the bedrock of intelligibility. The result was that investigation of any realm, living or not, was not considered satisfactory without attributing, rightly or wrongly, purposes to processes and phenomena of every kind, ranging from the fall of stones to the motion of the stars'.[14] For example, under the influence of the master Aristotle, until the seventeenth century AD a stone was thought to fall because, being base material, it longed for the centre of the Earth. This has led at least one writer (Jaki) to attribute the failure of scientific progress in classical and medieval times (and by implication the broader 'progress' resulting *from* successful science) partly to the over-exploitation and mis-application of the biological analogy of organic growth.

In terms of *history* we have already seen an intimation of its application in Aristotle. But we can also go back to Plato and before for the overall 'theory' that the polis (or Greek form of 'city-state') was in fact the culmination of a necessary, 'natural' process of development wherein the first form of social organisation was the family. This ('the seed') 'grew' into kinship groups organised into villages, which in time 'grew', through a 'natural' process of amalgamation and enhanced complexity, into city-states. The 'end' or 'telos' was, then, the city-state, but there is a strong sense in which, given the biological analogy, the city-state is *logically* 'prior' to the family and the village, since they are social organisations which must 'naturally' change and develop towards their 'pre-programmed' end-point.

Yet not only was the biological analogy of purposive growth applied to the emergence of nations and city-states; it can also be detected in how many Greeks conceived of the arts, the practical sciences of agriculture and animal husbandry, and general cultural sophistication, as the natural culmination of a progressive development from more 'barbarous' times. Some, regarding their own civilisation as the zenith (or 'telos') of humankind's development, exhibited a certain complacency, even smugness. The analogy of biological change and growth towards a fulfilled apex contained a powerful message, after all. It told them humankind was *meant* to live in city-states and was *meant* to achieve the culture and life-style enjoyed by (better born) citizens of Hellenic city-states. In short, it was *natural*, because things had 'grown' to be as they were – and insofar as, for example, the *polis* was natural, it was 'right' – and insofar as it was right, it was 'good'. Here we encounter perhaps the origins of the perennial equating of 'rightness' with 'the natural', and of both with 'the good'. The key to this familiar equation, however, is that underlying the notion of 'the natural' is the analogy of *biological growth* with its attendant notions of purposive ('teleological') change.

But history has of course moved on. The polis no longer exists, and markedly different civilisations or 'cultures' succeeded those times. Humankind is not, then, 'meant' to live as it did in, for example, fifth-century BC Athens. Does this mean those Greeks and Romans who saw historical change in this way were wrong? Or were they right to apply the analogy of purposive biological growth to historical change, and only wrong where they believed their *own* societies represented the *maturity* of human life? Let us not forget the other side to the principle of growth – namely, decay. There is logical room to argue that the fact of succeeding, different civilisations does not necessarily give the lie to those who regarded their own times as the apex of humankind – later times could simply represent gradual decay. And, as we shall see, this is indeed how many in the Renaissance interpreted history, looking back with admiration to the 'golden age' of classical civilisation and culture and hoping for a 'rebirth' of European societies (a fittingly *biological* metaphor) by following its model. Alternatively, there is logical room to argue the Greeks and Romans were not wrong in their 'biological' thinking, but only mistaken in placing their *own* civilisations at the apex of human development. And indeed, using a 'theory' not altogether dissociated from the classical pre-occupation with the principle of growth and teleological change, the nineteenth-century philosopher, Hegel, did just that, as we shall see. He proposed the view that humankind had in *his* times reached its ultimate 'meaning', 'nature', or 'perfection' in the socio-economic, political, and religio-philosophical forms of dominant post-revolutionary European countries. Not only this, later in this book we shall encounter the view put forward in our *own* times by Fukuyama (leaning on an interpretation of Hegel), that the collapse of Soviet communism at the turn of the 1990s has *at last* signified 'the end of history' in the sense that humankind has reached the zenith of its historical 'growth' – namely, a world now dominated by capitalist economies functioning through liberal-democratic political institutions.

Returning to classical times, however, we should observe that the notion of purposive historical change through the analogy of biological growth was one of the most important ways in which the course of history was made not only *intelligible* but also *meaningful*. Underneath the seemingly arbitrary play of immediate historical events, a pattern analogous to genesis, growth, and maturation in the organic world was discerned in the broader history of civilisation. This pattern endowed history with intelligibility. More than this, because the pattern was that of natural biological growth, it endowed history with meaning. History is not aimless. Although such ideas were not, so far as we know, put into a systematically worked out 'philosophy of history', the notions of intelligibility and meaning, however ill-formed, introduce ingredients essential to the subsequent emergence of just such 'speculative' philosophy.

Decay, and 'the ages of man'

We have already noted that one phase of the biological principle of 'growth' is its nemesis – decay – but have had little to say about it so far. When thinking in broad terms of the history of civilisations, some Greeks and Romans, as we have seen, were more concerned to point to the achievements of their societies than to contemplate the 'downside' to the biological analogy (although Polybius did warn of it in the case of Rome's triumphant rise to prominence).[15] But there were two other strains of thought which *did* concentrate on the notion of decay in their view of history and change.

The first is an ancient view, retold in some detail in Hesiod's myth of the races of men, and appealed to in one form or another by many subsequent Greek and Roman philosophers and poets. This idea was that over a huge time-span there had been a succession of different 'ages of men', and that each age was worse than the previous. Using a metaphor from metallurgy (which has some correspondence in archaeology), the first age was the famous 'golden' one in which men lived simple, peaceful, technologically uncomplicated, moral lives. This race of men disappeared, however, to be succeeded by the age of silver, where men were warlike, quarrelsome, and wicked – 'in no way like the first, in body or mind'.[16] This age was succeeded, in turn, by the age of bronze, in which the obsession with war grew to such a pitch that the race destroyed itself. In Hesiod, this age of bronze is followed by a race of military 'heroes' who, although warlike, were morally superior because of their uprightness and bravery. (This fourth age, 'metallurgically' unspecified, seems to interrupt the overall tale of decline – in Hesiod, it corresponds to the time and people of the Trojan war, and may thus be his way of paying tribute to a widely revered 'national myth' – indeed, those 'heroes' not killed in battle were awarded eternal life on the Isles of the Blest). The fifth, and final, age is the age of iron – their present age in which men's lives were full of oppression, labour, injustice, and other evils.

Thus the myth of 'the golden age', which people would look back to and, thinking cyclically, hoped would reappear following the destruction their own 'iron' age was inevitably headed for. Although not rationally explicated in Hesiod's *Works and Days* (and earlier mythologies), the idea of a Golden Age succeeded by progressive decline echoed on as a strain in the classical mind-set regarding the overall course of the history of mankind, alongside and perhaps contrary to the belief in 'growth'. But we should not look for too much consistency. To the extent that the myth of 'the ages of men' derived from, or was combined with, the notion of cyclical change, there is room in it for a return to 'the Golden Age'. Likewise, where the notion of cyclical change was associated with the biological analogy of 'growth', not only does that analogy decree decay – it also decrees a rebirth from new 'seeds'. In short, we have a set of notions flexible enough to engender apparent or even real inconsistencies, and one needs to see which notions were chosen, and how they were used, in any particular case. The myth of 'the ages of men' was usually interpreted pessimistically as signalling man's inevitable decline from a pristine happiness, simplicity, and morality. Yet, for example, one present-day commentator, Nisbet, abandoned this standard interpretation of the myth, claiming to find in Hesiod's famous version much that optimistically speaks of the *progress* of mankind (that is, without resorting to belief in a cyclical return to the 'golden' age).[17] *The principle of growth* (the biological analogy), on the other hand, was often used optimistically to praise the achievements of mankind and laud the present. Its darker implications – the inevitability of decay following the zenith of maturity – were underplayed. And even so, the analogy could be extended to include the notion of rebirth and reinvigoration from new 'seeds'. As for the third component of this set of notions, the notion of *historical cycles* – it could be used in conjunction with the biological analogy to give meaning and purpose to human history. On the other hand in classical times there were those who saw historical change as ultimately meaning*less* precisely because they saw history as one unfolding, endlessly repetitive cycle.

Political cycles

The other strain of thought which utilised the 'decay' dimension of historical change is that found in notions of *constitutional* change. Here the focus narrows from ideas about the course of humankind's overall history to the more immediate historical consideration of changes in forms of government in the recent experience of Greek and Italian city-states. As will be apparent, the notion of cyclical repetition played a strong part in classical *political* thought. So also did the idea of decay, although how far the common-place cyclical notion of constitutional change was associated with the *biological* analogy of growth, decay, and rebirth is more difficult to judge. It could be argued that the dynamics of political change in the 'standard' account were so based on common-sense and observation (157 constitutions, in Aristotle's case) as not to require resort, either deliberate or unwitting, to any analogy taken from another area of study.

Although the way in which political change was often understood has been the object of close scrutiny by political theorists and historians of political thought, whose detailed explorations engender different versions and diverse interpretations, it is sufficient here to abstract its general outlines. Pre-figured in Plato and given a more elaborate treatment in Aristotle's *Politics*, (and appealed to in one form or another by philosophers and political thinkers until beyond the sixteenth century AD) the 'standard' account suggested an inevitable cycle of constitutional change. The dynamic principally responsible for this was the notion of degeneration from an initally sound 'starting point', leading to a change of constitution. 'Starting' at monarchy, this initially healthy form of rule by a king who cares for the common good and judiciously balances the contesting ambitions of different groupings, begins to degenerate as the king becomes corrupted by power or greed, or if his successor lacks the skills, morality, and foresight to manage the complexities of statecraft. A point is reached where the better-off, responsible, influential, and well-born minority of the citizens take control of the city-state, thereby instituting an aristocracy. Initially a healthy form of rule, aristocracy itself begins to degenerate as jealousy and ambition within its ranks cause rival factions manoeuvring for power. The needs of the bulk of the citizens become ignored as corruption grows and public order and safety is diminished. As the aristocracy degenerates (into what Aristotle called 'oligarchy'), a point is reached where the general body of disillusioned, public-spirited citizens throw off the rule of the now selfish minority and themselves take power, thereby instituting a 'democracy' (or 'polity').

But the same principle of 'decay' inexorably begins to operate. What begins as the sensible government of the city-state, where wealth and property are respected and justice is strictly observed, degenerates through envy, ignorance, and selfishness into such disorder that government collapses. 'Anarchy' or mob-rule takes over, threatening the very existence of the city-state by subverting people's confidence in law and order and inviting foreign aggression. Out of such dangerous chaos emerges a ruthless dictator or tyrant who rescues the city-state by imposing despotic order, careless of the citizens' rights to life and property. The populace submit to tyranny, however – some willingly, given the alternative; others because they have no choice. Order is restored, but at a terrible price. As affairs settle down, however, the tyranny moderates ('deteriorates'?). It no longer needs to govern so draconically. It becomes to its advantage to cull the favour and cooperation of its subjects. A point is reached where tyranny either reforms itself into monarchy, or is succeeded by a monarch rather than a tyrant, or may even be overthrown in a revolution, to be replaced by a monarch. Whichever way this stage is achieved – (and the reader will see the manifold possibilities in actual history as to the rich variety of mechanics for *all* of these constitutional changes) – the circle is now complete. We are back at our 'starting-point' of monarchy, and the whole cycle begins again.

Apart from the fascination such a 'theory' might have had for political theorists and the tantalizing possibilities it offered for historians in their accounts of real events, what concerns us here is the common dynamic underlying this notion of constitutional change – the theme of decay or degeneration (or if 'degeneration' is over-suggestive of the biological analogy, 'deterioration') from an initially healthy 'starting-point'. I say 'starting-point' because the emphasis is clearly on the process of subsequent *decline* rather than on any process of *growth towards* a healthy form of state. An example of where attention *was* paid to the latter idea is Polybius' account of the 'growth' or development of Rome to its political pre-eminence. But here the 'standard' account is precisely set aside, for he argued that Rome was exceptionally well-favoured in its political stability because its institutions had 'grown' into a constitution remarkable for being a *mixture* of monarchy, aristocracy, and 'democracy'. In short, the Rome of the second century BC was exceptional amongst states *because* it was an exception in constitutional development. But this apart, the 'normal' or 'natural' course of political change was construed as a cycle driven by *deterioration* (even when things 'improve', as in the 'deterioration' of tyranny).

Unchanging 'human nature'

If we look further into this dynamic of deterioration we find another notion common to the classical 'understanding' of historical processes – namely, that human nature never changes. It is *because* it never changes that the political cycle turns inexorably. Although (apart from the beliefs of some Stoics) this does not mean a repetition of the same actual events, it does mean that in similar situations people, both individually and *en masse*, will act in the same way, thereby producing similar outcomes. Quite how this unchanging 'human nature' was construed is difficult, if not pointless, to specify but easy enough to imagine. As Aristotle insisted, men are neither gods nor beasts – we can take him to mean they are neither perfect in their virtues nor bestial in their vices. They have the light of intelligence and the balm of morality, but can be deceived by ignorance and appearances and corrupted by selfishness. Amongst their 'natural' attributes are love of family and fatherland, but also a self-love which invites greed, envy, and a capacity for violence. The natural urge for justice can be overwhelmed by the desire for vengeance. Although nature produces some individuals of unblemished character, given enough pressure most of humankind will put their own interests first, blame others for their own shortcomings, and en masse will seek scapegoats and be fickle in their political loyalties. Thinking as much of the history of the Roman Republic as of his own times, we shall find Machiavelli (in the sixteenth century AD) exploiting the notion of an unchanging human nature in the construction of his lessons of statecraft, and the picture he paints of it is famously cynical – or realistic – depending on one's point of view. But he was elaborating upon notions apparent amongst Greek and Roman writers, including many historians – namely, that we have to be realistic about human nature; that it never changes; that acquaintance with it helps to understand history; and that political lessons can be learnt from it.

That the notion that human nature is always the same is contradicted by the myth of 'the ages of men', in which it precisely is said to have changed from a race of 'golden' men, should not surprise us. We have outlined a number of different notions underlying attitudes towards the past and the course of human events (both long-term and more immediate) in the classical world. As broad presuppositions and/or tendencies of thought, it would be wrong to expect the kind of overall consistency found in later explicit attempts to construct a 'philosophy of history'. An exception to this could be the aforesaid Polybius. Many of the notions singled out in this chapter are interwoven into his Histories, particularly Book VI, making for instructive reading. Yet he wrote as an historian, not as a philosopher in the 'technical' sense of the term, and his employment of these various notions – for example, 'fortune', cycles, the biological analogy, and constitutional change – is eclectic rather than logically consistent, as so ably demonstrated by Trompf in the opening two chapters of The Idea of Historical Recurrence in Western Thought. Yet perhaps as much because of this eclecticism as despite it, Polybius' Histories is a valuable second century BC source for the mix of presuppositions and more explicit notions which coloured Greek and Roman attitudes towards the past and their understanding of the course of history. These continued after Polybius (doubtless partly because of him), variously reflected in poetry, philosophy, political thought, mythology, and the writings of classical historians.

Comments

Conflicting views on the idea of 'progress' in the Classical world

Given it was not until around the seventeenth century AD (with the possible exception of Augustine, discussed in the next chapter) that explicit 'speculative philosophies of history' emerged, which deliberately attempt to find an overall intelligible pattern – even 'purpose' or meaning – in history, what do we make of the less systematic yet suggestive classical ideas treated above? Fate, Fortune, cycles, repetition, decay, degeneration of mankind from a 'golden' age, the growth of culture and civilisation to its 'natural' zenith, an unchanging human nature, hopes for a new 'golden age', an ordained moral order – the reader may be forgiven for thinking this a mixed, even contradictory, bag. Is it right to conceive of the possibility of 'human nature' changing over the course of history (e.g., for either better or worse), or have human-beings always had basically the same nature, (and will they continue to) despite enormous changes in their circumstances? Is 'fate' or 'fortune' simply a device for expressing ignorance of causes and marking exceptional events, or does 'it' actually operate 'underneath' historical development, ultimately flouting all human attempts to fashion their own history? Again, does a fate-governed history render humankind's history meaningless, or reassure us that justice prevails, despite human failings? And perhaps most exasperating of all, should we conceive of history as progressive, as if humankind were like an individual growing from infancy, accumulating skills and learning from experience, all the while maturing towards a perfection of civilisation, knowledge, and culture? Or is human development caught in the grip of cyclical forces whereby, either through a necessity of decay (following the biological analogy) or through some 'flaw' in human nature which causes inevitable deterioration from healthy high-points, it is unrealistic to think in terms of unilinear progress?

It is this latter dichotomy which has particularly captured attention in modern scholarship. In 1920, J. B. Bury's *Idea of Progress* was published. Although not the first to make the claim, he insisted the classical world of the Greeks and Romans had no idea of 'progress'. Mesmerized by a world which was fundamentally unchanging because it was part of an endlessly wheeling cosmos, the classical mind submitted fatalistically to the ultimate pettiness of human affairs and aspirations. Many followed Bury in arguing that this world-view precluded any belief in the idea of human progress (understood as extending cumulatively in a linear direction). Indeed, this is one of the reasons given for the claim that speculative philosophy of history did not begin until the seventeenth century AD, since only then did the belief in human progress appear – the supposition being that a necessary condition for speculative philosophy of history is the holding of such a belief.

However, in 1980 R. A. Nisbet – who had already grappled with classical ideas in an earlier study of Western theories of social development[18] – directly confronted, and attempted to refute, this view of the classical mind in his *History of the Idea of Progress*. His method is to give numerous examples from classical literature where the notion of human progress *is* apparent, and to reinterpret writings which were in his view wrongly taken to deny its possibility. He does not deny the classical propensity for cyclical thinking, but even so:

> the point should not be lost that what eventually is to become decline and fall commences as genesis and progress . . . [and] whatever amount of

cyclical thought there may have been in classical antiquity, there was also a solid and fertile substance of belief in linear progress – from remote past to distant future.[19]

He reinforces this by making the following clarion-call for a revision of the view which alleges the absence of any idea of progress in the classical world-view:

> [t]he supposition, so widely repeated in even the best of modern and contemporary interpretations of Greek political thought, that time and change were regarded as enemies, that reality lay in the permanent and unchanging, and that everything must be seen as dictated by Fate – that supposition should be laid to rest forever.[20]

Some few years earlier, however, S. L. Jaki had reached the opposite conclusion in chapter 6 of his *Science and Creation* (1974). Concerned primarily with the history of *scientific* thought, Jaki is also deeply interested in the notion of human progress. Indeed, we might say it is the latter which is his ultimate concern, and that his interest in the history of science stems from his belief that scientific inquiry and progress is the key to human progress in general. His method is similar to Nisbet's insofar as he finds numerous examples from classical writings to demonstrate, in this case, the *lack* of the possibility of any worthwhile idea of human progress. Particularly critical of what he takes to be the dominant strain in classical thinking – the belief in cyclic recurrences – and especially of Aristotle's application of 'the biological cycle' to *physical* processes, which he claims held back progress in scientific thought, Jaki lays much of the blame for the lack of any commitment to human progress in classical thought to a mind-set oppressed by

> the inhibitory impact of the belief in cyclic recurrences. The treadmill of perennial returns not only generates pessimism by its spectre of the inevitable decay of man's achievements but it also invites the setting of a complacently low ceiling on attainable goals.[21]

Again, 'preoccupation with the idea of universal cyclic recurrences leads naturally to the weakening of a concept of time which gives to each human action a unique character and unequivocal meaning. More concretely, the meaning of historical succession and what is based on it, the concept of progress, would in such a framework lose their significance and, more specifically, their inspirational value'.[22] Such a preoccupation 'hardly encouraged conviction in the rationality of nature, nor did it enhance man's readiness to dominate nature. It did not generate intellectual curiosity or appreciation of experiments aimed at controlling nature. In particular, the belief in eternal cycles imposed on thinking a concept of time which could only be cyclic, therefore fundamentally repetitive and ultimately meaningless'.[23]

'Progress' and philosophy of history: special pleading?

The contrast between these two positions could not be clearer. Both are argued passionately and with impressive erudition. Yet it is what the two *agree* on which should particularly interest us. Despite their disagreement on classical thought both authors are intimating that the very idea of (and hence belief in) human progress must be grounded on a uni-directional rather than cyclical history; more, that the project of *philosophy* of history must be grounded on the notion of linearity and progress; and finally, that without such presuppositions history has no *meaning*, and (speculative) philosophy of history is impossible. In short, the disagreement highlights an alleged symbiosis between belief in human progress and the very rationale of speculative philosophy of history. And this may help account for what appears to be an alarming conflict of views. When we look at each book as a whole we find the above intimations brought out as, in fact, strongly held convictions. In Jaki's case (indeed, as his concluding words) he wants to insist on the Christian truth of 'the Creator and . . . a creation once-and-for-all . . . – a firm faith in the only lasting source of rationality and confidence, the Maker of heaven and earth, of all things visible and invisible'.[24]

Nisbet advances what appears to be a similarly religiously inspired viewpoint, for after complaining his contemporary Western culture has lost all sense of its historical identity and continuity, and its sense of religion – where '[t]he present becomes a scene composed of the absurd, the irrelevant, the demonic', and where 'the result of ceasing to believe in God is not that one will then believe nothing; it is that one will believe anything'[25] – he concludes his book by claiming that in such an atmosphere belief in the idea of progress 'is bound to remain moribund. . . . Only, it seems evident from the historical record, in the context of a true culture in which the core is a deep and wide sense of the *sacred* are we likely to regain the vital conditions of progress itself and of faith in progress – past, present, and future'.[26]

In short, both authors are engaged in special pleading, and where this happens distortions, exaggerations, forced interpretations, and partial selections of examples, are common dangers. This does not mean these books should be dismissed – on the contrary, they contribute greatly to our knowledge, and we are grateful to revisit them in the following chapters. But it does mean we should take into account the special pleading underlying their construction. Thus, to revert to the marked disagreement between Jaki and Nisbet on the classical world-view, it may be safe to assume that each side has exaggerated its case, and has selected examples less than impartially. The latter is all the more easy to do, of course, when dealing with a period in history so long (even if we limit it to *c.* 500 BC–*c.* AD 100) and so rich in diverse schools of thought. I suggest we should rest content with that mixed, even contradictory bag, summarised above as a more likely account of classical speculations on history.

4

THE CHRISTIAN CHALLENGE TO GRAECO-ROMAN HISTORICAL PERSPECTIVES

Introduction

After a period of turbulence which culminated tellingly in Julius Caesar's career, the Roman Republic (already with a considerable empire) gave way during the reign of Octavian (declared 'Augustus' in 27 BC) to the ensuing Principate, or system of Imperial rule. Under a long succession of Emperors, some as famous as others were infamous, the Roman Empire was extended and consolidated. Its power was unrivalled, its greatness unchallenged, its stability apparently ensured. In AD 330 the Emperor Constantine moved its capital to Byzantium (renamed Constantinople, and since 1930, Istanbul), facilitating the formalisation (by the 400s) of the Western and Eastern Empires. 'Rome' spanned the 'civilised' world, and where it also included 'uncivilized' regions, attempted to restrain, if not encompass, them. Yet by 476 the Western Roman Empire had collapsed, its last Emperor, Romulus Augustus, being deposed by the Goths. Although the Eastern (Byzantine) Empire survived until the Ottoman Turks sacked Constantinople in 1453, 'Rome' – 'the eternal city' – increasingly became a memory, oft despised in the Christian West, until many of its culture's ideals were revived in what we call 'the Renaissance'.

Roman historical ideas

The 'Four World-Monarchies' myth

Because of the constitutional stability and, until near its demise, the domination of the Roman Empire, that earlier Hellenic and subsequent Graeco-Roman (or Hellenistic) fascination in the constitutional changes city-states undergo increasingly lost its relevance. Correspondingly, although not abandoned, the underlying assumption of history as an endlessly repeating cycle underwent a shift in focus. Now entrenched in a system of hereditary Imperial rule, pagan thinkers turned their attention away from theories of constitutional change within the complex histories of individual city-states. Instead, they reflected on the larger (thus potentially more speculative) theme of the rise and fall of entire states and, indeed, empires. And it is clear that, partly influenced by the importation of Middle Eastern ideas (in particular, probably the Book of Daniel's prophecies), one of their approaches to this theme centred on a belief that world history consisted of the succession of four world-monarchies, or great empires – with a possible fifth, eternal, empire to come. Open to diverse interpretation, writers in Imperial times used this broad formulation variously. But their common concern was to assess the status of the Roman Empire itself. In some versions Rome was the fourth world-monarchy, succeeding the earlier empires of Babylon (or Assyria), Persia, and Greece (or Macedonia), each of which had inevitably declined and succumbed to the next. For some, as the fourth empire, Rome was the last, and would thus persist eternally. Others believed it would go the way of the previous empires, to be succeeded by a different, fifth, eternal empire. Yet others saw Rome *as* the *fifth* empire (succeeding the Assyrian, Median, Persian, and Macedonian Empires) and hence eternal – while at least one writer, Dionysius,[1] also marked Rome as the fifth world-monarchy, but still doomed to eventual oblivion.

Cycles

Irrespective of the various interpretations put upon the 'theory' of four or five successive world-monarchies, three features emerge relevant to our topic of the presuppositions informing how Roman history was made sense of in the culture of Imperial Rome. The first is that the doctrine of successive world-empires remains strongly suggestive of that *cyclical* thinking so prevalent in earlier Greek and Graeco-Roman approaches to history, except that now it was applied to the rise and fall of great empires rather than constitutional change within separate city-states. Adopting the notion of the inevitable eventual collapse of empires, a variety of explanations was offered, ranging from a Stoical 'superstition' centred on fate, or 'the Great Wheel of Fortune', which ensured the impermanence of all things as they were subject to necessary dissolution and subsequent eternal recurrence, (sometimes linked to the belief in *cosmological* cycles), to more rational or secular explanations couched in political and/or moral terms. Thus, for example, the eventual fall of empires was construed as 'necessary' because of their natural propensity to expand beyond manageable size – or relatedly, the emergence of political divisions so severe as to lead to radical disunity – or the increasing arrogance and aggression of overwhelming power, leading to risky ventures and the breeding of both foreign and domestic hostility. The moral undertones of this latter 'mechanism' were even more explicit in those who identified the growth of *luxury* as sounding the death-knell, since it engendered *moral degeneration* into idleness, vanity, and jealousy, (a theme echoing down the centuries and, for example, one that informed Rousseau's pessimism regarding Enlightenment 'civilisation' in his *Discourse on the Arts and Sciences*). Not surprisingly, some who saw the fall of empires as resulting from *moral* decline linked this to those earlier, comforting notions about the retributive nature of Fate whereby, ultimately, Divine justice rules the world.

A further version of the 'degeneration of morality' mechanism of inevitable fall of empire was proffered – particularly after Constantine converted to Christianity in AD 413, ending the persecution of Christians and giving them official State recognition. This version claimed that the departure from the Empire's religion – the abandonment of its gods – signalled its inevitable collapse, (not a uniquely Roman theory!).

Using, and sometimes combining, these arguments, (pagan) Roman historians, philosophers, and statesmen gave substance to the 'theory' of the 'four world-monarchies' by drawing parallels between Rome itself (their real interest) and earlier empires (about which, apart from the Greek, they had little information). But as noted earlier, not all were pessimistic about Rome itself. Some excepted Rome from a decline similar to previous empires without abandoning the overall 'theory' about their otherwise inevitable collapse. Variously, 'Rome eternal' was exempted because of its culture's particular virtues, or the exceptional qualities of its statesmen, or the ingenuity of its constitutional arrangements (even under the Emperors) – or because it was construed, in straightforward wishful thinking, as that fifth world-monarchy prophesied to be eternal. Leaving this last notion aside for the moment, we may now turn to the second feature of this underlying view of history.

The demise of Empire

If the first was the persistence of 'cyclical' thinking, the second is the effort to find large 'laws' of historical development. Speculative as such efforts had been earlier, people now living from around the 300s AD had much more concrete historical information about the Roman Empire gleaned over numerous generations – and some, as we have seen, inspired (or fooled) by the myth of the 'four world-monarchies', embarked on an embryonic 'comparative' history to make sense of their history and prospects for the future. The question for them was, would the Roman Empire go the way of all the others? It is true that in their search for common causes underlying the fate of great empires those employing the 'four monarchies' myth did not engage in sophisticated theorising about the mechanisms driving historical development – for example, none of their explanations relate specifically to *economic* factors. Also, the belief in cosmological cycles sometimes played a part in their thinking. Yet rather than be anachronistic we should recognise that, apart from politics, what we know as the 'social sciences' (economics, economic history, sociology, developmental studies) were unavailable to them – and partly because of this the study of history itself was far more narrowly based than today's. What they did contribute to, despite their lack of investigatory tools, was the notion that large, long-term forces, 'factors', or 'laws' operate to cause the collapse of great empires – and they opened the debate as to whether these were invariable, (and thus that all future dominant empires would inevitably collapse), or whether there could be an exception (naturally, their *own* Empire!). Given the collapse of the Roman Empire itself, and the later fates of, for example, the Spanish,

British, and Soviet Empires, this is not an inconsiderable theme for contemplation, and it should come as no surprise that contemporary scholars muse over the fate of 'the *American* Empire'! Doubtless many in the Western world, similarly inspired by a combination of 'superstition' and common-sense analysis, harbour the supposition that 'sooner or later' the latter will 'in its turn' go into fatal decline, to be succeeded by a new, different 'world power'. Is this what Paul Kennedy, in his *The Rise and Fall of the Great Powers* (1988), is hinting at when, discussing China's potential to upset the world balance of powers, he concluded, 'It is only a matter of time'?[2]

'Rome Eternal'

Such considerations, however, bring us to the third feature of interest in the Roman employment of the 'four world-monarchies' schema – namely, the possibility of an alleged 'fifth' (or, metaphorically, 'perfect') Empire which would escape the recurrent forces of decline and last 'forever'. We have already noted, confusingly, that some Romans thinking in these terms identified Rome as the fourth Empire, and did not believe it would be superseded by a fifth – that it *was already* the 'fifth' in the sense that their Rome was, indeed, 'Rome eternal'. Other optimists, more in line with the letter of the myth, simply identified four great Empires *prior* to Rome, and held Rome to be the prophesied eternal fifth. (Here we encounter the familiar syndrome that where events are seen as fulfilling 'signs', Providence, or prophesy, *any* can be so 'interpreted' or manipulated – in other words, history can be 'recast' so that what the 'signs' portend actually occurs). Here, then, we find the notion of the possibility of an *end* to further large-scale historical development – in short (to coin a contemporary phrase), 'the end of history'. But we should note that those who used the four world-monarchies myth to support their belief in 'Rome eternal' did not base their hopes on much substantive theorising about the driving forces of historical change. Certain features already mentioned, such as the constitutional nature of Imperial rule or the special wisdom of Roman statesmen, were appealed to, but in this version of 'the end of history' superstition rather than reasoning prevailed. Nonetheless the belief in an eventual settled, perpetual world-order was not only subscribed to by others in Roman times (in particular, by Christians who looked forward to 'the millennium', of which more below), but also echoed down the ages, most famously in the (different) theories of history proposed by Hegel and Marx. In these latter cases, however, this was presented not as belief but as the product of complex reasoning about the forces governing historical change. And in our own times, partly prompted by the collapse of the Soviet Empire, the idea has resurfaced in Fukuyama's book, *The End of History and the Last Man*.[3]

Escape from cycles?

But let us return to our Romans to make an important observation about those 'pagans' who, on the basis of the four world-monarchies myth, believed in 'Rome eternal'. It would be misleading to call them 'millennialists'. They were pagans (thus their belief lacked the special religious significance it had for Christians). They did not place 'the end of history' in the future, (they thought they were living within it). They did not prescribe a period of a thousand years (unlike Hitler's rhetorical hopes for the Third Reich). And perhaps above all, their belief in 'Rome eternal' was not premised on a *developmental* account of world-history whereby the 'fifth' monarchy emerged from a long line of intelligible *unilinear* change, inevitably progressing towards and presaging a final world-order. To take just one version, Assyria did not *pave the way* for a markedly *different* empire, Media – and neither did the latter for Persia, nor Persia for Macedonia, nor Macedonia for Rome itself. Rather, each previous empire was simply subject to the same recurrent process of decay. In short, we should not be misled into thinking that those believing in 'Rome eternal' because of the four-monarchies myth had thereby abandoned the governing belief in history as endlessly repeating cycles. Rather, paradoxical as it might be, they simply exempted Rome.

It is true that logically this does mean abandoning the term 'endlessly', and to this extent we might doubt their logic. But more to the point is that their underlying conception of historical change remained cyclical – and we may perhaps accommodate this by suggesting that a 'theory' of history proposing the possibility of escape from cyclical change is premised precisely *on* cyclical recurrence as the model of historical change. It could be argued that the same paradox is met in Marx. 'All history is the history of class struggle', the opening words of *The Communist Manifesto*, preface an analysis of historical development which, although sophisticated, offers a recurring cycle of class struggles as the driving force of history. Yet Marx predicts a *future* in which the cycle is escaped from. It might thus be difficult to present Marx's history as one, unilinear, continually developing story, culminating in a 'millennium' which history prepared for itself. But we must look again at Marx later. For the moment the point should stand – the notion of escape from repeating historical cycles does not necessarily imply abandoning the supposition of history as recurring cycles – and it certainly does not imply the necessary substitution of the latter by a 'unilinear' theory of historical change, just as it did not for those Romans who, influenced by the four-monarchies myth, believed in 'Rome eternal'.

The 'body–state' analogy

If, in their concern to analyse the prospects of the order under which they lived, some (pagan) 'Romans' (including Greeks, North Africans, Near and Middle Easterners) were influenced by prophetic or mythical suppositions, others thought about the Empire's history, its present dispensation, and its future in terms of what Trompf calls the 'body-state' analogy. As he observes,[4] this way of looking at history was probably an adaptation of that earlier Greek biological principle of genesis, growth, maturity, and decay previously discussed. In Roman hands this was expressed in less sophisticated, more 'practical' terms specifically related to *human* development – namely, from birth, through adolescence, to maturity and old age, and Romans applied the analogy to the rise and decline of states and empires, with results corresponding to their different perceptions and hopes. For example, after identifying Rome's infancy with Romulus, and discussing her boyhood and adolescence as she gained strength and territory, Seneca (in the first century AD) identified the civil strife involved in the pre-Imperial expansion of Julius Caesar's times as Rome's 'first old age',[5] after which, Imperial times came unflatteringly as a senile reversion to second childhood. Later, less pessimistically, Florus employed the analogy to suggest that Rome under Augustus had reached her proper manhood, and that although this was succeeded by old age, the invigorating Emperor Trajan revitalised her back to her prime rather than allowing her to complete the normal process of lapsing into a senility otherwise only relieved by eventual death. Whether Florus advanced this charming apologetic solely to flatter his own Emperor, Hadrian (Trajan's successor), or whether he was seriously subscribing in his own way to the notion of 'Rome eternal', may be difficult to judge. But he was clearly not alone in exploiting the 'body–state' analogy not only to make sense of Roman history through putting it into the perspective of the different stages of growth of the typical (male!) individual – involving notions such as wilfulness, extravagance, recklessness, and caution, judgement, and maturity – but also to suggest that Rome would not die. Trompf tells of the pagan Ammianus, who (writing in the second half of the fourth century 'under an empire fast becoming Christian') identified his own time as that in which Rome, having spent her adulthood in Imperial expansion, had now settled down to a more peaceful 'old age'. Although marked by 'a certain declining and slackness',[6] this was compensated for by a 'stability and venerableness' ensuring its Empire was 'destined to live so long as men shall exist'.[7]

How far such uses of the 'body–state' analogy were meant *literally* is perhaps impossible to judge. Clearly it was less credible in those cases where, as in 'Rome eternal', death was averted, but even here it was exploited as an 'explanation' by ingenious notions such as a second childhood or late reinvigoration. But what is equally clear is that many used the analogy as a convenient way of 'making sense' of Rome's long, varied history. It made it possible to identify distinct *phases* in it; to *simplify* it through the historian's necessarily selective treatment of events; to allow the making of moral judgements; to make change *intelligible* without reference to any special 'laws' of social, economic, or historical 'science' (unavailable to them); to permit both *assessment* of the present and *predictions* for the future; and even to extract some kind of *meaning* in the overall flow of history in the sense that, in relating to the familiar experience of the human life-cycle, people could recognise its 'naturalness'. In facilitating all this we might say that, in the abstract, the 'body–state' analogy furnishes an ideal organising principle for any historian! And if we add that it neither excluded a narrative approach, nor that venerable Graeco-Roman belief in fate and 'cycles', and even its interweaving with cosmological movements, we might answer our query whether Roman historians took the analogy literally by appealing to Dr Johnson's observation that, in the affairs of men, it is remarkable how 'interest smooths the path to faith'.

If, then, it was not taken literally it was taken seriously, and there may be nothing strange in that. How often, today, we encounter the politics and histories of states discussed seriously in anthropomorphic terms! New states are 'born', others are 'young' (with corresponding energy yet inexperience), some are described as 'mature' (as in 'a mature democracy'), whilst others are reckoned to be 'on their last legs' (the 'moribund' USSR of the 1980s). Again, for example, we talk of China as the 'sleeping giant', of certain countries being 'quarrelsome', 'ambitious', 'bullying', or 'evil', and of governments 'feeling' threatened, tired, or slighted, 'approving' this, 'disliking' that – and, of course, of electorates (or even 'peoples') 'choosing' this and being 'fickle' about that. On reflection we might recognise our lapse into analogical language, but still insist it should be taken 'seriously' – (after all, didn't the electorate 'desire' a change of government?). Does this tell us that we ourselves have suppositions underlying the way we make sense of history not so different (albeit less formalised) from the Romans' appeal to the 'body-state' analogy?

Other presuppositions

Other presuppositions also informed the way Romans 'understood' their own Imperial history and wider 'world history'. Trompf reminds us that the notion of 'fortune' retained its grip, inviting that comforting idea of 'moral retribution', and also the idea of history as an eternally recurring sequence of similar events. These notions were a continuing legacy from some of those outlined in the previous chapter, just as was the effort to *periodise* history. Yet if ancient versions of periodisation centred on poetic notions about the different 'Ages of Man', some Romans adopted the notion more historically and conceived of history as being divided into 'Ages' or recurrent 'periods of time', which some (for example, Seneca[8]) reckoned in terms of five human generations (and from which our rather meaningless but convenient unit of 'a century' was derived). Linked to the idea of successive 'ages' was the notion that as an 'age' came to its end, signs such as disease, famine, and other natural catastrophes signalled its demise and the dawning of a new one – a notion still subscribed to both by religious and secular 'doom merchants' in our own day who talk of 'troubled times'. Additionally, especially in the latter days of the Western Roman Empire, cosmological 'theories' regained currency within such thinking, possibly as a reaffirmation of fundamental 'Roman' beliefs against the growing challenge posed by an alternative ideology – namely, Christianity.

Graeco-Roman historical ideology summarised

Difficult as it might be to generalise and summarise 'the Roman' way of looking at 'history' (and related topics such as politics, morality, and philosophy), it seems many of their presuppositions and more explicit ideas were inherited from that earlier Hellenic/Hellenistic culture discussed in Chapter 3. Equally, we saw how in its turn that was partly a legacy, albeit dramatically recast, of even earlier primitive 'mythopoeic' intuitions. Just so, as Romans developed their own culture, rather than cast off Hellenistic ideas, they modified them to suit their practical needs and intellectual preoccupations. We might almost put this as a general rule underlying the history of *all* large-scale 'cultural' mind-sets – that they *evolve* from earlier (not necessarily less sophisticated) cultures, rather than start from a clean sheet. This, after all, is no more than an example of perhaps the one lesson all can agree history teaches – namely, the paradox that although there would be no history at all if nothing 'new' happened, history also tells us there is 'nothing new under the sun'.

Thus it is that many scholars still characterise Roman fundamental intuitions as 'Graeco-Roman', although noting various amendments and additions the more practically preoccupied Romans brought to their Greek heritage. Of special relevance to us is the claim that the 'Graeco-Roman' mind saw the passing of time as essentially cyclical or circular. Because of this fundamental idea (derived from belief in the determining astronomical forces of the great wheel of the cosmos and/or from the universality of the biological life-cycle of birth, growth, zenith, and decay), it is argued that the Romans saw themselves as in the grip of the natural, inevitable cycle of endless historical recurrence. Such a fundamental presupposition, strongly implying an ultimately directionless history, engendered at base a resigned fatalism, whatever the temporary excitements and achievements within a particular time-span. If the history of any state or empire is ultimately part of, or an example of, an overall world-history predestined to repeat itself in circular patterns, history (or human endeavour) is essentially meaningless. Great city-states, empires, and cultures might be founded, but ultimately to no avail since fate (whose sister 'fortune' might endow certain events with moral meaning) unmovingly decreed their decline and replacement by another state similarly doomed. We have seen how it was only by special pleading, or possibly in bad faith, that some Romans tried to exempt their own order from that fate. Hence it is that, if the aesthete and philosopher typify the 'Greek' view of the world, perhaps above all the *Stoic* remains the abiding image of 'the Roman view of the world' – a figure resigned to the dictates of Nature and Fate, determined so far as it is in him to live a life 'according to reason' whereby trivial pursuits and the temptations of desire are relinquished in the interests of a disciplined serenity gained through contemplation of his place in the greater scheme of things – a scheme in which time, governed by a remorseless, repetitive Fate, is endless.

The Judaeo-Christian alternative

Jewish apocalyptic ideas

The previous chapter already encountered the view, and its counter-arguments, that this Graeco-Roman perspective precluded any idea of *progress* in history. Yet this is only one aspect of a broader claim made about Roman presuppositions regarding time and history – namely, that they were fundamentally different from an alternative set of ideas uniquely characteristic of the Judaeo-Christian tradition. What, allegedly, was so different about the latter's assumptions?

Perhaps unsurprisingly, at the heart of this is the *religious* difference between Judaeo-Christian *monotheism* and paganism. From the earliest books of the Old Testament it seems the nomadic Israelites rejected that 'mythopoeic' view of nature which characterised dominant surrounding cultures. Instead they believed nature, the world, and the cosmos were subject to one *single* and *transcendent god*, Yahweh. Far from deifying nature by peopling it with gods, the only deity was the single Lord of all, construed as a 'Person' governing everything with ineffable power. (It was not until considerably later, according to Jaki around the time of Solomon in the tenth century BC, that this God was also called 'the Creator', as having created everything *ex nihilo*). For the Israelites, this Person demonstrated his purpose through his mediation with Abraham, whereby he would lead them to enduring multiplicity and blessings in the world he had made, so long as they held fast to their recognition of, and willing obedience to, him. The tribulations of 'the Chosen People' are told within the Old Testament, and as early as the eighth century BC apocalyptic prophecies featured in Jewish culture, whereby 'out of an immense cosmic catastrophe' involving a retributive period of 'famine and pestilence, war and captivity' a Day of Judgement would occur, casting down renegade Jews and heathen nations. Then the vengeful Yahweh would 'become the Deliverer. The righteous remnant . . .will be assembled once more in Palestine' in which Yahweh 'will reign from a rebuilt Jerusalem, a Zion which has become the spiritual capital of . . . a harmonious and peaceful world' in which material prosperity and justice will ensure that all live 'in joy and gladness'.[9]

Similar prophecies arose in the period of the Maccabaean revolt by the Jews against persecution by the Syro-Greek Seleucids, when around 165 BC that same Book of Daniel, in which a version of the 'four world-monarchies' was propounded, prophesied Israel's overthrowing of the last (in this case, Greek) 'evil empire' and its replacement by the everlasting dominion of 'the Son of Man'. As Cohn observes, 'for the first time the glorious future kingdom is imagined as embracing not simply Palestine but the whole world'.[10] When Pompey annexed Palestine in 63 BC the Jews fell under Roman rule and continued their struggle for independence until finally suppressed in AD 131. Apocalyptic propaganda (e.g., Ezra) played its role in their struggle and increasingly 'the Son of Man' (previously either a supernatural individual or Israel itself) was identified as the Messiah, 'incontestably a man, a warrior-king endowed with unique, miraculous powers' who 'will rout and destroy the armies of the enemy; he will take captive the leader of the Romans' and 'put him to death; he will establish a kingdom which shall last until the end of the world . . . an age of bliss . . . in which pain, disease, untimely death, violence and strife, want and hunger will be unknown and in which the earth will yield its fruits ten-thousandfold'.[11]

Early Christianity

In the meantime, Christianity had begun its spread into the Roman Empire, and it is not surprising the early, persecuted Christians' beliefs were influenced by Jewish apocalyptic ideas. Sayings attributed to Jesus of Nazareth could be, and were, interpreted according to the tradition from which he emerged. For many Christians up to the fifth century, Christ 'the Messiah' would make a triumphant Second Coming, in which, according to a popular interpretation of the Book of Revelation (written around AD 90), the Roman state ('the beast') and its priesthood 'were cast alive into a lake of fire burning with brimstone' . . . and 'the souls of them that were beheaded for the witness of Jesus . . . and who had not worshipped the beast . . . lived and reigned with Christ a thousand years'. After this, the Millennium, would come the Last Judgement when, apart from those cast out forever, the dead would be resurrected and the New Jerusalem would descend from heaven to become the new, eternal habitude of mankind in which 'God shall wipe away all tears . . . and there shall be no more death, neither sorrow, nor crying, neither shall there be any more pain . . .'.[12] Later versions of this apocalyptic outlook came, for example, from Montanus (who in AD 156 inspired a movement which spread throughout the Empire), Irenaeus towards the end of the second century, Tertullian in the third century, Lactantius in the fourth, and Commodianus in the fifth.[13]

Such apocalyptic religious beliefs and movements, Judaeo-Christian or otherwise inspired, have continued to resurface ever since, of course – but our present topic is not eschatology, millennialism, or apocalyptics as such, but the specifically Christian part of the Judaeo-Christian culture as it relates to presuppositions about the course and meaning of history. And there is a sense in which the early Church Fathers themselves can be understood as voicing the same distinction, for as the Church became more established under the Empire from the third century onwards, they were increasingly critical of the weight their uneducated followers put on apocalyptic ideas in their Christian faith.

First, as Christians became more integrated into Roman civic life, that obvious propaganda value of apocalyptic ideas for an oppressed people not only became increasingly irrelevant, but politically damaging. Second, although early Christians often saw themselves as an (oppressed) *national* people, Jesus' message was that of salvation for all mankind, irrespective of race, language, nationhood, or (current) religion. (Nisbet claims it was not until around AD 200 that the idea of 'humankind' as one genuine unity, with an historical past and potential for future actualisation, was actively propagated by Christian thinkers now eager to reach even beyond the Roman Empire – he further claims that 'this conception is peculiar to Western civilisation').[14] Third, many Christian leaders (including Origen, third century AD and culminating in Augustine) worried that to historicise (however fantastically) the notion of salvation by linking it to some forthcoming age in which new orders of justice, peace, virtue, and material prosperity would emerge was dangerously to miss the point of Christianity.

Augustine (354–430)

These ideas, and many others, were assembled in Augustine's ingeniously ambiguous masterwork, *The City of God*. Rome was sacked in AD 410, and this was taken as proof of the likelihood of the collapse of Rome and its empire. Pagan Romans blamed the establishment of Christianity in the Empire for its parlous state, and Augustine initially conceived his book as a defence against this accusation, carrying this out in its earlier parts by trying to show the Empire's ills as the fault of pagan Romans' misgovernment and factiousness. However, partly prompted by dissatisfaction with fellow Christians who also tried to defend Christianity's role in the Empire, but did so by claiming it had bestowed blessings on Rome, and even hinted at the order of Pax Romana turning into a (historically real) new era of universal Christian order, Augustine then turned to tackle the vexed question of the relationship between Christian doctrine and actual life as lived out in history. People have argued about what he meant ever since (as we shall see), but it is doubtless fair to say that the finished work 'moulded more than any other book by a Christian author the spirit of the Middle Ages. Its pages were as many wellsprings of information and inspiration for the emerging new world of Europe about the meaning of mankind's journey through time'.[15] Despite the diverse interpretations of Augustine's book, certain key points seem clear. First, with even more emphasis than previous Christian thinkers, he rejected the idea of cosmic and historical cycles endlessly recurring. Rather, he denied an eternity stretching either backwards or forwards in time. Instead he insisted on the monumental importance of the 'truth' that God *created* the world *in* time, and that the world was finite according to God's plan for mankind – in other words, that history is linear. Second, he stressed that the world God had knowingly created was *good* – that it was created for the benefit of all mankind. Third, he insisted that rationality and purpose therefore infused the whole of Creation, both in its physical and its temporal ordering, quoting from the Book of Wisdom, 'Thou hast ordered all things in number, and measure and weight'.[16] Fourth, (again in stark contrast to any last vestiges of a 'mythopoeic' outlook) he re-emphasised the utterly transcendent power of God, to whom all creation was subject. And fifth, premised on belief in the One God who created the universe and lovingly created mankind to unite in brotherhood and peace in willing fulfilment of His transcendent plan, he urged that the Christian message was essentially a *spiritual* message about the purity of the individual soul – that true happiness derived not so much from temporal circumstances as from an abiding belief centred on utter confidence in the beneficence of the Maker.

It is particularly this last point regarding the spiritual significance of Christianity and what it does or does not imply regarding actual, temporal life, which has been open to much interpretation ever since – a debate of signal relevance to our theme of 'making sense of history'.

The Graeco-Roman/Judaeo-Christian ideological divide

But before surveying the issue let us pause to identify from the previous passages the (alleged) seminal differences between the Graeco-Roman and Judaeo-Christian attitudes towards time and history. Numerous scholars[17] have argued that one of the most fundamental of them centres precisely on their attitudes to time. Whereas the Greeks and Romans had a cyclical approach to time and history, the Christians inherited from the Jews a *linear* approach. For the Greeks and Romans, time was infinite and circular, a closed system of eternal recurrences governed, ultimately, by inexorable cosmological laws. For the Jews and Christians, on the contrary, time has a beginning (with the Creation) and progresses in a straight line (as does history within it), through God's dealings with man, to an end. For the Greeks and Romans, then, history is endlessly repeatable, whilst for the Jews and Christians it is always unique. For the former, history is thus ultimately without purpose, and to that extent is meaningless. For the latter, on the contrary, history has a direction – it is the purposeful moving towards an end-fulfilment; in short, history is meaningful. For the former, an underlying fatalism colours their attitude towards history, since whatever temporary triumphs may distinguish a city or culture, nothing of unique, lasting, forward-looking significance can be achieved by men entrapped in the giant circle of cosmic existence – there can be nothing truly 'historical'. For the latter, on the contrary, an underlying hope pervades their attitude towards time and history. Bolstered by belief in the loving guidance of a transcendent, powerful, wise God to fulfil His purpose through His command of time and history, the forward, irreversible movement of mankind gives man an ultimate confidence in the future. Whatever disasters may occur, however arduous or puzzling the path may be, the history of both man and the cosmos is not to be dismissed as an infinitely wheeling cycle of unintelligible natural necessity, but to be affirmed in all its contingencies as the created, once-and-for-all gift of the supreme, rational Mind.

We appear to be confronted by a vast ideological divide between the two 'traditions, not only in religion, but derivately, in their respective assumptions about history – in short, by different 'philosophies of history'. Such, allegedly, is the magnitude of this latter divide alone that it is not surprising different scholars have either questioned its truth or speculated on its significance. In the latter case some extraordinary claims have been made not least about 'philosophy of history' itself. It is therefore salutary to look first at those who cast doubt on just how large a contrast in fact existed between the two traditions.

The dichotomy questioned

Perhaps the most exhaustive work on this theme, especially as it relates to ideas of time and history, is G. W. Trompf's *The Idea of Historical Recurrence in Western Thought*. Referring to the dichotomy in the two traditions he repeatedly warns that 'such a contrast should be eyed with caution'.[18] He tells us that 'the making of a sharp distinction between Christian linearity and classical cyclicism has undoubt-edly hindered rather than facilitated careful investigation' into the relation between Graeco-Roman and Christian assumptions about history, especially from the Church Fathers onwards into medieval times.[19] Not that Trompf thinks the famed dichotomy is entirely a fallacy:

> Admittedly, we have long been asked to believe that Christianity effected a decisive triumph for historical linearity over cyclical modes of thought, and certainly the Judaeo-Christian understanding of history excluded any doctrine of eternal recurrence, whether of worlds or inter-cataclysmic periods . . . . But that only tells one part of a complicated story.[20]

He then devotes much space to showing that 'Christians made no mean use of their Graeco-Roman heritage',[21] thereby reminding us the early Christians lived within a Graeco-Roman world. Trompf gives numerous instances, from as early as Luke's Gospel, where Christians employed distinctly Graeco-Roman notions in their presentation of history – particularly the ideas of historical recurrence and re-enactment (thereby showing they were not averse to approaching a cyclical interpretation of phases of human history so long as it was not taken to imply an *eternity* of *cosmological* cycles) – and various periodisations of history into different 'Ages of Man' (although where Christians appealed to this notion, as did Augustine, the 'ages' were presented as progressive, not circular). His researches into writings from Classical times through to the Renaissance and into the Reformation permit him to summarise that 'we have sought to undermine the well-known yet superannuated linear-cyclical dichotomy, and to explode the false opinion that recurrence views of history have been endemic to paganism but mortifying to monotheists'.[22] He reminds us that 'the persistence of Graeco-Roman themes was to be the inevitable result of Christianity's adaptation to a Gentile world'; that some of these 'are actually found in the Bible, the most sacred if misused tome of Western culture'; and in a well-judged aside complains that 'Interestingly, modern Christian scholars are still running away from the *falsi circuitus* of the classical philosophers without having any precise ideas as to the theories from which they flee'.

Regarding his central theme of *historical recurrence* (which he is careful to differentiate, where possible, from historical cycles *per se*) Trompf concludes that 'Jew and Christian have little to fear from ideas of historical (as against cosmological) recurrence, and that indeed they ought to acquaint themselves with these ideas if they intend to go on giving meaning to life',[23] for,

> in their capacity to interlock with such important (if apparently contradictory) ideas as progress, degeneration, fortune, necessity, and providence, they formed the tissue of a basic conception which lies close to the heartbeat of Western culture, and which goes back in its origins, with those ancient myths of eternal return, to the primal substructure of civilisation itself.[24]

Trompf cites other scholars who also challenge the linear-cyclical dichotomy[25] but, unsurprisingly, not Nisbet. For if Trompf's challenge stems from his argument that Christian thinkers did *not* so dramatically reject many Graeco-Roman ideas, including cyclical-type ideas of historical recurrence, we have already seen Nisbet arguing that Graeco-Roman thinkers were not dominated by such ideas in any event – that on the contrary they were perfectly comfortable with such *linear*-type ideas as growth, development, cultural transmission, and above all, progress. Thus Nisbet also challenges the dichotomy, but from the other side.

The dichotomy denied?

Going further than Trompf's reminder that Christians 'adapted' themselves to Graeco-Roman culture, Nisbet claims that, in addition to Judaism, 'the other source of Christianity is Greek'. He continues,

> The Jewish followers of and missionaries for Christ were obliged to learn Greek if they were to be able to communicate the Good News. And in learning the language they also learned ideas: such Greek ideas as natural growth, of change conceived of as the unfolding of potentiality into actuality, of fixed stages of the advancement of knowledge and mankind.[26]

Recalling his insistence that the notion that Greeks regarded everything as determined by Fate and had no idea of progress 'should be laid to rest forever',[27] it is no surprise that although Nisbet believes Christians built upon and *added to* Greek ideas of progress, he does not identify the notion of *linear* as opposed to cyclical ideas of history as an addition. Rather, he points to the *spiritual* dimension.[28] Although he sees the Christian notion of the millennium as referring to the hope of the eventual spiritual perfection of mankind (its ultimate meaning for Nisbet), he recognises that early (pre-Augustinian) Christians fused the idea of a *material* earthly paradise into their millennialist notions. Here, it seems for Nisbet, is the fundamental Christian contribution to civilisation.

> No other element of Christian thought has had as profound and far-reaching effect upon the entire world, not merely the West, as has its millennialist vision. We should be hard put to account for the social utopias of ... especially the Marxists ... were there not a long and powerful tradition of Christian millennialist utopianism which could be, in some degree, secularised, with its apocalyptic intensity left undiminished.[29]

Not, it seems, that Nisbet approves of such secularisation. Complaining (in 1980) of a debilitating lack of self-confidence, hope, and sense of direction in Western civilisation, he claims 'the reason for this ... is our lack of a true culture. And fundamental to this lack is the disappearance of the sacred'.[30] Thus it is, that in reply to his own question regarding the future of the idea of progress in the West, he responds: 'Any answer to that question requires answer to a prior question: what is the future of Judaeo-Christianity in the West?'[31]

Nisbet's overall view, then, is that belief in progress depends on a *unilinear* 'philosophy of history', and this in turn requires belief in 'the sacred'. As he puts it, 'there is no possibility whatever of dealing with "world history" in . . . unilinear fashion . . . apart from the use of an omnipresent, omnipotent Providence conceived as author and executor of a design within which all human cultures . . . fit smoothly',[32] and 'only . . . in the context of a true culture in which the core is a deep and wide sense of the *sacred* are we likely to regain the vital conditions of progress itself and of faith in progress – past, present, and future'.[33]

Here, then, are two writers who almost simultaneously challenged the view that a fundamental gulf separated the Graeco-Roman and Judaeo-Christian assumptions regarding time and history – namely, that the former had a cyclical, the latter a linear, view. Yet they approach the issue from opposite sides and draw correspondingly different implications regarding 'philosophy of history'. Nisbet approves of the linear approach, stresses the 'sacred', and believes both are essential for 'philosophy of history'. Trompf, on the other hand, believes the prerequisites for 'philosophy of history' do not depend on a linear approach – and that the linear approach was not, and need not be, so endemic to Christianity as modern scholars claim. Indeed, in a head-on collision with Nisbet's thesis, Trompf expresses some sympathy with those modern (Graeco-Roman orientated) political theorists who, equating Christian linear thinking with an *apocalyptic* belief in *spiritual* salvation which renders actual history unimportant, claim that Christian doctrine cannot truly accommodate real 'philosophy of history'. It seems Trompf would agree with them, were that equation accurate. Fortunately for Christians, however, Trompf argues such scholars are wrong about Christian thinking on history. Not only has it not always centred on apocalyptic theories, it has by no means even been exclusively *linear* in its assumptions. Hence his encouragement to them, as to anyone else, to stop fearing Graeco-Roman cyclical notions 'if they intend to go on giving meaning to life'.[34]

The dichotomy affirmed?

This has been quite a complex confrontation of views between two writers who otherwise *agree* that the well-known dichotomy between Graeco-Roman and Judaeo-Christian views on time and history is false. It has been worth outlining because of the dramatic implications each draws regarding its overall relevance to (speculative) philosophy of history. As for those scholars who *do* insist on the giant dichotomy, they often draw no less dramatic implications. For example, Bultmann proclaims:

the Jewish-Christian understanding of history . . . was dependent on eschatology. The Greeks did not raise the question of meaning in history and the ancient philosophers had not developed a philosophy of history. A philosophy of history grew up for the first time in Christian thinking, for Christians believed they knew the end of the world and of history.[35]

Another example takes us back to Jaki's *Science and Creation*. Although the focus of his extensive scholarship is on the 'philosophical' presuppositions shaping *scientific* thought, much of what he writes relates to philosophy of history. This is because Jaki sees the history of *progress* as substantially dependent on the emergence and (complex) development of scientific rationality. The suppositions underlying the latter thus intertwine with those involved in *historical* thought. This is nowhere more clear than in those numerous passages where Jaki insists upon a stark dichotomy between the Graeco-Roman (and previous cultures') cyclical view of time and history and the Judaeo-Christian linear view. Arguing that scientific thought was variously still-born, perverted, or delayed wherever the Christian rejection of cyclical assumptions was absent or ignored, he concludes, 'All great cultures that witnessed a stillbirth in science within their ambience have one major feature in common. They were all dominated by a pantheistic concept of the universe going through eternal cycles. By contrast, the only viable birth of science took place in a culture for which the world was a created, contingent entity'. And like others on this theme, Jaki draws lessons for the present and future.

Doubtless mindful that the vistas opened up by contemporary science are as astonishing as they are problematic – that they confront us with material, moral, and spiritual issues of genuinely historical proportions – he fears we may make the wrong choice 'between two ultimate alternatives: faith in the Creator and in a creation once-and-for-all, or surrender to the treadmill of eternal cycles'. Although unstated, we can assume that the latter belief is for Jaki both a cause of, and evidence for, a culture's lapse into moral indifference, loss of purpose, and ultimate hopelessness bred of fatalism and superstition. If, on the contrary, we are to stride forward to make a meaningful history in this age so dominated by science, 'The past and present of scientific history tell the very same lesson. It is the indispensability of a firm faith in the only lasting source of rationality and confidence, the Maker of heaven and earth, of all things visible and invisible'.[36] For those who may puzzle as to where the monotheistic *Islamic* faith figures in this theme, Jaki offers his own perspective, at least with respect to the times of Muhammad:

> the Koran did not provide the necessary mental encouragement and guidelines for a rational approach to the universe. The reason for this lies in the overly voluntaristic and moralistic tone of the Koran, and more particularly, in its emphasis on the will of the Creator . . . no conspicuous effort is made to tie the sovereign decisions of God to His nature, that is, to His rationality. In other words, the will of God [Allah] seems to be above any norm . . .[37]

Augustine, the philosopher of history?

Augustine's two 'cities'

Such, then, are some of the perspectives on what many urge as a fundamental innovation in the way time and history was understood – the alleged dichotomy between cyclical and linear 'theories' of history. Some have denied the dichotomy, although it has not stopped them drawing dramatic conclusions regarding the theme. As for those who insist on the dichotomy, some claim the Graeco-Romans were not interested in history because of their belief in cycles: others claim the Graeco-Romans *were* interested in history precisely *because* of their belief in cycles (that is, they hoped to learn lessons by charting them): others claim only *Christians* were interested in history, because of their belief in progress: whilst others, finally, claim Christians were *not* interested in history because their eschatology concerned an essentially *spiritual* state which rendered actual contingent historical circumstances ultimately irrelevant.

Thus the reader, whether monotheistic, Christian, or of no religion, may be forgiven for thinking this a confusing scenario. That it *is* so can partly be attributed to the legacy of St Augustine, about whose ideas in *The City of God* it has (somewhat dubiously) been said, 'With every reason, Western philosophy can be declared a series of footnotes'.[38] Because Augustine was 'the rhetorician, the epigrammatist, the polemicist, but not the patient, logical, systematic philosopher',[39] his ideas afford considerable scope for diverse interpretations. Additionally, not only is *The City of God* a long work serving a variety of purposes, it is only one of a large corpus of St Augustine's output. Again, within these writings it is more than likely he changed some ideas (e.g., his views on whether, and how, the *State* should deal with heretics – subsequently 'the subject of extended, and sometimes sharp, controversy').[40] But perhaps most of all, one of the central themes he addressed involves inherently ambiguous notions whose 'real' meaning may be impossible to reach scholarly agreement on – namely, his famous distinction beween 'the City of God' and 'the earthly City'.

Augustine employed these terms to highlight the difference between a life centred on involvement in our 'actual' circumstances as distinct from being centred on the spirituality of the individual's experience, whatever those circumstances. The former life is lived entirely within 'the earthly City', where aspirations for 'the good life' (wealth, pleasure, health) are defined by the managing of one's affairs in the busy surrounding world. The latter 'life', on the other hand, aspires to be lived in 'the City of God', where the value of one's being is measured not in terms of 'actual', earthly circumstances but in terms of the *spiritual* qualities of perfect love, justice, mercy, and faith. The truly 'good life' is, then, not determined by how the external world impinges on one and how one manages it to extract the desired life-experience. Rather, the good life is the maintenance of that 'spiritual' or psychological state of mind centred on an unqualified love of God and of one's neighbours, irrespective of the 'external' contingencies thrown up by actual circumstances – for example, poverty, ill-health, rivalries, hatreds, wars, betrayals, and other such trials.

Augustine is, then, contriving a kind of parable. The 'City of Earth' is a 'place' which, despite many attractions and possibilities for not only pleasure but also virtue of a kind, is inevitably a trap for those seeking the truly good life – God's kingdom, after all, is 'not of this Earth'. The earthly City is tainted by sin – the greed, brutality, and self-interestedness of fallen Man. The City of God, on the other hand, is a 'place' of like-minded 'saints' in spiritual communion with each other and God.

Obviously we are all born in, and thus 'into', the 'earthly City', but Augustine claimed that if one were a Christian, hopeful of salvation through God's grace, one should regard 'this' life as merely a *journey through* 'the earthly City' – indeed, as a *pilgrimage* – towards one's goal, the City of God. Like anyone journeying to a destination, the places in between are not important in themselves – one should neither tarry over-long, nor get involved, in them. It is this aspect of the 'parable' which has inspired many to claim that Augustine's perspective is 'other-worldly' – that he is suggesting Christians should not concern themselves with 'earthly' affairs, but respectfully and/or resignedly lower their heads and travel as trouble-free as possible, trying not to get involved in the turmoil of the busy streets they have to traverse. This interpretation was later exploited by the elites of medieval societies (including the Church itself) to preach to ordinary folk a message of obedience to authority. But more directly for our purposes, it has also been interpreted as meaning that for Augustine (and to that extent, for Christian thought), *history* is *irrelevant* both in the grand scheme of things and in its significance in our own life-times. Why? Because whatever dreams and schemes might hope to be fulfilled through manipulating and reorganising 'external' circumstances – for example, democratising government, defeating foreign rule, revolutionising the economy, or reforming social structures – they are futile, stuck as they are in the ultimately worthless dimension of 'the earthly City'. Logically, such a perspective does not necessarily deny that the course of history may be 'intelligible' – but inasmuch as history charts the 'busy streets', it lacks real 'meaning'. And being thus ultimately irrelevant, it is difficult to see the rationale for any kind of *philosophy* of history.

The irrelevance of history?

This interpretation of Augustine can, then, lead to the view, paradoxically, that despite God's once-and-for-all creation of the world and its finite, linear history (in contrast to the cyclical eternal history of the pagan Graeco-Romans), that same history is irrelevant and meaningless to man (apart from certain Divine happenings such as the Resurrection). For example, Trompf reminds us that despite Augustine's various versions of human history (always composed with a polemical purpose), his overall perspective on the history of 'the Earthly City' was that it demonstrated 'the mutability of the human estate',[41] that 'wars, diseases, sorrows, and famine had been with men always', and that one would ultimately search in vain for any evidence that God's justice was exemplified in His having instilled into the Earthly City's history any principle of moral retribution or inherent plan of spiritual progression.[42] Inasmuch as his own times presaged a new order in which the City of God may be established, not only was Augustine vague about how soon this would happen, neither did he conceive of the eventuality as emerging from, and because of, the previous course of secular human history. As another scholar, Deane, puts it, 'If we confine our attention only to the history of this world and do not look beyond it to the future kingdom of God's saints, we cannot call Augustine a believer in historical progress'.[43] In short, the City of God is not the product of human history – it is radically a-historical.

The same conclusions concerning Augustine's logic are drawn by Fortin, who argues that 'the rationality of the divine plan is not in the materials used. No analysis of [historical] events will ever lead to the discovery of an end which is at once present and operative in the process from the beginning and destined to be progressively actualised through it. It follows that the future course of human history is totally unpredictable. History will come to an end at the appointed time . . . because God will have chosen to bring it to a close . . . . Its completion is in no way related to emergent political structures or the general state of human affairs at any any given moment'.[44] He adds weight to his interpretation by arguing that Augustine rejected contemporary hopes that a new *Christian* Rome would necessarily bring temporal and material rewards with it.[45] Rather, the affairs of men are inevitably unregenerate, and inasmuch as the City of God is entangled in the Earthly City, its role cannot be to reconstruct the latter along lines of perfection. On the contrary, without the evil which must pervade ordinary society, the virtue of the saintly is meaningless – 'the function of virtue is not to do away with evil but to conquer it'.[46] Thus Fortin interprets Augustine as rejecting any notion of a realised Christian society functioning according to the morality of the Gospels. No temporal community can achieve this. Some may be better than others; some marvellous innovations may emerge. But there is no guarantee that a particular society will not be replaced by a worse one, nor that innovations will always be used for good rather than evil. In short, for Augustine there is no reason to believe that any 'actual' or temporal society 'is at all capable of fulfilling man's longing for wholeness'. The 'historical' goal of which Augustine writes in his *City of God* 'remains transcendent and wholly independent of any observable improvement in the political sphere'.[47] Fortin thus concludes that 'one is entitled to ask what, if anything, the modern philosophy of history owes to him?', to which a radical reply might be that, logically, it owes him nothing, since interpreted along these lines Augustine's thinking precludes the very idea behind 'philosophy of history'.

History as relevant?

Others, however, have interpreted Augustine along opposite lines. For them, Augustine sees human history (guided by God's design) as moving inevitably towards the destruction of 'the Earthly City' and its replacement by 'the City of God' – and the latter is here interpreted as, indeed, a totally reformed *temporal* world (presaged in Augustine's present times, his 'sixth Age', and eventually actualised in a forthcoming 'seventh Age' bearing all the hallmarks of an earthly millennium – after which, the world would be destroyed, ushering in the final, eternal, eighth Age). For example, Jaki claims that 'what the medievals learned [in *The City of God*] . . .was, above all, the proposition that the physical universe and human history both had their origin in the sovereign creative act of God, which also established a most specific course and destiny for both'.[48] He describes Augustine's book as the 'vehicle for a confidence which centuries later made possible the emergence for the first time of a culture with a built-in force of self-sustaining progress',[49] and praises Augustine for recognising that 'the Christian pursuit of happiness' must be protected from any 'relapse into the monotony of cycles undermining man's sense of purpose', from any 'anti-intellectualism disdainful of the attainments of reason', and from 'considering as something evil the material world'. Jaki's interpretation suggests the view of a human history unfolding in a linear fashion towards a reformed temporal world – and that despite some possible eventual extinction, the history of humankind is, or *can be*, one of continual progress towards the perfected Christian world-society. I say, 'can be', since from the above it seems that, for Jaki, much depends on people 'having the right attitude' (namely, the correct Christian beliefs). Yet whether they do or will is another matter, since Jaki adds that for Augustine, 'most importantly, the pursuit of happiness *rested on man's* grasp of his own and of the material world's fundamental contingency, as *everything rested on a sovereign, creative act of God*'.[50]

Quite what this implies is difficult to discern. Is the course of human history, then, one of unilinear progress, and hence meaningful? And if so, however, does this *depend* on people's 'right thinking', such that without it history would be chaotic and meaningless? Or if mankind and its world is fundamentally 'contingent', is the course of history up to God? If so, the only reason to be hopeful for continued progress in the reform of 'the Earthly City' is to rely on God's goodwill rather than on our own beliefs and powers, or on any inbuilt dynamic in the workings of history. Perhaps Jaki realises this is where his logic leads, for he stresses Augustine's message that God's ordering of material and human history can be trusted to be both intelligible (unlike, according to Jaki, the Muslim concept of God) and beneficent because His 'fingerprints were evidenced by the disposition of everything according to weight, measure, and number'.[51] The reader may be forgiven for thinking Jaki wants it both ways. On the one hand it would seem the course of history is at the mercy of God's will, which could (despite Jaki's and Augustine's protests) be arbitrary (the perennial theological problem of evil and suffering looms large here). On the other hand, it would seem that how human beings handle their world is of central importance in determining whether their history is one of progress and meaning. Yet whether human-beings are bound (by God or anything else) to conduct their affairs progressively, or bound not to, or not 'bound' at all, is another matter – another perennial theological problem looms here, namely, that of free will. There are, then, ambiguities in this presentation of Augustine's views on both the course and the importance of human history, although it is clear enough that, for Jaki, what happens in 'the Earthly City' does matter – implicit in his hopes for historical human progress there is a connection (albeit never spelt out) between the 'Earthly' and 'Heavenly' cities. However 'spiritual' the latter may be, it would appear to have distinct temporal implications in Jaki's interpretation.

Far less equivocal is Nisbet's interpretation of this aspect of Augustine. After arguing that the early Christians' idea of reform and regeneration encompassed not only spiritual but also 'material, political, and social improvement',[52] and choosing passages in which Augustine praises humankind's capacity for material progress, Nisbet refers to Augustine's notion of 'the education of the human race' over time, in which Augustine 'sees the progress of mankind, the material progress we have already found to shine so brilliantly in his account, as akin to a long process of cumulative education in a single human being'. This process of 'a single, unified mankind . . . advancing in accordance with an immanent design' is an historical process, despite 'the actual multiplicity and particularity of recorded history' which tends to obscure the 'reality' of the progress of mankind 'toward fulfilment of all that was good in its being'.[53] Aware that many have interpreted Augustine as being strongly opposed to all notions of an earthly millennium, Nisbet nonetheless argues 'there are grounds for belief that Augustine foresaw a progressive, fulfilling, and blissful period ahead, *on earth*, for humanity'.[54] Further, Nisbet somewhat mischievously notes that even Augustine's version of the New Earth which is, apocalyptically, to succeed the destruction of our temporal world, 'has a decidedly earthly, human flavour' including, in Augustine's own words, 'life, health, nourishment, and plenty, and glory, and honour and peace, and all good things'.[55]

In short, Nisbet offers an Augustine who, almost irrespective of his metaphor of the 'Earthly City' and the 'City of God', conceived of and bequeathed a 'philosophy of history' premised on the view that the course of human history is necessarily one of continuing progress, not only spiritually, but mundanely in terms of political, social, economic, and cultural improvement. If, then, by 'the Earthly City' is meant this temporal world, then what happens in it – namely, its history – is of the most intimate significance. In his version of Augustine, not for Nisbet the bowed head of the resigned pilgrim, ignoring as far possible his mundane surroundings as he travels in hope to a 'place' of a different order altogether!

Interpreting Augustine

Examining these large claims made of, and about, a central ideological divide between how the Graeco-Roman and Judaeo-Christian cultures viewed history (partly derived from the clash between pagan and monotheistic religions), we have devoted considerable space to Augustine – or rather, to differing interpretations of him. This is because his writings (particularly *The City of God*) crystallised the cultural clash between Christianity and Graeco-Roman ideas at a crucial time in the history of the Roman Empire. As such, combined with the extensiveness and stature of his writings, Augustine's legacy stretched over the ensuing centuries we call 'the Middle Ages'. Not only did he influence people's attitudes towards the course and meaning of history – his legacy is no less important in the related field of political thought. Yet, as we have seen, even now it remains a thoroughly ambiguous inheritance whose implications are nonetheless huge whichever interpretation of his ideas one adopts. (This has been a powerful contributory factor to his enduring influence, since neither scholars nor enthusiasts are prone to let ambiguities lie).

On the one hand, the implications of Augustine's doctrines are that mundane earthly history is a meaningless kaleidoscope of petty material struggles, triumphs, and disasters – that on its own, it is going nowhere, and nothing of lasting worth can be found in its past or be expected in its future. (Ironically one is reminded of precisely that alleged pagan doctrine of an ultimately meaningless repetitive history which Augustine is so concerned to refute). No amount of zealous reformism, social engineering, or political restructuring can bring about a 'City of Earth' which progressively fulfils 'the human good'. Rather, the latter is radically dissociated from temporal, earthly life, being instead a 'spiritual' state of mind and/or some transcendental New Order ('the City of God) subsequent to the apocalyptic destruction of human life on earth as we know it. That human history will eventuate in such a manner has been determined by God, irrespective of man's free will to fashion his own history. The best use of free will is to follow Christian morality, loving one's neighbour and God, rejecting the challenges and temptations of 'the Earthly City', in hopes of achieving a kind of 'virtual reality' of 'the Heavenly City' prior to its actual institution by God's judgement. As we have seen, interpreted so it is difficult to see any sense in which Augustine's doctrines offer a 'philosophy of history' – that is, a set of ideas which help make sense of, and thereby possibly give meaning to, human history by explaining what internal mechanisms or dynamics determine its course. If for some Graeco-Roman minds history was one of unmitigated gloom, at least they offered explanations for this. The only 'explanation' to be extracted for Augustine's view (to the extent it *was* his view) is a paradoxical intermixture of God's will and the free will of Fallen Man, where one is reminded of Spinoza's observation that to refer the inexplicable to 'the will of God' is 'truly, a ridiculous way of expressing ignorance'.[56]

On the other hand Augustine has been presented as the first great philosopher of history, whose ideas originated the notion of the linear, meaningful, progressive history of mankind towards fulfilling its potential towards unity, justice, and happiness. It has been claimed that Charlemagne's ambitions for a 'Holy Roman Empire' at his doubly symbolic coronation by the Pope on Christmas Day 800 were inspired by an Augustinian vision of a re-formed united Christian 'Earthly City',[57] and there is a hint in one recent commentator's mind that this 'worldly' version of Augustine, whereby the One Church is to be God's instrument for man's earthly salvation by extending its influence throughout the globe, remains a Catholic ideal disputed by Protestants who lean towards a more 'other-worldly' interpretation of Augustine – in short, that Catholics think more in terms of history, Protestants more in terms of souls.[58]

Some heuristics of the history of thought

From the above, it is clear that much of the problem in interpreting Augustine's views on history centres on this issue of 'worldliness' and 'other-worldliness'. Just what the role of Christianity in the actual affairs of the world should be – whether it should have any role 'in' history at all – remains ambiguous, just as whether 'earthly' history itself should be relegated to a meaningless flux or, on the contrary, be the focus for rational belief in the inevitable march of human progress towards the perfect society. Because, as your 'guide', I have highlighted opposing interpretations of Augustine, readers might think I should now try to settle the matter. However, I do not think it is possible to do so – rather, in a work, *The City of God*, so suffused with rhetoric (including polemic) because devoted to achieving practical objectives, I would almost say it is impossible to expect either philosophical consistency, intellectual honesty, or 'good faith'. I have elsewhere[59] attempted to explain what is involved in recovering a writer's thinking – that is, what is involved in doing 'the history of thought'. Where, by constructing his book, a writer is trying to achieve some *practical objective*, he is not concerned to explore and argue the truth for the sake of the truth. Rather, what he writes is chosen, *through* persuading his reader of the truth of what he says, to achieve some purpose external to the matter ostensibly under discussion – for example, to follow this religion, join that political movement, behave in this way, or believe in that way. There is nothing 'wrong' with practically motivated writings – but they are different from *theoretically* motivated ones. The latter occur where the writer has no (practical) axe to grind, being concerned solely to explore, argue, and communicate the truth on a matter, irrespective of any practical consequences. In this sense the *historian* as well as, for example, the scientist, critic, and philosopher, can and should be a 'theoretician'. This does not mean that theoretically motivated writings do not contain errors, or that practically inspired writings never say anything true. Nor does it mean that parts of a practically inspired book cannot be theoretically inspired, and vice-versa – (the point is to identify what is going on at any particular point). What it does mean, however, is that where a piece of writing is practically inspired, those criteria of logical consistency, objectivity, and open-ended pursuit of the truth necessary to theoretical writings are replaced by the criterion of efficiency in achieving the writer's practical objectives. Accordingly, opponents' views are often distorted, the writer's points overstated, 'inconvenient' facts ignored, and chains of reasoning directed to pre-chosen, 'appropriate' conclusions. (Another, less satisfactory, term for such writings is 'ideological').

Thus it is that where we encounter such writings it is not so much futile as a misunderstanding of their nature to assume the writer must be able to be made philosophical sense of, that inconsistencies and ambiguities must be capable of being cleared up, if only we, the poor readers, had the intelligence to do so. Later in this book we will encounter Vico imploring his contemporaries to stop believing that ancient writings must, by their nature, contain hidden wisdom – that whilst this attitude prevails, no true 'science' of the past is possible. Just so, albeit on a less general level, we might urge people to stop assuming that 'great thinkers' must have been aspiring to explore truth for the sake of truth, and that it is up either to us or to commentators and historians of thought to make consistent philosophical sense of what they 'must' have 'really' meant. Rather, the message is that history of thought approached in such a manner is pre-scientific, and will continue to be wherever we ignore its first rule – namely, to recognise books and other pieces of writing as more or less complex artefacts deliberately constructed by thinkers, and thus to ask, 'what is it that they are trying to do, both by the book as a whole, and in any particular part of it?'. All else follows, and as stated, I have explored the heuristic implications and techniques elsewhere. Our point here is that the distinction between theoretical and practically inspired writings is a telling one, and that because Augustine's *City of God* exemplifies the latter, those who insist on trying to interpret it as offering a consistent, unambiguous 'doctrine' are mistaken. And as for those who accept that he did bequeath a confusing legacy, but might suggest this is simply because, despite his genuine intentions, Augustine was confused, or wrote badly, or was simply unable to articulate certain 'inexpressibles', again I suggest they are mistaken, and that the more likely explanation is that he did not 'seriously' address the very issues they hope, by 'interpreting' him, to find him solving – in short, that his notions of 'the Earthly City' and 'the City of God', and their implications for the nature of human history and the role of the Christian in the temporal world, were not the product of theoretical thinking (thereby offering the expectation of some intellectually coherent philosophy), but were practically inspired and practically argued, and hence (particularly given the complex issues addressed) were unlikely to achieve a level of intellectual coherence never intended in any event.

It is beyond our brief to demonstrate, from his writings, what I have suggested about Augustine's *City of God* (although some indications may have emerged in our exposition of the controversy it has provoked). Rather, in line with what I have said about 'practically inspired' writings, we might want to attend to the following points: Augustine was educated as a pagan, and then during his twenties fell under the influence of the teachings of the Persian prophet, Mani. But he later renounced Manichaeism, employing his increasingly renowned rhetorical skills to refute the 'heresy'. Around 387, having been attracted to Neo-Platonist ideas, and then under the influence of (St) Ambrose, the Bishop of Milan, he converted to Christianity, and by 395 was made Bishop of Hippo (in North Africa). 'Never one . . . to hide his light under a bushel',[60] his renown as a winner of arguments, hounder of 'heresies', and indefatigable preacher spread, such that when the Goths sacked the city of Rome in 410, and Christianity was held to blame for the Empire's sorry demise, it was Augustine whom a Christian representative of Roman officialdom asked to refute the charge. Hence (although it took from 413 to 426 to complete) his famous *City of God*. None of these points in themselves prove, of course, the claims I have made about his ideas – but they do contain tell-tale signs of where practically motivated writings, rather than earnestly considered attempts to arrive at truth for its own sake, are more likely to be found.

Summary comments

The Christian challenge

Clearly, an important part of the Christian challenge to Graeco-Roman culture focused on its rejection of the doctrine of eternally recurring cosmological and historical cycles – and we have seen that for many scholars, let alone Christians, this (alleged) gulf has momentous implications for man's understanding of time, the course of history, his own place within it, and his expectations from it. Some have seen the originally Jewish insistence on the linearity of history, adopted by the early Christians, as providing the very foundations for 'philosophy of history'. Hence the surely extravagant claims made for Christianity in particular, along the lines that once it was committed to seeking a universal constituency it thereby 'invented' the concomitant notions of a meaningful history and belief in human progress; we are consequently urged to 'maintain (or regain) the faith' if humankind is to face the future with confidence rather than lose itself in doctrines and attitudes which, blind to the message of history, portend a future for humanity as meaningless (according, allegedly, to those doctrines and attitudes) as its past has been.

Cyclical and linear history

There are several problems with this point of view. First, in the abstract, neither linear nor cyclical 'theories' of history in themselves point to either the presence or absence of *intelligibility* in history. In microcosm, a linear sequence of events is no more intelligible *by its nature* than is a (recurring) cycle of events. That events do not repeat themselves does not mean the course they take is therefore 'meaningful'. Rather, we might tend more to the opposite view – namely, that where they do repeat themselves we are more likely to find some principle of intelligibility, or extract some meaning, in such an historical process. But still, in neither case is such meaning *necessarily* implied. What *is* true, however, is that to describe history as *either* cyclical *or* linear is to say something meaningful *about* history. But this is where confusion can arise, because to say something meaningful about history is not necessarily the same as saying history is meaningful. (By analogy I could describe someone's behaviour as repetitious, or observe that every life has a beginning and an end. Respectively, I am saying something meaningful about his behaviour, or her life. But this is far from saying that his behaviour, or her life, are meaningful). Now, when we refer to 'philosophy of history', which do we mean? If we mean 'saying something meaningful about the course of history', then the cyclical no less than the linear approach contributes to 'philosophy of history', (and Christianity loses its alleged uniqueness). If, however, we mean 'showing that history is meaningful', then neither the cyclical nor the linear approach *necessarily* imply this, (again, confuting those alleged *logical* grounds for claiming Christianity's pre-eminence in providing the only grounds for 'philosophy of history' through its adherence to linear rather than cyclical history).

But of course there is more to this claim, on behalf of Christianity, than its insistence on history's linearity. It is only linear *because* it is the fulfilling, through time, of God's *design*, or *purpose*. It is this which ensures not only that 'meaningful things can be said about history', but more powerfully, that 'history is meaningful'. The 'secret', then, in the momentous claims made for Christianity is that it is not its linear as distinct from the (pagan) cyclical approach which makes it 'unique' in the sphere of 'philosophy of history' but, mundanely enough, its concept of God.

The Christian deity and history

This invites a second observation. The Christian concept of God which furnishes a linear approach to the course of history is (following the Jews) that of both a *transcendent* deity and, to make history progressive, a *caring* deity. The latter point seems more a matter of belief, even wishful thinking (although some theologians and philosophers offer explanations) than the former, more metaphysical, idea. The significance of a *transcendent* deity is that, being 'above' or 'apart' from the universe (unlike the 'mythopoeic' notion of the universe as animated, or later pantheistic versions of God's, or gods', immanence *within* the universe), such a deity thereby has control over the universe. It is its creation and it determines what happens in it. God's transcendence is here seen as the condition of His determination of the course of history, since absolute power requires absolute disentanglement from that which is controlled. Logically, this seems sound. However, this scenario is contradicted by Christianity's insistence on human free will (although theologians tell us it is merely *complicated*, rather than contradicted, by free will – hence many a tortuous treatise trying to reconcile the necessity of a God-determined world with free human agency). It is not our brief here to explore the general philosophical problems which ensue, but it is relevant to comment where they impinge directly on the validity of those particular claims regarding Christianity's 'foundation' of philosophy of history. We have encountered the strident view that a progressive future history for humankind depends on the continued (or renewed) Christian belief in a linear, meaningful past history – in short, the huge claim that mankind's future depends on people adopting the 'correct' philosophy of history which, amongst other things, rejects any cyclical theories as otherwise consigning us to entrapment in a random, meaningless future. Yet this means the future progress of mankind depends on man, not God. Further, it means it depends on how people *think*, on their attitudes and beliefs. By implication, does it also mean that the course of (*past*) history has been linear, meaningful, and progressive *not* because it has been determined by God, but because of how free human beings have *thought* in the past?

Many conceptual problems surface here, threatening to render the claims made for Christianity's contribution to philosophy of history unintelligible. For example, what of the aeons of history prior to Christianity? Was their history also determined by how free human-beings thought? If so, their thinking could not have been along Christian lines, the very condition, it would seem, of linear, progressive history! In short, those who make such bold claims about the significance of Christian beliefs both for the 'foundation' of philosophy of history and for history's future course are caught in both a dilemma and a paradox. The dilemma is that to the extent their perspective demands we 'keep the faith', then the course of history is up to us, not God. And the paradox is that, in their logic, history is only meaningful because of this *immanent* process centred on human beliefs – beliefs, however, which precisely centre on the contrary notion of a *transcendent* God who determines the course of history! Such ingenious self-contradictions suggest that those generous claims we found about the Christian challenge to Graeco-Roman attitudes to history are less coherent than they might be, and contemporary Christians may think twice before endorsing them.

The temporal and spiritual lives

A further comment on the Christian 'alternative' philosophy of history returns us to Augustine's ambivalent legacy of the difference, and the relation, between the 'heavenly' and 'earthly' cities. We may safely translate this great metaphor of Christian thought as referring to the difference, and relation, between the temporal and spiritual side of life. Here we might wish to rescue Augustine somewhat from my 'accusations' of ambiguousness and lack of intellectual honesty, since the theme is inherently ambiguous in any event. It is also important, particularly for those religions *and* philosophies which recognise the spiritual or 'other-worldly' dimension to human experience. Unlike, for example, wealth or health, 'happiness' ('the good life', 'salvation') is clearly a state of mind. The question is, however, whether this 'state of mind' is the *product* of one's mind or the product of one's material circumstances (indeed, including wealth and health). Many religions and philosophies appear to adopt the former position whereby one is urged not to seek happiness in 'the things of this world' (that is, in temporal affairs) because any such happiness is fleeting (being at the mercy of chance) and illusory (because ultimately insatiable). Instead, 'true' happiness is said to be the product of a mind internally disciplined towards correct ideas and values, irrespective of 'the slings and arrows of fortune' and/or the vicissitudes of history. Images of the determined Stoic, serene Buddhist, or contemplative mystic spring to mind here, as well as the devout Christian. But wherever such a view has dominated, the question has arisen as to what one's relation with the actual (temporal) world should be. Should one ignore it as far as possible, or indulge it at least to be sociable, or combatively engage with it in pursuit of the ideals one's religion or philosophy teaches? Part of the answer is that it depends what those teachings are – or, more often, how they are interpreted. Therevada Buddhism, for example, recommended withdrawal from society in favour of 'the contemplative life', whilst Mahayana Buddhism urged the 'enlightened' to live and engage in society in hopes of improving it. Plato's famous cave analogy suggests the philosopher who has escaped into daylight ('truth') will not be welcome back amongst the slaves 'underground' unless he pretends to be like them. Having envisaged the perfect society in Book Two of his *Utopia*, Thomas More then wrote Book One, however, as an exploration of whether there is any point trying to realise such ideals in the real world. Later the philosopher Hegel, perhaps believing himself to be echoing Spinoza, claimed that for those of the contemplative mind, philosophy 'is the rose in the cross of the present', granting them the serenity afforded by insight into Reality, however unsatisfactory the actual world – and consequently insisted it is not the task of philosophy to try to change the world we live in,[61] a notion famously rejected by Marx.

Many other examples abound of thinkers, before and after Augustine, grappling with the overall problematic of the relation between the 'spiritual' and the 'temporal' life, or between the world of Ideal Truth and the actual, mundane world, or (in some treatments) between 'theory' and 'practice'. The problem even has resonance within the field of psychiatry, for can an unhappy state of experience only be corrected by changing the actual life-circumstances which (allegedly) cause it, or are the latter irrelevant, the cure being to 'rethink' one's way into a different state of mind (through psychotherapy and/or drugs)? Returning to Augustine, then, the question regarding his 'philosophy of history' is whether what happens in the mundane, actual world has anything to do with 'true' human happiness. Should one strive to change the real world, to refashion socio-economic and political structures in order to get rid of poverty, disease, oppression, exploitation, and injustice? Or is happiness a state of mind we have to *think* our way into by changing, not reality, but our ideas – in short, by 're-thinking' reality, in this case via 'converting' to Christian faith? If the latter, then (as often observed of much subsequent medieval historiography) the only relevant aspect of actual, mundane history is the history of the Universal Church because of its role as mentor of the flock and guardian of the faith (although military Crusades also have a place). If the former, on the other hand, then the full panorama of what we call 'history' comes into play. As seen, Augustine is open to either interpretation. Indeed, we can use his metaphor of the two cities to posit extremes, either of which he was probably striving to avoid. We can think of the 'pilgrim' self-absorbedly travelling through an alien land, selfishly aloof to the sufferings and injustices around him. Or we can think of the 'pilgrim' as an enlightened outsider, outraged by what he sees around him, determined to put things right in the alien land he is journeying through. As suggested, Christianity is not alone in proffering the dichotomy between the 'spiritual' and 'temporal' life, and in differing circumstances various 'kinds' of Christian have veered more to one side than the other. More usually, however, the religion has presented an 'orthodox' eclectic middle position whereby it neither aspires to take charge of temporal affairs in the hope of fulfilling an historical destiny for mankind, nor, however, stands mute and aloof on the sidelines of a temporal history reckoned to be irrelevant to 'salvation'. How far this is an inherent ambivalence which was simply (and unwittingly) translated into the ambiguities of Augustine's 'philosophy of history', or whether the latter *contributed* to an ambivalence in Christianity not in fact a *necessary* feature of it, is a difficult question – and whilst it remains so the contribution of Christian thought to philosophy of history, and its relation with it, remain problematic.

5

A CHANGING CONSCIOUSNESS OF HISTORY

The Renaissance and Machiavelli

Introduction

The 'Middle Ages'

Trends in recent scholarship have challenged the idea that the collapse of the Western Roman Empire provoked a radical change from classical Roman culture to a markedly different, now 'otherworldly' Christian culture. Rather, for example, the latter's 'intrusion' sparked an exciting 'cultural dynamic' in which 'new value-structures, new subjects worth writing about', and 'a whole new literary language' emerged from an interaction continuing into the seventh century.[1] Likewise, the 'standard' notion of the subsequent 'Middle Ages' as a long period unchanging in its basic intellectual assumptions has been robustly challenged in certain areas (e.g., the notion of an outburst of humanist literature in the High Middle Ages, as masterfully described by Southern).[2] But despite these revisions it remains true to say that regarding time and history the Augustinian heritage (including its ambiguities) dominated medieval presuppositions. Although those tensions implicit in the distinction between 'the City of God' and 'Earthly City' – between the spiritual and temporal dimensions to life – formed the backcloth to much dispute in *political* thought, they were neither resolved nor superseded by any new perspective on the significance and meaning of the course of history. Where novelties occurred they originated in one-sided interpretations of Christianity whereby an individual, sect, or 'heresy' emphasised a notion of 'heaven on earth' (that is, a *temporal* realisation of 'salvation') – or, alternatively, emphasised the opposite, whereby the temporal, earthly life was so reviled as to encourage, in the most extreme cases, group suicide pacts.

Historical monotony?

Thus it is, that, despite recent historiography showing 'the Middle Ages' replete with change and diversity rather than a static period stretching from the fifth to the fourteenth centuries, from our perspective of 'speculative philosophy of history' the platitude that 'people's eyes were turned towards Heaven' – that their intellectual interests centred on eternal verities, and their speculative instincts on attaining individual spiritual salvation – remains applicable. In this climate nothing innovative arose in terms of a new outlook on the significance of human history. Rather, it would seem, people in the Middle Ages were simply not interested in speculating beyond the Biblical version of history and Augustine's tutelage (via his famous metaphor) on how to understand what it meant or implied. This has led many, particularly in the light of the subsequent 'Renaissance', to characterise 'the medieval mind' as lacking any properly *historical* consciousness of their own past and of the diverse nature of other cultures. In short, the supposition is that they saw themselves as living in a basically changeless society, finding no inspiration for change through looking at their own or anyone else's history, and no inspiration for *progress* in particular because society neither did, nor needed to, change. Salvation was the goal of the individual. Temporal history did not matter.

The irony is that, arguably, this lack of historical consciousness was precisely the product of a *heightened* sense of *philosophy* of history (albeit of a 'negative' kind) – i.e., that it was just because the medieval mind was encouraged (by orthodox Christianity) to take a 'speculative' perspective on human history that it spurned genuine interest in real temporal history, whereas those later times (beginning with the Renaissance) which *did* demonstrate a lively historical consciousness of their own and other societies have largely lost that *speculative*, 'philosophical' approach whereby an overall sense of history's significance could endow their lives with 'spiritual' meaning. In its absence, interest in actual history thrives along with its paradoxical partner, *anomie*.

In raising this as a possible perception we encounter the intriguing possibility of an inverse relationship (both historically and logically) between belief in 'speculative' philosophy of history and interest in 'actual' history – in short, that they repel each other. If true, this should not be so surprising. After all, if in good speculative mode one 'knows' what history 'is all about', one is less likely to be curious about its 'details'. Wars, revolutions, migrations, and other 'large' past events are seen as confirming the substantive 'meaning' of the course of history, whilst 'lesser' events are dismissable as insignificant contingencies. Alternatively, if in good *historian's* mode one is fascinated in the discovery and understanding of past events, one is less likely to be attracted to some pre-determined pattern into which they 'must' fit since, apart from anything else, it undermines historians' motive of the instinct of curiosity.

Aquinas

But, however relevant to this 'guide' as a whole, let us return from such reflections to 'the Middle Ages'. It seems that throughout that period basic presuppositions about history and its course remained unchanged – that in having their eyes trained on 'Heaven', temporal affairs (however pressingly important in practice) were relegated to relative insignificance in people's perspective on the 'larger' questions of life, and that consciousness of and interest in *history* were perhaps particularly subject to this. One of the effects, of course, was that their underlying assumptions about the 'meaning' of history were far less likely to be challenged by the uncovering of new historical facts. In short, in this intellectual climate historical ignorance was self-reinforcing.

Significantly, part of this historical ignorance extended to intellectual and cultural history. With the downfall of the Western Roman Empire, numerous classical writings in mathematics, philosophy, poetry, drama, history, politics, and the other liberal arts, were lost to that part of Europe 'which became a cultural unit thanks to the Germanic invasions of the Roman Empire',[3] either literally through the effects of war, plunder, and destruction, or figuratively through neglect and indifference. It would seem that even when there was a major intellectual innovation in medieval thought – namely, the 'rediscovery' of Aristotle's philosophy and its integration into Christian thought in the thirteenth century – however else this affected people's way of thinking about life, it did not shift the Augustinian perspective on the place of 'history' in it. Vastly impressed by, and under corresponding pressure from, Aristotle's astonishingly comprehensive (albeit 'pagan') corpus of philosophical, scientific, and metaphysical writings, medieval scholars and theologians set about the task of reconciling his system with Christian thought, culminating in the mammoth synthesis achieved by Thomas Aquinas' *Summa Theologica* (1273). The tone underlying Aquinas' reconciliation of the two systems of thought is often summarised in his famous dictum, 'Nature is not destroyed by Grace, but perfected by it', meaning that earthly things ('Nature') are not utterly unregenerate, base, and corrupt (as could be interpreted from Augustine), but do have a value. There *is* beauty, truth, and virtue to be found in this temporal life. The fact of God's heavenly perfection ('Grace') does not relegate earthly things to a totally opposite corruption. On the other hand, the value which *is* to be found in earthly things is nevertheless incomplete – the temporal, earthly life is insufficient on its own, and needs the spiritual dimension to perfect its possibilities. '[T]he aim of a good life on this earth is blessedness in heaven'.[4] (Christian) faith in the perfection of God's heavenly world is required to properly make the best of what the earthly life offers – it is, so to speak, the necessary 'icing on the cake'. Without it, earthly things would indeed be abandoned to total meaninglessness and corruption. Reason needs to be accompanied by faith.

'Scholasticism'

Although this perspective put a more favourable light on temporal matters, opening up new topics and lines of enquiry hitherto ignored or deliberately shunned, it seems it was insufficient to effect any basic shift in presuppositions about the meaning and significance of history. Indeed, it could be argued that so 'intellectual' was Aquinas' synthesis that, unlike Augustine's combative ideas, his philosophy was not attuned to making much practical impact on *any* of people's entrenched ways of thinking and behaving. Where it *did* have a 'practical' impact was in the *intellectual* world. Monks and scholars, encouraged by Aquinas' staving off of the threat of an unanswerable, pagan, secular-orientated Aristotelianism (Aristotle was regarded as offering the epitome of a rational explanation of existence) busily set about the task of researching, publicising, and teaching the now 'Christianised' Aristotelian system. And it is here, in part, that we rejoin our theme of speculative philosophy of history, for what emerged was a formalised set of studies we call *scholasticism* (from the Aristotelian 'schools' of philosophy'), one replete with obscure Aristotelian technical terms and rendered more so for being Latinised. This is part of our story because the dominance of the 'schools' was no mean contributor to that new movement or period which did at last offer an alternative 'way of thinking' about the course and meaning of history – namely, 'the Renaissance'. It did so by helping provoke the beginnings of a culture *counter* to 'medievalism', partly centred on those such as Petrarch (1304–1374) who, inspired by *contempt* for 'scholasticism', encouraged a return to the study of the literature and ideas of the classical, Graeco-Roman world – what they referred to as 'the liberal arts', or *studia humanitatis* ('study of the humanities', from which we derive our concept of 'the humanities'). By the fifteenth century these (principally Italian) like-minded 'humanist' scholars (since referred to as 'the Renaissance humanists') began to impose their ideas on a rapidly changing society only too willing to listen. In schools and universities the new *humanist* curriculum of studies competed increasingly successfully with the late medieval *scholastical* curriculum. The scene was set, the intellectual world was now equipped, to at last induce some new presuppositions about the nature and meaning of 'history'.

Renaissance humanism and the 'Middle Ages'

Before we explore the broader implications of the Renaissance, and of Renaissance humanism, for speculative 'philosophy of history', we should note that the Renaissance humanists had a more direct impact on how people thought about history – and one of singular relevance to this part of our 'guide'. It was they, no less, who invented the very notion of 'the Middle Ages', or 'medievalism'. With a boldness perhaps necessarily characteristic of any who attempt to re-periodise existing historical conventions (e.g., many eighteenth- and nineteenth-century philosophers of history), Petrarch and those following him turned upside down the medieval (sic) notion of history's division into two basic periods – that of darkness before, and light after, the virtually simultaneous birth of Christ and foundation of the Roman Empire. Instead, the Renaissance humanists were remarkably successful in preaching a new, contrary understanding of the course of history, whereby the classical period of Greece, Rome, and the Roman Empire – *Antiquity* – was one of light, followed by a period of darkness (the 'dark ages' of barbarism, ignorance, and cultural desolation) they called '*the Middle Ages*', which extended from the fifth century AD until the dawning of their own 'new' age in the fourteenth century, an age of high culture 'reborn' from, and remodelled upon, Antiquity's dazzling achievements.

Although it was not until 1855 that the French historian, Michelet, coined it, there is no doubt they would have found the term '*the Renaissance*' perfectly suited to their thinking. And this is how, in a roundabout way, the innovative outlook elaborated by Aquinas, although not itself producing any shift in medieval assumptions regarding history's course and meaning, nevertheless eventually played its part – albeit negatively. The Renaissance period owes part of its origins and characteristics to the humanist movement, and the latter's identity owed much to their disillusion with the failed hopes of the optimistic twelfth and thirteenth centuries. In those times, hopes for a new universal order of peace and prosperity eventually came to be underpinned by Christian-Aristotelian philosophy, science, and political economy. The latter spawned an intellectual system – 'scholasticism' – of which, when the hopes proffered by the late Middle Ages came to nought, 'the details all appeared intensely repellent. No books have ever been written that gave less invitation to study . . . their illegible script, crabbed abbreviations, and margins filled with comments even less legible than the text, invite derision'.[5] In scorning their recent past and its ideological bulwark, 'scholasticism', Renaissance humanists looked back admiringly to classical literature and the cultural ideals it expressed – and in so doing, began to turn men's eyes from Heaven back towards earth, to an appreciation of *human* life in its temporal and secular setting.

Effects on historical consciousness

This very boldness in re-periodising history by inventing the notion of 'the Middle Ages' already evidences a willingness to move away from medieval presuppositions about history – a move which became increasingly explicit as the Renaissance humanists extended their classical studies and developed their thoughts. However, it would be wrong to suggest Renaissance humanism came up with an alternative (speculative) 'philosophy of history' by offering some new, systematic, overall coherence to the course and meaning of human history. Indeed, although there were Renaissance humanist *philosophers*, such as Lorenzo Valla (1407–1457), many scholars agree with Paul Kristeller's assessment that, at least given a more narrow, professional definition of 'philosophy', it is not possible 'to define Renaissance humanism by a set of specific philosophical ideas shared by all humanists, or to regard humanism exclusively as a philosophical movement'.[6] In short, no particular philosophical system characterised 'the Renaissance', nor its humanist scholars, let alone a particular 'philosophy of history'. Rather, without producing the latter, the Renaissance humanists nevertheless opened up the path for changes in the way people 'speculated' upon history and its meaning. They effected this in two ways.

First, and more directly, their promotion of the new curriculum, the *studia humanitatis*, meant replacing the scholastic curriculum which revolved around the disciplines of logic, law, pure mathematics, science, astronomy, and metaphysical (Aristotelian) philosophy. These disciplines were mostly directed towards the eternally fixed verities of nature, existence, and the universe – that is, 'towards Heaven'. Instead, the humanist curriculum studied the changing things of this human world: grammar (the correct rules, understanding, and use of language); rhetoric (the ability to articulate persuasive arguments based on a perceptive practical sense); 'poetry' (meaning the study of *classical* poetry to appreciate and replicate the 'liberal-humanist' culture and sensibilities of 'Antiquity'); *moral* philosophy (the study of justice in conduct and virtue in character, inspired by such 'greats' as Plato and Cicero, rather than the 'drier' technical and metaphysical components of Aristotle's philosophy); and, indeed, *history*. Primarily the latter meant reading the classical historians and, through imitation, and for good vocational reasons, learning how to write histories of their own cities and biographies of their dignitaries.

But more broadly, amongst the best scholars it fostered what we may call a properly *historical* consciousness whereby the 'otherness' of societies in the past was recognised. As Rice and Grafton explain, 'Since the medieval historian had believed that his own historical epoch went back to the reign of Augustus (27 BC– AD 14), he had been unconscious of the intellectual and imaginative gulf that had to be crossed if the ancient world was to be understood . . . He regarded the Romans as his contemporaries'.[7] Now, Renaissance humanists recognised that the Roman Empire, and periods preceding it, were long past, different societies, the meaning of whose cultures, *mores*, and languages had to be recaptured by paying attention to the contexts in which they flourished. Much work of the humanist scholars involved the re-translation of ancient texts to render their true historical meaning, as well as the avid discovery and historical interpretation of hitherto unknown or neglected writings. Forgeries (e.g., the famous 'Donation of Constantine') were uncovered, misunderstandings pointed out, stupidities exposed – perhaps above all, that air of unmovable authority which characterised the views and pronouncements of the leaders of the medieval world was ruthlessly and gleefully undermined.

Although it would be wrong to exaggerate the historical accuracy and expertise of humanist scholars, as well as to concur wholeheartedly with their contempt for (and, maybe, concept of) 'the Middle Ages', their contribution to the foundations of the modern, objective, source-respecting discipline of history cannot be over-estimated. But from our particular perspective of 'speculative philosophy of history', in challenging the medieval framework within which people had been taught to think about history, the emergence of this 'historical consciousness' (or sense of the 'historicity' of the past) opened up people's imaginations, a crucial step towards shifting basic presuppositions about the significance and meaning of 'history'. In short, it is difficult to see how later increasingly reflective, deliberate attempts to 'make sense of history' (i.e., the project of 'speculative philosophy of history') could themselves make any sense without the prior emergence of 'a sense of history'.

The humanists and 'secularism'

The second way in which the Renaissance humanists effected the opening up of changes in the way people thought about the significance of history, introduces us to some of those more general features of the Renaissance. The most important of these is that they helped, so to speak, turn people's eyes back towards this earthly life. Here we may elaborate upon the humanist curriculum. Inherent in the disciplines mentioned is a ('reborn') emphasis upon and interest in actual nature and human life 'on this earth', of which 'historical consciousness' is but one component. The study of the structure and meaning of language (increasingly including Greek) directs attention to human life, thoughts, and intercourse; the study of prose and poetic literature directs attention to the beauty and intricacies of nature, and the range and subtlety of human emotions; the study of 'rhetoric' to the capacity of man to perceive, reason, argue, make judgements, and influence others through persuasion rather than through unthinking, bluntly 'authoritative' pronouncements; and the study of moral philosophy directs attention to the (human) problem of free will in action, to choice between good and evil, to an understanding of what is virtuous conduct between friends, parents and children, rulers and subjects – and yes, between the individual and God.

The latter is important to mention because although the orientation of these disciplines is so clearly 'humanist' – directed away from the eternities of 'Heaven' towards the varying, contingent, complex *human* world – it does not mean Renaissance humanists were, in the main, anti-God (or atheistic) or even anti-religion. It is probably true that some (e.g., Machiavelli) were atheistic, and certainly true that some were sufficiently emboldened to become critical, if not contemptuous, of the (Catholic or 'Universal') Church, culminating in the savage critiques of such later figures as the famous Christian humanist, Erasmus, and his equally famous contemporary and initiator of the Protestant Reformation, the humanistically trained Luther. But the very mention of these two names reveals that humanist criticism of the Church was more likely, and more effective, when motivated by concern *for* religion rather than from those who, although not rejecting God, disdained religion *per se*.

This latter type of humanist was represented by those who, without rejecting God, nevertheless scorned a life dominated by religious belief and enthusiasm, (the life of the numerous clerical orders, and of the poor, especially in the countryside), and instead devoted themselves to the busy demands of an active urban life, pursuing careers in business, commerce, banking, town planning, architecture, administration, the arts, and government. Proud of their cities, wealthy enough to have disposable income and time, and excited at the prospects of achieving public recognition, they energetically pursued the good things of life – that is, a secular life. They are sometimes described as 'civic humanists', were often republican in their political ideals,[8] and became 'fashionable'. Whether their new, *secular* values were *inherently* atheistic is a matter of philosophy, not history.[9] More to the point is how they themselves viewed God and religion, and here we must recognise that in the fourteenth, fifteenth and sixteenth centuries one would never publicly disclose blatant atheistic views, so we cannot judge. But what seems likely is that many 'civic' humanists were simply not interested in religion nor, possibly, in God – not an uncommon position today. It is this equation which, for some, still links Renaissance 'humanism' with what the term means in today's world.

Broader Renaissance securalism

In the preceding paragraphs we have outlined how the work of the Renaissance humanists prompted changes in the way people thought about the past. But the impact of the Renaissance on such intuitions was not restricted to that of the humanist movement. It was a much 'larger', more amorphous movement, (perhaps better denoted as a 'period' or 'era'). That is, not all 'Renaissance' figures were 'humanists', especially if we restrict the latter primarily to scholars. Rather, the latter brought to consciousness, but also reflected, important aspects of those broader features which characterised Renaissance culture as a whole – and it is to where those broader features relate especially to a shift in historical presuppositions that we now turn.

Of such features, that shift to a *secular* outlook (so clear in humanist writing) is basic, and is evidenced in numerous other areas. As people's eyes 'turned back' towards man and nature, nowhere could this be seen more literally than in the realm of the fine arts and architecture. Foreign visitors (including invading armies) to Italian cities were astonished at the new style of church and civic building (and elegantly designed town squares and gardens), so much more ornate, 'this-worldly', and 'human' in the scale of their proportions and the interest of their decorations than the Gothic style dominant elsewhere in Europe. Also, Renaissance *sculpture* expressed the naturalness, beauty, and emotional nuances of the human form with astonishing skill and sympathy, whilst *painters* revolutionised their art by learning how to portray perspective and manipulate colour in order to make paintings of people, animals, and nature *lifelike* to a degree never thought of, let alone attempted, in symbolic medieval iconography, because it was not relevant from their other-worldy viewpoint.

Economic activity and secularism

This new, intense interest in the nature and possibilities of secular, temporal life was also manifested in a new outlook on *economic* activity. With a simultaneous rapid increase in population and prosperity from around 1500 in many parts of Europe, economic activities such as manufacture, commerce, international trading, and banking expanded. Entrepreneurship, business know-how, public financing, and the expansion of economic enterprises, became routine features of the fast-developing 'civil societies' which increasing numbers of towns and cities became during the Renaissance, spreading northwards from Italy into the rest of Europe. The merchant and businessman, eyes turned very much 'towards earth', became respected figures. Their perspective on life differed markedly from those of the two leading medieval classes of the religious clergy and the lofty aristocracy. Hard work, thrift, the rational pursuit of self-interest, concern for efficient and fair civil administration, the production of wealth, and the respectability of an ordered family and home, became a set of values (often, since, called 'bourgeois') which made sense to increasing numbers of people. In short, a crucial component of the new *secularisation* of society which differentiated Renaissance culture was the development of (pre-industrial) capitalistic practices and attitudes. We have only to recall Marx's brief sketch of the development of capitalism – it opened up the world to an extent unheard of before[10] – to recognise the importance of such innovative economic activity in both evidencing and promoting a fundamental shift in people's consciousness regarding the value, significance, and potential of this life on earth.

'Individualism'

Another feature of Renaissance culture in general which helped clear the ground for new perspectives on the 'meaning' of history was the growth of '*individualism*', a term used by Burkhardt to capture not only the emergence of certain people remarkable for the variety of their talents and interests – the famed 'Renaissance man' such as Leonardo da Vinci (1452–1519) – but also a more widespread individualistic spirit amongst people in general. Increasingly those in the developing commercial cities of Europe, loosened from a previously church-dominated rural way of life, began to think for themselves. This is already evident in the work of the humanists. But the latters' challenge to the intellectual dominance of medievalism was only part of a more general attitude which challenged the authority of tradition. The old ways of doing things, the old social attitudes, the old set of religious and moral beliefs, were increasingly abandoned by urban populations conscious of living in 'new times'. In modern parlance, a 'buzz' circulated, invigorating people to explore new ideas, try out new inventions, open themselves to new art, pursue the latest fashions in dress and modes of speech and social conduct, and purchase the new commodities increasingly available through the voyages of discovery, growth of international trade, and technological innovation. The individual, if he was prepared to *be* an '*individual*', alert to new ideas and opportunities, prepared to think for himself rather than submit to tradition, lucky enough to have an up-to-date ('humanist') education, and self-seeking enough to find patronage where necessary, could make his own way in the variegated, bustling city context, leaving behind the close-knit, tradition-bound, communal-based mode of rural, agricultural life.

Such, it seems, is the typical 'sociology' of urban culture, at least since 'the Renaissance' – namely, the emergence of *individualistic* values. Having mentioned 'capitalism' above, we should add that *its* typical 'sociology' is also frequently cited as 'individualism' – but we should note this is somewhat misleading since the idea that capitalism breeds 'individualism' was initiated in the nineteenth century as a hostile (socialist inspired) judgement where it meant an ethic centred on selfishness, competitiveness and anti-socialness characteristic of a greed and fear-driven exploitative socio-economic system spawning 'alienated' 'individuals' struggling to survive in a 'society of strangers'. This is not to say the 'individualism' of *Renaissance* culture was nothing to do with the emergent capitalism of the period – neither that the two 'individualisms' are not thereby connected. But it is to say that the 'individualism' attributed to Renaissance culture is different from today's often ideologically charged meaning. Applied to the Renaissance, its 'individualism' is usually presented as one of the most positive, progressive, civilised, and humanising aspects of its culture. Here we may return to Marx, for while (as above) we find him implicitly praising capitalism in its formative stages, we know what, according to him, capitalism grew to become. Perhaps the same applies to 'individualism'.

'Cultural relativism'

The final general feature of the Renaissance era which prepared the ground for a shift in people's perspective on time and history was the emergence of a new awareness of different societies and cultures – 'cultural relativism'. Again, although the humanist movement made an important contribution by reawakening an *historical* sense and producing both classical and contemporary histories, other factors also played their part. Not least was the revolution in *geographical* knowledge effected initially by the early fifteenth century 'rediscovery' of Ptolemy's second century AD maps and texts (brought from the Byzantine Empire), and subsequently by the Portuguese and Spanish voyages of discovery. Although Ptolemy's geographical knowledge was limited to Europe, North Africa, and Asia, unlike medieval 'world-maps' stylised around Biblical fantasies, Ptolemy's information was sufficiently objective and accurate for people to build upon during the fifteenth century so as to produce increasingly realistic representations of the oceans and continents, until the point was reached where geographers such as Mercator (1512–1594) simply left Ptolemy behind. In Mercator's case, he had by then the benefit of the knowledge gained by the spectacular achievements of explorers.

Beginning early in the fifteenth century, Portuguese discoverers in search of sea access to African gold and slaves went further down the west coast of Africa (as well as inland). Successful, by the 1480s their ambitions shifted to finding and rounding the southern tip of Africa, to travel east across the seas to India to create a sea-route to compete with the ancient (partly) overland spice trade from the Far East. In 1487 Dias duly rounded the Cape (appropriately named 'Good Hope'), and eleven years later Vasco da Gama reached the southwest coast of India via the Indian Ocean, paving the way for the rapid development of the Portuguese Empire in the East. Not to be outdone, however, by the 1490s the Spanish authorities were sufficiently convinced by Columbus (1451–1506) to finance the search for a direct route *west* across the Atlantic to the riches of the East, leading to his famous discovery of the Caribbean islands, after which, by the 1530s 'the New World' of the Americas had been settled by Cortes' intrusion into Mexico and Pizarro's into Peru. Prior to this, despite Columbus' undying belief that he had in fact discovered 'the East Indies', it was clear the New World was undoubtedly a whole continent standing between Europe and eastern Asia, and by 1521 Magellan had discovered the straits near the southern tip of South America leading into the 'calm' sea he called 'the Pacific', hoping the shores of the Far East would be but a short sail further west. In the event, his voyage, ending in the Philippines where he died, (the overall circumnavigation being completed some eighteen months later), showed how vast the Pacific Ocean is, and further revised understanding of the geography of the globe.

In less than 150 years, starting from the early 1400s, the Renaissance impulse for discovery, adventure, entrepreneurship, and worldly wealth had opened up not only 'the New World', but *a* new world. Rather than the cramped, Biblically slanted medieval notion of three continents (Europe, Asia, Africa) divided from each other by three great 'rivers' and surrounded by a circular ocean, the world was now seen as a collection of great continents connected via traversable oceans. This new world not only changed people's ideas about geography – it introduced them to different societies with 'novel' cultures and their own distinct past. Atlases and travel books became standard reading as people's imaginations were excited and their curiosity stirred. Gone forever was the narrow vision of European societies as the culmination and centre of the human world and its history. Rather, already stimulated by humanist writings, 'cultural relativism, one of the distinctive characteristics that differentiate modern from traditional culture, was powerfully reinforced by the European discovery of non-Western societies'.[11]

Printing

The other factor facilitating the growing awareness that peoples 'are the products of an ever-changing flow of events and that . . . all human values, ideas, and customs are contingent products of time and place',[12] is one that underlies everything else we have selected from 'the Renaissance', and without which it is doubtful it could have reached out to fashion the dominant features of the new era. This was the invention of printing in the West (the Chinese had invented their own techniques before AD 200). Although it is disputed whether Western printing was invented in Holland, France, or Germany, Johann Gutenberg (c. 1395–1468) of the Rhineland city of Mainz is traditionally regarded as producing the first printed books from 1450 (his famous Bible in 1455). Initially limited to religious writings and to imitating the aesthetic qualities of previous manuscript books, the printed book rapidly spread to a growing European urban market of consumers eager to learn and be entertained – for instance, by 1500, Venice alone had over 400 printers (and by 1539 it reached the New World, in Mexico City).

Typically, as it spread, emphasis upon religious books was superseded by the more secular interests of the Italian Renaissance. Not only religious subjects (and not only in Latin but also in the vernacular tongues), but books of history, law, mathematics, and secular stories – books on science, popular Latin classics, atlases – architectural drawings and engravings of paintings – poured off the presses to feed the educational, practical, and entertainment needs, as well as intellectual curiosity, of the growing middle classes of European towns and cities. In the first fifty years of printing (up to 1500) more than 6,000 separate works were published, involving the production of 'about six million books in approximately forty thousand editions, more books, probably, than had been produced in Western Europe since the fall of Rome'.[13] This phenomenal growth of the printed word in the fifteenth century – nothing short of *a communications revolution* – gave an enormous boost to the popularising of humanist writings and secular subjects, and it is little short of providential that in 1453, almost simultaneously with the invention of European printing, Constantinople, the seat of the Byzantine (East Roman) Empire fell to the Ottoman Turks, prompting a mass emigration of scholars to the West bringing numerous classical works unknown to medieval Europe to further boost the humanist project.

Overall, given that 'cultural relativism' is intimately dependent on the availability of knowledge and its reliable dissemination through a widely accessible system, it is difficult to over-estimate the impact of printing in broadening people's minds and loosening their preconceptions during the Renaissance period. The possibilities of a 'new age' in which human intelligence and knowledge could be expanded and communicated to open up the potential for a fulfilling, worthwhile temporal life characterised by the creative, tolerant interchange of different cultural and social ideas was clearly felt by optimistic Renaissance spirits.

Limitations of the Renaissance 'Cultural Revolution'

We have outlined the impact printing had in disseminating the secularism, individualism, and cultural relativism of the Renaissance, and the role the humanists and explorers played in forming this ethos, including a greatly heightened historical awareness – and taken all together, we might thus describe the Renaissance as a 'cultural revolution'. However, as with what many might see as an analogous 'postmodern' cultural revolution in *today's* world, fuelled by an analogous 'communications' and 'globalisation' revolution (IT), we should be cautious not to exaggerate the extent or beneficence of its impact.

First, as for the printed book, it did not reach down to ordinary labouring people, not only in the country but in the towns and cities, who had neither the 'know-how' to use them (i.e., they were illiterate), the education to appreciate them, nor the means to purchase them. And relatedly, the skills generated by familiarity with book-learning and its associated social and cultural graces were irrelevant to the working life and practices of the lower orders. Also darkening an otherwise rosy picture is the twin legacy of propaganda and censorship in fifteenth century Europe. As far as both the religious and temporal authorities were concerned, the new medium of printing could be used for subversive propaganda purposes. If unchecked, religious, moral, and political 'heresies' could be spread. The demon of 'the demos' could be unleashed. Arguably, this is precisely what happened as the new medium first made widespread the criticism of the Universal Church from cultured, respected figures such as Erasmus early in the sixteenth century, and then enabled a veritable explosion of highly charged pamphleteering which fuelled the Protestant Reformation from the 1520s onwards. But even prior to this explosion, 'the systematic censorship of books, little practised in the Middle Ages, appeared very soon after the invention of printing, and spread with it'.[14] By the 1530s both church and state (Protestant and Catholic) had drawn up lists ('indexes') of prohibited writings, continually revised and updated, such that 'by 1560 censorship of books in all its forms was universal in western Europe'.[15] 'The sword' was applied to 'the pen', but with as little eventual success as some hope, others fear, regarding censorship of the Internet.

Similar reservations apply to the other features which contributed to a growing fundamental shift in people's assumptions about the meaning and significance of history – namely, *secularism* and *individualism* and (to the extent it can be separated from these) Renaissance *humanism*. If printing encouraged a 'cultural relativism' which figures such as Erasmus hoped would make for a tolerant, civilised, peaceful and purposeful European community of peoples, by the 1530s it had also spawned ugly, divisive, religious propaganda and censorship, and an ensuing period of ignorance, superstition, and intolerance which threatened to plunge European populations into an intellectual barbarism more real than that which the Renaissance humanists thought had been left behind in 'the Middle Ages'. Many scholars agree that without printing the Reformation could not have happened.

Similarly, if geographical discoveries also contributed to 'cultural relativism', by those same 1530s they also spawned the growth of African slavery and the ruthless slaughter, enslavement, and 'conversion' of the Mexican Aztec and Peruvian Inca peoples of 'the New World'.

As for 'individualism', we have already commented upon a possible theory of how it was to grow from refreshing, benign, creative origins in Renaissance times to become an alleged Frankenstein's monster accompanying an increasingly rampant, inhumane capitalism some two hundred years later.

Similar mixed effects have been attributed to the rise of 'secularism', most obviously the notion that beneficial, progressive, and humanising as was 'the turning of men's eyes back to the things of this world' after centuries of static 'otherworldliness', it nevertheless sowed the seeds for later periods in which 'spirituality' or the sense of the 'sacred' gave way to a morally bankrupt materialism and soul-less atheism incapable of giving meaning to life. Some argue this began to occur as an effect of the 'Scientific Revolution' of the succeeding seventeenth century, whilst others point to the French Enlightenment of the eighteenth century as the crucial point at which 'secularism' turned sour. (Indeed, although from an opposite value-assessment, Michelet claimed that such Renaissance features as 'secularism' only reached their *fulfilment* in the French Enlightenment).

Finally, as for Renaissance humanism, although the effects we have discussed were real enough for brighter and more independent minds, for many it meant little more than learning the classics by rote and an uncomprehending acceptance of their relevance and significance – in short, a slavish and superficial following of fashion. And even at the properly intellectual level, the alleged superiority of the humanists' cultural and philosophical norms inherited from 'Antiquity' were to be challenged in the seventeenth century by the new proponents of the 'Scientific Revolution' and the associated new philosophy of 'scepticism' and 'empiricism', which rejected the learning of Antiquity as overblown and erroneous, correspondingly regarding humanist culture as presumptuous, narrow, and outmoded.

Continuing relevance of 'the Renaissance'

Such, then, are the *caveats* surrounding our presentation of 'humanism', secularism, individualism, and cultural relativism as those features of the Renaissance which, combined, we claim as principally responsible for initiating a fundamental shift in the way people thought about the meaning of human history. Some, if not all, of these *caveats* may be true. Certainly, consideration of them in other contexts casts salutary shadows upon an otherwise sunny perspective from which the above formative features are seen as such positive characteristics of Renaissance culture.

However, regarding the 'meaning' of time and history, because people's intuitions or presuppositions have not (empirically) been subject to either large or frequent variation – and because neither should we *expect* them to since they plumb the very depths of what and who human beings think they collectively are (i.e., the 'philosophical' question, 'what are we here for?', or 'what is life about?') – then we are dealing with alterations in people's mind-sets which can take centuries to 'filter' in. Today we are prone to overestimate the pace of some change in earlier history as well as perhaps exaggerate it in our own times. This is because certain changes, particularly technological ones, can have rapid *practical* effects. But changes in the way people think and behave regarding the larger questions of life take longer to become established, and even longer to work out their full effects.

For example, it is little over a generation ago in the West that 'the sexual revolution' began, partly prompted by the contraceptive pill. It is seen as provoking a rapid change in moral attitudes, as well as in sexual equality. The associated 'liberation' of women has significantly impacted upon their role in the workforce, with already felt effects on the institution of marriage and 'traditional' family norms. In short, it seems a rapid 'change' in society. Yet I venture that historical experience tells us 'we haven't seen anything yet', and that only after another hundred or so years will this fledgling 'change' have come to full fruition in a sexual-value and family culture unimaginable to us now. During this long period of gestation and unfolding of consequences numerous other changes in technology, attitudes, and behaviour will occur, such that it may be increasingly difficult to continue maintaining that 'the sexual revolution' began in the 1960s. Indeed, the whole concept of 'the sexual revolution' may be subsumed under some different 'change', or even be dropped altogether by future historians.

It is for these reasons that in treating of people's presuppositions about how they 'make sense' of history itself, I have chosen those 'conventional' features of humanism, secularism, individualism, and cultural relativity which play a part in the 'standard' account of 'the Renaissance', even though the *caveats* pointed out might (rightly) muddy the water when used to analyse other aspects of Renaissance times. Indeed, not only have such *caveats* (and others) served to revise people's notions of the Renaissance's connections with earlier periods and its significance for subsequent ones, some even doubt whether we should continue to use the notion of 'the Renaissance' at all in periodising European history. And a logical consequence of this, of course, is that the Renaissance humanist invention of 'the Middle Ages' is *also* brought into doubt, as demonstrated by the following current historiographical trends:

> Conventional chronological markers which since at least the time of Jacob Burckhardt delimited the end of the Middle Ages have . . . been dissolved in recent years. Both Renaissance and Reformation are liable to be appropriated by medievalists; alternatively the idea of an 'Old Europe' persisting until the convulsions of the French Revolution and Napoleonic wars can enfold both medieval and early modern Europe into a single pre-modern, or pre-industrial period.[16]

Again, there are doubtless many caveats which have rightly prompted such probings, in this case into the very *architecture* of our historical periodisations – yet, for those reasons given above, particularly centred on the nature of shifts in people's presuppositions about 'what history is', I do not think an account of their nature and chronology is misdirected by employing the concepts of 'the Middle Ages' and 'the Renaissance'. On the contrary, it is perhaps just in the context of changes in speculative assumptions about 'the meaning of history' that these periodising concepts are *substantively* useful, (going beyond Julia Smith's sensible conclusion, which she might also apply to 'the Renaissance', that if 'in neither geographical nor chronological terms is the notion of "the Middle Ages" neutral, value-free and unproblematic', nevertheless 'for all its faults, it remains in common usage, and will assuredly continue to do so. Part of its usefulness is simply its fuzziness, hallowed by five centuries of historical tradition').[17] To conclude this section on historiographical '*caveats*' which might otherwise threaten the integrity of this part of our 'guide', we can add two observations not only of direct relevance to the above considerations but also to our overall theme of the way people 'understand' the course of history.

'*Movements*'

First, in managing the kaleidoscopic flux of past events one of the more 'advanced' things we do, as distinct from constructing narratives of individual conduct vis-a-vis a political episode, military campaign, or writing a book, is to identify '*movements*' in history such as 'the Industrial Revolution', 'the Enlightenment', and, indeed, 'the Renaissance'. A 'movement' is, then, a 'large' phenomenon, and does not share the sharp resolution of other large-ish historical phenomena such as wars and specific *controversies* such as 'the Reformation'. (Elsewhere, in analysing their nature I have suggested 'movements' are the largest historically reconstructable, 'real' discrete phenomena).[18] Given their multifaceted nature, they are threateningly amorphous because made up of a collection of features and events otherwise with lives of their own, but which originate from, inter-transmit, and exemplify a movement's defining characteristics. As such, quite when and why 'movements' begin, where their parameters extend as they develop, and why and when they end, are difficult questions. Correspondingly, their validity as real phenomena is particularly vulnerable to destructive 'de-construction'. 'The Renaissance' offers a good example of all these points.[19] But it is just *because* of these *inherent* characteristics of 'movements' that their defining features are almost necessarily overstated, oversimplified, and over-generalised. Since they cannot be described or narrated with the accuracy of less complex historical phenomena, they are *denoted* by (more or less abstract) key concepts such as 'the rise of individualism' and 'the turn towards securalism' in the case of the Renaissance, or 'the critical application of reason to tradition and convention' in the case of the Enlightenment. Further, where a 'movement' spans maybe a hundred or more years, its *name* can be used to *periodise* history, denoting, for example, 'the Age' of the Industrial Revolution, or 'the Age' of the Renaissance. Potentially, this further obscures the real nature of any movement, for much of what occurred, for example, in fifteenth- and sixteenth-century Europe had little to do with 'the Renaissance', and this only serves to exacerbate the vulnerability of 'movements' to revisionist critiques.

However, none of this should persuade us there are not such things as historical 'movements', or that they can be easily revised by picking on some alleged determining feature. Rather, the point is to appreciate *why*, because of their nature, their features are 'overstated', 'oversimplified', and 'over-generalised'. It does not mean these movements were not 'real', or that their features were something radically different from how they are denoted. The critical historian should of course look closely at how a movement is explained, but if (because untutored regarding their nature) he is not appreciative of why *all* 'movements' are necessarily overstated, he runs the risk of throwing the baby out with bathwater as he undermines, amends, rejects, or otherwise 'revises' a movement out of recognition or out of history altogether. Equally, however, in the effort to recognise or extract discrete, identifiable phenomena from the kaleidoscopic flux of the past, neither should the historian 'invent' historical movements willy-nilly or idiosyncratically (as did a number of nineteenth-century thinkers[20]) – and this brings us to the second observation.

Even where a case can be made for fundamentally revising the commonly accepted notion of a particular movement, or for abandoning it altogether, people do not happily concede. This is even more the case where, as mentioned above, a particular movement is also used to *periodise* history by depicting an entire 'age' or 'epoch'. Having argued why 'the concept of the Italian Renaissance . . . has in my opinion done a great deal of harm in the past and may continue to do harm in the future', Lynn Thorndike adds:

> But what is the use of questioning the Renaissance? No one has ever proved its existence; no one has really tried to. So often as one phase of

89

it or conception of it is disproved, or is shown to be equally characteristic
of the preceding period, its defenders take up a new position and are just
as happy, just as enthusiastic, just as complacent as ever.[21]

In short, people do not readily relinquish the 'standard' periodisations of history,
however fuzzy or misleading they may be. However, perhaps neither should they,
since the standard periodisations may be replaced by a bewildering array of
alternative schemes, each with something to be said for them, but leading to no
consensus – and in its absence people would feel lost in an historical vacuum. In
other words, whether people *should* be readily prepared to revise their ideas
of history's major 'movements' and periodisations is debatable. More to the point
for our purposes is that their very unwillingness is evidence of what I have claimed
– people simply do not quickly or willingly concede their 'impressions' or
'perceptions' of the course of history because underlying them is an 'understanding'
or 'intuition' of the meaning or significance of history which, in its turn, is a crucial
component in forming their sense (whatever it may be) of 'the meaning of
life'. (The same reluctance applies to individuals' own *personal* history). Rightly
or wrongly, then, but certainly understandably, shifts in people's presuppositions
about 'the meaning of history' or 'the message of the past' have been few and
slow, and there is no reason to expect this to change short of some extraordinary
(extraterrestrial?) discovery of unmatchable provenance and unanswerable
relevance.

Thus it is, then, that despite those many areas in which doubt can be cast on how
far the Renaissance represented a sea-change in history – and, indeed, on whether
we should still believe in a movement, let alone denote an entire *period* of history,
called 'the Renaissance', – nevertheless in the case of tracing shifts in 'speculative
philosophy of history', the notion of 'the Renaissance' maintains its relevance to
the changes involved. Variously prompted or contributed to by technological
change (printing), military events (the fall of Constantinople), voyages of
discovery, literary research and retrieval, and economic development, those longer-
term, necessarily abstract-sounding (because 'cultural' and 'philosophical') factors
of secularism, individualism, and consciousness of cultural relativity began to mark
a shift in the way people conceived the significance of history. As already noted,
it did not demonstrate itself in any explicit works of 'philosophy of history' during
the Renaissance. These appear later. But it is *apparent* in many writings which
evidence the influence of the factors we have discussed, and it is to a sample of the
most famous (albeit often for other reasons) of these that we now turn.

Thomas More's *Utopia*

Although More did not discuss history itself, nor present any speculations upon its
meaning, in his popular little book, *Utopia*, (written in 1513 when he was gaining
the reputation as a lawyer and man of letters which was to lead to his appointment

as Chancellor by Henry VIII in 1521, and his subsequent martyred execution in 1535), it nevertheless typifies much that we have discussed in Renaissance culture as relevant to our theme. His humanist background (obvious from other writings displaying his Greek scholarship and brilliance as a Latin stylist) is evident in his admiration for classical culture, for although the society he describes in Book Two is not only imaginary but 'pagan', the educated, civilised, and rewarding richness of the Utopians' secular culture has an obvious classical reference. Part of More's purpose was to use his imaginary society as a stick with which to beat his contemporary Europe and to open up people's imaginations to the possibilities of social and economic change in the context of the new autonomy of emerging independent sovereign states. The book is replete with radical examples, some humorously intended, others seriously, of 'foreign' social customs and moral values, designed to foster that sense of 'cultural relativity' discussed above. But unlike strictly secularly-orientated 'civic' humanists, More (like his friend Erasmus) was a devout *Christian* humanist, and this explains why some aspects of Utopian society are inspired by monastic ideals of disciplined communal living which, arguably, run counter to the Renaissance spirit of 'individualism'. However, More can be interpreted as showing his sensitivity to this when, alert to the complaint that Utopians have little individual freedom (for example, to work as they wish) he retorts that because Utopian social and economic organisation, with its six-hour working day, gives each citizen economic security and full access to the benefits of education and culture, the Utopian is far freer than his average sixteenth-century European counterpart, whose life can be described as slavery.[22] (Later, in the early twentieth century, the socialist/anarchist thinker, Kropotkin, was to draw a distinction between 'individualism', by then associated with the debilitating effects of capitalism on working people, and what he called 'individualisation', the ethical goal of a communistically organised society only *through* which all would at last be empowered to fulfil themselves as individuals).[23]

Another aspect of *Utopia* relevant to our theme is More's (neo-) Platonism, which not only further evidences his humanist background but also draws together those components set out above. Although Aristotle continued to be studied in Renaissance times, the humanists 'rediscovered' the philosophy of Plato. Compared to the dry and technical scholastical selection and presentation of Aristotle, his mentor's philosophy was humane, idealistic, and inspirational, and presented via lively, user-friendly dialogues. Rather than metaphysics and logic, Plato dealt with more intimate *moral* issues such as love, justice, friendship, duty, the human good, and the ideal state. Not only does More's *Utopia* reflect these human-scale interests of Platonism – in 'imagining' the *ideal* society it directly reflects Plato's philosophical approach and teaching. Put simply, if, for Plato, we call this action 'just' and that (different) action just, and another action less 'just' than yet another, and so on, then all these different actions partake, to some degree, in the same thing, 'justice'. But no *actual*, single action exemplifies 'justice', nor ever could, because 'true' or 'real' justice is a perfect idea, form, or 'paradigm'. Similarly, most people's ideas of 'justice' only approximate towards it, as if seeing the truth only

91

through a mist. It is the philosopher's task to penetrate that mist to the *reality* of the matter, to discover, for example, true, or 'real' justice, friendship, love, or beauty. The actual, material world is then but a shadow of reality. 'Reality' is 'ideal'. As said, most people recognise 'reality' only partially, although they have an instinctive awareness of it. Without the latter they would not even try to be just, or have any idea what love is about, (let alone 'true love'). We need our 'ideals', then, and will be the more capable of approximating to realising them the more philosophers can enlighten us about the ultimate truths of 'reality'.

This Platonic approach to understanding the nature of reality is but one example of that enduring and variegated philosophical tradition called 'idealism', which essentially denotes the view that *material* 'reality' is insufficient in itself and thus cannot be understood in its own terms, but is only explicable as in some sense derivative of a more ultimate reality constituted by ideas, or mind. Equally enduring and multifaceted, the philosophical tradition which rejects this is called 'materialism'. As should be apparent, the *popular* meanings of both these philosophical terms do relate to their technical meanings, particularly the former. What we popularly call 'an idealist' is someone who strives towards, if not a perfect world, then at least one that approximates more closely to the 'ideal' reality he believes 'exists'.

Thomas More designed his *Utopia* (meaning 'nowhere' or 'no place') as just such an application of Platonic philosophy, in this case dealing with the ideal *society*. Its details do not concern us here; rather, its importance for our theme is that, in addition to being a highly individualistic work displaying a radically imaginative awareness of 'cultural relativity', it seriously asked people to think of a better world, of refashioning (if not revolutionising) their economy, social structure, and value-systems. He even raises the question of whether *human nature* itself can be changed through 'social engineering', almost implying that it is not fixed, but simply a product of environment. To ask people to think in this way is to invite them to see their *future* history as a residue of possibilities for their own conscious manipulation of it – and by implication, I suggest, it invites them to shift their preconceptions of the meaning of *past* history from one which sees it either in quasi-mythical (often millennialist) terms derived from Biblical prophesies or as a monotony of ultimately insignificant happenings from which nothing can be learnt. In short, how one sees the future depends, so often, on how one sees the past. However More's enigmatically written *Utopia* was received (including his own reservations about the relation between theory and practice, and the practical limitations of radical change[24]), in its wide appeal it represented as much a *contribution to* a shift in presuppositions about the meaning and significance of history as evidence that this was already under way.

Niccolò Machiavelli (1469–1527)

Machiavelli's reputation

Given Machiavelli's notorious reputation from *The Prince*, and the complication of revisionist treatments which present his ideas in a *favourable* light, it is proper to preface a treatment of his contribution to speculative philosophy of history by attempting to lay ghosts which might otherwise haunt our understanding. Not only in *The Prince* (1513– c.1515) but also in his much longer political work, *The Discourses on the First Ten Books of Livy's History of Rome* (1513–1517), examples abound of violent and deceitful statecraft which Machiavelli praises. Repeatedly he advises 'princes' (i.e., anyone in political control) to disregard conventional (Christian) morality if necessary to secure the political well-being of the state. Torture, cruelty calculatedly inflicted, assassination, lying, the breaking of promises, utter ruthlessness, and moral hypocrisy are all legitimate instruments of statecraft for Machiavelli. As for foreign affairs, the manual to a popular computer war-game selects a typically chilling (albeit un-referenced) quote: 'There is no avoiding war; it can only be postponed to the advantage of others'.[25] The traditional view is that Machiavelli was therefore 'a teacher of evil'.[26]

Against this, the 'liberal' view argues Machiavelli was a virtuous individual dedicated above all to the security and welfare of people in society, (e.g., the great *moraliser*, Jean-Jacques Rousseau, referred to Machiavelli as 'a proper man and a good citizen').[27] This view is derived variously from his *Discourses*, where he makes clear his preference for republican rather than monarchical government; from his realism as a 'man of his times'; from an historical recognition of his appreciation of classical politics and secular modes of thought; and most recently from a beguiling presentation of the complexities and contradictions of Machiavelli's personality so well described and compiled by de Grazia.[28]

The truth lies somewhere in the middle if we accept the universal intuition (explicated by Hegel[29]) that 'evil' is qualitatively different from 'wrong'. The former issues from a disregard of humanity as a whole (the conscience-less psychopath), whilst the latter occurs where the wrongdoer, in pursuit of his objective, knowingly violates someone's rights. Yet sometimes the sheer awfulness of situations can make, or seem to make, wrong actions necessary and thus 'right'.

Machiavelli took himself to be studying the fates of states and nations, and it ill behoves us, after such Second World War events as Hiroshima, Nagasaki, and the firebombing of German cities, to underestimate the literally awful moral territory he was addressing. Disarmingly (and, many would add, courageously) he does so with open eyes. He is dealing with real historical facts (e.g., Hannibal's harsh regime over his army, probably modelled on Polybius' account)[30] which, like Hiroshima, will not go away despite wishful thinking. He is not an irresponsible, unreflective moral degenerate – rather, he is a serious thinker tackling actual scenarios without the moral hypocrisy with which his own writings have so often been approached. This does not exonerate him from running the risk of skewed priorities and recommending 'morally wrong' actions, but it does show he was *not* a teacher of 'evil'.

On the contrary, De Grazia indicates that Machiavelli had a clear sense of 'evil' – and that he detested it.

> Cruelty to large numbers of men . . . wrings from him the superlative, 'cruellest'. . . . The instance of Philip of Macedon in the *Discourses* is . . . instructive. History discloses that he shifted men bodily from region to region as herdsmen shift their herds. [Machiavelli] considers this a horror. 'These methods are the cruellest and the enemies of every way of life, not only the Christian but the human'. Niccolò here acknowledges a moral law . . . a norm common to humans everywhere. So great a destruction occurs also when entire peoples and their families move from one place, forced by either hunger or by war, and go in search of a new location, not to rule it but to settle in it and drive out or kill its inhabitants. . . . A war involving a migrating or invading population 'is the cruellest and most terrifying'.[31]

Here we are surely reminded of the many examples of 'ethnic cleansing' around the world today, and it is clear Machiavelli would have utterly condemned such 'statecraft' as *evil*. In summary, then, Machiavelli is not a teacher of 'evil' – he is no demon. On the other hand, the 'liberal' counter-view is also incorrect. He is no saint. Like most people most of the time, as uncomprehending of true evil as they are incapable of it, he can however commit 'wrong', if only, in his case, by recommending it. It is simply that, given the domain he was confronting, and being a writer, his ideas were (despite censorship) spectacularly public.

Machiavelli on history

Machiavelli's fascination for both classical and his more local, and contemporary, history is amply proven in his political writings and in his *Florentine Histories*. His abilities as an historian, however, are not our concern here. Rather, it is his assumptions and more explicit thoughts on the nature and significance of history which attract our attention. Although Machiavelli was not a 'philosopher' in the sense of setting out an overall reasoned argument by defining his terms and making one proposition follow logically from another, neither was he unreflective (or uncommunicative) about how he viewed the meaning of history in general. This is because, although interested in history for its own sake, his primary passion was for the maintenance of an orderly governed society – and crucially, he thought that in its pursuit people can, and leaders should, *learn from history*. This thought is already indicative of a 'philosophy of history' underlying Machiavelli's general ideas, and as we will see, it informed his thinking on politics, morality, 'the meaning of life', as well as on history itself. But *why* did he think people can learn from history? And *what* does it teach? And, ultimately, what do Machiavelli's answers to these questions tell us about the shift in presuppositions about the meaning and nature of 'history' which, even more directly than More's *Utopia*, his writings both evidence and promoted?

Learning from history

Machiavelli dedicated his *Discourses* to two friends who encouraged him to 'write up' the many thoughts on politics and history with which he entertained them, stimulated by his reading of Livy's *History of Rome*. He writes: 'I have endeavoured to embody in it all that long experience and assiduous research have taught me of the affairs of the world',[32] and then begins the First Book with the bold declaration that, 'animated by that desire which impels me to do what may prove for the common benefit of all' – ('evil' Machiavelli?) – he has 'resolved to open a new route, which has not yet been followed by any one'. This 'new route' will involve 'the discovery and introduction of . . . new principles and systems', based on 'my little experience of the present and insufficient study of the past'.[33] In short, he is claiming, amongst other things, to 'use' or 'view' history in a new way. He remarks on 'the wonderful examples which the history of ancient kingdoms and republics ['Antiquity'] presents to us, the prodigies of virtue and of wisdom displayed by the kings, captains, citizens, and legislators who have sacrificed themselves for their country'. But 'not the least trace of this ancient virtue remains'. Given that civil law and medicine were still based on the learnings of Antiquity, it is surprising that 'to found a republic, maintain states, to govern a kingdom, organize an army, conduct a war, dispense justice, and extend empires, you will find neither prince, nor republic, nor captain, nor citizen, who has recourse to the examples of antiquity'.

The chief reason for this sad state of affairs, Machiavelli suggests, is that in addition to 'the evils caused by the proud indolence which prevails in most of the Christian states', there is 'the lack of real knowledge of history, the true sense of which is not known, or the spirit of which they do not comprehend'.[34] In short, he is accusing his contemporaries of a political complacency and inefficacy born of historical ignorance. Yet the ignorance he means is not so much of historical fact – most of those who read it 'take pleasure . . . in the variety of events which history relates'[35] – but ignorance of 'the true sense' or 'the spirit' of the history they read. Although he does not elaborate on this crucial notion, he seems to mean people do not use their imagination to understand historic figures as real individuals produced by their times – they fail to empathise with the culture in which the history they read took place. The result is they never think 'of imitating the noble actions, deeming that not only difficult, but impossible; as though heaven, the sun, the elements, and men had changed the order of their motions and power, and were different from what they were in ancient times'.[36]

Interestingly, Machiavelli here presents us with the other side of the 'cultural relativity' coin, for if one side is that a lack of a sense of cultural relativity leads people to disregard 'alien' cultures – they are not cultures at all but simply bizarre 'wonders' of no relevance to their own lives – the inverse is where people *do* 'recognise' a cultural difference between past and present, but out of a mistaken understanding of what fashions different cultures, still see no connection between them and their own lives, (for example, that aspects of them might be worth adopting). In other words, if straightforward xenophobia is one effect of a lack of a sense of 'cultural relativism', the more complex case is where that sense *is* present but is distorted by superficiality, leading to the misunderstanding that differences in cultures are so radical as to be unsurpassable. Machiavelli thinks people are wrongly overawed by the historico-cultural gap between their own times and antiquity, such that, out of their failure to understand 'the true sense' or 'spirit' of history, it appears to them impossible to learn from it. 'Wishing, therefore . . . to draw mankind from this error', Machiavelli declares his intention to write about the history he finds in Livy in a manner which treats of 'all those matters which, after a comparison between the ancient and modern events, may seem to me necessary to facilitate their proper understanding'. He intends, no less, a *comparative history* – but not for its own sake. Its purpose is to extract lessons about statecraft, if not indeed construct a 'science' of it. This would seem to be what he means when he boldly adds that this 'should be the aim of all study of history'.[37]

Machiavelli, then, shares that defining Renaissance sense of 'cultural relativity' so important in altering presuppositions about the meaning of history. But he is adding something. If previous Renaissance humanist scholars had helped generate a consciousness of 'cultural relativity' by their historically sympathetic translations and new editions of classical writings, it would seem Machiavelli remained dissatisfied with the historical consciousness involved. In pointing to the historical and cultural gap between 'Antiquity' and the Middle Ages, and between both and the present, it was correct and beneficial. But left at that, it was not only incomplete; it was damaging – because if history is viewed solely as a succession of different 'times', it can lead to the idea that they are so different that history is no more than an entertaining read; i.e., history is history, full-stop. There is nothing to be *learnt* from it. Further, there is no 'point' in history itself – that is, the *course* of history – for if societies are so radically dissociated by time that there are no connecting threads between them, then the course of history is devoid of any useful meaning for humankind.

Machiavelli does not believe this to be the case, and thus wants to inject into historical consciousness the salutary notion of the *connectedness* of history overall. This, as we will see, does *not* mean for Machiavelli that history is one single, meaningful 'story' unfolding through, for example, 'Providence' or divine planning. But it does mean that within the course of history men can find lessons, guidelines, and principles (he does not call them 'laws') which can be applied for the benefit of mankind. He views history as a (yet unopened) treasure-store of practically applicable experience, and intends to make a start at unlocking it. But people's presuppositions about the nature of history – their 'historical consciousness' – need shifting before it is worth their attending the opening.

96

Principles underlying history – unchanging nature and human nature

As mentioned, Machiavelli does not gather together the various 'principles' he sees as underlying history as a philosopher would. Rather, they emerge (and are repeated) in various parts of both the *Discourses* and *The Prince*. The passages quoted above have already revealed two. The 'order of nature' does not change; in men's perennial confrontation with the natural environment to secure safety and material well-being, the forces of nature remain the same. Geographical differences pertain, but within a given region, modern peoples face the same natural structures and forces their ancient predecessors had to deal with. Second, *human* nature does not change either. The way people handle their affairs and the ideas they have may differ from place to place and from earlier to later times, but this is not because the fundamental characteristics of human beings actually *change*. The remoteness of past times is not due to there having been a different natural order and different human nature. The same driving forces, the same fears and hopes, and the same range of emotions have always characterised human beings, and Machiavelli is famous for the cynical, or realistic, manner in which he views human nature in general. More accurately, however, because of his overriding interest in statecraft and government, the numerous and unflattering remarks he makes relate as often to how human nature *should* be viewed *for the purpose of government* rather than representing some overall view.

> [W]hoever desires to found a state and give it laws, must start with assuming all men are bad and ever ready to display their vicious nature, whenever they may find occasion for it. . . . Men act rightly only upon compulsion: but from the moment that they have the option and liberty to commit wrong with impunity, then they never fail to carry confusion and disorder everywhere.[38]

> [N]ature has created men so that they desire everything, but are unable to attain it; desire being thus always greater than the faculty of acquiring, discontent with what they have and dissatisfaction with themselves result from it.[39]

Also, men have 'the love of novelty, which manifests itself equally in those who are well off . . . For . . . men get tired of prosperity'. This 'love of change' makes men fickle and easily influenced, and if they are to be managed, the fundamental principle that 'men are prompted in their actions by two main motives, namely, love and fear', must be exploited, fear being the most reliable lever.[40] Finally, 'the great majority of mankind are satisfied with appearances, as though they were realities, and are often even more influenced by the things that seem than by those that are'.[41]

Machiavelli gives this latter thought particular prominence in *The Prince*, where, as an extension of his views on human nature (again, for *political* purposes), we see him dividing humanity into three groups. First there is the vast majority of ordinary people, 'the vulgar', who simply have to be manipulated in one way or another, as above. Hypocrisy (or 'public relations', 'spin-doctoring') is both necessary and effective, 'for men in general judge more by the eyes than by the hands, for every one can see, but very few have to feel. Everybody sees what you appear to be, few feel what you are . . . the vulgar is always taken by appearances . . .'.[42] The second, much smaller group, are 'the few' who, not deceived by appearances, know what actually goes on, including appreciating the art of manipulation. (A nice anecdote tells of a cynically smiling Machiavelli – one of the 'few' – standing at the back of a crowd, studying the charismatic preacher-politician Savanorola holding 'the many' in the palm of his hand). The third, even smaller group, are those actually in power, particularly the *individuals* involved. All three groups are brought together in Machiavelli's chillingly economical statement, '. . . the world consists only of the vulgar, and the few who are not vulgar are isolated when the many have a rallying point in the prince'.[43]

Nature does not change her ways – neither does humankind change its ways. 'Reflecting now upon the course of human affairs, I think that, as a whole, the world remains very much in the same condition, and the good in it always balances the evil'.[44] What, then, makes for change? (for without it, there would be no history at all). Machiavelli's answer is to add, 'but the good and evil change from one country to another'. After the fall of the Roman Empire, he tells us, the extraordinary concentration of good that characterised it was 'scattered among many nations', some of which do themselves an injustice in praising their past more than their present. Not so, however, for Italy and Greece, in whose past 'there are many things worthy of the highest admiration, whilst the present has nothing that compensates for all the extreme misery, infamy, and degradation of a period where there is neither observance of religion, law, or military discipline, and which is stained by every species of the lowest brutality'.[45] So things *do* change, and, according to Machiavelli, in finding what causes change we will find the other 'principles' or 'factors' which underlie history.

'Education': law, role-models, and religion

The most frequent explanation he gives for a country's changing circumstances and character is 'education'. He does not mean 'education' in the formal sense of schooling, but in the broader sense of the (moral, political, and religious) *culture* instilled in the people. Instilled in several ways, the most important for Machiavelli are the public effect of the laws *and* of their upholding; the propaganda value of great actions by 'virtuous' men; and the character of religion. The 'vulgar' need inspiration and fear to maintain that public-spiritedness which is the backbone of a healthy state – and any state naturally begins to lose its early vigour. Thus, regarding law and its observation in the Roman Republic:

> Even if we had not an infinity of other evidences of the greatness of this republic, it would be made manifest by the extent of her executions, and

the character of the punishment she inflicted upon the guilty. Rome did not hesitate to have a whole legion put to death according to a judicial decision, or to destroy an entire city, or to send eight or ten thousand men into exile. . . .[46]

As for the exemplary actions of great men, not only is it crucial for their sake that they receive appropriate public honours, the official celebrating and story-telling of their great deeds is also an excellent instrument of cultural education by providing the 'vulgar' with inspiring role-models.

Finally, as for religion, because it is 'the most necessary and assured support of any civil society',[47] . . . 'everything that tends to favour religion (even though it were believed to be false) should be received and availed of to strengthen it', and thus it is an essential duty of rulers 'to uphold the foundations of the religion of their countries, for then it is easy to keep their people religious, and consequently well conducted and united'.[48] Also, to claim divine authority and miraculous intervention in favour of a constitution (or founding system of law) adds immeasurably to its credibility with the people. Where a country's religion begins to weaken and stray from the vigour of its original principles, this will cause important changes in people's attitudes, morality, and political culture, thereby constituting a major factor, for Machiavelli, in provoking historical change. He makes no secret of his contempt for the state of the Christian religion in his own day; 'Nor can there be a greater proof of its decadence than to witness the fact that the nearer people are to the Church of Rome, which is the head of our religion, the less religious they are'. It has strayed so far from its founding principles that 'her ruin or chastisement is near at hand',[49] and much of the parlous state of Italy must be laid at its door. In addition to the general effects of the religion's decadence, in practice any religion's educative role is most immediately and effectively transmitted in its daily rites and frequent festivals. These 'set the tone' of a people's value-system and are thus a powerful historical instrument. In his own day Machiavelli complains that the Christian religion,

> glorifies more the humble and contemplative men than the men of action. Our religion, moreover, places the supreme happiness in humility, lowliness, and a contempt for worldly objects, whilst the other [the ancient Roman religion], on the other hand, places the supreme good in grandeur of soul, strength of body, and all such other qualities as render men formidable . . . These principles seem to me to have made men feeble.[50]

Although Machiavelli does not propose ditching Christianity for the secular advantages of Roman paganism (not that he would have any theological objection in my view), there are many examples of his wish that Christian rites, ceremonies, and spectacles were more enthralling and awe-inspiring – even ferocious and bloody.[51]

The role of individiuals

If 'education' is one factor explaining why things change (i.e., 'what drives history'), another returns us to the actions of great (or infamous) individuals – but now *directly* for their role in historical change rather than for their *educative* effect. No reading of Machiavelli can fail to reveal that he considers individual human agency, particularly of those in power, as a major determinant of (historical) change. Wrongly underplayed in much recent historiography and historical thinking because of a misguided disdain for narrative (and a consequent preference for using abstract 'factors' in historical analysis), the role of individuals in 'making things happen' is so obvious to Machiavelli that he does not feel any need to defend or explain it. After all, the world consists only of the vulgar, the few who are not vulgar, and 'princes'. Constantly, in all the lessons he extracts from his 'new route' of comparative history, he focuses upon the actions of those in power. Whether they succeed or fail, or are 'virtuous' or evil, how they perform has potent effects either for good or ill.

Although his thinking is restricted principally to the political and military aspects of history because of his fascination in statecraft, this does not mean he is not interested in the broader topic of *cultural* changes (e.g., religious change). Rather, it would seem they can be subject to the determining skill of 'princes'. In short, apart from his fascination in power *per se* (its acquisition, exercise, maintenance, expansion, and loss), implicit in Machiavelli's approach to history is an instinct akin to Aristotle's notion of politics as the master-science – namely, that in addition to those special techniques intimate to the practice of 'politics' in the narrow sense, 'politics' is not simply one area of expertise or 'techné' amongst others (medicine, warfare, agriculture) but is the overarching umbrella which embraces all aspects of society. This is because, from its unique overall perspective of *governing* society, it determines the relative importance of society's components. Rightly or wrongly, then, there is a larger logic to Machiavelli's belief in the importance of individual agency in history than simply his fascination in power. The exercise of statecraft, necessarily by those *individuals* in political power, is for him one of the principal causes of *change*.

'Fortune'

This said, however, there is a further force which contributes to change for Machiavelli, and it as often conflicts with the energies of great individuals as assists them – namely, *fortune*. Potent as the actions of strong political leaders may be, fortune can overturn their hopes and achievements. Alternatively, fortune can provide the circumstances, otherwise incapable of being fashioned by men, in which great leaders can fulfil their potential despite the odds. We have earlier encountered the *classical* notion of 'fortune', and it is no surprise that Machiavelli means the same, particularly where it refers not to mere chance but to a definite *force*. Quite what he thought this 'force' was is difficult to say, but from his frequent references to it (and his explicit treatment of it in Chapter 25 of *The Prince*) it is clear it is something tangible for Machiavelli, rather than a metaphorical way of pointing to the uncertainties which dog human affairs. As a distinct 'agent' in history, he presents 'fortune' as immensely powerful and unpredictable. Occasionally it may act as the deliverer of moral retribution, but that is not Machiavelli's dominant theme – usually (though not always) fortune is vindictive and destructive. Often he seems to equate it with 'the character of the times', or, alternatively, suggest the latter are *caused* by it. Either way, irrespective of anything people can do about it, there are good times and bad times, propitious times and threatening times, fast-moving times and slow-moving times. 'Fortune' determines the times we live in, and can rapidly change them so that those who, by chance or intelligence have prospered by adapting to 'the times', can be ruined if then unable to change their ways to meet the new. Repeatedly, Machiavelli stresses that, given fortune's power over 'the times', adaptability is the key to success. Famously, the only way to manage the caprice of fortune is, poetically, to treat her as a woman, boldly and fiercely rather than 'coldly' and rationally, for although she cannot be defeated, she may *let* herself be subdued by the young and impetuous.[52]

Finally, there is one further way in which fortune's governance of history can be challenged. It seems to Machiavelli that 'fortune is the ruler of half our actions, but that she allows the other half or thereabouts to be governed by us'. In a non-too consistent passage, Machiavelli compares fortune to 'an impetuous river that, when turbulent', causes chaos. But the river can also be quiet (fortune *chooses* to withdraw from governing the affairs of men?), and when this occurs, men can build dykes to restrain the river next time it tries to flood. Just so with fortune; when quiet (approximately half the time?), people can prudently take measures to minimise its return.[53]

Given this account, what exactly is this 'force' Machiavelli believed in as a potent determinant of history? Leaving aside the metaphors of the flooding river and the wilful woman inviting passionate seduction, we should recognise a rational core in what Machiavelli intuits about 'history' from this somewhat uncertain set of ideas. Clearly humankind has never been in control of its own circumstances and, thus, history. There are 'forces' man cannot control. Increasingly, through scientific research in its broadest sense, we have at least come to recognise what some of these forces *are*, and may even learn how to control, or at least restrain, them – stock-market crashes, economic movements, population expansions, class-structures, diseases, the causes of political alienation and terrorism. But there are others we know of but can do little about, such as climatic changes. *Knowing* the nature of such 'forces', we may fear them but do not refer to them as 'fortune' (or 'fate'). Where, however, 'things happen' of a totally unforeseen nature – epidemics, natural catastrophes, startling political and social developments due to 'changing times' – we have to admit there are 'forces' unknown which, with apparent capriciousness, help determine history. This is what Machiavelli means, except he gathers 'them' into one ('poetical', classical) 'force', namely, 'fortune'.

In his day, however, the state of scientific, economic, sociological, meteorological, and medical knowledge was miniscule compared to today. To Machiavelli and his contemporaries, then, so many of the forces we know, or think, help determine history (and thus make it intelligible) were unrecognised. In modern parlance, they must have felt alienated from history, relatively powerless before its march. It is in this light we should appreciate not only what Machiavelli *means* by 'fortune' (and why he refers to it so frequently), but also what he says about it. Here, rather than see him as a fatalist, obsessed by fortune's power over history, he appears in a more positive light, for he is attempting to lift a corner of the veil of ignorance concerning history's determinants. In the 'political science' he constructs from his 'comparative historical' studies, he is uncovering how 'politics' and 'statecraft' work, to show how men of the right calibre can take matters into their own hands. It is true that 'fortune' can still intervene, but if men *understand* the art of government (including warfare) they can at least manage affairs better when fortune strikes, and at best craft a viable state whilst it is dormant. In short, Machiavelli starts the 'scientific' task of revealing the 'forces' underlying the course of history. Limited as it is in scope (i.e., 'politics'), and inadequate as its conclusions might be, his analysis is tangible evidence of an approach not only reflecting but extending the shift in presuppositions about 'history' achieved in the Renaissance – one built upon by subsequent thinkers on history.

Cycles

We may conclude this exploration of the 'principles' which Machiavelli thought underlie history by briefly assessing two further (alleged) 'factors' in his thinking – the notion of historical/political cycles, and the role of God. Regarding the first, there are those who interpret certain passages from the *Discourses* and the *Florentine Histories* as showing Machiavelli straightforwardly subscribing not only to Polybius' notion of recurrent political cycles but also to the larger notion of history as an eternally recurring circle along cosmological lines. For example, Jaki includes Machiavelli in noting that the Renaissance saw (in some) a renewed interest in and acceptance of the basic cyclical theory of history, because Machiavelli offers 'a classic description of history as an ever recurring treadmill'.[54] Predictably this permits Jaki to include Machiavelli as one of those who failed to make any contribution to the idea of human progress. We may also revisit Nisbet, who adopts the same line on a Machiavelli who 'sees in history nothing but ups and downs, cyclical returns',[55] and therefore contributes to and confirms Nisbet's predictably revisionist, but here extraordinary, view that there are no 'ideas of progress to be met with throughout the whole Renaissance'.[56]

Trompf, however, by virtue of a detailed examination, adopts a less straight-forward interpretation. Although doubts linger over Machiavelli's access to the actual texts, 'during the sixteenth century the Polybian cycle of governments makes a dramatic reappearance in the pages of Machiavelli'.[57] However, not only does Machiavelli take an eclectic approach to its details, he removes that element of 'naturality' (which alluded to some kind of unknowable 'divine' or 'supernatural' force) driving the cycle, seeing it driven instead by the human-scale interplay between men's actions and the necessities of situations. Historical circumstances can repeat themselves, with similar outcomes, but the factors which produce this 'are neither supernatural nor extrahuman. . . . History remains the domain of human action'.[58] In Trompf's hands, then, although we would expect Machiavelli to be interested in this famous classical theory of inexorable political cycles, he uses some parts of it and abandons others, and most particularly, removes any 'superstitious' notion of 'the wheel of fortune'.

If we were to add that the recognition of historical repetition can be viewed as neither novel nor 'philosophical', but as a common-sense idea which occurs to anyone, (*pace* Trompf's special interest in the topic), then we move even further away from the view that a belief in 'supernatural' inevitable cyclical returns was an important factor in Machiavelli's approach to understanding the forces determining history. And (in a later analysis) this, indeed, is precisely where de Grazia takes us. Regarding the Polybian cyclical theory he tells us that Machiavelli, '[h]aving presented the theory (note that he calls it an opinion). . . . Niccolò takes it apart, gently, quickly, wittily'.[59] De Grazia observes that 'if cycles exist as Polybius would have them, the lessons of history would be restricted', and 'most of Niccolò's study and experience would be good for little except contemplation'.[60] In short, Machiavelli does *not* subscribe to a theory of inexorably recurring political cycles. Running counter to the grain of his activist, interventionist approach to (political) history, '[t]he theory of political cycles appears early in the *Discourses* and, in effect, is then discarded'.[61]

We may comment that this, of course, is not to say that history does not have its ups and downs, or even less that history is, for Machiavelli, purposefully *linear*. 'Fortune', as we have seen, is a powerful 'force', but even where he refers to it popularly as a 'wheel', this neither means Machiavelli believes in the classical theory of political cycles nor even that, as a 'wheel', fortune ensures eternal historical *repetition*. More typically he uses the metaphor to capture the notion of fortune confounding, or *overturning*, the plans and just deserts of men. It would seem, then, that de Grazia is the more correct and that those who interpret Machiavelli as believing in history 'as an ever recurring treadmill' have been misled by some general passages where he (unremarkably) reminds us of the ups and downs of history, and by confusing his notion of the role of 'fortune' (particularly as a 'wheel') with the classical idea of cyclical repetition. Rather, history is neither cyclical nor linear – it is, simply, threateningly chaotic.

God

Finally, in this examination of what drives history for Machiavelli, what about the role of God? The answer seems to be that God has no role. There is no overarching 'divine providence' planning the course of history. We cannot even be sure what Machiavelli's real thoughts were on 'God', although we know what they were on *religion's* role in society, and on the state of the Christian religion in particular. He probably did have some sort of 'belief in God', but in keeping his references to Him uncontroversial, general, and brief, he can be read in different ways – either as merely paying lip-service to a God in whom he believes but regards as unknowable and whose operations in history are not evident, ('that our free will may not be altogether extinguished')[62] – or as paying lip-service to a (Christian) God in whom he does not believe – or even, between the lines, as advocating atheism. As ever, we must recognise the power of censorship in the sixteenth century, both to endanger writers and deprive them of a hearing; and also that, irrespective of the times, many individuals sensibly wish to keep their deepest thoughts to themselves. Whatever the case with Machiavelli, it is clear he omits 'God' as one of the factors behind history. He does not ask us to bring 'Him' into our presuppositions regarding the meaning of history, even where he appears to. He opens the famous Chapter 25 of *The Prince* by saying, 'It is not unknown to me how many have been and are of opinion that worldly events are so governed by fortune and by God, that men cannot by their prudence change them . . .'. He then embarks on a discussion, reviewed above, of 'how much fortune can do in human affairs and how it may be opposed'.[63] Not accidentally, 'God' is not mentioned throughout the remainder of the chapter.

Summary comments

As noted, the complex, controversial period of 'Renaissance' did not produce its own distinctive 'philosophy of history'. But it would be absurd to ignore the Renaissance contribution to 'philosophy of history' on such grounds. As we move forward to later explicit and elaborate 'philosophies of history', one rationale of this 'guide' is to show they did not simply appear from nowhere. On the contrary, the very grounds on which they stood – an appreciation of the 'historicity' of the past; the linking of culture, religion, politics, and, latterly, class and economics, into a holistic appreciation of historical societies; the preparedness to question authority and generate new notions of 'what history is about'; and the urge to identify and understand the causes and/or 'forces' of historical change – were uncovered during and because of those features of Renaissance culture we have surveyed. And although this 'guide' does not purport to be a history of 'philosophy of history', the preceding chapters make clear that neither, in *their* turn, did these Renaissance shifts in assumptions about the nature and meaning of history simply appear from nowhere.

So many of the features making for these Renaissance shifts were reflected and (sometimes unpalatably) extended by Machiavelli that it is fitting this survey of relevant Renaissance trends should culminate in his ideas – (indeed, de Grazia goes so far as to refer to Machiavelli as 'our philosopher of history').[64] His writings exemplify, deliberately, the *consciousness* of a new approach (his 'new route'); individualism; alertness to 'cultural relativity'; and perhaps above all, his marked *secularism*. This latter feature (also famous in debates over his morality) invites comment, particularly in the light of that theme which has already emerged as integral (for some) to speculative 'philosophy of history' – namely, the question of human *progress*. Machiavelli can be viewed as a *frighteningly* secular thinker. As a precursor of the moral vacuum many felt the later Scientific Revolution's 'cold philosophy' spawned, (e.g., in Hobbes), there is no 'superhuman', or 'ideal', underpinning to morality for Machiavelli. Symptomatically, from what he writes (or omits to write), 'God' plays no role in humankind and its history. *Belief* in deities, however, plays a crucial role for Machiavelli insofar as the organised religions it generates may be more or less manipulable for the political projects of originating stable societies via 'authoritative' legislative frameworks and maintaining a politico-moral culture favourable to the security of the state. In short, religion is simply ideology – and the better the function and dynamics of ideology are understood, at least, by 'princes' and those of 'the few' who advise them, the more effectively can 'the vulgar' ('the masses') be managed. Yet, sinister (or realistic) as this may sound, the purpose of this aspect of statecraft – managing 'the vulgar' – is not to oppress them, nor exploit them for economic gain. Rather, as for *any* aspect of statecraft, it is to secure those minimal conditions essential for all in a society to extract what value they can from their particular lives. The latter is up to them, but without effective law, without an administrative system to tackle plague, drought and starvation, and without security from invasion, genocide, rape, plunder, and forced migration, the value this life may offer is aborted. And it would seem that, for all 'practical' purposes, there is only this life, here on earth, for Machiavelli.

As the 'cold' observer *par excellence*, he writes more than once that he is no 'idealist', no wishful thinker. Not only is he open-eyed about the selfish-interestedness, fickleness, gullibility, and moral hypocrisy of mankind – (he accepts it, and advises on how to make the best of it, for everyone) – he is equally open-eyed about 'history'. There is no divine plan for, or underneath, it. Neither is there any inbuilt dynamic making history *progressive* for humankind. Not a 'believer' in human, or historical, progress in general, he believes that in the ups and downs of history, 'virtuous' leaders can carve out the above minimal conditions for a human life and, with luck and foresight, sustain them long enough for the the fruits of a civilised society to ripen – hopefully to the extent of achieving glory in the annals of history for both that society and its leaders.[65] There is no higher reward – not salvation, nor human perfection, nor the perfect society, nor assured human progress into the future. There are simply human-beings, fixed in their nature, on an earth fixed in its nature. To that extent we are lost, save for the energy, intelligence, and courage we can muster to *make* our own history. 'History' itself is not going to help us – not being directed, it has no direction. But it does provide a storehouse of experience we can learn from, rather than approach it with irrational, erroneous suppositions about its 'meaning'.

Although not a nihilist, there are respects in which Machiavelli prefigures the twentieth-century existentialists. Although lacking their *psychological* sense of detachment, the notion that 'existence precedes essence' – that there are no blueprints men 'must' follow – pervades his historical thinking. (Even to the extent his beloved Roman Republic *does* provide a 'blueprint', it is one they forged for themselves). And as for the consequent – that we are thus '*condemned* to be free' – there is indeed an unsettling starkness about Machiavelli's view of the relation between history and humankind. Relatedly, this is also apparent in his *moral* thinking, for if by pointing to his clear attachment to the secular ideals of *classical* moral thought one rightly dismisses those who call him 'immoral', one nevertheless feels he *chose* them as the most 'appropriate' or 'effective' rather than their imposing themselves on his conscience. From this 'proto-existentialist' perspective it is difficult to separate his moral from his historical assumptions, or to see which determined which.

But our final comment must be that, in opening the door to modernity, Machiavelli went further than his contemporaries. We would overestimate, 'over-modernise', the contribution of the Renaissance period to the development of 'philosophy of history' were we to take Machiavelli as *representative* of Renaissance changes in historical assumptions. Rather, in *epitomising* its possibilities his ideas were in some respects *untypical*. If the predominant tone of Renaissance culture was one of self-praise and hopes for a more civilised future, Machiavelli's contempt for his own country's times, in terms of its 'political culture' – (for him, that which determines all else) – knew no bounds. And if the most important contribution of the Renaissance to altering ideas on the nature and meaning of history was its secular emphasis, most people (including intellectuals) remained not only religious but 'superstitious', for instance believing in magic and witchcraft, and holding 'pre-scientific' notions on cosmology, alchemy, and medicine. No doubt Machiavelli subscribed to some of this himself, but in respect of the cool, neutral rationality he brings to his consideration of statecraft and the nature of history he shows himself unencumbered by much of the baggage cluttering his contemporaries' clarity of vision. In short, if a major feature of Renaissance culture was to turn men's eyes back to earth, Machiavelli went further – he also opened their eyes, too wide for most, to what they saw. As it happened, they did not have to look. The corner of the veil, which Machiavelli's probings had lifted on the nature of history, fell back into place as even before his death in 1527 Europe plunged into a period of politico-religious turmoil and reactionary intellectual sterility. The secular impulse of the Renaissance, promising so much in the humanistic understanding of history, and bearing fruit in Machiavelli, was stopped by the Reformation. The project of a rational attempt to 'make sense of' history was not to be resumed for many decades, and not to be attempted comprehensively and systematically (but then for the first time) until the early eighteenth century by the then obscure, but now increasingly famous, Giambattista Vico.

6

AN INNOVATIVE INTERLUDE

From Machiavelli to Vico

Introduction

Despite the claims made for St Augustine as the 'first philosopher of history',[1] with good reason most scholars agree that Giambattista Vico (1668–1744), from Naples, better deserves the title. This is because he was the first thinker to produce an overall 'theory' of the course and meaning of history derived from objective study and the conscious application of abstract principles. Unlike Augustine, Vico's motivation was not primarily ideological. He was principally concerned to investigate 'the truth' about human history for its own sake, (although, as we will see, this did not preclude him from reaching prescriptive conclusions). In these respects we may compare Vico's to Machiavelli's 'scientific' thinking about history. But whereas Machiavelli was no philosopher, in the sense that he did not construe his ideas on history from abstract principles brought to light and defended, Vico's project was explicitly 'philosophical'. As he tells us in his *Autobiography*, he laboured for many years in comparative solitude to find the key to unlocking numerous problems in understanding the logic of the course of history – and it is clear he was open-minded enough to change his mind over certain issues on occasions.

Vico's originality

In these senses, then, Vico is recognised as a 'philosopher' in today's parlance – and, moreover, as the first philosopher of *history*. In itself this would establish his claim to originality. But in addition, numerous scholars have remarked that Vico's thought is also *intrinsically* astonishingly novel. There is much to be said for this, but it would be wrong to conclude our first real philosopher of history's ideas sprang from nowhere. Although the directions Vico's thinking takes were very much his own, the issues he addressed were neither invented nor discovered by him. Rather, he was responding to intellectual developments, both current and recent in his times (which spanned the latter part of the seventeeth, as well as nearly half the eighteenth, century). We finished the last chapter with Machiavelli, the High Renaissance, and the beginning of the Reformation, and now seem to be bridging some 150 years to reach Vico. Did nothing important to our theme occur between?

The answer is that, far from a period bereft of significant and relevant intellectual development, the intervening years were replete with innovation in the domains of philosophy, science, religion, political theory, law, literature, and history – such that the very foundations of the modern European mind were laid. Vico was far enough away from, yet still close enough to, this giant formative process to benefit from a perspective which generated an astonishingly wide scope and synthesising impulse in his thought. Thus it is that exploring those intellectual currents which Vico was responding to involves outlining many of the principal features of post-Reformation and seventeenth-century European thought – features the reader might fear were being neglected by our shift from Machiavelli to Vico. That this is no mere ploy of exposition on your guide's part is partly confirmed by Vico himself, for it is clear he conceived his major work, *The New Science*, as not only what we now call a philosophy of history, but as nothing less than a comprehensive 'new science' which would disentangle, correct, and make new sense out of numerous of the intellectual currents flowing from the Renaissance – in short, a synthesis of philosophy, historico-cultural studies, and politico-legal theory which was not only grand but so innovative that Vico regarded his work more as a *superseding* of previous knowledge than a synthesis. Having explained what is wrong with previous ideas, breathtakingly he tells us that 'for purposes of this inquiry, [into no less a topic than the understanding of world history, culture, and politics!] we must reckon as if there were no books in the world'.[2] Thus Vico's sense of his own originality; and it must therefore be with some irony that we have to insist that for the purposes of *our* enquiry (into what Vico's ideas were) we must precisely 'reckon with' the 'books in the world' which preceded his, since if we do not know what he was responding to we will not understand his thinking even if we 'understand' what he writes.

Vico's intellectual inheritance

The Scientific Revolution

We have claimed that Vico's philosophy of history, explicit in his *New Science* (final edition, 1744), is the product of his reflections on major intellectual movements developed since the Renaissance. Of these, arguably the most significant was what (since the eighteenth century)[3] we call 'the Scientific Revolution'. Indeed, it has been claimed that this movement 'outshines everything since the rise of Christianity and reduces the Renaissance and Reformation to the rank of mere episodes'.[4] From previous history, the revered authorities of Aristotle and Ptolemy had said the Earth does not move, and is at the centre of the universe. The Bible said the same, adding the huge moral gloss that the Earth is so placed as fitting for God's supreme creation, Man. Born in 1473, the Polish mathematician and astronomer, Nicolaus Copernicus, had by 1530 worked out a radically new theory which instead placed the sun at the centre of the universe, and claimed the Earth revolved around the sun (as did the other planets) annually, and that it rotated daily (swaying slightly as it did so). Although a largely mathematical, even hypothetical, construct which retained other (false) features of the old 'geocentric' theory of the universe, Copernicus' revolutionary new 'heliocentric' theory stimulated other astronomers and 'natural philosophers' in the second half of the sixteenth century. By the 1590s the German astronomer, Johannes Kepler (1571–1630), began publishing his own theories derived from the Copernican system, culminating in his discovery of the laws of planetary motion (Kepler's Laws) and his explicit defence of Copernicus in his textbook *Epitome of Copernican Astronomy* (1621). From the 1630s many more astronomers and 'natural philosophers' were thereby converted not only to the Copernican system but to the broader scientific and philosophical implications of this challenge to traditional learning. But such 'conversions' were not without their dangers, as the career of another epoch-breaking early 'scientist', Galileo (1564–1642), was famously to demonstrate.

By the 1590s this remarkable Italian champion of science and intellectual freedom, already a convert to Copernicism, began to design his own scientific instruments such as the pendulum, and scorning mere speculative hypothesis, combined mathematics and empirical experimentation to uncover and formulate the fundamental laws of motion and mechanics so essential to physics. His work convinced him that 'matter is unalterable, i.e., always the same, and . . . because of its eternal and necessary character it is possible to produce demonstrations of it no less straight and neat than those of mathematics'.[5] He was aware, of course, that such a statement concerned not merely physics but also held enormous philosophical and theological implications because it subverted both the authority of Aristotle and the Catholic Church. But by 1613, some three years before the authorities declared a ban on Copernican ideas, Galileo had used the telescope he had designed to empirically demonstrate the falsity of traditional ideas. Increasingly under threat for heresy by both the Church and academics, Galileo tried to avoid controversy but kept on with his scientific work, eventually entering the public fray again with a work in 1625 which the Church censors at Rome allowed to be published in 1632 as the *Dialogue on the Two Principal World Systems*. In this work (on the respective merits of Copernican and traditional Ptolemaic astronomy) Galileo himself summed up the reasons for resistance to the emerging new 'science' by having one of his characters say, 'this way of thinking leads to the subversion of all natural philosophy ['science'] and stirs up confusion and disruption in heaven, on earth, and in the whole universe'.[6] Despite such manoeuvrings (and official permission to publish), he was sentenced a year later by the Inquisition to life imprisonment for heresy. Living out his years, in fact, under house arrest he continued working, thereby contributing further stimulus to what we now call the properly scientific approach to natural phenomena. In less than fifty years after his death, the English mathematician and physicist, Isaac Newton (1642–1727), brought the synthesis of mathematics, physics, and astronomy to a famous summation in his *Principia* (1687), which demonstrated the law of universal gravitation.

If the Scientific Revolution originated in astronomy and physics, it was not limited to them. As early as 1605 the English philosopher-statesman Francis Bacon (1561–1626) published *The Advancement of Learning* in which he critically considered the present state and achievements of knowledge – a theme he revisited in his 1620 *Novum Organum* in which he poured scorn on purely 'theoretical' approaches to the natural world, and even more so on traditional ideas about it. Instead he insisted on the value of observation and experiment in order to reach reliable, objective knowledge (what came to be known as 'the experimental philosophy' or 'empiricism'), and would have been delighted when some twenty years after his death a group of like-minded individuals formed a scientific society along the lines he had proposed, not only to promote learning but to make for a better world, which became the Royal Society in 1660. This famous institution, amongst whose members were Boyle, Hooke, and Newton himself (who became its President in 1703) was matched by the founding of the Royal Academy of Sciences in France in 1666, whilst elsewhere in Europe other such societies emerged during a seventeenth century in which increasing numbers of intellectuals were fascinated by, contributing to, and convinced of the validity of 'the new learning'. The societies published numerous papers on new inventions in, for example, mechanics, clockwork, agriculture, and navigation, as well as research into medicine, optics, statistics, astronomy, geography, and mathematics.

Thus by the later seventeenth century, when Vico was a young man, the Scientific Revolution was well under way and the claims for the 'new learning' were well-known. Amongst these was the notion that, far from being heretical, the increasing revelation of the laws of the natural world was bringing people closer to God by discovering the true workings of His marvellous creation. However, others in addition to the Catholic Church were disturbed by what they saw as the replacement of their traditional beliefs about the cosmos and the natural world by a cold, mechanistic philosophy which offered neither spiritual solace nor moral certainty in a universe now no longer conceived of as finite and meaningful but as an infinite complex of, simply, 'matter in motion'. In short, the Scientific Revolution was far more than a 'revolution' in 'science' – it offered a new way of looking at the universe, a new set of presuppositions regarding the natural world and man's place in it, which sat antagonistically not only with the received wisdom of the ancient classics and of the Catholic Church but increasingly with the classics-orientated *humanist* heritage of the Renaissance. Although the contributors to the Scientific Revolution were of course interested in the *natural* world and cosmos rather than theories about *history*, we have already seen in preceding chapters how closely earlier ideas about the course and meaning of human history intertwined with both religion and ideas about Nature. Sooner or later the connection, already intuited by many enquiring minds, would be made again – but now by a thinker, Vico, consciously set on working out an explicit theory of history which would coherently reintegrate these diverse components. But before we see how Vico responded to the emergence of 'science', we must look at another major intellectual movement of the post-Reformation sixteenth and the ensuing seventeenth century which he was also responding to – namely, developments in *philosophy*.

Seventeenth-century philosophy

Nowadays, apart from its loose popular meaning, we regard 'philosophy' as a distinct academic discipline generating a specialised vocabulary and limited to considering only certain issues. But until modern times the term had a much broader connotation derived simply from its Greek origins as 'lover of knowledge', whereby the distinctions between, for example, the study of law, theology, medicine, political constitutions, astronomy and astrology, and even history, were subsumed under the generic term, 'philosophy'. In particular, the modern distinction between *science* and philosophy did not apply, the former being referred to, even in the eighteenth century, as 'natural philosophy'. Thus it is that many of the above-mentioned 'scientists' who contributed to the Scientific Revolution were called 'philosophers'. And so they were, in the primary sense that they studied 'the nature of things'. However, for a complex of reasons including the Renaissance humanists' rejection of scholasticism, the expansion of the known world through voyages of exploration, technological innovation, and a freer intellectual atmosphere in some now Protestant countries, the seventeenth century witnessed the beginnings of a disentangling of what we now call 'science' ('the natural sciences') from the general amalgam of 'philosophy'.

Vice-versa, however, the same began to happen to 'philosophy' itself, as it began to disentangle itself from that same amalgam. Thus it is that if Galileo was the father of modern *science*, in this same seventeenth century modern *philosophy* (i.e., 'philosophy' in its narrower sense) was fathered by René Descartes (1596–1650). Both are still described as 'philosophers and scientists', and rightly so. This is because of the seeming paradox that 'science' and 'philosophy' only became distinct from each other by initially sharing the same characteristic of wishing to begin anew the study of 'the nature of things'. Thus Galileo the scientist needed a new method of approaching knowledge (i.e., needed 'philosophy') to support his ideas, while Descartes the philosopher needed an open book on 'the nature of things' (i.e., needed 'science') to complement his ideas. These two stimuli came together in the seventeenth-century intellectual achievement of 1) detaching the physical world as a field of study which 2) required its own form of knowledge. In short, that the origins of both modern science and modern philosophy occurred together in time is no coincidence.

'Empiricism'

We have already noted how as the sixteenth turned into the seventeenth century some inquisitive minds had become thoroughly impatient – indeed, contemptuous – of traditionally received knowledge regarding particularly the *physical* world. A century earlier, of course, the Renaissance humanists had already rejected the medieval scholastic approach to learning. But apart from showing interest in the classical materialist/atomic theories of Democritus, Epicurus, and Lucretius (but even here, because of their *moral* ideas), the Renaissance humanists did not focus their attention on the study of the *natural* world. Rather, their invaluable researches were directed on the 'liberal arts'. By contrast, the exponents of the 'new learning' of the seventeenth century focused their thinking on the natural world. They thus found themselves not only at odds with medieval (and religiously inspired) scholastical thinking and methods (as had the Renaissance humanists) but also with *classical* (Aristotelian and Ptolemaic) theories of 'natural philosophy', which derived less from observation and experiment than from speculatively rationalising the remnants of earlier 'mythopoeic' concepts of nature. After all, if one could now *show* that 'things in motion' do not have an 'appetite to rest', but that the laws of physics determine in exact degrees that a thing in motion has to be prevented from continuing in motion because of measurable forces – or that the sun and moon are not perfect spheres but spotted and cratered purely material phenomena – then the facts could speak for themselves.

Thus a school of philosophical thought emerged, prepared to re-open the book of Nature because it was discovering a new set of presuppositions based on the *methodology* of actual *observation* combined with repeatable *experimentation* – in other words, *empiricism*, the taking of one's starting point for knowledge from the observed, tested facts. Such a method, 'way of knowing', or *epistemology* ('logic of knowledge') would correct errors and discover new truths. This empiricism did not necessarily lead to any new *overall* synthetic or comprehensive theories of nature – in fact, it was antipathetic towards such 'theoretical' constructs. But it did imply a new 'theory' or 'explanation' of knowledge itself (involving philosophical propositions about the nature of the human mind and the 'objectivity' of external phenomena) which was brought explicitly to reflection, argument, and defence in various works of philosophy. Notable amongst these was *Essay Concerning Human Understanding* (1689) by the Englishman, John Locke (1632–1704). This work tells us that to form 'true' ideas about the world we should recognise no other authority than what the senses actually perceive of it, combined with purely logical reasoning 'after the event' to make sense of this empirical source of knowledge. Indeed, much of the Royal Society's work (including prior to Locke's *Essay* and his own membership) was premised on this philosophy of 'empiricism', its long-serving Secretary, Henry Oldenberg, being much vexed by more 'speculative' frameworks which 'the experimental philosophy' generated in others. A salutary 'empiricism' has since remained a strong feature of particularly the Anglo-American philosophical outlook (including the approach to the study of history).

Seventeenth-century 'rationalism'

The other seventeenth-century principal innovation in philosophy is now called 'rationalism', whose original exponent was the Frenchman, René Descartes

(1596–1650). After moving to the Netherlands in 1628, Descartes wrote a number of scientific and philosophical works amongst which (in his *Philosophical Essays*, 1637) was his deeply influential and controversial *Discourse on Method*. Here again we encounter a philosopher/scientist deeply sceptical of traditional and 'received' knowledge, not prepared to consider any idea as true unless he was satisfied that the method of acquiring knowledge was indisputably correct. In other words, like the empiricists, he started his philosophy by enquiring into the nature of knowledge itself. But unlike them, Descartes did not start from the (alleged) truth of sense-experience. Instead he was convinced the only statements or ideas which are indisputably 'true', are those which partake of the certainty demonstrable in propositions arrived at through the process of deduction which is *innate* to the mind. As such, geometry and mathematics were the archetypal examples of clear reasoning untainted by the intrusion of mere opinion, sense-impressions, or 'received wisdom'. Hence Descartes' method was to doubt everything and start from some indisputable beginning (such as 'I think') – and then deduce step by step only what logically followed (in this case, according to him, firstly 'therefore I exist').

It was in this manner that the ancient Greek mathematician Euclid had uncovered the laws of the triangle, amongst which was his 47th Proposition demonstrating that for any right-angled triangle, the sum of the squares of the sides must equal the square of the hypotenuse. A famous anecdote tells of the English philosopher Thomas Hobbes' (1588–1679) astonished disbelief at reading this proposition. Hobbes therefore read back through the propositions from which the forty-seventh followed and was not only thereby convinced of its truth, but more importantly, of the indisputable certainty of that *method* as the *only* way of reaching true conclusions about *anything*. ('This made him in love with geometry').[7] Later, in the 1630s, Hobbes travelled in France and met with Descartes and other 'rationalists', and despite disagreeing with some of Descartes' ideas (particularly his exemption of mind from the world of matter) never wavered from his belief in the 'rationalist', inductive method of acquiring truth. Indeed, because Hobbes developed the view that *all* aspects of existence are solely *material*, he went on to construct one of the most sustained 'rationalist' explanations known in literature, not of objects in nature, but of no less a topic than the nature of man and the state – his *Leviathan* (1651). In order to ground the work on a method which would provide 'true' statements, Hobbes insists that '*true* and *false* are attributes of speech, not of things', and because 'truth consisteth in the right ordering' of what we say, then:

> By this it appears how necessary it is for any man that aspires to true knowledge, to examine the definitions of former authors; and either to correct them, where they are negligently set down, or to make them himself.[8]

Reasoning is the process of drawing out the logical implications of definitions. Hobbes calls the kind of knowledge gained 'science', and says 'this is the knowledge required in a philosopher; that is to say, of him that pretends to reasoning'.[9]

Our final example of 'rationalism' in seventeenth-century philosophy was written by the Dutchman and excommunicate Jew, Baruch Spinoza (1632–1677). Strongly influenced by the rationalist epistemology of Descartes and Hobbes, (although disagreeing with other elements of their respective philosophies), and motivated by a spirituality as sublime as it was unorthodox, Spinoza finally organised his philosophical thinking about 'God', the universe, man, and his ultimate good, into what some judge as among the most profound books ever written, his *Ethics* (*c.* 1674). Significantly, the full title of this masterpiece of deductive reasoning is *Ethics Demonstrated with Geometrical Order*, and accordingly it is rigorously organised in terms of Definitions, Axioms, and Propositions – and each of the latter are followed by Proofs, referring to earlier Propositions and Axioms, and ending 'QED' ('that which was to be demonstrated'). Echoing, but extending, Galileo's beliefs about the nature of the *physical* universe, and even more closely Hobbes' methodology, Spinoza tells us:

> nature's laws and ordinances, whereby all things come to pass . . . are everywhere and always the same; so that there should be one and the same method of understanding the nature of all things whatsoever, through nature's universal laws and rules. . . . I shall, therefore, treat of . . . [human] emotions according to the same method, as I employed heretofore in my investigations concerning God and the mind. I shall consider human actions and desires in exactly the same manner, as though I were concerned with lines, planes, and solids.[10]

And it is in another work, *On the Improvement of the Understanding*, that having insisted that 'before all things, a means must be devised for improving the understanding and purifying it, as far as may be at the outset, so that it may apprehend things without error, and in the best possible way',[11] Spinoza gives an extended ('rationalistically' argued) treatment of the inherent power of the human mind to deductively apprehend truth and avoid error, based on the notion that in doing so man 'tunes in' to God's 'thinking' (at least in relation to the logical and material aspects of Existence).

As intimated, these examples of seventeenth-century 'rationalist' philosophers differed significantly in the *overall* philosophies they produced. Yet they shared views on the *question* of method – (it should eschew 'empiricism' and rely on truth being discoverable by the innate operations of the mind) – as well as on the *importance* of method as the foremost key to true knowledge; ('philosophy' must begin with epistemology). This latter view they shared, of course, with the empiricists, with whom in other respects they had no sympathy – and this returns us to the fundamental point that the novel and diverse developments in *philosophy* in the seventeenth century grew from a common and radical source – namely, an increasingly outspoken rejection of traditional and Revealed knowledge, particularly regarding the nature of the cosmos and the workings of the natural world. In doing this, however, they developed distinctive theories of knowledge which were later extended to matters *other* than the physical world. When Vico entered the intellectual world (the later seventeenth century) the two pillars of modern philosophy, empiricism and rationalism, were recent innovations which could neither be taken for granted nor ignored. Their close association with the Scientific Revolution (and consequent focus on the physical world and cosmos) has been indicated, and although modern *philosophy* was beginning to broaden its focus by the end of the seventeenth century, neither from that direction nor from 'science' had any implications for the meaning of *history* been drawn. Rationalists might agree with Hobbes that 'history' is simply 'the register of *knowledge of fact*' (divided into 'natural' and 'civil' history – the former embracing empirical information of 'metals, plants, animals, regions, and the like', the latter of 'the voluntary actions of men in commonwealths'), whereas 'science' or 'philosophy' are *reasoning* disciplines which produce '*demonstrations* of consequences of one affirmation, to another'.[12] Empiricists, on the other hand, might have no methodological aversion to studying history, but would be as opposed to deducing any 'speculative' or 'theoretical' framework regarding its course as they were regarding anything else. Part of Vico's originality, however, is that he did take careful account of the modern developments in philosophy in order to substantiate his own 'theory' of *history* – and that in doing so, he proposed his own independent response to methodological theory (or epistemology) which accorded with neither empiricism nor rationalism. But before exploring what this was, we can indicate another leading aspect of seventeeth-century thought Vico responded to in his work – namely, developments in *political* theory.

Seventeenth-century political thought

The previous chapter concluded in the early sixteenth century with the famous political thinker, Machiavelli, whose noted cynicism, realism, apparent amorality and irreligiosity contrasted sharply with contemporary political ideology. Although the Renaissance humanists had opened up new ways of thinking, and the feudal political order of 'Christendom' was giving way to the early-modern (dynastically driven) form of independent, sovereign European states – a vast, lengthy process assisted by the religio-political turmoil of the Reformation – in Machiavelli's times most political thinking was dominated by medieval ideas. The civil and Church authorities still propounded the notion that through God's will (discovered via reason and Revelation) temporal order was sustained by an hierarchical order whose authority was, ultimately, God-ordained. 'Rights', privileges, or prerogatives of both ruled and rulers in the diversely ordered, parochial feudal system were understood to reflect an ordering of society according to 'natural law'.

The Reformation (hardly begun by the time of Machiavelli's death in 1527) did generate lower-order, quasi-'democratic', sometimes millennialist movements which disturbed this consensus on the nature of political society and civil authority. But as the sixteenth century progressed, the climate of Reformation and

Counter-reformation hardly conspired to produce any fundamental shift from the *religious* basis to political thought. Political theory remained moribund, bound up with the immediacy of events. It was not until the 1570s that a new departure was forged by the Frenchman, Jean Bodin (1529–1596), who, although deeply immersed in Court politics, achieved the necessary detachment in his *Six Books of the Commonwealth* (1576) to reflect anew on the principles underlying political society. Mindful that France had suffered some thirty years of intermittent religious civil war between factions of Protestants and Catholics, amongst which occurred the horrors of the St Bartholomew massacre in 1572, Bodin resolved to set down principles to demonstrate the need for any society to be governed by a single source of authority (the *sovereign* power) to which all, irrespective of social rank or religious persuasion, owe the absolute obligation of obedience. This sovereign power (Bodin argued it was best vested in a single individual – i.e., a monarch) cannot logically be accountable to any higher power (other, that is, than facing God's judgement) nor, through any constitutional form, to any constraint from its subjects – for in either case (Bodin argued with perhaps tautologous logic) it would no longer be 'sovereign', since sovereignty means the absolute right to rule. And where a sovereign power is absent, Bodin crucially argued, a 'state' ('commonwealth', or 'republic') cannot exist, for *any* state must have a sovereign power at its head, otherwise it would lose its unity and relapse into the threatening anarchy of unchecked families at war with each other. In short, law is the foundation of political society; the power to *make* law (the sovereign power) must therefore be absolute; the sovereign power is therefore indivisible (i.e., it cannot be shared amongst different bodies), inalienable (i.e., it cannot be given away to some other body or authority), and unaccountable (i.e., cannot be obliged to make laws which either other powers or its own subjects might wish). Although Bodin's mode of arguing mixed up appeals to 'traditional wisdom', the Divine Will, the natural order, and deductive reasoning, it seemed sufficiently religiously based to avoid giving offence, (although some religious enthusiasts thought it elevated the needs of political order above the claims of 'true religion', and thus contemptuously named Bodin's circle 'les politiques'). On the contrary, his book underwent numerous editions and retained a currency for at least fifty years. But this was not only because its arguments seemed steeped in traditional modes of argument – it was also because it was saying something *new* which reflected and made sense of the new political order emerging throughout Europe – namely, the actual emergence of sovereign, independent states. Indeed, for those today who still think that 'sovereignty' is the hallmark of statehood, Bodin remains relevant – for he 'invented' the notion.

As we move into seventeenth-century political thought, Bodin's new statehood/sovereignty message not only retained its currency – for many its relevance was heightened as political structures in Europe grappled with large problems associated with class tensions endemic to early capitalism, religious dissent, ambitious monarchs, and embryonic 'democratic' impulses. To use the 'body–state' analogy outlined in an earlier chapter, the gestation and birth of 'the modern state' were rarely easy processes throughout early-modern Europe (to be followed in the nine-teenth century by a further, 'adolescent', phase of development as states turned into 'nation-states'). One of the chief responses to these testing political times in the seventeenth century (sometimes now called 'the age of crisis') was advanced by Hobbes in the midst of civil war in England in the aforementioned *Leviathan* (and earlier writings). Not only did he retain Bodin's concept of 'sovereignty', he sharpened it by honing away even those few restraints on its absolutist message that Bodin had tried to retain principally through the religious overtones he employed (whereby a sovereign power 'ought' to govern benignly and honourably). Hobbes did this by omitting religious and moral arguments altogether, instead employing his purely *rationalist* (and *materialist*) approach to argue the same message. Famously, he claimed men's emotions and moral sensibilities are reducible to a species of pain and pleasure, presenting a world of human experience governed, whatever our illusions, by the purely *utilitarian* consideration of whether a thing pleases or harms us. Moral considerations disappear, to be replaced by the notion of the pursuit of *interest*, for Hobbes insists that 'whatsoever is the object of any man's appetite or desire, that is it which he . . . calleth *good*: and the object of his hate and aversion, *evil*'.[13]

Here, Hobbes is evidence of what some scholars[14] argue is a new cynicism underpinning much seventeenth-century political thought, whereby traditional, historically established notions of civic and feudal loyalties, and the reciprocal obligation of rulers to behave morally, give way to a belief in the kind of amoral power-politics propounded a century earlier by Machiavelli. But whereas the latter did not argue his views rationalistically (nor in any other specifically philosophical guise), Hobbes sought a new understanding of the nature of civic duty and the powers of the state based entirely on the *rational calculation of interest*. The result was his famous political theory whereby, from the premise of a pre-political 'state of nature' peopled by necessarily self-seeking competitive individuals in which life is 'solitary, poor, nasty, brutish, and short',[15] he deduced the logic of the 'social contract'. This erected a (Bodin-type) absolutist sovereign power to escape the 'state of nature' by enforcing its subjects' rational will to 'do as you would be done by'. In short, that which should determine the relation between rulers and ruled, the obligation to obey the law, the limits and prerogatives of the sovereign power, and all other aspects necessary to the secure existence of political societies, is derived from the logic of a rational 'social contract'. It is not tradition, morality, religion, nor history (nor any combination of them) which explains and validates political order – its rationale is located solely in logic.

Later in the century, John Locke, objecting to illiberal, absolutist political theories (whether from Hobbes or from more traditional sources), proposed an alternative understanding of political society in which individuals' 'natural rights' to life, liberty, and property are protected from arbitrary invasion by the authorities. In his *Two Treatises on Civil Government* (1690) he propounded a theory of the state in which its very rationale is to secure these individual rights – and this is achieved by a state in which the final (legislative) power is held by society itself, through its majority, rather than by an independent, unaccountable sovereign power above society. Although much of his argumentation is evasive, inconsistent, and eclectic, as an 'empiricist' Locke eschewed the rigours of Hobbes' rationalist approach to political theory and instead based his ideas on 'common-sense'. Yet, to reach conclusions opposed to Hobbes he nevertheless employed the same framework of a 'state of nature', and proceeded to derive the *logic* of a 'social contract' as the basis of political society.

Other seventeenth-century writers (including Spinoza in his unfinished *Tractatus Politicus*) also adopted the 'state of nature/social contract' framework for understanding the nature of political society, such that in Vico's lifetime it was a well-known theory. As indicated, it could be supported by different philosophical approaches and be used to reach different conclusions. Yet it demonstrated two common features – an imagined and/or 'rationally' derived concept of 'the state of nature', and a logically derived 'social contract' providing the rationale of political society. And these combine to force the observation that this approach was radically non-historical. The 'state of nature' was either unhistorical, because not based on historical knowledge but simply imagination, or a-historical, because logically deduced from some axiomatic notion of 'human nature' in the raw. And by the same criteria 'the social contract' was both unhistorical and a-historical because based on what we might call an early version of 'game theory' – the theory which constructs strategies and outcomes in interpersonal situations entirely according to logic (given certain axioms about individuals ideally calculating their interests), irrespective of their personalities, times, culture, or social circumstances.

In short, one of the major features of seventeenth-century political theory, associated with scepticism and cynicism about earlier religion-based political ideas and structures, was the attempt to understand political society in the abstract and fictive terms of social contract theory. The actual *history* of societies was not merely neglected – it was deliberately ignored in 'explaining' or validating the nature of political society. Since Bodin himself (who, although not employing a 'state of nature/social contract' framework, neither grounded his theory of 'sovereignty' in any real historical development) political society, now construed in the form of 'the state', was not approached as the product of any *actual, historical* process. Indeed, it could be argued that at no time before or since the seventeenth century was political theory more detached from all connection with any sense of a larger meaning and/or process in the course of human history (i.e., 'philosophy of history'). As we shall see, it was just this feature of political theory which Vico was interested in, and his independent, critical response to it was to form an integral part of his 'philosophy of history'. But there are yet two further features of later sixteenth- and seventeenth-century thought we need to appreciate before turning to Vico, because his response to them formed another crucial part of his thinking – namely, the interaction between new developments in historical methodology and religion, which combined in a new preparedness to engage in Biblical criticism.

118

The discipline of history

In the previous chapter, amongst the Renaissance humanists' achievements, we discussed their new sense of the *historicity* of a past they recognised as different and long-gone, the spirit of which could often only be recaptured through the process of retranslating ancient texts to recover their meaning. To a certain degree this same scholarly approach was taken to *Biblical* texts by figures such as Erasmus and Luther. Innovative as this was, it would, however, be wrong to suppose this resulted in new, critical histories of classical times, or in histories of more recent times which demonstrated anything approaching the meticulous apparatus of today's historians, with their critical awareness of sources, references, evidence, interpretation, and the issue of objectivity. The same can be said for Biblical scholarship. In both cases Renaissance humanists engaged more in a (valuable and necessary) process of correction of previous errors than in finding a better methodology for establishing historical truth in general.

Later in the sixteenth century, however, a number of (principally French) thinkers, including Bodin, built upon the approach of the earlier humanists to formulate basic rules for internal criticism of historical method in order better to reach the truth of events.[16] This effort was partly prompted by the urge to understand Roman law better, for they were sceptical of the meaning, authority, and universality it was alleged to have for their own times. As a result the foundations of modern historical practice were laid, whereby rules were set down to judge the reliability of historical sources and how to respect evidence. Thus historians were now urged not to interject their own religious, social, or patriotic prejudices into their accounts – to avoid anachronism when studying the distant past, and to maintain a detachment when studying recent events – to stick to the facts rather than invent them – to be aware of political or religious influences constraining previous historians' and others' accounts of events, or of their converse in attempts to flatter particular figures and/or the authorities – and to write in a sober manner appropriate to a dispassionate account of the past rather than seek to gratify readers' tastes for literary entertainment.

In addition to the further development of such internal rules of modern historiography there was 'from the fifteenth to the eighteenth centuries of our era . . . certainly no lack of developments, external to the craft and discipline of history itself' which conspired to improve the quality, scope, and expertise of historical writings.[17] Amongst these were the diverse influences of the many 'national' struggles over religion and dynasty ensuant upon the Reformation; the continuing discovery and colonisation of the non-European world; the growth of urban commercial societies with more educated citizens expanding the market for the printed word; the new outlook on the natural world generated by the Scientific Revolution; and (despite censorship) a growing preparedness to challenge traditional knowledge and superstition. As a result, many aspects of the national histories of e.g., Italy, France, Spain, England, and the Netherlands were explored, as well as attempts at compendia and comparative histories, and the devising of more accurate basic chronologies. The best of these demonstrated a sharpening of the critical historical faculties, a heightening of historical alertness, and an enquiring sensitivity into the causes of historical events. Thus it is that by the beginning of the eighteenth century the (modern) discipline of history was becoming established as a specific form of literature rich in variety and, even at its most blandly 'empirical', replete with both overt and implicit explanations of historical change – food for thought for anyone interested in the more speculative enterprise of *making sense* of history. Vico *was* just such a figure and many passages in his *New Science* show that his reading of (and frequent disagreement with) recent historians contributed to his thinking.

Religion and Biblical criticism

The final aspect of later sixteenth- and seventeenth-century thought Vico was responding to in the grand synthesis of his philosophy of history is the large theme of religious belief in general, and the narrower theme of Biblical criticism in particular, including the belief in Divine intervention and miracles. As for the former, since the beginnings of the Reformation both the theological and the more popular arguments about the nature of 'true' religion thundered throughout the century, their reverberations continuing well into the seventeenth, such that despite the secular impulse behind much Renaissance thought, consciousness of religion (even if not religious consciousness) was again as inescapable a factor in intellectual thought as it had been in medieval times. Initially a controversy between traditional Catholicism and the new 'protestants', by the middle of the sixteenth century the former attempted to regroup itself through reform, and the latter, having opened the floodgates for a degree of freedom of religious thought, began to schism as attempts were made to close them again. Of the numerous issues involved in this prolonged and heady atmosphere of religious enthusiasm, controversy, and persecution, we shall mention only those which contribute to understanding Vico's philosophy.

First, on the larger theme of religious belief in general we have already indicated how the Scientific Revolution raised severe doubts about traditional Christian ideas in many minds. As one author puts it, towards the end of the seventeenth century, Isaac Newton's gravitational theory had shown that:

> the universe turned out to be a Great Machine, made up of material parts which all moved through space and time according to the strictest rules of mechanical causation . . . no room was left for supernatural agencies, whether divine or diabiolical.[18]

This did not necessarily mean a denial of the existence of God (something virtually impossible), but it raised huge questions about the nature of God and His role in the world. Was He, as some have interpreted Hobbes and others as implying, simply the great watchmaker who made the world, wound up the spring, set it going, but then played no further role in history, nature, and human affairs? In itself this is not an irreligious view, and can also accommodate some notion of God's Providence insofar as, by analogy, He has designed how the watch ticks away over time. But such a view could not but prompt more thinking minds to query not only the veracity of *miracles* but also that which was at the heart of Christianity, the role and significance of Jesus Christ. Was Jesus a miraculous intervention in history? If so, why was this necessary, and how is it consistent with the 'watchmaker' view of God's relation to the world?

Second, the *rationalist* school of philosophy also could not but raise fundamental questions about religion, and Christianity in particular. Descartes, we recall, vowed to doubt everything, including the existence of God, until it could be 'proved' through the demonstrative certainty of deductive reasoning. For those who subscribed to this rationalist notion of 'truth' it implied that much that was said in the Bible about God, and natural events, was radically problematic. A common way out of this difficulty was prefigured by Galileo's insistence that where the indisputable truths uncovered by science conflicted with the word of God in the Scriptures, then the former should prevail, since words (even those inspired by God) are subject to the limited power of human understanding, as well as often being ambiguous in meaning. Just so for subsequent rationalist thinkers where the indisputable truths uncovered by *logic* conflicted with Biblical statements. Their escape from accusations of blasphemy, if not atheism, lay in the defence that the Bible used human language to express ideas, and therefore need not always be taken literally. Indeed, this position was expanded by Hobbes into a more full-blown defence which implies that since language is anthropocentric, anything said about God is anthropomorphic. Thus, in 1642 we find Hobbes railing against, not the Bible, but those philosophers and theologians who use statements about the nature of God to reach conclusions on any number of topics ranging from whether the universe is infinite in time and space to whether God is the cause of evil.

> Personally, while I hold that the nature of God is unfathomable, and that propositions are a kind of language by which we express our concepts of the natures of things, I incline to the view that no proposition about the nature of God can be true save this one: God exists, and that no title correctly describes the nature of God other than the word 'being' [*ens*]. Everything else . . . pertains not to the explanation of philosophical truth, but to proclaiming the states of mind that govern our wish to praise . . . God. Hence those words 'God sees, understands, wishes, acts, brings to pass' . . . display, not the Divine Nature, but our own piety . . . who desire to ascribe to Him the names most worthy of honour among us . . . Neither propositions nor notions about His nature are to be argued over, but are part of our worship . . . .

Thus for Hobbes, because true 'philosophical / scientific' ideas are solely the product of logical propositional reasoning, we cannot use what the Bible says about God (or much else?) as the basis for discovering truth, 'for, as I said, the words under discussion are not the propositions of people philosophising but the actions of those who pay homage'.[19]

Another, different, example of the critical application of rationalist principles to religion is Spinoza's aforementioned *Ethics*. Appearing to contradict Hobbes' insistence on God as 'unfathomable', Spinoza employs a strictly deductive method to actually determine the nature of God, such that after the eight definitions, seven axioms, and thirty-six propositions of Part 1 he tells us, 'In the foregoing I have explained the nature and properties of God'.[20] During his exposition Spinoza tackles the problem of God's 'freedom' to do anything, and typically employs as an example of incontrovertible *truth*, that 'from the nature of a triangle it follows from eternity and for eternity, that its three interior angles are equal to two right angles'. His critics read this as meaning that Spinoza was thereby denying the freedom, and thus omnipotence, of God, since it implies that not even God can change the angles of a triangle. Spinoza anticipated such criticism by arguing it stems from the error of attributing to God what are merely human qualities – in this case, intellect and will, neither of which 'appertain to God's nature'.[21] In this important respect, then, Spinoza agrees with Hobbes, frequently complaining that most of what is said of God, and the plethora of religious rules taken to follow from His 'utterances', derive from speaking *more humano* – that is, in the manner of human beings, or anthropomorphically. From today's viewpoint, that Spinoza and Hobbes had to argue this at all demonstrates the depths of religious superstition, closed-mindedness, and fear of the authorities still abounding amongst intellectuals in the times Vico was born.

Third, and despite this, such views contributed to a developing seventeenth-century trend to rethink the status of revealed (i.e., Biblical) and theologically derived religious truth – in particular, to make more of the fact than did the Renaissance Christian humanists that the Bible is a series of written documents. This led to a new kind of Biblical criticism based not only on accurate translation but also on recognising the *anthrocentricity* of the language used. From this it is but a short (and logical) step to treat the Bible 'merely' as an historically conditioned set of writings, even if in some sense 'divinely' inspired. And this is precisely what Spinoza did in his *Tractatus Theologico-Politicus* (1675), thereby scandalising fainter hearts (and slower intellects) who shrank from what they took to be the clear atheistical message behind this approach. Spinoza frequently points to where Biblical passages need to be re-understood in terms of the historical and human context behind the meanings of the words used. Also, what real *history* the Biblical books recount has to be recovered by such techniques – and here we can see the clear link between the study of *history* and *linguistic analysis* presaged in earlier Biblical criticism and implicit in Spinoza's thinking. Yet up to this point there is no evidence that Spinoza was interested in the methodology of *secular* history, or history in general. Tragically, he died two years later aged only forty-five, thereby depriving the world of the possibility of one of its finest intellects perhaps applying its genius to the study of history – and, given its bent, possibly to theorising about its course and meaning.

As for Hobbes, although interested in history (he made a translation of Thucydides in his early life, and attempted a history of the English Civil War, *Behemoth*, in later life), we have already noted the scant attention he paid to the topic of historical *methodology*, relegating history to the empirical study of 'fact' undeserving of the epistemological underpinnings he insisted on for 'science' or 'philosophy'. As for 'philosophy of history' itself, Hobbes would have regarded the very idea as a contradiction in terms – history (as well as theology) is absent in his schemata of the 'philosophical' or 'scientific' disciplines.[22]

Yet this only highlights that much which was innovatory in the intellectual context of the later sixteenth and the seventeenth century – the Scientific Revolution, empiricism, and rationalism – appeared to have nothing to do with the study of *history*, let alone invite new insights into its overall course and meaning. Particularly in the wake of the Reformation, however, a potential link *did* appear over the manner in which these developments impinged on *religious* ideas. These factors, combined with the nurture of methodological discipline in history, generated both the willingness and ability to engage in a new kind of Biblical criticism. At the minimum this involved closer enquiry into the meaning, both literally and philosophically, of much Biblical language. And at its heights, as in Spinoza, it pointed to nothing less than a reconstructing of how to understand the Bible by accepting its *historicity*. Thus the Bible itself should be approached *historically* as a mixture of voices communicating the mind-set of ancient peoples in their own language. Also, if the Bible is in that sense 'historical', it is also (in part) directly a work of history. But the history it teaches must therefore *also* be seen as 'historical' – that is, as needing to be reconstructed via the same historico-linguistic techniques. Thus it is that in Spinoza's *Tractatus Theologico-Politicus* (in which, significantly, he also made a famous plea for freedom of speech) a clear methodological connection was made between language and historical interpretation of the Bible, including Biblical history itself. And to the extent the latter involves not only Christianity but also Judaism, this connection expanded the grounds for exploring the nature of religious ideas in general. Now, by the later 1600s, not only could traditional religious ideas be subjected to philosophical criticism from rationalist philosophers and natural scientists – they were also subject to the different, more empirically orientated, criticism based on historico-linguistic evidence.

In this manner, then, varied strains of later sixteenth- and seventeenth-century thought, many of which seemed to have no relevance to history, let alone philosophy of history, began to be drawn closer together – namely, over the question of religious truth. History, at least with respect to the *Bible* (regarding its meaning, its history, and the history in it) appeared as a potentially powerful, reformed discipline no longer restricted to accounts of events but bearing the possibility of *interpreting* the past – and thereby bearing 'philosophical' implications inasmuch as it could occupy as respectable and fruitful (albeit different) a role in debating religious truths as 'philosophy' or 'science'. To this extent, then, it might be said that the discipline of history becomes a tool of philosophy. But why limit the 'philosophical' significance of history to the question of Biblical truth? We have noted the apparent irrelevance history had for those post-Renaissance/Reformation rationalists, empiricists, and scientists who were rethinking so many traditional ideas not only regarding the natural world (and religion) but also in the areas of politics, law, morality, and human nature. If history could be a legitimate tool for furthering 'philosophical' enquiry into Biblical/religious issues, why not for these other areas also?

Conclusion

We can usefully preface our exposition of Vico's philosophy of history by claiming his response to the above questions would have been, 'Exactly! And that is the whole point of my *New Science*!'. We have already noted his extraordinary boldness in claiming that 'for purposes of [his] enquiry, we must reckon as if there were no books in the world'.[23] The subject of his book is indicated in its full title, *Principles of New Science of Giambattista Vico Concerning the Common Nature of the Nations*. In other words, the subject of his study is 'the civil world',[24] a term embracing all aspects of *human* life as organised into *societies* – family, property, language, customs, law, political forms, religions, morality, the arts, cultural norms, and 'mind-sets' or 'mentalities'. An alternative title was *New Science Concerning the Principles of Humanity*, which captures far better the sheer scope of what Vico understood as his subject-matter. In these same passages he 'beg(s) the reader to consider what has hitherto been written concerning the principles of any subject in the whole of gentile [non-Hebrew] knowledge, human and divine', and urges that the reader 'will perceive that all that has so far been written is a tissue of confused memories, of the fancies of a disordered imagination; that none of it is begotten of intelligence . . .'.[25] In other words, (and to retrace those principal aspects of his intellectual heritage outlined in this chapter), he thought that the Scientific Revolution was mistaken in some of its claims and he was uneasy over its direction; that the critical innovations in philosophy, particularly the epistemological theories of both empiricists and rationalists, led away from the path to the true understanding of anything; that seventeenth-century political and legal theory, particularly that based on the 'state of nature/social contract' theory, and on Bodin's explanation of 'sovereignty', was completely fallacious; and that the new breed of more expert historians laboured under huge misapprehensions about the larger aspects of human history. The only part of his intellectual heritage which must have seemed promising to him was the kind of *historico-linguistic* analysis Spinoza engaged in. But (publicly reviled by our seemingly 'orthodox' Vico), Spinoza had only made a beginning, and rather than use it to further the true understanding of 'the principles of any subject in the whole of gentile knowledge', had restricted the technique to the Bible, the one source of 'knowledge' Vico wished to *appear* to exempt from criticism!

Instead, Vico sought to recast all knowledge about 'the civil world'. The key to this reconstruction lay in extending those historico-linguistic techniques prefigured by Renaissance humanists and applied to *religion*. For Vico, a true understanding of *where things come from* removes all sorts of illusions – but this involved his rejecting much of what seventeenth-century philosophers had said about how to uncover true ideas, and instead propose his own theory of knowledge. It is just this grounding of his ideas in his own (distinctive) theory of 'truth' which makes his work explicitly *philosophical*, and was partly in his mind when he entitled it a new *science*. But he also called it 'new'. This was because the central focus of its subject-matter was nothing less than the origins and development of the principal 'institutions' of human societies – an *historical* study undertaken according to explicit methodical presuppositions. As such, his 'history' is inspired by theory. But vice-versa, his theory (or 'science') 'concerning the principles of any subject in the whole of gentile knowledge, human and divine' is *historical*. The key to understanding *any* aspect of the human world (i.e., not just the *history* of this or that) is to uncover its origins and trace its development in real history, rather than to hope to find true knowledge (of, for example, justice, or 'the ideal society', or moral rectitude) by some process of logical deduction, empirical observation, philosophical speculation, or reliance on some 'received wisdom' from past tradition. This approach to settling the diverse issues surrounding human living in society is nowadays often referred to as 'historicism' – an approach using 'history' as method, whereby history becomes the tool of 'philosophy' or 'science'. Equally, however, the latter become enslaved to their servant.

Thus what we encounter in Vico is not simply some new account of human history, to compete with previous ones. Nor is it simply some new 'theory' of human history, competing with those explored in our preceding chapters. (It turned out to be both.) Rather, we are at last in the hands of a formidable and independent thinker for whom history, which *should* teach us the historicity of things, provides the true foundations of 'theory' or 'philosophy' – but also for whom 'theory' or 'philosophy' provides the true foundations of history. It is this explicitly argued inseparability of history and 'philosophy' which raises Vico above previous attempts to 'make sense' of human history. Indeed, his own audacious estimation of the *significance* of his book was that it represented more than a (new) theory of the course and meaning of human history. Although *incorporating* history, it was however an entirely new 'science' or 'philosophy', which he was convinced would revolutionise 'the principles of any subject . . . human and divine'.

This introduction to Vico's thought has been a necessary prelude in order to explain the complex intellectual heritage to which he responded. Also, in allowing us to recount some of the intellectual history between the times of Machiavelli and Vico, it has gone some way to explaining why this intervening period (however eventful otherwise) did not itself include any significant contribution to philosophy of history. Nevertheless, it did provide that complex of ideas which provoked, in Vico, the first explicit philosophy of history. By this I do not mean to suggest it could not have emerged at some earlier period, or that it was bound to emerge in Vico's time. But neither, it could be argued, was the time of its genesis accidental. We may suppose as preconditions a certain sophistication behind the discipline of history, thought-provoking innovations in philosophy, and an atmosphere of challenge towards the dominant ideology (in this case, religious truth). But we also need the *individual* whose particularity conspired to fulfil their potential.

Because Vico is still relatively unknown compared to famous philosophers and political thinkers – and because his principal text, *New Science*, appears formidable reading at first acquaintance – the ensuing guide offers a combination of some detail and frequent quotations better to familiarise the reader with the ideas and style of his work.

7

VICO'S PHILOSOPHY OF HISTORY

Introduction

Vico's intellectual development

Born in 1668 into a bookseller's family in Naples, Vico had a sickly, introverted childhood devoted much to reading. After a typical classical and Catholic education he attended the University of Naples to study civil and church law, a popular career path. Through his twenties, although working as a private tutor to a country family outside Naples, he kept up with the city's lively intellectual circles, for as one commentator puts it, 'despite his self-image of the solitary thinker [in his *Autobiography* of 1728] . . . Vico was not unclubbable'.[1] Amongst other intellectual societies, he associated with somewhat subversive intellectuals in an academy called the 'Investigators'. They were regarded with suspicion, and some prosecuted, by the Inquisition because they were proponents of the 'new learning' of rationalists, empiricists, and scientists, many of whom were regarded as 'atheists', particularly by a Catholic Naples (under Spanish rule) somewhat removed from the centres of European intellectual life. The Investigators' purpose, however, was partly precisely to keep in touch with the latter, and thus they found themselves engaged in the then European-wide controversy over the relative merits of ancient and modern learning – the 'Quarrel between the Ancients and the Moderns'.[2] The Renaissance humanists had of course claimed pre-eminence for the philosophies and literary graces of the 'ancients' (the classical world), but as the seventeenth century progressed this was increasingly challenged by the 'new learning' in science and philosophy and, especially in France, by those who argued that in the separate field of the humanities (including poetry, prose, and history) 'the moderns' not only matched but surpassed 'the ancients'.

As one scholar puts it, 'this conflict between the new and the old was undoubtedly the most exciting intellectual event in the Naples of Vico's youth',[3] and he kept abreast of the issues, joining the Palatine Academy, which continued the Inquisitors' modernizing impulse. In 1698, now thirty, Vico became Professor of Rhetoric at the University of Naples. This post (held until his death in 1744) obligated him in teaching and research into classical authors, and ceremonial duties of delivering public orations and writing poetry and some histories. Thus placed, as an educationalist Vico could not have avoided 'the Quarrel' even had he wanted to. Rather, he devoted much thinking to the issues during the early years of his post. Some of this is reflected in a work comparing the 'modern' approach to education with the traditional learning on the classics (*On the Study Methods of Our Time*, 1708), and in a work which urged, against Cartesian claims that ancient literature was worthless as a source of knowledge, that the ancient Romans' writings should not be neglected, but do need re-studying in terms of the origins of the languages and myths from which they had evolved in order to arrive at the 'real' knowledge they contain, (*On the Most Ancient Wisdom of the Italians*, 1709).

What emerges is that Vico equivocated between different aspects of the ancient and new learning. He could not gainsay the superior methodologies of modern philosophy in establishing mathematical, logical, and scientific truths, and was as impressed as anyone with the associated practical-technical achievements of the Scientific Revolution (an admiration he never abandoned).[4] Yet he was increasingly uncomfortable with the notion that modern philosophy and science held the superior key to understanding *everything*, particularly in the 'humanist' areas of history, law, morals, and other human 'institutions'.

Rather, to think (as some 'moderns') that the wealth of classical humanist literature contained no insights about life contradicted Vico's intuitions. However, so various were the perspectives offered by the classics on the vast terrain of human and civil affairs, it seems Vico could at least appreciate the moderns' scepticism. An intricate and entertaining garden in which one could endlessly wander, the 'ancient learning' was also untidy and unplanned, demonstrating no *commonality* of either method or focus for understanding human affairs. In contrast, the 'new learning' was methodical, organized, and progressive.

Vico's 'great discovery'

A fresh outburst of the Quarrel (in France) from around 1710 further prompted Vico's ideas, since it revolved around the nature of ancient 'poetry' – especially Homer's, the (alleged) ninth-century BC 'father' of Greek literature. French Cartesians, battling for the 'moderns', refuted traditional claims that the *Iliad* and the *Odyssey* were unsurpassable expressions of philosophical and human wisdom set down in matchless poetry. Instead, they argued, the Homeric epics were riddled with ignorance, superstition, and disgraceful praise of barbaric behaviour. Homer's defenders, however, stuck to their view of Homer as the teacher of profound philosophical and historical truths. The dispute continued into the 1720s, and although it is likely Vico had for many years been independently mulling over the issues it raised – an alleged ancient wisdom, the interpretation of the nature of poetry, and the appropriateness of the learning of ancient cultures to modern times – there can be little doubt he knew of the row over Homer and that it added focus to his thinking.

This is because it was in relation to Homer that towards the end of the second decade Vico found his 'master key' which (according to him) unlocked the path to nothing less than the true understanding of the course and meaning of human history. This 'master key' derived from reinterpreting ancient writings by locating the meaning of the language they used in terms of the cultures from which they emerged. Narrow and specialised as this methodology might seem, it was inspired by Vico's growing perception that the 'literature' of a people (drama, poetry, philosophy, history, mythology, legal codes, and other proses) should not be read 'literally', as from a modern standpoint. Neither (where it is poetic and/or mythical fiction) should it be read metaphorically, or cabbalistically, as if it was some sort of code for a hidden, pristine wisdom. Either approach made the huge mistake of assuming that earlier peoples were so like later peoples, that the 'knowledge' contained in their diverse literary products could be judged by the same criteria modern Europeans applied to themselves. It was not just a question, for Vico, of recognising that earlier peoples lived in different times – the Renaissance humanists had brought that to light.

Rather, his 'great discovery' was that ancient peoples had a *general mentality* or mind-set profoundly *different* from that of subsequent periods. His contention was that ancient peoples did not view the world from a rational, objective standpoint, but from a fundamentally emotive, imaginative perspective which he called 'poetic'. This notion has strong affinities to that 'mythopoeic' outlook we discussed in Chapter 2, and Vico is at pains to stress the difficulties 'civilised' man has in empathising with this mentality and thus 'understanding' what it utters through its literature (or 'philology'). Ancient peoples viewed the world figuratively, with a kind of 'poetic' consciousness focused on concrete, expressive, individual features which they used, via vivid imagination, to describe their world by transposing them from one thing to another. Thus, for example, if dark clouds portend gloomy rain a *poet* might refer to a troubled man as having clouded brows – or use a metallic quality to describe someone courageous as 'a man of steel'. 'Modern' poets know when they speak like this – ancient men knew no other way, Vico suggests. In that sense they were not 'being poets' in their utterances – rather, they *were* 'natural' poets, and thus what they said about things has to be taken *literally*, but only once one has understood what they are referring to. This requires combining painstaking research into the 'poetic' references their language expresses with an historical-imaginative reconstruction of the world *they* experienced themselves as inhabiting. Only if we engage in this will we understand the knowledge (the '*poetic* wisdom') their 'philology' contains.

This, then, was the 'great discovery' which, according to him, Vico had been working towards for twenty years, and which he must have experienced as a moment of enlightenment, for in the early 1720s he began the exposition of his basic ideas on history precisely in relation to Homer's epics.

Vico's 'master-key'

For Vico, this 'great discovery' was a *master-key*, since it impelled him towards that reconstruction of the course of human history he set out in his *New Science*.

129

(Although he had already written a massive work, *Universal Right*, in 1720 – an intriguing precursor to his versions of the *New Science*, yet only available in English translation since 2001, thus inviting much scholarly interest[5] – he prepared the first edition of the latter work in 1725, and continued revising it intermittently until his death, a second edition appearing in 1730, and the final one in 1744). It achieved this because his theory about Homer held momentous implications for Vico. Not only did it 'unlock' Homer. In relating the language and 'letters' of peoples to their mentalities, and their mentalities to a (partly imagined) recovery of the world they inhabited, it opened up a methodology whereby Vico thought he could retrace distinct historical stages through which *all* 'human institutions' have passed. In addition, his linguistic ('philological') researches convinced him that although all 'nations' traverse the same stages, they do so independently rather than their cultures stemming from some single original source later transmitted to them. In its turn, this convinced him that all 'human institutions' *must* have passed through the *same* stages, and that therefore his work uncovered nothing less than the universal laws governing the history of 'nations' (or 'gentes') – what he variously called the 'ideal eternal history', 'the common nature of nations', or the 'principles of humanity'. Further, his researches also led him to believe that a certain stage had been *repeated* in European history, and thus to hint (albeit obscurely) that history is cyclical overall.

Thus we find Vico claiming that to properly understand the nature of human societies and all the issues of 'philosophy' involved (e.g., methodology, epistemology, political theory, moral philosophy, comparative law), 'we must reckon as if there were no books in the world' up to now which have been of any use. This is because all scholars, classical and modern, had failed to appreciate the truly radical historicity of more ancient times and mentalities which Vico's work had uncovered. They therefore held distorted views on the origins of society. And since, for Vico, there is a strong sense in which the 'origins' of a thing equate with the very 'principle' of a thing, then nothing of what they said about human affairs 'is begotten of intelligence'. Scholars had consequently either praised the ancients for some alleged esoteric philosophical wisdom or regarded them as unworthy of attention from a modern age.

Instead, Vico viewed ancient writings as *evidence* from which he *inferred* their 'poetic wisdom', itself *evidence* of a different mentality. From there, one could proceed to *infer from the evidence*, rather than merely imagine, the actual circumstances in which human beings generated the first 'institutions' or 'principles' of society, and from which all else followed. And as we will see, Vico did not restrict his analysis to the first societies. As societies developed over the ages, human consciousness or 'mentalities' changed. Yet significant vestiges of the *language* of earlier times lingered on with modified meanings, but still relatable to earlier circumstances. Thus various seminal documents such as the early legal codes and historical mythologies of the Greek and Romans were not only hopelessly misunderstood by *later* scholars, but were often inherently confused themselves, often misappropriating words and terms from an earlier age. Vico displays a special fascination in tracing such vestigial meanings in later literatures and employing the insights gained to better understand (i.e., 'scientifically') not only ancient but also succeeding epochs of human history.

Hopefully this exposition of both the general and more immediate origins of Vico's *New Science* will help in the reading of Vico's final (1744) version, otherwise a somewhat challenging experience partly because he is responding to those large and diverse themes outlined in the previous chapter. Not least amongst that complex, as we have seen, was the philosophical issue of *method* for achieving *true* knowledge. Reflective on the issue, and sensitive to its primary importance, Vico had his own ideas – of profound significance to his philosophy of history.

The question of true knowledge

The earlier Vico

Vico grappled with this issue from as early as 1708, and a good case can be made for claiming he altered his views on it[6] by the time he worked on the *New Science* (especially from the 1730 version onwards). Nonetheless, aspects of his earlier theory of knowledge continued to play a part in the latter. In his (1709) work *On the Wisdom of the Most Ancient Italians* Vico elaborates his theory that 'the true' (*verum*) is 'the made', or 'that which is done' (*factum*). By this he means to refute the Cartesian notion that 'truth' is simply the property we ascribe to *statements* which follow *logically* from *definitions*.[7] Rather, if we want to *know* or understand a thing *truly* we have to be aware of how it was made or done. Everything which exists (from natural phenomena and happenings to human events, institutions, and the arts and sciences themselves) is the product of 'making' or 'doing' (*factum*). Since this is the very foundation of all reality, it is also the very foundation of 'the true' (*verum*). All else is fiction or fantasy. Thus, if only that which is 'made' or 'done' is the true, equally, only that is 'the true' which is 'the made' or 'the done'.

On this basis Vico evaluated the 'truth' status of the various branches of human knowledge. But this exercise was premised by his insistence on the religio-philosophical notion that God made Nature (including man), and that God did this out of nothing other than His own intellect. Put simply, Existence in all its forms is the manifestation or 'product' of God's thinking – not, then, that God forged the things in Existence from some *pre-existing* primeval elements, but in the literally *radical* sense of conceiving everything *ex nihilo* from His own mind. Now (according to the pre-*New Science* Vico), the nearest human-beings can approach such 'making/doing' is found in mathematical reasoning, because here they engage in creating ideas and drawing conclusions from them solely from their own minds. Since, then, the 'knowing' and the 'doing' coincide in the mind of the mathematician, this is 'making' *par excellence*, such that mathematical knowledge achieves that equation of 'the made' (*factum*) and 'the true' (*verum*) nearest to Divine knowledge. It is the most 'true' or 'certain' knowledge. Next in order of certainty is physics. It shares the exactness and clarity of mathematical reasoning, yet in dealing with the laws of *matter* the physicist is not creating ('making') the elements he is thinking about – (God, not the physicist, made Nature).

From this Vico constructs a descending order of disciplines. The more entangled a subject-matter is in the contingent externalities of the world, the further removed is the knowledge of that subject from the abstract clarity of mathematical principles. It is true that the problems of 'knowing' things external to the mind can be mitigated through the process of experimentation, whereby to an extent we replicate natural processes. Such work was common in physics, and chemistry was also beginning to benefit from it. But on both counts – their contingent externality and the difficulty of conducting repeatable experiments – certain topics remain relatively inaccessible to 'knowing', and Vico places 'ethics' at the bottom of the list. By 'ethics' he means that venerable and extensive area of (humanist) enquiry into knowledge of 'the good', encompassing justice, morality, and law (and thereby political institutions). Perhaps to our surprise, then, it is just the study of human *mores*, laws, and institutions which is the furthest removed from a 'knowing' validated through the equation of 'the made' with 'the true'. In short, for the earlier Vico, knowledge of what he later called 'the civil world', or 'the world of nations', is the least 'certain' or 'scientific'.

Yet over time Vico altered these views to the point where he implies it is precisely knowledge of the above subject-matter which we can put *most* trust in, *if* we follow the principles he proposes in his *New Science*. As a change of mind, however, it is clear it emerged from these interesting earlier reflections on epistemology.

'True knowledge' in the New Science

Principally in paragraphs 119 to 164 of the *New Science* (1744 edition), Vico set out his considerably revised views on the truth status of knowledge in a set of propositions which 'are general and are the basis of our Science throughout'[8] and which, 'just as the blood does in animate bodies, . . . will . . . course through our Science and animate it in all its reasonings about the common nature of nations'.[9] We have already noted his bold dismissal of all previous attempts to gain proper knowledge of human affairs, and he begins by saying that 'the inexhaustible source of all the errors about the principles of humanity' is the propensity whereby, when man is 'lost in ignorance', he 'makes himself the measure of all things'.[10] This spawns two fallacies – first, 'the conceit of nations', whereby each nation mistakenly believes that 'it before all other nations invented the comforts of human life and that its remembered history goes back to the very beginning of the world'.[11] This leads to interpreting cultural history as originating in a single source, from which it was subsequently transmitted to other nations – a grievous error leading historians, philosophers, and linguists into illusion and confusion. The second is 'the conceit of scholars', 'who will have it that what they know is as old as the world'[12] whereby in trying to give their own ideas a spurious authority they allege an esoteric and pristine wisdom existed in ancient times, to which their own ideas accord. Since no such ancient wisdom existed, Vico insists, this is equally grievous an error since it generates a complete misreading of ancient cultures, and thus of history itself.

These remarks already suggest a more confident approach to knowledge of the human world than in his earlier epistemology, for now he is saying the deficiencies of such knowledge are not *intrinsic* to the subject-matter, but are explicable in terms of those common errors exposed above. Once avoided, he can proceed to establish the bases for a 'true' understanding of the human world. They are as follows: God created the world, and thus knows it absolutely 'since in God knowledge and creation are one and the same thing':[13] men can approach such true knowledge through 'science' or 'philosophy', which 'contemplates reason, whence comes knowledge of the true'.[14] Yet such (logical) reasoning deals only with *abstract fictions* of the human mind such as the 'points, lines, surfaces, and figures' *invented* by geometry (still an archetype of this kind of knowledge for Vico). In this sense, although philosophy discovers (logical) truth, its knowledge is deficient to the extent that it deals with abstractions rather than *real* things. Where, however, such 'scientific' or 'philosophical' reasoning *is* applied to real things, two problems continue to undermine the truth status of the knowledge gained. The first remains intrinsic, and is where the subject-matter is the *natural* world (e.g., physics, mechanics) – for man has not made the natural world, and so natural science, however expert, must ultimately remain incomplete knowledge. The second is where the scientist-philosopher, even when contemplating real things rather than abstractions, does not take sufficient care over the *empirical* details of his subject-matter (e.g., misperceiving it because relying on previous assumptions). This can still be a fault in the natural sciences, which is why Vico so much approves of Francis Bacon's 'method of philosophising, which is "think and see"'.[15] But the philosopher-scientist can also contemplate the *human* world, and it is here in particular that Vico believes their knowledge has 'failed by half'[16] through lack of attention to the empirical facts.

So 'scientific' or 'philosophical' reasoning, 'whence comes knowledge of the true', gives the certainty of *logical* truth and can be applied to both the natural and the human world. But in both cases it must get its *facts* straight. The facts in the natural world are made by God, and thus there is a limit to natural science's grasp of its subject-matter, although observation and experiment can achieve great insight. The facts in the *human* world, however, are 'made' in the immediate sense by *men*. *Knowledge* of these facts is what Vico calls 'philology', by which he means 'all the grammarians, historians, critics, who have occupied themselves with the study of the languages and deeds of peoples: both at home, as in their customs and laws, and abroad, as in their wars, peaces, alliances, travels, and commerce'.[17] Now the knowledge or consciousness of *fact* is not the same kind of 'knowing' as that of the philosopher-scientists. They construct 'knowledge of the true', whereas knowledge of *fact* is what Vico distinguishes as 'consciousness of the *certain*'. He tells us that 'men who do not know what is true of things take care to hold fast to what is certain'.[18] Knowledge of fact, (i.e., empirically based knowledge), thus bears the stamp of 'certainty' rather than the hallmark of logical validity (the different province of philosophy/reason/science).

Now, logically speaking, there seems no reason to restrict knowledge of 'the certain' to the *human* world. After all, natural scientists-philosophers must also get *their* facts straight – and this must involve them in knowledge of 'the certain', which seems to be what Vico praises Bacon for. Yet Vico glosses over this, wanting to restrict knowledge of 'the certain' solely to knowledge of the *human* world. Thus where he introduces his distinction between knowledge of 'the true' and 'the certain' he writes: 'Philosophy contemplates reason, whence comes knowledge of the true; philology observes that of which human choice is author, whence comes consciousness of the certain'.[19]

Whether or not this constitutes an error in Vico's thinking, it evidences a distinct shift from his earlier epistemology – a shift crucial to the entire logic of his *New Science*, and which he therefore impresses on the reader. Now, in the *New Science*, 'the civil world' has been made by men, and can therefore come to be 'known' in a manner superior to the philosopher-scientist's knowledge of the natural world. Vico writes that it is 'a truth beyond all question: that the world of civil society has certainly been made by men, and that its principles are therefore to be found within the modifications of our own human mind', and complains of the fact that 'the philosophers should have bent all their energies to the study of the world of nature, which, since God made it, He alone knows; and that they should have neglected the study of the world of nations, or civil world, which, since men had made it, men could come to know'.[20] Again, 'this world of nations has certainly been made by men. . . . And history cannot be more certain than when he who creates the things also narrates them'.[21] He thus suggests that his 'Science', because dealing with *real* things created by *men*, is (potentially) superior to natural science in respect of its truth status.

Thus the outlines of Vico's (new) epistemology – so much at the heart of his philosophy of history – become clearer. But as his response to seventeenth-century epistemological debate, what is Vico suggesting about the kind of method and knowledge his book contains? In our *modern* terms, is it 'science' or 'philosophy' – or in *seventeenth-century* terms, is it simply another example of 'philosophy-science' (applied to human institutions)? This is all the more important an issue because, in approaching the first example (in today's parlance) of explicit 'philosophy of history', it raises the vexed question of its disciplinary status or integrity. But Vico's answer seems clear. Rather than his *New Science* contributing to or combining any existing disciplines, for him it seems that (what we now call) 'philosophy of history' is nothing less than a new, independent discipline *in itself*, which his book *establishes*.

This is because Vico wanted to supersede the debates between 'science' and 'philosophy' and between rationalism and empiricism. For Vico, we can call knowledge of 'the true' equally 'science' or 'philosophy, so long as we mean knowledge derived from abstract logical reasoning. Knowledge of 'the certain', on the other hand, is empirical knowledge of fact, but he restricts its reference to those matters of fact of which *men* are 'makers' and 'doers'.

Here we *can* properly 'know' the facts of the *human* world, but such empirical knowledge cannot stand on its own as a comprehensive *understanding* of that world, since its mode of knowledge does not involve knowledge of 'the true'. In short, the facts of the human world still need to be interconnected through the process of logical reasoning (science/ philosophy) in order to arrive at 'the truth'. Thus for Vico 'the truth' must be a mixing of 'the certain' and 'the true', and is, then, *more* than either factual knowledge ('empiricism') or science/philosophy ('rationalism') – it supersedes both. Vico calls it 'new science'. But above all let us note that for Vico this ultimate form of knowledge is *intrinsically* and *exclusively* knowledge of civil or human affairs, and thus in the broadest sense of the term, *historical* knowledge. By this we do not mean (merely) knowledge of history, but a method of knowing something comprehensively through making sense ('the true') of the facts – ('the certain').

And the only things amenable to such complete knowledge are those 'facts' made or done by men. This, however, is a huge area incorporating customs, languages, all kinds of institutions, legal codes, religious beliefs, social structures, and the arts, sciences, and philosophy – in short, nothing less than human *culture* in its broadest sense, or in his words, 'the principles of humanity'.

Thus we find Vico complaining how, in respect of the human world, 'the philosophers failed by half in not giving certainty to their reasonings by appeal to the authority of the philologians, and likewise how the latter failed by half in not taking care to give their authority the sanction of truth by appeal to the reasoning of the philosophers'.[22] When the two approaches are fused, according to Vico, the resulting knowledge is not merely a (now correct) understanding of this or that detail of civil affairs. Rather, it contributes to the understanding of 'this world of nations in its eternal idea'.[23] This is the final summit of his 'new science', achieving what he calls 'an ideal eternal history traversed in time by the history of every nation',[24] such that we discover 'the eternal laws which are instanced by the deeds of all nations . . . even if . . . there were infinite worlds being born . . . throughout eternity'.[25] In short, that which is 'known' by Vico's 'new science' – the object of its knowledge – is nothing less than the universal laws governing the history of all humanity, whichever cultures, nations, or peoples it is comprised of. It would appear to be the *only* object of his 'new science', just as his 'new science' can only 'know' one subject – the universal principles of mankind wherever instanced through men organising themselves into the societal world.

In his own mind, then, Vico was not simply offering a revised version of human history on the basis of his discovery of new facts. Rather, he is highly aware of the radical status of his approach to knowledge – (like blood circulating the body, it 'courses through our Science') – and is equally anxious to publicise the fact: 'Hence we could not refrain from giving this work the invidious title of a *New Science*, for it was too much to defraud it unjustly of the rightful claim it had . . .'.[26] It is this feature of his work which, perhaps above all, justifies the claim that he is the first explicit *philosopher* of history, and not surprisingly it is the feature which most continues to interest philosophers and historical theorists.

Vico's 'ideal eternal history'

Mankind's origins – the 'age of gods'

We may now proceed to Vico's actual account of the course and meaning of human history, beginning with its origins. From his reading of Homer, Vico claims that early men (i.e., before the dawning of classical Greek culture) had a profoundly different mentality from their more civilised successors. Being brute ignorant, having neither language or reason, living in dire straits, and prey to urgent fears, their consciousness was supersensitive to the immediately perceptible qualities of things they encountered, such that their awareness of the world was solely (and highly) figurative and imaginative. Initially mute, the earliest kind of language to emerge amongst these feral beings was, Vico suggests, 'singing' (see below). This evolved into the first spoken words, but these did not denote the common properties of things (as in our languages). Rather, they marked a thing's most importantly sensed impact, irrespective of its other features. And where something else provoked the same effect, the same word would be used to signify the thing.

It is this propensity to construct imaginative, figurative language that Vico calls 'poetry'. Interestingly, Vico thinks children's mentality is the perfect analogy. 'In children memory is most vigorous, and imagination is therefore excessively vivid; . . . this . . . is the principle of the expressiveness of the poetic images that the world formed in its first childhood'.[27] Again, 'Children excel in imitation . . . they generally amuse themselves by imitating whatever they are able to apprehend; This . . . shows that the world in its infancy was composed of poetic nations, for poetry is nothing but imitation'.[28] Vico delights in peppering his *New Science* with examples of how the meaning of words in use at a later time can be traced back to their initial figurative source. For example, referring to the Latin word *lex* ('law'), he writes:

> First it must have meant a collection of acorns. Thence we believe is derived *ilex*, as it were *illex*, the oak (as certainly *aquilex* means collector of waters); for the oak produces the acorns by which the swine are drawn together. *Lex* was next a collection of vegetables, from which the latter were called *legumina*. Later on . . . when . . . letters had not yet been invented for writing down the laws, *lex* . . . must have meant a collection of citizens, or the public parliament; so that the presence of the people was the *lex*, or "law" . . . Finally, collecting letters, and making, as it were, a sheaf of them for each word, was called *legere*, reading.[29]

The reader of Vico will find numerous such treatments of the origins of words (etymology), and the point here is not so much their accuracy but the rationale of

136

the exercise. For example, we know the word 'companion' derives from the *concrete* notion of 'sharing bread' (*com – panis*). Similarly, imagine a distant future in which space-travel is common and in which the term 'docking' persists. Then imagine how enlightening an account of where the term came from in the twentieth century (i.e., ships 'docking') would be. The next step, of course, would be to see where the *twentieth*-century term itself originated by consulting an etymological dictionary.

This is the significance Vico attaches to etymology. It tells us where ideas came from, and thus evidences the manner in which earlier cultures perceived the world – and, in turn, how *it* impinged on *them*. It persuades Vico that when language emerged from 'the earliest antiquity' and was eventually put into writing (initially signs and hieroglyphics rather than 'sheafs of letters'), the first men's knowledge of the world was comprised of what he calls 'poetic wisdom'. However, this 'poetic wisdom' has no connection with the (later) *rational*, analytical apprehension of things in terms of abstract genera. Rather, it is the expression of the heightened alertness to the striking features of things, creatively applied through a highly imaginative 'imitation' to identify and describe the surrounding world, and (as in Homer) it can reach 'sublime' heights. Although not 'rational', such 'knowledge' is thus essentially creative, and characteristically Vico traces the meaning of the word *poet* (in Greek) to *creator* or *maker*.

With these insights into 'poetic wisdom', Vico proceeds to construct the fundamental developments in human history since the Flood. Elaborating on the Biblical account, Vico claims that in Mesopotamia, after the Universal Flood, Noah established the Hebrew people[30] which, through keeping faith with the true religion of God, continued thereafter on a separate path from all other subsequent gentile nations (of which more below). But the descendants of Noah's three sons gradually renounced their religion and dispersed into three different races and areas of the world. The immediate post-Flood world, Vico claims, must have been covered in damp, dense forest full of wild beasts, and as the peoples of Ham, Japheth, and Shem dispersed throughout it, individuals must have become separated. In this precarious situation, fleeing from wild beasts, and pursuing women who themselves must have become increasingly wild and fearful, all vestiges of their previous culture disappeared.

> Mothers, like beasts, must have merely nursed their babies, let them wallow naked in their own filth, and abandoned them for good as soon as they were weaned; . . . [W]ithout ever hearing a human voice, much less learning any human custom, [these generations] descended to a state truly bestial and savage.

Vico then suggests these feral creatures developed physically, 'excessively big in brawn and bone, to the point of becoming giants'[31] (much talked of in ancient fables), and it is from 'these first men, stupid, insensate, and horrible beasts',[32] that the history and institutions of all (gentile) nations emerged.

So (gentile, post-Flood) history began with an age of 'giants', horrifyingly and almost unimaginably sub-human in their brute natures. The stronger 'giants' naturally took to the drier safeholds of mountain-tops with caves – and such would have remained the condition of humanity were it not, according to Vico, for a dramatic event. After some hundreds of years of drying out, the earth at last produced sufficient vapour to cause the first thunder and lightning. Never witnessed before, and of such an awe-inspiring nature, it terrified and traumatized our feral giants, and none more so than those frequenting the mountain heights. Unaccustomed to pay attention to the sky, they now became aware of it, and,

> because in such a case the nature of the human mind leads it to attribute its own nature to the effect, and because in that state their nature was that of men all robust bodily strength, who expressed their very violent passions by shouting and grumbling, they pictured the sky to themselves as a great animated body. . . . who meant to tell them something by the hiss of his bolts and the clap of his thunder.[33]

This is the origin of gentile religion, whereby our 'giants' believed in a terrifying power 'speaking' in/from/as the sky, later called Jove. This event must have been replicated many times and to the same effect – such that 'every gentile nation had its Jove',[34] with correspondingly numerous names. Later, 'the first theological poets created the first divine fable, the greatest they ever created: that of Jove, king and father of men and gods, in the act of hurling the lightning bolt; an image . . . its creators themselves believed in . . ., and feared, revered, and worshipped . . . in frightful religions'.[35]

The first effect of this traumatic experience of a 'voice' in the sky was to terrify the 'giants' into retreating into their caves, and 'to check their bestial habit of wandering wild through the great forest of the earth',[36] making them remain within a settled territory. This is the very seed from which subsequent social developments sprang, and without which there would be no societies in the (gentile) world – such that Vico puts religion as the first 'institution' of every nation. The essence of this 'religion' was, from fear of Jove's authority – (they had never felt 'authority' before) – to try to 'divine' what the signs made by Jove meant, leading to the auspices, oracles, and sacrifices of these 'frightful religions'.

The second effect was to restrain

> their bestial lust from finding its satisfaction in the sight of heaven, of which they had a mortal terror. So it came about that each of them would drag one woman into his cave and keep her there in perpetual company for the duration of their lives. Thus the act of human love was performed under cover, in hiding, that is to say, in shame . . . In this guise marriage was introduced, which is a chaste carnal union consummated under the fear of some divinity.[37]

In this manner the first *proper* families emerged – that is, where the offspring's parentage was certain. Since Vico insists all nations originated in families, marriage is thus the second fundamental principle of any society.

The third is burial. Surprisingly, all Vico says to explain this is that it came from the belief 'that human souls do not die with their bodies but are immortal'. But he also links it to the emergence of family lands (property) whereby 'by long residence and burial of their dead they came to found and divide the first dominions of the earth, whose lords were giants, a Greek word meaning "sons of earth"'.[38] Be this as it may, Vico observes that 'all nations, barbarous as well as civilized, though separately founded because remote from each other in time and space, keep these three human customs: all have some religion, all contract solemn marriages, all bury their dead'.[39] One might wonder at the prospects for our contemporary Western societies, in which all three 'fundamental institutions' are increasingly disrespected through, respectively, atheism, the 'sexual revolution', and 'spare part' body donor practices!

There is a sense in which Vico adds a fourth fundamental institution, for he says these first families cleared the forests around them and made fields. In short, property was introduced, whereby territory was delineated on family lines, put to economic use, and its boundaries defended.

In this initial stage, then, some 'families' were established, restrained by religion into the practices of marriage, burial, and settlement. These first cultivated fields were burnt clearings in the forests, and here we may give another example of Vico's intriguing use of etymology as evidence of features of ancient antiquity. These fields were called *luci* by the Latin peoples,

> in the sense of an eye, as even today we call eyes the opening through which light enters houses. The . . . phrase that 'every giant had his *lucus*' [clearing or eye] was altered and corrupted when its meaning was lost, and had already been falsified when it reached Homer, for it was then taken to mean that every giant had one eye in the middle of his forehead.[40]

This, then, for Vico is the origin of the myth of the Cyclops, the race of one-eyed giants, and we can see how he uses it both to arrive at the *historical facts* he claims underlie it and to explain their passing into 'mythical' form through the corruption of time. In this case, at an earlier age when the imagery of 'giants/fields/eyes' was a genuine perception of the figurative/associative 'poetic' consciousness, it denoted a true state of affairs. But in later times the different associations of such figurative language generate misunderstandings and myths whose meanings have to be interpreted – but not on the basis of some esoteric, hidden philosophical wisdom. Rather, the meaning and use of words has to be related both to where they *originated* and to the *present* mind-set of the culture now employing them. Their changing meanings over time are not only a potent clue to their *original* meaning but also to the historical circumstances and mentalities of the *succeeding* cultures who use them in their own way. He was especially proud of how his etymological/

philological researches into the earliest documents (Homer – 'a vast store-house of knowledge' – in Greece, and the Roman Law of the Twelve Tables) at last revealed and proved (according to him) the hitherto unknown or purely fantasised history of 'the lost times'.

Vico called this first age 'the age of gods' or 'the age of giants'. As we have seen, some of these 'giants' became subdued by 'Jove' and settled into the first form of social organisation, which Vico calls 'the family state'.[41] But other 'giants' (less 'noble')[42] remained in the forests, and 'impious . . . , continued the infamous promiscuity of things and of women'.[43] Eventually, however, their miserable circumstances (akin to Hobbes' 'fierce and violent men'[44] or Pufendorf's 'Big Feet' giants[45]) drove them to seek succour in the enclosed 'fields' or 'asylums' established by the god-fearing 'giants' already organised into family states. But the latter did not accept these wretched 'refugees'[46] as equals. Rather, they killed the more violent newcomers and took the remainder under their protection as inferiors obliged to work and defend the land (belonging exclusively to the 'nobles'). Vico variously refers to their status as like that of prisoners-of-war,[47] day-labourers,[48] slaves, 'clients',[49] or plebeians.[50] It was this development which 'gave a beginning to society in the proper sense', since although a prior 'society' had prevailed in the family state of the noble giants, it had only come about through their being 'driven thereto by religion and by the natural instinct to propagate the human race . . . and thus gave a beginning to noble and lordly friendship'. But, importantly, it seems Vico denies that 'friendship' or 'sociability' is the basis for 'society in the proper sense'. Rather, the latter only begins when formed from *practical* motivations. Society 'proper' fulfils practical need, not altruistic yearnings. Thus it was not until the subsequent stage, when 'base and servile' refugees 'came out of a necessity of saving their lives', that society began 'in the proper sense, with a view principally to *utility*'.[51]

The 'age of heroes'

Thus we arrive at Vico's second age, the 'age of heroes', in which society proper began. During this age the small family-states of noble giants evolved into cities, or city-states, often expanded through military conquest. The form of government common in the heroic age was necessarily (given its origins) 'most severely aristocratic'.[52] The descendants of the first noble 'giants' retained their ownership of land through their status, guaranteed via the integrity of their lineage, and ruled their 'plebeians, being considered of bestial origin',[53] with what from a *later* perspective was barbarous cruelty. Vico does not minimise the brutal aspects of 'heroic' natures where, 'being as yet incapable of reason', the only law initially was that of force. But the outcome of force was regarded as a divine judgement and therefore just. It was 'the law of Achilles, who referred every right to the tip of his spear'.[54] Thus issues between the noble families would often be settled by bloody duels, whilst any issue between noble heads of families and their dependents (servile 'plebs' *or* their own children) would be ruthlessly dealt with by the noble head who exercised a 'divine' right of life and death.

But barbarous as were these early aristocracies of 'the age of heroes', Vico insists we must understand and judge the 'heroic' mentality in terms of its own times, not ours. The noble families saw themselves as descended from a special lineage which had maintained its integrity through pious observance of the religious heritage of their god-like ancestors. Indeed, so intimate and integral had been their ancestors' communion with Jove (and with all the other gods they invented by 'ascrib[ing] to physical things the being of substances animated by gods'),[55] that they saw themselves as Jove's descendants, and jealously guarded their knowledge of the mysteries, rites, auspices, sacrifices, judgements, and modes of divination from their plebeian underlings. (Vico thus describes the first city-states as 'priestly aristocracies'). Given this mentality, (and the awe in which at least the first generations of refugees held their lords) a different morality from ours held sway – the virtues of 'heroism'. Order was ruthlessly maintained through the sword, and right amongst equals, including 'international relations' between different 'nations' or city-states, was established by appeal to divine judgement via force of arms (sometimes via duelling rather than all-out conflict). Reminding us of the equivocation in Machiavelli's notion of 'virtue', Vico similarly talks admiringly of the 'heroic' virtues, despite their seeming barbarity. Thus,

> the strong, with a fierceness born of their union in the society of families, slew the violent who had violated their lands, and took under their protection the miserable creatures who had fled from them. And above the heroism of nature which was theirs as having been born of Jove . . . , there now shone forth preeminently in them the heroism of virtue. In this heroism the Romans excelled all other peoples of the earth, practising precisely these two aspects of it, sparing the submissive and vanquishing the proud.[56]

Large sections of the *New Science* are devoted to explaining this 'heroic' mentality of barbarous times, the essence being that these peoples had intellects 'incapable of abstracting forms and properties from subjects',[57] but attended only to the striking *particulars* of matters, generating that vivid and imaginative 'poetic' consciousness described earlier. Combining this fundamental intellectual deficiency with 'their recent gigantic origin', Vico outlines their inextricably linked psychological character – 'the heroes were in the highest degree gross and wild . . . very limited in understanding but endowed with the vastest imaginations and the most violent passions. Hence they must have been boorish, crude, harsh, wild, proud, difficult and obstinate . . . and (yet) easily diverted'. But they must also have been 'bluff, touchy, magnanimous, and generous, as Homer portrays Achilles, the greatest of all the Greek heroes'.[58] Vico also believes that despite, or because, lacking the capacity for reason, they must have had exceptional memories, and that prior to the emergence of written language (at the end of their age) they preserved the memory of important events (related to their society's origins and development) in figurative signs, later transposed into 'poetic' song as verbal language took shape. But we must understand that these 'songs' were not 'poetic' because they were *songs*. Rather, the first verbal language was 'poetic' because it emerged from 'a fantastic speech making use of physical substances endowed with life and most of them imagined to be divine'.[59] And it was 'song' because 'mutes utter formless sounds by singing', and 'men vent great passions by breaking into song' – thus 'the founders of the gentile nations, having wandered about in the wild state of dumb beasts . . . were inexpressive save under the impulse of violent passions, and formed their first languages by singing'.[60]

These first 'songs' were thus histories of their societies, but posed in the necessarily 'fabulous' terms corresponding to their 'poetic' consciousness. Yet this does not mean the 'fables' containing their history were untrue. On the contrary, Vico insists 'the fables in their origin were true and severe narrations',[61] and that they preceded the first *written* histories which after 'the long passage of years and change of customs'[62] distorted their meanings, which were 'altered, subsequently became improbable, after that obscure, then scandalous, and finally incredible'.[63] This corrupting process was well under way even before Homer,[64] (whom Vico doubted as an historical figure, claiming that he stood for a tradition of mythical narration spanning centuries of Greek 'heroic' culture), such that the history of earlier times which his great myths recount requires a radical reconstruction in the light of Vico's method.

In short, what Vico employs in his 'discovery of the true Homer' is a highly suggestive, complex technique which uncovers the 'heroic' mentality and circumstances, which are themselves a product of the earlier, entirely mythopoeic mentality and circumstances of the 'age of giants'. Both 'spoke' poetically, but the latter's poetry was 'theological' and spoke only the truth (albeit in its own way), whilst 'heroic' poetry became increasingly fantastical in terms of the 'history' it related (although its meanings and referents can still be recaptured).

In practice (since, lacking speculative reason, they were nothing if not practical in their mentality) the 'heroic' peoples were concerned with what Vico refers to as the 'utilities and necessities of life' – territory, fields, corn, inheritance, boundaries, family lineage, authority, and terms of protection. Vico uses this notion to help disentangle the meaning of the words they used. Thus he found the (Roman) Law of the Twelve Tables especially illuminating. It is the other major 'document' he uses to complement the analysis of the 'heroic ages' he derives from Homer. But mention of this Roman source introduces us to the third age Vico identifies, 'the age of men', for in his opening 'Chronological Table' he dates the Law of the Twelve Tables at around the time when in Italy the 'age of heroes' had run its course. Appearing on the cusp of epochal change, the Twelve Tables are thus of seminal interest as a source both of the age from which they emerged and of that which was dawning. According to his Chronology, the same significance attaches to Homer, for his epics appeared around the time this same epochal change occurred in Greece – some three hundred years before Italy.

The 'age of men'

What, then, is 'the age of men', and how did it come about? Vico uses the term to denote the age in which men became recognisably 'human' in their mentality. The fierce, passionate, unreflective 'heroic' nature dissipated, along with its purely imaginative, 'poetic' consciousness, to be replaced by 'human nature, intelligent and hence modest, benign, and reasonable, recognising for laws conscience, reason, and duty'.[65] Correspondingly, the 'age of men' sees the origins of articulate speech and written words, denoting things in terms of the genera to which they belong. In short, it witnesses the birth of philosophy and science, in which the world is now construed rationally by language denoting the properties of things according to the abstracting of universals. For example:

> after the poets had formed poetic speech by associating particular ideas, the [human] peoples went on to form prose speech by contracting into a single word, as into a genus, the parts which poetic speech had associated. Take for example the poetic phrase 'the blood boils in my heart' . . . They took the blood, the boiling, and the heart, and made of them a single word ('I am angry')[66] . . . [By these means] the minds of the people grew quicker and developed powers of abstraction, and the way was thus prepared for the coming of philosophers, who formed intelligible genera.[67]

Interestingly, Vico claims the emergence of this 'human' language was hugely significant in *political* terms, for whereas 'hitherto [in the 'age of heroes'] . . . the nobles, being also priests, had kept the laws in a secret language as a sacred thing', 'human language' used:

> words agreed upon by the people, a language of which they are the absolute lords . . . whereby the people may fix the meaning of the laws by which the nobles as well as the plebs are bound . . . Hence, . . . once the laws had been put into the vulgar tongue, the science of laws passed from the control of the nobles.[68]

In short, a feature of the benign 'age of men' is that ordinary people appropriate the language. (Here we may be reminded of those concerns expressed today about scientists – and perhaps Internet users – speaking a different 'language', such that many people feel deprived of the ability to participate in crucial areas of public policy-making!).

Vico closely associates the gentleness of people in 'the age of men' to this dawning of reason. As he puts it: 'The people had finally come to understand that the rational nature (which is the true human nature) is equal in all men'.[69] If the mentality, form of language, and human nature were transformed in 'the age of men', so were other aspects of their culture, including their socio-political organisation – and a brief examination of how the latter came about will help account for the demise of 'the age of heroes'.

Back in the first age (of gods/giants), order over the first 'fields' was maintained by the few pious giants, who governed theocratically via the taking of auspices and consulting oracles.[70] But as 'refugee' giants fled to these asylums for protection, over time these settlements grew in number and size, as did the number of the original 'pious' giants. A point came when the latter banded together better to guard their lands and authority against the growing numbers of 'plebs' they had taken under protection. The 'age of gods' was giving way to the 'age of heroes'. In short, 'commonwealths' or city-states emerged, under a now aristocratic form of government which Vico often describes as 'severe'. Once established, in these 'heroic or aristocratic governments, . . . in virtue of the distinction of a nobler nature ascribed to divine origin, . . . all civil rights were confined to the ruling orders of the heroes themselves, and the plebeians, being considered of bestial origin, were only permitted to enjoy life and natural liberty',[71] whereby they 'shared only the labours of the heroes, not their winnings, and still less their glory'.[72]

As these noble aristocratic commonwealths became established, (the nobles themselves often organised under kings they could not control), 'at last, after a long period, [the plebs] grew weary of being obliged always to serve their lords' and thus 'laid claim to the lands and rose in mutiny . . . and revolted against the heroes'. Some defeated rebellious bands,

> committed themselves to the hazards of the sea and went in search of unoccupied lands. . . . This is the origin of the migration of peoples already humanized by religion . . . By means of such colonies. . . . the human race was spread abroad in the rest of our world by sea, just as by means of the savage wanderings a long time before it had been spread abroad by land.

Vico insists these colonies must have been small, because reached by sea; were nothing to do with a non-existent empire (allegedly) acquired by the heroic aristocracies; nor with reasons of trade (with unoccupied lands!) – but were established because 'heroic law made it necessary for such bands of men . . . to abandon their own lands, a thing which naturally happens only under some extreme necessity'.[73]

The majority of rebellious plebs, however, remained at home and began to extract concessions regarding the ownership of land and terms of service from their noble overlords.

The 'age of heroes' was drawing to an end, both in political and in broader cultural terms, eventuating in the emergence of 'popular commonwealths'. The barbarous modes of 'heroic' government and mentality were supplanted by 'the age of men' (or 'human times'), in which 'in virtue of the equality of the intelligent natures which is the proper nature of man, all are accounted equal under the laws'.[74] Reason now prevailed, and was applied to the practical needs of the (now free) citizens in such a manner that 'universal legal concepts abstracted by the intellect' brought the citizens 'into agreement upon an idea of a common rational utility'.[75] This new 'practice of wisdom in affairs of utility' provides the basis for the 'mild law'[76] which characterizes 'the age of men', and Vico even suggests that the actual process by which popular assemblies first achieved this 'coming to agreement in an idea of an equal utility common to all of them severally' (as in Athens) prompted Socrates to 'adumbrate intelligible phenomena or abstract universals by induction'. In short, 'laws came first and philosophies later',[77] suggesting that the very rationality which lies at the core of 'human' men was not so much a product of some sudden intellectual revolution, but of changes in men's material circumstances. Yet it is clear from Vico's account that prior to the beginnings of actual philosophical reasoning (in Socrates), the mentality of ordinary people had already changed from the 'heroic'. It is just this interplay between 'mentality' and material circumstances which runs like a thread through Vico's analysis of the origins, development, and demise of all three different 'ages', and is one of the reasons (in addition to Vico's emphasis upon 'class-conflict') the more erudite Marxists find in him a precursor to Marx's 'historical materialism'.[78]

Monarchy in the 'age of men'

Taking his cue from classical history (especially the rise of the Emperor Augustus in Rome[79]), and yet happy to generalise from it, Vico claims the 'free popular states' characterising 'the age of men' are not its only political form. In principle, better even than such republics are monarchies. His reasoning is that ' in the former the citizens have command of the public wealth, which is divided among them in as many minute parts as there are citizens making up the people who have command of it' (even in republics not *all* are citizens). This can work, but given that 'love of ease, tenderness towards children, love of women, and desire of life' characterises today's strivings towards the 'utilities and necessities of life', then 'men are led to attend to the smallest details which may bring their private utilities into equality with those of others'. In other words, (to use modern terms), individualism and competitiveness always threaten neglect of the public good because individuals' concern for their own private good 'is the only reason of which the multitude are capable'.[80] Thus, just as happened in the Roman Republic where, 'finally, as the free peoples could not by means of laws maintain themselves in civil equality . . . but were being driven to ruin by civil wars, it came about naturally that . . . they sought protection under monarchies',[81] monarchy is the other, better, and 'natural' form of government for free, rational, 'human' men.

In such monarchies, 'the subjects are commanded to look after their own private interests and leave the care of the public interest to the sovereign prince'.[82] Lest this seem 'undemocratic' in today's terms, Vico has a different view, for he construes monarchy in 'the age of men' as *having* to best represent the common good of citizens, and thus as 'by nature *popularly governed*: first through the laws by which monarchies seek to make their subjects all equal; then by that property of

145

monarchies whereby sovereigns humble the powerful and thus keep the masses safe and free from their oppressions; further by . . . keeping the multitude satisfied and content as regards the necessaries of life and the enjoyment of natural liberty'.[83] Thus in monarchies 'there are needed a few men skilled in statecraft to give counsel' regarding the conduct of affairs of state, whilst 'a great many jurists' are needed to regulate citizens' arguments over their private affairs.[84] In short, despite the benign tones in which Vico describes the 'age of men', he has a somewhat Machiavellian view of 'the multitude' as 'naturally' concerned in their own selfish interests. Thus, for Vico, 'monarchy is the form of government best adapted to human nature when reason is fully developed'.[85]

The potential demise of 'the age of men'

There is, then, a certain equivocation in Vico's views about human nature in 'the age of men' – although essentially 'intelligent, . . . modest, benign, and reasonable',[86] Vico's insistence on the self-interestedness of 'the multitude' and their unsuitedness to affairs of state is less than flattering. In fact, it seems Vico construes the 'properly human nature' of the 'age of men' as eventually departing from its optimistic origins to a point where the latter's very continuance is threatened. Again he appeals to classical history (especially Rome), but also generalizes from it. Essentially, 'the popular states became corrupt'.[87] In the case of Rome and other 'popular commonwealths', the common-sense of the (now reasonable and free) citizens initially determined that responsibility for governing should (via the census) rest with 'the industrious and not the lazy, the frugal and not the prodigal, . . . the magnanimous and not the fainthearted – in a word, the rich with some virtue or semblance thereof, and not the poor with their many shameless vices'.[88] But there came a point 'when the citizens were no longer content with making wealth the basis of rank', and encouraged by the 'false eloquence' of trouble-makers, 'strove to make it an instrument of power . . . [and thereby] provoked civil wars in their commonwealth and drove them to total disorder'.[89] In the case of Rome, the institution of monarchy under Augustus solved the problem – but clearly not permanently, and it seems that for Vico, whether 'human government' is under a republic or a monarchy a process of corruption is likely because of a natural evolution of the 'human' nature of people away from its benign beginnings.

He expressed this in two passages generalising from all three 'ages'. Thus, 'Men first feel necessity, then look for utility, next attend to comfort . . .'. But he continues, 'still later [they] amuse themselves with pleasure, then grow dissolute in luxury, and finally go mad and waste their substance'.[90] Presumably these latter are still features of human beings in 'the age of men', but they clearly point to a *deteriorating* scenario. The second passage follows immediately and in similar vein. Corresponding to the three different ages, '[t]he nature of peoples is first crude, then severe, then benign . . .' – but then he adds, 'then delicate, finally dissolute'.[91] Should we doubt what these cryptic additions really mean, Vico elaborates on them in the concluding passages of his book. We have noted his claim that 'popular states became corrupt'. This corruption can reach a stage where peoples 'become naturally slaves of their unrestrained passions – of luxury, effeminacy, avarice, envy, pride, and vanity – and in pursuit of the pleasures of their dissolute life . . . [they fall] back into all the vices characteristic of the most abject slaves (having become liars, tricksters, calumniators, thieves, cowards, and pretenders) . . .'.[92]

This *moral* decline, whereby 'such peoples, like so many beasts, have fallen into the custom of each man thinking only of his own private interests and have reached the extreme of delicacy, or better of pride . . .' is matched by an *intellectual* decline where that *reason* which dawned in man after the age of heroes becomes abused. Thus, 'as the popular states became corrupt, so also did the philosophies. They descended to skepticism. Learned fools fell to calumniating the truth. Thence arose a false eloquence, ready to uphold either of the opposed sides of a case indifferently'.[93] If unchecked, this intellectual decline leads to:

> the misbegotten subtleties of malicious wits that have turned [men] into beasts made more inhuman by the barbarism of reflection than the first men had been made by the barbarism of sense. For the latter displayed a generous savagery, against which one could defend oneself or take flight or be on one's guard; but the former, with a base savagery, under soft words and embraces, plots against the life and fortune of friends and intimates.[94]

How far these purple passages are evidence of Vico's disappointments at being neglected (e.g., Isaac Newton never acknowledged the first [1725] version of the *New Science* Vico sent him) is a matter of conjecture. Not so, however, his clear account of the gradual moral and intellectual failings of our 'benign' and 'rational' nature in 'the age of men', derived partly from his reading of classical history, but also elevated to being a general principle of 'human' nature. We, (if we can presume to be living in an 'age of men') will 'finally go mad and waste our substance'!

The recourse of history

The idea of 'recourse'

In Vico's account of (gentile) human history we have reached where the 'age of men' is threatened by the moral and intellectual 'corruptions' which Vico presents as integral principles of 'human' nature as it slides from benignity and rationality into 'delicacy', casuistry, and dissoluteness. His primary *historical* model for this is the transition from republican Rome to the 'monarchy' of Augustus – (his brief remarks on the subsequent downfall of the Roman Empire do *not* exploit this model[95]) – but he clearly believes the same happened elsewhere in the classical world of 'the age of men'. The institution of monarchy is one of the 'three great remedies'[96] which can (possibly) correct 'the perfect tyranny of anarchy'.[97] A second remedy is that 'corrupted' societies 'become subject to better nations, which, having conquered them by arms, preserve them as subject provinces' and their inhabitants as 'slaves'. Again, although thinking of historical examples, Vico sees them as exemplifying general principles of historical development. 'Herein two great lights of natural order shine forth. First, that he who cannot govern himself must let himself be governed by another who can. Second, that the world is always governed by those who are naturally fittest'.[98]

The third remedy is the most interesting – and the most chilling. It is this:

> But if the peoples are rotting in that ultimate civil disease and cannot agree on a monarch from within, and are not conquered and preserved by better nations from without . . . [then] through obstinate factions and desperate civil wars, they shall turn their cities into forests and the forests into dens and lairs of men. In this way, through long centuries of barbarism, rust will consume [their previous moral and intellectual faults, such that] stunned and brutalized, [they] are sensible no longer of comforts, delicacies, pleasures, and pomp, but only of the sheer necessities of life. [Thus driven (as if in some appalling post-nuclear holocaust)] the few survivors in the midst of an abundance of things necessary for life naturally become sociable and, returning to the primitive simplicity of the first world of peoples, are again religious, truthful, and faithful.[99]

And from this return to the beginning of (gentile) history, 'the nations . . . , like the phoenix, rise again'.[100]

It is, then, in this account of the third, most dreadful, remedy that Vico's notion of 'recourse' appears, and we need to be as clear as to what he is *not* saying as to what he *is* saying.

First, by 'the recourse' of history he does not so much mean the point where a 'nation' might have plumbed the very depths and has to start again, phoenix-like. Rather, he means that *if* a nation is subjected to this third remedy, *then* its re-growth will 'recourse' the same history of the succeeding ages of 'gods', 'heroes', and 'men' – but even here, only all other things being equal. Specific circumstances may intervene (as, for example, he suggests of the American Indians, who 'would now be following this course of human institutions if they had not been discovered by the Europeans'[101]). This is why Vico claims his 'science' is of 'an *ideal* eternal history'.

Second, (unlike earlier cyclical theories), it is far from clear that *all* societies will inevitably undergo a 'recourse'. Although it seems all will eventually reach that point of corruption in their 'age of men' described above, the return to primitive beginnings is only the *third* 'remedy'. They may be rescued from this by monarchy or conquest – although whether the monarchy or conquering power itself would eventually degrade into a corruption requiring the third remedy is another point. If it would, it looks as if Vico is indeed proposing a full-scale cyclical interpretation of past and future history. Yet he does not say so. He claims his 'science' demonstrates what 'the course of the institutions of the nations had to be, must be, and will have to be . . . even if infinite worlds were born from time to time through eternity, which is certainly not the case'.[102] This 'ideal eternal history' is 'traversed in time by the history of every nation in its rise, development, maturity, decline, and fall'.[103] He does not add, 'and its rise again'. In short, the 'ideal eternal history' does not mention 'recourse', and the most we can say is that whether 'recourse' is inevitable for every society in history remains unclear in Vico's logic.

'Recourse' in post-Classical European history

What *is* clear, however, is that for Vico 'recourse' is not only a theoretical possibility for some societies, but has actually happened in history – and his model is nothing less than the 'dark' and 'middle' ages of European history. He calls them 'the period of the second barbarism' and notes that 'in countless passages . . . we have observed the marvellous correspondence between the first and the returned barbarian times'.[104] He proceeds to bring these observations together in his sketchy Book Five called 'The recourse of human institutions which the nations take when they rise again'. Emerging from the confusions caused at the collapse of the (Christianised) Western Roman Empire, 'when so many barbarous nations began to inundate Europe and Asia and Africa', some Christian leaders in Europe held together their communities, and became akin to the kingly 'theocratic' family leaders of the first 'age of gods', fighting barbarous religious wars against like-organised pagan nations. In these recurred 'divine times', slavery, duels, raids, and reprisals re-appeared, and since 'everywhere violence, rapine, and murder were rampant, because of the extreme ferocity and savagery of these most barbarous centuries', new 'asylums' appeared where people 'in fear of being oppressed or destroyed betook themselves to the bishops and abbots, . . . as being comparatively humane in the midst of such barbarism, and put themselves, their families, and their patrimonies, under their protection'.[105]

Then, for the same reasons as in the *first* 'age of gods', Europe evolved into those feudal institutions of the high Middle Ages, where powerful 'lords', barons, and petty kings formed aristocratic states better to protect their lands and control the lower feudal orders of serfs and vassals (the equivalent of the first 'plebs'). The 'age of heroes' was back, and Vico delights in drawing correspondences between its institutions, mentality, and customs and those of its predecessor. Feudalism, even where organised under nominal monarchies, was essentially aristocratic and culturally 'heroic'.

But just as the first 'age of heroes' evolved to a point where pressure from the plebs combined with factious civil wars amongst the nobles brought it to an end, so in many parts of Europe the second 'age of heroes' was supplanted by a second 'age of men', as feudal aristocracies turned into either 'free popular commonwealths' (i.e., republics) or 'perfect monarchies'. Rightly, Vico is not too specific about where and when this epochal change occurred, since it replicated itself amongst separate nations at different times. Also, the process was still incomplete by the time he was writing. For example, he claims that France 'now' has become a 'perfect monarchy'

– that Sweden and Denmark remained heroic aristocracies 'until a century and a half ago' – and that Poland still is one, although he adds that 'in time, if extraordinary causes do not impede its natural course, Poland will arrive at perfect (that is, at absolute but enlightened) monarchy'.

The inevitability of 'recourse'?

What seems clear, then, is that Vico sees much of his present Europe as having entered, or being in the process of entering, a second 'age of men'. Whether he also already sees signs of its *demise* – and may thus be incorporating some political message into his writings – is another matter, best left to our concluding remarks. But it does graphically raise the question of whether 'recourse' is inevitable. By this, I do not mean whether, *if* a recourse occurs, it will run an inevitable course of repetition of 'the three ages of men'. Vico clearly affirms it would. Rather, does 'recourse' *have* to happen to all historical societies? Since we have seen Vico's *logic* leaves it unclear, we might try answering this by returning to his account of how the first, *actual*, 'recourse' came about.

That recourse began with the collapse of the Roman Empire in the fifth century AD. Logically, this means the Roman Empire, despite being under monarchy, must have reached that point of corruption and dissolution described above, from which (in its case) the third (dreadful) remedy emerged, involving a return to primitive times, succeeded by a 'recourse'. And some such standard notion of the reasons for the Empire's collapse seems to be in Vico's mind. Yet he says surprisingly little about it. Having explained why all preceding 'ages' with their corresponding institutions inevitably change, he does not conclude his account with any hint that 'monarchy' in the 'age of men' must itself eventually decline and collapse. If he had, then indeed his logic points to 'recourse' as the inevitable outcome of the history of societies – and thus Vico would be subscribing to a full-blown cyclical theory of history. It is possible that he did, because elsewhere he does occasionally refer to the instability of 'perfect' monarchies. As different emperors succeeded Augustus (the founder of 'perfect monarchy' in Rome), the citizens became increasingly indifferent to politics to the point where, having become 'aliens in their own nations, it becomes necessary for the monarchs to sustain and represent the latter in their own persons'.[106] In short, 'in proportion as the free peoples relax their hold the kings gain in strength until they become monarchs',[107] who, 'by force of arms, take in hand all the institutions and all the laws, which, though sprung from liberty, no longer avail to regulate and hold it within bounds'.[108] Eventually, then, true 'monarchs' achieve absolute power. Now we have already seen Vico arguing that 'in spite of their unlimited sovereignty . . . the very form of the monarchic state shall confine the will of the monarchs . . . [to] the natural order of keeping the peoples content'. But closer reading shows that this 'natural order' does *depend* on two factors.

First, 'without this . . . content of the peoples, monarchic states are neither lasting nor secure'[109] – in other words, *if* monarchs follow their *own* interests by attending to the *peoples'* interests, then they can maintain their states indefinitely. But this leads to the second condition hidden under Vico's apparent confidence in 'perfect monarchy' – the monarch must be of sound mind! And much earlier in the book, in one of his few references to the downfall of the Roman Empire, Vico blames 'the dissolute and shameless madmen, like Caligula, Nero, and Domitian' for having *themselves* overthrown the Roman monarchy through their actions.[110] It seems Vico was returning to this notion in his brief reprise of the major historical stages in his Conclusion, where as an example of events turning out contrary to agents' plans, he says: 'The monarchs mean to strengthen their own positions by debasing their subjects with all the vices of dissoluteness, and they dispose them to endure slavery at the hand of stronger nations'.[111]

Thus we finally arrive at Vico's surprisingly brief admission that monarchy itself, despite being 'the form of government best adapted to human nature when reason is fully developed',[112] is inherently vulnerable. The Romans, he tells us, 'clung to the monarchy as long as they could humanly withstand the *internal and external causes which destroy that form of state*'.[113] It is true that even here he is not saying *all* monarchies are *inevitably* doomed, but if we add the preceding scattered references, a strong case can be made for claiming this as his real view. If it was, then by his own logic it would seem that recourse in history is inevitable, and that Vico *was* therefore advancing a cyclical theory of history. Yet this would require a theory of the *inevitable* and *cataclysmic* downfall of 'perfect monarchy' (and/or 'popular commonwealths') which, although hinted at, is not to be found in the *New Science*. The theme of the decline of the Roman Empire could have provided Vico with the opportunity to exemplify such a theory, and yet so far we find only one minimal reference to it (i.e., the madness of Caligula *et al.*).

One's puzzlement might be compounded, then, when we add the only other reference, and that the most sustained, which Vico makes to the topic, for in introducing his analysis of the actual recourse represented by the Middle Ages, he says:

> When, working in superhuman ways, God had revealed and confirmed the truth of the Christian religion by opposing the virtue of the martyrs to the power of Rome, and the teaching of the Fathers, together with the miracles, to the vain wisdom of Greece, and when armed nations were about to rise on every hand to combat the true divinity of its Founder, he permitted a new order of humanity to be born among the nations in order that [the true religion] might be firmly established according to the natural course of human institutions themselves.[114]

Vico continues; 'Following this eternal counsel, he brought back the truly divine times, in which Catholic kings everywhere . . . founded military religious orders by which they re-established in their realms the Catholic Christian religion against the Arians . . . and numerous other infidels'.[115]

Here, then, the Roman Empire's downfall occurs when God, having established the Christian religion, saved it from foreign hordes by 'permitting a new order to be born', in which 'the truly divine times' (of 'the age of gods') were brought back, thereby instituting a 'recourse'. Here, whether the downfall of the 'perfect monarchy' was natural or not, its drastic replacement by 'recourse' cannot be read as 'natural'.

But perhaps these very passages help settle the issue. They introduce the religious dimension which we have yet to address. For the present, the textual evidence suggests that Vico's otherwise curious reticence to complete his theory of history by clearly stating and analysing the inevitable downfall of 'perfect monarchy' can be accounted for in terms of his unwillingness to be seen as subscribing to a *cyclical* theory. The evidence suggests he *might* have done (certainly, numerous commentators assume unproblematically that he *did*), but that he shrank from declaring it, and even from including those prior considerations (on monarchy) which would properly lead to it. It is this latter exclusion which smacks of deliberation, suggesting that he did indeed subscribe to cyclical history, but knowingly concealed it. The immediate reason for doing this was simply that cyclical conceptions of history were regarded as pagan. The standard Christian notion of history was linear, with a beginning, middle, and end, as so fiercely insisted upon by Augustine (to whom Vico makes a few respectful, yet neutral references in his book). At the very least, then, the text suggests that Vico deliberately presented his theory of history in such a manner as to leave open the possibility of defending it from Inquisitorial and other public accusations of heresy. We might read him as a 'cyclicist', but his text makes it difficult to *prove*! And as for reading him as a *pagan*, that is clearly the last interpretation Vico wants, so numerous and obsequious are his expressions of Christian piety and devotion! But what part did religion really play in Vico's thought?

Religion and the meaning of history

The above reminds us that fear of religious persecution and of thus not being published were factors in many intellectual's minds in eighteenth-century Europe, even in more tolerant countries, let alone a Catholic Naples subject to the Spanish Inquisition. (Indeed, even a century after Vico's death, in 'free-thinking' England, such concerns were partly responsible for Darwin's twenty-year delay, until 1859, in publishing his On the Origin of Species). Thus we have to be careful not to accept at face-value what (particularly independent) thinkers wrote impinging on religion. Various techniques were employed, ranging from simple circumspection to hidden esoteric messages, to evade the wrath of the religious establishment (as well as public hostility and political persecution).[116] This does not mean, however, that we should *automatically* distrust writers' words and seek to uncover alternative, devious meanings. But it does mean we are entitled to query those words when their import is obscure, or inconsistent with other ideas they advance. Vico's *New Science* is a case in point. He had a powerfully independent mind, lived and worked in Catholic Naples, desperately wanted to be not only published but lauded, and yet found himself writing on no less a theme than the meaning of human history, bristling with religious implications! He presents himself in all his writings as a devout Catholic, and actually presents the *New Science* as a new and unique *proof* of that religion, as if that were his prime motivation.

Indeed, for those who take Vico at face-value, his *New Science* is one of the most sustained theodicies ('explanation of the ways of God to man') ever written – and they may be right.

With these provisos in mind, let us explore what he wrote about God, gods, truth, God's Providence, and the role of religions in human history.

Biblical history and the Hebrews

Describing 'the true God' as 'creator of the world and of Adam the prince of all humankind',[117] throughout the *New Science* Vico excludes the Hebrews from his principles of historical development because 'the entire first world of men [i.e., after the Flood] must be divided into two kinds: the first, men of normal size, which includes Hebrews only; the second, giants who were the founders of the gentile nations'.[118] Those Hebrews who remained true to their faith were distinct from all other nations because they correctly 'thought God to be an infinite Mind beholding all times in one point of eternity' whereas 'the gentiles fancied bodies to be gods'.[119] The Hebrews were correct because 'the Hebrew religion was founded by the true God',[120] and were equally correct in believing that they 'had extraordinary help from the true God'[121] who 'either Himself or through the angels that are minds or through the prophets to whose minds God spoke, gave notice of what was in store for His people'.[122] Because of 'the particular assistance which a single people [the Hebrews] received from the true God',[123] there is then a 'fundamental difference' between the principles governing Hebrew and gentile history.[124] 'The Hebrews were the first people in our world', and Vico insists that 'in the sacred history they have truthfully preserved their memories'[125] of 'over a period of more than eight hundred years [of] the state of nature under the patriarchs'.[126] This includes the times when, 'since the Hebrews had lost sight of their natural law during their slavery in Egypt, God himself had to reinstitute it for them by the law he gave to Moses on Sinai'.[127]

Therefore Hebrew history is unique – and since their religion and institutions were never taught them by any outside culture,[128] and nor did they themselves teach other cultures,[129] their history should be excluded from consideration of the principles governing gentile history. It is the latter the *New Science* is concerned with. The former have had the benefit of the true religion, and of God's extraordinary help. The latter have had to make do with God's 'ordinary' help – 'providence' – a notion to which we must shortly turn. First, however, what does Vico say about Christianity?

Christianity

For Vico, 'God founded the true religion of the Hebrews, from which our Christian religion arose'.[130] The divine mind is 'understood only by God' – but men can know of it to the extent it 'has been revealed to them. To the Hebrews first and then to the Christians, this has been by internal speech to their minds as the proper expression of a God all mind; but [also] by external speech through the prophets and through Jesus Christ to the Apostles, by whom it was declared to the Church'.[131] By these means the Christian religion 'inculcat[es] an infinitely pure and perfect idea of God and command[s] charity to all mankind'.[132] Apart from the Hebrew and Christian religions, there are only two other 'primary' religions, and they are both false – the gentile (or pagan) religion which believes 'in the divinity of a plurality of gods, each imagined as composed of body and of free mind', and 'that of the Mohammedans, who believe in the divinity of one god, an infinite free mind *in an infinite body*, for they look forward to pleasures of the senses as rewards in the other life'.[133]

As human reason emerged in ancient Greece in the first (pre-Christian) 'age of men', certain philosophers (particularly Pythagoras and Plato) 'by virtue of a most sublime human science . . . exalted themselves to some extent to the knowledge of the divine truths which the Hebrews had been taught by the true God'.[134] This process of confirming religious truth through human reason has been extended in Christian times through Platonic philosophy and the Aristotelian tradition 'insofar as it conforms to the Platonic',[135] as well as through the other 'most learned philosophies of the gentiles' which the Christian religion has appealed to in its effort to 'unite a wisdom of [revealed] authority with that of reason, basing the latter on the choicest doctrine of philosophers and the most cultivated erudition of the philologists'. Because 'Christian Europe is everywhere radiant with humanity, . . . ministering to the comforts of the body as well as to the pleasures of the mind and spirit', Vico adds that 'even for human ends, the Christian religion is the best in the world'.[136]

In these ideas Vico is 'orthodox' enough. But a problem looms. If the Hebrews are exempted from Vico's 'science' of historical development because of the 'extraordinary' help God gave them, what of the Christians? Subscribing to the true religion, do they also have 'extraordinary' help from God? If so, then most of what Vico says about European history since the downfall of the Roman Empire must also be exempted. And if that is exempted, then his theory of 'recourse' becomes incoherent. But if the course of European history through the Dark and Middle Ages down to Vico's present *is* a 'recourse' based on what governed historical changes from ancient antiquity to the fifth century AD, (excluding the Hebrews), then most of it is a 'recourse' of a *gentile* history, where God played no 'extraordinary' role – in which case, does God have no special role in *Christian* history?

Alternatively, if God *does* play a special role in Christian history, how can that history (principally of the Middle Ages) be seen as a 'recourse'? Yet Vico uses the content of this 'recourse' to *support* the general principles of historical development he claims are exemplified in ancient and classical (gentile) history! In short, whichever way he has it, it seems Vico is treading on dangerous ground. Not only might his theory of historical development be accused of an un-Christian belief in cyclical repetition; it raises fundamental questions about Vico's beliefs about God's role (if any) in history.

'Providence'

Earlier, we noted Vico's important claim that God made Nature (which thus remains ultimately unknowable) but that men have made their civil societies (whose nature and history can therefore be known). Does this mean, for Vico, that God plays no part in the course of human history? On the contrary, Vico insists. Perpetually at work through the actions of free men is God's providence, which beneficially ensures the emergence of those institutions and practices which enable men to live together happily and constructively. In addition, it would seem, God occasionally intervenes in particular times with special, explicitly 'supernatural' help. Let us explore Vico's thinking here.

In what they do, men have free choice[137] – this is 'by its nature most uncertain', but rather than rendering human actions arbitrary, 'human choice . . . is made certain and determined by the common sense of men with respect to human needs or utilities'.[138] In other words, practical motivations amidst practical constraints determine the broad direction of man's exercise of free will.

Knowing what is *best* to do is a kind of wisdom – an idea of 'good and evil'. But such knowledge was originally prohibited to Adam by God, and it was on this basis that 'God ordained his true religion for Adam',[139] 'from which our Christian religion arose'. Meanwhile, the (pagan) gentile peoples tried to acquire this knowledge of what is best to be done, which they believed their gods had, by using the art of 'divination', (taking the auspices and consulting the oracles).[140] The *original* 'divination' was, as we have seen, the constraining effect of the first giants' experience of thunder and lightning.

Religious belief, then, can/does affect how people behave – a point we shall return to. For most of the time people seek the necessities and utilities of life, and this causes 'ferocity, avarice, and ambition, the three vices which run throughout the human race'. And yet 'out of the passions of men each bent on his private advantage . . . , which could certainly destroy all mankind on the face of the earth', orderly societies have emerged.[141] This, Vico claims, proves that 'this world without doubt has issued from a mind often diverse, at times quite contrary, and always superior to the particular ends that men had proposed to themselves'.

This is what Vico means by 'providence' – the notion that there is a mind (God's) which, by making means of the 'narrow ends' of men 'to serve wider ends', thus employs the former 'to preserve the human race upon this earth'.[142] This 'providence' is most clearly shown at each critical stage of the course (and recourse) human history has taken through the three ages of man.

Let us be clear here. Vico is not saying that providence works in extraordinary ways. On the contrary, it works through the very nature of things, including human nature rather than being an external 'force' such as 'fate' or 'fortune' governing history. It is thus not (God's) mind *behind* history and nature, controlling them from 'outside'. Rather, 'this world . . . has *issued from*' mind, such that the way the world works when *left to itself*, i.e., naturally, guarantees the continuous survival and sociality of human life. The analogy of the watch and the watchmaker is *not* helpful here – rather, we might think of the watch and the watch *designer*, for if the watch is the human world and its history, and the designer is God, the watch*maker* is man himself, as Vico so often stresses. It follows, then, that providence is not concerned with the fate of *individuals*. For Vico, it would be pointless for any troubled individual to pray for relief either *from or by* Providence, for providence is simply the way things turn out *collectively* in the natural order of things as (often unintended) consequences of the interaction of people's behaviour.

But finally, if providence is 'simply the way things turn out', it seems this by no means diminishes its significance for Vico. On the contrary, he not only claims that 'providence' proves the goodness of God, he comes close to claiming *his* theory of providence is a proof of the very *existence* of God. First, since God is infinitely wise, and since providence is what God has designed, then that design must, 'in its entirety', be one of *order*. Second, since God's will is 'immeasurabl[y] goodness', then that design 'must be directed to a good always superior to that which men have proposed to themselves'. Third, since God as designer is omnipotent, the design 'must unfold . . . by means as easy as the customs of men'.[143] Thus, if we properly understand human history, we have to conclude it demonstrates 'the eternal goodness of God', who has by such easy means so beautifully ordered its course that there is no way 'human society could be better conducted and preserved'.[144]

Insofar, then, as Vico's theory of history demonstrates God's providence, and in so doing His omnipotence, wisdom, and goodness, it also attests to the very *existence* of God. Vico complains that previous philosophers have either failed to see human history as evidencing mind or providence, or alternatively have ignored history and sought to confirm God's mind by studying the laws governing the *physical* universe. But they ought to have confirmed it by studying it 'in the economy of civil institutions' in order to 'divine' therefrom 'what providence has wrought in history'. *Divination* properly means 'to understand what is hidden *from* men – the future – or what is hidden *in* them – their consciousness', and Vico's 'science' does just that, he claims. It is 'a history of the institutions by which, without human discernment or counsel, and often against the designs of men, providence has ordered this great city of the human race'.[145] And Vico implies that the study of history (if conducted via his methods) is a *surer* proof of God's mind than the study of natural science, because in tracing what men have *themselves* made, the knowledge involved cannot be more certain. In his discovery of 'the ideal eternal history traversed in time by the history of every nation', Vico is thus implying that his 'Science' is grounded in *fact* (knowledge of the certain), and is nothing less than a proof of the Divine Mind,[146] contemplation of which will give the reader 'in his mortal body a divine pleasure'.[147]

Divine grace

If Vico attributes God a pre-eminent role in the course of historical development through 'providence', he also refers (much less frequently) to the operation of 'divine grace'. By this Vico means those occasions when God intervenes in *miraculous* ways, unlike the operation of 'providence' which is (simply) the natural order of things. As Vico puts it, 'man has free choice, however weak, to make virtues of his passions; but . . . he is aided by God, naturally by divine providence and supernaturally by divine grace'.[148] We noted Vico's claim that 'besides the ordinary help from providence, . . . the Hebrews had extraordinary help from the true God'[149] in the form of 'particular assistance'[150] – and a similar reference relating to early Christians:

> When, *working in superhuman ways*, God had revealed and confirmed the truth of the Christian religion by opposing the virtue of the martyrs to the power of Rome, and the teaching of the Fathers, *together with the miracles*, to the vain wisdom of Greece, and when armed nations were about to rise on every hand destined to combat the true divinity of its Founder, he permitted a new order of humanity to be born among the nations in order that [the true religion] might be firmly established according to the natural course of human institutions themselves.[151]

Vico nowhere else refers to this 'extraordinary, supernatural, superhuman' action in the course of human history, and we should note that in both instances God employed it to establish and/or defend 'the true religion' (of the Hebrews, then the Christians). It would appear, then, that 'the true (Judaeo-Christian) religion' has been a literally *miraculous* phenomenon, not emerging in the natural order of things (i.e., via providence) like the other (false) religions. Now, we have seen that Vico exempts the Hebrews from his 'science' precisely because 'divine grace' intervened in their history. Does it now seem he wants to exempt Christian nations as well? If so, this would seem to nullify his account of the Middle Ages as a 'recourse' of the natural (providential) development of ancient and classical history. In short, although the operation of 'providence' is no threat to Vico's theory of history – on the contrary, he deems it crucial to it – the (sporadic) operation of 'divine grace' seems to stick out like a sore thumb!

Before deciding on this, let us examine the only other two references Vico makes to 'divine grace'. A recurrent point Vico is concerned to make, to solve an old dispute, is whether man is naturally sociable. His answer is that 'man is not unjust by nature in the absolute sense, but by nature fallen and weak'. But in addition to God's 'normal' aid through providence (i.e., the logic of the natural order), 'the Catholic principles of grace' are demonstrated, which 'give[s] effect' to man's potential for good works.[152] Although a sparse remark, Vico probably had in mind that (Catholic) doctrine propounded by Aquinas that 'Nature is not destroyed by grace, but perfected by it'[153] – in other words, he takes the opportunity to conform to (Catholic) orthodoxy.

His final, longer and more interesting, reference to 'divine grace' forms part of his concluding remarks summarising the *New Science's* achievements. He tells us his book shows that those who believe chance governs human history are wrong (citing Epicurus, Hobbes, and Machiavelli) – similarly with belief in fate (citing Zeno and Spinoza). Vico claims 'the facts' show that 'providence directs human institutions', and praises those 'political philosophers, whose prince is the divine Plato', (and including Cicero) who agree with this. Both were non-Christian – but no matter, like the (pagan) Roman law-makers, they insisted on belief in 'providence' as the 'first principle' for the organisation of society. In short, they saw *religious* belief as essential. The fact that their religions were fierce, dreadful, and linked to barbaric practices – and even more to the point, were '*false*' in their knowledge of God – is not the immediate issue. Rather, they saw that 'if religion is lost among the peoples, they have nothing left to enable them to live in society'.[154] Thus, says Vico, those who think like Polybius, 'that if there were philosophers in the world, living in justice by force of reason and not of laws, there would be no need in the world of religion',[155] are deluded. Equally deluded are those who, like the French rationalist philosopher and religious sceptic, Pierre Bayle (1647–1706), argue 'there can be nations in the world without any knowledge of God'. Rather, 'religions alone can bring the peoples to do virtuous works by appeal to their feelings, which alone move men to perform them; . . . the reasoned maxims of the philosophers concerning virtue are of use only . . . for kindling the feelings to do the duties of virtue'.

Vico is clear, then. Any religion (however false its knowledge of God) is better than none, for religions appeal to the feelings, and thus to the senses – whereby even the mute, bestial 'giants' actually originated the course of human (gentile) history. But Vico adds:

> There is, however, an essential difference between our Christian religion, which is true, and all the others, which are false. In our religion, divine grace causes virtuous action for the sake of an eternal and infinite good. This good cannot fall under the senses, and it is consequently the mind that, for its sake, moves the senses to virtuous actions. The false religions, on the contrary, have proposed to themselves finite and transitory goods, in this life as in the other (where they expect a beatitude of sensual pleasures), and hence the senses must drive the mind to do virtuous works.[156]

(Does this imply that doing good 'for its own sake' is miraculous, and reserved to Christians?).

Again, then, we encounter that same logic in Vico implying (intentionally or not) that the Christian religion is literally miraculous, for having earlier claimed that its *institution* was through 'divine grace', he now implies its *truth* is based upon its capacity to move men to virtuous action through the intellect – and that this is 'caused' by 'divine grace'. Without it, we have to presume Christianity would be just one more 'false' religion emerging through the ordinary nature of things ('providence'). That it is true is not a matter of philosophy (natural human reason) nor of 'providence' (which underlies all religions) – it is a 'special, supernatural, extraordinary' matter provided by 'divine grace'. With perhaps an appropriate logic, then, Vico is appealing to a *deus ex machina* to substantiate his claim that the Christian religion is 'true'!

Was he sincere in what he says about 'divine grace' and Christianity's truth? And more to the point for us, does it matter in relation to his philosophy of *history*?

Religion and history in Vico

The answer is surely not. Logically, the notion of 'divine grace' is not only redundant to his theory of historical development – it actually interferes with its coherence. Likewise with the question of the 'truth' of Christianity. Both interfere with the whole point of his 'science'. But, as seen, Vico includes these otherwise literally 'extraordinary' notions, even 'conceding' that the Hebrew and Christian histories are exempt from his 'universal history'.

From this we have the probability of a Vico who merely pays lip-service to the orthodox (Catholic) Christianity of his day. If this is true, of course, it does not make Vico a closet atheist. On the contrary, there is no reason for disbelieving his sincerity in claiming his *New Science*, particularly in its treatment of 'providence', as a confirmation of the existence of God. Also, in praising certain philosophers' attempts to rationalise the nature of God, there seems little doubt he believed the Judaeo-Christian notion of God is along the right lines. But there is also no reason to suppose that Vico, like millions before and after him, kept his own deepest 'religious' views to himself, even if it involved his having to jeopardise the outward coherence of his cherished 'science' with arguments as ingenious as they are disingenuous. In short, unless we are to believe Vico was deeply confused in his thinking, we should perceive his *New Science* as a classic and extreme case of that self-censorship so prevalent in the history of thought. Arguably, only through such a recognition can the true meaning of his overall theory be revealed and its coherence be restored. It also removes obstacles otherwise obscuring the *political* dimensions intrinsic to his philosophy of history.

Political dimensions

Cyclical depression?

Our claim that Christianity's *truth* is irrelevant for Vico clears the way to discovering those political implications which are to become so allied a feature of modern 'philosophy of history'. We have noted the ambiguity surrounding whether Vico's theory of history is inherently *cyclical*. Many have taken his phraseology (e.g., 'the ideal eternal history'), particularly in conjunction with his idea of 'recourse', as straightforward proof that Vico did believe in a human history which endlessly repeats its developmental stages and thus leaves no role for politics to be the vehicle for the 'fulfilment' of mankind. But that would be a simplistic reading of Vico. What *is* true is that Vico's own religious views did not oblige him to subscribe to the Judaeo-Christian *linear* theory of history, culminating in some kind of millennium. But neither do they oblige him towards classical cyclical fatalism.

Repeatedly, (as seen), Vico attacks those thinkers who believe in 'fate'. There is 'mind' or 'design' in the course of history – God's 'providence'. And what it provides is not some endless, meaningless repetition of stages of human history. Neither, however, for some unilinear progression towards human perfection or 'the millennium'. Rather, it provides for the formation, from bestiality, of *society* amongst men, and its continued re-formation through fundamentally changing times – in short, what we call 'civilisations'.

However, we know that according to Vico the first 'age of men', or 'human times', succumbed to collapse, followed by a 'recourse' of the three ages culminating in a second 'age of men'. The huge question (for Vico as well as for those attracted to his theory) is whether this second 'human' age is inevitably doomed to similar collapse, to be followed by a third cycle of 'recourse'. To the extent Vico answers this, we must look in his writings rather than arbitrarily extrapolate from his logic. And what seems clear is that he nowhere claims that 'providence' *decrees* the collapse of each different 'age'. Their decline (including the first 'human' age) happened principally as a result of that self-interestedness and assertiveness of human nature which generates class-conflict between those controlling power and wealth and the rest of society. Not the work of 'providence', it is the result of a 'flawed' human nature which has free choice. Were the chaotic collapse of a society's order and culture the work of 'providence', then God would not have been a benevolent designer. But if not providence, neither is it clear that 'human nature' *necessitates* it. The point for Vico is that societies *have* succumbed to fundamental disintegration in the past, and that *when* this occurred, *then* 'providence' decrees their re-formulation in a different mode. In short, the collapse of a form of 'society' is not a determined necessity of history (as in classical cyclical fatalism) – it is not the providential design. But the *resurrection* of 'society' (albeit in a new form) *is* the work of 'providence' – i.e., the existence of *some* form of 'civilisation' (however unattractive to those of a later period looking back anachronistically) *is* a 'determined necessity' of history – that is, it is 'inbuilt', irrespective of human choice and intention.

But such solace as this may afford in the abstract must be counterbalanced by two factors: first, we have seen Vico describe the dissolution of the 'age of men' in particular as an horrendous eventuality where 'peoples . . . rotting in that ultimate civil disease . . . live like wild beasts in a deep solitude of spirit and will'. Only after 'long centuries of barbarism' are they eventually 'brutalized' back into that elementary common sense of 'the sheer necessities of life' which forces them to become 'sociable and . . . [return] to the primitive simplicity of the first world of peoples'.[157] Second, it follows that a long process of 'recourse', through the three ages, would have to be undergone before a properly worthy 'human' civilisation were regained.

Stopping the rot?

This focuses attention on what Vico thought of his own times. For Vico, man can do nothing to frustrate the 'force' of providence – but neither should he want to, since it is solely benevolent. It ensures 'society'. It does not decree its corruption. But can man do anything to *supplement* the help of 'providence'? Translated into Vico's own times, this means asking whether men can prevent a collapse of their society and institutions, which promise so much in this 'age of men'.

We have seen Vico's sketch of the historical possibilities. Once that decline endangers society's very fabric, it can be stopped by the strong hand of a new 'monarch', able to restrain the corruption. The only other possibility – conquest and rule by another nation – would hardly be *deliberately engineered* by a people to maintain its culture. The only other political development Vico mentions – but not in connection with salvaging a corrupt nation – is the formation of 'leagues, whether perpetual or temporary' between sovereign powers. But rather than see such unions as progressive (we might think of contemporary enthusiasts for European political union), he sees them as akin to new 'aristocratic states into which enter the anxious suspicions characteristic of aristocracies', and interprets them as a *regression* analogous to the first 'aristocracies of the fathers'.[158]

This said, however, we must recognise that Vico says little forward-looking or judgemental about his contemporary European political scene. Possibly circumspect, it is, however, certain that his focus was elsewhere than on the immediacies of European political affairs. Thus in response to our large query as to whether men themselves can do anything to maintain and promote the 'age of men', it is not surprising he offers no immediate political prescriptions. Rather, his focus was the much longer one of the *philosopher of history*, contemplating in his case huge, holistic, cultural shifts in human history. He thought European nations had comparatively recently embarked on a second 'human' age, and given the epochal time-scale he finds exhibited in previous fundamental historical change, contemporary political comment is not part of Vico's remit.

But he is prescriptive in longer-distance terms – and characteristically, his messages for his time's future revolve around that very notion of 'mentality' so prominent in his holistic historical thinking. Given he clearly judges 'the age of men' as superior to other 'ages' (despite his otherwise markedly impartial 'cultural relativism'), and that its decline is *not* providentially decreed, a case can be made that Vico has two prescriptions – one more concerned to *stave off* those (human) causes for decline, the other to *promote* the second 'human age' to *new* heights.

Regarding the former, we noted Vico's prognosis for the way 'the age of men' tends towards decline as men deteriorate from being 'benign' to being 'delicate', then 'dissolute', leading them to 'finally go mad and waste their substance'. Although Vico does not comment on whether this disintegration of a people's mentality can be halted, his obvious respect for much of the (prior) 'heroic' mentality provides food for thought. Frequently Vico writes admiringly of the bravery, honesty, and straightforwardness of the 'heroic' outlook on life. It is true they also behaved with 'barbarity', consulting their feelings rather than their (undeveloped) 'reason', but Vico is more often understanding than condemnatory, because of their perceptive sense of reality. One senses it is precisely this grip on reality which Vico fears can get lost, eventually, in the 'age of men', and that he sometimes uses his notion of the 'heroic' mentality as a stick with which to beat its vices – vices linked above all to the disappearing of 'common sense'. By analogy, many parents today gladly send off their teenage child to be enlightened, informed, and fulfilled by what the world of education and work can offer – but also in the fervent hope that amidst all the marvels and distractions the child will hang on to its common sense. Quite what Vico would have made of the present state of European and North American 'civilisation' is of course beyond us, but it is interesting to compare it with some of the 'heroic' features Vico asks us to compare even to *his* times! 'Luxury, refinement, and ease were quite unknown':[159] 'the [heroic] education of the young was severe, harsh, and cruel, . . . whereas the indulgences with which we now treat our young children produces all the tenderness of our [modern] natures'.[160] Another example is irresistible in the light of Vico's own observation that his wife was not really interested in house-keeping and child-minding. Is it perhaps *ruefully* that he remarks that in 'heroic' times, 'children [were] acquired and wives saved for the benefit of their husbands and fathers; not, as nowadays, just the contrary'?![161]

In short, a case can be made for saying Vico thinks that if his 'age of men' is to progress rather than decline, it might need 'stiffening up' with some of the 'heroic' attitudes. He would be the last, of course, to suggest one could simply transplant the heroic mentality into the 'age of men' – but he asks us not only to understand it better, but to respect it more and possibly even learn something from it. Some of the flavour of this is apparent in an oration Vico gave to incoming students to the Royal Academy of Naples in 1732. Entitled *On the Heroic Mind*, amongst other things Vico tells the students not to study in order to become rich or powerful, nor for the narrow purpose of love of learning for its own sake. Rather, he enjoins them to be 'heroic' and raise their eyes to the purpose of 'lay[ing] foundations of learning and wisdom for the blessing of the human race'.[162] Significantly, he urges students to an *interdisciplinary* approach, and not to be deterred from being ambitious by 'scholards with petty minds'.[163] 'This world is still young . . . countless possibilities still remain, so 'apply yourselves to your studies with heroic mind. . . . Prove yourselves to be heroes by enriching the human race with further giant benefits'.[164]

A new age?

These passages provide a useful transition to that other aspect of our query as to Vico's thoughts on his second 'age of men' – namely, in addition to preserving it from corruption, can men go further and actually *promote* its possibilities? The tone of the above Oration suggests they can – interestingly enough, *if* they adopt an 'heroic' spirit. But a more substantial case has been made by those who find a positive message embedded in the internal logic of the *New Science* itself, and perhaps occasionally hinted at explicitly by Vico. This is nothing less than the view that Vico looked to a *higher* phase of 'the age of men' – maybe a new age altogether – in which societies would be in conscious control of their own development. Just as the natural sciences' discovery of the laws of the physical world enabled its increasing manipulation to the betterment of mankind, so (it is suggested) Vico thought his 'new science' offered men the opportunity to increasingly control their own societies through the new understanding of the *social* world it offered. After all, it is suggested, Vico is the very one who insists that *men make* their own history, and that because of this the workings of the social world can be *understood* (better, even, than the natural world). It is true that, up to now, 'providence' has seen to it that societies exist in some form or other, often at variance with the uncoordinated, uninformed designs of men. But now Vico has uncovered the logic 'providence' has implanted into human affairs. The scene is set, then, for a step advance by humanity towards at last being in control of its future through the conscious determination of its present.

Such is the interpretation put upon Vico's *New Science* by some, particularly those intellectual Marxists who see in the relationship Vico proposes between 'philosophy' and 'philology' a precursing of Marx's notion of 'revolutionary praxis'.[165] The Marxian notion of a 'pre-history', in which men not in control of the very societies *they* make, is to be succeeded by 'human history' where they are at last able consciously to create themselves, looms large here. As one commentator puts it (reminding us of Vico's equating 'poet' with 'creator' or 'maker'), 'it is precisely because the first men were poets and hence *made* their world that this world can be *known*. As a science of "the principles of humanity" the *New Science* is a science of creativity, of man *qua* creator'.[166]

Although these are speculations both about Vico's real intentions and the meanings (intended or not) which can be extracted from his work, they may not be wild. Yet problems remain. For example, it is not clear from *his* 'science' whether 'human nature' can *itself* be subject to such conscious re-formation. Some allege there are *two* 'human natures' in Vico – that which forms the unchangeable substratum of humanity at any time (be they 'gods', 'heroes', or 'men'), and the 'nature' which changes from one 'age' to another, culminating in the 'human' nature of people in the 'age of men'. If a correct reading of Vico, this would presumably impose limitations on man's capacity to re-fashion *himself*. A related problem is whether Vico believed that man can ever 'know' his mind. It has been argued that the earlier Vico believed man could *not*, since even though man 'makes' his own history, he does not 'make' his own mind – but that he altered his view by the *New Science*, implying that in understanding previous minds (mentalities) we retrace the making of our own minds – i.e., as insightful 'new scientists' we *do* 'make' our minds.[167]

These are but some of the disputed meanings extracted from Vico's logic, and if nothing else, such weighty themes demonstrate the continued appeal of Vichian studies. But the other issue is what Vico himself *intended* to mean about the prospects for the (second) 'age of men', with its larger implications for his entire philosophy of history. This takes us back to the text itself – but no longer, I suggest, to its internal details. Rather, we will answer our query better by considering the rationale of the *New Science* as a whole. Why did he write it? We know there were earlier 'versions' before the first edition of 1725, and that for the rest of his life he kept on revising it. What is the overall point he wanted to make?

It is clear Vico thought he had something of great importance to communicate; namely, nothing less than the 'logic' of human historical development – and that this 'new science' at last provided the answers to those numerous fundamental questions about society, justice, human nature, morality, and government which philosophers, historians, and political theorists had grappled with over the millennia. But he did not write his book solely to enlighten others. We have already found him dismissing study solely for the sake of learning. He clearly believed that the knowledge conveyed by his 'science' (confessedly incomplete) could not only solve matters which had puzzled others for centuries, but that it should have *practical implications* for the way people handled their societies and civil institutions in the future. Quite what they were he did not spell out in any detail – but perhaps he could not be expected to. Rather, it seems he hoped for the kind of large-scale, long-term improvement in the social, political, and cultural affairs of human-beings which he thought the approach of scientists such as his beloved Bacon presaged for their physical, economic, and medical welfare.

If this estimation of Vico's intentions is correct, it would seem wrong to propose that his theory consigns nations to some inevitable deterioration as they progress further into the 'age of men', ultimately to start their civilisations again in a 'recourse' of their previous developmental stages. The pessimism underlying such a prospect sits uneasily with the optimistic sense of discovery and intellectual urgency Vico conveys in his *New Science*. Rather, his commitment to his project is more suggestive of the notion that he meant his theory of history to be a *transformative* 'science' or 'philosophy' which could not only prevent a ceaseless recourse of cycles of human history, but also help fulfill the promise inherent in the 'human' age of reason. As such, his philosophy of history assumes an ambition as vast as its scope – a feature, it would seem, endemic to 'philosophy of history' itself as we now proceed to those subsequent thinkers who also put their minds to it.

Summary comments

Nowadays, students and scholars will find a wealth of literature exploring whichever parts of the labyrinth of Vico's thinking interests them. Accordingly, it seems appropriate to limit our comments to 'seeing the wood for the trees' – and this, I suggest, returns us to Vico's *method*.

Essentially, Vico re-presented the course of human history in terms of its *origins*, and in doing so believed he made it 'make sense'. He devised an account of the very 'principles' which drive historical development and inform it with 'meaning' (in the sense that it is not arbitrary, but neither the product of human planning) – and he did this by claiming to have found an 'ideal' (or *model*) 'story' or 'course' through which all nations traverse (other things being equal).

Prior to examining the notion of a model 'story', in the first instance this draws our attention to the 'logic' of *individual* 'stories' taken by themselves. For Vico, the history of any 'nation' is not a random collection of disconnected 'ages' happening to succeed each, and neither does it endlessly elaborate around its starting point. Rather, it is comprised of remarkably different cultures corresponding to remarkably different 'ages', and yet a fundamental *continuity* is maintained precisely *through* this process of *change*.

This is the logic of 'stories', for any proper 'story' must feed on change, since if nothing new happens after the first event there is no story to be told. But equally, the different events in the story must emerge from each other, otherwise again there would be no story, but simply a random collection of different anecdotes. Thus it is that a story is a *single* thing, an identity, essentially constituted through *change*.

Further, a story is not knowable via logical deduction. Nor is it knowable via understanding each event discretely. Rather, the way we grasp the story is neither through rationalism nor empiricism, but through an *historical* consciousness which, in tracing a thing's continuity through change, understands its present dispensation in terms of where it came from.

So far, the analogy with the logic of 'stories' is sound enough in following Vico. Particularly apt is that feature whereby outcomes are the result, not of a necessary sequence of cause and effect, but of the 'free', yet intelligible, responses of human beings to the circumstances they encounter.

Now, if the story is *fiction* (e.g., a novel) the outcome at any point will have been *designed* by the *author* in such a way that it 'makes sense' by 'following' from the preceding events. Yet Vico, of course, does not believe his (hi)stories of 'nations' are fiction. The other kind of story is the factual 'story' – that is, history, where the historian is the discoverer, not the *author* or *inventor* of the 'story'.

Put in this way, we may ask how Vico stands in relation to these alternatives? It is clear he does not see the course of history as determined through 'scientific' cause and effect. Rather, it displays the logic of a 'story'. But it is not a story invented by him – i.e., it is not fiction. But neither does he present its intelligibility as an historian would – i.e., as simply inherent in the course of events, without the need for an 'author' designing it. Vico insists there is an 'author', or a 'mind', designing the 'story' – and it is understandable that he should therefore call the author 'God', for what other option could there be?

But *why* does Vico insist there is an 'author'? Why not simply say that, as an historian, he has found an intelligibility in what might otherwise appear a random succession of events? Why does he need 'God'?

The answer to this, I suggest, rests on the fact that Vico does not understand himself to be constructing some 'universal' history of humankind, in which the latter is the subject of *one single, ongoing* story. As we have seen, (unlike a *fictional* story), any *single* factual story does not need, or point to, a designer behind it. Had the 'course' each 'nation' underwent simply been different in each case, then one could present each 'story' as an historian, without the need to introduce deliberate design – i.e., 'God'. But what so excited Vico was his 'discovery' that, despite contingent differences, each 'nation' went through the same basic story, independently – in other words, that mankind's past consisted of *numerous* versions of the *same* story. And one can only wonder at how excited he must have been to 'discover' that this same basic story is not only to be found in different cultures, but has even *repeated* itself in a 'recourse'! This could not be chance.

Thus, had Vico only studied the history of the Roman people he might have found most of what he *did* find, but still not need 'God' to make the development of its society intelligible. But because he found the same basic 'story' in Greece and elsewhere (and 'recoursed' in Europe since the demise of the Western Roman Empire), the only way *he* could account for this correlation was the presence of mind, design, or 'God'. That Vico should propose, and mean, this is understandable – for he had stumbled on something then unknown in the intellectual world he inherited; what we call 'social science'.

Today's social sciences employ a variety of methods to understand the social world (Vico's 'the world of nations') – and the concept of *correlation* is important amongst them, inspiring the 'science' of *statistics* to invent the basic concept of '*significant* correlation', which discovers predictable regularities amidst the diverse social world. Also, in addition to a substratum of *historical* knowledge, social scientists employ quantitative analysis in graphs, flow charts, and logical models.

But even now, they still debate their fundamental methodology, and are subject to outside scrutiny on the same count. Is 'social science' the same as natural science? If not, should it aspire to be? Is 'social science' more than, or different to, *history*? What methods should social science employ? What is the epistemological status of its disciplines (i.e., their 'truth' value)? In short, *how* we study the social world remains problematic for some.

Now it is highly unlikely Vico had any concept of a 'significant correlation', let alone of how to calculate it. Also, many have commented on the substantial neglect of *economics* in Vico's otherwise holistic approach to understanding societies. Yet the 'sciences' of statistics and economics, let alone other 'social sciences', were hardly developed in Vico's day, nor the thinking that underlay them.

It is in this context that Vico nevertheless stumbled upon the basic problems of the 'logic' of 'social science' – he intuited that the study of the social world could not rest solely on history ('philology'), nor model itself on the methodology of the natural sciences ('science/philosophy'). Some new way (his 'new science') needed to be forged to properly understand the social world, and having worked towards it, he 'discovered' that the social world *must* be intelligible because both historically and holistically it exhibited 'pattern' or 'regularity'.

Many of today's social scientists, it seems, are happy enough to find such 'regularities' without asking *why* they occur, (e.g., the correlation between crime and poverty) whilst others seek to *explain* them, but often through what might be regarded as the blind alley of searching for what 'correlates' to the very correlation under scrutiny! But for Vico, in the absence of our idea of 'social science', his discovery of a pattern, or 'model story', would have been enough to evidence 'design' or 'authorship', and thus point to 'God'. That he also found the model story to be one which *benefited* mankind only served to encourage this view, to the point where he claimed his work provided an actual *proof* of the existence of God – a view as foreign to the 'social sciences' today as it felt natural then to Vico. We may only ask; although Vico's reliance on 'God' ('providence') in 'making sense' of the nature and history of human societies is out-dated, is the logic of 'significant correlations' any better? Presumably, when something is 'significant' it thus *signifies* something? Yet the logic of social science seems reluctant to engage in what Vico called the art of 'divination' to find out what.

8

SPECULATIVE PHILOSOPHY OF HISTORY DURING THE ENLIGHTENMENT

Introduction

Vico and the Enlightenment

Vico was severely neglected until the twentieth century – by which time his writings could only exercise academic interest (albeit increasingly enthusiastic since the 1960s English translations of *New Science*, and poised to continue since the 2000 English translation of *Universal Right*). Hence his ideas did not play a role in the intellectual history of his immediately succeeding generations.

One of the reasons for this neglect was the growing predominance of an (allegedly) new movement of European thought historians periodise as 'the Enlightenment'. In this they accept the movement's self-identification, beginning with the French from around the 1730s, and then spreading to other parts of Europe, the British Isles (notably Scotland), and North America, and culminating (arguably) in the American and French revolutions of 1776 and 1789 respectively. Inasmuch as we can characterise the movement as inspired indeed towards 'enlightenment' by a heady combination of rationalism, empiricism, modern science, and a belief in resulting 'human progress', we can see why (although he was still revising his *New Science* when he died in 1744) Vico's ideas sat uneasily with the developing intellectual fashion. After all, from the 1690s Vico had already been pondering these pinnacles of seventeenth-century intellectual achievement and increasingly developed his own complexly critical stance. There is a sense, then, in which Vico had already superseded fundamental tenets of 'Enlightenment' thought before that movement began – leading to the suggestion that 'the Enlightenment' is either rather a misleading periodisation of European thought (because its essentials belong to an earlier century), or at least that those who identified themselves as promulgating the movement were under the illusion of breaking new ground.

The Enlightenment

Be this as it may, let us accept 'the Enlightenment' as that period spanning much of the eighteenth century in which numerous intellectuals and interested laymen challenged the intellectual hegemony of the established elites (especially the church and nobility), and advocated radical reforms in what they perceived as their backward, tradition-bound, unjustly unequal societies. Thus, numerous aspects of society were subjected to radical criticism – the institutions of state for venality and inefficiency, the nobility for its reactionary privileges, and the church for its narrow-mindedness and authoritarianism. In addition, religion itself was subjected to rational criticism, and it was at last possible not only to think, but also publish, the unthinkable – namely, atheist beliefs. Relatedly, morals and customs were questioned and (as in Voltaire) subjected to ridicule where found 'lacking in reason'. Likewise, the economic structures and practices of society were criticised over their lack of efficiency, their failure to adopt new agricultural and scientific methods of production, and perhaps above all, as in Adam Smith's *The Wealth of Nations* (1776), for the prevalence of archaic monopolistic restrictions on freedom of trade and employment. In that same year Jeremy Bentham wrote his *Fragment on Government* which poured scorn upon the pretentious, tautological arguments used to defend the British Constitution, and later he exposed the injustices of the penal code. Also in 1776 the American War of Independence against the mismanagement and injustices of an arrogant British ruling elite's vested economic interests began the American Revolution, whilst thirteen years later the French revolution of 1789 shattered forever whatever complacency the European 'ancien regimes' had retained in the face of the upheavals fuelled (at least partly) by 'Enlightenment'. Indeed, in their Euro-centred periodisations of history, today's historians date the beginnings of 'modern history' from the 1789 French revolution and Napoleon's succeeding revolutionary wars, such were the political, economic, social, and intellectual changes involved, and to which the Enlightenment contributed.

The Enlightenment, then, was above all an age of criticism – and its practitioners understood this to mean the fearless application of *reason* to society's institutions, practices and beliefs. But we should comment that 'reason' is not as uni-directional an approach to knowledge as many think it is. It is true that it is worth distinguishing 'reason' (as a way of *acquiring* knowledge) from *belief* or *opinion*. Just as a statement based on factual error is 'unreasonable', so is one that purports to factual truth when based on mere belief or opinion. It is in this sense that *empiricism* – the grounding of knowledge on observed facts – is part of 'reason'. Likewise it is worth distinguishing 'reason' (as a way of *reaching conclusions*) from thinking which does not 'follow' logically, (e.g., 'the cat is on the mat and is therefore black') or which pretends to uncover new information via mere tautologies (e.g., 'a duty is that which one ought to carry out, since a duty is something one is obliged to perform'). In this sense *rationalism* is part of 'reason. However, there is far more to be said about 'reason' than these two aspects – and yet it seems that in their reliance on the power of 'reason' to criticise societies, Enlightenment thinkers meant little more than the above. Thus their reverence for the rationalist Descartes, the 'empiricist' Locke, and the practico-experimentalism of 'scientists' such as Bacon, all figures of the previous century.

169

However, if there was nothing fundamentally new about the philosophical *foundations* of Enlightenment thought, what *was* new was its intense focus on the character of *society* rather than on the abstractions of philosophy. This is famously displayed in the cutting satires by Voltaire (1694–1778) and in the work of other French Encyclopedists. The latter, under the editorship of Diderot (1713–1784), contributed numerous articles on the sciences, arts, morals, and practical activities, eventually constituting a thirty-four volume work which, begun in 1751 and completed by 1780, underwent many editions despite attempts at censorship. Not only a vast reservoir of the current state of knowledge, however, it constantly exhibited the Enlightenment's critical edge and its enthusiasm for reform, modernisation, and progress. And it is here, in its constant criticism of tradition, convention, the 'irrational', and the superstitious, that we can derive the sense in which the Enlightenment embraced a 'philosophy of history', for in criticising the past and present this implied things could be better (otherwise, what is the point of criticism?).

Enlightenment 'philosophy of history'

For the 'enlighteners', if only Reason could be applied to societies' problems, wars could be prevented by a tolerant acceptance of cultural relativism between nations (albeit backed up by a Western 'civilising mission' over 'underdeveloped' peoples), economic production could advance via the application of science and free trade, social justice could be achieved by the removal of the vested interests of the privileges of inheritance, free thought could prosper through undermining the reactionary power of organised religion, and political power could be revolutionised by being directed solely towards the benefit of all in society, so that (to use a phrase Lenin echoed in 1917) 'the manipulation of men would be replaced by the administration of things'.

In short, the Enlightenment believed above all in *progress*. As such, it rested on a broad consensus revolving around a critical (but also self-congratulatory) posture towards the present, a preparedness to examine other cultures (both contemporaneous and from 'mankind's history') for what could be learned, and a confident belief in the possibility of 'progress' – all this in the name of 'Reason'. Unsurprisingly, within this broad consensus, different views and theories abounded on politics, economics, religion, and morality – and intelligent and knowledgeable as were many 'enlightened' intellectuals, no singular, innovative, comprehensive works of 'philosophy' emerged to summarise, tie together, and dominate the field. Perhaps this was because the topics were so diverse. Indeed, in a positive light we might almost say that the *idea* behind Diderot's *Encyclopédie* (and many other eighteenth-century encyclopedias) represented precisely such a comprehensive philosophy in itself. Alternatively, however, it might be because the Enlightenment's intellectual foundations (the belief in 'Reason') were too insubstantial, or too simplistically derivative from previous theories of knowledge, to generate a new, all-encompassing, singular philosophy.

Be this as it may, part of the overall consensus of Enlightenment thought included philosophy of history. In seeing their own time as (at last) the Age of Reason, they looked back at history as the movement of humanity from its initial imperfections of ignorance, stupidity, barbarity, and superstition towards the eventual enlightened state of knowledge, intelligence, tolerance, and reason which offered the ultimate achievement of the perfectibility of humankind. Although not necessarily irreligious, it was a markedly secular outlook on the 'meaning' of history, since even for those who believed in a God who had given man Reason, history and the future were seen as in man's hands rather than pre-ordained. Earlier periods (and contemporary nations) were judged by how far they contributed to 'progress' for humankind. As such, for many, their interest in history shifted from the political histories of kings and constitutions towards a broader, more anthropologically orientated history of cultures and peoples, (albeit more often to discover different habits and customs which might be 'useful' to an enlightened life-style rather than from purely historical interest).

However, the same may be said of this Enlightenment 'philosophy of history' as of the broader agreement underlying Enlightenment thought in general. A consensus can be detected, and although more than one attempt was made to construct an explicit philosophy of history, none achieved the depth, comprehensivenesss, or impact which allowed us to identify earlier distinctive 'philosophies of history', or which compare with post-Enlightenment theories, particularly those of Hegel and Marx. One of those who *did* attempt an explicit theory was the Encyclopédist, Condorcet. But prior to examining his effort (which perhaps best exemplifies Enlightenment thinking on the meaning of history) we should not neglect the contribution within this field of a more famous Enlightenment figure, the enigmatic Jean-Jacques Rousseau.

Rousseau

The Discourse on the Arts and Sciences

One of the enigmas surrounding the complex life, personality, and ideas of Rousseau is that although he lived within Enlightenment culture and circles, much of his thought was diametrically opposed to its consensus – and perhaps this is nowhere more the case than in his ideas on the meaning of history.

Born in 1712 in the independent republic of Geneva, at sixteen he rebelled against being apprenticed as an artisan and ran away in the hope of improving his lot. This he managed under the tutelage and protection of a wealthy lady, the first of Rousseau's many intimate associations with supportive women in his life. Aged thirty, having acquired education and self-confidence he went to Paris in 1742 to seek fame and fortune in that most 'civilised' of cities. In the former task (albeit not in the latter) he was to succeed beyond his dreams, for by 1750 not only had he become friends with many future Encyclopédists including Diderot and his circle, he shot to fame (but also notoriety) by writing the prize-winning essay set by the Academy of Dijon that year. Reflective of the self-congratulatory Enlightenment tone, the Academy had posed the question, 'Has the restoration of the arts and sciences had a purifying effect upon morals?'. Directly contrary to the optimism of Enlightenment culture, Rousseau penned his answer emphatically in the negative – 'and from that moment I was lost. All the rest of my life and of my misfortunes followed inevitably as a result of that moment's madness'.[1] Although not denying progress in the arts and sciences, it 'has added nothing to our real happiness: . . . it has corrupted our morals'.[2] Doubtless influenced by his amused reception in smart Parisian salon society as somewhat of a rustic, Rousseau's basic argument was that the genuine cultural accomplishments of any society, past and present, were always accompanied by lesser minds' corruption into hypocrisy and superficiality. Impressed by the trappings of high culture, people who would be better off following ordinary, useful pursuits become seduced into a false refinement and urbanity of manners – 'in a word, the appearance of all the virtues, without being in possession of one of them'.[3] Mere wit replaces genuine wisdom. In order to impress others, 'we no longer dare seem what we really are, but lie under a perpetual restraint'[4] to appear what we are not. For example, 'the question is no longer whether a man is honest, but whether he is clever. We do not ask whether a book is useful, but whether it is well-written'.[5] Ensnared in a web of superficiality, hypocrisy, and egoistic competitiveness, 'jealousy, suspicion, fear, coldness, reserve, hate, and fraud lie constantly concealed under that uniform and deceitful vein of politeness, that boasted candour and urbanity, for which we are indebted to the light and leading of this age'.[6]

The constant theme is the contrast Rousseau draws between the damaging moral effects of the artificialities of 'civilised' society and the straightforward virtues of 'natural' man uncorrupted by the lure of luxury and sophistication.

Apart from this general effect, Rousseau blames two sources in particular. First, 'even from our infancy an absurd system of education serves to adorn our wit and corrupt our judgement; our youth are . . . instructed in everything but their duty'.[7] The other source is the intellectuals. Apart from those few geniuses – he cites Bacon, Descartes, and Newton – who genuinely shine above the rest of society, there are those 'respectable' scientists and philosophers who labour away at mathematics, astronomy, the mind–body relationship, biology, and the like. 'Answer me', says Rousseau, 'you from whom we receive all this sublime information, whether we should have been less numerous, worse governed, less formidable, less flourishing, or more perverse, supposing you taught us none of these things'. Rather, their effect is to breed idleness among people, and thus it is that 'the labours of the most enlightened of our learned men . . . are of so little utility'.[8]

But Rousseau reserves his highest contempt for 'that numerous herd of obscure writers and useless *litterateurs*' who, simply to please the corrupted taste of the public, produce specious works of critical pretension. In criticising, analysing, and pulling everything apart, these pen-pushers breed cynicism and scepticism in a population already out-of-touch with reality because lost to the artificialities of 'civilised' life. In disgust, Rousseau even appears to attack the invention of printing, asking us to 'consider the frightful disorders which printing has already caused in Europe'![9]

Profoundly out-of-tune with his own age, then, one can hardly imagine what Rousseau would have said of today's world of constant media outpourings which bombard people's thinking, tastes, and sensibilities. But more to our purposes, there is also in Rousseau's highly moralising piece an embryonic *historical* perspective which he was subsequently to explore much further. He opens the *Discourse* by appearing to praise the 'noble and beautiful spectacle' of 'man raising himself . . . from nothing by his own exertions; dissipating, by the light of reason, all the thick clouds in which he was by nature enveloped. . . . All these miracles we have seen renewed within the last few generations'. Referring to the Middle Ages, he claims that Europe, 'which is at present so highly enlightened', had 'relapsed into the barbarism of the earliest ages'[10], and was only rescued from ignorance by the influx of literature because of the fall of Constantinople in the fifteenth century, followed by the rise of the sciences and philosophical writings. It is immediately after this introductory nod to the Enlightenment, however, that Rousseau inveighs against the deleterious effects of this 'restoration' of the arts and sciences, claiming that those in power are only too happy because, 'besides nourishing that littleness of mind which is proper to slavery, the increase of artificial wants only binds so many more chains upon the people',[11] as they lose the virtues associated with the original simplicity of man in his natural state.

But he adds that this corrupting effect of the arts and sciences – ('as their light has risen above our horizon, virtue has taken flight') – is not unique to the Enlightenment, but that 'the same phenomenon has been constantly observed in all times and places'.[12] In short, Rousseau proposes a law of human development from 'the inductions we can make from history'[13], beginning with ancient Egypt. When it 'became the mother of philosophy and the fine arts', it was soon conquered repeatedly by a series of other nations, culminating with the Turks. The same happened to Greece, 'once peopled by heroes'. When the sciences progressed there, 'Greece, always learned, always voluptuous, and always a slave, has experienced amid all its revolutions no more than a change of masters'.[14] In particular, Rousseau contrasts Sparta, 'a city as famous for the happy ignorance of its inhabitants, as for the wisdom of its laws' as 'eternal proof of the vanity of science' by comparing it to the cultivated elegance of Athens where the kinds of vices complained of by Socrates – ignorance of the nature of the true, the good, and the beautiful – flourished. The same occurred eventually in Rome. Initially peopled by independent, hard-working peasants who loved their liberty, community, and country, 'culture' invaded and took command. The 'ancient Roman simplicity' succumbed to 'pomp and magnificence', and from this 'fatal splendour', Rome, 'once the shrine of virtue, became the theatre of vice, a scorn among the nations, and an object of derision even to barbarians',[15] to whom it inevitably fell. His final historical example is Constantinople, which in the Dark and Middle European ages 'seemed destined to be the capital of the world' because it was the 'refuge of the arts and sciences'. Instead, 'the most profligate debaucheries, the most abandoned villainies, the most atrocious crimes . . . form the warp and woof of the history of Constantinople'.[16]

For Rousseau, then, history teaches that people first lived close to nature in a pristine ignorance which enabled their 'natural' virtues of straightforwardness and honesty to flourish. Although 'human nature was not at bottom better then than now', the transparency and authenticity of human beings 'prevented their having many vices'.[17] But wherever the arts and sciences were introduced into these simple, virtuous societies, 'the effect is certain and the depravity actual'; minds are inevitably corrupted, for 'the evils resulting from our vain curiosity are as old as the world'.[18] Although sketchy and unsupported by any real analysis, Rousseau had set the basis for a closer look at the mechanisms by which, according to his intuitions, the history of humankind is one in which peoples, 'originally' or 'naturally' happy and virtuous (albeit ignorant), inevitably degenerate once embarked upon the path of 'civilisation'. The opportunity to fill out this sketch presented itself four years later when Rousseau responded to another Dijon Academy essay competition, which asked 'What is the origin of inequality among men, and is it authorised by natural law?'.

The Discourse on the Origins of Inequality

> . . . wandering deep into the forest, I sought and I found the vision of those primitive times, the history of which I proudly traced . . . I dared to strip man's nature naked, to follow the progress of time, and trace the things which have distorted it; and by comparing man as he has made himself with man as he is by nature I showed him in his pretended perfection the true source of his misery.[19]

Rousseau begins by distinguishing between natural inequalities of body and mind, and 'moral or political inequality'. He proposes to explore how the latter came about, (and whether they can be justified), by starting at man's 'natural', i.e., pre-social, pre-political, state – man 'in the state of nature'. Presumably ignorant of Vico's ideas, he claims 'the philosophers, who have enquired into the foundations of society, have all felt the necessity of going back to a state of nature; but not one of them has got there'. This is because they have 'transferred to the state of nature ideas which were acquired in society; so that, in speaking of the savage, they described the social man'. Instead, Rousseau proposes to construct a history (in the absence of the historical facts) derived from 'conditional and hypothetical reasoning . . . just like the hypotheses which our physicists daily form respecting the formation of the world'.[20] Referring to his previous Discourse's declamations against 'civilised society', he tells us that 'it is, so to speak, the life of your species which I am going to write', warning that its message will constitute 'a panegyric on your first ancestors, a criticism of your contemporaries, and a terror to the unfortunates who will come after you'.[21]

The 'noble savage'

There follows Rousseau's famous description of 'the noble savage', derived partly from Rousseau's imagination, partly from deduction by removing what he calls the 'supernatural' additions of 'civilisation', and partly from contemporary accounts of 'savage nations' such as the native Americans and the Hottentots of the Cape of Good Hope. Initially, man in the state of nature is little more than an animal, sharing the physical virtues of robustness, keen senses, health, and simplicity of purpose. But just as domesticated animals lose these virtues, so does man as he begins to 'advance' from his natural state. He is able to do the latter because, unlike the animal, which Rousseau sees as 'nothing . . . but an ingenious machine' governed entirely by instinct, man 'has some share in his own operations, in his character as a free agent'.[22] Relatedly, man has the 'faculty of self-improvement, which, by the help of circumstances, gradually develops all the rest of our faculties'.[23] It is because of this that man has a 'history' at all, whereas animals do not.

Before beginning this history, however, our noble savage's *moral* character is that of a deprived yet happy being. Leading a mainly solitary life (apart from occasional matings and motherhood), having no language, the savage would be devoted principally to looking after himself. But according to Rousseau the consequent inability to think very far and the absence of social life are precisely what gives the savage his moral strength. Because savages 'maintained no kind of intercourse with each other, [they] were . . . strangers to vanity, deference, esteem, and contempt'. Rather, they were motivated by the virtue of self-respect, as distinct from the 'civilised' vice of selfishness – and in the absence of the rational ability to think up the maxim, *Do to others as you would have them do unto you*, would live out the 'less perfect . . . but perhaps more useful' rule, *Do good to yourself with as little evil as possible to others*.[24] Rousseau insists this was because savage, unreflective man, although not by nature sociable, naturally feels compassion when he encounters others' suffering. It is only when he develops into a social mode of life that he can deliberately seek to harm others from malevolent motives, or take pleasure in gaining advantage from others' misfortunes. And as for being deprived of the power to think (i.e., much beyond his immediate needs), this is where Rousseau is at his most characteristically and deliberately controversial, for he says, 'If she [nature] destined man to be healthy, I venture to declare that a state of reflection is a state contrary to nature, and that a thinking man is a depraved animal'.[25] It is as if Rousseau is prefiguring the early twentieth-century existentialist notion that self-consciousness – the power to reflect – is an unbearable burden.

So much, then, for Rousseau's perhaps highly romanticised notion of 'the noble savage', except to say that he can see no reason why man should have wished to leave that state. Rather, the potential for self-improvement – indeed, perfectibility – inherent in 'natural' man could never have developed in itself, he suggests, 'but must require the fortuitous concurrence of many foreign causes'. He then turns to 'consider the different accidents which may have improved the human

175

understanding while depraving the species, and made man wicked while making him sociable'.[26] In Part 2, then, Rousseau attempts to reconstruct the origins and development of human society and civilisation – a history of whose meaning and significance he has left us in no doubt about what he believes.

The disastrous progress of mankind

The ascent of man from his happy pristine infancy began, Rousseau surmises, because 'difficulties soon presented themselves' in his circumstances – such as competition with animals, and population pressures, causing scarcity of resources – so that 'it became necessary to learn how to surmount them'.[27] Depending on their location, men invented hooks and lines to become fishermen, or bows and arrows to become hunters in the forests, or fur-skin clothes in cold regions. This process must have stimulated the mind to make elementary perceptions of the relations between things in terms of size, strength, and speed. Also, formerly leading solitary lives, 'experience' now began to teach the advantages of joining 'some kind of loose association' with others, 'that laid no restraint on its members' – sporadic groupings within which the rudiments of language would have begun.

After what must have been 'a multitude of ages . . . these first advances enabled men to make others' – in particular, Rousseau suggests, the increased use of primitive tools enabled them to make rude permanent dwellings – and this was 'the epoch of a first revolution' because it 'established and distinguished families, and introduced a kind of property'. These first proper families generated 'conjugal love and paternal affection', but also began to ascribe different roles to male and female – 'whose manner of life had hitherto been the same' – the women minding 'the hut and their children, while the men went abroad in search of their common subsistence'. This basic division of labour, coupled with the simplicity of their wants, enabled man 'a great deal of leisure, which he employed to furnish himself with many conveniences unknown to his fathers', whilst family-living must have advanced the use of language.[28] Rousseau then suggests environmental causes such as floods and earthquakes portioned off numbers of families, compelling them to live in common circumstances. This is another turning point since 'everything now begins to change its aspect', for 'at length in every country arises a distinct nation, united in character and manners, not by regulations or laws, but by uniformity of life and food', and language. In this greatly expanded social context,

> men continued to lay aside their original wildness . . . They accustomed themselves to assemble before their huts round a large tree; singing and dancing . . . became the amusement, or rather the occupation, of men and women thus assembled together with nothing else to do. Each one began to consider the rest, and to wish to be considered in turn; and thus a value came to be attached to public esteem . . . and this was the first step towards inequality, and at the same time towards vice.

This is because 'from these first distinctions arose on the one side vanity and contempt and on the other shame and envy'.[29] With the emergence of self-esteem, there 'hence arose the first obligations of civility even among savages', and what Vico might have called a 'severe justice' whereby 'every man punished the contempt shown him by others' with a 'revenge' that was 'terrible', 'bloody, and cruel'. Because there were as yet no institutions of law, 'the dread of vengeance had to take [their] place'.

By this stage of its history, then, mankind had moved some way from its 'natural' state, and clearly there are already significant respects in which for Rousseau – ever the moralist – the potential for 'decline' is present. And yet, perhaps curiously, for Rousseau this stage 'must have been the happiest and most stable of our epochs . . . altogether the very best man could experience'[30] – our Golden Age, if you wish – or as he put it, 'the real youth of the world', (giving the lie to the common perception that Rousseau most admired 'the noble savage' of mankind's origins). This is because of 'the expansion of the human faculties' achieved at this stage. Although the potential for future vice is implicit, it was a period which kept 'a just mean between the indolence of the primitive state and the petulant activity of our egoism'. So idyllic was this era, Rousseau suggests, that man 'can have departed from it only through some fatal accident which, for the public good, should never have happened'. But the 'accident' did happen – one that 'apparently [was] so many steps towards the perfection of the individual, but in reality [was] towards the decrepitude of the species'.

This second 'great revolution' was the invention of metallurgy and agriculture. Its 'accidental' nature, Rousseau suggests, rested on 'the extraordinary accident of some volcano which, by ejecting metallic substances already in fusion, suggested to the spectators the idea of imitating the natural operation' – and on what must have been their 'unusually advanced minds'. As for agriculture, he suggests the emergence of metal-working caused a shortage of people left to provide food, and thus prompted the development (helped by iron tools) of tilling the land to grow crops. But this was not just a revolution in technology. Rather, it was a revolution in humanity, because men lost their independence by becoming embroiled in the division of labour – and if there is one characteristic which Rousseau admired in the two previous eras, it was men's independence.

> But from the moment one man began to stand in need of the help of another; from the moment it appeared advantageous to any one man to have enough provisions for two, equality disappeared, property was introduced, work became indispensable, and vast forests became smiling fields, which man had to water with the sweat of his brow, and where slavery and misery were soon seen to germinate and grow up with the crops. . . . The poets tell us it was gold and silver, but, for the philosophers, it was iron and corn which first civilised men, and ruined humanity.[31]

The overall division of labour between agriculture and manufacture was exacerbated by further divisions within these activities – and these, along with the system of exchange of commodities they necessitated, further exacerbated whatever *natural* inequalities already existed. In addition, agriculture in particular required rules about property – and taken all together, Rousseau tells us, 'it is easy to imagine the rest'; the advancement of other arts and technologies, of language, and of the inequalities of riches. Men now lived their lives increasingly entangled with, and in need of, each other – and their own position in the socio-economic field became crucial to them. For Rousseau, the moral effects of this new situation were appalling. Because 'man must now have been perpetually employed in getting others to interest themselves in his lot', it now became the interest of men to appear what they really were not. 'To be and to seem became two totally different things; and from this distinction sprang insolent pomp and cheating trickery. On the other hand, free and independent as men were before, they were now, in consequence of a multiplicity of new wants, brought into subjection . . . to all nature, and particularly to one another; and each became in some degree a slave even in becoming the master of other men: if rich, they stood in need of the services of others; if poor, of their assistance'.[32]

The origins of political societies

Rousseau depicts this 'new-born state of society' in which equality disappeared as 'a horrible state of war' (as some – 'like ravenous wolves' – enlarged their possessions and powers at the expense of others driven to violence or slavery to survive), akin to Hobbes' famous picture of 'the state of nature'. But, as Rousseau had himself pointed out in criticism of such 'social contract' theorists, this was a state already far removed from man's 'natural' state. On the contrary, he saw the Hobbesian/ Lockean 'social contract' theory in a markedly different light, for far from rescuing man from an appalling 'state of nature', it introduced a new, devastating era into a situation where man had already left his natural state far behind but was not yet entirely 'lost'. Rousseau explains: The 'horrible state of war' ushered in a further development in man's history, for in his insecurity 'the rich man . . . conceived at length the profoundest plan that ever entered the mind of man: this was to employ in his favour the forces of those who attacked him'. He did this by devising 'plausible' or 'specious' arguments whereby, pointing out the horrors of the present anarchic situation, all should join together to 'institute rules of justice and peace, to which all without exception may be obliged to conform. . . . Let us . . . instead of turning our forces against ourselves, collect them in a supreme power which may govern us by wise laws, protect and defend all the members of the association . . . and maintain eternal harmony among us'. Because 'so barbarous and easily seduced', the rest agreed. 'All ran headlong to their chains, in hopes of securing their liberty', and as a consequence institutions of law and government arose. But for Rousseau, this 'specious' social contract was simply a confidence trick perpetrated by the rich (who currently had no right to their unequal status gained by force, cunning, and intimidation) upon the poor, who 'had just wit enough to perceive the advantages of political institutions, without experience enough . . . to foresee the dangers'.

The political societies which ensued 'bound new fetters on the poor, and gave new powers to the rich'; they 'irretrievably destroyed natural liberty, eternally fixed the law of property and inequality, converted clever usurpation into unalterable right, and, for the advantage of a few ambitious individuals, subjected all mankind to perpetual labour, slavery, and wretchedness'.[33]

'Such was, or may well have been, the origins of society and law', says Rousseau – and we can see, for him, how much this development revolved around property. (Indeed, in a rhetorical flourish opening Part 2 Rousseau had already declared, 'The first man who, having enclosed a piece of ground, bethought himself of saying "This is mine", and found people simple enough to believe him, was the real founder of civil society').[34]

Having reached this critical historical stage – 'the origin of political societies' – Rousseau devotes most of the remainder of the *Discourse* to speculating on the different forms of government which subsequently evolved. But things did not improve, because 'as it had begun ill, . . . the original faults were never repaired'.[35] On the contrary, Rousseau presents a rough, and typically pessimistic, theory of the development of political constitutions. Although initially loosely 'democratic' in form, eventually 'ambitious chiefs' began to 'perpetuate their offices in their own families', and thereby 'contracted the habit of considering their offices as a family estate, and themselves the proprietors of the communities of which they were at first only the officers'. These chiefs/magistrates thus began 'regarding their fellow-citizens as their slaves, and numbering them, like cattle, among their belongings'. This phase, 'which is the last degree of inequality', thus 'authorised . . . the condition . . . of master and slave',[36] and is the condition Rousseau implies has been reached in his own times.

The final stages

Sketchy and intuitive as is this 'history' – (unlike Vico, Rousseau offers no actual evidence) – Rousseau elaborates on his theory that different forms of government derive from degrees of inequality. There are many sources of inequality, but Rousseau asserts that 'wealth is the one to which they are all reduced in the end'. He claims that this is the measure for analysing a people's 'progress towards the extreme term of corruption' and for demonstrating what 'may appear in ages yet to come' regarding the nature of government. As money increasingly becomes the measure of all things, 'the rights of citizens and the freedom of nations' will be 'slowly extinguished', and in passages prescient of twentieth-century fascism and totalitarianism,

> from the midst of this disorder and these revolutions . . ., despotism, gradually raising up its hideous head and devouring everything that remained sound and untainted in any part of the State, would at length trample on both the laws and the people, and establish itself on the ruins of the republic.

Equally prescient, Rousseau predicts that 'the times which immediately preceded this last change would be times of trouble and calamity; but at last the monster would swallow up everything and the people would . . . have . . . only tyrants', such that there is a complete return to the law of the strongest, and so to a new state of nature, 'differing from that we set out on . . . [because of] the consequence of excessive corruption'.

This last stage in political evolution is, then, 'the extreme point that closes the circle', but it does not seem Rousseau therefore means to present a cyclical theory whereby mankind starts again on the disastrous path to 'civilisation'. Man at this last stage is, after all, totally different from the 'noble savage' or, for that matter, from man in the initial stages of society. Rather, Rousseau simply comments that at this last stage, where force alone 'justifies' rule, 'popular insurrection that ends in the death or deposition of a Sultan is as lawful an act as those by which he disposed, the day before, of the lives and fortunes of his subjects'.[37] Although he does not say so, such revolutions could hardly be likely to usher in some new, benign future for man, but rather to initiate permanent instability and continuing moral chaos.

Rousseau's philosophy of history

Such, then, are the gloomy results of Rousseau's efforts to 'retrace' 'the lost and forgotten road, by which man must have passed from the state of nature to the state of society'. He concludes by summarising the unfavourable comparison in scathing terms:

> In reality, the source of all these differences is, that the savage lives within himself, while social man lives constantly outside himself, and only knows how to live in the opinion of others, so that he seems to receive the consciousness of his own existence merely from the judgement of others concerning him.[38]

Inasmuch as this passage is a 'psychological' observation about man's consciousness of his being in the world, it introduces a modern slant into a philosophy of history otherwise distinctly slight on actual historical facts. What Rousseau has done is propose an understanding of human history which excludes God, 'providence', and supernatural teleology; avoids the notion of recurrable 'cycles' as much as it does some determinate unilinear future; does not deny the obvious fact of 'progress' in the arts, sciences, and technology, and yet still finds a 'meaning' or 'significance' of human history – not in such 'progress', but elsewhere; namely, in the nature of man's consciousness of being in the world.

Thus stripped of 'external' determinants of history, it is, then, a *materialistic* theory grounded on the bedrock of economic life. Economic necessity drove man to live in settlements, which expanded social intercourse and, correspondingly, language and intelligence. Then a technological revolution occurred as men accidentally discovered metallurgy, prompting the art of agriculture and the division of labour, thus making people more interdependent. Concomitantly, man's consciousness of his identity, worth, and role in life was increasingly mediated by the socio-economic nexus in which he functions. The first 'political societies' emerged, but essentially as confidence-tricks by the powerful and wealthy, leading eventually to societies where the mass of people are powerlessly entrapped in a complex web of economic relationships which encourage and feed upon the egoism, exploitation, and insecurity of all involved, having stripped them of all independence, self-respect, and genuine morality. Thus has man, through his history, become increasingly 'civilised'.

And as for the future? Rousseau was of course writing prior to the European industrial revolution and population explosion of the nineteenth century and to the stunning technological revolutions of the twentieth century. We noted his gloomy *political* intuitions – despotism, revolution, turmoil – and must assume he would have been even more gloomy to witness our 'progress' in economics and technology. But he would have been resigned to them and their consequences, just as he declared himself to be in his own day when, foreseeing Enlightenment satire that he wanted man to 'return again to the forests' to live in his 'natural' state, he dismisses the possibility and argues instead that we must do the best we can within our 'civilised' societies without, however, having any 'less contempt' for them.[39] And it seems this air of resignation constantly underpins his interpretation of man's history, for although there are stages where man would better have remained (particularly Rousseau's version of the 'golden age' of early *social* man), the equilibrium cannot hold. Prefiguring Hegelian dialectics, it is as if each stage of society breeds the very opposite factors which cause them to change – although in Rousseau's case, always to something worse. And, prefiguring Marxian dialectics, the chief of these factors is *economic* development linked to technological changes, which revolutionise the nature of societies and the 'moral' and 'psychological' character of men. Thus, although we have said that for Rousseau there are no 'external' determinants of human history – that man makes his own history – it would seem that man is not in control of that history, and thus of his own destiny as a being innately bearing the seeds of perfectibility. On the contrary, it seems that every time man takes a step further towards self-improvement (the development of language, social cooperation, political organisation, the arts and sciences, wealth creation) the economic factors on which these are based drive him ever further away from his 'perfection'. Instead, they lead to his increasing corruption as a being who, hopelessly enmeshed in an autonomous socio-economic nexus, further loses what it is to be 'human'.

Postscript on Rousseau – The Social Contract

Because of its celebrity (although falling somewhat out of our topic), we should note that only some few years after the resigned tone of his *Discourse on Inequality*, Rousseau *did* propose a positive solution to the current ills of society in his famous

The Social Contract (1762), a work of political philosophy. But our interest here must be limited to the question of whether it adds anything to Rousseau's theory of history just outlined, and the curious answer must be that in some important respects it actually contradicts it. Reiterating his complaints about exploitation and slavery, Rousseau argues that 'liberty' is essential for a person's actions to be truly 'human'. This is because man, unlike animals, has free will – and this, uniquely, allows him to choose between right and wrong. In short, man alone can be a *moral* being – but he can only realise this essential aspect of his humanity if he is free to choose his actions. As Rousseau puts it, 'Force is a physical power, and I fail to see what moral effect it can have. To yield to force is an act of necessity, not of will . . . In what sense can it be a duty?'.[40] Thus, to close the circle, because 'to remove all liberty from his will is to remove all morality from his acts', liberty is essential to being human, for 'to renounce liberty is to renounce being a man, to surrender the rights of humanity'.[41]

Now, given that people live in organised societies requiring rules, how can we construe such an organisation whereby, in obeying its laws, the citizen does so not because *forced* to, but, 'while uniting himself with all, may still obey himself alone, and remain as free as before'?[42] In short, is it possible to conceive of a political society in which it is possible to remain 'human'. Rousseau's celebrated solution revolves around what he calls 'the general will', whereby everyone gives up *everything* to the entire community, which then makes fundamental laws which all have a direct say in formulating. Thus gathered together, the people are 'the Sovereign', and in obeying the laws it passes (through each individual voting, entirely motivated by the good of the community rather than his private or sectional interests), they retain their freedom, since 'obedience to a law which we prescribe to ourselves is liberty'.[43] So far nothing said actually contradicts his *Discourse*. Rather, it seems to offer a welcome solution to at least the former work's *political* pessimism. However, Rousseau takes his thinking a stage further since, not only has he devised a way of *reforming* political society, he now tells us it is *only* in and through the political state (properly established) that humankind can achieve its perfectibility. And here he appears to contradict those thought-provoking intuitions underlying the *Discourse*'s philosophy of history.

Now, in *The Social Contract*, 'the passage from the state of nature to the civil state' *humanises* man by 'substituting justice for instinct in his conduct, and giving his actions the morality they formerly lacked'. Now, 'although . . . he deprives himself of some advantages which he got from nature, he gains in return others; . . . his faculties are . . . stimulated and developed, his ideas . . . extended, his feelings . . . enobled, and his whole soul uplifted'. What, then, of 'the noble savage'? Now, so great are the above advantages that, 'did not the abuses of this new condition often degrade him below that which he left', man should be ever grateful for being made into 'an intelligent being and a man, . . . instead of a stupid and unimaginative animal'. And returning to his philosophical definition of what it is to be 'human', he concludes, 'We might, over and above all this, add, to what man acquires in the civil state, moral liberty, which alone makes him truly master of himself'.[44]

Critique

This last phrase should rightly remind us of the crucial role a man's *independence* played in the moral ideas of the *Discourse*, and yet in that work this is increasingly *compromised* as man leaves the 'natural state', moving through early non-political societies, on into the political/civil state. Here, Rousseau appears to turn his ideas upside down. We have only to compare a passage already quoted from the *Discourse* with a further passage from the *Social Contract*. In the former work which lauds 'natural man' and condemns 'civilised' man, 'In reality, the source of all these differences is, that the savage lives within himself, while social man lives constantly outside himself'. Now, in the *Social Contract*, Rousseau emphasises that:

> He who dares to undertake the making of a people's institutions ought to feel himself capable . . . of transforming each individual, who is by himself a complete and solitary whole, into part of a greater whole from which he in a manner receives his life and being. . . . He must . . . take away from man his own resources and give him . . . new ones . . . incapable of being made use of without the help of other men . . . so that if each citizen is nothing and can do nothing without the rest, . . . legislation is at the highest possible point of perfection.[45]

Then, it seems, 'the general will' can properly function, and mankind can thereby not only rescue, but perfect, its human nature.

The ideas behind these contrasting passages are perhaps impossible to reconcile – but then neither should we necessarily try to, but leave room for thinkers to develop their ideas even to the point where they change their minds. But our interest is that these ideas in *The Social Contract* invite the comment that Rousseau perhaps underestimated the implications of that sketchy philosophy of history he presented in the *Discourse on Inequality*. There, he suggested his approach (which, *pace* Vico, he regarded as entirely novel) furnishes 'the solution to a number of problems of politics and morals which philosophers cannot settle'.[46] What he seemed to mean is that the grounding of the course of history on the practical matter of how, over time, the development of man's faculties, moral ideas, and modes of social organisation were determined by the *economic* facts of his material existence, demonstrates the futility of abstract philosophising about, for example, the moral nature of man or the ideal logic of the State. The centrality of the economic factors of property and the division of labour as determinants of man's history is clear. And yet when, in *The Social Contract*, Rousseau attempts to offer some positive solution to those problems of 'civilised society', it is one which ignores those inescapable economic mechanisms underlying historical development and focuses instead on some *a priori*, abstract, purely *political* notion of 'the general will'. (Ultimately, all we know about 'property' under this new dispensation is that 'the right which each individual has to his own estate is always subordinate to the right which the community has over all'.[47] In short, it is up to 'the general will', starting from a clean slate, to determine the nature of the economy). This can be seen as a phony solution which relapses into just that abstract political philosophising whose utopianism Rousseau had earlier criticised in the philosophy of history contained in his *Discourse on Inequality*.

Those earlier intuitions were later to find their expansion in Marx's historico-economic theory. On the other hand, the basis of the *Social Contract* – the concept of freedom of the will – was to be expanded (through an extraordinary philosophical historicisation) by Hegel. Thus in waving *adieu* to Rousseau we leave a thinker whose intuitions in the field of philosophy of history, as in other areas, pointed in so many of the different directions modernity was to explore.

Turgot

Rousseau's *Discourses* remain as testament to his reaction against that implicit Enlightenment consensus on 'philosophy of history' outlined at the outset of this chapter. Clearly, Rousseau was aware of this consensus which so closely linked the idea of 'progress' with an implicit 'philosophy of history', and he set out to attack both. But there was as yet no celebrated individual exponent to target – rather, he was attacking a general trend which was to find a systematic individual exponent only some twenty years after his death, in Condorcet's (1794) *Sketch for a Historical Picture of the Progress of the Human Mind* (which singled out Rousseau's two *Discourses* for attack). But if Condorcet's work summarised preceding Enlightenment sketchy efforts into 'a definite philosophy of history',[48] and 'was the form in which the eighteenth-century idea of progress was generally assimilated into Western thought'[49], the consensus it represented was already implicit by the 1750s, and perhaps no better example need be found than the scientist-statesman Turgot (1727–1781) – 'of the middle generation of the *philosophes*'[50] – who in 1750 delivered two lectures which 'framed a new conception of world history . . . and constituted the first important version in modern times of the ideology of progress'.[51] That Turgot befriended and advanced Condorcet, and that the latter admired him to the extent of writing his biography, exemplifies the basic similarity of their, and their numerous *philosophe* contacts', views on the meaning of history. Thus, to more closely explore the typical Enlightenment philosophy of history, let us begin by outlining Turgot's ideas on this theme, particularly as set out in Manuel's account in his stimulating book, *The Prophets of Paris*.[52]

On 'progress' and 'rationality'

Like other *philosophes*, Turgot passionately believed in 'progress', and this 'progress' was measured by, and depended on, the extent to which mankind could become ever more 'civilised' through applying 'reason' to achieve the fully happy life. To Turgot and many others of his generation the application of 'reason' meant following the ideas of Locke and Condillac, whereby all knowledge is derived from sense-experience. There are no innate, pre-existing ideas, concepts, or values.

Rather, all knowledge should be shorn of such mysteries and depend instead upon the gradual uncovering of reality through observation, comparison, and experiment. Other ideas – derived from imagination or superstition (including many religious ideas), or merely accepted on grounds of tradition and convention – are deeply suspect and lead to irrational thinking.

For Turgot this belief in 'progress' looked in two directions. First, it meant a belief in the inevitable triumph of reason governing human affairs in the (hopefully non-too distant) *future*, whereby mankind could finally realise its perfectibility in 'one enlightened world with a uniform culture' – indeed, 'one political world'.[53] Here, the irrationalities of war, economic deprivation, political oppression, ignorance, and exploitative inequalities, would be abolished, never to return because of the ineradicability of the accumulated knowledge of the physical and social sciences. Also, however, it meant understanding the meaning of all previous human *history* from this same perspective of 'progress' dependent upon the development of 'rationality'. This is how Turgot looked at, and what he sought in, the history of humankind. For him, human history was the long ascent from ignorance and the rule of passion to the reign of 'scientific' knowledge and reason. It was, he claims, what history itself tells us from the facts we can observe or otherwise rationally hypothesise. Although for him there may be some kind of divine providence underlying this encouraging history, more prosaically he construed the determining mechanisms behind the inevitability of 'progress' as being the utilitarian impulse of the search for pleasure and happiness, combined with the capacity to accumulate ever more, and more certain, knowledge through experience, observation, and reflection. In short, there is a 'law' governing human history. Sooner or later – in this nation or that – the law of the inevitability of 'progress' has prevailed (and will continue to do so).

But this is not to say 'progress' was easy. Rather, throughout history the spark of innovation is held back by the forces of *routine*. These negative forces are not so much some innate conservatism in human nature. On the contrary, Turgot believes the impulse to discover new knowledge and create new things is basic to human nature. Rather, they originate from established institutions which labour 'to stall man in the rut of sameness, . . . in a state of treadmill repetitiveness', to defend their vested interests.[54]

Thus Turgot's perspective on history focuses on the gradual development of the human mind, and he saw this process as evidenced primarily by the evolution of language and modes of thought. Initially, the ancients 'communicated their ideas as a sort of baby-talk', in 'metaphors and images'. This was linked to what Turgot saw as a basically 'theological' view of the world. But as the human mind developed, this theological approach to existence was replaced by the *metaphysical* approach, reflected in correspondingly more abstract language (e.g., the philosophical achievement of the Greeks and its subsequent heritage).

But the *third* (and final?) stage is the growing recognition of 'the real objective nature of things' achieved through the application of empirical, 'scientific' method, and it is at this stage that reason, in coming to fruition, increasingly begins 'to formulate . . . relationships [between things] in *mathematical* terms'.[55] Now, the metaphysical view of existence is superseded by the 'positive' view, and Turgot clearly meant by this the transforming (or 'reducing'?) of as many facets of existence as possible into the rational purity of mathematical relationships. Quite how far he thought this could be extended is difficult to say.

The monitoring of 'progress'

In his thoughts about history Turgot identified four general areas which interplayed in different ways and at different rates. Technological innovation was the most reliable and enduring of these. Closely linked were developments in speculative science. But if, for Turgot, 'science owed more to technology than technology to science', it was 'a relationship Turgot was prepared to see reversed by the imminent explosion of speculative science. . . . For the future the scientists were the unchallenged vanguard of the battalions of progress'. Another area in which 'progress' could be assessed was in the arts, but here Manuel tells us that 'Turgot modified his theory of limitless infinite progress' on the simplistic grounds that 'the fine arts aimed only to please'. Once good taste had established the proper parameters of aesthetic pleasure, and the properties of human psychology involved were understood scientifically, then the knowledge appropriate to the arts was achieved, and no further progress would be possible since 'a specific art object either obeyed . . . the rules or violated them'. Since Turgot's view was that artistic perfection had been achieved in the age of Virgil and Horace, the only question was whether the good taste involved could be recaptured, or imitated properly in different societies.[56]

The other area in which 'progress' could be monitored was that of moral behaviour, or put in modern terms, 'the social sciences'. Here, Turgot adopted a standard view of the cruel nature of early societies with their fierce natural religions and barbarous practices. Unlike some of his anti-clerical, even atheistic, fellow Enlightenment *philosophes*, however, he praised the achievements of Christianity in overcoming many pagan practices, and saw the church as 'one of the great civilising and moralising forces in the history of mankind'.[57] But he looked forward to further 'moral' progress towards the ideal of peace-loving, tolerant, just, prosperous societies in which 'reason' prevailed. Above all was his hope that the keys to unlocking the problems of how to organise society to maximise individual happiness with 'social order' could be found in the further application of reason to social science. And this, of course, meant 'the mathematicisation of the study of man', whereby 'moral problems would be removed from the disputes of the marketplace', where there would be 'no room . . . left for vagueness, for the exaggeration of enthusiasts, for superstition' and other baggage of the pre-scientific approach.[58] Then, whereas progress throughout (previous) history had often resulted from the clash between the forces of innovation and those of reaction and evil (thereby affording the latter a positive role nevertheless), future progress would be self-sustaining because based on the universal growth and application of educated rationality.

The direction Turgot's ideas were taking, particularly his view of the meaning of history from which they derived, is clear. But his increasing embroilment in French politics from the early 1760s, culminating in his office as Comptroller-General of Finance in 1774 and his downfall two years later, never permitted him to properly systematise his historical ideas or pursue his hopes for the 'mathematicisation' of the social sciences. Had he done so, Manuel for one believes 'he would have ranked with Vico as a creator of the "new science"'.[59] As it was, it fell to his protégé Condorcet to develop Turgot's typical Enlightenment philosophy of history into a systematic treatise.

Condorcet

Born in 1743 and educated by Jesuits, the young Condorcet achieved some distinction as a promising mathematician, a talent he kept in touch with and whose possibilities always fascinated him as he moved forward to achieve increasing eminence as a 'scientist-policy-maker', elected at the age of twenty-six to the French Academy of Sciences in 1779, and becoming its permanent Secretary in 1785. Involved in the fervour of the Revolution of 1789, he was elected to the Commune of Paris and then to the 1791 Legislative Assembly, which in recognition of his extensive intellectual connections and organising abilities commissioned from him a Report on Education – (a matter central to Condorcet's hopes for the future) – which 'was to have great influence on the revolutionary remodelling of the French education system'.[60] Then elected to the National Convention, Condorcet's downfall began as he fell out with the more extreme policies of the Jacobins. Denounced as an enemy of the Republic in 1793, he went into hiding in a house in Paris, and when some eight months later he tried to escape, was captured and died the next day in somewhat mysterious circumstances. During those eight months, as a kind of summation of his life-long involvement in scientific and intellectual matters and of his ideas as a *philosophe*, Condorcet wrote his *Sketch for a Historical Picture of the Progress of the Human Mind*, (the *Esquisse*).

In this work, Condorcet tried to collate the many observations and reflections he had indulged in throughout his life regarding the past development of human-kind and its future prospects. In short, he tried to make systematic sense of his (and other Enlightenment) views on the significance of human history, views in his case strongly influenced by his knowledge of the history of science. Also he was clearly influenced by Turgot's ideas regarding 'progress' in history and by the latter's intuitions about the prospects which a 'social art' based on 'positive' social science held for the future. However, he differed from Turgot in being unambiguously atheistic, and this perhaps allowed him a bolder view of history and a more radical tone – in addition, the circumstances under which he wrote the *Esquisse*, bereft of his home and library, concentrated his attention on the essentials.

For Condorcet, history should be a 'science', essentially like any other science. God and/or 'providence' can be removed from the study altogether, and to the extent that 'the history of man . . . is linked by an uninterrupted chain of facts and observations, [so that] the picture of the march . . . of the human mind becomes truly historical', then *philosophy* can also be taken out of the study. As Condorcet put it, 'Philosophy has nothing more to guess, no more hypothetical surmises to make'. History is a matter of gathering and ordering the facts, and then of showing 'the useful truths that can be derived from their connections and causality'.[61] That the latter exercise is surely a form of 'philosophy' (if only because, from our point of view, so obviously 'value-laden') Condorcet might have accepted – but in apparently relegating 'philosophy' in favour of 'science' he was primarily objecting to those, like Pascal, who insisted on a sharp distinction between the objects of scientific study (with its mathematical approach) and the objects of moral study (with their historical and philosophical approach). In that sense, for Condorcet, the study of the history of man should be a science rather than require an explicitly non-scientific, 'philosophical' approach.

But there is also a more radical sense in which Condorcet relegated 'philosophy' in favour of 'science'. If the *study* of history should be 'scientific' rather than 'philosophical', that same study demonstrates that, ultimately, the study of *anything* (including moral questions) should abandon 'philosophy' and become 'scientific'. In short, philosophy is not only inappropriate to the study of history. Rather, history itself teaches us that 'philosophy' was but one phase of human understanding of reality which should be superseded by 'science' in *all* areas of knowledge. For Condorcet,

> Metaphysicians and system-makers in all ages . . . were as inimical to progress as priests and religious enthusiasts. . . . True knowledge was restricted to . . . simple straightforward empirical science, preferably with a mathematical base . . . Philosophies were disguised religions and they invariably led to the decline of true science.[62]

In being a typical part of his overall interpretation of the sweep of human history, this idea can introduce us to the larger picture he drew.

Historical premises

According to Condorcet, the history of humankind can be divided into nine stages, with a tenth about to dawn. Similar to Turgot's approach, his underlying premises are that historical progress is basically accountable for in terms of man's capacity to receive knowledge through his sense-experiences, and accumulate and organise such knowledge in order to further his utilitarian impulse to achieve a more pleasing life. (Note an even more basic premise at work here – that 'history' *is* the history of 'progress'). Thus for Condorcet 'history' is basically the interplay between man's intellect and the fulfilment of his needs and desires, and progress occurs when intellectual innovations break down the resistance of traditional ways of doing things and change the way people live. The source of such resistance, rather as in Turgot, is the opposition of vested interests concerned to perpetuate the *status quo*. But unlike Turgot, in Condorcet's case it is not only superstition and convention that have upheld erroneous knowledge, but religion in particular – including, in the West, the Christian church. Also, 'philosophy' has perpetuated erroneous knowledge, particularly when it spawns 'schools' anxious to uphold their ideas against competing 'metaphysical' systems. Indeed, it would seem that for Condorcet there is little difference between superstition, religion, and philosophy as reactionary forces, although it is true that philosophy has sometimes stimulated 'scientific' ideas, the only source of truth. History, then, has been the grand battlefield between truth and error, and as such Condorcet construes its different stages in 'primarily intellectual and cultural' terms. Yet this is not because of any high-brow elitism on his part. Rather, it was because he was convinced – by his 'historical observations' – that 'scientific' progress led to political, economic, and social betterment, i.e., '*moral*' progress. Thus it is that, although Condorcet's stages of history often relate to economic factors in particular, he was (as Mazlish notes) 'basically not an economic determinist . . . [but] far more interested in the "moral relations"' of societies.[63]

The ten stages of history

Eschewing reference to Biblical accounts, or to philosophical constructions of a 'state of nature' (as in, for example, Rousseau), Condorcet identifies the first stage of human history as that in which people lived in small tribes and survived by hunting and fishing. The second stage is the change to an agricultural way of life, where even at this early stage (as indeed Rousseau had suggested) sufficient material welfare was achieved to produce a surplus – and this allowed the emergence of a 'priesthood' which, although it might have initially fostered new knowledge of, for example, astronomy, exclusively guarded its knowledge, partly by obscurantist language (as in Vico, whose ideas it is doubtful Condorcet or any other *philosophe* was properly familiar with). The third stage of history is the development within simple agricultural societies of the division of labour. This enhanced economy, in which the emergence of artisans and traders extended human communications, was assisted and encouraged by the invention of the alphabet. But it also spawned the feudal system whereby an hereditary nobility governed over 'a common people condemned to toil, dependence and humiliation without actually being slaves'.[64] Although Condorcet claims that feudalism is a feature (and a 'curse') in most societies' histories, rather than constituting one of his ten stages it spans some of them as a long-standing phenomenon where priesthoods and aristocracies hold back innovation by trying to maintain an ideological hegemony based on superstition and reactionary philosophy. This, combined with Condorcet's approach of identifying 'stages' in terms of *intellectual* progress, involves him in re-periodising European history, for (as Mazlish points out) he does not refer to 'the

Middle Ages', normally associated with feudalism. Rather, feudalism seems to encompass a broader span of time (and place) for Condorcet, and always to have been an underlying 'social' source of error and ignorance. Thus the fourth actual stage of history he identifies is that of the intellectual achievements of the Greeks, followed by the fifth, 'the progress of the sciences from their division to their decline' with the Romans. His sixth stage spans the period of 'darkness' from the decline of Rome up to the eleventh century, when the crusades provoked a revival of knowledge, and his seventh stage covers the restoration and further development of the sciences (preserved by the Arabs) to the invention of printing – i.e., the Late Middle Ages. Throughout these seven stages 'the human mind' had made obvious progress in scientific knowledge and technology despite the resistance of obscurantist religion and entrenched philosophical absurdities common to basically feudal overlordship. But the battle against error and illusions had been hard and erratic, as, for example, the enlightenment the Greeks fostered became but a flicker not to be relit until Europe began to recover its highlights from Muslim and Byzantine sources (in what we currently call the High and Late Middle Ages).

The eighth stage of 'the progress of the human mind' was greatly stimulated by the invention of printing in the West – (a good example of technological innovation causing rather than following scientific progress) – and coincides roughly with what we now call 'the Renaissance'. Printing vastly extended the variety and communication of ideas as well as facilitating the Renaissance secular impulse. In challenging the straight-jacket of religious authority and ideological dominance (including Aristotelian 'scholasticism' in philosophy), this stage prepared the way for the ninth epoch, where the foundations for a 'new enlightenment' were laid by such seventeenth century heroes of rationalism and empiricism as Descartes and Locke. In short, the ninth stage equates partly to what we now call 'the Scientific Revolution' (which, as we saw in an earlier chapter, had ramifications far beyond the realm of the natural sciences), but also to the Enlightenment itself, (where so many of those ramifications matured).

At last, 'reason' was emerging triumphant, not only in the understanding of natural phenomena but also in man's view of society, politics, and morality. The forces of reaction, holding up the progress of the human mind (and thus of progress in the utilitarian quest for a happier, fairer, more prosperous and fulfilling life for the masses of people) were on the brink of defeat. Irrational, speculative philosophies were being swept away by the fresh air of empirically based, rationally organised knowledge. Religious superstition and metaphysical absurdities were being exposed for what they were – lamentable errors exploiting the ignorance of the mass of humanity in the interests of outmoded elites. Yet the world-historic battle between truth and error, with all that meant for Condorcet for the progress of mankind, was not yet quite won at this ninth stage. But all the prospects of victory were there – the apparent dominance of Enlightenment ideas themselves, the American Revolution of 1776, and of course the French Revolution itself, were ample evidence. In addition, Condorcet's whole view of human history was that 'progress' is *inevitable* – and although he would be the first to deny any 'supernatural' determinant behind history, there is a strong sense in which the inevitability of progress is *itself* a force driving history. When the battle was won, then a tenth stage of history would be reached, where all vestiges of ignorance, superstition, and error would be flushed out of societies, and unhampered 'reason', based on 'science' now including a new *social* science (or 'social art'), would govern the bright future for mankind.

Overview of Condorcet's philosophy of history

We will explore this proposed tenth stage shortly, but since it concerned the future for Condorcet let us first review his philosophy of history so far. Perhaps primarily, Condorcet's nine stages do not seem to make for convincing history since there is clearly so much else 'going on' which he ignores. In short, we might agree with Mazlish that 'it is poor history . . . because it is so far removed from historical reality' – and that 'it is also bad, that is, non-instrumental or operational, science', because 'he has no notion at all about the actual, historical transitions – and the way in which they occurred'.[65] However, it could be argued that the details of Condorcet's stages do not matter so much as his overall idea. It centres on his identification of human progress in general with the progress of rational knowledge.

But what about the subject of history itself, irrespective of its narrowing down to 'the history of progress'? Condorcet's answer seems to be that as the 'progress of the human mind' approaches the full rationality of 'science', that very 'science' instructs us that the study of history itself should *also* be 'scientific' – that is, be divested of religious and philosophical notions and be subject to the same tests of empiricism and of the probability of hypotheses as any other science. This achieved, Condorcet finds that this new, 'scientific' approach suggests history is inevitably progressive regarding mankind's welfare, *and* that this progress is principally the product of man's *intellectual* development. In short, we might give Condorcet the benefit of the doubt by claiming he has proposed a coherent, self-supporting argument about the nature of history both as a content and as a discipline. The alternative is to suggest his approach to history derives from his prior interest in the history of *ideas* (especially the mathematical sciences), which he tautologically transposes into 'history' *per se* – in short, that only because he already sees history in terms of the history of ideas, his historical studies show him that history *is*, effectively, the history of ideas!

Whichever, it follows for Condorcet that, in becoming a 'science' of the progress of the human mind, history provides a lesson-book and its study should thus be useful rather than merely an academic exercise. As he put it, 'the history of the progress already achieved must be [the] foundation . . . [of] a science for predicting the progress of the human race'.[66] This exemplifies another aspect of Condorcet's approach to history – namely, that by comparing the histories of different peoples, his aim is 'to extract the hypothetical history of a single people',[67] by which he meant 'mankind' in the abstract. In itself this may appear a reasonable project to some, for how often does the term 'mankind' roll off the tongue! Yet it *can* imply, and seemed to unconsciously for Condorcet, a philosophical position which believes in the *reality* of this abstraction – and almost inseparably, believes 'it' (humankind) has some ideal (Platonic) form which demands and awaits ultimate 'realisation' in the future. This is hardly a 'materialist', 'scientific' conception, and probably points to a central inconsistency in Condorcet's thinking. From a 'scientific' point of view there is surely no such (*real*) thing as 'mankind'. There are only actual, empirical men and women. This must be even more the case for the *historian*, the object of whose study may be all men, all societies, all nations, but not a phantom being, 'mankind'?

This premise about 'mankind' relates to another feature of Condorcet's philosophy of history – its *teleological* character. Taking his cue partly from Turgot, what Condorcet's 'scientific' approach told him was that, whereas when 'science' examined the material universe it discovered 'the principle of recurrence' in its laws, when applied to 'the human order' it uncovered 'an antithetical principle – Progress'.[68] This principle is at work from man's beginnings, but not because of any divine plan or mysterious help from 'providence'. Rather, it derives from the combination of a 'sensationalist' theory of knowledge (whereby men, in perceiving the world through their senses, are able to build up ever more true and useful ideas through experience) and man's utilitarian instinct towards pleasure. This combination generates progress. Two more factors in Condorcet's mind added to this stamp of *inevitability* in the march of progress. First, knowledge is by its nature relentlessly cumulative. It is remembered, recorded, and built upon, despite wars and natural catastrophes. Looking to the future, Condorcet is even more sure of this, for in looking to a single whole world sharing 'enlightenment', nothing short of a global catastrophe could then extinguish the light of human knowledge already attained.

Second, Condorcet 'shared a widespread hypothesis among many eighteenth-century thinkers' that 'acquired characteristics were inherited'. Thus 'the intellectual and moral attainments of one generation could be passed on intact to its successor', a process which he presumably thought had occurred throughout history, and which he believed would accelerate as scientific knowledge (and manipulation?) of the human organism would be developed in the tenth stage. Thus, as Manuel expresses it, '[a]ny possible remnant of doubt about the inevitable and infinite progress of the human spirit was dispelled once the human organism was shown to be subject to biological perfectibility'.[69]

Perhaps none of these reasons sustaining Condorcet's teleological thesis are especially persuasive, despite his rejection of any supernatural influence. Indeed, one could claim that it is his very attempt to ground his teleology on aspects of man's naturality which provides the weakest of his arguments – namely, his reliance on man's *utilitarian* nature. Although the appearance of 'utilitarianism' falls outside our remit, it nevertheless attracts comment insofar as Condorcet embraces its outlook, and falls captive to its typical shortcomings. Fundamentally, as explained by Bentham in his *A Fragment on Government*, the utilitarian philosophy insisted that all human behaviour is reducible to the impulse to seek pleasure and avoid pain. It is, so to speak, as simple as that – an irreducible fact of life about which it is therefore as pointless to complain as it is futile to argue. Philosophical systems which contradict it are sophistries; moral theories which introduce transcendental concepts such as 'duty' and 'obligation' mystify matters; and ethical or social systems which conceive of 'the good of society' in any terms other than the straightforward aim of 'the greatest happiness of the greatest number' are not only erroneous, but mischievous. It can be seen how readily these tenets of utilitarianism fitted in with a 'scientific' attitude to both individual and collective life, and Condorcet agreed with them, especially the last in terms of the purpose of his proposed 'social art' – but even more fundamentally with the starting point, that human behaviour is determined by pleasure and pain. As we have seen, it is this to which he appeals in his naturalistic teleology. It is *because* man seeks a more pleasurable, less painful life that his mental abilities are used in such a manner as to promote 'progress'.

The problem with this 'utilitarian' idea is not that it is simple – rather, it is simplistic. In explaining everything, it explains nothing. It explains why I bought that bar of chocolate *and* why I gave it away to a beggar in the same terms – both actions 'pleased' me. Thus unselfish, principled actions are no differently motivated at base than selfish actions. By thus removing a multitude of otherwise diverse motivations in human conduct, we might say 'the principle of utility' is of no use whatsoever to, above all, the *historian*, who needs to take account, not of people's 'desires' and 'aversions', but of their principles, their religious ideas, their moral preferences, their sense of identity, their desire for respect, and other such 'non-material' factors, in explaining the complex interplay that goes to make up human history. To imply, instead, that people who commit heroic acts, unselfish acts, principled acts, loyal acts, even suicidal acts, are acting out of delusion is a profound insult to the subtle complexities of the human spirit.

To the extent, then, that man's fundamental 'utilitarian' nature provides a basis for Condorcet's belief in the inevitable 'progress' of mankind towards perfectibility, it is weak support indeed for his teleological theory.

The tenth stage

For Condorcet, his predictions about the *future* course of human affairs – a 'future-history', if that is not a contradiction in terms – are an integral part of his 'philosophy of history'. This is because, like many previous 'theories' of history dealt with in this book, it conveys a *message*. His message is primarily a socio-political one regarding the new future he sees for Europe and North America, and eventually world-wide, which the ethos and events of his *own* time presaged. It presaged it because all of Condorcet's philosophy of history pointed to it. The tenth stage *would* follow from the present ninth stage, since the seeds were already there. They just needed to be nurtured. In this tenth stage Condorcet looked to the final triumph of 'reason' governing the affairs of societies. The 'scientific' spirit would reign not only in technology and philosophy, but also in the 'moral' affairs of society. A 'perpetual and universal' scientific academy would hopefully emerge, eventually on a worldwide scale (using the universal, neutral 'language' of maths and symbolic logic), to whose organisational aspects he gave much thought.[70] Independent of governments, whom the 'universal republic of the sciences' would advise and whose plans they would review, a crucial area of practical and theoretical research would be the *social* sciences. Here, 'the social art' would research and devise ways of achieving political rights and equality for all, and the equitable distribution of wealth and income.

To achieve the former, the 'social art' would explore means of calculating the truth regarding public preferences. Theoretically, this attempt at calculating a neo-Rousseauistic 'general will' could approach something like the mathematics of 'game theory' through its 'calculus of combinations and probabilities'.[71]

To achieve the latter he looked to a capitalist, market economy tempered by institutions of a welfare state which, again via mathematical and statistical techniques, would fairly provide social security for all citizens. Above all, the general purpose of 'the social art' would be to advance the theory, and devise institutions, whereby the interests of each individual and those of society at large could be identified and reconciled in *all* spheres of life. The further dimension to his hopes/predictions for the tenth stage were that this new society, initially established in 'advanced' European countries, would be exported world-wide, such that ultimately there will be 'the abolition of inequality between nations, the progress of equality within each nation, and the true perfection of mankind'.[72] Fittingly, then, in this formulation we have the notion advanced by his predecessor, Turgot, of the emergence of 'one political world',[73] united in a common culture of harmony, justice, prosperity, and tolerance, infused with the 'rationality' of 'scientific' or 'positive' philosophy.

Politics and philosophy of history in Condorcet

Of course, it is not difficult to see Condorcet's philosophy of history as justifying the French Revolution and mapping out its future direction. As such, it might be claimed his philosophy of history is simply apologetics for 1789. However, this is to go too far, and to oversimplify this episode in philosophy of history. First, although the *Esquisse* was indeed written in unusual and ironic circumstances – by 1794 the Revolution was under dire threat from Robespierre's 'reign of terror', as was Condorcet himself – many of the essay's sources of inspiration reach back into Condorcet's earlier life (including Turgot's influence) and are scattered throughout his earlier writings. In this light, the *Esquisse* is much more a broad summation of Enlightenment 'philosophy of history' in general rather than mere contemporary political apologetics.

Second, there is surely much to be said for the common-sense perception that human history has indeed been a history of 'progress' – *and* that overall this progress has been *relentless*, however sporadic and unpredictable. Further, there is surely equally much in Condorcet's observation that this progress can principally be measured in terms of 'the progress of the human *mind*' as it accumulates knowledge and understanding of both the natural and human world. It is true that terrible counter-examples both to the belief in progress, and to the role the human intellect played in it, abound in history (including since Condorcet's times) and this can suggest that he was naively foisting his local Enlightenment optimism upon history as a whole.

However (and third), this would be to neglect the fact that Condorcet did not underplay the darker moments of history. Indeed, he also voiced serious worries about the future, for example about the exploitative nature of European colonisation and the troubles it was storing up for the future of international relations.[74] Far from ignoring negative episodes, he nevertheless remained optimistic – but not because of any thoughtless naivety. Rather, as Manuel observes, 'like many philosophers of history prior to Hegel, [he] made frequent use of a primitive sort of historical dialectic', whereby good grows out of, and because of, evil. For example, the Crusades (contrary to their religious aims) helped undermine superstition by opening up Arab knowledge of the sciences; the discovery of the destructive power of gunpowder enhanced the military role of ordinary soldiers at the expense of the nobility, and repelled the terrible threat of cultural annihilation from invasions by uncivilised barbarians.[75] In short, although as an atheist he does not present history as a theodicy justifying the existence of evil as part of God's plan for man's development, he was approaching that cast of mind which sees evil as *vindicated by history*. To return to the French Revolution, we can be sure Condorcet was as aware as anyone of its darker sides, and yet saw his uneasy present as historically justified.

For the above reasons, then, Condorcet's philosophy of history rises above mere manipulative 'ideology'. It was reflective; it was not *naively* optimistic; and its emphasis upon progress, and the role of the human intellect, cannot be dismissed out-of-hand. Yet this is not to deny that it *is* 'political' in the broad sense of the term, for its message is one of vindicating his present revolutionary times and of encouraging further intellectual and practical struggle. As such, it is highly politically-charged – and from Condorcet's times onwards the link between 'philosophy of history' and political philosophy took firm hold. The latter became 'historicised' in the sense that no respectable political philosophy from the French Revolution onwards could be sustained without the support of some accompanying 'philosophy of history' – whilst the former became 'politicised' in the sense that its exponents from then on derived explicit *political* messages from their efforts.

As we now turn to our final instance of philosophy of history in 'Enlightenment' times, we will find these closing thoughts on Condorcet vindicated by the example of Edmund Burke, for here was a figure whose most famous work, *Reflections on the Revolution in France*, was written some four years *before* Condorcet's *Esquisse*, and in which the symbiosis between political philosophy and philosophy of history is just as clear as in the latter work. Yet the message Burke drew was in stark contrast to Condorcet's.

Edmund Burke

Born in 1729 in Dublin, after graduating from Trinity College in 1748 Burke left Ireland to make his career in London. Making some headway as a writer, he nevertheless graduated towards a political career which found him elected to Parliament by 1766, where he stayed until retiring in 1794, three years before his death in 1797. As a Whig opponent of governmental maladministration, Burke defended the 1776 rebellion of the American colonies, spoke up for his native country when he sensed British policies reflected 'the malignity of the principles of Protestant ascendancy as it affects Ireland',[76] and objected to what he saw as the British exploitation of India through the East India Company. Thus he was a man of 'liberal' principles in today's loose sense of the term. Yet as French republican and revolutionary ideals fomented like-minded movements in England during the 1780s, a different side to Burke's thinking (that for which he has since been famous) was increasingly brought into play. Opposed to *radical* political thinking and its revolutionary practical import, this side of him was galvanised into action in the early months of 1790 as he articulated his detestation of the revolution that had broken out in France in his book, *Reflections on the Revolution in France*, published in November 1790. Because it contained theoretical arguments addressing general principles of politics and history far beyond the immediate context of the French Revolution, it has entered that rarefied catalogue of famous texts where often a book's reputation (and its author's) is more important than the real subtleties of both. In Burke's case, his *Reflections* have established him as 'the father of modern conservatism', because he provided coherent and persuasive arguments for those in modern society who are sceptical of radical political and social thinking and fearful of the sudden, drastic changes which would follow from taking it seriously.[77]

The argument of the Reflections

Burke was not of the cast of mind to present his ideas in logical sequence, but as your guide I will attempt to. We can best begin with his notion that societies (particularly by the eighteenth century) are immensely *complex* phenomena. They comprise political institutions, legal systems, economic structures and practices, and different social classes; religious beliefs, customs and habits, and moral ideas; families, schools, and industries; armed forces, priests, administrators, and private occupations; the fine arts, the natural sciences, literature, and popular culture and entertainment; diverse geographical features and natural resources; and human resources; and a language.

Usually, these complicated societies ('countries', 'nations') nevertheless manage to hold together these multifarious components, whose particular nature and interactions constitute their unique identities. Although societies may contain anomalies, irrationalities, even contradictory elements, they nevertheless continue to function in their way. Indeed, Burke specifically recognises that sentiment and indeed prejudice not only abound in any society, but are integral parts of its identity, significantly helping to make it what it is. The same is true of inequalities, even injustices. There must therefore nevertheless be something 'coherent' about societies, despite their complex intricacies. What lends them their identity and coherence?

To begin in the negative, Burke is clear that societies are not the product of deliberate human design. In this vein he reserves particular criticism for the seventeenth-century 'social contract' foundations of liberal political theory. For Burke this is simply non-historical fiction. Rather,

> [S]ociety is indeed a contract . . .; but the state ought not to be considered as nothing better than a partnership agreement in a trade of pepper and coffee . . ., to be dissolved by the fancy of the parties. It is to be looked on with other reverence. . . . It is a partnership in all science; . . . in all art; . . . in every virtue, and in all perfection. As the ends of such a partnership cannot be obtained in many generations, it becomes a partnership not only between those who are living, but between those who are living, those who are dead, and those who are to be born'.[78]

Similarly, he dismisses the related Benthamite utilitarian view that a society 'is a fictitious body, composed of the individual persons who are . . . its members'.[79] On the contrary (and to coin a phrase), for Burke there is 'such a thing as society'. And this brings us to his positive argument, for he insists that a society is a real organic unity whose identity extends beyond the people who live in it at any one point in time. The term 'organic' is important here, for he means to point not only to the intricacy of any society but also to the idea that it is a complex which has evolved over time. In short, societies are *historical* phenomena which have taken centuries to develop into what they are. They are the work, then, not of human contrivance but of ages of accumulated growth and adaptation to diverse, unforeseeable circumstances. The *immediate* mechanisms involved are the manner in which particular generations find means to respond to contingent problems arising in their society. And this has always been a *practical* matter – not only in itself but also, according to a Burke acutely aware of the unmappable complexities of a society's organic makeup, because it is usually achieved through trial and error. (However, as we shall see, a special kind of insight can also be applied).

> The science of constructing a commonwealth, or renovating it, or reforming it, is . . . not to be taught a priori. Nor is it a short experience that can instruct us in that practical science, because the real effects of moral causes are not always immediate; . . . very plausible schemes, with very pleasing commencements, have often shameful and lamentable conclusions. In states there are often some obscure and almost latent causes . . . on which a very great part of its prosperity or adversity may . . . depend. The science of government being therefore so practical in itself, . . . a matter which requires . . . even more experience than any

person can gain in his whole life, . . . it is with infinite caution that any man ought to venture upon pulling down an edifice which has answered in any tolerable degree for ages the common purposes of society.[80]

Thus societies are evolved phenomena, however 'untidy' the resulting ensemble. The *lessons* of this practical experience in maintaining the coherence and identity of a society are not to be found in any book on statecraft, political science, or ethics – and *certainly* not in the moral catchphrases of temporary dissaffected elements (e.g., 'the rights of man'). 'The pretended rights of these theorists are all extremes; and in proportion as they are metaphysically true, they are morally and politically false'.[81]

Rather, they are ensconced in the existing *traditions* and *conventions* of a society. These encapsulate the hard-won lessons of the past. That which has become conventional has done so because it *works*; likewise, a tradition is by its nature something which has stood the test of time. There is, then, no surer guide to the appropriateness of any particular arrangement in society than its having been *historically* established. For example, those who drew up the Petition of Right against Charles I 'claimed their franchises not on abstract principles "as the rights of men", but as the rights of Englishmen . . . derived from their forefathers. . . . (T)hey preferred this positive . . ., *hereditary* title . . . to that vague speculative right'.[82] It is in this immensely powerful sense, for Burke, that history vindicates the present. Things are as they are at any point in time because that is how they have come to be. In other words, there is 'reason' in history – but not the kind of abstract, scientific 'reason' so lauded by Enlightenment thinkers: rather, something not only different but more profound. And to the extent a society respects its traditions and conventions, it avails itself of this 'reason', this practical wisdom forged by time and circumstance. For a society to neglect this inestimable inheritance by pursuing some allegedly 'rational' principles derived from enthusiasts for radical change would therefore, in fact, be 'unreasonable'.

Does this then mean that a society should never embrace *change*? Burke's answer is clear. Inasmuch as societies have evolved over the ages, this has precisely involved their changing. But these changes have been *adaptations* to circumstances rather than the deliberate replanning of society through human design. And the essence of an adaptive, evolutionary process – in addition to change – is the maintaining of *identity* throughout the process. Any society incapable of change would sooner or later disintegrate in the face of new circumstances. But the slower such change can be, and the smaller in immediate impact, the better for maintaining the identity of that society, given the complexity of its interrelated features. Thus the art of the statesman is, not to resist changing anything, but to conserve the essential identity of society precisely *through* a careful management of change based on respect for the past's legacy. This means, first, that one should not automatically succumb to urges for change which emanate from only this or that present, localised discontent. Second, one should resist all philosophical, 'scientific', or 'rational' schemes for re-constituting society along the lines of some purported perfect model. 'When I hear the simplicity of contrivance aimed at and boasted of in any new political constitutions, I am at no loss to decide that the artificers are grossly ignorant of their trade'.[83] Rather, the art of the statesman depends on a largely intuitive grasp of the manner in which things have come to be as they are in their complex interconnectedness – i.e., on understanding the historical 'reason' in them.

Should readers nevertheless find this 'intuitive' knowledge rather mysterious, consider the analogy of 'knowing' an individual and of 'knowing' how to handle their interests. One does not want a 'scientific' (e.g., biological) account of the individual, nor some guru-guide to 'the perfect human-being'. Rather, one wants to know what makes *that person* tick, so that any proposals one makes about their present problems are indeed appropriate for *that person* (unless one has the audacity to wish to completely transform them into effectively someone else). What could be more suitable as the required knowledge of that person than knowing as much of their *history* as possible? The 'reason' that makes them who they are is contained in their history, and that 'reason' is appropriated by us insofar as we have insight into that history.

Just so with Burke's view of *societies*. Inestimably valuable, when it comes to handling their problems they are complicated phenomena for which 'scientific' or 'philosophical' knowledge is inoperational, despite the conceits of radical (and particularly, revolutionary) thinkers. Rather, it requires having one's finger on the *historical* character of society, whereby one understands the *reason* inherent in the present. Although primarily a political message (Burke's ultimate aversion is to radical change of the formal political constitution itself, as in 1789 France) it is intimately dependent upon a distinctive 'philosophy' of history, whose main features we can now summarise.

For Burke, the notion of 'a history of humankind' was a nonsensical rationalist abstraction. Each society's history is explicable in terms of an evolutionary process (which he sometimes refers to as 'divine', although it adds nothing to his idea) whereby, in adapting to new circumstances, change gradually occurs. For Burke, there is no millennialist perfection towards which history is inevitably moving. Neither is there any pristine 'golden age' to hark back to. Although there is a certain teleology implicit in the idea of an evolutionary process of adaptation, it is by no means clear that 'things get better' as the centuries roll on. All that is clear is that things *change*. And it would seem unlikely that, as of some *necessity*, things would change back to how they were at an earlier stage – so the notion of a history revolving in recurrent cycles is also ruled out in Burke's philosophy. And as for the role of human agency in determining the course of history, his position on this can hardly be overstated. Just as no animal determines its own evolution, (although Darwin's theory of evolution was of course unknown to a Burke long dead) so for Burke no society can determine its own 'evolution' over time. First, this evolution spans numerous generations and is thus unamenable to any one generation's manipulation. Second, since evolution proceeds because of new circumstances (some so apparently slight that they escape notice by those first affected), it is inherently unpredictable. Third, given the strictly *practical* nature of the complex interconnections within societies, no new 'science' could ever so encompass the *ensemble* as to render its development subject to human planning. What human agency *can* achieve, however, is to conserve the holistic identity of a society through the wise introduction of such modifications as are required to meet the contingencies of changing times and unforeseen events. As we have seen, for those who govern, this necessitates patience, restraint and, above all, that special kind of intuitive insight into the historic rationale of why things are as they are.

Thus, although Burke eschewed abstract philosophical concepts, his overall view of history is that societies do 'develop', and that there is a 'logic' underlying this. This 'logic' or 'reason' in history, however, would not seem to be some 'pure' or 'rational' logic (and thus graspable through science or philosophy), nor reducible to a simple formula such as 'the history of progress'. Rather, the 'logic' of history derives from the interplay between the given present identity of a society and the diverse, contingent circumstances it encounters and adapts to in practice. It is thus an 'untidy' logic, inherently unpredictable, and only chartable after the event. In one sense – that is, for the grand and illusory project of 'man' designing and fulfilling his 'destiny' – history thus tells us nothing. But in another sense – that of attaining what *is* possible – it tells us everything.

Conclusion

This last point provides our bridge to the following chapter on perhaps the most explicit and audacious attempt at (speculative) philosophy of history ever undertaken – that of Hegel. In his seminal *History of Political Theory*, Sabine rightly observes that Burke was no philosopher – that although his ideas 'have the consistency that is the stamp of a powerful intelligence and settled moral convictions', 'he could not have given systematic form' to them. Sabine goes on to say: 'But what Burke had taken for granted Hegel tried to prove: that the apparently fragmentary social tradition can be placed in a general system of social evolution'. This is fair comment and a good way of introducing Hegel's political and historical philosophy – but in adding that Burke never thought of this,[84] Sabine might have underestimated Burke's sense of the inherent 'untidiness' of the 'logic' of history. Burke had intuited that the much vaunted 'Reason' of the Enlightenment was as poor a vehicle as it was an arrogant one for understanding the 'logic' of society and the meaning of history. Thus, had he lived to witness Hegel's astonishing attempt to rationalise the 'logic' of history he would doubtless have thought it futile and vain because causing us 'to be entangled in the mazes of metaphysic sophistry'.[85] Whether Hegel's effort helps prove Burke wrong, or instead dramatically vindicates Burke's anti-rationalism, readers can judge for themselves as we now turn to explore Hegel's philosophy of history.

9

HEGEL'S PHILOSOPHY OF HISTORY

Introduction

The scope, rich complexity, and fascination of his ideas, and the profound influence he has exercised, bestow G.W.F. Hegel his reputation as one of the greatest of modern professional philosophers. Although his overall philosophy (incorporating his philosophy of history) generated hostility particularly from the Anglo-American empiricist tradition, it is still studied, argued about, and exploited. Perhaps unusually, Hegel's personal life is unimportant in accounting for his ideas. This may be because it was relatively quiet. He was born in 1770 into a modestly well-off family in the southern German city of Stuttgart, where he was schooled until he went to study theology at Tübingen University. There he pursued his interest in the classical world, and also caught the 'philosophical bug' from his friend Schelling. After graduating in 1793 Hegel worked as a private tutor for seven years – a period of intensive philosophical and religious reflection – before taking up a teaching post at the University of Jena in 1801, then one of the most stimulating centres of German intellectual life. But this same city was to be the battleground of Napoleon's defeat of Prussia in 1806, and when the university was closed under French occupation Hegel soon moved to Nüremburg, leaving an illegitimate son born to his landlady in 1807. Perhaps equally productively it was during these years in Jena that Hegel conceived his fundamental philosophy, publishing his first major work, *Phenomenology of Mind*, in 1807.[1] After eight years as a schoolteacher, during which he wrote *The Science of Logic* (and married, to become the father of three more children, one dying in infancy) he became Professor of Philosophy at Heidelberg University in 1816, a brief prelude to his prestigious appointment in 1818 to the Chair of Philosophy at Berlin University (in Prussia). He remained there, working at different branches of his philosophy until his death in 1831, having published *The Philosophy of Right* in 1821 and leaving copious lecture notes from which other works (including *The Philosophy of History*) were posthumously published.

The influence of Hegel's times

If Hegel's personal life was fairly uneventful, not so his times – and he himself recognised their role in the formation of his ideas. First, he was born at a high point in German philosophical culture, when the philosophy of Kant (1724–1804) exercised the minds of such contemporaries as Fichte (1762–1814) and Schelling (1775–1854). Influenced by Spinoza's ideas, Kant tried to show that reason governs the universe, and developed a *moral* theory centred on the notion of 'freedom', which he construed as individual self-discipline to follow the dictates of reason. He also famously argued that the empirical, material world is inherently unknowable – a mere 'thing in itself'. Otherwise following Kant, Fichte rejected the latter idea and hoped to find the basis for systematising all experience in terms of the confrontation between the freedom inherent in self-consciousness and the 'external' world. Schelling (Hegel's Tübingen friend) pursued these themes, adopting a theory which overcame the opposition between 'subject' (self-consciousness) and 'object' (the 'external' world), resulting in a notion of God as the universe, rather than transcending its laws. Later he altered his philosophy to argue that *human* existence is in fact the Absolute's (or God's) expression of its consciousness of *itself* – and that therefore creative freedom is the essence of humanity. Hegel's thinking matured, then, within a context dominated by these lofty themes of self-consciousness, freedom, the subject-object relation, the nature of ultimate reality, and its relation to our actual ('phenomenological') world (i.e., reality as it appears to us). All these themes are deeply embedded in Hegel's outlook, demonstrating that his thinking is far from original.

Second, an important yet complex influence was 'the Enlightenment' immediately preceding his times. No late eighteenth-century intellectual remained unaffected by its ethos, either to deplore its seeming simplicities or to be inspired (however critically) by its ideals of rationality and progress. Hegel was no exception. However, matters are more complicated because, although primarily considered a Franco-British movement, there was also during the eighteenth century a German 'enlightenment' – the 'Aufklärung'. Although, in particular, its proponents' *historical* approach differed from the French, and found its fulfilment alternatively in early nineteenth-century German romanticism and philosophical idealism (including Hegel and the Rankean school of history[2]), it has been urged that this should not exclude them from the Enlightenment, but encourage us to broaden our conception of it.[3] A complex matter for historians of thought, then, the point is that part of the ethos to which Hegel responded was the work of 'Enlightened thinkers in Germany', since 'the problems Hegel sought to resolve with the dialectical method were clearly posed, though imprecisely solved, by the scholars of the Aufklärung'.[4]

The third influential aspect of his times was their famously *eventful* nature. Hegel was nineteen, at University, when the hugely important French Revolution erupted. Like many Europeans he was enthralled by its ideals of Freedom, Reason, and Progress – inspirations he never abandoned, but within which he was later to find his own sometimes apparently opposite meanings. After its bloody birthpangs came 'the child of the Revolution', Napoleon, and we can only imagine with what fascination Hegel followed his career to its doom, having witnessed in awe the Emperor, 'this world-soul', at his defeat of the Prussian army at Jena in 1806, riding though the streets on his historic mission to change the world. These profound events surrounding his otherwise routine academic life offered Hegel not merely food for thought, but a gargantuan feast for reflection as to their meaning and significance – resulting in a lifetime of philosophical work pervaded by the notions of Freedom, Progress, Reason, portentous political and cultural change, the tragedy of greatness, and the march of history and its relation to ultimate reality – i.e., history's *meaning*.

Introduction to Hegel's thought

It is impossible to understand Hegel's philosophy of history without some grasp of his *overall* philosophical approach, yet this is famously difficult to understand fully. This is partly because his thinking functions at a markedly abstract level – namely, in the domain of ultimate Being, or 'ontology' – where behind the empirical realities we perceive is the higher realm of the logic or 'Reason' pervading existence. It is the bringing together of the world as we know it (its 'phenomenological' character) with this underlying ontological dimension of Absolute Reality, which Hegel calls 'philosophy'. 'Philosophy', then, is the key to understanding reality, for it is his abiding belief that what we call 'existence' or 'actuality' is imbued with Mind (or Reason). The task of 'philosophy' is to discover this Reason inherent in the world as we know it. We may call this Reason (or Mind), 'God', as does Hegel frequently. But he himself argued that *religious* notions of 'God' are but symbolic expressions of rational truths, so when he uses the term 'God' he means it philosophically as one term amongst others (e.g., 'the Absolute') to denote ultimate reality. The *religious* expression of this belief is the symbolic notion that 'God created the world', but even symbolically this is simplistic, vague, and possibly misleading. It is too *simple* because it suggests a one-off act of self-manifestation of Mind, whereas for Hegel 'creation' (i.e., Mind's objectification of itself in/as the actual world) is a process of *development* in distinct stages. It is too vague because it gives no indication of the mechanisms driving this developmental process nor of the instruments employed. And it is *possibly* misleading insofar as it suggests a transcendent Mind or agent, i.e., 'above and beyond' the world, in some undefined sense causing and governing it.

I stress '*possibly*' because this is a controversial aspect of Hegel's philosophy. The issue is this: is Hegel's 'God' or 'Mind' some *transcendent* force, or is it co-equal with the universe as the *immanent* principles of its constitution and workings? This latter theory – namely, equating God with His creation – is called 'pantheism' in theology, and is regarded as religious heresy by Christians. (Both Spinoza and

Schelling, for example, were accused of it.) It is important because, for many, it is the crux on which depends whether Hegel's philosophy is worthy of study or whether it should be dismissed as the indulgences of a philosophical dreamer. Why is this so? Many will think that, if construed as a *transcendent* Being responsible for willing and designing the universe, 'God' should be removed altogether from rational, 'scientific', explanatory discourse (the position of both classical and modern materialists, and atheists) on the grounds either that no such 'Being' exists, or that if it does, its disconnection from the universe other than through an unknowable, hence unintelligible, act of wilful creation makes it an absurd thing to appeal to in trying to *explain* existence.

The alternative is the *immanentist* position, which construes 'God' as synonymous with the known principles inherent in Existence. The analogy of a spontaneously evolved *system* may help. Such a system (e.g., the ecological system) is not designed by anyone, yet the interconnections between its parts can be explained (via cause and effect). Alternatively, however, the different laws interplaying *within* the parts of the system can be seen as implying an *overall* 'logic' which encompasses but is not exhausted by its component parts. In this sense the system is *more* than simply the sum of all its parts interacting individually. Now, the *immanentist* position on 'God' is analogous to construing the universe as 'a system as a whole', and to denoting this by the term 'God' or, philosophically, 'the Absolute', or 'Substance'.[5]

The point of this is that an immanentist concept of 'God' makes the universe far more amenable to *explanation* (both of what goes on in it and of its overall-ness) than the concept of a *transcendent* 'God'. If the latter, it may be good religion but as a philosophy it promises ultimately nothing in terms of rationally explaining existence, and should accordingly be derided (as many have Hegel's philosophy). If the former, however, the apparent absence of the supernatural, coupled with its potential for explanation of the whole (rather than only the interactions of individual things, as, arguably, in modern science), persuades many intellectuals to take such philosophies with the utmost seriousness, as many have Hegel's philosophy.

Whichever interpretation one puts on Hegel in this respect, above all our initial task must be to approach his thinking with this awareness that Hegel did profoundly believe in 'Mind' or 'God'. This so pervades his entire philosophy that, according to one scholar, it causes many to 'believe that in Hegel the profoundest thoughts of God became articulated in man';[6] in other words, that in exposing the nature and workings of 'Mind', Hegel's philosophy is nothing less than 'God' explaining himself *to* himself, i.e., through the vehicle of *Hegel's* thinking!

Mind objectifying itself

To understand Hegel, then, we need to grasp this central notion of 'Mind' objectifying itself. In one sense this is a familiar notion if we leave aside 'Mind' as 'God' or 'the Absolute' and think instead of an individual *human* mind. Here, we can say that any artefact created by an individual is the product of his mind. He has an idea, and 'objectifies' it by making an actual object. The object 'realises' or 'actualises' his idea. Two points can be added to this straightforward example.

To outsiders encountering the artefact, it is often obvious that it is the product of someone's mind. In other cases this may not be obvious, as in an abstract painting mistaken for an accidental spilling of paint. Here, it is up to the art expert to demonstrate it *is* the product of an artist's mind – and he does this by exposing the thought implicit in the artefact. Similarly, whatever topic Hegel gives a philosophical exposition of, be it Nature, history, or the State, in insisting they exemplify Mind he does not ask us simply to *believe* him, but instead to *attend to* his exposition of the 'logic' in things. Importantly, then, the notion that reality exemplifies Mind is not regarded by Hegel as an article of faith: rather, the proof of the pudding is in the eating.

The other point is that, in 'objectifying' his *idea* of something, as in a potter making a pot, that which he makes is *his*, in the double sense that it expresses or 'objectifies' both his idea of the pot and of himself as a potter. It is, then, part of his *self*, if by 'self' we mean that of which we are conscious when we describe ourselves as 'self-conscious'. This shows how the mundane fact of someone making an artefact can be expressed esoterically as an act of 'self-realisation'. The *point* of so trans-posing it is that, in introducing the notions of consciousness, self, objectification, and the subject–object relation, it enables deeper analysis. Let us now go further.

Dialectics

Let us suppose our potter initially only *aspires* to be such. He has yet to actually make a pot. At this point we have to make a supposition crucial to Hegel's approach – namely, that his first attempt to make a pot is a crude effort. For example, he gets the shape right, but in order to do so has had to make the body excessively thick. Thus, surveying his pot, he does not want to be pinned down by this object – it is not the full expression of his idea of the pot, and hence neither of himself as a potter. He considers it, to that extent, an alien object, not *his*. (In Hegelian terms, his act of self-objectification turns out to be an act of self-*alienation*). Thus he rejects (or 'negates') this first pot, and makes another which corrects its deficiency by making its sides less thick. But in doing so, the pot lacks the strength to sustain its original shape. Like the first effort, it also is a one-sided, incomplete objectification of his idea. What is required is thus a *third* pot which 'negates' the deficiencies of both the first and second, and instead synthesises their *positive* aspects, where shape and thickness combine successfully in a new effort. As such the third pot is not only different from both the earlier ones – it is more complex and more fully objectifies the potter's idea of a pot. But it has not sprung from nowhere. On the contrary, its 'logic' is precisely the product of that *prior* progression whereby the first pot generated the second, and the second the third. In that sense we may call it the *necessary* consequence of the *logical development* of the potter's idea, not only of the pot, but of himself as an actual potter.

To complete the analogy, we may suppose this third pot, although resolving the contradictions generated by the first two, is itself still less than the completely satisfactory actualisation of the potter's idea. For example, it may still be deficient in aspects of its functionality or of its external decoration. The third pot thus becomes a new starting point, (now from a higher stage), which through the same 'logic' of producing and resolving contradictions will achieve a yet higher, even more complex, stage – and so on, until the point is reached where *all* the apparently conflicting features of 'the perfect pot' are reconciled and superseded in the final creation. In surveying it, the potter at last takes satisfaction in his 'self-objectification' as a potter. This last pot is, then, a complex artefact which has worked out such apparently diverse features as shape, thickness, function, colour, and so on, into a coherent whole – i.e., there is more to 'the perfect pot' than meets the eye!

It is just this way of looking at things Hegel calls 'dialectics'. This term is reminiscent of its classical Greek usage referring to 'argument', where (like Socrates) one would establish the truth about something by raising a point, contradicting it, finding some common ground, then contradicting that, and so on, until all the apparently opposite perceptions would play their part in the full exploration of the truth. It is in this (now Hegelian) sense that our potter's pots are 'dialectical' in nature. Rather than given, fixed objects (examples of Being), each is replete with the tension of change. In other words, each is a manifestation of *Becoming*. The proper understanding of this or that pot requires, then, not only that we understand it *is* a pot rather than an arbitrary natural object – i.e., that it is a product of someone's mind. It also requires that we penetrate to the *idea* which the potter is trying to actualise, and thus see this or that pot as, so to speak, an unstable thing caught up in the process of the 'coming-to-be' of that idea which the potter aspires to fully objectify.

Impersonal 'Reason'

So far, in conveying Hegel's conviction of an underlying 'logic' to existence, we have used the potter analogy. This shows some of Hegel's meaning, including dialectics. But Hegel goes further. We may observe from our potter analogy that, although the dynamic driving his successive 'objectifications' comes from *him*, there is a sense in which he is not in control of the process because the implications of his idea of the pot seem to take over the process as *they* seem to determine his successive efforts. It is almost as if the potter becomes a prisoner of the process which he consciously initiated but unknowingly fulfils.

It is to just this *impersonal* level that Hegel moves, for in his philosophy the logic embedded in the actual world is not that which human-beings impose upon it through their activities. Rather, the mind endowing the world with rationality is a metaphysical entity, the 'World-Mind', the 'Absolute', (or 'God'). Thus we need to move from the analogy of a *human-being* creating an artefact to a more advanced one where the human mind (although involved as an *instrument*) plays no conscious role in the gradual unfolding of the logic behind reality, but where the 'Idea' being actualised belongs to impersonal 'Mind'.

Suppose two people, Peter and Paul, entirely in the abstract – neither has ever had contact with another person. Suppose they simply appear on an island, and meet. Initially each may like, dislike, or be indifferent to the other. Let us suppose that, at some time, they 'like' each other. Peter asks Paul to help him chop down a tree; (he expects Paul to help him because he knows Paul likes him). Paul, surprised, says 'No, I'm too tired'. Peter is offended and is thus unpleasant to Paul. Paul finds Peter's new antagonism uncomfortable since, after all, he had enjoyed Peter's company. Paul therefore apologises and helps cut down the tree. (Paul has realised his tiredness is not as important as their liking each other). Peter and Paul continue to meet, and help each other with their tasks. They thus begin to rely on each other's help, and get to know each other better, so that they feel they can take their mutual help and liking for granted. One day Peter is ill, and correspondingly ill-tempered. He tells Paul to do all his tasks for him that day. Paul, taken aback, says 'Don't *tell* me what to do! If you ask me, I'll do it'. Peter apologises, and asks Paul nicely. Paul does Peter's tasks, and cares for him while he is ill. Peter is truly grateful, the experience cementing their mutual respect, trust, affection, and support. They become life-long friends.

The point of this little fable is that at the beginning neither Peter nor Paul had even met anyone before, but at the end they were true friends. In understanding this outcome, at no point in the story was it necessary that either player knew what friendship is, nor aspired to it. Yet the 'logic' of their encounters and immediate impulses drew them on from merely 'liking' each other (a merely *implicit* idea of friendship) to a higher relationship which finally fulfils the complex requirements of 'true' friendship (i.e., making it *explicit*). It is true our little story contained two crisis moments, but it appears these were *necessary* to the further development of the players' relationship, and thus ultimately powerfully productive. To an extent, they also appeared as consequences of the previous (happier) situations, such that overall we might recognise an Hegelian dialectic at work, including 'the power of the negative'. And this is partly the point of the analogy.

But more than this, there is a sense in which the true subject of the story is neither Peter nor Paul, but *the idea of friendship*. This idea was not something Peter or Paul were either conscious of or intending to achieve. They were merely the instruments the idea employed to become actualised. Unlike our potter analogy, here 'the idea' being 'objectified' owes nothing to human intentions. Rather, it is part of a completely *impersonal* mind. Pre-empting his *Philosophy of History*, we can say that in its Introduction Hegel devotes considerable space to explaining (similar to Vico) that, although men's pursuit of their needs, passions, and convictions might seem to determine the course of history, these 'manifestations of vitality on the part of individuals and peoples, in which they seek and satisfy their own purposes, are, at the same time, the means and instruments of a higher and broader purpose of which they know nothing – which they realise unconsciously'.[7] Although Hegel does recognise certain exceptional people as 'world-historical individuals' (he cites Alexander the Great, Caesar, and Napoleon) even these 'had no consciousness of the general Idea they were unfolding'. However, they were remarkable for having 'an insight into the requirements of the time – what was ripe for development', and may thus even be excused for actions judged immoral by ordinary standards.[8]

These latter observations, however, go beyond the scope of our little island-story, to which we return to extract another of its implications – namely, that in demonstrating the true nature of friendship, the story only shows this at the *end* of what has been a dialectical process. Were we, without hindsight, to have stopped the story half-way through, we would not know what it was about – or rather, be under the illusion it is about Peter or Paul. But at the end one can say: '*Now* I see what this is the story of'. This insight enables one also to comprehend what was truly going on half-way through the story, removing one's previous illusions by showing what was irrelevant because devoid of significance in the dialectical unfolding of the idea of friendship.

Our little story is, then, markedly selective, and this exemplifies what might be seen as a problem endemic to Hegel's approach. Because 'philosophy' is the revelation of Mind at work in the world, then only those things which are dialectical moments of the 'objectification' of Mind are philosophy's concern. Other phenomena are mere 'appearances', which can be studied from numerous viewpoints – for example, what kind of tree did Peter and Paul chop down?, what was the nature of Peter's illness?, and so on. But such discourse is not philosophy because it is not cast in terms of revealing the operation of Mind. Thus numerous things are removed from 'philosophical' understanding and relegated to other discourses. Only that which is 'rational' (i.e., a manifestation of Mind) is 'real'; conversely, only that which is 'real' is 'rational' – a double dictum Hegel famously formulated.[9]

But it could be argued that this makes Hegel's philosophy one giant tautology, since to claim the world exemplifies Mind is only acceptable if the world can be so shown. But in Hegel only *part* of the world can be so shown – namely, that which suits the showing. The rest remains inaccessible to philosophy, which many think should explain all. Indeed, we will see him putting huge restrictions on what *historical* material is relevant to *philosophy* of history.

Alternatively it could be that, rather than presenting an empty tautology, Hegel is right to so differentiate things in the world. Let us not forget his own claim that he is not suggesting this a priori, but that the logic which pertains to (some) things is demonstrable – in just the same way as we claimed an observer can show that *this* object is, in fact, a pot whereas *that* object (e.g., a piece of mud) is meaningless – i.e., 'the proof of the pudding is in the eating'.

However one sees this, it as well to raise the issue now, when it already surfaces, since it is a problem from the outset and permeates all his subsequent arguments.

To summarise, then; the overall point of our little island-story is to suggest an analogy for Hegel's notion that ultimate reality is Mind, and that the logic pervading the phenomena of the actual world is the product of the inherent dynamic in (impersonal) Mind to objectify its nature and Ideas. The range and nature of these Ideas are expounded in different parts of Hegel's philosophy (whereby the corresponding features of the actual world are explained, including physical nature, consciousness, art, religion, politics – and, indeed, 'history'). When considering an aspect of the actual world, then, it is crucial to discern *what* Idea is being realised in order to comprehend the reality underlying its appearance.

But how one does this is difficult to ascertain, and here we should leave analogies and let an example from Hegel speak for itself. Perhaps the clearest exposition he gives of this exercise is his discerning of the Idea underlying *politics* in his *Philosophy of Right*. Also, because *The Philosophy of History* is most intimately related to the former work, it is doubly helpful to summarise his text.

Hegel's *Philosophy of Right*

Right, will, and freedom

In German, 'Recht' (Right) means both the (abstract) *moral* notion of 'right' and actual *law*. Law, then, is the *objective* form 'right' assumes in the real world. As such, it is inseparable from what we loosely call 'politics', and Hegel's *Philosophy of Right* is his political philosophy. Thus the aspect of the actual world under Hegel's scrutiny (i.e., politics) is clear enough, as (provisionally) is the sense in which it manifests an 'Idea' – i.e., the idea of right. But since 'any genuine philosophy must in Hegel's view form a systematically and organically developed whole',[10] it is crucial for Hegel not to take the idea of 'right' as given, but to show it as part of Mind. He had already done this in his *Encyclopaedia of the Philosophical Sciences* (1817), where he tried to show that Mind is driven to express its nature through a dialectical process which 'passes in its development from feeling, through representative thinking, to thinking proper'[11] – consciousness. From there, moving to sense-perception and on to self-consciousness, Hegel arrives at 'appetite' or 'desire' as the form in which *self*-consciousness is first objectified[12] – in other words, the *will*. The emergence of 'will' is a crucial stage in Mind's development.

Now, we may recall Rousseau arguing that *force* and *right* can have no connection, since a forced act cannot issue from a sense of duty. Thus, moral action must be an act of free will. Hegel exploits this. He tells us that 'the basis of right is, in general, mind'. Next, that 'its precise place and point of origin is the will' (i.e., exploiting the above). In other words, in understanding 'right' as it appears in the world, its *philosophical* referent (as stemming from Mind) is the *will*, as an aspect of mind. It is thus *this* aspect of Mind we need to explore in understanding 'politics' or 'right'. To continue: for Hegel, not unreasonably, the essence of 'will' is its freedom (i.e., compulsion is foreign to its nature). Thus he continues; '[t]he will is free, so that freedom is both the substance of right and its goal'. It therefore follows (returning to the actual world) that 'the system of right [the law and the constitution] is the realm of freedom made actual, the world of mind brought forth out of itself like a second nature'.

Here, then, is an example of how Hegel, in looking at an aspect of our actual world, derives what Idea is being 'objectified'. But our two analogies should remind us that, in Hegel, no Idea springs forth fully realised in the actual world. Just so with the Idea of Right. It is a complex idea requiring a dialectical process via which it manifests itself. This accounts for the diverse political systems in the actual world, whereby even primitive examples have some positive element in them, whilst that which *fully* realises 'freedom' is a complex of apparently contradictory features. But wherein lies this complexity?

The will is essentially free. It must contain 'the element of pure indeterminacy'. On the other hand, the will must will *something*, for otherwise it would remain an empty potential. Thus it is driven to will an object, (for example, 'I will that apple'). Yet in thus activating itself, it is now pinned down in the external object and (by analogy with our potter's first pot) is driven to recoil from its own 'objectification'. Thus because will is essentially free, its logic demands that it is not lost in that which it wills, but that it reflect back into itself, becoming 'indifferent to this determinacy' into which it entered. It must, in short, become *self*-determined, such that in willing this or that, 'it knows it as something which is its own, . . . by which it is not constrained and in which it is confined only because it has put itself in it'.[13] This implies that the will is driven forward (via negative moments) to find an 'object' which satisfies its nature as both *free* and *actualised* in the real world.

Having abstractly sketched these fundamentals of the complexity of the Idea of Freedom (or of Right – an unresolved ambiguity in Hegel), the remainder of the *Philosophy of Right* involves Hegel in correlating them with aspects of the world as we know it. Because Hegel's philosophy of *history* is so intimately concerned with 'Freedom' and its relation to *the state*, its proper understanding necessitates a résumé of these key ingredients in advance.

Property and crime

The most primitive expression of the will's freedom is where someone wills an external object (e.g., 'I will that apple'), and this is the basis of the individual's *right* to private property. Now, the individual can *contract* to trade his property for someone else's. This is crucial because it introduces a context where the object of a person's will is no longer simply an external object, but the other *person's* will. Both people will that each respect the other as property-owners – and 'this relation of will to will is the true and proper ground in which freedom is existent'. As a salutary example of human-beings being merely the unconscious *vehicle* of Mind's self-development, Hegel adds: '[r]eason makes it just as necessary for men to enter into contractual relationships . . . as to possess property. While all they are conscious of is that they are led to make contracts by need in general . . . the fact remains that they are led to do this by reason implicit within them, i.e., by the Idea of the . . . existence of free personality'.[14]

The problem with a contract, however, is that it can be broken. This introduces the notion of non-malicious 'Wrong', or even worse, where a person *forcefully* deprives someone of his property, 'Crime'. This is ultimately a self-contradiction on behalf of the criminal, because 'it is an expression of a will which annuls the expression . . . of a will'.[15] Such 'wrong' or 'crime' cries out to be corrected. (Indeed, Hegel claims it is the *right* of the criminal to be punished). But such corrections can take the form of individual *revenge* which, meted out differently by different people, can sometimes be seen as 'wrong' by others.

'Morality' and conscience

What people therefore yearn for is a *common* notion of right and wrong – what Hegel calls 'morality'. In short, we have arrived at a context where, via the unconscious vehicle of *men's* wills, *the* will now expresses itself in willing that *all* will the same – i.e., it 'wills the universal as such'.[16] Here, Hegel's referent in the actual world is that people have a *conscience*, or sense of what is morally good. Yet because conscience, albeit directed to the Good, is only a subjective, inward impulse, it can at the extreme deceive one into thinking the satisfaction of one's *personal* ends is the ultimate good. Not only does Hegel dismiss such thinking as self-contradictory, sophistical, and hypocritical,[17] he adds that it is 'potentially evil'. 'Evil', then, is qualitatively worse than 'wrong' and 'crime' since it is the *conscientious* dismissal of the *common* Good and, instead, the 'elevating above the universal the self-will of private particularity . . .'.[18]

Evil (just as 'wrong' and 'crime') cries out to be defeated. Now, because the potential for 'evil' emerges from the same source as conscience, (namely, a subjective conviction of 'the good'), it is precisely the *subjectivity* of conscience which has to be overcome. What is required (metaphysically) is that the Idea of Right is instead embedded in *objective* institutions which embody a moral structure. Mere conscience is not enough.

Ethical Life – the family

In turning to this *objective* arena of (moral) institutions, Hegel calls it 'Ethical Life', i.e., 'the objective ethical order, which comes on the scene in place of good in the abstract'.[19]

Because most natural and immediate, the first manifestation of this higher stage of Right is the family, which Hegel sees structured on (heterosexual) monogamy and the rearing of children. Here is an *objective* moral order where, 'in a family, one's frame of mind is to have self-consciousness of one's individuality *within* this unity . . ., with the result that one is in it not as an independent person but as a member'.[20]

211

The positive side to this is that 'the will' now has for its object an actual, concrete context made up of a *unity* of *wills*.

However, the family is *too much* of a unity since it restricts the development of each member's individual, subjective freedom. Given the bonds of duty, and as a practical environment, the family does not provide the context of individual ambition and the diverse opportunities needed for a person's particularity to blossom. Thus children, once 'educated to freedom of personality',[21] naturally leave the family and launch out into the wider world.

Hegel is referring to 'society at large' and calls it 'Civil Society'. Thus, 'civil society' may appear the supreme structure fulfilling individuals' freedom. Yet, in their turn, features of 'civil society' require negating, resulting in the highest structure of all, 'the State'. Why is this so?

Ethical life – 'Civil society'

For Hegel, civil society has two contradictory aspects. While giving full scope to the individual's freedom to pursue his own aims, this arena only functions precisely because everyone else pursues *their* own self-interest. Without each other, this arena would be an empty opportunity. Thus there is an implicit *universality* to civil society. This shows itself inasmuch as 'the entire complex is built up into particular systems of needs, means, and types of work . . . in other words, into class-divisions'.[22] These generate their own public organisations to promote their interests. This entire system of *inter*dependence thus requires a system of justice to enforce positive law regarding the rights of individuals and their organisations. Hence this implicit universality becomes completely *explicit* in a public authority to safeguard the system as a whole – and it is here that 'the sphere of civil society passes over into the state'.[23]

Without the state, civil society could become a turbulent arena of the assertion of self-interest where injustice, the power of the stronger, and even anarchy hold sway. Thus its logic paves the way for a separate, qualitatively superior organisation above the diverse components of civil society.

Ethical life – 'the state'

Metaphysically speaking, then, what Hegel calls 'the modern state' (by which he means some kind of constitutional monarchy) is the end-journey of the self-development of the freedom of the will. As Hegel puts it, 'self-consciousness in virtue of its sentiment towards the state finds in the state, as its essence and the end and product of its activity, its substantive freedom'.[24] Although referring here to *Mind's* self-conscious freedom, he also means that its final objectification is exemplified by patriotism, construed as peoples' willing and rational recognition that they belong, and have their ultimate duty, to their state.

212

Thus, in the actual world, a genuinely universal will with a genuinely universal object has emerged – the state – via the phenomenon of the patriotic citizen who feels his freedom realised (rather than restricted) in his dutiful obligation to the state. In words echoing Burke's disgust at 'social contract' theories of the state, Hegel says:

> If the state is confused with civil society, and if its specific end is laid down as the security and protection of property and personal freedom, then the interest of the individuals as such becomes the ultimate end of their association, and it follows that membership of the state is something optional. But the state's relation to the individual is quite different from this. Since the state is mind objectified, it is only as one of its members that the individual himself has objectivity, genuine individuality, and an ethical life.

The state, then, is the context where 'freedom comes into its supreme right', and accordingly it 'has supreme right against the individual, whose supreme duty is to be a member of the state'.[25]

If this last phrase seems ominous in the light of twentieth-century totalitarianism, the attentive reader will know better than to tar Hegel with this brush. True, he elevates the state above all other objective moral contexts, but we must bear in mind that, as we will see in his philosophy of history, he is lauding the *modern* state as the culmination of an historical process whose metaphysical 'truth' is the full realisation of *freedom*, not the ghastly twentieth-century experiments in extinguishing it. On this point, and also as a summary of his overall political theory, we may leave the *Philosophy of Right* with Hegel's own words:

> The state is the actuality of concrete freedom. But concrete freedom consists in this, that personal individuality and its particular interests not only achieve their complete development and gain explicit recognition for their right (as they do in the . . . family and civil society), but . . . they know and will the universal; they even recognise it as their own substantive mind; they take it as their end and aim and are active in its pursuit.[26]

Hegel's *The Philosophy of History*

Hegel had already outlined his views on philosophy of history in the closing section of *Philosophy of Right* (having indicated its metaphysical foundations as early as 1807 in the section on 'Spirit' in his *Phenomenology of Mind*). But it was only after the former's publication in 1821 that he prepared its systematic treatment. This was delivered as a lecture course throughout the 1820s, and published posthumously from his, and students', notes firstly in 1837, and then (newly edited) in 1840 by his son Karl.[27] It begins with a long introduction where Hegel explains the metaphysical basis of 'world-history', followed by chapters covering the different stages in actual history.

'*Spirit*'

Hegel's overall idea is that a *principle* underlies world-history which *determines* its course and displays its *meaning*. At its heart is what Hegel calls 'Geist', translated as 'Mind' or 'Spirit'. However, the latter is more useful in the context of Hegel's philosophy of history. What does he mean by 'Spirit'? We have seen that, for Hegel, existence manifests 'Absolute Mind' or 'Reason' – and have pursued one example of this, namely, the political world as the Idea of Right. Now, unlike the Idea of Right, which is a *specific* 'product' of Absolute Mind, 'Spirit' is an entire *dimension* of the latter's self-development; namely, when it arrives at *self*-consciousness. Here we need to recall Hegel's overall philosophical system of reality. This includes the properties of Matter which, according to Hegel, are governed by the principle of striving towards Unity. 'The essence of Matter is Gravity', says Hegel (and if Matter ever achieved its Idea – Unity – it would disappear, as it were, down a 'black hole' of gravity!).[28] But Matter is only one dimension of the objectification of Reason. From the first stirrings of existence eventually comes consciousness, and then *self*-consciousness, a qualitatively higher dimension of Being which Hegel calls 'Spirit'.

Now, 'consciousness of one's own being' is described by Hegel as 'self-contained existence' independent of anything external to it. It thus 'has its centre in itself', and 'this is Freedom, exactly'. The freedom that is Spirit, then, 'is to be displayed as coming to a consciousness of itself (for it is in its very nature, self-consciousness) and thereby realising its existence'.[29] It is this very journey which forms world-history.

It would be wrong, therefore, to regard self-consciousness as a static frame of mind. On the contrary, because 'Spirit *knows itself*, . . . it involves an appreciation of its own nature, as also an energy enabling it to realise itself; to make itself *actually* that which it is *potentially*'.[30] Seen in terms comparing humans and animals, this becomes clearer. For Hegel, animals are not 'free', for in lacking consciousness of self, they cannot make their own aims the object of their will and activity. Rather, they do not *have* their 'own' aims at all – they do not reorganise their world. As Hegel puts it: 'what I will I hold before my mind as an idea; it is the object of my thought. An animal acts on instinct, is driven by an inner impulse . . . , but it has no will, since it does not bring before its mind the object of its desire'.[31] A human-being, however, in being self-conscious, construes aims in accord with his idea of 'himself'. It is in *this* sense that human-beings manifest the freedom that is the essence of Spirit. (This allows us to appreciate Sibree, in his translation of *The Philosophy of History*, where he defends his choice of the word 'Spirit' rather than 'Mind' by quoting the Biblical passage, 'Their horses are flesh and not *spirit*').[32]

214

'Spirit' and World History

The above means there is a specific aspect of the actual world, intimately dependent upon the constructive energy inherent in humans' being self-conscious, which is explicable in terms of 'Spirit' actualising its essential nature – i.e., Freedom. What is this aspect of the actual world? It is nothing less than what Hegel calls World History, by which he primarily means its *political* history. An explanation of the term 'political history' should clarify matters.

First, it is *history* because (as already seen) no Idea or feature of Absolute Mind realises itself all at once. 'Spirit' is no exception. Its manifestation, in involving a process over time, is 'historical' in that general sense of the term. But it is also 'historical' in the *narrower* sense, where we restrict the term 'history' to the *human* world – for, as we have seen, 'Spirit' is solely manifested in *human* life.

Second, it is *political* history, because although human history incorporates numerous aspects of life, the essence of 'Spirit' is Freedom – and we have already established from Hegel's *Philosophy of Right* that this Idea is manifested in *political* structures. In short, the latter work explains the inner dialectical *logic* of the Idea of Freedom, culminating in the (modern) State. On the other hand, *The Philosophy of History* explains the *historical* progression of political structures, again focused on 'the State', but now in terms of its development from primitiveness to maturity.

In tracing this (earthly) history, Hegel thus understands himself to be revealing 'the destiny of the spiritual World', its 'final cause' (i.e., its teleology), which he finds 'to be the consciousness of its own freedom on the part of Spirit, and *ipso facto*, the *reality* of that freedom'. Thus, 'Universal History . . . is the exhibition of Spirit in the process of working out the knowledge of that which it is potentially'.[33] So Hegel insists that, in considering history *philosophically*, we should concentrate on the heart of the matter, the above 'sole aim of Spirit' – which is to actualise Freedom. Amidst the myriad of events intertwined in history, including tragedies and horrors, 'this is the only aim that sees itself realised and fulfilled; the only pole of repose amid the ceaseless change of events and conditions, and the sole efficient principle that pervades them'.[34] In short, we need to learn how to see the wood for the trees.

Hegel's method

For Hegel, then, world-history is the arena on which Spirit's self-consciousness is gradually realised through 'a series of increasingly adequate expressions' of its Idea of Freedom.[35] Although we have yet to explore how this relates to the actual *content* of 'world-history', we have identified the *general* area Hegel is referring to – political history, especially 'the State' – and why; namely, that this aspect of history can only come about because of that property in man we call 'self-consciousness'. We have seen why this overall idea seemed so obvious to Hegel – i.e., we cannot but take account of the *fact* of complexedly developed political systems (centred on law, duties, morality, rights) completely absent from animal life. The point is, what do we make of this fact? How do we account for it?

This returns us to Hegel's method. Having boldly announced that 'the only Thought which Philosophy brings . . . to the contemplation of History, is the simple conception of *Reason*; that Reason is the Sovereign of the World; that the history of the world, therefore, presents us with a rational process',[36] Hegel nevertheless says 'yet I am not obliged to make any such preliminary demand upon your faith'. Rather, he claims that the philosophical basis underlying history 'is only an inference from the history of the World', and as such is 'the *result of the investigation* we are about to pursue'. The notion that history is the rational unfolding of World-Spirit 'must present itself as the ultimate *result* of History. But we have to take the latter as it is. We must proceed historically – empirically'. The only reason that he, Hegel, knows or 'infers' the resulting philosophical framework is 'because I have traversed the entire field'.

He is claiming we should study history *empirically* – but that when we do so, certain facts will/should stare us in the face, crying out for explanation. In this case, it is the distinctiveness of 'the State' as a phenomenon in the world, and its historical progression. Thus the only *inference* which makes sense is that which Hegel draws – i.e., the facts prove his philosophical theory. Put in this way, he seems to be appealing to an empirical methodology of science – namely, that one begins with no presuppositions, but studies the facts, after which one construes the most likely hypothesis to explain them. Otherwise, if one *begins* with an hypothesis, the danger is one distorts the facts to 'prove' it.

However, this is not Hegel's position. Rather, prior to insisting he is not asking his students to accept anything on faith, he nevertheless expressed the hope that, 'If the clear idea of Reason is not already developed in our minds, in beginning the study of Universal History, we should at least have the firm, unconquerable faith that Reason *does* exist there . . .'.[37] This perhaps puts a different light on his subsequent protestations, and later in the Introduction he clarifies the matter by claiming the investigator into history should not simply uncover and register the facts, but that 'it is of importance that the essential should be distinguished . . . in contrast with the so-called non-essential'. This requires 'an intimate acquaintance with the Idea. The investigator must be familiar a priori (if we like to call it so) with the whole circle of conceptions to which the principles in question belong'.

So here Hegel accepts the need for a pre-existing analytical framework with which to approach 'the facts'. But he does not conceive of this framework as some kind of (a priori) hypothesis we need to accept on faith. Rather, he claims it derives from established principles gained from Philosophy, and cites the example of the scientist, Kepler, as an analogy. The latter 'must have been familiar *a priori* with ellipses, with cubes and squares, and with ideas of their relations, before he could discover, from the empirical data, those immortal "Laws" [of planetary motion] of his. . . . He who is unfamiliar with the science that embraces these abstract elementary conceptions, is as little capable . . . of understanding those Laws, as of discovering them'. The same applies to the study and understanding of history, says Hegel. Thus those who criticise him for introducing 'the so-called a priori method, and the attempt to insinuate ideas into the empirical data of history', are suffering from 'a want of acquaintance with the ideas that relate to' what is *essential*. This is, 'in view of the History of the World in general – the Consciousness of Freedom, and the phases which this consciousness assumes in developing itself'.[38]

In short, Hegel is claiming that just as everyone accepts that the physical world works according to 'laws', so does the historical world. And just as it is crucial to study the physical world empirically, so it is the historical world. But it is equally crucial to approach the physical world with an established abstract analytical framework – and so it is for the historical world. And this, I suggest, is for now as far as we can go in vindicating Hegel's methodology of studying, and understanding, 'history', (although we will revisit the topic in our Conclusion). The *logic* of his argument may deserve more respect than most hard-headed practising historians award it. After all, what is the *point* of studying history, and how *does* one separate the 'meaningful' ('the essential') from the surrounding kaleidoscope of events? On the other hand, the *substance* of his argument must remain dubious. The abstract principles Kepler employed were already 'proved', unlike Hegel's philosophy of Absolute Mind and Spirit's Idea of Freedom. Yet, with a confidence as inspiring to some as it is offensive to others, Hegel awards the principles of his overall philosophy the same 'truth' status as the tried and tested principles of Euclidean geometry.

The State and 'World History'

From the preceding it has become clear why, for Hegel, 'world-history' is *essentially* to do with 'Spirit', and why this implies focusing on 'the state' in history – 'Law, Morality, Government, and they alone, [are] the positive reality and completion of Freedom'. Yet in The Philosophy of History Hegel adopts a broader notion of 'the state' than in the Philosophy of Right, for in addition to the state's formal (constitutional) features is the entire moral ethos of a nation which has given rise to the state and which it, in turn, sustains. The state 'is the moral Whole',[39] and any particular state 'is an individual totality, of which you cannot select any particular side . . . and deliberate . . . respecting it in that isolated form'.[40] Rather, 'the State . . . is . . . the basis and centre of the other concrete elements of the life of a people – of Art, of Law, of Morality, of Religion, of Science'.[41]

Having thus broadened the significance of 'the state' to include a people's culture, and hence potentially expanded the historical content to be included in his philosophy of history, Hegel's insistence on 'the state' nevertheless causes him to list a series of exclusions which may invite incredulity from historians unless they happen to agree with his philosophical reason. Because the State is 'the basis and centre' of a nation's culture, 'in the history of the world, only those peoples can come under our notice which form a state'. Since 'nations may have passed a long time before arriving at this their destination' (statehood), it follows first that such 'ante-historical periods' must be excluded from World-history.[42] Thus those periods – 'centuries or millennia . . . which may have been filled with revolutions, nomadic wanderings, and the strangest mutations', fall outside of consideration. So, second, do records of 'family memorials, patriarchal traditions' and other matters 'confined to the family and the clan'.

Third, there are countries of his own time which Hegel excludes from having played any part in World-history because they never formed proper 'states'. India is a prime and interesting example in Hegel's mind, for he is respectful of 'the treasures of Indian literature', and of 'a land so rich in intellectual products, and those of the profoundest order of thought'. Yet he claims that the caste system, based solely on 'natural distinctions', prevented 'the element of morality' from developing in Indian political institutions.[43]

Fourth, Hegel boldly excludes two entire regions, the 'frigid' and the 'torrid' zones, where 'the locality of World-historical peoples cannot be found'. This is because peoples in these 'extreme zones' are unable to escape the 'pressing needs' of Nature, being 'constantly impelled to direct attention' to it. Thus, 'man cannot come to free movement; cold and heat are here too powerful to allow Spirit to build up a world for *itself*'. Authentic morality and ethical life (the preconditions of statehood) are unable to develop, and thus the peoples of these zones 'have to be excluded once and for all from the drama of the World's History'. Instead, 'the true theatre of History is therefore the temperate zone',[44] (and even here, Hegel restricts this to the northern half because, unlike the southern half which 'runs out into many points', as a continental mass it better enabled communication and migrations).

So far, then, it seems his insistence on 'the state' as the *essential* in World-history has persuaded Hegel to exclude a vast amount of historical content as 'inessential'. But more than this, he narrows his focus even further to only those 'states' which have played *significant* roles in world-history – namely, those which fully manifest a recognisable stage in the unfolding of the logic of Spirit, whose essence is Freedom. To see why this is so takes us now beyond the general principles of his philosophy of history to its actual historical content.

National Spirits

We have already noted Hegel's larger, holistic notion of a 'State' incorporating the 'culture' of a nation, and his notion that individuals' immersion in this context gives them their very being. He develops this further. Not only does the state award them their rights, but 'its natural features, its mountains, air, and waters, are *their* country'. Also, the history of their state – 'what their ancestors have produced' – constitutes 'their deeds' and 'belongs to them'. Because of this, Hegel refers to 'the spirit of *one* People', or 'the Spirit of the State', as being specific to them. It is 'One Individuality', including its religion, art, philosophy, science, and mechanical skills.

218

Taken together, these form the 'particular National Genius', and each 'is to be treated as only One Individual in the process of Universal History'.

Now, the 'boundless impulse of the World-Spirit'[45] is to successively realise the different stages of Freedom and is thus manifested, at each stage, by the most advanced 'national spirit'. Indeed, this notion draws him into ideas many regard as deeply unpalatable, because for Hegel the inexorable, impersonal nature of the project of the 'World-Spirit' appears to justify overriding 'ordinary' moral judgements. This is at its clearest in his *Philosophy of Right* where he says: '[t]he nation to which is ascribed a moment of the Idea . . .' (i.e., which represents a stage in the Spirit's development) '. . . is entrusted with giving complete effect to it in the advance of the self-developing self-consciousness of the world mind. This nation is dominant in world history during this one epoch. . . . In contrast with this its absolute right of being the vehicle of this present stage . . ., the minds of the other nations are without rights . . .'. And, 'the same consideration justifies civilised nations in regarding and treating as barbarians those who lag behind them in institutions which are the essential moments of the state'.[46]

It is with such ideas in mind that, having dismissed the 'frigid and torrid zones' from any significance in history (whether they contained states or not), Hegel also dismisses the native cultures of North, Central, and South America, Australia, and Africa. America, he tells us, 'has always shown itself physically and psychically powerless, and still shows itself so'. He claims the native Americans showed 'a mild and passionless disposition, want of spirit, and a crouching submissiveness', concluding that 'the inferiority of these individuals in all respects . . . is very manifest'. This enabled Europeans to dominate the native Americans, with the result that 'what takes place in America, is but an emanation from Europe'.

But he notes large differences between North America and the remainder of the continent. The former became one state and is prosperous, whilst the latter consists of numerous republics mostly dependent on military force, and 'their whole history is a continued revolution'. Hegel attributes this partly to the fact that Southern and Central America were conquered (by Spain) whereas North America was *colonised*. Also, the latter, 'although a land of sects of every name, is yet fundamentally Protestant', whereas the former are Catholic. This last may be the reason Hegel pays no further attention to South and Central America, since (as will become clearer below) a constant refrain in his historical and political writings is that Catholicism can no longer feature as the religion of more 'advanced' states, having been superseded by Protestantism.

The USA engages Hegel further, however. The European colonisers were industrious, and many had emigrated to gain religious freedom. From this arose a state based on the protection of property and religious freedom. But Hegel viewed this state as still undeveloped because these two features were *too* predominant. He describes as 'the fundamental character of the community – the endeavour of the individual after acquisition, commercial profit, and gain; the preponderance of *private* interest, devoting itself to that of the community only for its own advantage'. Relatedly, their belief in religious freedom led to 'unseemly varieties of caprice', causing 'the splitting up into so many sects, which reach the very acme of absurdity'. Thus the USA's immature political culture, the state being 'merely something external for the protection of property'. Also, (writing in the 1820s) he thought its further political development was inhibited because 'the immeasurable space which that country presents to its inhabitants' has so far rendered them 'exempt from that pressure' caused by the emergence of 'a distinction of classes, . . . when wealth and poverty become extreme', and which would otherwise have caused its people 'to be pressed back on each other'. But while 'the outlet of colonisation is constantly and widely open . . . the general object of the existence of this State is not yet fixed and determined, and the necessity for a firm combination does not yet exist'. Here, for the moment, we leave America – for although we will find Hegel saying more about its potential *future*, for him it did not signify in 'world-history' in his times.

Instead, 'dismissing, then, the New World' (including Australia),[47] Hegel turns his attention to 'the Old World – the scene of the World's History'.[48] But again he excludes another huge area, Africa. He divides it into European Africa north of the Sahara, the Nile valley region, and 'Africa proper', south of the Sahara. Of the latter, Hegel claims its tropical nature and geographical isolation combine to leave it 'beyond the day of self-conscious history, . . . enveloped in the dark mantle of Night'. He follows this with a deeply unpleasant characterisation of the African 'spirit' derived from his notion that 'in Negro life . . . [the] distinction between himself as an individual and the universality of his essential being' has 'not yet [been] attained'. In the absence of this consciousness, 'the Negro . . . exhibits the natural man in his completely wild and untamed state', there being 'nothing harmonious with humanity to be found in this type of character'. He claims African religion is simply 'sorcery' and 'fetishism', where 'the idea of a God, of a moral faith' is absent, man himself being 'regarded as the Highest'. With a perhaps curious logic, Hegel claims 'it follows that he has no respect for himself', and this explains (for Hegel) the Africans' 'perfect *contempt* for humanity', as exhibited in tyranny, cannibalism, slavery, 'want of self-control', and the non-existence of 'moral sentiments'.[49]

Given these views it is not surprising Hegel claims 'the entire nature of this race is such as to preclude the existence' of political constitutions (or 'states' proper). Only external, tyrannical force 'can hold the State together for a moment', and he then recounts selective dramatic examples of chaotic, barbaric African rule. He concludes by saying of 'the character of the Negroes', that 'this condition is capable of no development or culture, and as we see them at this day, such have they always been'. And thus 'we leave Africa, not to mention it again, for it is no historical part of the World'. Rather, it is 'the Unhistorical, Undeveloped Spirit, still involved in the conditions of mere nature, and which had to be presented here only as on the threshold of the World's History',[50] (i.e., the nearest Hegel gets to construing a 'state of nature' in either his *The Philosophy of History* or *Philosophy of Right*).

'History proper'

Thus Hegel has 'eliminated this introductory element'[51] – i.e., stateless peoples, India, the frigid and torrid zones, North, South, and Central America, and sub-Saharan Africa – from playing any role in the drama of 'Universal History'. Their histories, their states (if applicable), their cultures, their 'national geniuses', are inessential in Hegel's philosophical terms, since they fail to exhibit significant stages in the developing consciousness of Freedom. That process found its 'real theatre' in the 'Asiatic and European world', beginning in the former and culminating in the latter. How does this story unfold, and what are its counterparts in the actual historical world?

The Oriental realm

The process, then, does not begin with Africa. Rather, since 'the History of the World is the discipline of the uncontrolled natural will, bringing it into obedience to a Universal principle and conferring subjective freedom',[52] the journey of the World-Spirit *begins* with the initial achievement of a primitive, undeveloped consciousness of *universality*, where the 'uncontrolled natural will' first submits to an objective *order*. This first stage is that in which order and right (essential aspects of freedom) are objectively established in a political system, but where the universal will is focused entirely at a single point which, through its awe and majesty, extracts subservience from the remainder of the whole. This stage was manifested in the 'despotic' states of 'the Orient', China being a prime example. Because the emperor is regarded as 'the One individual . . . to which all belongs', then 'no other individual has a separate existence, or mirrors himself in his subjective freedom'. Rather, in such despotic states subjective freedom is simply absent. All revolves around, and issues from, the decree of the divine Emperor; and 'the subjects are . . . like children, who obey their parents without will or insight of their own'. Thus, the unity of the state is solely a product of 'unreflecting use and habit', rather than of the rational will of 'reflective and personal beings having a properly subjective and independent existence'. These latter features only emerge at a much higher stage of History, and elsewhere. Prior to that, 'the political life of the East', taking the form of 'the gorgeous edifices of Oriental Empires', 'is the childhood of History'.[53]

Where he goes into detail, he incorporates China, India, Persia, and Egypt in an overall westward movement. Although all manifest the same broad characteristics, as we move further west into Central Asia and beyond, individual differences are also identified as complex subdivisions within this first stage – for example, the disorganisation of the Persians, the 'voluptuousness and luxury' of the Syrians, the activeness and 'courage of the sea-braving Phoenicians', the 'pure thought' of one God in the Jewish religion, and 'the mental unrest of Egypt'. All these conspired progressively to make Spirit negate its lack of individual, subjective freedom and instead manifest itself anew at a higher stage, where the principle of 'free Individuality' arose to take centre-stage.[54]

The Greek realm

We thus arrive at 'the *second* main principle in human History', where the morality of a people now issues from 'the free volition of individuals', or 'the subjective Will'. The historical correlate of this was 'the Greek world', which Hegel admiringly calls 'the Kingdom of *Beautiful Freedom*'.[55] Now, 'advancing Spirit makes *itself* the content of its volition', and thus individuality is given full reign, prompting Hegel to say 'Greece presents to us the cheerful aspect of youthful freshness, of Spiritual vitality'.[56] Wonderful works of art and literature, the fabled 'democracy' of Athens and the fierce patriotism of the Spartans – all these epitomise the spirit of individuality and subjectivity underlying the ethos of Greek culture, qualitatively different from that manifested in Oriental despotisms. Interestingly, as in some earlier philosophies of history, Hegel uses the analogy of the *individual's* development from infancy to old age, usually applied to the rise and decline of individual states. Hegel, however, employs it to describe World-history as a whole! Since History proper began with Oriental despotisms, this represented 'the childhood of history', and as developing Spirit moved westwards into Central Asia, whose peoples 'no longer manifest[ed] the repose and trustingness of the child' but instead became 'boisterous and turbulent', this period was 'the boyhood of history'.[57] Now, in the Greek world, Spirit exhibits 'the period of adolescence, for here we have individualities forming themselves'. It is this youthful factor which makes classical Greece so attractive.

And yet in good dialectical fashion the positive features of Greek culture are matched by negative ones, requiring that the Greek world eventually be superseded. Hegel identifies four drawbacks. First, because of their precocious individuality the Greeks were divided into numerous city-states rather than making one political society. Second, despite its sophistication, even 'the beautiful democracy of Athens' displayed an immaturity common to Greek political forms, because 'the Greeks derived their final decisions from . . . quite external phenomena such as oracles, the entrails of sacrificed animals, and the flight of birds', rather than directly from a real will. This persuades Hegel that, with the Greeks, Spirit's 'self-consciousness had not yet advanced to the abstraction of subjectivity' where, 'when a decision is to be made, an "I will" must be pronounced by man himself'. (This relates to Hegel's insistence, in his *Philosophy of Right*, on a constitutional *monarchy* as the proper form of the modern state. 'This "I will" constitutes the great difference between the ancient world and the modern, and in the great edifice of the state it must therefore have its appropriate objective existence').[58] A third drawback is slavery, another sign of immaturity insofar as 'the due satisfaction of particular needs' (i.e., economic life) is not incorporated 'in the sphere of freedom but is relegated exclusively to a class of slaves'.[59] In short, there is no properly developed 'civil society'. The final drawback returns us to his analogy of 'adolescence', for he reminds us that 'youth . . . does not exert itself for a definite intelligent aim'. Rather, the typical youth is too busy exploring his individuality! By implication, then, Hegel saw the Greek world as charming, aesthetic, and sensitive, yet lacking in substantial purpose.

The Roman realm

Thus these deficiencies in the Greek world, symptomatic of Spirit's 'adolescence', had to be superseded by a yet higher stage of Spirit. Continuing his analogy, Hegel contrasts brilliant but shiftless adolescence to the stability of purpose and character of a full-grown man, who 'devotes his life to labour for an objective aim; which he pursues consistently, even at the cost of his individuality'.[60] Put abstractly, then, Spirit is driven to negate the extremes of subjectivity which it enjoyed, and instead focus on a truly universal purpose. This third stage was manifested in what Hegel calls 'the Roman world', where subjectivity is now restrained, and 'the Social aim absorbs all individual aims'. The Roman state had a universal aim – namely, its compulsive mission to imprint itself on the known world – and for this reason manifests 'the severe labours of the *Manhood* of History. For true manhood acts neither in accord with the caprice of a despot, nor in obedience to a graceful caprice of its own, but works for a general aim'. Individuals now 'have to merge their own interests' in 'the severe demands of the *National* objects'. However, this does not return them to the childlike obeisance endemic to Oriental despotisms. Rather, the universal aim of the Roman state is inculcated into its peoples' lives in such a manner that the Roman citizen 'realises his own private object only in that general aim'. Recognising its dependence on this, the Roman state extended 'definite rights' to its citizens (and to its conquered territories), thereby establishing them as proper *persons* rather than as slaves, or chattels of a despot, or as insignificant 'individuals'.

However, the dialectic is relentless, and Hegel constantly describes the Roman state as manifesting a universality which was (too) *abstract*. He means that Rome's aim was *power* for its own sake, since Rome used it to create a 'political Universality' which was relatively indifferent to its actual ethical content. Rome would 'crush' the 'national individualities' it conquered (just as its rule at home was, within the law, ruthless), but would then 'incorporate' their gods and other aspects of their culture into 'a homogenous and indifferent mass'. Because of this mixture of ruthlessness and liberality, 'Rome becomes a Pantheon of all deities, and of all Spiritual existence', and yet 'these divinities and this Spirit do not retain their proper vitality'.[61] Rather, in being absorbed into the Roman world they become part of a culture which does not have 'a concretely spiritual life, rich in itself'. Instead, the Roman citizens and territories are subject to 'the *abstractum* [abstraction] of Universality' whose object, 'which is pursued with soulless and heartless severity, is mere *dominion*, in order to enforce that *abstractum*'.[62]

We have seen Hegel comparing the Roman world to the stage of manhood in positive terms. But there is also a 'downside' to manhood – namely, that in devoting 'severe labours' to settling down to a fixed purpose, the grown man becomes *too* immersed in his role. There comes a time when the ties it imposes begin to chafe, and his individuality begins to assert itself in acts of caprice. Such sometimes bizarre expressions of individuality may remind us of 'mid-life crisis' – after which, many a man decides to continue 'doing his duty', but now with less unconscious devotion, and more an inclination to suit himself as much as possible!

Now, something like this extension of the life-cycle analogy may have been in Hegel's mind when he explains the fate of the Roman world. Its deficiency (in terms of Spirit's freedom) is that the universality it manifested was too 'abstract' – it lacked 'concrete' richness. According to Hegel, this displayed itself in a growing contradiction between 'the Aim of the State as the abstract universal principle' and the claims of individual personality. Initially in harmony, as time went on 'individuality gains the ascendant', and peoples' obedience, 'instead of being hearty and voluntary', becomes reliant simply on their 'contingent disposition'. In historical terms, this corresponded to the growth of quarrelling factions between the Roman aristocracy and the plebs. As this threat grows, 'the breakup of the community . . . can only be restrained by external compulsion', as a result of which the citizen is 'led to seek consolation for the loss of his freedom' by pursuing his own private ends. This only exacerbates the contradiction between state and subjects, and eventually one side of the contradiction, individuality, overcomes its other side (universality) even at the level of the state itself; i.e., the state became governed by the 'contingent' and increasingly capricious power of 'one despot'.[63]

This was the final phase of that stage of Spirit manifested in the increasingly chaotic Roman world. But its problem was endemic from its inception – in terms of Spirit, its *universal* principle was too *abstract*. In corresponding historical terms, the founding of the State involved 'the severest discipline and self-sacrifice to the grand object of the union. A State which had first to form itself, and which is based on force, must be held together by force. It is not a moral, liberal connection, but a compulsory condition of subordination, that results from such an origin'.[64] This underlying deficiency meant that, in its turn, 'the Roman world' was necessarily superseded by a yet higher stage of Spirit, 'the German world'.

The Germanic realm

Seen in terms of Spirit, the collapse of the Roman world equates with the depths to which Spirit had sunk in its dialectical development, where 'insatiable self-will'[65] evolved as its sole content. But in reaction to this, Spirit 'leaves the godless world, seeks a harmony in itself, and begins now an inner life'. Having been 'driven back into its utmost depths' from a world abandoned to the ravages of pure self-will, it now enters a higher phase of spirituality where 'the individual personality, instead of following its own capricious choice, is purified and elevated into universality'.[66]

The result is that Spirit achieves an inner reconciliation to the outside world, derived from its recognition of 'the unity of the divine nature and the human'.[67] Gradually the outside world is made to bear the imprint of the unassailable right of subjective Freedom, such that eventually it is brought into full conformity with it.

In referring to this new consciousness which recognises the essential unity between the human and the Absolute, Hegel sees this as the principle of *Christianity*. In good theological fashion he points to the overwhelming significance of Christ's *humanity*, as God being made flesh, exemplifying the ultimate unity between God, Man, and consciousness or Mind (i.e., 'Spirit') – expressed symbolically in the Holy Trinity. This final coming together of 'God', man, and the world *is* the grand project of *history*, and its final stage is dependent upon the Christian religion for its underlying principle. As Hegel puts its, 'The Idea can discover in Christianity no point in the aspirations of Spirit that is not satisfied'.[68]

Again he appeals to his analogy of an individual's life-path, comparing this fourth phase of world-history with 'old age'. He tells us, 'the Old Age of *Nature* is weakness; but that of *Spirit* is perfect maturity and strength, in which it returns to unity with itself, but in its fully developed character as *Spirit*'.[69] He does not elaborate upon this analogy. (It seems consolatory, even hopeful!). But more to the point, his consistent appeal to it perhaps suggests he relied on it more than he supposed – in other words, that although he grounded his philosophy on the ultimate reality of impersonal Mind, perhaps what he was actually thinking about was the psychology of human beings. Not only might this apply to his philosophy of history (i.e., from history's 'infancy' to its 'old age'), but also to his general philosophy of 'Spirit' (i.e., his distinction between humans and animals).

Be this as it may, 'the part assigned [the German world] in the service of the World-Spirit' has been to realise this final stage of Spirit's journey to Freedom, underpinned by the essential principle of Christianity. But again, this final stage did not unfold itself all at once. Rather, it went through different periods. And here, Hegel's *historical* account (i.e., the 'earthly' correlate to Spirit's unfolding) is perhaps as suspect as it is audacious – for it spans the entire time from the origins of Christianity, through centuries of the Roman Empire, then the 'Dark Ages', through the Middle Ages, then the Renaissance, to Protestantism and the 'modern' state of his own times.

The first period

The 'German World' began, then, with the origins of Christianity, for it was that religion which established the true principle of the reconciliation between individual freedom ('Subjective Spirit') and the Absolute ('Objective Spirit/Mind'). But Christianity 'needed eight centuries to grow up into a political form', by which he means the founding of Charlemagne's state in AD 800 – a symbolic restoration of the Roman Empire. Before then, although Christianity had introduced the full principles of spirituality, it had only done so through people's *retreat* from the 'barbarian Real World' into their own inner spirituality. Initially persecuted by pagan Rome, Christianity gradually managed to consolidate its ecclesiastical order despite the collapse of the (Western) Roman Empire and the succeeding three centuries of 'Dark Ages' of barbarian invasions.

The second period

The second period of 'the Germanic world' extends from Charlemagne's 'empire' to the sixteenth century. Its chief features were twofold: 1) the reorganisation of Europe into numerous feudal states. Because the feudal system was based on private obligations and loyalties, it gave the lie to the hopes for 'a kingdom of heaven on earth' which had been 'promised to follow in the wake of [the] reconciliation' between Church and State symbolised by the Pope's crowning of Charlemagne. Politically, Europe was anything but united. Rather, the hierarchy of superior and inferior states linked by complex feudal ties excluded 'a sense of universality', just as did feudalism *within* each territory. 2) The moral decline of the Church as it sunk 'down into every kind of worldliness', such that 'instead of a spiritual kingdom of heaven, the inwardness of the Christian principle wears the appearance of being altogether directed outwards and leaving its proper sphere'.[70] This brought the Church and the State into constant competition. But this antagonism was not only an opposition between the secular and the spiritual. Each side was also in opposition to itself – the secular because European states were devoid of the principle of universality (owing to their feudal organisation), and the spiritual because it appeared to have abandoned its true ground in pursuit, instead, of temporal ambitions.

The third period: The Renaissance

The overall antithesis between the spiritual and secular at last began to be resolved (for Spirit cries out for it to be superseded) by what we now call the Renaissance and the Reformation. This is the third period of European ('Germanic') history, and although Hegel dates this period as extending from the *Reformation* to his own times, he could not be clearer in referring first to the ethos of the *Renaissance* – (the term itself was yet to be coined) – as issuing in this third period.

For Hegel, the Renaissance brought an end to the Middle Ages because it was the time when, the Church having become desperately corrupt, 'Spirit, once more driven back upon itself, produces its work in an intellectual shape, and becomes capable of realising the Ideal of Reason from the Secular principle alone'.[71] In other words, rebelling against the corrupt spiritual realm, the secular world discovered within *itself* a new sense of spirituality centred on man himself. As Hegel puts it, '[s]ecularity appears now as gaining a consciousness of its intrinsic worth – becomes aware of its having a value of its own in the morality, rectitude, probity, and activity of man'.[72]

Although this was partly exemplified by the political collapse of feudalism and the emergence of sovereign, independent states (Hegel praises Machiavelli's ruthless views as necessary) he makes it clear this was far more than a political movement. Rather, he suggests it began with the new sense of spirituality exhibited by Renaissance *art*, which eclipsed the merely representational shallowness of medieval art and instead produced paintings 'rich in thought and sentiment', and sculptures, 'in looking at which, soul holds converse with soul and Spirit with Spirit'. He also praises the work of the Renaissance humanists for reviving Greek and Roman literature and thereby doing 'honour to the Human' by acquainting the West 'with the true and eternal element in the activity of man'. The invention of printing assisted this new consciousness, as (less obviously) did that of gunpowder (by 'democratising' even warfare). Finally, he singles out the voyages of discovery as exemplifying the 'urging of the Spirit outwards' – that is, the 'desire on the part of man to become acquainted with *his* world'.

In these ways, then, the secular world became imbued with a new spiritual consciousness, centred on the nobility of man himself. In summary,

> [t]hese three . . . [Renaissance arts, humanism, and global exploration] . . . may be compared with that *blush of dawn*, which after long storms first betokens the return of a bright and glorious day. This . . . is the day . . . which breaks upon the world after the long, eventful, and terrible night of the Middle Ages.[73]

The Reformation

If the Renaissance revitalised the secular world, in the early sixteenth century the spiritual world was revolutionised by the Reformation, 'the all-enlightening *Sun*, following on that blush of dawn'. Its significance, for Hegel, lies in 'Luther's simple doctrine . . . that the specific embodiment of Deity . . . is in no way present and actual in an outward form, but . . . is obtained only . . . in *faith and spiritual enjoyment*'. He claims the Catholic Church had sunk to the level of superstition, putting its faith in a *sensuous* 'embodiment of Deity', generating an 'absurd and childish' belief in miracles, the 'grossly superficial and trivial' notion that remission of sins can be 'purchased for mere money', and a 'slavish deference to *Authority*'.[74] Luther swept away such error, insisting instead that 'man sustain an immediate relation to [Christ] in Spirit' on an *individual* level. Objective religious truth (exemplified in Christianity) is thereby recognised as embedded in individual hearts and consciences, and 'this subjectivity is the common property of all mankind' rather than the exclusive possession of a priestly class.

In metaphysical terms, the *subjective* side of Spirit (so essential to Freedom) is no longer lost in particular, selfish aims, nor in erroneously abstract universal aims, but has finally achieved its proper end in 'the objective purport of Christianity, i.e., the doctrine of the . . . Lutheran Church'. Having repudiated the authority of the

Catholic Church and centred spiritual truth within men themselves (guided by the Bible), the subjective side of Spirit (manifested in people's *consciousness*) is no longer at odds with the objectively established religion, because the latter is now based on free, individual consciousness. 'Thus Christian Freedom is actualised', says Hegel. 'This is the essence of the Reformation: Man is in his very nature destined to be free', and since the early sixteenth century, 'time . . . has had no other work to do than the formal imbuing of the world with this principle'.[75]

The emergence of 'modern times'

The remainder of Hegel's *Philosophy of History* explains how Spirit increasingly exemplifies (in man) this full and conscious recognition of its ultimate 'divinity', and also how it *translates* this new stage of consciousness from the religious to the *secular* world. The Renaissance had already prepared the *secular* world for transformation, re-establishing its own independent sense of human worth. No longer was it 'regarded as evil only'. Now, with the Reformation, the breech between religion and the secular world is in *principle* resolved. This is because the Church is no longer confronted by a conscience-less secular world devoid of Reason – and vice-versa, the secular world feels that 'the Spiritual is no longer an element foreign to the State'. Thus, gradually during this third period of the Germanic world, 'the antithesis of Church and State vanishes. The Spiritual becomes reconnected with the Secular' such that, finally, 'Freedom has found the means of realising its Ideal – its true existence. This is the ultimate result which the process of History is intended to accomplish'.[76]

But again, as in all four principal stages of World-history and their own internal periods, this third period of the Germanic world is culminated only through a struggling dialectical sequence. Initially, the Reformation involved substantial religious reform in parts of Europe, often spilling out into the secular world where 'rebellion was raised against the temporal authorities'. However, 'the world was not yet ripe for a transformation of its political condition as a consequence of ecclesiastical reformation'.[77] Rather, that 'reconciliation between God and the World' which is the overall significance of the period from the Reformation to Hegel's own times, was first fought out in the consciousness of *individuals*. This took the form of peoples' 'painful introspection' into their sinfulness, combined with 'a tormenting uncertainty as to whether the good Spirit has an abode in them'. Thus 'Protestantism . . . was for a long time characterised by a self-tormenting disposition and an aspect of spiritual wretchedness'. This heightened belief in 'Evil' conspired, as also in Catholicism, to produce a superstitious belief in witchcraft, which was persecuted by dreadful means (including the Catholic Inquisition) throughout the sixteenth and seventeenth centuries. Indeed, referring to the public burning of a witch in 1780, Hegel remarks that 'we have not long been quit of this frightful barbarity'.[78]

Whilst the subjective side of Spirit adopted this unfortunate form, its objective side was developing the *secular* world towards the emergence of the modern state, characterised by its 'recognition of the universal laws of Freedom'. This political movement was principally driven by the creation of independent monarchies which 'no longer denote[d] a kind of private property, private possession of estates . . . etc.', but abandoned such feudal relations, which instead became the trustees of State-property, administered by a centralised system of law. Standing armies and centralised systems of taxation developed, and the previous feudal nobility were transformed 'into an official position in connection with the State'. But Hegel's primary interest in this formation of the early-modern state focused on the achievement of Protestant countries to attain independent statehood, involving such struggles as the Thirty Years' War, the Dutch wars against Spain, and the Seven Years' War. The latter consolidated the emergence of Prussia as an independent Protestant state under the rule of Frederick the Great at the end of the seventeenth century.

If the secular world in various parts of seventeenth-century Europe was moving towards the perfected form of the state, we left the spiritual world (albeit set on the right track by the Reformation) in an undeveloped state of gloomy introspection, obsessed by the idea of 'evil'. But this phase gave way to a deeper consciousness centred on the recognition that *all* existence (including our consciousness as well as the external world) exhibits fundamentally the same 'Reason'. This new movement – the recognition of the power of *thought* to understand everything as *rational* – blossomed into what Hegel (accepting the French and German terms) calls the *Eclaircissement* or *Aufklärung*. He is referring not only to what in English came to be called the (French, eighteenth-century) Enlightenment, but also to the preceding Scientific Revolution. He cites Descartes as laying its intellectual foundations (what we have called 'rationalism' in philosophy), and attributes to 'Experimental Science' (what we have called 'empiricism') the discoveries flowing from the recognition that 'Nature is a system of known and recognised laws'. But this combination of rationalism and empiricism was not restricted to the investigation of nature. 'Right and Morality' were also brought within the compass of *Eclaircissement*, in order to base them on the laws of reason rather than, as previously, on 'the command of God . . . written in the Old and New Testament, or appearing in the form of particular Right in old parchments, as privileges . . .'.[79]

The 1789 French Revolution

The most dramatic effect of this 'new world of ideas' on the secular world was, eventually, the French Revolution of 1789. Following his general principle that 'secular life is the positive and definite embodiment of the Spiritual kingdom', Hegel praises the Eclaircissement (and the role played by Kant in its German equivalent) for representing the raising of consciousness to the proper understanding of Freedom – i.e., (referring his readers to his *Philosophy of Right*) where 'the Will . . . does not will anything alien, extrinsic, foreign to itself . . . but wills itself alone'. As for the principle itself, he tells us that, partly because of their parlous political condition, it was the French who 'wished to give it practical effect . . . [and] set about realising it'.[80] The initial result was the 1791 *Declaration of the Rights of Man and the Citizen*, which began the world-historic mission of 'remodelling of the State in accordance with the Idea of Right'.[81]

But Hegel does not underplay the difficulties thrown up during the French Revolution, for example describing Robespierre's brief reign as 'the most fearful tyranny'. As usual, Spirit has to engage in arduous struggle to fully manifest its principles, and this last period of history is no exception. Napoleon 'knew how to rule, and soon settled the internal affairs of France' – and then, 'with the vast might of his character . . . subjected all Europe, and diffused his liberal institutions in every quarter'. Yet, it seems, the culmination of Spirit's long journey to actualise its full self-consciousness of Freedom (via the political institutions of the real world) was not to be completed via Napoleon himself. His defeat and (according to Hegel) spiritual desertion by the French people precipitated France into a 'fifteen years' farce' of constitutional monarchy, succeeded by another revolution (1830). At the time of his writing Hegel saw this as facing the problem of what he calls 'liberalism' – namely, the 'agitation and unrest' which is 'perpetuated' by the 'liberal' principle which maintains 'that all government should emanate from . . . the express sanction' of the people.[82] As previously clarified in his *Philosophy of Right*, the logic of the perfected (modern) state requires that public affairs should principally be in the hands of a professional administrative class, leaving only a limited role for popular opinion.[83]

The end of history?

The last point demonstrates that, for Hegel, even the French state of his own day still had imperfections – in other words, that Spirit's Idea of Freedom was not yet *completely* realised by that nation's political institutions. Rather, probably more as a nod of flattery, Hegel appears to reserve that honour for his present-day Prussia.[84] It had adopted the French code of Rights, but was a constitutional monarchy which reserved the monarch the authority to counteract pressures of public opinion. In any case, according to Hegel, the German people were not infected by 'liberalism'. Also, the Prussians were Protestant (unlike the French), and thus the potential for tension between religious and civic conscience – for Hegel a permanent feature of Catholic states – did not exist there. These observations might suggest that, in the Prussian state and culture, Spirit had at last fully objectified its Freedom.
This raises the huge question of whether, for Hegel, 'history' had reached its consummation – in other words, that his times were witness to the end of World-History – and if so, what this might *mean*.

Together with a grasp of Hegel's overall philosophy of history, a close consideration of the last few pages of Hegel's text should help determine this issue. What becomes clear, as he discusses contemporary France, Austria, Spain, and England, is that

Hegel does indeed see his own times as exhibiting in *principle* the features correlating with the final realisation of Spirit's journey to realise the Idea of Freedom. We must recall that the journey began thousands of years ago with the 'Oriental despotisms' of the East, and that since then Spirit had advanced through two qualitatively higher stages (the Greek world, then the Roman world) until it embarked on its fourth stage, the German world. Because Christian, this fourth stage was premised on a true consciousness of the relation between man and Absolute Reality (Mind, or 'God'). But its full implications had to be unravelled through a complex dialectical process culminating in the *religious* enlightenment of the Protestant Reformation and the *secular* emergence of properly independent states. But even then, a further process was required to clarify the spiritual truth of Protestantism, and for the secular world to independently discover the rational basis to the state and morality. The Eclaircissement achieved the latter.

The final denouement was to bring together the rational principles of the secular world with the purified spiritual consciousness of man, achieved in *principle* via the French Revolution (however imperfectly in *practice*). Hegel expresses this by saying that 'in its substantial import' the French Revolution was a 'world-historical' event, irrespective of its flawed details. This principle 'gained access to almost all modern states, either through conquest or by express introduction into their political life'.[85]

Broadly, then, it does not appear that there need be any further overall stages in Spirit's journey (i.e., a fifth stage beyond 'the Germanic world'), and there is nothing in Hegel's logic to suggest he thought otherwise. Also, each of the four stages of World-history undergoes its *own* internal dialectical development through different periods. The fourth stage has been no exception to this, being composed of three successive internal periods. And even its third period had to unfold through its *own* internal subdivisions, culminating in what Hegel calls 'Modern Times', originated by the French Revolution. Having reached this point, again it does not appear there is anything in Hegel to suggest the need for a further period (or subdivision) which would introduce qualitatively new features. Rather, actual examples of the modern state had emerged, as he had already argued in his *Philosophy of Right* – a veritable panegyric on the modern state as the realisation of freedom.

Loose ends

In this broad sense, then, both Hegel's logic and writings suggest he thought his 'modern times' were the 'end' of history – a fortunate phrase since 'end' also means 'telos' (i.e., the 'end' or 'purpose' of a thing). It is difficult to read Hegel any other way. However, it is equally difficult to read him as meaning that, in his time, the story was *completely* over. It is clear he thought there were some loose ends – i.e., that in practice there remained imperfections. And given the immensity of the overall time-scale Hegel has been working with, he may well have thought the required 'fine-tunings' could take a century or longer to come to fruition. Apart from a despairing reference elsewhere to the problem of the 'rabble' disaffected by poverty – 'the important question of how poverty is to be abolished is one of the most disturbing problems which agitate modern society' – [86] he indicates two features of 'the modern state' which he regarded as present flaws.

First, there is the problem of 'liberalism' already mentioned in regard to post-revolutionary France. For Hegel, so long as the state's constitution guarantees the principle of the universal or general will, then there is no necessity that it should constantly be expected to bow to pressure from 'the sway of individual wills' expressed in various interest groups and competing political parties. Yet this is precisely the expectation of 'liberalism', where 'the will of the Many expels the Ministry from power'. The Opposition then takes office, only in its turn to 'meet with hostility from the Many' and thus 'share the same fate. Thus agitation and unrest are perpetuated'. In short, the balance between the *responsibility of the state* for promoting the interest of all, as distinct from the role which what we now call 'democracy' should play, is a problem Hegel perceives. Presciently, he claims 'this collision, this nodus, this problem is that with which history is now occupied, and whose solution it has to work out in the future'.[87]

The problem of (excessive) 'liberalism' is, however, merely symptomatic of a more general threat to the modern state – namely, what Hegel calls the 'disposition' of its citizens. Reason requires that although 'there may be various opinions . . . respecting laws, constitution, and government, . . . there must be a disposition on the part of the citizens to regard all these opinions as subordinate to the substantial interest of the state'. He means there should be an underlying *consensus* on the sanctity of the constitution itself, and a corresponding genuine 'acquiescence in the laws', despite opinions otherwise critical of aspects of the nation's life. Here he singled out religion for special notice, insisting 'it must involve nothing really alien or opposed to the Constitution', and attacks the Catholic religion in particular, saying 'it is a false principle that the fetters which bind Right and Freedom can be broken without the emancipation of conscience – that there can be a Revolution without a Reformation'.[88] Thus he regards the Catholic states of Europe as either lost to the principle of the modern state or gravely compromised.

But Protestant states can also suffer from an imperfect 'disposition', and here he particularly cites England for its markedly decentralised system where 'every parish, every subordinate division and association has a part of its own to perform'. The persistence of these jealously guarded rights 'render a general system impossible', and thus, 'of institutions characterised by real freedom there are nowhere fewer than in England'. Additionally he points to the 'utterly inconsistent and corrupt' system of bribery associated with Parliamentary seats, but concedes that at least it produced men schooled from their youth to 'political business', and that 'the nation has the correct conviction and perception that there must be a government, and is therefore willing to give its confidence to a body of men who have had experience in governing'. Clearly somewhat bemused by the 'disposition' of the English, he concludes by wryly querying whether the forthcoming (1832) Reform Bill 'will leave the possibility of a government' at all![89]

These observations provide useful insights into Hegel's implied 'end of history'. As noted, they leave room for future 'fine-tuning' of the modern state. But also they remind us that in no sense does he imply that all states, or even a number of states, must assume the form which 'finally' realises the Idea of Freedom. On the contrary, throughout his account of its self-revelatory journey, 'Spirit' repeatedly exemplified each of its stages (and subdivisions) in only one 'State' at a time. Correspondingly, even when treating of his contemporary Europe, Hegel claimed many countries were left behind – and there seems no reason to doubt that, just as in previous historical periods, this is where Hegel thought they would stay. In short, there is nothing in his account of previous history to suggest that the 'end of history' should be manifested on a world-wide scale, or even encompass all European states. All that is (metaphysically) necessary is that Freedom be fully objectified in at least one instance.

The only alternative is to look not at his historical account of the world but at the *logic* of his argument. Does it imply something different when it comes to 'the end of history'? For example, is there anything different about this *final* period to suggest it should spread world wide? Donning a Hegelian hat, some may argue that his logic points precisely to that conclusion, since the principle of *universality* of will lies at the heart of Spirit's nature. This could imply either that most of the world's states evolve towards Hegel's model 'modern state' (or are brought to it by conquest) – or even more radically, that individual states will be subsumed under one world-state. Given the predominance Hegel awards 'the state' (and different 'national spirits'), particularly this latter might appear to stretch his logic beyond its compass. But does it? We should be reminded that, in logic, Hegel treated 'Rome' as one 'state'.

That we can reasonably raise such speculations about Hegel's implied 'end of history' suggests Hegel himself is not much help. Rather, he seems to have left us with a paradox, for on the one hand he has claimed to have exhaustively laid out the meaning and direction of history up to his present, which he has demonstrated as nothing less than the culmination of world-history. Yet we do not know what he thought this meant for his present world, and by implication for its future, either as its continuance, its eventual decline, or even some further *development*. Of these options, the last seems the least likely because ruled out by his logic. Spirit has, after all, finally realised its Freedom in the manifestation of 'the modern state'. Yet, extraordinarily, it is just this last option Hegel appears to point to as a possibility – and this returns to his view of the USA.

USA – the future?

We saw him earlier denying the USA any significance in world-history up to his times. Because of its still immense potential for further colonisation, 'the general object of the existence of this State is not yet fixed and determined'. But on the same grounds, Hegel announces that 'America is therefore the land of the future, where, in the ages that lie before us, the burden of the World's History shall reveal itself'. Extraordinarily, this suggests that History has *not* reached its consummation in the Europe of Hegel's 'modern times', but that some further stage(s) still beckon for Spirit's final realisation – and here, tantalisingly, we can revert to his analogy of the individual's life cycle. Elsewhere in his Introduction we saw Hegel liken the fourth stage of World-history (his 'German world') to Spirit's old age, followed by his insistence that, whereas 'the old age of *Nature* is weakness, . . . that of *Spirit* is its perfect maturity and *strength*'.[90] This reinforces the notion that, for Hegel, this fourth stage was the 'last' in History, (other than a fifth – death – which he ascribes to Nature but not to Spirit).

Yet describing America here as 'the New World', Hegel refers to the 'Old World' as indeed 'old', including Europe itself, saying that America 'is a land of desire for all those who are weary of the historical lumber-room of old Europe'. Quoting his hero Napoleon who supposedly said 'this old Europe bores me', Hegel then announces 'it is for America to abandon the ground on which hitherto the History of the World has developed itself'. Quite how these passages impinge on the integrity of Hegel's philosophy of history, especially its alleged 'end' or consummation, is difficult to judge – the more so since he then loftily dismisses the topic of America as 'a Land of the Future' and 'the dreams to which it may give rise' as falling outside the compass of *history* (i.e., 'that which has been, and that which is'),[91] and thus also outside the compass of *philosophy* of history. Rather, he reverts to his insistence that 'philosophy' is concerned with the Reason present in things. He reiterates this in the very closing passages of his book where, if he thought his philosophy implied a changing future derived from *further* self-revelations of Spirit, he might be expected to have said so. Instead, he leaves us on an ambiguous tone, saying of his times, 'this is the point which consciousness has attained'. And since 'the History of the World is nothing but the development of the Idea of Freedom . . . we have confined ourselves to the consideration of that progress of the Idea. . . . Philosophy concerns itself only with the glory of the Idea mirroring itself in the History of the World'.[92] This can be read as leaving open whether 'consciousness' has any further 'point' to 'attain'. If he *did* think some new stage beckoned beyond the 'old age' of Europe, he was hoisted on the petard of his own philosophy which prevented him from exploring it – for apart from anything else, in his *Philosophy of Right* he had already insisted on the futility of expecting 'philosophy' to raise hopes of changing the world – a message which many interpreted as emphatically conservative: 'Since philosophy is the exploration of the rational, it is for that very reason the apprehension of the present and the actual, not the erection of a beyond, supposed to exist, God knows where . . .'.[93]

Conclusion

Hegel's philosophy of history is extraordinarily audacious, and it is perhaps this very feature which renders its appraisal so difficult. Many historians abominate it as speculation of the worst kind, founded on abstract principles having nothing to do with history – this despite the fact that Hegel never claimed he was writing history, but was instead treating history 'philosophically'. So long as the history he does treat of is not empirically incorrect, he is exonerated from much criticism for omitting, and thereby potentially distorting, 'the facts'. Rather, the whole point of (speculative) philosophy of history for Hegel – as for anyone – is the endeavour to extract from the material of history some overall meaning or intelligibility. Thus we earlier saw Hegel insisting his theory depended on considering the actual historical facts, from which he was able to derive the *framework* into which they fitted. But equally he explained (using the analogy of Kepler's scientific work) that this framework did not spring newborn from the historical material but instead depended upon a previous set of established *principles* relevant to the topic of enquiry. However, this draws particular attention to what those principles *are*, and as your guide I suggest this is ultimately where each reader should settle accounts with Hegel's philosophy of history.

If, for example, Kepler needed familiarity with Euclidean geometric *principles* in order to derive, from his empirical studies of planets' movements, a framework for the laws of planetary motion, when it comes to the topic of world-history Hegel tells us we need to be familiar with the *principles* involved in understanding 'Spirit' in order to derive, from the historical facts, the particular *framework* world-history exhibits. Those principles, themselves part of a larger set concerning Existence and Reason, he had set out years before and revolve around notions involving self, consciousness, the objective world, will, freedom, and right. Hegel brought this rich philosophical heritage to what he took to be its consummation in his *Phenomenology of Mind*, and we have seen how he applies these principles to history.

Thus the challenge Hegel presents is not whether we 'believe' him, or in 'Spirit', as in some religious act of faith, but whether we agree history *is* fundamentally about what he calls 'Spirit'. To Hegel a number of things seem obvious: that there is a qualitative difference between human beings and animals; that in being *self*-conscious, humans introduce a revolutionary, fundamental principle otherwise absent from Existence – namely, that they are beings imbued with a self-directing energy to strive towards aims, however petty or ambitious; that this is the very *condition* of there being any 'history' at all; and that the logical heart of this human activity – will – seeks 'freedom', whose ultimate realm cannot but centre on individuals' relation to each other in terms of 'right' – in other words, the realm of the political organisation of 'the state' broadly conceived. Equally obvious to him was that different states and corresponding national cultures have arisen in history; and that, as much because of as despite dreadful setbacks, Freedom's general characteristics have been progressively made actual, as shown in certain parts of the modern world. Viewed as a whole, then, there would be no *intelligible* history without the phenomenon of Spirit, expressed via the fact of human self-consciousness. Therefore, without a prior understanding of what Spirit means and involves (i.e., its 'principles'), we cannot hope to *understand* history but can only record its facts and, wandering in the dark, make of them (or not) whatever erroneous 'framework' or meaning might occur to us.

Now, one could simply dismiss the notion that history has an intelligibility – or claim it does demonstrate one, but not that argued by Hegel – or, that history is indeed made intelligible by the notion of 'Spirit', but that 'Spirit' does not have the properties Hegel ascribes it. But in each case, one would have to give *reasons* for dismissing Hegel – and it is likely these would need to be philosophical rather than historical. In the light of the scientific, empiricist, atheistical suppositions underlying our times, the most likely objection to Hegel is not so much his notion of the essential 'spiritedness' inherent in human-beings, but his apparent *elevation* of this crucial feature into an impersonal, supernatural *force* or 'Being' – i.e., that his thought is simply religion posing as philosophy.

However, let us consider arguments which could salvage Hegel from this accusation. We take the force of gravity as 'real' – we see its effects distributed in the workings of the natural world. But no one has ever suggested it is a *personal* or human force, neither some kind of supernatural 'Being'. It is an impersonal, 'disembodied' reality which not only explains but shapes much of our actuality. Likewise, then, one might accept something like Condorcet's notion of 'progress' arising from the 'scientific' development of the human mind as a principle continually at work in the world. This principle (or 'force') obviously involves human beings. More than this, it *depends* on them. But the same can be said for Hegel's notion of 'Spirit' – it involves human beings inasmuch as it is *their* being self-conscious, hence 'willing', which manifests the principles underlying 'Spirit'. And thus it also *depends* on them for its working out in actual history. However, that a principle involves and depends on human actions – such as Condorcet's – does not mean that human-beings (or some 'supernatural' agent) must have *invented* it, nor make the realisation of the principle their conscious aim. In like manner, the laws of gravity involve and depend on the properties of material objects, but are obviously not their deliberate *product*. Rather, they remain an impersonal and 'disembodied' reality 'behind' material actuality.

This, then, may be a way of understanding Hegel's philosophy of history. Although recognising it involves some impersonal 'principle', it means we are no more transported to a 'supernatural' realm of fantasy than when we talk of gravity or any other 'principle' we see at work either in the natural or human world. That we never 'see' gravity, or Hegel's 'Spirit', does not matter. What matters is, do we see these 'principles' *at work*?

One mundane problem is that few people know enough of 'world-history' to feel confident of answering that question – a situation which can only worsen as even the *asking* of such a question (i.e., the effort to 'see the wood for the trees') is hardly encouraged by today's professional *historians*. In their antipathy towards searching for 'principles' underlying history (Hegel's or any others) they are often still influenced by a Western Cold War mentality which, in recoiling against both the horrors of Nazism and the threat of communism, opposed any approach to history which claimed to find 'meaning' in it. The perception was that such 'theories' spawned dangerously illiberal *political* ideologies which inspired mass movements to believe 'the inevitable march (or 'logic') of history' was on their side. Curiously inconsistent, the Western liberal-democratic tradition thus spurned the idea of a 'logic' to history, albeit happy to believe in the 'logic' of the impersonal forces of the free market – namely, Adam Smith's 'invisible hand of God' at work in the world, manifest in the beneficent, yet autonomous, operation of market economics.

But apart from such *political* suspicions some attach to *any* philosophy of history, there are many who reject Hegel's because they do indeed interpret his notion of 'Mind' and/or 'Spirit' as introducing the 'supernatural'. But is this Hegel's position? It is true that in *all* his writings Hegel gives the impression that, in being 'behind' reality, 'Mind' is separate from it, and yet in some mysterious sense determining it – an impression any guide finds equally difficult to avoid giving. Despite this, I have tried to suggest how Hegel's appeal to the operation of impersonal 'principles' underlying actuality need not imply transporting us to the incredible realm of some supernatural agent. More important, however, is that neither did Hegel think it implies this.

At one level he viewed such 'supernaturalism' as religion, which he saw as only the *symbolic* expression of rational thought. At a deeper level, however, he did not believe that the kind of philosophical idealism which proposes the *dual* reality described above – the one 'ideal', the other 'material' – was philosophically true. Rather, he thought the two are in fact an inseparable unity, which *we* make the mistake of separating because we are 'conscious' of 'reality'. This fosters the illusion of the 'ideal' world of consciousness as distinct from the 'real' world of material existence.[94] Instead, at the heart of Hegel's philosophy is his notion that Reality is Reason, which he tried to express as follows: '. . . existence and self-consciousness are the same being, the same not as a matter of comparison, but really and truly in and for themselves. It is only a one-sided, unsound idealism which lets this unity . . . appear on one side as consciousness, with a reality . . . over against it on the other'.[95] Applied to Hegel's philosophy of history, then, this seems to imply either that those who reject it because it demands belief in some supernatural agency directing the course of earthly history have misunderstood him – or that he misunderstood himself. Either way, this redirects attention to his *fundamental* philosophy, and is to an extent precisely the challenge we find Karl Marx accepting as we turn to explore the last grand example of speculative philosophy of history.

10

MARX ON HISTORY

Introduction

Marx was born in Trier in the Rhineland province of Prussia in 1818 to middle-class Jewish parents. He went to read law at Bonn University in 1835, from where he moved to Berlin University, mixing his formal studies of law with his own studies of history, literature, art history, and philosophy, culminating in the completion of his doctoral thesis (comparing the classical philosophies of Democritus and Epicurus) in April 1841. During these Berlin years Marx became familiar with the philosophy of Hegel (whose death in 1831 had left a powerful legacy), and associated with a group known as the Young Hegelians. These were radical intellectuals who, unlike their counterparts, the Old Hegelians, did not interpret Hegel as implying a staunchly conservative defence of the status quo in Prussia and other German states. Instead, they seized upon Hegel's 'Idea of Freedom' to use as a weapon of criticism against Prussian authoritarianism. A passage from Engels (1820–1895) who associated with the Young Hegelians in 1841 (and was from 1844 to become Marx's life-long friend and co-worker) gives a flavour of their idealism. '. . . Such is the power of the Idea [of Freedom] that he who has recognised it cannot cease to speak of its splendour or to proclaim its all-conquering might. . . . Let us not think any love, any gain, any riches too great to sacrifice gladly to the Idea . . .'.[1]

After leaving Berlin University Marx went to Cologne to edit a paper which became so radical in his hands that the Prussian authorities soon prohibited it, prompting Marx to resign. That same summer, in 1842, he married, and in the autumn moved to Paris to edit another German journal. There he wrote ever more radical articles which evidenced his increasing conversion to communism, until expelled in early 1845. He moved to Brussels, where he finally resolved his intellectual doubts about communism, a task which not only involved a critical examination of various socialist ideas gaining ground around Europe, but also (to use his own words) involved 'settling accounts' with Hegel's philosophy. Now intellectually confident of his own distinctive theory of history, economics, and politics, with Engels he set about working with embryonic communist movements to propagandise working-class, democratic, and socialist parties towards international solidarity along the lines of his 'scientific socialism', popularly expounded in their *Communist Manifesto* published in 1848. Expelled from Belgium that same year, Marx returned to Cologne to participate in the revolutionary events beckoning in Germany, but was soon expelled. The French authorities refusing to have him in Paris, he emigrated to London in August 1849, where (age 31) he settled.

After these 'watershed' years of European revolutions in 1848–1849, Marx spent most days in the British Museum's Reading Room, reworking his theory of the nature of capitalist economy and society (but also writing numerous essays and articles), which evolved to become *Das Kapital*, the first volume being published in 1867. Also, he played a dominant role in the organisation of the International Working Men's Association (The First International) in 1864, until its virtual disbanding in 1872. Thereafter, in addition to continuing his work on volumes two and three of *Das Kapital* despite deteriorating health, he took a particular interest in the development of the German Social-Democratic Party from 1875 onwards, until his death in March 1883.

I have slanted the above sketch to Marx's early years because it was during them that he undertook the intellectual journey which explains the theory of history he formulated by 1846. This remained essentially unaltered as the substratum to his subsequent economic and political writings, including *Das Kapital*. This journey, as indicated, involved Marx's extricating himself from the allure of Hegel's general philosophy, as well as from Hegel's philosophy of history in particular, to the point where he formulated his own apparently diametrically opposed historical theory. The latter has variously been called 'scientific socialism', 'scientific communism', 'historical materialism', or (of course) simply 'Marxism', and the journey towards its formulation is often described as marking the transition from the 'early' to the 'mature' Marx. Partly because many of Marx's writings from 1842–1846 were not published until after his death, some not even discovered until the 1920s, and only made available in English during the 1960s, this period of his thought has generated much interest, reflected in many books re-evaluating the 'philosophical' foundations of his thinking. Thus we now have a superior understanding of the philosophical underpinning to Marx's theories than was available both to those generations who subscribed to what they took to be 'Marxism' (or, Soviet-style 'Marxism-Leninism'), *and* to their critics. The (especially political) ramifications of this endemic 'misunderstanding' of Marx fall outside our theme. But the material exposing it – the transition from the 'young' to the 'mature' Marx – is central to it, for in addition to permitting us better insight into Marx's mind, it also reveals an early, embryonic philosophy of history preceding the 'historical materialist' theory for which he is most famous.

Philosophical foundations: the early Marx

As indicated, at university Marx was attracted to the Young-Hegelian radicals enthused by their master's 'Idea of Freedom'. Indeed, it was only shortly after leaving university in 1841 that we find Marx idealistically writing about 'human emancipation' and calling for people to have 'real freedom'. He attacked Prussian censorship, called for greater democracy, and criticised discrimination of the Jews. Last chapter we noted room left by Hegel for at least some 'fine-tuning' of the modern state, and Marx was amongst those who used Hegelian logic as a spear of criticism, arguing that the kind of 'freedom' we saw Hegel referring to – that of freely dutiful citizens of a state respectful of individual freedom within the context of a communal will – was yet to be attained in Prussia. But it must be noted here that Marx's critical stance in no way refuted Hegel's fundamental (philosophical) *idealism*. Rather, it precisely exploited the belief that history is driven by the Idea of Freedom – i.e., that there is an underlying meaning given to history through some determining (extraneous?) logic. (In the article already quoted, Engels anticipates 'the thousand-year reign of freedom'.)[2] The problem was, for Marx, that in the *real* world the modern state vaunted by Hegel radically failed to fulfil that Idea of Freedom. Increasingly, this led Marx to criticise Hegel himself, as in his *Contribution to the Critique of Hegel's Philosophy of Law [Right]*.

Written in early 1843, (although not published until 1927, in German), Marx's objective in this seminal but difficult work was to show that Hegel's concept of the modern state was deeply flawed. It purports to exemplify freedom, yet only does so at the level of citizenship of the state, which via its institutions claims to be the unifying factor manifesting the communality of will of freely obligated citizens. But Marx insists this universality of will and social purpose is phony because completely abstract. In the real world of work and the concrete organisation of society (i.e., 'civil society') below the state's institutions, numerous antagonistic divisions of wealth, status, class, religion, property, and power abound. This is where individuals live their real lives, and yet as (political) citizens they are all treated as 'equal', afforded the rights to private property, religious expression, equality before the law, and potentially (via universal suffrage) the right to political representation. For Marx, such 'citizenship,' is a purely abstract expression of man's communal nature – in fact, a contradiction to it, since

> in order to behave as an *actual citizen of the state*, and to attain political significance and effectiveness, he must step out of his civil reality, disregard it, and withdraw from this whole organisation into his individuality; for the sole existence which he finds for his citizenship of the state is his sheer, blank, *individuality* . . .'.[3]

Thus, far from experiencing his citizenship as his social participation in a genuine universality of will, his political existence 'as a citizen of the state is an existence outside his *communal* existences and is therefore purely *individual*'.

But what of the great advances towards 'freedom' which the French and American Revolutions apparently achieved in their institution of 'the universal rights of man and the citizen', whereby ordinary people were politically 'emancipated' from exploitation, inequality, and discrimination on grounds of religion, social standing, and property? Marx's reply (even clearer in his article, *On the Jewish Question*, written later in 1843) is splendidly ironic. These much-vaunted 'rights of man' characterising the modern state do *not* free people from the divisive inequalities in actual society. On the contrary, their very *function* is to copper-bottom in law the bases of social division by giving all citizens the right, for example, to freedom of religion and freedom to own private property. Thus, for Marx, although the modern state does offer *political* emancipation from religious and property discrimination (by permitting freedom of religion and removing property qualifications from citizenship), it does not free people from such discriminations in real society. On the contrary, it maintains and even exacerbates it. For example, if by abolishing property qualifications for the vote, 'the masses have won a victory over the property owners and financial wealth', this might mean the state has freed itself from property restrictions – however, this 'not only fails to abolish private property but even presupposes it'.[4] Likewise with other 'universal rights', e.g., 'man was not freed from religion, he received religious freedom . . . He was not freed from the egoism of business, he received freedom to engage in business'.[5]

Thus the problem with the modern state, for Marx, is that in *political* terms it establishes a coherently equal society in which the essential communality of man is no longer divided by wealth, rank, religion, birth, and other divisive distinctions. Yet it only does so by 'freeing' individuals to pursue their own merely individualistic aims without hindrance from social accountability (i.e., from 'political' control). In passages concerning previous *feudal* society Marx suggests there was at least something authentically *social* about it, now swept away by the modern state. It is true there were gross inequalities of rank, wealth, and power in feudal society. And yet at least these differences were given directly political expression in their hierarchical constitutions, such that the overall social organisation in which each individual lived was transparent to him. In *that* sense, there was an authentic society, governing itself *as* a society, rather than what Marx saw as the situation under the modern state, where *any* sense of social solidarity and communal consciousness was stripped from man in a 'civil society' left to the pursuit of self-interestedness. As Marx put it, '*egoistic* man . . ., the member of civil society, is thus the basis . . . of the *political* state. He is recognised as such by this state in the rights of man'.[6]

The solution, for the early Marx, is a society and 'state' where Hegel's ideal of 'universality' *truly* pertains. He refers to this variously as 'democracy', 'the genuine state', or the condition of 'human emancipation'. Quite what this means for the *form* of state under his ideal of 'democracy' is not spelt out. Yet this may be precisely the point, for Marx insists that 'in democracy the constitution, the law, the state itself, insofar as it is a political constitution, is only the self-determination of the people'.[7] In other words, in the 'genuine' state it is up to the people to decide what 'political' functions should exist and what form they should take – but crucially this is premised on people not being divided amongst themselves.[8]

This returns us to Marx's view of the phony claims of the modern state to exemplify 'universality' via its 'rights of man'. For example, regarding liberty, Marx complains: '[b]ut the right of man to liberty is based not on the association of man with man, but on the separation of man from man. It is the *right* of this separation, the right of the restricted individual, withdrawn into himself'. Similarly, the right to private property is 'the right to enjoy one's property and to dispose of it at one's discretion, without regard to other men, independently of society, the right of self-interest'.[9]

Like Robert Owen, the French 'utopians', and other socialists preceding him, Marx thus identifies individualism, egoism, and exploitation as endemic to modern society. But he goes much further than them by relating the modern *state* to this non-communal society, as being simply reflective and supportive of it. Marx's idealistic alternative is 'democracy', and we can see how he equates it with 'human emancipation' in the following passage: '. . . only when man has recognised and organised his own powers as *social* forces, and consequently no longer separates social power from himself in the shape of *political* power, only then will human emancipation have been accomplished'.[10]

Towards private property and the proletariat

So far we have seen Marx severely critical of Hegel's estimation of 'the modern state', yet not because he doubts Hegel's underlying philosophy centred on 'the Idea of Freedom'. But his thinking developed, resulting in an article published early in 1844 as an introduction to his earlier *Contribution to the Critique of Hegel's Philosophy of Law*. Here, he turns from 'the state', and instead focuses on the reasons why *civil society* is so fractious. To do this, he turns to primarily *economic* factors, claiming that 'the relation of industry, of the world of wealth generally, to the political world is one of the major problems of modern times'.[11] In one of the earliest indications of his subsequent 'class' theory of history, he focuses on the connection between private property and classes or 'estates', claiming that periodically in history a certain class emerges which, in order to emancipate itself from subjection to higher classes, presents itself as the saviour of the whole of society, and is indeed 'perceived and acknowledged as its general representative'. He claims the bourgeoisie played exactly that role in the French Revolution, in its struggle against the classes which represented 'all the defects of society', namely, the French nobility and clergy. He even anticipates the time in French history when, as 'the role of *emancipator* therefore passes in dramatic motion to the various classes of the French nation', it finally passes to a class which will 'organise[s] all conditions of human existence on the presupposition of social freedom'[12] – a vague formulation which nevertheless suggests that changes in the fundamental *economic* organisation of civil society, involving the displacement of previously dominant classes, may produce a civil society no longer riven by egoism and divisions, but instead provide the conditions necessary for that 'democracy' he had described earlier. Indeed, referring to 'modern nations' other than Germany (which he regarded as laughably backward), he looks forward 'to the *height of humanity* which will be the near future of those nations'.[13]

Tantalisingly, however, he then leaves France aside, and asks what the possibilities of such a movement are in *Germany*. Scathingly, he says that in Germany there is neither one particular class which marks it as 'the negative representative of society', nor one which has 'the breadth of soul that identifies itself, even for a moment, with the soul of the nation', such that the political progress apparently possible in France and elsewhere seems impossible. This prompts Marx to ask, '[w]hat, then, is the *positive* possibility of a German emancipation?', and he answers that in Germany's case the only solution is 'the formation of . . . a class of civil society which is not a class of civil society', a class which 'claims no *particular right* because no particular wrong but *wrong generally* is perpetrated against it', a class which has a genuinely 'universal character by its universal suffering', and which therefore 'cannot emancipate itself without emancipating all other spheres of society'. This class is the proletariat. It is unique because premised on *not* resting on *any* share of private property (i.e., ownership of national wealth and resources) – and it is a definite *class* because it is not 'the *naturally arising* poor' which feature as flotsam in any society, but rather is the specific product 'of the rising *industrial* development',[14] i.e., an integral part of the functioning of society. Marx claims 'the proletariat is coming into being in Germany', and that its demand will be 'the negation of private property'. Although he does not elaborate on this here, he makes it clear that the logic of the proletarian demand – a civil society no longer based on the previous class divisions symptomatic of differing degrees of ownership of private property – equates with those necessary conditions of 'democracy', 'freedom', or 'human emancipation' he earlier derived from his (critical) interpretation of Hegel.

The other theme emerging in this piece reflects Marx's increasingly uneasy relation with idealist philosophy, both of Hegel himself and its radical interpretation by the Young-Hegelians. Marx begins to display impatience with philosophical criticism which does not recognise and incorporate the need for *practical* change – i.e., a transformation of the nature of civil society. For example, after famously referring to religion as 'the opium of the people', he argues that '[t]o abolish religion as the *illusory* happiness of the people is to demand their *real* happiness. The demand to give up illusions about the existing state of affairs is the *demand to give up a state of affairs which needs illusions*'. Thus, speaking of political theory in general, it follows that 'the criticism of speculative philosophy of law turns, not towards itself, but towards *problems* which can only be solved by one means – *practice*'.[15]

In this article Marx wrote about Germany specifically, and yet in the course of his analysis he stumbled upon the principal ingredients of the version of communism for which he became famous – for within a few months, in his *1844 Economic and Philosophic Manuscripts*, he generalised these thoughts on class, private property, the proletariat, and 'human emancipation', to *all* modern societies. No longer concerned with Hegel's theory of the state, he concentrates on criticising the capitalist basis of modern civil society. Capitalist society is deeply divided, contradictory, and fundamentally inhumane, as evidenced most sharply by the situation of the proletariat (the industrial wage-labourer). Marx observed that 'the worker becomes all the poorer the more wealth he produces', that 'with the *increasing value* of the world of things proceeds in direct proportion the *devaluation* of the world of men'. This is because 'labour produces not only commodities: it produces itself and the worker as a *commodity*'.[16] From here, Marx elaborated his now famous theory of 'alienation', deriving from that Hegelian notion of 'self-objectification' explored in the previous chapter.

Marx first adapts the notion to man's *labour* generally, saying that 'the product of labour is labour which has been embodied in an object, which has become material: it is the *objectification* of labour. Labour's realisation is its objectification'. Yet in the actual world of capitalist economic relations, 'this realisation of labour appears as *loss of realisation* for the workers; objectification as *loss of the object*: . . . as *alienation*'. This, however, is not merely a *subjective feeling* on behalf of the worker. Rather, in the actual world, 'the more objects the worker produces the less he can possess and the more he falls under the sway of his product, capital'.[17]

Marx then extends this notion to the *activity* of work itself, for he claims that because the worker confronts the objects of his labour as 'alien' to him, then the very activity of producing the object is also 'alien' to him. 'If then the product of labour is alienation, production itself must be active alienation, the alienation of activity . . .'. This is demonstrated by the fact that in his work, the worker 'does not affirm himself but denies himself, . . . does not develop freely his physical and mental energy but mortifies his body and ruins his mind.' He 'therefore only feels himself outside his work, and in his work feels outside himself'. The key to this is that labour is *forced* upon him by someone else (the capitalist), and thus, not being 'his spontaneous activity, . . . it is the loss of his self'. Indeed, Marx observes that 'man (the worker) only feels himself freely active in his animal functions – eating, drinking, procreating . . . and in his human functions he no longer feels himself to be anything but an animal. What is animal becomes human and what is human becomes animal'.[18]

This takes us back to Hegel's distinction between humans and animals, and Marx elaborates upon this in order to bring his moral objection to capitalism to its dramatic culmination. For Hegel, (self-)consciousness differentiates man from animals. Just so for the early Marx. He asserts that the character of the human species is 'free, conscious activity'. According to Marx, 'the animal is immediately one with its life activity. It does not distinguish itself from it', whereas 'Man makes his life activity itself the object of his will and of his consciousness; . . . his own life is an object for him', and because of this, his activity is *essentially* (i.e., in principle) 'free activity'.[19]

In other words, the essence of being human is *freedom*, the necessary condition of which is *self-consciousness*, by which man can make his own life an *object* of his *will*. The italicised words are precisely the terms in which Hegel explained 'freedom'. But what Marx has done is unequivocally to transfer this Hegelian logic from 'Spirit' to *man*, and his complaint is that under an economic system in which capital employs labour, 'man' is alienated from his essential human nature, because that nature is freely productive work. Under capitalism, work is imposed by others (for selfish ends) upon men who are thereby deprived of the capacity to make their lives the object of their will. Instead, in a cruel reverse, men are forced to sell what should be their human-affirming activity simply to keep alive.

Marx's 'immature' philosophy of history

If such ideas might appear over-dramatised, we should recall that Marx was referring specifically to the plight of the industrial wage-labourer (the 'proletarian') of the early decades of the nineteenth century, during which it has been claimed, for example, that one generation of northern English mill-owners would run through three generations of mill-workers. However, in these *1844 Manuscripts* he generalised his analysis to imply that 'man as such' has become radically alienated from his human essence. This is because Marx conceives of man's *history* as a process whereby, through his productive activity ('work'), man has progressively 'objecti-fied' or 'realised' himself in the actual world, altering it in accordance with his *human* needs. The combination of modern industrial production and the natural sciences, however, has enormously accelerated this process of mankind's self-expression, whereby 'the nature which develops in human history . . . is man's *real* nature'. Marx claims that 'we have before us the *objectified essential powers* of man in the form of *sensuous . . . useful objects* . . . displayed in *ordinary material industry*'. Nature has become increasingly 'humanised', such that 'history itself is a *real* part of *natural history* – of nature developing into man'.[20] And yet the huge irony, for Marx, is that as man 'duplicates himself not only, as in consciousness, intellectually, but also actively, in reality, and therefore . . . contemplates himself in a world that he has created', he does not recognise himself in that world. Why? Because 'in tearing away from man the object of his production, . . . estranged [alienated] labour tears from him his *species life*, his real objectivity as a member of the species'.[21]

The *private* ownership of the means of production thus exemplifies this giant irony of 'alienation' in human history. For Marx it seems that just as, via modern industry and science, humanity is approaching conditions which promise its full self-objectification, it has never been more cut off from experiencing its self-fulfilment. This is because of the modern system whereby capitalists (the property owners) pay others (the property-less proletariat) a wage to work the means of production so that they (the capitalists) can make a profit by the sale of the proletarians' work. Thus the almost mystical significance of 'the proletariat' for Marx. As claimed in his earlier article, on the one hand it is a distinctive class because integral to the functioning of modern industrial society, but also there is a sense in which it is *not* a class because, unlike other classes, it occupies no rank whatsoever in property-holding, but is merely a commodity to be variously exploited by them. By a plausible, even elegant, logic it follows for Marx that the only 'class-interest' of the proletariat is to abolish private ownership of economic resources altogether. But in removing the very basis for *its* existence as a class, it would also be removing the basis of *any* classes in society, since their existence derives from a civil society organised around private property.

The logical result, then, of the proletarians' interest is a classless civil society characterised by the *social* ownership of the means of production. These would no longer be worked to make a profit (for capitalists), but be worked to meet the agreed needs of society. In short, we arrive at the practical basis for that 'universality' of will underlying Hegel's notion of freedom – and this is why Marx refers to the proletariat as providing 'the key to the riddle of history'. Its unique destiny is to emancipate not only itself but, in so doing, the whole of society by realising the universal will of man. Marx refers to this new society as 'communism', and describes its significance in thoroughly Hegelian terms. It is 'the *positive* transcendence of . . . *human self-estrangement*, and therefore . . . the real appropriation of the *human* essence by and for man'. It is 'the *genuine* resolution of the conflict between man and nature and between man and man – the true resolution of the strife between existence and essence, between objectification and self-confirmation, . . . between the individual and the species'. Moreover, still thinking in Hegelian terms, Marx suggests that the movement towards 'communism' is in fact nothing less than the meaning of world-history displaying itself.

> Communism [is] the complete return of man to himself as a *social* (i.e., human) being – a return accomplished consciously and embracing the entire wealth of previous development . . . Communism is the riddle of history solved, and it knows itself to be this solution. The entire movement of history [is communism's] *actual* act of genesis . . . [and] also . . . the *comprehended* and *known* process of its *becoming*.[22]

Here, then, in these abstract formulations, is nothing less than an (undeveloped) 'philosophy of history' from an early Marx clearly indebted to Hegel, despite being centred on the self-realisation of 'man' rather than on that of Hegel's ambiguous 'World-spirit'. However, another revealing feature of the *1844 Manuscripts* is Marx's increasingly ambivalent attitude towards Hegel's *fundamental* philosophy. Although captive to Hegel's logic regarding 'freedom', 'universality', 'self-objectification', and 'alienation', we have already seen Marx's growing impatience with abstract philosophising which ignores practical reality. This reappears immediately after the above 'philosophical' passages on the movement of history as 'the return of man to himself', for Marx adds: 'It is easy to see that the entire revolutionary movement necessarily finds both its empirical and its theoretical basis in the movement of *private property* – more precisely, in that of the economy'.[23] This suggestion – that *economic* factors underlie the movement of history – is of course thoroughly un-Hegelian, since for Hegel it is Spirit's impulse towards self-consciousness of its essence, Freedom, which underlies world-history. Marx's thinking, it seems, may be losing its coherence just at the point where he attempts to formulate his own philosophy of history. Why was this so?

Feuerbach and 'materialism'

A key factor in explaining Marx's philosophical difficulties in these 1844 texts is Feuerbach's strong impact on his thinking. Ludwig Feuerbach (1804–1872) was until 1839 a follower of Hegel's philosophical idealism, believing that reality is infused with Reason. But he then radically altered his ideas, and propounded a *materialist* philosophy based on sense-perception. Now, for Feuerbach, reality consists solely of the material world, whose nature is apprehended through the senses. The reality of the material world of objects is irreducible and unsurpassable – there is no 'logic' behind it. Existence is not the Hegelian fusion of Being and Thought, of the 'real' and the 'rational'. 'The real in its reality . . . is the real as an object of the senses; it is the sensuous. Truth, reality, and sensation are identical'.[24]

What, then, becomes of 'God', (or of Hegel's 'Mind')? Feuerbach's answer is that God is simply man's idealised image of man himself. 'God is nothing other than the original and the model of man; corresponding to how God is and what he is, man must be and wants to be or at least hopes to be in the future'. . . .[25] This is because 'the essence of a being is recognised . . . only through its object. . . . Thus, the object of the eye is neither tone nor smell, but light. In the object of the eye, however, its essence is revealed to us. . . . He who cultivates the soil is a farmer, he who catches fish is a fisherman'. He observes that 'God is an object . . . only of man', and thus 'what is expressed in the being of this object [God] is merely the peculiar essence of man'.[26] Thus, God 'is man's own essence and goal conceived as a real being'. This explains the attributes of God in theology – e.g., omnipotence, omnipresence, and omniscience. They are simply man's own consciousness of the capacities of *mankind's* nature.

And yet because man's actual possibilities have historically been limited, man idealises his nature into a transcendent, unapproachable being – 'God' – and bows down in self-abnegation before his own fetish. 'Where else than in the pains and needs of man does this being who is without pain and without needs have its ground and origin? . . . Only in man's wretchedness does God have his birthplace'.[27] In short, man alienates himself in religion.

From this standpoint Feuerbach launches his fundamental criticism of Hegel's idealism. He tells us that 'the culmination of modern philosophy is the Hegelian philosophy', and yet 'it is . . . nothing other than theology . . . transformed into philosophy'.[28] But he, Feuerbach, has rumbled Hegel, and instead proposes a new philosophy which will at last emancipate man from the debilitating influence of (religious) alienation and Hegelian 'speculative' philosophy. This new philosophy rests not on 'God' or (philosophically) on some disembodied Reason. Rather, 'it rests not on a beingless, colourless, and nameless reason, but on reason saturated with the blood of man'. Repeatedly, Feuerbach stresses that man is a sensuous being of flesh and blood, and therefore the new philosophy 'corresponding to the needs of mankind and of the future'[29] 'declares that only the human is the rational; man is the measure of reason',[30] – man, that is, as the species, for 'the single man for himself possesses the essence of man neither in himself as a moral being nor in himself as a thinking being. The essence of man is contained only in the community and unity of man with man'.[31]

Feuerbach, Marx, and Hegel

Marx was impressed by Feuerbach's ideas, and in the *1844 Manuscripts* he furthered the task of criticising Hegel's philosophy at its very heart – i.e., idealism. Marx's essential complaint is that instead of viewing self-consciousness as a property of human nature, Hegel regards human nature as 'a quality of *self-consciousness*'. Because of this mystification, in Hegel man is essentially 'regarded as a *non-objective, spiritual* being'.[32] It follows, for Hegel, that if in his actual material life man does not feel fully objectified (i.e., is alienated), then the solution lies in re-arranging his consciousness, i.e., in 're-thinking' himself, rather than re-arranging his material conditions – akin, arguably, to psychotherapeutic theories which purport to solve psychological problems on the couch, through altering one's consciousness via a revised self-knowledge, rather than addressing the actual circumstances causing the psychological problem.

But for Marx, (as Feuerbach had argued), 'Man is directly a natural being . . . a corporeal, sensuous, objective being', and this means that 'he has *real, sensuous objects* as the object of his being or of his life, or that he can only *express* his life in real, sensuous objects'. Thus, because Hegel's philosophy depends on the notion that material reality (including human history) is the expression of disembodied Mind, it is fundamentally flawed. According to Marx this entraps Hegel into the notion that *all* materiality, whatever form it takes, is an alienation of Spirit and thus ultimately something to be spurned by 'self-consciousness' – akin to the mystic's rejection of the actual, material world and his retreat into his self. As we have seen, Marx's view is different. If one is alienated by one's actual circumstances, then it is those circumstances which need to be changed.

The importance Marx attaches to man as an *objective* being, a part of Nature, is thus clear enough. However, this does not mean man is like any other animal, for we have already seen Marx stress his uniqueness in being self-conscious. He returns to the point. 'But man is not merely a natural being: he is a *human* natural being. That is to say, he is a being for himself. Therefore he is a *species being*, and has to . . . manifest himself as such both in his being and in his knowing'. What does this imply? Again, Marx reverts to that embryonic theory of *history* expressed earlier:

> [t]herefore, *human* objects are not natural objects as they immediately present themselves, and neither is *human sense* . . . immediately . . . *human* sensibility . . . Neither nature objectively nor nature subjectively is directly given in a form adequate to the *human* being. And as everything natural has to *come into being*, *man* too has his act of origin – history –

which, however, is for him a known history, and hence as an act of origin it is a conscious self-transcending act of origin. History is the true natural history of man.[33]

These are difficult passages, but taken in conjunction with his previous references to labour as man's objectification, and to 'communism' as the solution to the riddle of history, we can reconstruct Marx's thought. Having dismissed both Hegel's 'Spirit' and Hegel's man as fantastical non-beings because non-objective, Marx is arguing that man is nevertheless unique in being self-conscious. This permits man to produce his own conditions, by changing the world given him in nature. In his activity of changing the world, man is thus 'producing' himself, and is conscious of that 'self' as imprinted on, or expressed in, the world he produces. In this sense, then, history is the process of human self-realisation – the process of man's 'coming-to-be'. Yet although this giant process of world-history has made huge strides particularly since the Scientific Revolution and the increasingly cooperative nature of productive activity, man fails to *experience* his increasing self-fulfilment and 'species nature' because of the alienating impact of private possession of the economic resources which underly class-divisions. The industrial proletarian, whose working life is merely a commodity, is the supreme exemplar of this alienation. And this is why 'communism, as the supersession of private property, is the vindication of real human life as man's possession'[34] – that is, 'communism' provides the objective circumstances, through social control of the productive process, for the realisation of man's potential to experience the world as his own, thus 'solving the riddle of history'.

This, then, is the embryonic philosophy of history amongst these disorganised *1844 Manuscripts*. For Marx, history is nothing less than the process whereby a species whose essence is self-consciousness undertakes the long journey of fulfilling its self (its nature) via the mediation of 'objectifying' itself in the real world. Both the concepts and the logic of this theory derive directly from Hegel, revolving as they do around the interplay between a subjective consciousness and the external, objective world it engenders, and how in experiencing this 'self-objectification' as alien to itself, it progresses (dialectically) to overcome this defect. And yet the influence also of Feuerbach is dramatic, for whereas in Hegel this being is Mind or 'Spirit', for Marx this being is 'man' – and 'man', moreover, who although indeed self-conscious, is an objective, natural, sensual being of flesh and blood. Man's project (the meaning of history) is to 'realise' his nature via a process of mediation between his consciousness and the external world – and he does this by 'objectifying' himself in productive activity. But whereas for Hegel (at least, according to Marx) the external world manifested by 'Spirit' is *always* alien from that of pure Self-consciousness, such that the latter must always transcend it and return to its self as 'Mind', this is not the case with 'man'. Because 'man' is an objective, natural being, the objective 'external' world is *not* alien to him. It is true that as raw nature it is alien – it does not reflect human nature. But in his work in/upon the external world, man constantly alters it to accommodate it to his bodily and mental needs. Thus, 'objectification' is not ultimately alienating (as in Hegel), but is in principle direct 'self-realisation'.

However, that the world man creates is not *experienced* as self-realising, or 'human', but as alienating, is because of the divisive factors of power and property relations which reduce most of mankind's productive activity to the status of a commodity. This perverts the living experience of the affected class not only 'subjectively' in terms of how they feel but objectively insofar as they are poverty-stricken, insecure, and powerless amidst a land of plenty – and (it is fair to assume from Marx's comments) it is equally alienating for the rich and powerful who, although materially comfortable, have an equally perverted consciousness of what it is to be 'human' in their exploitative, egoistic lives.

The resonance of Marx's 'immature' philosophy of history

Although much interest in this early, neo-Hegelian, philosophy of history by Marx centres on its relation to his later theory of 'historical materialism' (treated below), its scope and audacity merit considering it in its own right despite its sketchy nature. Noticeable first is the obvious moral dimension the concept of 'alienation' introduces into it, reminiscent of Rousseau's strictures on 'civilised' society. Second, the theory continues that 'politicisation' of philosophy of history we noted as a feature developing in the Enlightenment. In Marx's case this clearly revolves around the reconstructing of a civil society no longer based on private-property-based economic and social relations – ie 'communism', ('practical humanism', or 'true democracy'). Today this belief in 'communism' can seem outdated, although what Marx meant by it in the *1844 Manuscripts* is extremely general – but even as such, seems far removed from its controversial twentieth-century versions. (Neither is it clear that in this early theory Marx saw 'communism' as historically inevitable.)

Rather, it is another feature of Marx's theory which resonates in today's world – namely, his notion of the overall meaning of human history as the process of altering the external, natural world to accommodate it to our human nature – i.e., that history is man 'humanising' the world. We now know Marx was merely on the threshold of the advances since made in 'man's conquest of nature'. And even now, these advances promise to accelerate at a pace and encompass a scope unheralded in history, such that increasing numbers of people question the wisdom of the process. Ecological concerns abound as human activity deliberately or otherwise alters the planet's systems. Medical possibilities raise increasingly fundamental dilemmas regarding our notions of how, and how long, we live our lives. And perhaps above all, genetic engineering, not only of plants and animals, but of human beings, raises into the starkest relief the issue of what it is to 'be human'.[35] In short, if in Marx's day, questions regarding what it actually *means* to 'humanise' the world could be judged rather speculative, in today's world it beckons to have literal import. In this light it is worth revisiting the efforts Marx made to directly address this question as central to his early philosophy of history.

His thinking on this begins with his notion that 'in his *work upon* inorganic nature, man proves himself a conscious species being, i.e., as a being that treats the species as its own essential being. . . . [a]n animal only produces what it immediately needs for itself or its young, . . . whilst man produces universally'. What Marx means is that man's productive activity is not limited to his individual physical needs, but reflects the multifarious attributes of his species, sensual and intellectual. Thus, 'the universality of man appears in practice precisely in the universality which makes all nature his *inorganic* body', but a body 'which he must first prepare to make [it] palatable and digestible'.[36]

Further on, Marx tries to explain what the truly *human* experience of the objective world should be. Ideally,

> [m]an appropriates his comprehensive essence in a comprehensive manner, that is to say, as a whole man. Each of his *human* relations to the world – seeing, hearing, smelling, tasting, feeling, thinking, observing, experiencing, wanting, acting, loving – . . . are in . . . their *orientation to the object*, the appropriation of that object; . . . their orientation to the object is the *manifestation of the human reality*.

Ideally, then, 'all *objects* become for him the *objectification of himself*, become objects which confirm and realise his individuality. . . . The manner in which they become *his* depends on the *nature of the objects* and on the nature of the essential power corresponding to *it*'.

What does this mean? Marx explains that any *individual's* experience of the world depends upon what 'essential' powers he has. For example, 'the most beautiful music has *no* sense for the unmusical ear', and this is (presumably) simply a 'natural' misfortune. However, any such block to the possibility of *human* experience pales into insignificance compared to the damage caused by the alienating effects of a private-property based society and culture. 'Private property has made us so stupid and one-sided that an object is only *ours* when we have it – when it exists for us as capital, or when it is directly possessed, eaten, drunk, worn, inhabited, etc. – in short, when it is *used* by us'. Referring to man's 'essential' powers, Marx complains that because of this utilitarian attitude to the world, 'In place of *all* these physical and mental senses there has therefore come the sheer estrangement of *all* these senses – the sense of *having*'. (We might today gloss this as the 'commodification' of experience in our 'consumer' societies).

Instead, he looks forward to a time when, via 'the transcendence of private property' 'all human senses and attributes' will be 'emancipated'. This emancipation is based upon a new society where 'need or enjoyment has . . . lost its *egotistical* nature, and nature has lost its mere *utility* by use becoming *human* use'. In this new situation, man's senses will 'relate themselves to the *thing* for the sake of the thing', by which Marx means that one will be able to find in the thing or object that which stimulates our *human* sensibilities. For example, 'For the starving man it is not the human form of food that exists, but only its abstract existence as food. It could just

251

as well be there in its crudest from' – or, '[t]he dealer in minerals sees only the commercial value but not the beauty and the specific character of the mineral'.[37]

Finally, however, we return to Marx's theme of the 'universality' of man, for he claims the most pervasive block to *human* experiencing of the world has been because individuals live in circumstances which alienate them from their species-consciousness. We have already noted Marx's rejection of egoism and individualism, and he seems to suggest that such a 'non-social' consciousness blunts the capacity for *human* sensitivity because individuals are unable to benefit from an openness to the multifarious 'essential' capacities of mankind. For this reason, 'the *senses* of the social man *differ* from those of the non-social man', and it is in elaborating on this apparently bizarre claim that his assorted ideas on human experience and the meaning of history reach their summation.

> Only through the objectively unfolded richness of man's essential being is the richness of subjective *human* sensibility . . . either cultivated or brought into being' – that is, 'a musical ear, an eye for beauty of form – in short, senses capable of human gratifications, senses affirming themselves as essential powers of man.

He continues: 'For not only the five senses but also the so-called mental senses, the practical senses (will, love, etc.), – in a word, *human* sense – comes to be by virtue of its object, by virtue of *humanised* nature. The *forming*[38] of the five senses is a labour of the entire history of the world down to the present'.[39]

Sufficient has been said to justify our claim that in the *1844 Manuscripts* Marx sets out the principles of a 'philosophy of history'. Indeed, given his interest in Hegel it is difficult to see how he could have avoided doing so. However, his ideas only amount to a framework of key concepts. The reader cannot fail to notice that Marx has not offered any actual *history* as yet! However, we can see the direction his mind was taking. Shortly after the above passages on history as the 'objectification' of man and the 'humanisation' of nature, he says that if we wish to trace this formative process we must look at man's work or industry, since then 'we see how the history of *industry* . . . [is] the *open* book of *man's essential powers*, the perceptibly existing human *psychology*'.[40] Clearly, then, although the framework of his (1844) philosophy of history was infused with aspects of Hegelian philosophy, its *empirical* content would have been markedly different because it would have focused on man's productive activity – 'the history of industry' – rather than on (Hegelian) changing phases of Self-consciousness. And this is precisely what his 'mature' theory of history is to focus on. However, having argued that 'history is the true natural history of man', Marx added, 'on which more later'.[41] But he does not fulfil this intention. Instead, in the few remaining pages of the *1844 Manuscripts* Marx returns, like a dog worrying a bone, to criticising Hegel's concept of Mind and the alienation of Self-consciousness, at which point he abandoned the *Manuscripts*, unfinished. When, more than a year later, he returned to flesh out his theory of history, that theory appears to have undergone a transformation.

Marx's revised theory of history – 'Historical Materialism'

From 'philosophy' to 'practice': Marx's epistemology

The reason Marx abandoned the *1844 Manuscripts* (only written for self-clarification in any event) was partly that he had argued himself into a blind alley. In talking of history as man's self-objectification, throughout the *Manuscripts* he employs the concept 'man', meaning the abstraction 'mankind'. But when he posed the question, 'how . . . does man come to alienate his labour?', suddenly this abstraction 'creates the domination of the person who does not produce'[42] – a confused answer because somehow real, class-divided men have emerged as if produced by 'mankind'. As he explored this further, he realised the need to abandon such 'philosophical' abstractions as 'man', and talk only of actual *men* (i.e., real men and women). But this was no mere technical point for Marx. On the contrary, it persuaded him there was something fundamentally wrong with 'philosophy' itself insofar as, at least in its idealist tradition (exemplified by Hegelianism), it sets up abstractions and treats them as real things. Hence the blind alley he had encountered when asking how 'man' came to alienate 'himself'. In short, it may be reasonable to talk abstractly of 'mankind' as comprising both masters and workers, but it is as difficult to see how a 'mankind' *solely* comprised of workers can somehow become a real *agent* and *produce* masters as, presumably, also part of 'mankind' – and an 'alien' one at that!

By 1845 Marx's doubts about the efficacy of (idealist) philosophy to talk sensibly about reality crystallised into his *Theses on Feuerbach*, where he laid the basis of 'historical materialism' as an alternative approach to understanding the world. Now, Marx not only dismissed Hegelian idealism, but also criticised Feuerbach on the grounds that his materialism was in fact just another species of idealism. This issue gets to the heart of the 'mature' Marx. He complains that all previous materialist philosophies (including Feuerbach) are incorrect because they believe in the self-sufficient reality of 'objective' things in nature – i.e., they assume there 'really' *are* 'trees', 'rocks', 'horses' existing as such, and which the human senses straightforwardly perceive as if the mind were like a mirror, reflecting a given reality. Marx calls this 'contemplative materialism', and says it is erroneous. Rather, our ideas of things in the external world are not simple 'reflections' but are mediated by how those things impinge upon our *practical* experience as beings in that world. As beings of flesh and blood (rather than pure intellects) we notice things and their properties insofar as they are relevant to us 'in practice'

This can be explained by some simple examples. Imagine the proverbial caveman bumping into something hard, which hurts him. He will therefore notice 'it', and let us suppose he calls 'it' a rock. He has become aware of 'rocks', but all he means by 'a rock' as yet is something hard which hurts if one bumps into it. 'There are such things as rocks' – this idea about the world, albeit crude, is at least some help to him. Now suppose he bumps into another thing which is hard, but it drops fruit he can eat. He will thus notice this object, and rather than call it a rock, distinguish it by calling it, e.g., a tree. There are now such things as 'rocks' and 'trees', but their meaning is established through man's experience of them *in practice*. By the word 'rock' our cave-man now means something which is not only hard and can hurt, but something which does not bear fruit. This is how we can conceive the development of human consciousness of the external world, whereby through 'practice' (i.e., the *manner* in which we respond to 'objects') we extend our 'understanding' of that world's nature. Whether there are 'really' such things as 'rocks' or 'trees' is a meaningless question. The point is, are they useful ideas in practice? (Let us note it was not until the 1960s that people became aware of 'teenagers', and not until people flew airplanes that they became aware of 'air-pockets'. Does this mean that teenagers, or air-pockets, did not exist in previous history? Alternatively, does this mean that teenagers and air-pockets will always exist?)

Thus we see the force of Marx's assertion that 'the question whether objective truth can be attributed to human thinking is not a question of theory but is a *practical* question. Man must prove the truth, i.e., the reality and power, the this-worldliness of his thinking in practice. The dispute over the reality [validity] or non-reality of thinking which isolates itself from practice is a purely *scholastic question*', (e.g., such futile 'philosophical' questions as 'how many angels can stand on the head of a pin'). All such erroneous thinking stems from the fallacy whereby 'things, reality, sensuousness are conceived only in the form of the *object, or of contemplation*, but not as *sensuous human activity, practice . . .*'.[43]

The trouble with Feuerbach, according to Marx, is that despite talking of 'real, living' men, he is still wedded to the abstract concept, 'man'. Hence, although he gets as far as to see 'man' alienating himself in religion, he attributes this to the 'essence of man' as an abstract category, and thus fails to explain why this 'man' alienates himself. But now, for Marx, just as there is no such reality as 'the essential' rock or tree, so there is no such thing as 'the essence of man'. There are only real, actual men and women, and their nature or 'essence' is no more than how, in practice, they relate to each other. 'The essence of man is no abstraction inherent in each single individual. In its reality it is the ensemble of social relations'. Thus, if 'man' is alienated in religion, we should recognise that this is a property, not of 'the human essence', but of actual men who 'belong in reality to a particular form of society' – i.e., religion 'is itself a social product'.[44]

Just so, then, with 'man's self-alienation' in the *productive* process. It is not a property of 'man'. Rather, it is a feature of actual, real men who live in the particular social relations which produce alienation.

A crucial implication of this new approach was that Marx abandoned belief in 'truth' as some kind of philosophical absolute, and instead judged the validity of ideas in terms of their efficacy in practice. Two things followed regarding socio-political thought and its role in historical change. First, people can imagine or philosophically 'deduce' whatever ideas they like about society, justice, freedom, and the like – but unless these are grounded in the actual nature of material reality they are barren. If new, they are likely to be utopian because merely wishful thinking disassociated from the realities of the actual world. But, second, it also follows that where new ideas derive from a practical awareness of how reality is *actually* impinging upon people in a new way, then these new ideas will have a genuine currency whereby they can indeed 'prove the truth. i.e., the reality and power, the this-sidedness' of their thinking 'in practice'.

This latter thought finally released Marx from the last restraint he felt Hegel imposed, for Hegel had famously said of his book of political philosophy, that 'as a work of philosophy, it must be poles apart from an attempt to construct a state as it ought to be'. Rather, what philosophy achieves is 'to recognise reason as the rose in the cross of the present'.[45] This gigantically conservative judgement on the point of political and social 'philosophising' – that it cannot lead to bringing about a better world – had impressed and perhaps restrained the young, radically-minded Marx, despite the preparedness of his less intellectually conscientious radical colleagues simply to ignore it. Indeed, we have just seen that a part of Hegel's stricture was to remain integral to 'historical materialism' – namely, Marx's lifelong battle against 'utopianism', begun back in 1842 when he voiced scepticism over French socialist and communist ideas.[46]

Historical materialism: The German Ideology

The *Theses on Feuerbach* thus represent a distinct shift in Marx's thinking. Rather than continue 'philosophising' about the 'essence of man' and alienation, Marx turned to seeking explanations of problems by looking at people's actual circumstances, especially their social organisations at any particular time. Indeed, so marked is this shift in approach, and so certain was Marx of its validity and significance, that he set about writing *The German Ideology* with Engels in late 1845. The intention was to publish his new outlook and to roundly criticise those 'radicals' who continued to base their thinking on Hegelian premises. Amongst them he now included Feuerbach, because he 'never arrives at the actually existing, active men, but stops at the abstraction, "man"'. This is a 'relapse into idealism'.[47] Marx calls his new theory, 'the materialist conception of history', and in a head-on clash with Hegel and his philosophical legacy, contrasts it to 'the idealist conception of history'. But as already hinted, there is now a sense in which for Marx *all* 'philosophy' is 'idealist' to the extent it relies on the efficacy of pure thought, dissociated from the concrete social mediation in which it arises, to 'objectively' understand reality.

For this reason, in expounding his basic theory of society and history, Marx's tone is scathing about the claims of 'philosophy' to speak sense. His first point is that there would *be* no human history without the existence of actual human beings in their real historical circumstances – and these human beings have first and foremost to survive, which involves 'eating and drinking, housing, clothing . . .'. Human beings, unlike animals, do this by *producing* the means to satisfy these basic needs, and thus this production is the first properly *historical* act.[48] Already we see how Marx's views have changed, for whereas a crucial notion in the *1844 Manuscripts* was that 'man' is distinguished from animals by self-consciousness, now Marx says: '[m]en can be distinguished from animals by consciousness, by religion or anything else you like. They themselves begin to distinguish themselves from animals as soon as they begin to *produce* their means of subsistence'.[49]

His next point is that in producing to meet their needs, new needs are generated, and he reminds us that the productive process 'today, as thousands of years ago, must daily and hourly be fulfilled merely in order to sustain human life', a fact he deplores historians and philosophers for neglecting.[50] This is because, 'by producing their means of subsistence men are indirectly producing their material life' – and at any one time, how men produce (i.e., the 'mode of production') not only keeps them alive: 'Rather it is a definite form of activity . . . , a definite form of expressing their life, a definite *mode of life* on their part'. Having dismissed all philosophising about the nature of 'man' as so much verbiage, Marx completes the point by saying: 'As individuals express their life, so they are. What they are, therefore, coincides with their production, both with *what* they produce and with *how* they produce. Hence what individuals are depends upon the material conditions of their production'.[51]

His next point is 'that men, who daily re-create their own life, begin to make other men, to propagate their kind'. In short, some kind of *family* structure pertains, and this is a cooperative context involving a division of tasks. Alongside this, other forms of cooperation emerge to facilitate the activity of production, such that,

> it follows from this that a certain mode of production, or industrial stage, is always combined with a certain mode of cooperation, or social stage, and this mode of cooperation is itself a 'productive force' . . . hence, the 'history of humanity' must always be studied and treated in relation to the history of industry and exchange.

Within these basic 'premises' underlying history, Marx has so far ignored consciousness, or the role of ideas. This is because he argues that consciousness is from the beginning a product of those material conditions of human life already outlined. He links it to the origins of language, which itself emerges 'from the need . . . of intercourse with other men' in the productive process. Thus from its origins, 'language is practical, real consciousness that exists for other men as well', and thus 'consciousness is . . . a social product, and remains so as long as men exist at all'. Marx claims that initially men's consciousness was thus only a limited awareness of each other (and hence of themselves) because of the restricted social relations in primitive modes of production – 'mere herd-consciousness'. Also, 'because nature is as yet hardly altered by history' and thus 'confronts man as a completely alien, all-powerful . . . force', men's first religion is that mere 'natural religion' in which nature itself is animated.[52]

However, because population growth generated an increase in needs and greater productivity, cooperation extended – and these conditions promoted a development of men's consciousness to the seminal point when 'a division of material and mental labour appears'. Indeed, Marx claims it is only then that division of labour truly becomes established, when 'ideologists' separate themselves from material labour and become 'priests'. In scathing terms Marx claims that from this point, 'consciousness is in a position to emancipate itself from the world and to proceed to the formation of "pure" theory, theology, philosophy, morality, etc.', and that it can now 'flatter itself that it is something other than consciousness of existing practice, that it *really* represents something without representing something real'. But, for Marx, 'it is quite immaterial what consciousness starts to do on its own'. This is because it is only possible for it to propose ideas at odds with the world around it – 'all this trash' – insofar as that real world itself exhibits contradictions. The latter arise because 'intellectual and material activity, . . . enjoyment and labour, production and consumption, devolve on different individuals',[53] and this is due to the division of labour.

Division of labour

'The division of labour' is a key concept in Marx's theory of society and historical change. Although practised in varying degrees for millennia, the concept was famously brought to prominence by Adam Smith, who opened his *Wealth of Nations* (1776) by showing how the productive process – (he used the example of pin-making) – is enormously enhanced by dividing the separate actions involved in production between different individuals, thus allowing specialisation and saving time (and also facilitating the use of machinery). This extends from the operations involved in manufacturing a single article to the division between different occupations, and as Smith pointed out, it is primarily due to the division of labour that, relieved from having to produce everything for themselves, individuals enjoy vastly increased wealth. As such, 'the division of labour' seems a solely technical matter of the efficient deployment of work-activity.

For Marx, however, although 'the division of labour' indeed means the above, it also means much more. This is because of the economic and social implications inseparable from it in actual history. Marx claims the first division of labour was in the family, 'where wife and children are the slaves of the husband'. This was 'the first form of property', for although crude, 'even at this stage it corresponds perfectly to the definition of modern economists, who call it the power of disposing of the labour-power of others' – (i.e., by 'property' Marx, like economists, is not referring to mere personal possessions). Even at its inception, then, the division of labour implies 'the *unequal* distribution, both quantitative and qualitative, of labour and its products'.[54]

The division of labour extended beyond single families to a division of labour between different families, and then into the tribe. Later, as nations emerged, it led 'at first to the separation of industrial and commercial from agricultural labour, and hence to the separation of town and country . . . Its further development leads to the separation of commercial from industrial labour'. Subsequent divisions of labour within these different branches result in different relative positions of groups depending on 'the way work is organised in agriculture, industry, and commerce'.[55] At each stage, however, these further divisions of labour are not merely technical improvements in the organisation of productive capacity. Rather, because 'division of labour and private property are, after all, identical expressions',[56] then 'the various stages of development in the division of labour are just so many different forms of property', which 'determines . . . the relations of individuals to one another with reference to the material, instrument and product of labour'.[57] In short, historically any mode of production functions through a particular division of labour, and thus generates a certain set of social relations based on the 'labour-disposing' powers of private property. In this sense, all societies have been 'class' societies, where different classes occupy different positions of relative inequality and privilege.

The state

Marx then extends this analysis to the *political* aspect of societies. Overall, the division of labour helps generate a society's total production by which its members are sustained. But the society is divided into unequal parts, and therefore there is a 'contradiction between the interest of the separate individual . . . and the common interest of all individuals who have intercourse with one another'. This 'common interest' exists 'as the mutual interdependence of the individuals among whom the labour is divided', yet individuals are unable to relate to this genuine common interest because restricted, in their unequal societies, to seeking '*only* their particular interests'.[58] Because of the threat of continual discord, the 'common' interest has to be asserted, and this is exactly the function of 'the state'. Yet Marx distinguishes between the *genuine* and the *illusory* 'common' interest, claiming that in reality the state only asserts the latter. Why? Because 'the state is the form in which individuals of a ruling class assert their common interests',[59] and thus it functions to maintain the property-relations which correspond to the division of labour. Being therefore always the agent of the dominant class (apart from tumultuous revolutionary times), it is not surprising that numerous individuals should experience the so-called common interest asserted by the state as 'alien' to them.

In a rare contribution to this part of *The German Ideology*, Engels puts its clearly: 'Out of this very contradiction between the particular and the common interests, the common interest assumes an independent form as the *state*, which is divorced from the real individual and collective interests'. It is only 'an illusory community', and 'it follows from this that all struggles within the state . . . are merely the illusory forms . . . in which the real struggles of the different classes are fought out'. As such, the state is always the creature of 'civil society', reflective of the power and property-relations within the latter – just as the latter has in its turn been shaped by the productive forces which underlie the whole edifice of 'state' and 'society'. Engels' complaint, that 'of this the German theoreticians have not the faintest inkling'[60] is generalised in Marx's conclusion that 'we see that this civil society is the true focus and theatre of history, and how absurd is the conception of history held hitherto, which neglects the real relations and confines itself to spectacular historical events'. Marx is not only criticising 'mere' empiricist history, but also the Hegelian approach to history. For Marx, 'alienation' is now clearly the effect of private property and the division of labour, which with its further development through history ensures that individuals 'become more and more enslaved under a power alien to them'. This power is in fact 'the world market', but for the Hegelians is 'a pressure which they have conceived of as a dirty trick on the part of the so-called world-spirit'![61]

Superstructure and ideology

So far, Marx has argued that at the basis of any society is its mode of production and the attendant property-relations which its division of labour generates. He has also argued that, because the *state's* function is to fix and defend the existing privileges of the dominant propertied class, then the *political* dimension to societies is merely a superstructure emerging from the 'true theatre of history', namely, civil society. According to Marx, this realisation should amend much of the way history is understood, for it means that political struggles have not *caused* historical change, but are rather the *effects* of changes ultimately traceable to *economic* factors.

But Marx is not only concerned to downplay the role of politics and state-activity in historical change. He also wants to downplay the role of *ideas* – i.e., widely construed as all the products of consciousness. Although particularly concerned to attack Hegelianism as the most extreme version of the illusion, he generalises this to all approaches which elevate 'consciousness' into a determining factor in historical change. Instead, he insists that his conception of history – 'historical materialism' – which starts 'from the material production of life itself' and explains the nature of 'civil society', also shows how the latter in its turn explains 'how all the different theoretical products and forms of consciousness, religion, philosophy, morality, etc. arise from it'.

To justify this huge claim (as influential as it has been controversial) Marx reminds us of his fundamental proposition that 'life is not determined by consciousness, but consciousness by life', and that therefore the correct approach to history 'does not explain practice from the idea but explains the formation of ideas from material practice'.[62] Elsewhere using the term 'ideology' to encompass all modes of thought, Marx is therefore insisting that the ideological dimension to any society is, like its politics, merely superstructural – i.e., that it is explicable via the nature of 'civil society', itself made up of social relations dependent upon the mode of production. Thus, for Marx, philosophy, legal ideas, morality, and even art, do not even generate their *own* self-contained history, let alone determine history's course, but should be explained in terms of their origins in practical life.

For example, regarding philosophy, he claims that when 'the reality' of 'the practical process of the development of men' is described, then 'a self-sufficient philosophy loses its medium of existence'.[63] This completes that growing disillusion over the nature and function of 'philosophy' we noted as a feature of Marx's intellectual development. It implies that one may philosophise as much as one likes about e.g., the nature of justice, love, or God, and construct a 'history' of how these ideas have been differently construed over the ages by philosophers – but the only worthwhile questions are, not 'what is justice?, 'what is love'?, 'what is God'?, but first, what was *meant* by these terms in ancient Athens, or in Renaissance Florence, or in the writings of Plato or Hegel? – and second, *why* did they construe these meanings? This latter question resolves into an enquiry into the social relations pertaining at the time in order to explain why these ideas made sense, or 'worked' for them, (or alternatively, was being challenged by alternative notions by those for whom the present understandings did *not* help make sense of *their* actual experience).

In short, to understand Marx's theory of ideology it is worth reminding ourselves of his epistemological dictum, 'The question whether objective truth can be attributed to human thinking is not a question of theory but is a *practical* question'. On this basis, then, Marx attacks the tendency 'common to all historians, particularly since the eighteenth century', to attribute historical change to changes in ideas and values – i.e., 'ideology'. For Marx, they have got matters upside down, and he exposes their error as follows:

> If . . . in considering the course of history we detach the ideas of the ruling class from the ruling class itself and attribute to them an independent existence, . . . without bothering ourselves about the . . . producers of these ideas . . . and world conditions which are the source of these ideas, then we can say, for instance, that during the time the aristocracy was dominant, the concepts of honour, loyalty, etc. were dominant, during the dominance of the bourgeoisie, the concepts of freedom, equality, etc., [were dominant].[64]

And in repeated sections of the *German Ideology* Marx reserves special scorn for the extreme version of this error – the Hegelian philosophy of history – for it is precisely this 'trick' which the Hegelians exploit, for

> once the ruling ideas have been separated from the ruling individuals and, above all, from the relations which result from a given stage of the mode of production, and in this way the conclusion has been reached that history is always under the sway of ideas, it is very easy to abstract from these various ideas "the Idea" . . . as the dominant force in history, and thus to consider all these separate ideas and concepts as "forms of self-determination" of the Concept developing in history

thus leading to the ludicrous conclusion that 'the philosophers, the thinkers, have at all times been dominant in history'.[65]

The course of history: historical change

For Marx, on the contrary, the history of states and of ideas has always been merely reflective of what *really* determines historical epochs, namely, the economic basis to actual material life. The final component which completes his overall theory of history is his theory of historical *change*.

In *The German Ideology* Marx claims that the motor behind major historical changes is the repeated emergence of a *contradiction* between 'the productive forces' (i.e., the mode of production) and 'the form of intercourse' they generate, (i.e., 'the relations of production', or property-relations). For Marx, 'the conditions under which individuals have intercourse with each other' are 'the conditions under which alone these definite individuals . . . can produce their material life and what is connected with it'.[66] These conditions, because generated by the mode of production, are appropriate whilst it prevails as the dominant form of a society's productive forces. There is thus a period of comparative stability where the social relations, political system and legal code, and the ideological superstructure, efficiently correspond to the fundamental mode of production. However, there comes a point where the existing productive forces become held back from further expansion because they begin to outstrip the 'social relations' appropriate to them up until now. A huge contradiction develops, and is only resolved by a period of revolutionary turmoil during which the social/property relations are transformed into new 'forms of intercourse' which correspond to the new mode of production harbingered by the further development of the productive forces.

In short, there comes a point where the relations of production and corresponding superstructure become a straightjacket, rather than a cosy glove, for economic development. They become 'fetters', and it is their transformation into a new set of social/property relations necessary for the expanding mode of production which is the very stuff of history. 'Thus', Marx writes, 'all collisions in history have their origin, according to our view, in the contradiction between the productive forces and the form of intercourse'.[67] The motor of history is driven forward as 'an earlier form of intercourse, which has become a fetter, is replaced by a new one corresponding to the more developed productive forces . . . – a form which in its turn becomes a fetter and is then replaced by another'.[68] This, then, is a process 'which . . . has occurred several times in past history', and 'necessarily on each occasion burst out in a revolution, taking on at the same time various subsidiary forms, such as all-embracing collisions, collisions of various classes, contradictions of consciousness, battle of ideas, political struggle, etc.'.[69]

Historical sketch

Having set out this overall theory, Marx devoted considerable space in *The German Ideology* to therefore sketching out the principal periods of history in terms of how the productive forces generated their specific property and class relations via the division of labour. He begins with 'tribal property', which 'corresponds to the undeveloped stage of production' revolving around hunting, fishing, cattle-raising, and primitive agriculture. The division of labour is 'still very elementary', being merely an extension of that in the family, such that 'patriarchal chieftains' exercise power over the tribe and its slaves. The next stage of society was classical antiquity (i.e., exemplified by Greece and Rome) based on what Marx calls 'ancient communal and state property'. This emerged 'from the union of several tribes into a *city*', which is the communal property of its citizens, via which they 'hold power over their labouring slaves'. But gradually these societies based on 'communal private property' were undermined by the development of 'immovable private property', whereby patrician families began to own parts of what had been common land farmed by 'the plebeian small peasantry'. Marx claims this process of the decay of communal private property 'began very early in Rome . . . and proceeded very rapidly from the time of the civil wars' (amongst the patrician class of Rome) 'and especially under the emperors' (i.e., beginning with the fall of the Republic in AD 30). He suggests that one of the effects of 'the concentration of private property' was 'the transformation of the plebeian small peasantry into a proletariat' – in other words, as with (later) *industrial* private property, a property-less, wage-labouring class – but that 'owing to its intermediate position between propertied citizens and slaves', this class 'never achieved an independent development'.[70] In this important respect, then, the 'proletariat' of the classical world was unlike the modern proletariat because there existed a class below it – the slaves.

Feudalism and the Middle Ages

If classical antiquity was based on the city (and its surrounding agriculture), the succeeeding form of society was based on the country, and here Marx is referring to the Middle Ages following the decline of the Roman Empire. This decline, coupled with 'conquest by the barbarians, destroyed a considerable part of the productive forces'. Industry 'had decayed for want of a market', trade had been violently disrupted, and coupled with 'the influence of the Germanic military constitution' of the invaders, these conditions led to the development of 'feudal or estate property'. This form of society was based primarily on the rural agricultural economy and, according to Marx, was, 'like tribal and communal property . . . also based on a community'. But in this case 'the community' was that of the landowning nobility, which held power over 'the directly producing class', namely, 'the enserfed small peasantry' – still, then, 'an association against a subjected producing class', but different to antiquity 'because of the different conditions of production'. This feudal landed hierarchy 'had its counterpart' in the 'feudal organisation of trades' in the towns of the Middle Ages – again, a kind of communal private property in which 'the gradually accumulated small capital of individual craftsmen' was organised into guilds which controlled the employment and training of journeymen and apprentices, and protected the merchant/industrialists against 'the robber-nobility' and from 'the growing competition of the escaped serfs swarming into the rising towns'. Marx summarised medieval rural and town organisation by saying it 'was determined by the restricted conditions of production – the scanty and primitive cultivation of the land', (the strip-system), 'and the craft type of industry'. Although the overall social/property division into hierarchical estates was 'strongly marked' – 'princes, nobility, clergy and peasants in the country, and masters, journeymen, apprentices and soon also the rabble of casual labourers in the towns', the actual modes of production involved 'little division of labour in the heyday of feudalism'.[71]

Pre-industrial capitalism

For Marx, what began the break-up of medieval, feudal society was precisely a development of the division of labour. Whereas in medieval towns those who manufactured also promoted and sold their goods, in the Renaissance era there 'was a separation of production and intercourse, the formation of a special class of merchants'. The effects of this crucial development in 'commercial communications' were that the merchants extended trade 'beyond the immediate surroundings of the town'; 'new tools are brought from one town to another', which now enter into reciprocal relations, generating a further division of labour whereby each individual town 'is soon exploiting a predominant branch of industry'. This greatly expanded the forces of manufacturing production, indeed to the point where the guild-system and its accompanying property-relations were 'outgrown'. Whilst this economic expansion was initially limited to the home market in England and France, in Italy and Flanders it took off because of 'intercourse with foreign nations', and it is this latter eventuality which Marx calls 'the historical premise for the first flourishing of manufactures'. He observes that this depended upon an increase in the concentration of capital both in the private hands of the merchants and, 'in spite of the guild regulations', in the guilds themselves, (symptomatic of their decline). He points to a symbiosis between the growth of trade, the merchant class with its capital, and the development of manufacture as a mode of production, because 'the kind of labour which from the first presupposed machines, even of the crudest sort, soon showed itself the most capable of development'. Weaving became the principal manufacture because of factors which gave it 'a quantitative and qualitative stimulus, which wrenched it out of the form of production hitherto existing'. In addition to country peasants who began to make weaving their primary rather than merely secondary occupation, 'there emerged a new class of weavers in the towns', serving domestic and foreign markets with increasingly luxurious goods.

All this depended upon the gradual transformation of fixed, immovable capital (i.e., 'natural capital' as ownership of land in the country and guild-property in the towns) into *movable* capital (i.e., the fluid mobility of investment *money*). The capital of the merchants was of the latter kind from the beginning, and the second impulse for its growth was manufacture itself, 'which again mobilised a mass of natural capital, and altogether increased the mass of movable capital as against that of natural capital'. (The enclosure of land for pastoral farming, resulting in a leap in vagabondage, is a well-known example of this process, and was complained about by Thomas More in his *Utopia* in 1513). Technical as this may be, for Marx it was a crucial economic, even historic, development, for it transformed property and hence class relations. Above all, increasingly 'the relations between worker and employer changed' from the patriarchal relation between journeyman and master in the guilds into the purely 'monetary relations between worker and capitalist'. Although feudal relations persisted in the countryside, increasing numbers of peasants fled from their landlords to the towns, which were already becoming more important than the countryside as powerhouses of production.

One of the chief features of this period spanning the fifteenth to the seventeenth century was that 'manufacture and the movement of production in general received an enormous impetus through the extension of intercourse which came with the discovery of America and the sea-routes to the East Indies'. Countries 'entered into competitive relations . . . fought out in wars, protective duties and prohibitions', and 'the masses of gold and silver which came into circulation' stimulated the growth of a world-market dependent upon an expansion of commerce, manufacture, and movable capital.[72] Nevertheless, Marx claims that compared to later periods, 'the movement of capital . . . still remained . . . relatively slow' because of the protectionist policies of the manufacturing and trading nations. Correspondingly, merchants rather than manufacturers were the dominant new class. Nonetheless, this 'mercantilist' attitude did not prevent 'the beginning of money-trade, banks, national debts, paper money, speculation in stocks and shares . . . and the development of finance in general',[73] thus preparing the conditions for an ever greater transformation of capital from its 'natural' form in physical resources into infinitely mobile capital, i.e., pure money.

Industrial capitalism

Sometimes the above is described as the era of 'pre-industrial capitalism', and this captures Marx's approach, for he claims it was succeeded by what became a qualitatively different period, 'the third period of private property since the Middle Ages', namely, the era of large-scale industry characterised by 'the application of elemental forces to industrial ends, machinery, and the most extensive division of labour'. Because of the special 'concentration of trade and manufacture in one country, England', which thus developed a 'relative world-market' for its goods, a point was reached when the demand for its manufactures 'could no longer be met by the industrial productive forces hitherto existing'.[74] This circumstance provided 'the motive power' for the emergence of large-scale industry, the chief mode of production of Marx's own times, and in addition to the scientific and technological advances involved, it also depended on the development of freedom of competition within nations (i.e., a market economy) – something that 'had everywhere to be won by a revolution – 1640 and 1688 in England, 1789 in France'.

For Marx, the emergence of large-scale industry as the dominant force of production had dramatic effects upon the nature of societies. Increasingly, it 'universalised competition' within and between countries, which 'forced all individuals to strain their energy to the utmost'. It 'established means of communication and the modern world market', which 'produced world history for the first time, insofar as it made all civilised nations and every individual member of them dependent for the satisfaction of their wants on the whole world'. It 'subordinated trade to itself, transformed all capital into industrial capital, and thus produced the rapid circulation . . . and centralisation of capital' – in other words, it created the big bourgeoisie and the modern industrial proletariat, removing from the division of labour, and from labour itself, 'the last semblance of its natural character . . . as far as this is possible', by destroying 'the crafts and all earlier stages of industry where it gained mastery'. In creating 'the modern, large industrial cities which have sprung up overnight', it 'completed the victory of the town over the country'. In creating 'everywhere the same relations between the classes of society', it 'thus destroyed the peculiar features of the various nationalities', creating 'a class [the proletariat] which in all nations has the same interest and for which nationality is already dead'.

Although elsewhere Marx was to lavish praise upon pre-industrial and then industrial capitalism for opening up the world and gigantically expanding the productive forces of society, in the above passages he has stressed the negative effects in an almost wistful way. As noted earlier, Marx thought that in previous eras there was at least something 'natural' in people's relation to their work-activity, however restricted (e.g., the medieval craftsman) – and something authentic about their social relations, however unequal, because based on more 'natural' communal distinctions (e.g., feudal relations of reciprocal obligation between lord and serf). We have even seen him distinguishing between 'natural' (immovable) capital based on physical property, and money capital. The latter is completely indifferent to its use so long as profit is made, and it is this feature of the era of industrial manufacture and its attendant social relations and ideological superstructure that prompts Marx to summarise the effects of industrial capitalism as follows: it 'resolved all natural relations into money relations', thereby producing an ethos which 'destroyed as far as possible ideology, religion, morality, etc. and, where it could not do this, made them into a palpable lie'.[75]

The moral dimension

Without such passages involving *moral* evaluation, the tenets of 'historical materialism' could be regarded as a purely 'scientific' approach to human history – i.e., as an objective theory not dependent upon 'philosophical' assumptions or any particular moral values. And so it has often been viewed, and indeed also utilised in academic areas ranging from political history to economics, from cultural history to the history of thought, and to sociology (which partly originated from Marx's insights). However, it is not only the hyperbole of the above passages which shows that 'historical materialism' was not conceived as 'value-free' by Marx. On the contrary, a moral position runs throughout the whole text, and directs it to a dramatic consummation of his theory of history – namely, the call for and prediction of a communist revolution.

Not surprisingly, this moral dimension harks back to those earlier 'humanistic' writings associated with Marx's *first* attempt at philosophy of history. There, he emphasised 'alienation' as a grim feature of human history, and proposed the moral ideal of escaping from it in order to achieve the realisation of the human species, construed in the neo-Hegelian terms as 'freedom' – i.e., man's experience of full 'self-objectification' in his being-in-the-world. Then, in *The German Ideology*, we saw him spurn such 'speculative' philosophising, not least because of the (to him) risible philosophy of history underpinning it. But Marx's *volte-face* did not involve ditching his moral ideals – rather, they were recast into a different conceptual framework and language. In the *1844 Manuscripts* he had posed the question as to 'why man alienated himself' through his work, but had aborted the attempt to answer it because it was a purely 'philosophical' question resting on a-historical notions of 'the essence of man'. In *The German Ideology* the problem is redefined. Now it is the situation of real individuals, as they function in their productive context and relate to others in their community, which is the focus of Marx's moral attention – and he singles out *the division of labour* as the prime culprit.

Ideally, then, the division of labour needs to be abolished, for it has transformed all 'personal powers . . . into material powers' over which individuals have no control, such that they cannot feel fulfilled in their lives. This dire situation 'can only be abolished by the individuals again subjecting these material powers to themselves and abolishing the division of labour'. But, Marx insists, this is not possible without the formation of a genuine community. He tells us that 'in the previous substitutes for the community, in the state, etc., personal freedom has existed only for the individuals . . . of the ruling class'. It was an 'illusory community' made up of 'one class over against another', which bore down particularly on the lower classes, since it was 'for the oppressed class not only a completely illusory community, but a new fetter as well'. What is needed is a 'real community', for it is only *within* such that 'each individual [has] the means of cultivating his gifts in all directions; hence personal freedom becomes possible only within the community'.[76]

The prediction of 'communism'

Put like this, this 'real community' (Marx's 'communism') might be no more than an abstract ideal following from Marx's *moral* preferences. As such, his vision of communism would have little to do with our theme, philosophy of history. Rather, we could rest content with 'historical materialism' solely as a theory of the past historical development of societies. However, Marx is emphatic that 'communism' is, for him, not merely a *moral preference* – rather, its actual coming-to-be follows directly from his philosophy of history. 'Communism is for us not a *state of affairs* which is to be established, an *ideal* to which reality will have to adjust itself. We call communism the *real* movement which abolishes the present state of things. The conditions of this movement result from the now existing premises'.[77]

In other words, Marx is claiming that history has *once again* developed to a point where the conditions for another new era are in place, thus presaging an overall 'revolution' in the political, social, and ideological nature of societies. As such, this coming upheaval will again come about through the same determinants of previous epochal change – namely, the releasing of the accumulating productive forces from the property/class relations which have become 'fetters' on the development of the mode of production. In this case, the contradiction is between the wealth of productive forces harbingered by modern industrial manufacturing and the extension of a world-market, and the capital-labour, property/class relations presently pertaining. As in previous revolutionary transformations, this will involve ousting the ruling, propertied class from its control of the means of production, and thus be driven by class-struggle.

However, for Marx there is a crucial respect in which the forthcoming upheaval will be different in its outcome, and of the utmost significance in world-history. This is because, whereas all previous transformations have replaced one form of class-rule with another, the coming revolution will abolish class-divided societies altogether, and instead usher in societies where the means of production will be owned and controlled, not as some form of private property, but at last by the 'real community', no longer divided into separate classes. This will be truly 'world-historical' because 'in history up to the present . . . individuals have . . . become more and more enslaved under a power alien to them, . . . a power which has become more and more enormous'. The coming (communist) revolution will at last put a stop to the paradoxical dialectic whereby, as men increasingly master and 'humanise' the world through their productive activity, they are increasingly dominated by the very world they are creating, and consequently feel increasingly 'dehumanised'. Instead, the communist revolution will, from the logic of the premises which have made it imminent, transform this powerless dependency 'into the control and conscious mastery of these powers, which, born of the action of men on one another, have till now overawed and ruled men as powers completely alien to them'.[78] Years later, in referring to the significance of the new era beckoning, Marx expressed the idea as follows: 'The prehistory of human society accordingly closes with this [new] social formation'[79], paving the way for history proper, i.e., a new world-order in which human-beings consciously (freely) make their own history as their own deliberate creation.

As noted, Marx is emphatic that the above is not simply a wished-for ideal, but follows from the 'laws' of historical change he has set out, such that his prediction of the new era is an integral part of his theory of history. Why is this so? The answer reverts to those first intimations he expressed in 1843 about the proletariat's uniqueness. His view then was that, specifically in relation to Germany, the only class which could 'emancipate' German society into 'true democracy' was its developing proletariat, because it was not suffering a particular wrong done to it by a higher class, but was suffering 'wrong generally' in that its total lack of property, power, and status epitomised the negative aspects of private-property based society. Its class demand could only be the abolition altogether of private ownership of the means of production, thereby abolishing the very basis of class-divided society. We saw Marx generalise this idea in the *1844 Manuscripts* to apply to *all* modern countries. Yet he was still under the allure of the Hegelian concept of 'the universality of will'. His theory about the proletariat derived directly from deducing what the achievement of that 'philosophical' ideal would imply.

When, however, in *The German Ideology* he came to abandon Hegelianism (and, arguably, 'philosophy') altogether, he did not abandon this theory of the proletariat. On the contrary, he incorporated it into 'historical materialism'. In the latter work he advances the notion that the 'subsuming of individuals under definite classes cannot be abolished until a class has evolved which has no longer any particular class interest to assert against a ruling class'.[80] Now, historical development has generated precisely such a class – the proletariat. Unlike the serfs, who when they broke from their feudal servitude, 'did not free themselves as a class' and 'did not break loose from the system of estates, but only formed a new estate, retaining their previous mode of labour even in their new situation, and develop[ed] it further by freeing it from its earlier fetters', Marx claims that,

> for the proletarians, on the other hand, the condition of their life, labour, and with it all the conditions of existence of modern society, have become something extraneous, something over which they, as separate individuals, have no control, and over which no social organisation can give them control, [i.e., as a class].[81]

Indeed, whereas 'all earlier revolutionary appropriations were restricted', the proletariat's plight is such that 'things have now come to such a pass that the individuals must appropriate the existing totality of productive forces, not only to achieve self-activity, but, also, merely to safeguard their very existence'.[82] Likewise, Marx claims, 'in all previous revolutions the mode of activity always remained unchanged and it was only a question of a different distribution of this activity, a new distribution of labour to other persons'. Here again the logic of historical development dictates the uniqueness of the proletarian situation, because,

> the communist revolution is directed against the hitherto existing *mode* of activity, does away with *labour*, and abolishes the rule of all classes with the classes themselves, because it is carried through by the class which no longer counts as a class in society . . . and is in itself the expression of the dissolution of all classes . . . .[83]

In short, then, the laws of historical development have generated the situation where modern industrial-capitalist societies are on the cusp of epochal change to 'communism', construed as, amongst other things, classless societies, 'stateless' societies (i.e., in the sense of being 'true democracies'), and societies where the forced division of labour is abolished, along with 'labour' itself, (i.e., productive activity as a commodity to be bought and sold).

Later developments

The historical imminence of 'communism', then, is the dramatic consummation of Marx's 'mature' theory of history first worked out in 1845 in *The German Ideology*. Not published until 1932, aspects of it were instead exploited by Marx in subsequent works published at the time of writing – for example, in *The Communist Manifesto* in 1848, and in *Das Kapital* in 1867 as well as in his unpublished extensive preparatory notes to *Das Kapital* since published as *Economic Manuscripts of 1857–58*[84] (in both of which latter works Marx includes sections analysing in greater detail the origins of capitalism itself) and in politico-historical works analysing key episodes of recent and contemporary French history in class terms.

But as a theory of history he did not change it. Rather, it is the bedrock on which he developed his further political, historical, and economic ideas, (for as he tells us himself, it had achieved its 'main purpose – self-clarification' after his earlier wrestlings with Hegelianism). For example, because of its obvious *political* message he frequently simplified the role of class in history – e.g., 'The history of all hitherto existing society is the history of class struggles',[85] this despite the fact that in the *German Ideology* we saw him saying that when epochal revolutions occur because of contradictions 'between the productive forces and the form of intercourse', then these collisions take on 'at the same time various subsidiary forms, such as . . . collisions of various classes, contradictions of consciousness, battle of ideas, political struggle, etc.'.[86] In other words, class-struggle is but a *part* of these huge movements. Likewise, for good propagandist purposes Marx was wont to declare that the victory of the proletarian revolution was inevitable, whereas nowhere in *The German Ideology* did he claim such a cast-iron necessity. Rather, although the economic determinants of a society are crucial, so is the more subjective factor of the degree of class-consciousness and initiative. 'Both for the production on a mass scale of this communist consciousness, and for the success of the cause itself, the alteration of men on a mass scale is necessary, an alteration which can only take place in a practical movement, a *revolution*'.[87] It is true Marx did see capitalist society as on the threshold of epochal change towards 'communism', and thus in that sense as historically determined or inevitable. However, there is a certain tension between his saying, in the *German Ideology*, that the abolition of private property is *necessary* because 'only in a revolution' can the proletariat 'succeed in ridding itself of all the muck of ages and become fitted to found society anew',[88] and the notion that such a revolution is *inevitable*, and will *inevitably* succeed. The term, 'necessary', could be read as referring to the *logical* necessity of the abolition of private property as the 'only' way of overcoming class division, given the logic of 'historical materialism'. This is different from claiming an empirical or 'scientific' necessity, whereby an event is indeed construed as *inevitable*.

Although Marx was to use the latter language on later occasions, it was far more a feature of *Engels'* formulations. Engels developed his own version of Marx (called 'dialectical materialism') in which historical development is presented in unambiguously mechanistic terms, as if social change followed autonomous 'laws' akin to the scientific laws governing the natural world. As noted by the best commentators,[89] this was not Marx's position, since in his more subtle approach human beings play an active, constitutive role in historical development, albeit often deluded in their consciousness about the world. Thus (rather as with Vico) for Marx, human beings make history (albeit under definite conditions), not some autonomous 'laws' of social development. A certain latitude is therefore justifiable where Marx in later writings seems to present the transition to communism as *inevitable*. Whilst it is true that his theory in *The German Ideology* indeed looks to the collapse of the capitalist society *he* was familiar with, quite how and when this would happen is not predicted in historical terms. And quite sensibly so, we might judge, considering that (like Hegel before him) Marx was working out a theory of history that analysed huge changes which often took centuries to work out all their manifestations.

In this light it is instructive to note Marx's relative openness over the actual manner in which capitalism would be replaced, and the time-span involved. For example, when he first formulated his (mature) philosophy of history in 1845, many European countries were deeply embroiled in their particular nationality problems, in facing strident calls for 'democracy' from large radical movements, and in confronting the ubiquitous problems of poverty, unemployment, and urbanisation known then as 'the social problem'. This heady mixture was to lead to 1848, that 'watershed' year of European revolutions, and later in his life Marx admitted that he and fellow radicals thought they were 'witnessing the death-throes of capitalism', only to find that what they were actually witnessing was its 'birth-pangs'. Indeed, it was partly this shock (along with his own assessment of 'the new stage of development which this society seems to have entered with the discovery of gold in California and Australia')[90] that encouraged Marx to engage on a close 'scientific' study of capitalism (leading to *Das Kapital*) from the 1850s onwards. Similarly, in his *political* thinking, it was not until the Paris Commune of 1871 that he construed the notion of a transitionary phase from capitalism to communism via 'the dictatorship of the proletariat'. In addition he came to speculate that a *peaceful* transition might, unusually, be possible in Britain and the USA. Such observations, then, should encourage us better to understand the epochal perspective from which Marx was viewing history than has many an impatient, dogmatic Marxist since, as well as many a scornful critic alleging that history has shown Marx wrong. Feudalism, after all, lasted centuries, and took centuries to be discarded – and even now, not globally.

Comments

'Progress', 'determinism', and inevitability

Having already remarked on his early, 'immature' philosophy of history, I will mainly restrict comment to 'historical materialism' – firstly as an example of 'philosophy of history' in general, and secondly to its status as either 'philosophy' or 'science'.

Regarding general observations, first it is clear that in both his earlier and 'mature' theories, Marx did not see history as cyclical. This is not to say, however, that distinct forms of society do not collapse, particularly in his mature ('historical materialist') theory. On the contrary, history moves through epochal changes. (Perhaps confusingly, these changes are called 'revolutions', a term suggestive of history 'going round in circles').

Second, is history driven *forward*? i.e., is it *progressive*? Marx's answer (apparent in both his theories) is in the affirmative, yet the matter is not straightforward. This is because history is not *unilinear* for Marx. Rather than a relatively uncomplicated march of progress, integral to Marx's theorising was the notion that as some things get better others necessarily get worse, precisely leading to fundamental upheaval ushering in a new era. This is reminiscent of Hegel's notion of *dialectical* change (through thesis, antithesis, and synthesis). In Marx, however, the dialectical nature of change stems from practical, not logical, contradictions – and even here, was later presented too mechanistically by Engels and 'orthodox' Marxists. Rather, it was a general framework of explanatory and predictive value – for example, his graphic notion that capitalism produces its own gravediggers by generating the proletariat. Third, it is clear that for the atheist Marx there is no 'God' or immaterial 'Mind' behind the course of history. However, this does not exclude its course being *'determined'* by factors (outside of human design) which shape a discernible pattern to the major outlines of historical development. But just how far this lends an *inevitability* to historical change and its direction has often been overstated by Marxists and critics alike.

Perhaps a clear way to address this much-debated theme is, first, to ask: could the course of history have been different as far as Marx was concerned? The answer must surely be 'yes'. For example, there is nothing in his theorising to suggest the Scientific Revolution was 'inevitable', nor that it should have made the particular discoveries it did. (Likewise with the new discoveries of gold whose significance we saw Marx noting in the 1850s). Without it, however, we can assume the large-scale industrial manufacturing mode of production would not have emerged. More to the point for Marx is that, once it *did* emerge, many changes in class-structure, property relations, political systems, and ideology/culture did indeed come about *necessarily*, 'inevitably', or were 'determined' (i.e., to use these terms interchangeably). But their exact nature and timing is not something Marx's theory ever purported as 'inevitable'.

Second, then, we may ask; could the *future* course of history Marx predicted be different as far as he was concerned? The answer to this hot potato is surely to be found in the remarks just made. Marx did regard the collapse of capitalism as historically inevitable. In one sense, given the scope of speculative 'philosophy of history' this eventuality should occasion no surprise to anyone, whether of a Marxist persuasion or not, since the alternative is to suggest that the remainder of the world's history will permanently be restricted to 'capitalism'. One hardly needs a 'theory' of history to express astonishment at such a lack of imagination.[91] But Marx did not base his prediction on such obvious historical instincts. Rather, he claimed to find present reasons (further researched in *Das Kapital*) in the make-up of capitalist societies which not only spelt their demise but also 'determined' what, in broad terms, would replace them – i.e., 'communism'. However, 'capitalism' is a term used by Marx to denote the *social relations* of modern society, not its *mode of production* – and according to 'historical materialism' it is because of changes in the *latter* that capitalism will be discarded by the course of history.

This puts a different complexion on whether, for Marx, that course could be different from what he predicted, for it depends not so much on the nature of capitalism as on movements in the nature of modern productive forces. In his own times, Marx was witnessing the rapid development of large-scale industrial manufacturing as the predominant 'mode of production' in modern societies. His predictions about capitalism were not based on the *demise* of industrialism, but on its future expansion and development, potentially, he believed, to where poverty could be eradicated (eventually world-wide). Modern production was becoming ever more highly 'socialised' in its exploitation of resources world wide, including the work-activity of human-beings. Yet the means of production were still owned as private property, and worked by wage-labour to make a profit for the capitalists. It was this contradiction which prompted Marx's prediction that, as in all earlier epochs, the relations of production were becoming fetters on future development, and would inevitably be broken by the sheer needs of those suffering most from their disadvantages. This was what Marx saw as 'inevitable', or 'determined' by the course of history.

But since his death in 1883, it could be argued that a second 'industrial revolution' began towards the end of the nineteenth century, incorporating electricity and petrochemicals, dramatically altering numerous aspects of society, albeit still under capitalist relations. (Lenin was not alone in suggesting the latter were significantly altered through the growing internationalisation of capital and the new wave of 'imperialism'.)

Again, it could be argued that in the third quarter of the twentieth century a third major development in the 'mode of production' of advanced countries was the growing automation of industrial processes, changing working lives beyond recognition compared to Marx's day. Finally, it is now suggested we have entered the '*post*-industrial' era, dominated by 'service industries', electronic technology, pharmaceuticals, and the new economies based on the 'information technology revolution'. (And bio-engineeering beckons!) Yet it is true that capitalism, understood as competitive commodity production by privately controlled interests employing the labour force, survives as the predominant socio-economic system under which these contemporary forces of production operate. In that fundamental sense it could be argued nothing has changed since Marx's times, despite economic 'globalisation'.

For some this suggests not only that Marx's *predictions* have been proved wrong but that the persistence of 'capitalism' through vastly expanding and altering 'modes of production' disproves the entire principles of 'historical materialism'. Others, however, have argued that the course of history since Marx's death has exemplified these principles in ways obvious to any thinking person. It is true that 'capitalism' has not yet succumbed to pressure from the disadvantaged 'classes' it produces, but this is because it has *still* yet to reach as far as Marx himself saw as a necessary precondition of its demise. When he first formulated his theory in 1845 he made clear that amongst the material, practical premises of the coming of communism was the necessity for capitalism to have 'rendered the great mass of humanity "propertyless", and moreover in contradiction to an existing world of wealth and culture'. This necessitates the 'universal development of productive forces' such that 'a *universal* intercourse between men' would be established, which 'produces in *all* nations simultaneously the phenomenon of the "propertyless" mass (universal competition), making each nation dependent on the revolutions of the others, and finally puts world-historical, empirically universal individuals in place of local ones'. He concluded from this that communism (and hence the collapse of capitalism) 'is only possible as the act of the dominant peoples "all at once" and simultaneously, which presupposes the universal development of productive forces and the world intercourse bound up with them'.[92] It is because, in 1845, he saw capitalism already (and necessarily) developing on these lines that he said the premises for communism were already present.

Whether this universalisation of capitalism he stipulated is nearing completion after its fearsome battles of the twentieth century is conjectural, although one cannot fail to reflect on our present terms, 'global capitalism' and 'the world economy'. But what is beyond doubt is that Marx could not have been expected, and never claimed, to predict the actual events and time-scale it would entail. Also, from the perspective of the 'philosophies' of history we have been examining, the course of history moves far more slowly than its prophets like to think – which might prompt us to suggest (Marx notwithstanding) that the attempt to use 'philosophy of history' for *political* purposes has been, and will continue to be, ludicrous. Along these lines, then, it is not that with hindsight Marx would have predicted some alternative course of history, as if its principles of development had suddenly changed. Rather, he might have congratulated himself on the accuracy of his prediction of the world-reach of capitalism, but have been as fascinated as anyone by the actual historical events involved. And as for his prediction of 'communism', there would seem no reason to suggest he would jettison it in principle, although many reasons to suggest he would amend what little he predicted about its concrete nature and manner of coming about.

'Science' versus 'philosophy'

It is perhaps appropriate that now our final comments on Marx's theorising about history should coincide with ending the first Part of this guide, devoted to 'speculative philosophy of history'. This is because, ironically, Marx understood himself to have dealt this branch of philosophy a death-blow. Arguably he was right, insofar as it could be claimed that since his writings no new, great speculative philosophy of history has been conceived. But however much this is attributable to his impact, it is also the case that towards the end of the nineteenth century 'science' increasingly replaced 'philosophy' in the explanation of numerous aspects of social reality.

In this light it is worth commenting upon whether 'historical materialism' is indeed part of 'speculative philosophy of history' or, instead, 'science'. As far as Marx was concerned, from 1845 he stopped writing 'philosophy'. Instead, he is always translated as claiming 'scientific' status for what he called 'the materialist conception of history', even though the term 'science' in translation rarely appears in The German Ideology, and is in any event ambiguous in the German: 'Where speculation ends, where real life starts, there consequently begins real, positive science, the expounding of the practical activity, of the practical process of development of men'.[93] Indeed, when famously distinguishing his version of socialism from others in The Communist Manifesto, the term is not used at all. Rather, the language is as follows:

> The theoretical conclusions of the Communists are in no way based on ideas or principles that have been invented, or discovered by this or that would-be universal reformer. They merely express, in general terms, actual relations springing from an existing class struggle, from a historical movement going on under our very eyes.[94]

The emphasis upon 'historical materialism' as a science, meaning the model of natural science whereby things happen through the iron necessity of 'laws' independent of human control, came later from Engels, particularly in his dabblings with the natural sciences in his Anti-Duhring of 1875, (where Marx never dabbled) and later, more famously, in the very title of his work, Socialism – Utopian or Scientific?, which was the most influential popular exposition of 'Marxism', running through numerous editions and translations. It was perhaps from this work most of all, especially in its English title,[95] that readers derived the view that the march of history was viewed by Marx as 'scientifically inevitable', the exact impression Engels wished to make.

Thus questions arise as to how far Marx meant to afford his 'theory' or 'conception' of history the status of 'science' in that strong sense defined above, or meant something nearer to what we would call a 'philosophy', despite his rejection of the term. The answer lies partly in semantics. For centuries, in different languages, what we translate as 'science' and 'philosophy' were used as interchangeable terms for 'knowledge'.[96] Even when the specifically factual, empirical knowledge we call 'scientific' began in the seventeenth century to be detached from a priori conceptual thinking, it was often called 'natural philosophy'. There are also the related terms, 'a theory' and 'to theorise', with their own contradictory meanings. Such ambiguities demonstrate that we are far from having a uniform, clear, vocabulary to denote the status of 'knowledge', and that particularly as we go back into history caution is needed in ascribing what writers mean when they employ such terms, their contextual use often being a surer guide than dictionary definitions.

In Marx's case it seems clear that when *attacking* 'philosophy' he is attacking thinking which proceeds purely through deduction from logical categories. This is not to say he dismissed the power of logic – rather, he rejected the validity of treating universal terms such as 'man' as if they denote real phenomena. In this he was following earlier 'nominalist' thinkers (such as Hobbes) as distinct from the 'realists' who thought otherwise. By his day, this traditional dispute was couched in terms of 'materialist' versus 'idealist' philosophy, and thus when attacking 'philosophy' it could be argued Marx was only attacking *idealist* philosophy (i.e., particularly Hegel). However, we also saw him attacking *materialist* philosophers (including Feuerbach) on somewhat similar grounds – namely, their belief that in talking of *material* things (rather than logical categories) they were talking of things whose reality, meaning, or nature was objectively fixed through sensual perception as by some external *diktat*. For Marx such thinking was equally flawed, for it still believed in things having fixed *essences*, despite being apparently grounded in empirical, material reality rather than abstract concepts. It is in this larger sense that Marx attacked both idealist and materialist 'philosophy' as a mode of apprehending and understanding the world.

Instead, Marx's proposed new method, 'historical materialism', was 'scientific' in the sense that, for him, it was derived from the facts of practical reality rather from fixed or a priori concepts. It was also 'scientific' in the sense that, from this 'real actuality', it proposed a general 'conception' or framework of central tenets which explained the connections between things – akin to the role 'scientific laws' play in explaining nature. However, unlike the latter, the subject-matter of 'historical materialism' was not nature, but the *human* world – and this distinguishes it from the model of the 'hard' physical sciences, since the 'laws' governing the development of societies are not some extraneous 'principles' directing how things function, but are what he calls 'premises' derived from straightforward practical reality, (e.g., the production of means of subsistence). In understanding the human world, then, we must be 'scientific' in the sense that we should begin from its strictly *material* 'premises'. History must be understood *materialistically*. So, we might say, must natural science. However, it is equally important that this materialist basis to human life must be understood *historically* – i.e., as subject to continuing alteration over time, partly (but significantly) because of the impact of human activity itself – and this is not a feature of natural science. Put simply, then, in 'historical materialism' it is as important that human life be approached *historically* as that it be approached materialistically. 'History' thus becomes integral to the understanding of social reality, as *method*, rather than being merely something whose facts might interest one.

It is just this restricting of the scope of 'historical materialism' both to *human* affairs and to their *historicity* which prevents Marx's theory from being 'scientific' in our contemporary sense of the term.

But how far is his theory of history 'scientific' in what *he* meant by the term? Some have argued that, whatever he meant by claiming he was not 'philosophising' but was instead being 'scientific', he failed because of the inclusion of *moral* judgements in his historical theory. Similar doubts are raised about the 'objectivity' of his specific theory about economics in *Das Kapital*, a work so clearly fired by the same moral impulses present twenty years earlier in *The German Ideology*. The argument is that, whatever we mean by 'scientific' knowledge, it must at the minimum eschew the intrusion of moral evaluations about its subject-matter. If not, it is being 'philosophical' rather than 'scientific' because introducing ideas unamenable to empirical verification. On these grounds, Marx's theory of history is 'philosophy'. Moreover, it could be claimed that it is 'philosophy' in *bad faith* because it purports not to be philosophy. This is because Marx himself appears to dismiss 'moral' ideas as simply reflections of different material (class) interests. An important achievement of 'historical materialism' is, after all, to explain where moral ideas come from, thus stripping them of any claim to universal 'truth'. But by these same criteria, then, the moral impulse underlying Marx's *own* theory relegates it to 'mere ideology' – certainly not 'science', and arguably not even 'philosophy' because the latter, where value-orientated, is supposed to *argue* its values rather than assume them as given.

The demise of 'philosophy of history'?

Such arguments raise considerable questions about 'historical materialism' as a method of understanding the course of history. However, a case exists for suggesting they arise from false expectations derived from the belief that Marx understood himself to be proposing a rigidly determinist 'science' of history. I have tried to indicate that this is a false reading. No 'science' *or* 'philosophy' of history can ignore the role human needs, desires, illusions, and ambitions play in human history. That is, after all, what makes it *human* – or put the other way round, is what makes it *history*. Marx was acutely aware of this, as demonstrated firstly by his turn away from Hegel's 'Spirit' as the central figure in historical development, replacing it with 'man' – and then his turn away from (Feuerbach's) 'man', replacing it with actual men embroiled in and responding to their material circumstances. He undertook this intellectual journey – away from 'philosophy' towards 'real' knowledge – better to understand the grand scope of history. But making that journey did not involve his abandoning his previous thinking *in toto*. His earlier, merely general, notion of history as the process of human self-objectification through productive activity is strongly present in his (mature) historical materialist theory, albeit stripped of its abstract connotations. Likewise his earlier notion of 'alienation' continues to resonate in his mature theory, except that the abstract ideal of 'freedom' is transposed into the more prosaic ideal of individual fulfilment within the context of a fully enabling mode of social and productive organisation. Also, the centrality of private property, class division, and the proletariat in his earlier 'philosophising' about history persists into his mature theory, but now as real operative factors in explaining actual historical epochs and their changes. It is true that a moral standpoint underlay this overall conception, from his earliest 'philosophising' to the 'scientific' claims of historical materialism. But Marx never made any secret about it, nor felt the need to apologise for it on the grounds that it might invalidate his theory.

Perhaps one reason for his lack of concern was that the moral views he expressed were not, as far as he was concerned, intrinsic to any particular class-interest, and thus not narrowly 'ideological'. Rather, it is a morality which reviles any limitation upon individuals' ability to explore and fulfil their capacities because their activity is treated simply as a means to be commandeered and exploited for others' selfish ends. As such, it is a 'general' moral value which may be expressed differently, and involve surmounting different problems, throughout the history of societies – but one that, for Marx, has doggedly shown itself throughout the practice of human beings' history. And it is this latter observation which perhaps provides a more satisfactory explanation for why Marx never flinched from incorporating his moral perspective into his thinking and writing. By doing so he was hoping to insert his ideas, including their moral imperative, as a factor in people's understanding of the world – because it is *human beings* who, in their thoughts and actions, are the stuff of world-history. But the corollary to this (which Marx's own logic dictates) is that it is up to *them*, through their continuing activity in history, to 'prove' whether the meaning he claims to find in that history is valid. 'The question whether objective truth can be attributed to human thinking is not a question of theory but is a *practical* question'.[97] Have better historical understanding, or subsequent events, consigned Marx's theory of history to the proverbial dustbin, or is the jury still out?

Part II

ANALYTIC PHILOSOPHY OF HISTORY

11

ANALYTIC PHILOSOPHY OF HISTORY

What is it and why study it?

Analytic philosophy of history

As explained in Chapter 1, 'philosophy of history' has two branches; speculative and analytic. Part I of this book offered a guide to the former. This Part treats of the latter branch, *analytic* philosophy of history – and again, does so in the form of a 'guide'. This means that it is neither offered as an exhaustive treatment of the subject, nor as a particular contribution towards it (although even as a 'guide' it is on occasions impossible to avoid engagement in the issues because they relate to the very premises underlying thinking). Rather, its purpose is to familiarise readers (especially students of history) with the principal features of this area of study, and to incorporate some critical awareness of the issues raised.

We should begin elaborating upon the brief account already given in Chapter 1 of what analytic philosophy of history is, and by addressing those same questions we asked of speculative philosophy of history – namely, how far is it relevant and worthwhile for students of history to get involved with?

Whereas its speculative branch treats of history as past events and circumstances (i.e., history as 'content'), analytic philosophy of history enquires into history as the *discipline* (or 'form') which discovers and understands that past. Its enquiry is 'analytic' because it critically analyses the thinking behind the ways in which historians undertake their discipline. For example, what conditions must be met for a statement about the past to be 'true'. Is there an exclusively 'historical' way of explaining the past as distinct, for example, from a *scientific* way? Is *narrative* a satisfactory vehicle for historical knowledge? Do historians implicitly rely on certain 'laws' of human behaviour in their understanding of history? If so, what are they, and are they valid? How far are an historian's perceptions and judgements an extension of his or her own 'unconscious' or ideological views – in other words, can the historian reach *objective* truth, or is he or she captive to *subjective* accounts?

Historical methodology – an important distinction

The above might suffice as a general indication of the nature of analytic philosophy of history, but to stave off potential confusion it is worth distinguishing between it and *historical methodology*. Many history students will have been introduced to the latter, generally by practising historians rather than by philosophers. Partly because the topic is addressed by, and clearly relevant to, working historians it tends to deal with the more intimate 'nuts and bolts' issues which arise in the actual practice of researching, understanding, and constructing writings in history. For example, where is it appropriate to use statistical data, and what pitfalls await such use? How reliable are oral accounts as evidence and/or proof of events? Likewise regarding film. What is the distinction between 'primary source material' and secondary sources, and can it become blurred? Are State papers and other official records unusually reliable as documentary evidence, and/or do they require special techniques of interpretation? How might one best approach 'non-traditional' kinds of history, such as women's history, the history of the media, or the history of sport? What should be the focus of 'social' history? How should one judge between different historical accounts of the same events?

If dealing with these more 'technical' questions of direct practical relevance to actual historians is one reason for distinguishing between historical methodology and analytic philosophy of history, the other reason is allied to it – namely, the latter asks more abstract, general questions which focus not so much on how 'best' to engage in the existing practice of being an historian, but rather on 'what *is* the discipline of history?'. Here the meaning of '*is*' is ambiguous, however, because the analytic philosophers, although concerned with the straightforward empirical answer to the question, also mean 'what *should* the discipline of history 'ideally' be?', and 'does the discipline of history make sense?'. The difference, then, between historical methodology and analytic philosophy of history exemplifies that between the *practical* (or 'technical') and the *theoretical* (or 'critical') study of an activity, generating the different sorts of questions posed above.

The difference between historical methodology and analytic philosophy of history

Because this is not only a difficult distinction, but also a controversial one for some, it is worth elaborating on by means of an example. Let us take the activity of building a house. Our 'methodologist' will critically study the problems involved, examine the techniques used, judge the suitability of the materials used, and assess the skill and qualifications of the builders. In short, he studies the practical aspects of house-building. Unless something is radically wrong with the normal results of 'house-building', then in his capacity as 'methodologist' he will be exercising his critical faculty *within* the existing practice of house-building and *within* the existing notions of what a 'house' is. He is not involved in re-examining what 'houses' are, nor in revolutionising the activity of house-*building* on the grounds that the existing practice is fundamentally flawed, or even senseless. The same applies to our historical methodologist. The activity he is studying is the discipline of history. But as practically inspired, his study invites only certain questions and excludes others. His thinking proceeds within the 'normal' parameters of the discipline. His practical stance does not invite fundamental questions regarding what the past is, neither to what extent the discipline of history makes sense.

The case is different with a *theoretical*, rather than practical, study of an activity. Returning to 'house-building', our analytic philosopher of house-building adopts the properly 'philosophical' stance of 'astonishment' at the activity. Eschewing existing ideas of it which emanate *from* the practice and are thus 'captive' *to* it, he wishes to understand what this activity called 'house-building' 'is'. For example, what 'is' a house? Is it a functional thing, and if so, are its functions sensible? Could the same functions better be served by some other structure, or in some other way? Does it matter what it looks like? Is a 'house' different from a 'flat', a 'tent', a 'hut'? What makes 'the ideal house'? Regarding *building* 'houses', is the character of houses determined by building techniques? Could one envisage a more efficient way of 'building' them? Is house-building a worthwhile activity, or might resources be used better elsewhere?

We can see from this, then, how the theoretically inspired study of 'house-building' differs from its practical study. Now, just as 'house-building' is an activity, so is the discipline of history, and thus the same principles apply. It can be studied practically – that is, *historical methodology*; and theoretically – that is, *analytic philosophy of history*. The two approaches differ, generating different sets of questions.

The blurring of the difference

This said, however, the difference between the two *can* become blurred. Why can this happen? This can be shown by returning to 'house-building' and observing there are times when it undergoes significant *changes*. This may be because of some revolutionary technology which transforms building techniques (making possible 'houses' unthought of before), or because ideas of what a house 'is' shift radically from existing norms, (for example, because of new ideas regarding life-styles, or new circumstances such as population pressure or change of habitat). In such periods of radical transformation we can expect a certain coming-together of the kinds of questions posed by both the practical and theoretical study of 'house-building'. Its practical study no longer has a sure 'norm' from which it emanates, for the new technology raises unprecedented challenges and possibilities which generate those more abstract questions usually reserved to the *theoretical* study of house-building. For example, in the absence of any existing norms, the issue of how best to incorporate electronics into the building of houses brings to the fore the question of the function of 'housing' – is a 'house' a place for working, or is it 'home', or can both functions be incorporated, and if so, what is the best way to tackle it? Similarly, if 'house-building' is changing because of new life-styles involving a radically different concept of a 'house' – the practical study of 'house-building' will again have points of intersection with its theoretical study. For instance, what exactly is it the builder is supposed to achieve?

But if there are pressures which can broaden the practical study of 'house-building' towards issues more theoretical, so the same pressures work in the other direction, 'narrowing' the scope of its *theoretical* study towards *practical* issues. For example, where the nature of house-building is radically altering then the theoretical study of it, *simply to understand what is in front of one*, is drawn more closely than usual to the details of its practice. The theorist, now bereft of a traditional norm to criticise in terms of its presuppositions, instead needs to look closely at the 'nuts and bolts' of what house-builders are doing simply to discover what its presuppositions actually are, (which he wishes to critically explain and assess). For instance, why do these house-builders include so many cable-layers and electronics engineers – what is their significance?

Thus it is particularly in the context of rapid and/or fundamental changes to an activity, I suggest, that its practical and theoretical studies approach more closely together in the kinds of questions they ask. Returning to the discipline of history, there have indeed been times when just such a relative coming-together of historical methodology and analytic philosophy of history has occurred, appearing to confuse them. One such was during the sixteenth century when a variety of thinkers began to put together the very foundations of the modern discipline of history. Partly prompted by a growing scepticism regarding the relevance, meaning, and historical authority of the Roman Law, their ambition was to change the way in which history was studied, not only to make it make more sense but also to make its study more 'useful'. Through adopting a comparative approach they hoped to find some universal patterns and lessons within the legal, cultural, and political histories of nations, and this involved them in some 're-thinking' of history both in terms of what the discipline should aspire to and in terms of the 'nuts and bolts' of a proper methodology designed to achieve that end. Not least among them was the French philosopher, jurist, and political theorist, Jean Bodin. Dissatisfied with the way history was studied, written, and read, in his *Method for the Easy Comprehension of Histories* (1566) Bodin advanced ideas which 'approach a genuine system of internal criticism' of historians and historical sources, and contributed significantly to 'the first extensive formulation of the rules and conditions of historical belief'. For example, he recommended that the 'good' historian needs to be neither too close nor far away in time from the events he recounts. He should be honest, avoid value-judgements altogether, and any bias which might arise from his patriotic or religious feelings – i.e., he should strive to be objective. He should not invent speeches, nor use flowery language, for his purpose is not to entertain but to render the truth of events; and we should take care, in reading historians, that they were not writing under constraint of persecution or in response to bribery.[1]

Elementary as Bodin's ideas might now seem, (although then radical in the light of previous historical writings), the point is that they demonstrate a perspective on the discipline of history which exemplifies that intermixing of the concerns of historical methodology with the more theoretical ones of analytic philosophy of history; and I am suggesting that this is hardly surprising given the context of major change in which the thinking emerged. It would appear another such period of change is with us now, when again the (present) foundations of the discipline of history are under attack by the so-called 'postmodernists'. Their thinking radically challenges the very possibility of viable historical knowledge, involving critiques aimed both at the *methodological* procedures of historians and at their broader presuppositions of a knowable past, thus tending to merge concerns of historical methodology with analytic philosophy of history.

The relevance of analytic philosophy of history

Having explained the approach of 'analytic philosophy of history' and distinguished it (in principle) from 'historical methodology', we may now ask of it what we asked of 'speculative philosophy of history' – namely, what (if any) is the *relevance* of analytic philosophy of history for historians? *Should* historians be concerned by the 'philosophical' analysis of how they think about their subject? The initial response may be that historians should indeed be interested in studying how they themselves 'think'. Does what historians tell us make sense? – what *kind* of sense? For instance, can they be said to be thinking scientifically? If not, are they instead engaged in their own ('historical') way of thinking? Can the way historians think and write be trusted in terms of truth? – and (a separate matter) in terms of objectivity? Are there necessarily hidden ('unconscious') assumptions influencing how historians construct or recover the past, (for instance, a reliance on 'human nature', on 'laws' determining the behaviour of organisations and institutions, and on cultural norms)? If so, are these assumptions valid? Is it *possible* to avoid 'assumptions'? Should historians be focusing on issues different from those they normally address (i.e., the origins and consequences of things)? Are there certain topics which cannot by their nature be the subject of a history, or does 'anything go', such as a history of racism, of the Atlantic Ocean, or of beauty?

The supposition is, then, that historians who are critically aware of the thinking processes they engage in will be that much more thoughtful, perceptive, and confident of the value of what they do, making them 'better' historians. This, however, is a rather simplistic answer, and in addition is unlikely to convince those historians who are antagonistic towards such 'philosophising', preferring to get on with their work without such outside interference. The more satisfactory answer as to why historians ought to reflect on their own thinking-processes is longer and somewhat different.

We may begin it by observing that the short answer given above suggests the historian should, so to speak, pay occasional health-giving visits to the foreign terrain of analytic philosophy of history, thereby returning refreshed to his own native terrain. One problem with this is that, as with visiting any health-clinic, one needs to trust the doctors there. But a more fundamental flaw is the assumption that reflective analysis of the assumptions underlying his own thinking is *not* an integral part of the historian's task *as an historian* – that it is, indeed, *foreign* terrain (however

285

beneficial a visit might be). This is an assumption of some historians, and it is as false as it is damaging. Why? The answer revolves around the fact that the discipline of history is a 'theoretical ' activity rather than a 'practical' one, and should therefore intrinsically involve reflection on one's thinking. History is a *theoretical* subject. What does this mean?

Theoretical and practical studies

The difference between studying something theoretically and studying something practically rests on the motivations of the enquirer. For example, one may study a neighbour's activity in her garden to understand what she is doing. One does not understand what she is up to, and is curious to find out. Why is one curious in this instance? Simply because one is averse to not understanding what one is observing – one is puzzled. Alternatively, one might recognise she is planting potatoes, but still be simply curious as to how she goes about it. In both cases one wants to understand what one is observing solely for the sake of understanding, as an end in itself. One is not observing her in order to achieve some purpose or objective, for which understanding her actions is a *means*. This *latter* 'kind' of understanding or study is *practically* inspired, as, for example, wanting to understand what she is doing in order to check on her state of mind, or because one hopes to learn how to plant potatoes. The same distinction between theoretical and practical understanding can apply to numerous objects of study. For example, one may study politics simply to understand it better, (theoretical study) – or to learn how to become a politician, or to bet on an election, or stage a coup, (practical studies).

The same applies to the study of history. For instance one may study past events in Ireland solely to understand them (in terms of what happened and why, how they originated, and what their consequences were). Such a study is history proper and is, then, 'theoretical'. Alternatively, one may study past events in Ireland in order to find support for one's political views, or to produce a flattering biography for publication, or to prepare a revolutionary manifesto. Such studies are practically inspired, not seeking understanding for the sake of it, and are consequently *not* examples of the discipline of history, but variously exercises in propaganda, rhetoric, or ideological literature. It is not that such studies are *poor* history; they are not history at all. It is true there can be better and worse history, but different criteria are involved in *that* distinction. Far more fundamental is the distinction between the discipline of history and other studies of the past, and it rests on the difference between the theoretical and practical approach to the past.

'Observing' things

Why is this difference fundamental and what are its effects? The original meaning of the Greek verb 'to theorise' was 'to observe'. This meant that, as observers of things, we are not part of them. We neither hope for, nor expect, anything from them. We simply observe them 'from a distance' in the hope of making sense of them. In solely wishing to understand them, with no practical objectives to realise *through* understanding them (such as making money, achieving fame, or learning a skill), we are essentially *dis-interested* in what we are observing (however fascinated we may be by it), and *dis-interested* in the *results* of our observing other than how adequate or true our understanding is. For instance, one may attend a pop-concert simply as 'an observer', wanting to understand what goes on for the sake of it. One is not there in order to enjoy the concert, nor because of a crush on a member of the pop-group, nor for any other self-interested motivation. In short, one is not a *participant* involved in what one is observing. Neither does it affect one's interests *what* understanding one gains of the event – for example, one has not attended to find out how to become a successful pop-star, or how best to organise a concert. The essence of the 'observer' (or 'theorist') is that he has no axe to grind either about *what* he is 'observing' (or 'theorising'), or about the *conclusions* he reaches in his effort to understand what he observes. Further, in his stance as 'observer' there is thus nothing to influence either *what* he studies in the pop-concert, or whether he rejects or approves whatever *ideas* he forms as part of his understanding of the event.

This is not so with a practically motivated study of the pop-concert, because the practical objective (whatever it might be) affects what one chooses to examine – much of what is happening is irrelevant to one's purpose, and is consequently neglected. Similarly with *how* one studies the pop-concert in terms of the thinking one pursues – some lines of enquiry will be ignored because they are irrelevant to, or even interfere with, what it is one needs to think about to achieve one's objective.

Thus a practically motivated study of something is *partial* both in the sense that it does not study its material fully but only those 'parts' relevant to its objective – and in the sense that the thinking involved demonstrates a 'partiality' towards lines of thinking and conclusions appropriate or 'convenient' to one's purposes. Although this does not mean the understandings achieved will necessarily be false (although such a danger threatens), it does mean the study, as angled towards the ends sought, will be 'distorted'.

A *theoretically* motivated study, on the contrary, is 'impartial', because as the disinterested 'observing' of something, any and every of its aspects is open to enquiry, however obscure it may appear. It is also 'impartial' in the sense that, as a non-participant in that which he studies, the observer ('theorist') does not 'take sides' in his thinking. Having no aim other than understanding, no lines of enquiry or ideas reached can be 'unwelcome' or 'inconvenient'. The only 'unwelcome' idea would be one that was untrue; the only 'inconvenient' conclusion one that did not follow. The theorist simply seeks 'the truth' – or more accurately, in seeking understanding solely for the sake of understanding, what else can this mean than seeking *true* ideas about something? (Although this is far from meaning the theorist's conclusions must always be true – mistakes can be made). Unlike the practical study of something, where the relevance or usefulness of the ideas reached provides the rationale of the exercise, the only rationale of a theoretical study is the adequacy or truth of its ideas. Further, *this* is why an integral aspect of the theoretical study of something is that the 'theorist' reflects on his *own* thinking, both in terms of whether there are aspects of the object of study he has neglected, and whether the direction his thinking has taken and the conclusions reached are logical and unsullied by 'partiality'. Reflexive thinking, or 'thinking about one's thinking', is, then, a *crucial* feature of theoretical study because the latter, as directed towards the truth or intellectual adequacy of its conclusions, demands one checks one's thinking for logical consistency, accuracy of facts, and ill-founded or unexamined assumptions.

Thus it is, then, that integral and crucial to the discipline of history, inasmuch as it is a theoretical study of the past, is the historian's perpetual preparedness to revise his ideas, approaches, reasoning, and conclusions via an ongoing critical awareness of his own thinking. Insofar as this part of his work constitutes 'analytic philosophy of history', the latter is, then, an important part of the historian's *own* work. It is not foreign terrain to be visited occasionally like a health-farm. It is native territory.

'History proper'

I will make two further observations on the overall issue of the relevance of 'analytic philosophy of history' to historians. First, the reader may think the above reasoning amounts to a circular argument – namely, 'history is a theoretical discipline – theoretical disciplines involve critical awareness of the thinking involved – therefore integral to the discipline of history is historians' self-critique of their reasoning'. In other words, the conclusion is implicit in the premise, for having initially defined history as a *theoretical* subject the rest follows. This is fair enough, although it is far from the case that nothing is gained by exploring the implications of what a 'theoretical' approach is. Nevertheless, the spotlight does turn upon the fundamental premise, that 'history proper' *is* a 'theoretical' discipline. I have asserted it, but in showing what it means I have implicitly shown what the alternative would imply, and I invite any who challenge its 'theoretical' nature to defend that alternative. I believe they would not only be defending something deeply contrary to historians' impulse towards 'impartiality' but also something which would disintegrate into such piecemeal sundry discourses that all hopes of rescuing the foundations of a coherent discipline would be lost.

Foreign territory?

The second observation returns us to the analogy of visiting a health-farm. We noted it matters whether the doctors know their business. But I have argued that the analogy is misleading in any event because the terrain of analytic philosophy of history is *not* foreign territory for the historian. He or she should be their *own* 'doctor' as an integral part of their work. But, it may be asked, surely the doctor at the health-farm is the expert, whilst the patients are amateurs? In other words, is not the job of critically analysing historians' thinking best left to the professional (analytic) philosophers of history, rather than demanding that historians, who are at most amateur 'philosophers', do it themselves? But this is where the analogy breaks down. Analytic philosophers of history are not, in the main, historians; they are philosophers. And insofar as it is in fact *they* who are visiting foreign territory – namely, the discipline of history – when they engage in analytic philosophy of history, we could just as well say it is *they* who are the amateurs. Do they *know* what they are trying to talk about? The historians, on the other hand, are in home territory; we should assume that if anyone is entitled to talk about the way historians think it is the historians themselves from their own intimate knowledge of what they do.

It is in this manner that arguments can be turned on their head, and it is fair to remark that the indifference of some historians towards the critiques from analytic philosophers of history stems from a scepticism regarding how far the latter have a genuine acquaintance with the discipline of history. Equally, however, philosophers can have a point when they expose inconsistencies or other inadequacies in an historian's thinking. But the truth surely lies somewhere in the middle. It is not unreasonable to expect the analytic philosopher to be acquainted with the discipline he is analysing (i.e., history). Equally, however, it is not unreasonable to expect the historian to be capable of critical analysis of his own thinking – in other words, to engage in 'philosophy'. If, then, the analytic philosopher of history runs the risk of 'amateurism' regarding the discipline of history, so the historian runs the risk of 'amateurism' regarding 'philosophy'. Both risks are avoidable, but particularly the latter once we recognise that 'philosophy' is not some mysterious, exclusive 'way of thinking', but simply reasoned argumentation regarding questions inaccessible to established disciplines.

In the above exposition of what analytic philosophy of history is about, I have given a number of examples of the questions around which it focuses – for example, how generous can the subject-matter of 'history' be? How do we judge the truth of an historical account? Are there 'hidden' assumptions interweaved into understanding past events? These questions alone generate numerous ancillary issues (often treated independently in journal articles) such that there is a danger of becoming so immersed in the minutiae of complex arguments that the larger purpose of analytic philosophy of history escapes the reader. This would be all the more regrettable for students of history, for whom this guide is written. Therefore I have collated (without academic references) what I take to be the most recurring and relevant issues under just two general chapter headings, within whose broader scope they are treated. Given its contemporary resonance, I have reserved treatment of the postmodernist position to a separate chapter (opening Part III), which may serve as both a continuation of this 'guide' to analytic philosophy of history, and (as now specifically focused) as an example of some of its specific argumentations.

12

THE 'WHAT *IS* HISTORY?' DEBATE

Introduction

For students of history the considerable, often complex, and apparently diverse subject-matter of analytical philosophy of history is best made accessible by subsuming it under two general enquiries – 'what *is* history?', and 'what is history *for?*', (i.e., 'history' as *discipline*, not 'content').

My intention is not to give detailed accounts of particular contributions to these questions, nor to explain where and why such debates originated. Rather, the aim of these two chapters is best met by a general presentation of the issues, unencumbered by academic references and excursions from the highways down the sometimes intricate byways (amply covered by the reading list).

Just as *objectivity* is one of the issues related to the nature of historical writings, so it is for theorists' writings. Thus it is appropriate to make clear that the following account of what analytical philosophy of history is about is based upon an earlier attempt I made to expose the theoretical underpinnings of history as a discipline (undertaken, incidentally, better to see how far 'the history of *thought*' is a viable subject).[1] Although in itself this need not concern the reader, it is fair to remark that where in the following I offer specifically *critical* points and/or refer to other theorists, these mainly derive from those arguments and references.

This chapter comprises five sections, beginning with some preliminary observations necessary to clear the ground, followed by four sections reflecting the principal areas of discussion involved in theorists' closer reflections on 'what is history?' – namely, *types* of history, the *epistemology* of history, 'historical *explanation*', and historical *subject-matter*.

Theoretical preliminaries

'*Actual*' and '*ideal*' history

The question 'what is history?' is two-faced. On the one hand it could simply be asking 'what *is* history' as a straightforwardly empirical matter – and the obvious answer would be to say 'what historians actually do, today'. (If they used to do something different, that would simply answer the question, 'what *was* history?').

On the other hand, in asking 'what is history?' one might really mean, 'what *ought* history to be?' – in other words, what should someone called 'an historian' (ideally) be doing in order to properly qualify as such? What *in principle* should the subject of history entail?

Understandably, these two sides often become entangled, since the dichotomy is not unique to the question 'what is history?'. For example, if asked 'what is marriage?', many would be hard-pressed not to combine an idea of what it *actually* is in their present society with some idea of what marriage is *in principle* (i.e., what it *ought* to be). And if 'marriage' might seem a special example, it is not – for one might say the same about questioning what *anything* 'is'. What is a car? A Mini is a car, and so is a Ferrari. But isn't a Ferrari more of a '*real*' car? The same problematic applies to any 'thing', both natural and man-made (e.g., 'what is a tree?', 'what is a chair?'), for in every case some idea of what a certain thing is *ideally* probably intrudes into our answer. (In Western philosophy this dichotomy began with the different approaches adopted by Plato and Aristotle towards 'the nature of things').

The question, 'what is history?', then, is not unusual in inviting answers which combine both the empirical and idealist approaches. It is true that some practising historians are likely to restrict themselves to an empirical answer, whilst it is equally evident that some analytic philosophers of history seek some idealised paradigm of history as a discipline, yet to be practised or attempted. But the thinking of most historians *and* analytic philosophers of history, however varied or even confused their answers might be, commonly reflects both sides to the question. For example, however dissatisfied we will find some philosophers are with the notion that *narrative* is an important element of history, they recognise it as an empirical fact (however reluctantly) and include a critical exploration of narrative in their considerations of 'what is history?'.

Words and 'reality'

These considerations straight away confront us with a dilemma, for it seems those even posing the question, 'what *is* history?', are immediately cast into philosophical issues. However, this dilemma of what we *mean* by the question can be, if not solved, at least diverted by adopting the following approach: the word 'history' (i.e., the academic subject) is but a word. Whatever else we might say about words (such as their fascinating etymological origins, their changing meanings), like any word, it was contrived by human-beings to denote or 'single out' something in the 'world out there' worth noticing and distinguishing from other things. Now, the reasons humans have had for thus 'noticing' this or that are as numerous as their interests (material, practical, emotional, aesthetic, scientific, *et al.*). For example, for us it is worth noticing things we can comfortably sit on. We call them 'chairs' to distinguish them from things we notice for other reasons – e.g., 'trees'. We use words, then, to map out our experience of 'the world out there' in terms of the relevance, and hence noticeability, of the differences we find 'out there'. And it is fair to assume that intelligent beings with other senses from humans might find, from *their* experience of 'the world out there', 'things' unknown to humans – just as *within* the human world, different cultures and different times have generated (to a degree) different 'perceptions' of the world. The ancient Romans had no concept of 'an air-pocket'. There are societies today which have no concept of 'teenagers'.

This shows that the meaning of words reflects the ways in which the myriad aspects of the world impinge upon us – and the question of whether chairs, trees, teenagers, or air-pockets 'truly' or 'really' exist, such that when these concepts emerge we have in some sense 'tuned in' to objective, pre-existing 'truths' about the world, does not arise. Rather, the point is, do the distinctions we make about 'the world', which are denoted by the different meaning of words, 'work' for us in practice? Are they reliable? Can I 'drive' a 'chair'? Can I 'eat' an 'air-pocket'? Are 'teenagers' 'right-angled'? Will 'taking a holiday' 'refresh' me? Is it 'dangerous' to approach 'snakes'? What is the 'cause' of this 'war'?

All this is not to say that 'things' do not 'really' exist – that the world is simply our idea of it. For of one thing we can be sure: if there were not (what we call) 'the world out there', and were we not beings for whom (what we call) different 'things' were relevant, then we would have no ideas and thus no words. But neither is this to say that 'things' *really* do exist, as if chairs, trees, and teenagers were in some sense pre-existent, meaningful 'things in themselves', rather than simply words denoting our experience.

The word 'history'

Now, applied to 'what is history?', we can say that in their experience of the world humans have found it worthwhile to distinguish things called 'activities' (separating them off from other things such as emotions, objects, qualities and so on). And they have also found it worthwhile to distinguish *different* 'activities' – e.g., skiing, reading, courting. Amongst these numerous activities are *intellectual* activities, and one of these they have thought worth differentiating is 'doing history'. In other words, the word 'history' has been used not only to refer in some general way to 'the past' as a vast arena of events and circumstances no longer present to us, but also to denote the (intellectual) *activity* of establishing and studying the details of this 'past'. From this viewpoint, the question of the nature of 'history' becomes sensible and manageable, for it neither invites the trite notion that 'history' is simply the catch-all of the various things 'historians' do, nor philosophical flights into a fantasy world of some 'ideal' existent or 'essence' called 'history', which 'really' exists if only we poor mortals could see it clearly – (an occupational hazard of historical theorists). This latter notion is the (idealist) philosopher's conceit, and misdirects many a poor soul's attempt to understand 'what history is'.

Rather, the question of 'what is history?' divides into two: first, what is it about the activity we call 'history' that has made it worth noticing and distinguishing from other (intellectual) activities? And second, how useful or 'workable' is this distinction?

History as 'the study of the past'

All theorists agree that the subject called 'history' studies the past. On this there is no room for debate, (except to ponder whether this excludes those who, in the guise of historians, discuss both the present and the future – an issue reserved for the following chapter on 'what is history *for?*'). 'The study of the past', however, is too broad a notion with which to define 'history' very usefully. On the one hand 'the past' simply means any and every thing which ever was or happened, and on the other hand 'the study of' means any and every thing which can be *said* about this 'past'. It is when we start to narrow down this profligate notion of 'history' as simplistically meaning 'the study of the past', to make it more manageable and useful, that the work of analytical philosophy of history begins and the debates develop.

The catch-all notion of 'the past', (meaning so little because embracing so much), thus needs slimming down. And it seems that the first step, recognised in conventional wisdom, is to restrict the discipline of history to the (past) world of *human* affairs. It is true the term, 'history', has also been used (and still is) in relation to the *natural* world. For example, the identification and classification of species of animals and plants used to be called 'natural history', and nowadays we are familiar with the notion of 'the history' of the Earth's geological formation, 'the history' of its climate, and so on. However, we recognise the difference between these latter 'histories' and what is conventionally meant by 'history'. Tellingly, in dealing with the natural world their accounts are presented in terms of cause and effect; in other words, the understanding they offer is 'scientific'. This, at least for most historians and analytic philosophers of history, clearly distinguishes such 'histories' from what *they* mean by the discipline of history – and this immediately suggests something important, for it implies that the kind of understanding historians engage in is not structured in strictly cause/effect terms.

It is true that the *language* of 'cause and effect' appears frequently in historians' writings – however, I suggest it is rarely meant in literally scientific terms. Rather, where they say such things as 'the assassination of President Kennedy caused numerous conspiracy theories', or 'the introduction of income tax was the effect of the Napoleonic Wars', they are using 'cause' and 'effect' in the same way most of us do when we say, for example, 'my friend's plight caused me to lend him my car', or 'his decision to leave town was the effect of his having lost his job'. In these cases we use the language of cause and effect simply as an alternative to saying 'he did this *because of* that' – i.e., as a way of formulating *why* something happened or was the case. In ordinary conversation, where rigorous analysis is out of place, such terminology does not matter. However, if we are seriously concerned to explain something, we all recognise the difference between eating contaminated food *causing* one to be ill, and one's friend's plight 'causing' one to assist him. In the former, we mean strict 'scientific' causation – a determinate process over which we have no control. In the latter we do not mean this – we recognise the role of human choice or 'response'. The difference, then, between 'natural' and 'human' history is telling since it suggests the latter (as 'proper' history), because limited to *human* affairs, does not *literally* offer scientific accounts and explanations of the past. (We have yet to see if there is, instead, a 'kind' of account and/or explanation special to history).

But apart from this *difference*, equally telling is something *shared* by both 'proper' history and 'natural history', at least in the latter's more contemporary guise of tracing e.g., climatic and geological 'history'. Rightly or wrongly, these topics are called 'histories' because they not only focus on past natural processes, but also on *change* over time – and it is this latter feature which correlates with an important notion behind the concept of (human) history, since it suggests that essential to the notion of 'history' is the notion of 'change', whether in the human or natural world.

So far, then, in refining the initial notion that the discipline of 'history' studies 'the past', we have restricted its compass to *human* affairs, and noted the importance of the notion of *change* over time. Although both these restrictions may appear sensible and may accord with what most people are differentiating by pointing to a thing called 'history', further exploration of their implications has not courted universal agreement, (maybe even casting doubt on their viability in the first place), but has instead provided a rich arena of argument amongst analytical philosophers of history. To see why this is so, we can now turn to the first of those four broad areas of discussion generated by theorists' closer reflections on 'what is history?'.

'Types' of history

Descriptive history

One of the more obvious yet controversial implications stems from the second restriction just mentioned – namely, the focus on *change*. If an important element in differentiating 'history' is that it specifically deals with a *changing* past, then it follows that to *describe* or *identify* some past scene or artefact is not enough to fully qualify as 'doing history'. This is because to describe, e.g., London in 1666, or to identify, e.g., the remains of a Roman villa, is to talk about something *static* in time. One is dealing with a 'circumstance', not with change. It is true that in order to trace change (e.g., the development of London during the seventeenth century, the origins of the Roman settlement of the North of England) it is essential to know what was the case at particular points in time. But if one's discourse is restricted solely to this – describing/identifying moments in the past – why call it 'history'? Why not call it 'antiquarianism' or, often, 'archaeology'?

The counter-argument is that this criticism is outrageous, for it implies that the painstaking research into details of the past – sometimes literally unearthing artefacts, or identifying manuscripts, or meticulously recovering the details of an organisation, or establishing the class background to a religious movement – is not 'doing history'. Indeed, it would be easy to find many, disappearing to obscure places and recondite archives and returning to present in invaluable articles the information they have uncovered about the past, who would be grossly offended at the suggestion they were not engaged in the discipline of history. On the contrary, they may even retort that *theirs* was the *real* historical work, all else written about the past being mere idle talk of one sort or another!

However, does this answer the point? Although it may indeed be outrageous to suggest they are not being historians, is it not fair to remark that their activity is only a *part* (however essential) of what is involved in 'doing history', and that if all their careful research is left at the production of descriptions, identifications, and accounts of things *in stasis*, then they have fallen short of actually producing 'history'. In short, what is the point of their work if left at the level of *describing* some past situation or circumstance? Although we will be addressing the *general* question of 'what is the point of history?' in the following chapter, does not the notion of 'history' demand that, for example, our historian of art goes further than describing different paintings and/or painters, to *link* them into some notion of painting changing over time, or that our historian of a religious movement goes further than collating the class-composition of its members at any one time, and *link* this information into part of an account of *change* (e.g., origins, development, decline)?

To do justice to such work, however, perhaps it is better not to press the point any further, but to suggest instead that, insofar as it is so intimately concerned with discovery of aspects of the past, it be called 'descriptive history' and accorded the massive respect it deserves. But from a philosophical perspective, it can still be argued that its only claim to be a distinctive activity rests on its connection with 'the past' (which is too general a claim), since to *describe* something is hardly unique to writing history. In short, not all information about the past, nor all that is said about the past, is *ipso facto* 'history'. We mean to differentiate something more specific by the term, such that 'descriptive history' is at the least inadequate, and at worst an oxymoron.

Analytic history

The implication of the above is that 'history' goes beyond describing how things were – and this is indeed the case with many students of the past, for in addition to (or instead of) describing something past they also *analyse* past circumstances or situations. By this I mean the work and thinking that goes into attempts to *generalise* from particulars in order to arrive at useful notions about past phenomena. By a process of analysis, certain common features of things and situations otherwise unique can often be abstracted to show in what respects they were predictable in character and/or behaviour. For example, analysis of different medieval courts may indicate something common about their composition: the aims and methods of different Victorian craft-unions may indicate something common about their character: the economic status of different Renaissance sculptors may indicate some common insight into the nature of their artistic works. Such analytic work (so long as it is reliable) provides useful knowledge of the past because it provides us with generalisations which enable us better to 'understand' past phenomena. Such notions as 'the typical Victorian craft-union', 'the typical medieval court' and 'the typical Renaissance sculptor', afford a kind of short-hand which not only helps describe this or that particular thing but also helps *explain* some of its features. It does so insofar as to identify any 'common type' of a thing is, in a sense, to explain why any *particular* example of it is as it is, or behaves as it does. For instance, to refer to a particular sculptor as 'a typical Renaissance artist' may indicate not only *that* he is male, works to commission on both religious and secular topics, and uses certain techniques such as perspective, but also 'why'. The 'reason' is that he was a typical Renaissance sculptor, and analysis has not only shown they shared these features, but in doing so, has also implied a *reason* for this. To this extent, then, the hard analytic work which goes into abstracting instructive generalisations about past phenomena contributes towards making aspects of *particular* individuals, organisations, and so on, more *intelligible* than they might otherwise be; and to make something intelligible is, of course, to go beyond describing it. It is to 'explain' it.

This said, however, there are two reasons for caution regarding the explanatory power of what I have called 'analytic history'. It is true that to discover significant and reliable regularities in past phenomena (including otherwise particular 'events' such as wars, revolutions, partitions, treaty-making, peace-keeping, and so on – the realm of what is called 'comparative history') is to offer valuable insights into 'why things were as they were', or 'why things happened as they did'. But first, generalisations not only vary enormously in their precision, e.g., from the simple term 'medieval' to the notion of 'a typical late-nineteenth century French career diplomat'; even such detailed generalisations as the latter rarely if ever bear the stamp of scientific certainty. In history, we might say, when explaining things we should not only respect the particular, but almost expect it. Second (and from a philosophical viewpoint, more importantly), in what sense, exactly, does a generalisation explain something particular? I can notice several pieces of furniture in my room, all individually different. Yet three of them share features worth noting. They have legs supporting seats. They are 'chairs'. My little boy points to the largest of the three and asks why it has legs. I reply, 'because it is a chair, and chairs have legs'. I have used a generalisation to explain a particular circumstance. It is 'reasonable', 'intelligible', or 'explicable' that this thing has legs, because it is an example of the generalisation, 'a chair'. Chairs have legs because they need to seat someone above the floor-surface. That is (part of) the rationale of 'chairs'. It 'explains' them in general, and therefore in particular examples.

What can be overlooked, however, is that when I say that 'this thing has legs because it is a chair', I have not explained why this thing has legs. Rather, I have explained why, in having legs, it is *called* 'a chair'. I have explained (part of) the meaning of the word 'chair'. And to revert to our earlier discussion of words, we recall that any word denotes something which is *from our point of view* worth differentiating from other things 'out there'. The 'reason' which is *in* 'a chair', then, is in fact *the reason we have* for differentiating or noticing it. Things 'in themselves' have no 'reason'. They are radically non-explicable. What we *can* explain is why, in having certain features, they are denoted by this or that word – namely, in giving the meaning of the word we reveal why we have differentiated a particular class of things.

Thus, I have not explained why this particular object has legs by saying 'because it is a chair'. Rather, I am suggesting that (some) particular things are predictable in terms of their characteristics and (where relevant) their behaviour.

There is a strong sense, then, in which to subsume particular things under a generalisation is *not* in fact to explain why a particular thing is as it is or behaves as it does. And this is one of the dangers of 'analytic history' – that the concepts or generalisations it produces are appealed to in order to explain individual circumstances, as if for instance one could explain some particular feature of English society in 1660 by saying that 1660s England was 'a typical pre-industrial capitalist society'. We should bear in mind that 'the typical pre-industrial capitalist society' (like 'the typical Renaissance artist' or 'the typical chair') is an abstract concept, and that as such it could never have 'caused', contributed to, or even influenced any actual thing, situation, or event. To be sure, analytic history can provide a rich and changing harvest of concepts, some more useful than others in terms of their reliability and fecundity, which are strongly *suggestive* of how this or that particular thing might be explained. But the concepts themselves cannot explain any actual circumstance, situation, or event. That task requires that each past phenomenon be studied in its actual particularity: i.e., that one appeals to 'facts', not concepts.

These cautionary notes demonstrate the kind of arguments which analytic philosophers of history get involved in. However, even more central to the issue of whether 'history' is best construed as *analytic* in approach, is another of the latter's features – and this returns us to the notion of the relation between 'history' and *change*. Analytic history is not essentially concerned with a changing world. An expert who analyses different medieval villages, different industrialising societies, or different Renaissance artists, is not so much concerned to trace *change* in this medieval village, that industrialising society, or this Renaissance artist's work. Rather, he either wants to analyse (e.g.) this medieval village on its own merits, or abstract features from several which they share in common, in order to arrive at some insightful notion of 'the typical medieval village'. In either case, just like *descriptive* history, it is not intrinsic to his project to deal with a changing phenomenon. On the contrary, even where the analytic historian is dealing with *events* (where, as we shall see, 'change' is intrinsic to understanding them),once he has discovered common features to, for example, different revolutions, religious revivals, or economic slumps, he will (so to speak) stop the film rolling and set his mind to constructing a suggestive general rationale to the way revolutions, religious revivals, or economic slumps happen. Rather than concerning himself with change his hope must be that, whatever concept he constructs of, e.g., 'the typical religious revival', it will remain applicable despite changing particulars. In short, his project is concerned precisely to *supersede* changing circumstances rather than focus on tracing a changing world.

Because of this, we might view 'analytic history' similarly to 'descriptive history' – namely, that to claim it equates with what we mean by 'the discipline of history' is at the least to go too far, and at worst to mislead. This is because, as an activity, it is only distinctive insofar as it studies *past* phenomena – (too general a feature) – and only does so by 'analysing' them – (again, too general a feature, since just as the discourse of 'description' has no intrinsic connection with either the past or with change, neither does the process of 'analysis'). Again, although to suggest that those engaged in the demanding work of analysing past phenomena fall short of 'doing history' may be a notion which outrages them, the philosophical point needs to be made. Although there is indeed a loose sense in which 'doing history' encompasses such things as describing and analysing past phenomena, it is that same loose sense which permits not only *whatever* is said about the past to be called 'doing history', but even includes *reading* history books! If left at that, there is nothing left for the philosopher of history to say about 'what is history?', for in being nothing more nor less than anything which, willy-nilly, is said or even read about the past (with the proviso that it be 'true'), the subject of 'history' defies further analysis.

Doubtless there are some content to construe 'history' in this markedly generous sense, appealing to the way the word is often used in practice. But even here, there is an aspect to the word's use which hardly needs esoteric reflection to bring it to prominence – namely, that however vaguely the term can be used, 'history' not only purports to tell us 'what it was like', and try to explain why, but it also tells us 'what *happened*'; i.e., historians have always concerned themselves with *events*. Events may require explanation: they may lend themselves to analysis as in comparative history: but first and foremost they have to be *apprehended* – and the only way to do this is to piece together a sequence of happenings into a *narrative*. Narrative discourse (as distinct from descriptive or analytic discourse) is uniquely the form of following and articulating 'what happened' – and inasmuch as 'history' (even in its vaguest sense) is perhaps above all about *change*, it feeds upon 'what *happened*'. This intimate connection with narrative thus promises far greater and more precise insight into 'what is history?' than either 'descriptive' or 'analytic' history, or both taken together.

Narrative history

The connection, then, between what is even loosely meant by 'history', and narrative, is accepted as a fact of life even by those who (as we shall see) regret it.

However, as suggested above, there are good reasons in any event for claiming it is precisely in the area of *narrative* history that the intellectual challenge of 'slimming down' the otherwise profligate notion of 'history' can most satisfactorily be met. But this does not mean that all problems are thereby suddenly solved, since the exploration of narrative generates its own controversies.

Let us begin by clarifying what is meant by 'narrative history'. A 'narrative' is an account of 'what *happened*', understood as a *sequence* of occurrences. Essentially, then, a narrative is structured in terms of 'this happened, then that happened, then that happened', and so on. It is, in other words, the familiar form any *story* takes. (The proviso that narrative *history* should be a 'true' story rather than fiction is a separate matter considered later, and does not affect this fundamental feature of any narrative or story).

We should immediately notice three things from this. First, narrative feeds on things which *happen*. It is not focused on describing an object, circumstance, or state of affairs, nor on analysing (e.g., explaining, comparing) objects, circumstances, or states of affairs. As already seen, neither description nor analysis is essentially to do with happenings. Narrative, on the other hand, cannot but be structured on 'things happening', and in that strong sense, on *change*. (And we might want to say that if nothing ever changed, there would be no history).

Second, a narrative does not deal with single happenings, but links two or more happenings by the formula 'this happened, then that'. A single happening is simply expressed by the appropriate *verb* – for example, 'he *ran* down the street', or 'Little Red Riding Hood *entered* her grandmother's cottage'. Now it is true that when we denote a single action or happening (by a verb) it could be argued that the action itself can be broken down into 'he did this then did that'. For example, in 'running' one puts one leg forward, and *then* the other leg, or in 'entering' a room one moves from not being in the room, to *then* being in the room, such that a single action/happening seems to express a *changing* situation. However, I believe closer analysis shows that this is an illusion. When we say someone is 'running' or 'entering' (or 'loving' or 'thinking', and so on) we do not mean to differentiate a *changing* situation from the myriad of situations 'out there'. Rather, the way we apprehend a *changing* situation would be, for example, to say 'he ran down the road and *then* entered the house'. In short, we do not *narrate* a single action/happening. We simply identify it via a verb. Narrative, on the other hand, only comes into play when we put different actions into a *sequence* of 'doing this then doing that', thereby denoting a changing situation. I have explored elsewhere the apparent paradoxes of the interplay between single happenings and narrative, elaborating on the point that any 'single' action can indeed be broken down into a narrative sequence – indeed, much history is focused precisely on doing just that (e.g., 'Cromwell invaded Ireland'!). But it remains important to demonstrate that amongst the various ways in which we differentiate 'the world out there', apprehending a single happening or action is *different* from apprehending a changing situation. When we do the latter we cannot but use a different form of apprehension – namely, the *sequencing* of different actions into 'this happened *then* that happened', which is the essence of narrative.

What this shows, then, is that one of the ways we make sense of 'the world', in addition to singling out different objects, qualities, relationships, and indeed happenings/actions, is to single out a class of things which might technically be called 'narrative identities', or more suggestively, 'story-objects'. The story, or narrative form is ubiquitous in all human language and experience, from the most trivial – 'he came out of the house and then walked down the street' – to the most complex. The form of discourse corresponds to the nature or 'structure' of that which we are apprehending when we 'see' an intelligible sequence of happenings/ actions. In short, it is no more an arbitrary matter that we 'see' story-objects than that we 'see' physical objects. And as urged earlier in our remarks on the relation between 'reality' and words, where we dismissed the question of whether 'this chair' *really* exists, the same can not only be extended to single happenings/actions – ('was that *really* 'running'?) – but also to 'story-objects'. They are as 'real' as the different objects, actions, and qualities which we differentiate in 'the world out there' – which means that to ask of the 'story' that 'he came out of the house and then got into his car', is this 'story' *real?*', is a non-question. It is the same as asking whether 'this wedding' or 'that war' (or, indeed, 'weddings' and 'wars' in general) were 'real things'. The point is, does singling out this sequence 'work'?; is it a relevant and reliable understanding? (Notice that we are not here addressing the issue of 'truth'. This will be dealt with below, but suffice it to say here that the question, 'is it *true* that this is a chair?', is answerable simply in terms of whether what is stated as the case is in fact the case. 'Truth' applies to statements, not things. Just so, then, with the question, 'is it true that he came out of the house and then got into his car?'. The statement is either true or false, not the sequence itself).

If it is true that not all analytic philosophers of history would agree with the preceding analysis of what constitutes 'narrative' – (in the extensive literature on 'historical narrative', readers will find either different analyses of narrative, or discussions *about* narrative based on an unexplored, impressionistic notion of what it is) – most would agree with the *third* point we should notice; namely, that a narrative is different from a *chronicle*. A chronicle is the ordering of a class of phenomena in terms of their dates, from the earlier to the later. They may be Acts of Parliament, the battles in a war, the models of a make of car – indeed, any class of things whose instances can be put into *succession*. Thus a list is produced in 'chronological' order; i.e., this (then) this (then) this, and so on. As such, a chronicle tells one no more nor less than when a thing was, or happened, and when the next instance occurred, and so on. It is not identifying something specific 'out there', but remains a self-confessedly abstract exercise.

The case is different with a narrative. In identifying/apprehending a *sequence* it is doing something different from ordering things into a *succession* of 'this (then) that'. Rather, what is crucial in a narrative is that 'this happened and *then* that happened', or 'he did this and *then* he did that', whereby the force of the term 'then' is transformed from its operational muteness in a chronicle – 'this (then) that' – into a *meaningful linking* of 'prior and subsequent' – 'this *then* that'. In short, a narrative is pointing to something intelligible 'out there' – (a sequence or 'story-object') – whereas a chronicle is not. This difference between chronicle and narrative also reinforces the fact that although chronicles can list virtually anything (objects, situations, and happenings), the operational force of the term '*then*' in a narrative is only *meaningful* when it links *happenings* ('actions', or 'occurrences'). For example, it makes no sense to say, 'his trousers were grey and *then* he ran down the street', or 'he ran down the street and *then* his trousers were grey'. Narrative *must* link *occurrences* – 'he left the house and *then* ran down the street' – such that if there were *no* occurrences in the world, *or only one*, narrative would be impossible. In the former case, where nothing ever *happened*, 'the world' would be changeless – and this, I suggest, would preclude the possibility of *history*. In the latter case, where only one thing had ever happened, the same applies – nothing would actually *change*; history would not arise.

Thus this analysis suggests there are inextricable links between 'things happening', narrative, and change – and thus between all three and 'history', (unless we are happy to construe 'history' as simply the description, and/or analysis, and/or chronicling of objects, situations, or circumstances). To the extent this is correct, 'history' therefore revolves around narrative – that is, the apprehension of situations which *change* because of things that *happen*. Or put another way, narrative is not some extra technique or type of discourse we might or might not choose to employ in 'doing history'. Rather, it is a way of 'seeing' and saying 'things about the past' which is sufficiently distinctive to differentiate, from within that broad field, something we call the discipline of 'history' in an identifiable, manageable, and relevant sense of the term.

But even if these arguments hold, they do not answer all the issues involved in 'what is history?'.

The epistemological status of 'history'

Apart from 'types' of history, another debate which emerges in analysing 'history' is the problem of the *status* of knowledge of 'the past'. Here, we do not need to restrict 'history' to a narrative, descriptive, or any other approach to the past. Rather, all analytic philosophers of history, and historians themselves, recognise there are special problems regarding the credibility or 'truth' of what historians say about the past. The problem arises primarily because the past is no longer present, and therefore we cannot 'know' a past phenomenon directly, as when we see an object before us or witness an event taking place. 'History', then, as (at the minimum) 'knowledge of the past', is a discipline which must partly be identified in terms of its *epistemological* specialness; i.e., the special problems it has (as distinct from many other disciplines) both in acquiring 'knowledge' and trusting its veracity. What are these problems, and what issues do they raise?

Acquiring knowledge of things past

Because what was, and/or what happened, in the past is no longer 'visible' to us, there appear to be only three ways of acquiring 'knowledge' about something past. First, one can either be *told* it by hearsay or (hopefully better) by a history book. In the former case one is at liberty to mistrust 'memories', either individual or collective – and in the latter case, although history books may be more reliable, reading them is merely consuming knowledge already acquired.

A second way now available is to watch and/or listen to actual recordings of past circumstances and events, (sometimes professionally collected in film and sound archives). Clearly, such recordings can only deal with that portion of the past since this technology became available, and to that extent its applicability is limited. However, there is a case for claiming that, unlike verbal or written accounts of the past, whose reliability is always open to question, there is a qualitative difference to the information captured in contemporary recordings because they transport us back 'directly' to the circumstances which pertained and the events which happened.

However, both theorists and historians have argued about the nature of the information thus acquired. For example, that film and/or sound recordings are not simply a 'mirror' of what they record, but are *produced* by those doing the recording, suggests to some that their reliability as a source of information from the past is, in principle, as 'tainted' as oral or written accounts based on memory, although partly for different reasons. For example, although the camera does not 'lie', it nevertheless has to be pointed by someone. What it records is therefore restricted in content, *and* selected. Indeed, in practice, most film and sound material is also edited after the event. Again, even where a recording shows a demonstrable 'fact' – for example, the famous film of President Kennedy's shooting in Dallas, or film of the First World War trenches – the 'facts' recorded still have to be 'interpreted', and often establish less than we think. In Kennedy's case, the film shows him being shot. But whether it was an accident, a murder, or an assassination is another matter. Perhaps the neutral term, 'a killing', is the most we can safely say the film tells us. But even that is not the case, since he did not die at that point. On the contrary, many suspicious things might subsequently have happened (not on film) before he actually died! Similarly, although First World War recordings might help recover 'what it was like' in the trenches, in practice the information is again both limited and partly pre-selected.

Such reservations about the role of recorded (contemporary) information are, then, understandable, and have occasioned considerable ambivalence regarding their relevance to 'what is history?'. From our theoretical stance, this is perhaps most interestingly displayed in the issue of whether a recording should be viewed directly as a 'source' of information (i.e., as conveying 'facts'), or only as *evidence* which needs to be 'processed' into 'fact'. And this leads us to the third way in which we get to 'know' things in the past – namely, the reliance on *evidence*.

Evidence, inference, and facts

Both historians and theorists recognise that in order to establish some fact about the past, the historian must go through the mental process of *inferring* information from the evidence. This means regarding things we can experience here and now as *evidence* of things of which we cannot be immediately aware because they are past and gone. And the essential technique or mental process involved is *inference*. For example, we infer from these stones and other objects present to us that there used to be a bridge here: or we infer from this 1860s Irish Fenian newspaper present to us (e.g., preserved in a library) that, although it does not say so, it regarded such-and-such as the movement's main enemies, was indifferent about a possible alliance with socialists, and so on. Inferences thus produce 'facts' from the past – i.e., statements of 'what was the case'. And as indicated earlier, any 'fact' is either true or false depending upon whether what it states to be the case is, or was, the case. Where a fact derives from an inference, then, it is clear that the 'truth' or reliability of that 'fact' depends on the inference – and inferences vary in their strength. For example, from seeing smoke pouring from a gun-barrel I infer that someone has recently fired it. I thus propose 'the fact' that someone fired the gun, even though I was not there to witness the happening – and this 'fact' (i.e., statement of what was the case) is unlikely to be wrong. But it *could* be, as must be the case with any inference. Why?

Let us suppose another case, where I infer from a piece of pottery I find at a certain site, that there used to be trade between this and that town. Here, the inference is more speculative, and we would feel it needs to be supported by other evidence from which we can infer the same 'fact'. What this shows is that, with *any* inference, some unstated 'theory' or hypothesis about 'the way the world works' is at play in the mind of the historian, prompting him to link one thing to another intelligibly. In short, because of what he knows about the particular matter in hand, be it bridge-building, Irish politics, firearms, or trading, he assumes that one thing follows from another within how these things 'work'. This brings into play the historian's own assumptions about 'how things work' – including, of course, human psychology on numerous occasions – and for some theorists this at the least raises questions about the 'facts' historians employ (since most are inferred), and at worst renders 'the facts' inherently biased or distorted because of this or that historian's 'way of looking at the world'. If the historian is white, middle-class, male, and American, might this not lead him to make inferences which 'unconsciously' depend on his particular way of understanding what is relevant in a certain area, and how things 'work' within it? The point can be compounded by noting *my* selection of 'white, middle-class, male, and American', for why did I not select a 'ginger-haired, slim, and sporting person' as an example? Clearly, because given the topic in hand – namely, 'bias' – *my* understanding of 'how things work' in that area is based on certain 'theories' or 'assumptions' about the kind of characteristics which produce bias!

The reliability of 'facts'

As we will see later, although it is more usually whatever historians *do* with the 'facts' they uncover (e.g., describe a medieval village, analyse the membership of a Victorian craft-union, narrate the origins of the Vietnam War) which raises issues about the truth, objectivity, and general status of historical knowledge, it could be argued from the above that *even before* they proceed to incorporate them into a 'history' of this or that, the 'facts' themselves are suspect in terms either of their truth or their objectivity. In short, because so much historical information is inferential, then the very foundation of history – 'the facts' – loses credibility.

This, however, would surely be to go too far. Rather than destroying our faith in the factual foundation of history, it should merely make us more aware of this feature of its epistemology so that we can exercise scepticism *where justified*. The above analysis of the process of 'inferring from evidence' has shown something interesting and instructive about historians' thinking – namely, that the vital process of inference does not involve any distinctive kind of knowledge which may be called 'historical'. On the contrary, we have seen that inference depends upon the accepted or 'conventional' understandings of 'how the world works' in relation to whatever matter is at hand. If I infer, from seeing my friend arrive unexpectedly in a new car, that she has come into some money, I am using an 'ordinary' set of assumptions about money, spending, and life-styles. Similarly with the Irish newspaper – I employ an 'ordinary' understanding of political matters, as I did above regarding psychology and sociology and their relation to bias.

This shows that the historian does not need some special 'historical' technique of 'knowing' the past – indeed, one wonders what such a uniquely 'historical' set of assumptions could be, despite attempts to identify just such a 'mode'. Rather, to make his inferences he needs to know about, e.g., military affairs if he is to pursue military history, political affairs if he is to uncover political facts, human psychology if he is to focus on biography, and so on. And in all these and other possible areas, he will do best to employ their 'ordinary' ideas rather than some obscure 'theory' of his own. This is because their 'ordinariness' evidences their reliability. It is true they may be proved incorrect or inadequate at some future date, and be successfully supplanted. But until that happens, I suggest that to the extent historians employ conventional assumptions about 'how the world works' (as applied to any particular matter), then we should not be unduly pessimistic about the 'factual' foundations of historical knowledge. Only where assumptions of an unconventional nature (deliberately or 'unconsciously') underlie his inferences should we feel justified *prima facie* in doubting the reliability of the facts an historian uncovers.

Proof *and* 'sources'

In addition to such reassurance there is of course a further reason for confidence – namely, that (where they can) historians look for *proof* of the truth of what they infer. For example, I might infer from this stonework that there used to be a bridge here. I may find other evidence from which the same inference can be drawn. This strengthens it, but still cannot 'prove' it correct. However, I may find a map, drawn at the time, which indeed places a bridge on the spot. This map is *present* to me (even though drawn centuries ago) and can be seen to *prove* the correctness of my initial inference; that is, it shows the (inferred) 'fact' that there used to be a bridge here to be true; (whether we *believe* the map is a separate matter). The point about proof, then, is that it derives from something *present* to us which we construe as proving some inferred knowledge of something *not* present to us.

Although this shows that to infer a fact from evidence is to do something different from proving a fact to be true, it also demonstrates there is room for confusion between the two procedures. Our map can be seen as 'proof' of inferences. But we may also view this old map as *evidence* from which to infer knowledge about the past which it does *not* contain – e.g., that a military build-up was underway, or that trade increased between two districts.

The above is important because it draws attention to the equivocal nature of what historians call 'the sources', and upon which they lay such emphasis in explaining and, if necessary, defending the nature of their discipline. To recoup a little, the status of historians' knowledge is influenced by being of things past, no longer present to us. Rather than rely on hearsay or imagination, they find things *present* to them (buildings, objects, preserved documents) which they view as *evidence* from which to *infer* things about the past. They also find things *present* to them which they view as *proof* of inferred facts. In both cases, that which is *present* to them is called a 'source', or 'source-material'. Although in theory perhaps anything present is potentially a 'source' (either as evidence or proof of something), in practice it is of course those things which have *survived* from the past into the present which most naturally offer themselves as 'sources'. And amongst these, again in practice, *written* 'sources' are the most sought after – for example, letters, parliamentary and legal records, parish registries, trading inventories, rules and membership lists of organisations, autobiographies, newspapers, and so on. 'Sources', then, are the invaluable bedrock upon which historians both infer and prove 'facts' from the past (again, irrespective of what they go on to do with 'the facts' – i.e., describe, analyse, explain, or narrate past phenomena). That they deal in 'facts', and that these 'facts' are supportable and sometimes verifiable by 'sources' open to examination because they are present to us, lends the same kind of credibility to what historians say about the past as does the production of tangible pieces of *evidence* and *proof* in a court of law.

This said, there are however two kinds of limitations to the knowledge acquired, and here we may be reminded of our earlier remarks on the usefulness of surviving *film and/or sound recordings* as ways of finding out about past situations and incidents. In fact, we can now see that such recordings constitute *sources* in just the same way as, for example, parish records, except that the former are on film whilst the latter are written – and in principle the same two drawbacks we ascribed to the former also apply to the latter.

Written sources: their limitations

First, written records are restricted in what we can either infer or prove from them because of the limited *forms* they take. Just as the camera and microphone have to be pointed by someone, *written* sources only convey or suggest the kind of information appropriate to the form or rationale of their construction. For example, much can be gleaned about a village population from a surviving parish register of births, marriages, and deaths. But equally, there is much we might want to know for which that source, by its very nature, is useless. The same can be said for parliamentary records, or the minutes of meetings, and so on. In short, generous and varied as is the written word as a fund of sources, its capacity to communicate information is nonetheless restrained (like film) by its nature as a medium. To a certain extent, 'the medium is the message'.

This may be an obvious point, but it is worth setting out because it tells us something about the epistemological scope of history. *Because history is source-based*, historical knowledge is limited to what sources are available. Indeed, in practice, much history is produced *because* such-and-such sources are available, rather than 'the past' offering itself, so to speak, as an open area simply waiting to be explored by enterprising historians. Some even see this as the tail wagging the dog, and thus complain of the restricted scope of historians' attention. For example, it could be argued that so much history until recent decades – and still much today – was *political* history simply because political matters have been so prevalent amongst written records (i.e., *sources* such as parliamentary debates, cabinet minutes, diplomatic notes, international treaties, newspaper reports); and that because of this, many a poor soul grew up to equate 'history' with *political* history, and even worse, with his or her *national* political history!

The second drawback to written sources reverts us to the parallel with film and/or sound recordings as sources. In the latter case we noted the potentially serious 'criticism' that a film is *produced* by someone. Because the filmer selects what to film, then even though what is filmed is indeed 'true' (e.g., President Kennedy is shown being shot), the motivations of the person wielding the camera raise issues about the objectivity of the information the film conveys – issues ranging from the simple practical inability to capture 'everything' relevant to the incident, to the more threatening one of the deliberate (or unconscious) intrusion of the filmer's own assumptions and prejudices into *what* he films and *how* he films it (e.g., close-ups, camera panning, exploitation of lighting, and so on). Leni Riefenstahl's filming of the 1936 ('Nazi') Olympics is a classic, because extreme, example of such deliberately manipulative techniques used for 'ideological' purposes.

Less obviously, such drawbacks also apply to *written* sources, because (in addition to taking some or other *form*) they also are of course *produced* by the writer. We are not here thinking of cases where a written source *obviously* bears the writer's influence (as, for example, any autobiography). Rather, some analytical philosophers of history have raised the issue even in the case of the most apparently

306

'innocuous' written records used as sources. For example, parish records had to be produced, and we have noted their form partly determines what kind of information they contain. As with a film, they do not record 'everything' about the parishioners, (nor ever could). But also (as with a film) it is possible that, even with the information which *is* selected, (e.g., births, marriages, and deaths), details which should be included are omitted or otherwise 'distorted' because of the recorder's assumptions and/or prejudices (e.g., illegitimate births, ethnic minority marriages, deaths through sheer poverty). It is not difficult to see how the same doubts can be raised about other apparently 'innocuous' sources such as economic statistics, written recordings of court cases, prison files, and so on. Indeed, where 'records' are literally produced as such, particularly 'official' records, we might say they are by their nature 'tainted'. In addition, some have argued that where documents of one kind or another are later assembled into an *archive* or *collection*, similar questions can be raised about the unspoken focus and motivations of the archivist.

Now it could be argued that, because written 'sources' are so intrinsic to the 'nuts and bolts' of their work, practising historians are perfectly aware of these two potential drawbacks. As such, discussions of particular historians' employment of sources fall more properly under *historiography*, whilst awareness of the various techniques and precautions involved in using them falls under *historical methodology*, rather than the more 'abstract' approach of analytical philosophy of history. Without recapping the distinction between the latter and the former discussed in the previous chapter, the reason these issues arise here is that, although they are indeed the meat and drink of much historiography and historical methodology, neither of the latter usually question the very nature and use of 'sources' *per se* as the foundation of the discipline of history. Analytic philosophy of history, on the other hand, takes a step back to theorise on the *general* significance of the fact that *any* 'historical' knowledge is 'source-based', however that is handled in particular cases. And as we have seen, such consideration opens the opportunity for differing degrees of scepticism regarding the possibility of grounding history on 'objective' and 'true' *facts* at the outset. Some theorists (see Chapter 14) appear to have lost faith altogether in the 'factual' basis to history, which leads them into correspondingly strange territory when grappling with 'what is history?'.

One can see the force of such complaints. For example, it is true that in practice much historical research is chosen because of the ready availability of particular sources. There may be lessons to be drawn here, although in recent decades some historians have been more imaginative in construing things as sources. Also, it is probably true that some historians are insufficiently critical of the potential for bias and/or distortion in apparently 'innocuous' source-material, and perhaps 'sources and methods' courses should be even more alert to that possibility.

One lesson which should *not* be drawn, however, is that because of the limitations imposed upon history by 'the sources', its claims to objectivity are invalidated *in principle*. Rather, we should insist that history remain source-*based*, but avoid being source-*driven*; and that where a 'source' is the product of a human being (from the most harmless parish registrar to the most meticulous statistician, from the most scrupulous clerk of court to the most clinical documentary film maker), that should always be taken into account *if justified*. The alternative would appear to throw the baby out with the bathwater – and although some analytic philosophers of history might threaten just that, it is surely a position which is as regrettable as it is exaggerated.

'Historical explanation'

So far we have discussed different 'types' of history, and the epistemological foundations of historical knowledge. But these are not the only considerations involved in reflecting on 'what is history?'. Many analysts have proposed that a major part of this enquiry should focus on how historians *explain* past phenomena. Is there anything 'special' about the way historians explain things? And even if there is not, the way they do it still requires a critical understanding in order to give further insight into what 'history' is.

This topic ('historical explanation') would take us into much difficult and recondite territory, at least if we were to believe those who propose that there is in fact a specifically *historical* way of explaining things. Rather, let us proceed as clearly as the topic allows, and defer consideration of the latter claim until the appropriate place, beginning instead with less esoteric notions. The question is, do (or should) historians explain things in a particular manner? Or put the other way around, does 'history' as the *content* of the past (i.e., rather than the discipline) require a particular 'kind' of explanation because of its nature?

Scientific causality

At first view there appear to be three possible approaches to this question. First, we know that one of the commonest ways we *explain* something is to employ the notions of 'cause' and 'effect'. We have already commented on this, noting that the terms *can* be used loosely simply as a substitute for 'because' – e.g., 'her distress caused me to comfort her'; 'I comforted her because she was in distress'; or 'the huge waves were the effect of a hurricane'; 'the waves were huge because of a hurricane'. However, we also noted the paradigm of science, where 'cause' and 'effect' are appealed to as a strictly determinist framework articulating the physical laws governing the universe. Most theorists agree that, although historians may need on occasions to exploit this strict scientific meaning of 'cause' and 'effect', it should not be a model which generally characterises their explanatory discourse. There can be two reasons for this. Either it is thought that, even if *in principle* everything is indeed ultimately only explicable in terms of the workings of a material universe, it is simply impossible in practice to do this for the kaleidoscopic multitude of events and circumstances which make up the panorama of history (i.e., understood here as 'content'), or it is thought that the scientific model of causality is *in principle* inapplicable to history understood as focused on humans' interaction between themselves and between them and their surrounding world. (We have already noted, and approved of, this latter position when distinguishing between human and 'natural' history, without at that point, however, suggesting any alternative way of explaining things appropriate to history).

'Covering-law' models

The second possible approach to 'historical explanation' is to suggest that what some have called 'covering-laws' underlie the multitudinous particulars of (human) history, which therefore provide a general 'model' or template followed in the historian's explanatory discourse. Although a somewhat vague claim in the abstract – (indeed, there seems no reason to suggest 'scientific causality' is not just such a 'covering-law') – what its proponents seem to mean is that the diverse and particular actions, events, and circumstances of a (past) scenario are not explicable with reference to their individuality in each case, but need subsuming under some general 'laws' which 'govern' or feature in *all* history. What these 'covering-laws' *are* may vary from one historian to another; and it is far from clear whether our analysts actually approve of historians using them, irrespective of what particular covering-law (deliberately or unconsciously) is allegedly in operation. Rather, their point is that, in their view, 'historical explanation' relies on 'covering-laws' of one kind or another, whether historians realise this or not.

Perhaps the clearest example of a deliberate use of 'covering-laws' is Marxism, particularly in its more vulgarised sense as described in our Chapter 10. Here, the formulae that 'the mode of production determines the relations of production, which in turn determine the superstructure of any society', and that 'all history is the history of class-struggle', provide the underlying backcloth or framework into which the diverse particulars are assimilated, thereby 'explaining' them. But the same can be said for the great *bulk* of that *speculative* philosophy of history explored in Part I of this book, of which Marx's 'historical materialism' is only one example – for what is a backcloth, framework, or imposition of overall *meaning* to history, other than a 'covering-law', (in these cases made *explicit* via argument)? We explored Hegel's complex framework, and how he employed it to explain not only 'world-history' as a whole but numerous episodes within it (e.g., Hellenic Greece, the Protestant Reformation). Far less specific, but nonetheless operational, were classical theories of eternally recurrent cycles, or Christian ideas of 'history' being governed by God into one huge, *linear* 'story', from Creation, through the Fall of Man, to the eventual 'millennium' of the Second Coming. However, in all these and in other examples of speculative philosophy of history, the fact that they might be called different examples of 'the covering-law model of historical explanation' adds as little to understanding them as, I suggest, it does to understanding 'historical explanation' by claiming it is modelled on 'covering-laws'.

The vagueness of the latter notion is compounded by the fact that it can also be used – and has been – to suggest that even where historians do not subscribe to any explicit overall 'theory' (or 'speculative philosophy') of history, but instead understand themselves to be explaining particular events and circumstances in their individual discreteness, they nevertheless (usually unconsciously) exploit some 'general laws' about human behaviour. Put together and made explicit by analysis, the 'covering-laws' used by this or that historian can thus be identified and, if necessary, criticised. However, other analytical philosophers of history have criticised, not this or that example of such 'covering-laws', but their use at all in historians' explanations. Their argument is that to explain something by implying it is an instance of a 'covering-law' is therefore to derive or *deduce* the event or circumstance from some abstract principle – and to do this is thus not only to neglect the particular in circumstances, but also lends them an *inevitability* which sits uneasily with what they take to be the forum of historians' attention, namely, the contingent and unique.

The latters' rejection of the 'covering-law model' for 'historical explanation' implies, then, not just the possibility, but the necessity, of the historian explaining things without 'covering-laws', and debate has ensued as to how to do this ever since the latter were claimed (in the 1940s) as an inevitable feature of historians' thinking.

However, how far this debate actually offers insight into whether history is (partly) characterised by a distinctive way of explaining things – and if so, what it is – must remain dubious. The problem is that insofar as the notion of a 'covering-law' can extend from explicit speculative philosophies of history to implicit 'assumptions' about human behaviour, for example, it says nothing of any value. As a catch-all notion one is reminded of Edward Bernstein's observation (in criticising the emphasis crude Marxists put upon 'the theory of surplus-value') that the atomic theory of matter, true as it might be, can give no insight into the beauty of a vase. Just so with the (logically) profligate notion of a 'covering-law'.

But if, as its critics imply, the alternative is for the historian *not* to have any 'covering-laws', but to deal with each matter (event, circumstance, action) separately, this is straightforwardly unrealistic – for as we have seen, even the process of *inference* involved in *establishing* 'the facts', never mind *explaining* them, can only function through assumptions about 'how the world works'. Thus, if all that is ultimately meant by 'covering-laws' is, at the minimum, having assumptions about how the world works, then their very pervasiveness – from (e.g.) Marxism to (e.g.) the assumption that people try to avoid pain, or like to help their friends – renders the notion non-operational in any realistic or distinctive sense; i.e., it is of no use, in practice, in identifying *different* features of the way past phenomena can be explained.

'Explaining' things

Rather, let us adopt a third possible approach to the question of whether historians do (or should) explain things in a particular way, by abandoning the above terms of reference and, in better philosophical fashion, begin at the beginning. This means starting with what it is that analytic philosophers are trying to explain – and in this case, it is the notion of 'explanation' itself! This should put one in a better position to see what sense, if any, attaches to the notion of *historical* explanation.

From earlier discussion of 'words' and 'reality', we can say that one of the things people have found worth singling out from 'the world out there' is the (mental) activity denoted by the verb 'to explain'. To see what it is 'to *explain* something' we need only consult the dictionary for a clarification of what is *meant* by the word, (i.e., there is no paradigmatic 'real thing' called 'to explain' which we poor mortals may or may not manage to apprehend; rather, it is a term used by us *for* us, better to manage an aspect of our experience – in this case, our *intellectual* interests). The list of meanings in the 1989 *Oxford English Dictionary* includes 1) 'to make clear the cause, origins, or reason of; to account for', and 2) of the phrase 'to explain oneself', 'to make one's meaning clear and intelligible . . . also, to give an account of one's intentions or motives'. A little reflection, I suggest, shows the common core to these definitions, which is that 'to explain' something is to show how what is to be explained '*follows on*'. For example, in (2), 'to explain one's conduct' is to show how it 'follows' from one's intentions or motives – or, 'to make one's meaning clear and intelligible' is to show how what one has said does indeed 'follow on' from one word to the next. Likewise with the first definition, (1), the notion of one thing 'following on' from another is at the core. For example, it *follows* that if 1+1 = 2, then 2–1 = 1; that if one uses Newton's laws of gravity, it *follows* that an unrestrained object will fall downwards towards earth, and at a predictable rate of acceleration; or, finally, that given the sequence of occurrences outlined in (someone's) history, it followed that war broke out in 1914. I have included this last somewhat tendentious example to highlight the point that common to any *explanation* is the notion of one thing 'following on from' another.

Now it is true that in the above examples things are construed as 'following on' for different reasons (via logic, or scientific causality, or via conventional assumptions about human conduct). But these are differences *in* the way things 'follow on', not differences which imply that 'explaining' a thing sometimes involves the notion of 'following on', but at other times does *not* involve this notion but some other operative principle instead. The cardinal principle at work when we 'explain', 'understand', 'reason about', or 'account for' *anything* (terms often, and under-standably, intermixed in dictionary definitions) is that propensity of the human mind to think in terms of 'one thing following on from another'. This is the way the mind works, from the reason it 'makes sense' to the paranoic to kill his family, to Einstein to claim E = MC squared, to the banker to charge interest, to me to take an umbrella when it looks like rain. And what we do when we 'explain' something is to *demonstrate* that it 'follows on'.

Having said this, our concern, then, is that the concept of 'historical explanation' implies there is a class of things which 'follow on' *historically*, such that when we 'explain' them we are doing so 'historically' rather than in some other (alleged) way – hence, 'historical explanation'. But this is a chimera. Just as things do not *fall* scientifically, biologically, mathematically, or historically, then in *explaining* why a thing falls we do not explain it scientifically, biologically, mathematically, or historically. It is true that things may fall quickly, slowly, noisily, silently, but these adverbial qualifiers denote merely contingent features of what is essentially happening, and moreover have to be applicable to that kind of occurrence – i.e., they could not be applied to 'loving'.

Thus with things 'following on'. They may do so more nearly or distantly, or more obviously than other things which also 'follow' – but not noisily, nor historically. Just so, then, with the process of *demonstrating* that one thing follows another – i.e., of *explaining* something. One may do it clearly or confusedly, lengthily or succinctly, conventionally or originally – all contingent features of the same essential phenomenon. But one cannot do it 'historically'.

Historical accounts

Instead, the most which can be said is that distinct topics and activities often generate their own terminology or frame of reference. For example, in explaining why an engine has a flywheel one is to an extent captive to the topic of mechanics – i.e., one shows how the need for a flywheel 'follows' from the way the laws of mechanics are exploited in engine design. From this, there is nothing wrong in referring to a 'mechanical' explanation so long as one does not mean there is a 'mechanical' way of explaining things. Similarly, in explaining the course of the First World War one can give a military account of it, since any warfare is clearly amenable to military terms of reference. Also, of course, one can give an *historical* account of the First World War (albeit not a mechanical or biological account), but what does this mean? Does it mean the war is somehow explained 'historically'?

What we mean by 'an historical account' of (e.g.) a war is simply that, given it was a sequence of events, we can demonstrate how those events 'followed on' from each other. We may need on occasions to use military terms of reference, but also economic and political ones. But overall, there will be no *single* special terms of reference applicable to accounting for or 'explaining' what happened 'in that war'. Rather, what characterises the *historian's* account or explanation is simply that it consists of making an intelligible continuity from numerous and diverse events and circumstances. In short, then, an explanation is 'historical' simply and solely inasmuch as it deals with *any* occurrences by putting them into an intelligible sequence, whereby one thing 'follows from' another, be it the outbreak of a revolution, the invention of a medicine, or (in principle) my visit to the cinema last week. As such, the term 'historical' is an unusually *broad* term denoting that a thing is treated within the reference of 'sequences of occurrences', just as the term 'scientific' (unlike, e.g., 'mechanical', 'biological', or 'geographical'), is an unusually broad framework denoting a thing's treatment within the reference of causal law-determined phenomena, be it the composition of a planetary system, the strength of a bridge, or the course of an illness. The crucial difference between 'historical' and 'scientific', however, is that these latter phenomena, despite their diversity, are amenable to explanation *exclusively as causally determined*, whereas the things historians explain are not. They are 'simply' construed as one event following from another, and how this linking is construed takes us to what I have already suggested is the distinctive character of history proper – i.e., *narrative*.

Narrative and 'explanation'

We have already said something about the structure of narrative, but now need to probe a little further into its characteristics, (whose fuller complexity, however, I have explored elsewhere, and at greater length than we need indulge in here). We should recall the seminal difference between a narrative (both factual and fictional) and a chronicle, and above all the crucial operational force of the term 'then' in the basic formula of narrative, 'this happened and *then* that happened and *then* that happened' and so on. What lies behind this formula is the notion that what happened *next* (or 'then') happened *because of* what had gone on *before*. In other words, occurrences are put into a *sequence* where one occurrence 'follows from' another in terms of 'prior' and 'subsequent', or 'this *then* that'. What this achieves is that an occurrence ('happening', 'action', 'event') is 'explained' as *following on from* a previous occurrence. For example, 'Mr. Brown entered the room, and then felt cold, and then turned on the fire'. In this elementary narrative, its very *form* as narrative implies he felt cold because he entered the room, and he turned on the fire because he felt cold. It is in this manner that 'explanation' is built into the very structure of narrative – i.e., we do not have to interrupt the narrative to add some separate (e.g., analytic or scientific) form of discourse to explain why he turned on the fire. Rather, his action 'makes sense' given he felt cold.

If this is clear enough – (after all, to 'explain' things via narrative is so common as to be 'natural' to us; 'why did you come home so late last night?', 'why did Britain go to war in 1939?') – three points remain worth adding.

The logic of narrative sequences

First, in any narrative, however exhaustive in detail, not every occurrence is included in the sequence articulated by the narrator. Not only would this be impossible in practice, (although the ideal of science might be to say '*a* caused *b*, which caused *c*, which caused *d*', etc.) in *narrative* it is both unnecessary and irrelevant. In short, narrative does not proceed from *a*, then *b*, then *c*, then *d*, and so on. (Mr. Brown's actions in turning on the light *could* in theory be spelt out in terms of his moving towards the switch, raising his hand, extending his finger, grasping the switch, and so on – and any one of those actions could in theory be broken down again into a sequence). Rather, narrative at its starkest moves from an initial occurrence *a*, ignores potential *b*'s and *c*'s, etc., until it reaches that point (say *k*) which would *not* be understood to 'follow' from *a* ('Mr. Brown came down to breakfast and *then* braked his car violently to avoid a stray dog'). *a* then *k* would not 'make sense'. But *a* then *j* still makes sense ('Mr. Brown came down to breakfast, then got into his car to go to work'). So, of course, does *j* then *k* (Mr. Brown got into his car to go to work, and then braked violently' etc . . .). After this, point k is treated like another point a. Thus, at its most basic, this is how the principle of selection and omission of occurrences works in the narrative form: not a, b, c, etc., but $a \ldots j,k \ldots s,t \ldots y,z$, etc. In this way, occurrences are put into a sequence which makes each explicable at any point in the narrative/story, without requiring a potential infinity of detail. (*Within* that essential structure all sorts of games can of course be played, as they are in fiction to achieve various contingent effects such as to convey information about a character, or build up tension. And the same can be done in a factual narrative, but if so, it must always be to achieve *more* than simply to 'explain' a sequence of events – but let us postpone examination of this possibility until the next chapter, which includes the various purposes to which factual/historical narrative are put).

Narrative and conventional understanding

Having witnessed narrative's ability, embedded in its very form, to 'make sense of', or 'explain', occurrences, the second point to add is, what *kind* of sense is involved here? And the answer is that the 'sense' or 'explanation' implicit in narrative is *conventional* to whatever the topic might be. By 'conventional' I mean our 'ordinary' understanding of how one occurrence or action leads to 'the next'. We have seen it would not make sense to say, for instance, that 'the young Hitler sold one his paintings in the streets of Vienna and then invaded Poland'. Too many intervening 'nexts' are omitted for the conventional way in which our minds link up actions into an intelligible sequence. But to say that 'Hitler had a long discussion with his generals, and then invaded Poland', or 'Hitler saw all was lost and then committed suicide', are examples where the 'next' action can be understood to be conventionally contiguous to the 'previous' action. These conventional understandings on which narrative feeds range from psychology to economics, from military matters to political insight, from the amorous life to family relations, and so on – and this reinforces the point that no special kind of understanding need be at work (although if the topic is inherently technical, the conventional understanding of that topic's special terminology may come into play, but only for that topic). Rather, we are back to the reliance on conventional understandings of 'how the world works', from Mr. Brown's choice to turn on the fire when he felt cold, to Hitler's choice to commit suicide, having judged all was lost. Indeed, so 'instinctive' or 'natural' is it to not only explain things via a narrative, but also to employ 'ordinary' rather than 'specialist' assumptions in doing so, that we might rightly be sceptical of an historian whose narrative sequences require us to share some unconventional and/or special assumptions if we are to make sense of it – for example, a particular theory of psychology when dealing with human motivations.

These 'conventional' assumptions about 'how the world works' may of course change slowly over time, and may be suspect, if not indeed wrong. However, they have the advantage that they are flexible and do not require justifying in each case as one moves forward in a narrative.

Indeterminacy in human conduct

Third, there is one more feature of narrative worth noticing. Narrative (insofar as it deals with human conduct) does not offer a rigidly *deterministic* explanation of occurrences and actions. Rather, if Mr. Brown felt cold and then turned on the fire, this does not mean his action was 'caused' in the sense that it could have been no other. He might have left the room instead, or put on a pullover, or put up with feeling cold. We do not know. We do know, however, that he turned the fire on, and we see this as his *response* to feeling cold. In short, narrative leaves room for the notion of 'free will' or 'choice', despite the philosophical problems involved. But here, narrative form simply reflects the conventional view, no worse for being conventional, that human beings respond rather than *react* to situations (e.g., as machines, or conglomerations of chemicals). In short, we arrive back at the point that narrative discourse is different from scientific discourse – but can now appreciate perhaps even further the peculiar appropriateness of narrative for the discipline of history, given we mean human rather than 'natural' history, and given that 'the study of past events in the human world' includes *explaining*, or *accounting for*, their occurrence (as it surely should).

Summary

Having clarified and commented upon not only the *manner* in which narrative is explanatory, but also what *kind* of sense or explanation it offers, let us conclude these considerations by returning to what instigated them, i.e., the notion of 'historical explanation'. What the historian is doing when he constructs a narrative is to give an account *of* a sequence of events. In so doing he or she is accounting *for*, or 'explaining', the occurrences involved. Thus historians know how to 'explain' their material, aware as anyone else that this involves demonstrating that one thing follows from another. But they are wary of the notion that they are explaining things 'historically' – or more to the point, that in relying on narrative they are, according to many analysts, thereby *failing* to explain things 'historically'. Many analytic philosophers of history, and some historians, have been hostile to *narrative* history precisely because they claim narrative (or 'story-telling') is either *non*-explanatory *per se*, (a blatant error), or at most offers only 'weak', simplistic explanations (as if narrative were inherently incapable of incorporating e.g., sociological insights into history!). Instead, for decades they have thus gone off in search of some 'ideal' mode of understanding and/or discourse they call 'historical explanation', a search which has dominated much analytic philosophy of history – which is why, as your guide, I have devoted such space to the topic, if only to reassure students of history who visit that literature that, if their instincts are likely to rebel against it (as have many practising 'historians'), not *all* theorists find it illuminating either.

'Historical explanation' restored? – 'explication'

Having considered the notion of 'historical explanation' and found it wanting so far, there is, however, an alternative sense in which the term may be awarded some credence – but this derives from *another* meaning the dictionary gives for 'explain' (i.e., in addition to those we have used above), and also focuses on a further property of *narrative* history in particular. One of the meanings of 'to explain' is 'to make [something] clear or intelligible with detailed information'. Used in this sense, the term is interchangeable with a more technical term, namely, 'to explicate', meaning 'to develop the notion of something', or 'to unfold' or 'make explicit the nature of something'. Here the emphasis is not on explaining what caused a thing, or where it came from, or some other sense of *why* something is as it is, but on 'explaining' (or 'explicating') *what* the thing is (or was). Now, if (as we have seen) one of narrative's properties is that it 'explains' *why* happenings occur – 'this happened *then* that happened' etc.) – another of its properties is to 'explain' (or 'explicate') the *nature* of those things I earlier called 'narrative identities' or 'story-objects'; in other words, those 'things' which comprise *sequences* of happenings.

For purposes of exposition, let us now use the term, 'an event' no longer as interchangeable with an 'occurrence', 'happening', 'incident', or 'action', but as meaning that which *results* from their connecting together (via narrative logic) into an intelligible *sequence* of happenings. I have already proposed that in addition to our apprehending different *physical objects* in 'the world out there', we also apprehend or single out 'occurrences' and/or 'actions'. And I have claimed that when we use a word to denote an occurrence (e.g., he is 'swimming'), then 'to swim' is no more nor less 'real' a phenomenon than, e.g., 'a chair'. Pursuing this logic a little further, in the case of physical objects it is clear that many things posited as single objects can in another light be seen as made up of a *collection* of *other* objects. For example, we can talk of 'a rose', 'a lawn', or 'a pond' as separate, individual objects. But we can also talk of 'a garden', which incorporates these otherwise separate things. A 'garden' is no more nor less 'real' a thing than, e.g., a 'lawn'. And in its turn a garden may be part of *another* single thing, namely, 'an estate', just as (vice-versa) a lawn can be seen as a *collection* of otherwise separate individual things (blades of grass, moss, soil). In short, there is an (almost?) infinite dialectic between physical objects denoted as singular things and as breaking down into other singular things, or as forming part of other (larger) single things – all of which 'things' are as 'real' as any other, ranging ultimately from 'the universe' to 'an atom'.

We noted the same logic applies to single occurrences and/or actions, in the example of 'switching on' a light. This action can be broken down into other 'contributory' actions – e.g., extending an arm – or itself could be part of a 'larger' action of, e.g., 'setting up' a studio. Again, none of these actions is more nor less 'real' than any other. But we should also note that when an occurrence or action is 'broken down' into its 'parts', what this actually entails is putting different actions into a *sequence*. And this is precisely what narrative does. It singles out a sequence of otherwise individual occurrences and thereby 'describes' a phenomenon as 'real' as anything else – namely, an intelligible sequence of occurrences, for which we can give the generic term 'an event', meaning anything which is conventionally understood to be *explicitly* comprised of different occurrences (linked via the narrative logic of 'this happened *then* that happened'). Numerous 'events' are uniquely their own 'stories' which thus require individual narration. However, other 'sequences of occurrences' ('events') share sufficient common features as to have been classified via different 'event-nouns' – for example, 'a war', 'a revolution', 'an election', 'a love-affair', 'a slump', 'a cricket-match', 'a wedding'.

Thus we can now see more clearly the sense in which narrative 'explains' or 'explicates' the very nature of phenomena – phenomena, I repeat, no more nor less 'real' than physical objects, actions, qualities, and so on. In the case of narrative, the phenomena whose nature it explains are 'events', i.e., intelligible *sequences* of occurrences/actions. If we want to know in concrete terms, for example, 'what the First World War *was*', we need to be told its 'story'. The narrative of that war will 'explain' ('make explicit, or unfold, the nature of', or 'develop the notion of') that war. Now, in relation to '*objects*', when we put hundreds of them together and perceive e.g., 'an estate', we may differ as to what to include in it, and where it 'starts' and 'stops' – but (unless we are to lose our senses) we do not therefore suggest it does not 'exist', or is not a 'real' thing. Likewise with 'events'. Because the First World War was complex, because its 'story' can be told differently, this does not mean 'it' did not happen, or was not 'real'. It is true that the connecting of occurrences can be misapprehended, even to the extent that 'an event' is proposed/constructed which never actually happened. But this is rare in factual narrative, apart from the *lie*. Rather, what is far more common is where 'events' which *did* take place are denied, particularly by governments and others with vested interests who, wishing to avoid embarrassment or exposure, have throughout history engaged in 'cover-ups'. Attested (single) *occurrences* are often harder to deny – e.g., USA bombs falling on Cambodia; individual killings in Bosnia. But a *war*?! An *ethnic-cleansing campaign*?! 'There was no such thing', some insist in each case! Of this syndrome, Holocaust denial is surely the most (in)famous example.

A crucial achievement of the narrative form, then, is that in addition to 'explaining' *why* this or that occurrence took place, in a different sense of the word it also 'explains' ('explicates') the *nature* of this or that 'event' (i.e., an identifiable or meaningful *sequence* of occurrences singled out from the otherwise kaleidoscopic anarchy of things 'going on'). This latter achievement seems sufficiently distinctive, and so much the natural territory of those we call 'historians', that it may warrant being called 'historical explanation'. But the reader should note that, given *this* meaning, 'historical explanation' consists in giving an account *of* an intelligible sequence of occurrences (i.e., an 'event') – but it does not account *for* it; i.e., it does not 'explain' it in the sense of saying *why* it took place. Rather, it 'explains' it in the sense of laying bare its nature. Put another way, an 'event', 'story', or 'sequence of occurrences' is something made up of change. But in *itself* it is not a thing which changes. What the explicatory property of narrative does is to give an account *of* a thing made up of change by explaining the process of change *within* it ('this *then* that'). But it does not account *for* the sequence as a whole. To expect that it could is to enter unchartable territory, for by example of Mr Brown entering the room, and then feeling cold, and then turning on the fire, it is like asking 'why did Mr Brown enter the room, and then feel cold, and then turn on the fire?'. This is a question which goes beyond the form of narrative to answer – and, I suggest, beyond *any* form of answer we could imagine as empirically based. Rather, it could be argued that the quest for such an answer transports us to the realm of *speculative philosophy of history*, which precisely tries to make sense not of this or that occurrence, but of the grand sweep of huge 'events' – i.e., making *them* parts of a quasi-narrative. Interesting efforts have ensued, as explored in Part I of this book. But they are not examples of the discipline of history, and never claim to be. They are 'philosophy'. And yet it is just this expectation that sequences of occurrences, already made intelligible by narrative, have *themselves* somehow to be explained in terms of *why* they existed, which appears to have preoccupied some theorists' search for what they call 'historical explanation'. Not satisfied, or sometimes not even aware of, the explanatory and explicatory power of narrative, they look elsewhere for some 'special way' historians 'explain' (or *should* explain) the past as part of their search for what distinguishes 'history'. For our part it seems more appropriate to praise what narrative historians *do* achieve – namely, meticulously revealing the nature of past 'events' as well as 'explaining' the occurrences they comprise in ways which everyone can understand – rather than bewail their 'failure' to explain the categorically inexplicable, (unless, that is, one confuses 'history' with speculative philosophy *of* history).

Historical topics

'Anything goes?'

There is, finally, a further issue involved in pondering 'what is history?', and this is whether history should study *anything*, or whether only certain things or 'topics' lend themselves to the historian's scrutiny. By necessity our previous sections have at least *begun* to answer this, insofar as we have already addressed the truism that history deals with topics *in the past*, and the perhaps less certain truism (for some) that 'history' deals with the *human* world to the exclusion of 'natural history' (the domain of science).

In the abstract, these elementary parameters to *what* history studies may suffice for some. On the one hand, why should we stick to the traditional topics of 'history', (politics, warfare, economic development, revolutions – i.e., affairs of state)? In recent decades 'social' history has achieved some prominence, whilst many of today's historians grapple with new topics such as womens' history, media history, black history, and the history of sport. And let us not forget *intellectual* history. The history of social and political thought, and the history of philosophy, have long flourished, and have been joined more recently by the history of scientific thought. Thus (one could say), not only should we welcome these topics into the purview of 'history', we should hold the discipline open to explore any and every area where human activity and endeavour have a past, from sex to cannibalism, from stamp-collecting to space-travel.

Put more theoretically: what *principles* can be found, within the parameters of the human past, for claiming that some aspects of that past *cannot* be studied, or are at least less worthy of attention than others, and thus *ought* not to be studied? *Prima facie* it seems difficult to conceive what these principles could be, such that those bold spirits who claim that 'anything goes' as a topic of historical enquiry (so long as it concerns the past world of human concerns) are vindicated in their generous view.

Alternatively, it could be argued that it is indeed only in the abstract that 'history' has such generous parameters, and that such a vast area of study cries out for refinement, which has been carried out in practice in any event. But where do we start to conceive of what principles might underlie this refinement? This seems difficult to do *ab initio*, such that the supporters of 'anything goes for history' may have a point. Indeed, it seems incontrovertible if we include what I have called 'descriptive' and 'analytic' history, for on what grounds can we say something from the human past is *in principle* either incapable or (at least) 'unworthy' of being described or analysed? Philosophically speaking, none, since there is nothing in the logic of description or analysis to limit their subject-matter – a position which contributes to the notion that 'history is anything, willy-nilly, which is said about the past'.

Narrative parameters

The case is different, however, with *narrative* history. Here, the practice of that art does generate limitations for what topics are studied, *and* for what is treated *within* a topic or field of enquiry. Sufficient has already been said about the logic of narrative to recognise one major constraint upon its subject-matter – namely, it only treats of 'events', i.e., intelligible sequences of occurrences. This implies that narrative history, in addition to being applicable only to occurrences, 'happenings', or actions, is further restricted to only those which can be linked into genuinely operational temporal relationships of 'this *then* that'. By analogy, millions of *physical objects* are located in the space occupied by a house, but only some are 'noticed' as parts of the house – and even within that discrimination the *spatial relations* some exhibit to each other are crucial in making up 'a house', (e.g., the walls and the roof). Just so in any *temporal* space (i.e., a period of time) a myriad of occurrences happen, but only some are relevant to a particular topic, and of these, only some bear that special *temporal* relationship of 'this *then* that' which makes up an (intelligible) *sequence*. This seemingly abstract point has practical import for the discipline of (narrative) history, for it dictates that even where the historian limits himself to the (human) world of past *happenings* – ('history is what *happened*') – the 'branch' or 'subject-area' of his study must be one where genuine narrative sequences (or '*events*') are sufficiently prevalent to allow a properly historical treatment. The danger otherwise is that a random juxtapositioning (or worse, even a chronicle) of different occurrences all related to a subject-area is presented as 'history'. For example, in any given period of time there was a myriad of occurrences specifically relevant to women, or to an ethnic group, or to 'society'. But their arbitrary recounting would hardly constitute 'women's history', 'Black history', or 'social history'. Such histories can only properly become such by their material being amenable to the tracing of intelligible processes of *change* through time – articulated, of course, via the narrative form. This is not to say, for example, that 'womens' history' is not a viable undertaking. Such a view would be difficult to defend on any a priori grounds. But it does mean that its practitioners can only be convincing in defence of the 'historicality' of their topic to the extent that they can extract genuine 'events' from the (sometimes alarming) breadth of otherwise discrete aspects and occurrences they deal with. The alternative is a kind of 'pseudo-history' which again threatens the 'history is anything, willy-nilly, which is said about the past' syndrome (even where restricted to things that *happened*).

Highways and byways

As noted, then, none of the above suggests any a priori grounds for dismissing topics, subject-areas, or 'branches' involving human activity from the purview of (narrative) history. As such it remains a sufficiently generous set of 'restrictions' on what topics history 'should' deal with for enterprising spirits to continue to innovate into unexplored parts of the past and even develop new branches of history. But it does suggest some of the reasons why recognised areas of interest become established amongst historians – namely, they are those areas where we are most likely to 'notice' events (or 'stories') and thereby benefit from understanding 'what happened' in terms of meaningful sequences of occurrences. Here we return to the observation that 'events' are no more nor less 'real' than other kinds of 'things' we apprehend – i.e., it is not their 'reality' which somehow imposes them on our consciousness. Rather, it is their relevance and workability for *us* in our experience of 'the world out there'. And what this comes down to is the mundane observation that 'events' in some areas of human activity are regarded as more *important* than those in other areas – and, to an extent, these can vary over time and culture. For example, religious history used to predominate (and still does) in societies where religion was an important factor in peoples' lives. Political history has always been a major topic of historians' work, although where political division is less pointed this has inclined some to suggest that politics is far less influential than many suppose – (e.g., compare Great Britain to Northern Ireland, or USA to Israel) – and prompted them more towards economic history, or social history, or even to develop new topics such as 'media history', or 'the history of globalisation'.

There are, of course, other factors at play in the emergence of established areas of historical focus. We have already mentioned the possibility of a subject-area being source-driven, and will in the following chapter consider the influence which ideology and, indeed, 'fashion', can exert. But these are contingent factors, I suggest, compared to the otherwise mundane factor of perceived 'importance' proposed above. Not only this, however, the latter also helps explain why even *within* a given topic or subject-area the historian's focus narrows down to certain events rather than others – i.e., it helps us probe further into what conspires to make 'history' restrain its field of scrutiny. This returns us to our analogy with the spatial connections between things in a house, where we claimed that numerous of them are pure chance, having nothing to do with the logic of the house. The other side to this, however, is that some of those which *are* integral to the house are more important than others. For example, the spatial relation between the foundations, walls, and the roof, is more important in understanding or 'explicating' the house than, for instance, that between the front and back door.

Likewise with the *temporal* relations between occurrences within a given subject-area. Any given occurrence may form part of numerous *different* sequences or 'stories', many of which have no bearing on the subject-area. (We have all met people who, in recounting an event we are interested in, get sidetracked by intermixing other stories set off by one of the occurrences they have narrated as part of that event.) Some of the sequences, however, *are* relevant to the topic, and amongst these, some more so than others. The topic may be political or maritime history, or the history of art – and what we are suggesting is that within that topic attention focuses first upon those sequences of occurrences ('events') which are conventionally regarded as relevant to it; but that then a further discrimination generally operates, whereby the historian focuses upon those events which relate more directly to what we might call the principal pillars of the topic's architecture – for example, the make-up of government, legislation, elections, revolutions, organs of public opinion, in the subject-area of political history (earlier dominated by the individual dynastic careers of monarchs). And this is because where occurrences following on from each other involve the more important or formative features of a topic, the more likely it is we will find the dynamic behind intelligible change. We can remind ourselves of the platitude that, where nothing changes, there is no history to be told. And thus we find historians within a certain subject-area narrowing down their attention to those events or 'story-objects' which most directly articulate how the overall 'eventscape' they are interested in changed over time.

Summary comments

This chapter has incorporated four of the areas of debate which fall under analytic philosophy of history, on the grounds that they each relate in their different ways to one of the *overall* questions it addresses – namely, what *is* 'history' (as a discipline). To summarise, these four areas are: what *kind* or *type* of discourse is history?; what kind of *knowledge* lies at its foundation? (i.e., history's epistemological status); what things does history *explain*, and how? (i.e., 'historical explanation'); and to what extent (and why) are the topics or subject-matter of 'history' limited in character? (i.e., can history be about *anything* in the past?). Readers will not fail to have noticed that, as your guide to these theoretical issues, in each case I have prompted them towards narrative as offering the best direction to take in considering them – and further, that because this prompting is *common* to all four areas, it is suggestive of an overall coherence which might be achieved in reflecting on 'what is history?'. Readers will also have noticed that a more general 'philosophical' position, centred on the nature of 'reality' and the function of words, underpins these suggestions. In short, as your guide I have found it neither fruitful, nor hardly even possible, to give an exposition of these issues without suggesting where they might be at least be clarified, if not resolved – i.e., it seems as futile to analyse the discipline we call 'history' without central reference to the logic of *narrative*, as it would be to attempt understanding the nature of what we call 'travel' without central reference to *movement*.

However, readers will of course make up their own minds as they further explore the differing approaches of analytic philosophers of history, and hopefully this chapter (either despite or because of the direction it prompts) at the least demonstrates the relevance of these four issues and helps simplify the sometimes complex and/or technical ways they are articulated in the genre of analytical philosophy of history.

The following chapter explores the second of those general headings under which I suggest the reflections contained in 'analytic philosophy of history' are subsumed – namely, if the first is 'what is history?', the second is 'what is history *for?*'. Although intimately related to the first question, it generates sufficiently different issues to warrant separate treatment.

13

WHAT IS HISTORY FOR?

Introduction

In the previous chapter we explored the issues analytic philosophers of history raise in relation to the question, 'what is history?'. Properly, we treated this as a *philosophical* question because there is no other 'discipline' which has ready answers, and in the sense that the philosophical attitude is that of 'astonishment' at anything – not only at the obscure, but also things otherwise taken for granted because so familiar and thus apparently 'obvious'.

It is in this light that analytic philosophers of history also pose the question, 'what is history *for*?' – i.e., what is the *point* of history? The same two-facedness attaches to this question as to 'what *is* history?'. This is that the philosophical approach straddles between empirical observation of what the point of history 'is' as it appears to those who engage in it, and critical notions of what the point of history *ought* to be for anyone. Now, this latter form of the question implies some *ideal* motivation for the study of history, and may thus appear a curious, even presumptive, question. What does it matter what motivates an individual to study history, so long as he or she does it well enough? A possible reply, however, is that the sting is in the tail of that complaint, since there is a case for claiming that, as with many things we do, we do them well or badly depending on what motivates us. In the extreme case, we may fail altogether in our effort to undertake an activity because the expectations we have of it, which *motivate* us, distort how we go about it. For example, if I play football simply to impress my girlfriend, this is likely to make me play badly – maybe to the point where I am sent off for, as they say, 'not playing the game'! Applied to 'what is the point of history?', we shall amongst other things explore whether, how far, and why one's *motivation* in studying history may distort the 'history' one does, possibly to the point that one is not 'doing history' at all, but something else – for example, political propaganda.

What this implies is that where the thing in question is a *human activity*, there is a symbiosis between the *nature* of an activity, (as in 'what is history?'), and its *purpose*, (as in 'what is the point of history?'). This may remind readers of Aristotle's notion that the definition of a thing should include its *telos* (or 'end' – see p. 35 above), except that (more realistically) here we are limiting the notion to human activities, where intentionality is not a metaphysical supposition but clearly actually present. In short, if one does not know what the point of e.g., 'washing up' is, or of 'history', then how can one undertake these activities? So much is this the case that we might almost argue that the question of the previous chapter, 'what is history?', should have been approached by *first* asking, 'what is history *for*?' – in other words, one could try to establish the *nature* of an activity by asking first and foremost what people who engage in 'it' are trying to *achieve*, and why.

Persuasive as this might be, however, it does not allow us to escape the philosophical dilemma of trying to straddle empirical and ideal notions. This is because, in asking what people are trying to achieve by 'doing history', their answers might differ to the point where we can find no significant common ground. Consequently, 'history' is either indefinable or simply a catch-all term for *different* things people do. The implication of this is that in asking what people are trying to *achieve* by 'doing history', we *first* need at least some idea of what 'history' *is* – i.e., we are brought full-circle, thereby emphasising the symbiosis between the *nature* and the *point* of recognised human activities.

On a separate note, so far we have treated 'history' strictly in terms of the activity undertaken by practising historians, and have had cause to comment that *reading* history books (or 'consuming' lectures, and so on) is not 'being an historian' – rather, it is 'merely' studying the *product* of 'history' as a discipline. This may dismay many hard-working students who believe they are indeed undertaking the discipline of history rather than merely studying its products! However, for the purposes of examining 'what *is* history?' the distinction was essential. But now, in addressing the question, 'what is history *for*?', it is proper to include the study of 'history' as *communicated to us* by practising historians – i.e., the *reading* of history books and articles. Here, these latter are not 'sources' of historical knowledge (used as evidence and/or proof of historical facts), but actual *versions* of historical knowledge (referred to as 'secondary sources' to distinguish them from the former, *primary*, sources). In practice, 'the study of history' of course more often refers to this reading of, and thinking about, the knowledge produced and communicated by historians, rather than the practising historians' activity itself – and despite the severe distinction it was necessary to draw between the two in the previous chapter, no denigration of the latter meaning of 'studying history' is intended. This would indeed be strange in a book written for 'students of history', by which I mean both practitioners *and* readers of history.

But additionally, it is now appropriate to include both meanings of 'doing history', because in asking 'what is the point of history?' we must note that, even if the question was restricted only to the practise of working historians, part of their work is to *communicate* their knowledge, and thus their expectations of how readers might profit from it is integral to understanding at least part of the motivation behind their activity – i.e., it is part of 'what history is for' for them. And as for history *readers*, it would be strange if the point of reading history for them was different from the reasons historians had for presenting them with the material to read! However, not only can this be the case, it is possible to conceive of the respective motivations of writer and reader even to be contrary – for example, an author may write in order to make his readers *think* about a problem, whilst some may read him in order to get the answer to it!

Such disconsonance between writer and reader over 'what is the study of history *for*?' would be bizarre, and therefore reinforces the notion that in addressing this question, the expectations of both parties should not only be incorporated, but that a strong kinship 'ought' (ideally) to prevail in their motivation for 'doing history'.

In the following, then, we will explore the issue of the *point* of the discipline of history both from the historian's and the reader's (or student's) viewpoint. However, as in the previous chapter, some 'clearing of the ground' is necessary.

Theoretical preliminaries

Because this aspect of analytical philosophy of history focuses on what the *purpose* of historical study 'is' and/or 'should be', the general ground of this enquiry relates to peoples' *motivations* in what they do. As such, it might be objected that there already exists a discipline which deals with this – namely, psychology. Also, it might be objected that people's motivations, even in practising or studying history, could be so varied and individual that it is a fruitless line of enquiry for the purpose of any useful generalisations. Both these objections are sound, but only insofar as one is addressing *individual* motivations. Psychology studies what a person's motivation is, not what motivation is. We, on the other hand, are not here concerned with the individual motivations at play when people do this or that (e.g., play football or study history) – but not because of the potential blind alley it invites us down. Rather, our focus is on the *ground* of motivation in general, where a useful overall distinction *can*, and needs to, be made. The distinction is that between doing something for its own sake, and doing something as a means to an end. Because this distinction is central to the ensuing arguments over 'what is the point of (studying) history?', it is worth clarifying in advance.

When we do something 'for its own sake', we undertake the action or activity (comprising a number of related actions) for the sake of experiencing doing it. We do it for the experience *of* it, rather than as a means to some (other) end. The doing of the action is, thus, an end-in-itself. As such, it must be presumed we do it because we enjoy it. Here, semantics can confuse matters, since the same point is sometimes expressed in terms of doing something *in order to* enjoy it. But this is misleading, because when we do something for its own sake we do not do it 'in order to' experience it. This suggests the doing of it and the experiencing of it are two separate things, the former being a means to the latter end – whereas in reality the doing of it *is* the experience of it. Where, then, one does something for the sake of (the experience of) doing it, rather than as means to some (other) end, let us call this a 'final' action.

The other ground to people's motivation is where they do something *not* 'for its own sake', but as a means to achieve some objective separate from, and beyond, the action itself. For example, I switch on the light *so that* I can see better. Actions (or activities) so motivated, where they are engaged in to effect some separate end, may be called 'practical' actions – and here the term 'in order to' has its proper place, for in switching on the light *in order to* see better, or getting on the bus *in order to* get to work, we are positing two separate situations, the first *ordered to* achieving the second. *Different* actions are put in an order which (eventually, hopefully) achieves the situation desired. Thus an entire *chain* of different actions may be undertaken in the 'practical' spirit, all ordered to achieving a single objective. Unlike 'final' actions, then, none of them are undertaken for the experience of undertaking them – they are purely 'practical' actions.

Before drawing out the relevance of this distinction to 'studying history' (either as practising historian or student), it is important to point out that, perhaps despite appearances, *in the abstract* any action or activity can be undertaken *either* as practically motivated, *or* for its own sake. In other words, no actions are either 'practical' or 'final' simply in virtue of what they involve. For example, I may engage in housework either in order to achieve a clean and tidy house, or because I enjoy that activity (i.e., I do housework 'for its own sake'). One may engage in sexual intercourse either in order to conceive a child, or to enjoy it. Indeed, this latter example shows there are many occasions where both kinds of motivation are simultaneously involved! It is true there are numerous actions which, simply in virtue of what they involve, would *appear* to be merely 'practical', and probably are in most cases. For example, it is difficult to conceive of tying one's shoelaces as an action which is not practically inspired (i.e., to secure one's shoe) – however, in theory we should leave room for the odd individual who really enjoys tying shoe- laces. Vice-versa, it may be difficult to conceive of playing a game, not as a way of 'enjoying oneself', but as a *means* towards some (separate) objective. Nonetheless, it could be the case (as with our show-off footballer). A few activities, indeed, seem so obviously either 'practical' or 'final' that the language denoting them reflects this. 'Making love' is an example of the latter, whereas 'mating' exemplifies the former. But far more often, the terms used to refer to actions and activities denote their 'objective' character, leaving the grounds of their motivation open. For example, 'having a conversation' refers to people talking with each other, but whether one or more are doing it 'for its own sake' or, alternatively, in order to e.g., impress the company, or in order to ingratiate themselves, is left an open question.

This seems to confirm that there is nothing *in principle* decreeing that this action is, by its very nature, a 'practical' action, or that that action is, by its very nature, a 'final' action. However, it is reasonable to suppose that, although most of the objective characteristics of an activity remain the same irrespective of whether it is undertaken practically or for its own sake, closer attention to the *manner* in which it is performed often betrays which ground of motivation is in play. Tell-tale signs relate to each, derived from the logic of their motivation. Because practically motivated actions are dedicated to achieving some external objective, they are not desired in themselves but are merely necessary labour. As such, the sole criterion of their performance is efficiency (incorporating e.g., speed, economy, and minimum effort, and above all, effectiveness in achieving the desired outcome), and in an ideal world one would pay someone else, or invent a machine, to do them. (Largely gone are the days when the 'wealthy person's' every practical need was taken care of by a retinue of servants, down to tying their masters' shoe-laces!). On the other hand, where an activity is undertaken 'for its own sake', efficiency is not a relevant criterion for its performance, since it is not undertaken to achieve any extrinsic purpose. Rather, since what is at stake is the enjoyment of doing the activity, we wish to perform it *well*. We, so to speak, *indulge* the activity so that we can benefit from the experience it offers us. Another way of putting this is that when we perform an activity for its own sake, we 'do justice' to the activity. It is not practically motivated, so there is no pressure to cut corners, save time, substitute a more efficient activity, or (least of all) get someone else to perform it for us. In these respects, the signs of whether an action is undertaken as a means to an end or for its own sake are not only different – they are antithetical.

Thus, as an example, I may see someone gardening. That she is gardening does not in itself tell me whether she is doing it as a 'final' or a 'practical' activity. But closer observation of the *manner* in which she gardens may reveal which. She is hurried, neglects areas difficult to reach, and rushes indoors at the slightest sign of rain. For her, it is simply a means to an end. *What* that end is for her may be one of many – e.g., to keep fit, to keep up appearances with her neighbours' gardens, or even to put herself on display to attract the boy next door – and maybe still closer observation will reveal one of these to be the case. Alternatively, the manner in which she gardens may reveal that she is doing it 'for its own sake'. She is appropriately attired, she is thorough, spends much money on it, and is not unduly hurried – indeed, she lingers longer than 'necessary' over certain tasks. And I have noticed that she not only gardens frequently; she even does it when it does not 'need' doing. These signs suggest she is gardening because she enjoys it. Not surprisingly, the *product* of her activity – her garden – is high quality, and part of the reason for this is that, as a 'final' activity for her, she has 'done it justice'.

I will add only one point before drawing out the relevance of this discussion for our topic. The last remark might be taken to imply that, when something is undertaken for its own sake, the result will be superior to when the same thing is undertaken simply as a means to an (extrinsic) end. 'Theory' might indeed imply this, but the real world often confounds it. Much as my neighbour may love gardening, she may be a poor gardener – for instance, she may lack a true eye, plant at the wrong time of year, and have no colour sense. Vice-versa, the gardener she employed to look after her garden while she was away – a man who hated his job – may present her with an excellent garden on her return, such is his skill. The moral is that whether one does something for its own sake, or 'merely' as a means to an end (e.g., that huge area of activity undertaken in order to earn money), does not *necessarily* mean that, judged by their results, the former performance will be superior to the latter.

Let us summarise: put simply, there are things we do because we *like* doing them, and there are things we do because we *have* to in order to achieve an extrinsic objective, (and sometimes we can combine both motivations). Although in practice common-sense often suggests that certain actions are 'by their nature' simply means to an end, whilst others are done 'for their own sake, *in principle* this difference does not attach to the things themselves (i.e., actions/activities). Rather, it can often be observed from the *manner* in which we do something, where either efficiency in achieving the (separate) objective dictates how we do something, or where 'doing justice' to an activity dictates how it is done. Although *in principle* it is reasonable to expect a thing done 'for its own sake' to be done *better* than when it is done merely as a means to an end, in practice this is somewhat dependent upon individual aptitudes. Thus where an action or activity results in a tangible product, (e.g., a garden, a meal, a book), that product need not necessarily display in what spirit it was produced.

Thus, I can have a cup of coffee 'for its own sake', or in order to e.g., refresh myself; I can play football 'for its own sake', or in order to e.g., keep fit; I can have a drink with colleages 'for its own sake', or in order to e.g., clinch a deal; I can have sexual intercourse 'for its own sake', or in order to e.g., reproduce.

The same applies to *mental* activities. Just as I can *remember* things 'for their own sake' (i.e., indulge in nostalgia), *or* in order to, e.g., find my keys, so with *understanding*. I can study e.g., politics 'for its own sake', *or* in order to e.g., win an election. I can enquire into something 'for its own sake', *or* in order to e.g., solve a pressing problem. In short, I can seek to understand something 'for the sake of' understanding, *or* in order to *effect* something via and extrinsic to understanding it. It is precisely this difference which is at stake when we ask what the study of history is *for*, (as applied now not only to the thinking of the practising historian but also to the student's reading of history books).

The other mental activity relevant to 'what is the point of history?' is that of *communicating*. Here again, I can communicate my ideas (verbally or in writing) 'for their own sake', *or* in order to e.g., titillate the audience. Because, of course, 'history' has to be *produced* by historians, it is this difference which is at stake when we ask what 'is' (or 'should be') the point of *writing* history.

This approach – i.e., what 'are' the motivational grounds for the study and writing of history, and how do they affect the discipline as an activity? – will give us a relevant and useful perspective from which to cover most of the otherwise disparate issues analytical philosophers of history raise in discussing 'what is history *for*?'.

The practising historian

Here, our concern is with the practising historians' study of the past. The *communication* of the knowledge thereby acquired (i.e., historians' *writings*) will be treated in another section, as will the history *students'* study of those writings (i.e., *reading* history).

Following our introductory framework, it must be possible for the historian to engage in the activity of uncovering 'what happened' in the past *either* 'for its own sake', *or* in order to achieve some extrinsic purpose beyond 'simply' that of discovering past events and explaining/ understanding their constituent parts. (We are of course referring here to narrative history, but the same applies to 'descriptive' and 'analytic' history). Let us consider the latter case first.

Practically motivated historical work

Just as in our example of studying politics *in order to* e.g., learn how to win an election, rather than 'for its own sake', so an historian can work at uncovering and understanding some past event(s) *in order* to effect something via and beyond the knowledge gained. In other words, the historian can be practically motivated, and we need to explore the general implications of this, whatever the individual motivation might be. Let us suppose, for example, the objective is to demonstrate that women played an important role in the origins and development of the (British) Campaign for Nuclear Disarmament (CND). Here, we have to assume the historian has *already* formed his view, but is seeking *evidence* to substantiate his case. Because of this, there will be much about the history of the CND which will not interest him because it is irrelevant to the role of women. His focus will be restricted to important moments in the CND's history, and to discovering and assessing the role women played in them. Hopefully for him, he will find sufficient evidence from which to make the reasonable inference that their role was important, and he may even find proof in hitherto unknown contemporary documents attesting precisely to this. So far, so good. The problem is, what if he does not find such evidence and proof of the case he *wants* to make? The danger is that, to the extent he has already prejudged the case and is now concerned to demonstrate it, he may thereby either deliberately or unconsciously – (often more of a sliding scale than a clear difference) – neglect certain 'inconvenient' facts and important episodes, and exaggerate others. In short, he may give a biased account.

Because the questions of 'bias', 'objectivity', and 'truth' are rightly regarded as important factors in the study (and writing) of history, it is worth exploring the above more closely. Let us suppose our historian did succumb to the dangers just outlined. As said, this implies his understanding is 'biased'. But what does this mean? It does not *necessarily* mean that he has had to falsify 'the facts' – rather, it means he has selected those which support his case, and ignored others. In two senses of the term, then, he is being 'partial' in his work. First, because he is only interested in the role of women, his account of the CND is 'partial', ignoring many other features of its history. Second, in a related sense of the same term, because he has a certain axe to grind he 'angles' his account (already 'partial' in the first sense of the term) towards the conclusions which fulfil his objective. But he does not have to give a 'false' account. Only if he was unconcerned to give his case the authority of 'history' might he so distort his account to the point of actually telling lies.

To generalise from this, we see that where the historian engages in his work of uncovering the past in order to achieve some (extrinsic) objective, he does less than 'justice' to that activity because of his 'partiality'. This does not preclude him, however, from 'telling the truth', for other historians with no axe to grind on the matter *might* find his work and judgements perfectly sound. Nevertheless, as suggested in our 'theoretical preliminaries', even in this case tell-tale signs of the practical basis to our historian's motivation should be apparent. The difference (which may range from subtle to glaringly obvious manifestations) can be shown by contrasting the above case, where the historian has an (external) objective directing his work, to the case where an historian is *asked* the question, 'how important was the role of women in the history of the CND?'. It is true that, in setting to work to respond to the question, the historian's focus has been narrowed to a particular aspect of the CND's history and might therefore warrant being called 'partial' in our first sense of that term. But this is an illusion, since in that sense answering *any* detailed questions asked about the past would imply a 'partial' account. Rather, the point is to assume our hypothetical historian is not practically motivated in answering the question and therefore engages in a full examination of what was important in the CND's history before focusing on, and assessing, the role of women in important episodes – all this without either a pre-formed view, or by jumping to conclusions half-way through.

The moral of this discussion of *practically* motivated historical work is that, both in the direction of its focus and (relatedly) in the 'picture' it develops, the thinking behind it is 'partial' because *directed* towards demonstrating something about the past (which may or may not have been true). The 'facts' it employs need not be false, nor the 'conclusions' it proffers by the story it tells or by the scene it depicts. But there will always be the uneasy feeling that an historical enquiry undertaken for a practical motivation is thereby 'tainted', however excellent it might turn out to be. This is because the *suspicion* is *always* justified, that a degree of 'distortion', or 'angling' (conscious or otherwise), characterises such an historian's thinking, leading to the danger of his 'misrepresenting' the past.

Should we therefore say that, where practically motivated, the historian is betraying his discipline – that 'this is not what history is *for*?' – that he or she is thus *not* an historian, but merely adopting the *guise* of being an historian in order to lend his or her accounts of the past the *authority* of 'truth' and 'objectivity'? The answer to this surely depends on whether we think the discipline of history should bear the hallmark of striving for 'objective truth' in what it says about the past. If we do think this, then practically motivated 'history' is not 'history as it ought to be'.

Alternatively, some theorists argue that objective truth is an impossibility, and that to believe it does (or 'should') characterise the historian's thinking (as do many historians themselves) is to be deluded. If this were indeed the case, then our practically motivated 'historian' is not betraying his discipline, since the threat of 'bias' or 'partiality' is somehow integral to it, making it pointless to complain, and meaning that those who do complain have simply misunderstood the nature of the discipline.

Much, then, hangs on whether 'impartial', 'objective' thinking is a possible undertaking, or whether *all* thinking is *necessarily* somehow 'angled' or 'distorted'. (We shall encounter in a later section the arguments of those who take the latter view, where in particular we will explore the notion of 'ideology', its alleged ubiquity, and how it impinges on the question of 'what is history *for?*'). In turning now to examine the case where the historian is *not* practically (neither 'ideologically') motivated in his work, but instead engages in the discipline 'for its own sake', we will find this issue reappearing.

Historical work 'for its own sake'

The notion of enquiring into the past 'for the sake of it' derives from our 'theoretical preliminaries' where we argued that all actions and activities can be undertaken either as means to an (external) end, or 'for their own sake' (sometimes combining elements of both motivational grounds) – and that intellectual activities, the discipline of history included, are no exception. But what exactly does it mean to engage in historical work 'for its own sake', and how does this affect (if at all) how the practising historian goes about his work? Most of the answers to these questions can be found in the contrast between such activity and that of our practically motivated 'historian'.

First, we mean that it is possible to enquire into an aspect or episode of the past for no other reason than that one enjoys the activity involved. As with anything else done 'for its own sake', it is done for the experience of doing it – and as we have seen, it would be curious if this did not imply that one *enjoyed* doing it. Thus, one engages in the activity of finding out 'what happened' (or 'what it was like') and why, not *in order* to achieve anything 'external' by the outcome of the activity – such as demonstrating a political point, destroying a colleague's academic reputation, or writing a best-selling history book. The only sense in which something might be *achieved* by the activity is the acquisition of knowledge and understanding. But this is the *intrinsic* rationale of the activity, not some external objective influencing how it is undertaken. (*All* actions and activities have an intrinsic 'objective' simply in virtue of being sequences of 'movements', from switching on a light to gardening, from uttering a sentence to solving a chess problem). But even here, it follows that if one is 'doing history' for its own sake, then whatever pleasure the historian might get from finding out about some aspect of the past, the pleasure is in the activity of finding out, not in the knowledge gained. If it were the latter, then one might as well pay someone to find out that knowledge rather than bother oneself with the work.

Second, because of the absence of a practical motivation directing his focus, the historian will (as we have put it) 'do justice' to the activity of enquiring into the past. Although individuals may differ as to how competent they are at the activity, in principle this means they will explore *all* avenues of their topic, none being 'irrelevant' or 'inconvenient' because of some exterior objective – and will consider *all* angles from which it might be understood. This, after all, is what it *is* to 'enquire' into and seek to 'understand' something solely for the sake of it. There are no foregone conclusions to be reached, no 'embarrassing' facts to omit, no 'angles' to be stressed. Rather, the thinking involved will be 'objective' or 'impartial'. However, in itself this does not *guarantee* that either the 'facts' the historian infers or the conclusions he reaches will be *true*. Impartiality is not a sufficient condition for saying things that are true. 'Honest' mistakes can be made – e.g., mis-identifications, illogical reasoning, and simple lack of knowledge. Neither is impartiality even a *necessary* condition of saying true things, for we have already noted that the 'facts' a biased historian uncovers need not be false, nor the conclusions he reaches. To this extent, then, impartiality and truth are *separate* features of intellectual work, allowing the possibility that an historian may be proposing false 'facts' and absurd conclusions, yet thinking with impeccable impartiality.

Left at this, although impartiality is a necessary feature of the thinking involved in studying the past 'for its own sake', it might appear a disappointing attribute in terms of the difference it makes, since all it means is that the historian has not concocted lies and has not skewed his account. The question of 'truth' remains.

There is, however, a third attribute to any study done 'for its own sake' (including historical study), and here we can again refer to the notion of 'doing justice' to an activity. When we think about something solely to understand it, it is difficult to see how this does not equate with the urge to arrive at *true* ideas about it (i.e., to reach the point where one is confident that what one thinks is the case, *is* the case, 'truth' being a property of statements, not of things themselves). Indeed, 'truth' is so integral to 'understanding' that where something has been misunderstood we mean it is not true – a false understanding is a *mis*understanding. Put another way, it is not conceivable that one should wish, in understanding something, that one should construe false ideas. 'Doing justice' to the effort to understand something thus involves the deliberate effort to ensure that the ideas one conceives are true. For the historian this involves checking his 'facts' rather than assuming them, and checking that whatever conclusions he may draw are logical. It also involves checking that, even where logically correct, the chain of his reasoning has *not* been influenced by any extrinsic objective, as in practically motivated thinking, which may so distort his reasoning as to guide him towards unsound conclusions – e.g., exaggerations, misrepresentations of potential objections, and so on. Thus, for example, however surprising, unconventional, 'politically incorrect', or unpopular the understanding of a topic he conceives from his work, he should offer no resistance to what he sees as true. Vice-versa, he should be open to change his mind if new 'facts' or arguments conflict with his accounts.

What all this amounts to is that the historian, like anyone else studying something 'for its own sake', is 'dis-interested' in (i.e., impartial about) what he studies – and this involves *thinking about his own thinking*, not only to rid it of errors but also to guard against its direction being 'skewed' by external motivation. It is in this sense that, as suggested in Chapter 11, the historian who 'does justice' to the activity of historical work because doing it 'for its own sake', is in that manner a 'theorist', since the principal marks of 'theoretical' thinking are precisely that it has no axe to grind and is *reflexive* – i.e., it reflects on itself to guard its adequacy.

Where, then, an historian enquires into some aspect of the past 'for the sake of it', the search for objectivity and truth are integral to his work – and because of this, some may assert that only where the discipline of history is undertaken in that spirit is it '*truly*' history. In short, historical work 'is' ('ought to be') objective and true. Indeed, this position will commend itself to many, and there seems nothing wrong with it so long as one is not implying that the discipline of history 'really' exists as some paradigm 'above' us which historians 'ought' to aspire and bow down to. Rather, objectivity and truth are not god-given criteria for historical work – they are simply what most people expect from it and *mean* by the term. And contrary to those who claim that such 'history' is an impossible ideal precisely because neither objectivity nor truth are possible – (e.g., because of the intrusion of 'ideology', a claim considered later) – we have seen that such historical work *is* possible to the extent that it, like any other activity, can be done 'for its own sake', the properties of objectivity and truth happening to be necessary offshoots rather than some 'extra' demand added on in the name of an allegedly hopeless idealism.

The *communication* of history: the history 'book'

The other aspect to the practising historian's work is *communicating* its results. This is mostly done in books and articles, but also in lectures and occasionally in 'documentary' films. Although these different media to a certain extent lend themselves to different purposes (e.g., the introductory textbook, the detailed article, the 'blockbuster' documentary series), for the purposes of argument let me combine them under the generic term, 'the book'. And the question is, what 'are' history books *for?* – i.e., what 'should' they be for? The historian has engaged in his enquiry, (which the last section discussed); he now proposes to communicate its results; what, as an *historian*, 'should' he or she be trying to achieve? What 'is' the point of 'the history book'?

The obvious answer is that it is to communicate knowledge about some aspect of the past. However, this is simplistic, because communicating knowledge of the past is *intrinsic* to history books. But it may not be the point behind writing them. Thus our question might just as well be, 'what is the point of communicating knowledge about the past?'. And in this form it can be seen more clearly that the question has two aspects: why communicate *knowledge of the past?*, and why *communicate* knowledge of the past?

In exploring this, we take it for granted that 'the book' does not represent the thinking of the historian, as if it were the facsimile or record of all the thinking he did in the course of his enquiries. Rather, 'the book' is the *product* (carefully *made*) of that thinking, and as such can be viewed as *evidence* of what was going on in the historian's mind. And this allows us to adopt the same approach towards the writing of history books as we did to the activity of historical enquiry – namely, to treat the issue of the *motivation* of the historian in terms of the difference between having a practical objective and doing it 'for its own sake'.

Practically motivated historical writings

By 'practically motivated' historical writings I mean, then, those produced as a means to some end. As explained before, it is not relevant (and hardly possible) to explore the numerous diverse objectives individuals may have when they do things as a means to an end – and this applies equally to the writing of history books. What we can say, however, is that insofar as it involves communicating *knowledge of the past* these different purposes can sensibly be related more closely to the 'normal' possibilities the activity offers. For example, servicing a car might be undertaken for its own sake, but when done as a means to an end, we would normally expect that end or purpose to relate more immediately to the obvious possibilities the activity offers. In this case, the purposes would appear to be markedly limited – namely, in order to make the car go faster, and/or more economically, and/or more safely, and/or to maintain its market value, and/or to prolong its working life. A more 'distant' purpose might be to avoid the wife indoors, and many others can be imagined!

Applied to writing history books, however, although we might imagine such vicarious objectives, the intrinsic nature of the activity (i.e., communicating *knowledge of the past*) offers a wide enough range of possible objectives immediately related to it. 'History' can be written in order to *entertain* the reader (e.g., to fascinate, titillate, horrify, amuse). In Chapter 6 we saw Machiavelli complaining that (even if a history was not written with that purpose in mind) this was what many *readers* anticipated – and it is clear that 'knowledge of the past' is an area offering ample opportunities for those who wish to write history for that purpose, and has been so written. The 'popular' biography is often a case in point.

History can also be written *in order to* generate controversy through upsetting peoples' longstanding impressions of important past episodes or circumstances (possibly as a means for an ambitious historian to 'make his mark'). The obvious genre is that of 'revisionist' historical writings, where it is important to judge whether their alternative accounts are deliberately devised as such (i.e., are practically motivated), or happen to be the way an impartial historian clinically sees things.

Another way in which 'history' more obviously offers itself to be written as a means to an end is that of *political persuasion*, where the historian devises his account in such a manner as to invite the reader towards some political commitment – for example, 'official' histories sanctioned, vetted, and financed by the state, *in order to* foster a sense of national confidence or even triumph. But apart from these, there are histories written *in order to* justify the aims of revolutionary and nationalist movements, by trying to show the justice of their historical grievances and, by implication, the continuing resonance of their cause. As such, these histories (like any written as a means to an end) are as much an engagement with the present as with the past, and it would be naive to take them at face-value as 'history'. Rather, the information and judgements they contain are 'suspect' (albeit not necessarily 'untrue') for the reasons already outlined.

Such *political* objectives can be subsumed under a wider genre, namely, that of writing history *in order to* convey a message which can broadly be called 'moral'. For example, a writer might wish to highlight social deprivation, racial discrimination, or the position of women, as issues rooted in the past and, by implication, still needful of being addressed. Women's history, Black history, minority 'culture and heritage' histories are examples where it is reasonable to ask whether they are written to achieve a moral end or, as is perfectly possible, 'for their own sake'.

In all these examples, where communicating knowledge of the past can be allied to an external objective which that activity more obviously invites (i.e., as distinct from more 'vicarious' objectives), we have made these observations on the basis that the writer is perfectly aware of his or her objective. However, this need not necessarily be so, for many have made the case that historical writings can be produced by those who believe they are writing them solely 'for their own sake' (an eventuality explored below), but demonstrate a 'bias' (and thus imply a 'moral' message) of which the writer is unaware. (Some, indeed, insist that *all* historical writings *necessarily* share this feature). Although this might be a possible feature of *any* practical 'motivation' (namely, that the agent might be unaware of its practical bent), our concern here is with what is usually referred to as 'ideology' and the manner in which it can intrude into and affect the history 'book'.

The nature and role of 'ideology' in communicating history

'Ideology' is a term which arose in the late eighteenth century (as we saw in Chapter 10, later to become in particular an integral part of Marx's theories about history and society) used to express the notion that many of peoples' ideas can be accounted for, not as the 'free' product of their thinking, but as stemming from the position they occupy in society, particularly in terms of its associated material interests. Although a source of much debate ever since, we can say that 'an ideology' is a more or less coherent set of ideas about the world which serves the *function* of making that world *intelligible* for the purposes of *action* and/or *commitment*. In short, when we act we do so on the basis of how we view or understand the relevant features of our world (and no more so than when we act in the *social* field, comprising our duties and obligations, our notions of justice, vice, and virtue, our political activity and moral aims). That view or understanding needs to reflect or 'make sense of' our world in such a manner as to *accommodate* the pursuit of our interests rather than conflict with them – for how else can we *act* in the world, as

335

distinct from merely observing or contemplating it? (There is even the case where action involves doing things otherwise disadvantageous to us, as when, for example, the Christian acts contrary to his immediate interests – e.g., turning the other cheek – *because* he believes in an ultimate justice ensured in resurrection.)

Further, the working assumption of those who employ the notion of 'ideology' is that because people occupy *different* positions in society, they will have correspondingly different 'understandings' or views of social life which reflect the interests associated with that position. As such, although an ideology may be unique to an individual, the term is more usually meant to apply to recognisable *groups* in society – e.g., different classes, different age groups, the genders, cultural, 'racial', and national minorities – who will share the same 'world-view' as others in their group.

Thus, it is proposed, 'women' look at many aspects of the world differently from men; the working class have different assumptions about e.g., work, family, and politics from the middle class; poor Blacks see the world in perhaps radically different ways from rich, professional Whites.

The further assumption is that these different ways of looking at the world (which make sense of that world for the purposes of appropriate social and moral action) can not only be consciously held and indeed deliberately propagandised in order to promote the relevant group's interests, but that they can also form sets of *unconscious* assumptions which permeate peoples' thinking. In short, individuals may believe themselves to be viewing things 'fairly' and 'objectively', but in fact may be biased because of unwitting assumptions they hold, constitutive of this or that 'ideology'. If this is the case, then their thinking is 'ideological' rather than impartial – and because of this, when they communicate statements about the world they are, without intending it, promoting a practical agenda, supportive of the position and aims of the group to which they belong.

To the extent this is a realistic notion about what can be a feature of peoples' consciousness, it presents a special, albeit potentially ubiquitous, case of what I have called 'practically grounded motivation': special (indeed, almost paradoxical) because the motivation is unintended, and potentially ubiquitous because everyone occupies some position in society vis-a-vis others, linked to different 'interests'.

The final point – and it is a worrying one responsible for much of the heated controversy over the notions of 'ideology' and 'ideological thinking' – is the claim by some that ideological thinking is not merely a feature which *may* attach to peoples' understandings of the (social) world, but that it is an *inevitable* feature which we can *never* escape. In short, some claim that *all* thinking (at least related to human affairs) is 'ideological', and is therefore, in something like the sense explained regarding 'practical' thinking, somehow 'skewed' or 'distorted', such that it is impossible to make 'true' statements about human affairs – or even, perhaps, that this raises queries over the very *nature* of 'objectivity' and 'truth' themselves, as conventionally applied to our hopes when we wish to 'understand' something.

This claim, which applies to a variety of disciplines, will be considered below, but it should come as no surprise that one of the prime candidates for the 'accusation' of being 'ideological' in content (either in particular cases or always necessarily so) is the *history* 'book', since its intrinsic rationale is precisely to communicate knowledge and understanding of (past) human affairs. Thus the history 'book', in addition to offering ample opportunities as a means to some extrinsic end, or as a vehicle conveying an explicitly held 'ideological' world-view designed to persuade readers towards some moral, social, or political committment, also particularly offers itself as a forum in which, far more insiduously, distinctive but *unconscious* socio-political values infiltrate the apparently impartial accounts historians give of past events and circumstances. Where the latter occurs it is all the more threatening if the particular ideology unconsciously held by the historian is also unconsciously shared by the readers, since they will fail to notice it, assuming instead that they are reading history which is 'objectively true'. Where, on the other hand, the ideology permeating a history book is *different* from that of the reader (or where, despite claims that it is impossible, the reader does not think 'ideologically' at all), there is more chance of the reader detecting its influence and thus being suitably cautious, even 'suspicious', about the 'history' he is reading.

Sufficient has been said to explain what people mean by 'ideology' and how, like other species of practically motivated thinking, it impacts upon the forming and communication of knowledge, to see that historians (as well as some other disciplines) do need a grip on the concept if they are to be self-confident both as practitioners and readers of history. Because of the potential complexity of the notion, and the issues raised in the preceding treatment of more straightforward types of the practically motivated history 'book', it is useful to conclude this section by positing a simple analogy and drawing out the principal points. Let us suppose a little child wants to understand what a razor-blade is. Her father tells her it is an extremely sharp and dangerous kind of knife, for shaving his face. Now, what he has said is true, but it is only a *partial* account of a razor-blade – 'partial' in those two senses of the term pointed out earlier. First, it is partial because he has omitted so much else that could be said about a razor-blade – e.g., its other uses, what it is made of, why it has that shape, and so on. Yet the father has only mentioned one or two things about the razor-blade, and it is not difficult to see that this is because he wishes to protect his daughter from the danger it poses to her. This, then, is the second sense in which the understanding he offers is 'partial' – i.e., it is 'biased' or 'distorted' towards achieving the objective of making his daughter wary of touching razor-blades. In short, it is an example of practically motivated communication of understanding. It is not an impartial account of a razor-blade. However, this does not mean what he says is therefore not true. Rather, to use a legal expression, it is not 'the truth, the whole truth, and nothing but the truth'.

Further, if he wished to enhance his warning about razor-blades, he could of course invent some grim 'fairy-tale' to further persuade his impressionable daughter. But in the case of *writing history* for a practical purpose, one would think such 'myth-making' might undermine one's purpose because of the danger of being caught in a lie – not, however, that this has prevented practically motivated 'historians' from doing just this (particularly where they are using 'history' for explicitly ideological political ends), nor from getting millions to believe them (if only for a time).

Returning to the caring father's explanation of what a razor-blade is, it would be extravagant to call this an example of 'ideological' thinking if the case begins and ends there. Rather, it is simply one example of someone purporting to offer a 'true' and 'objective' account of something, but doing so as a means to an end, and thus being 'partial' in what he says. He may be perfectly aware of this – and the only relevant criterion of his performance is how *efficient* it is at achieving his objective of protecting his child from playing with razor-blades. On the other hand, it is possible that he is not aware of his 'bias', his account of razor-blades seeming perfectly 'natural' and 'obvious' to him. But as *observers* of the interchange, we should be able to see the tell-tale signs of his practical motivation, just as (in principle) we should be able to in the case of 'the history book'.

Let us now extend the analogy to incorporate the notion of 'ideology'. Here we would have to posit the case where what the father offers as the understanding of a razor-blade forms but part of a larger set of ideas which make up a more or less coherent 'outlook' which underpins many of his actions. In this case, let us posit that they centre more immediately around his understanding of marriage, the family, gender and age differences, and fatherly obligations, within which his duty to care for his daughter fits consistently. As stated, he may be perfectly aware that this set of ideas serves a *prescriptive* function rather than merely being *descriptive*, and that other people situated differently have different understandings of that aspect of life. On the other hand, as stated, he may believe he is simply 'telling it as it is' when he explains what a razor-blade, a family, a father, and so on, are.

Also, we could add that his coherent set of ideas on these matters might themselves be but part of an even larger 'ideology' which embraces more general social and political views, or which derives from this or that religious outlook – and it is indeed often this larger reference which those concerned about 'ideology' mean by it. However, rather than extend the analogy further to encompass this, it is more important to recognise that, *if* we know what 'ideology' an individual subscribes to, we might almost predict the ideas he communicates, whether he is doing so in full knowledge that he has a practical objective, or in the more complex case where he is unaware that he is offering ideas which derive from his (or his group's) interests.

Alternatively, although we might recognise an utterance is practically inspired (as in 'razor-blades are sharp and dangerous instruments'), if we do not know whether this is part of an 'ideology' or a one-off statement, the more we hear of what *else* the father says the clearer it should become, such that *if* he is speaking 'ideologically' we can see how his various ideas fit together to form a prescriptive framework. In short, both in the case of straightforward practically inspired communications of ideas, and in the related but subtler case of 'ideology', it is to be hoped that careful reflection by a reader will recognise those various signs which reveal whether the knowledge being communicated is offered 'for its own sake' or in order to realise some objective in the author's mind (including, possibly, his 'sub-conscious') – and if the latter, the reader can adopt that cautionary stance towards 'objectivity' and 'truth' appropriate to such writings.

Three questions

Before concluding this section on the practically motivated history 'book', three questions need answering. First, is such 'history' *useless* as history? Clearly, when written deliberately to serve a practical purpose, the *author* does not regard 'the book' as useless. On the contrary, he hopes he will achieve his ends. But his ends, whatever they are, are not the communication of historical knowledge. More to the point is whether such 'books' are useless as history *for the reader*. On the one hand it is tempting to say they are, because they do not meet the expectation that 'history' should be communicated impartially and truthfully. However, this could be regarded as harsh, since we have seen that, although biased, the practically inspired history 'book' at least does not need to tell lies. By analogy, the little girl learned something true, and nothing false, from what her father told her about razor-blades. Just so, a practically inspired 'history book' may contain much original and fascinating material, all of which is 'true', and knowledge of which is useful to any student of history. The extreme case is where, like our paid gardener, the professional historian writes a book to make money or to court fame. However, even here there must remain an unease over such books (and other forms of communication), since the issue of 'truth' will not go away.

I have argued that 'truth' is a property of statements rather than of 'things themselves'. In this sense, the statement that a razor-blade is a sharp and dangerous instrument is clearly 'true'. But when we read history we are not being given a list of individual statements. Rather, we are given 'accounts' of events and circumstances – and to ask of an *account* of something (involving *numerous* statements of fact) whether it is 'true', is to use the word 'true' in a slightly different, albeit closely related sense, compared to when we apply it to single statements. In the latter case it means, 'is what is stated to be the case, the case?'. If so, the statement is true. But when we ask if an *account* is true, we do not mean, 'are all the statements within it true?', but is the account as a whole 'true'? By 'true' here we mean, does it give a 'fair' account which all can agree with from whatever 'angle' they may approach it, or does it omit things which are clearly relevant, include things which are not, and exaggerate other things? If it does, we are wont to call the account 'untrue' rather in the sense that an arrow, when not straight, is called 'untrue'. Thus, although we have earlier rightly separated the criteria of 'truth' and 'objectivity', we see how, and in what sense, they re-combine when it comes to considering 'the history book'. Although its numerous statements are factually true, the overall 'impression' it gives is not, just as when the father asks his son what life is like as a student, the reply may well be 'untrue' despite no *individual* statements involved being untrue! This even applies to our skilled professional historian who writes history to serve some practical objective rather than as 'a labour of love'. How many corners have been cut? What questions have simply been left aside because difficult? How clearly have things been thought through? How scrupulously has he/she checked their facts? (Some believe that, as in other academic disciplines, professional pressures have led to there being far too many history 'books', many being 'pointless' in the real advancement of historical knowledge. Perhaps the fairest retort to this complaint is to remind ourselves that people can, within the same activity, intermix practical motivation with performing it for its own sake, such that within an individual 'book' there may be as much gold as there is dross, or vice-versa).

But apart from the more straightforward case of practically motivated history 'books', what about the subtler case of their being *ideologically* driven, particularly where the historian is 'unconscious' of it? Does this so distort his 'book' as to make it useless as history? Here, the same judgements apply as those just offered above, except in 'ideological' history the point about 'truth' applied to the *account as a whole* particularly comes home to roost, for we would expect an ideological bias to demonstrate itself consistently, and in different ways, throughout the diverse material contained in an account. In short, it is particularly in history which is unconsciously 'ideological' that we need to be alert to the overall 'impression' it conveys. Not apparent to the historian himself, it may not be apparent to us as his readers, since in all good faith the historian believes his 'book' represents a true and objective account of something in the past.

The second question is: are practically motivated 'history books' *reprehensible*? Some who care about history object to them on the grounds that such works betray the discipline they love. The more obvious such 'history' (e.g., as in Holocaust denial literature), the more some express their anger and contempt at it – albeit misdirected when grounded in a motivation which is in fact as 'ideological' as that which they are attacking, rather than in concern for 'genuine' history. However, even where grounded in the latter, we have already shown that practically motivated history (and its close relation, ideological history) are far from necessarily 'useless', and to that extent are not outright betrayals of the discipline.

But perhaps more to the point, we should remind ourselves that such 'history books' are simply a species of communicating knowledge in order to achieve an objective (i.e., with the exception of 'unconscious' ideological works), and it is difficult to see why such activity is, in itself, reprehensible. If the father wishes to warn his little girl of the danger of playing with razor-blades, what is 'wrong' about that? If the 'historian' wishes to write a thoroughly *entertaining* account of something in the past in order to profit from a best-seller, what is wrong with that? If the 'historian' wishes to influence people's political or social views by writing about the past in such a manner as to engage their sympathies for a cause, what is wrong with that? Insofar as such history may not meet the criteria of objectivity and 'truth', it may be a disservice to 'history' – but 'history' is not a *sentient being* which can suffer from being shown lack of respect, or from exploitation, or some other form of morally reprehensible treatment. Rather, the question is more sensibly put in terms of whether, in writing such history, it harms the *readers*. And here the reply must surely be that where such history is a deliberate practice in deceit, because purporting to be objective and 'true', its practitioners are indeed engaging in reprehensible conduct, but only to the extent that the father knowingly 'angles' his description of a razor-blade to his suggestible little girl. But students of history should *not* be naive, and thus there is an onus on them to adopt a critical attitude to what they read, take from it what is valuable, and not moralise about 'biased' history. The alternative – of simply rejecting it out-of-hand in a fit of moral *pique* – would mean ignoring what can be learnt from works as various as those written in order to highlight the unequal position of women throughout history, to those written in order to expose the endemic evils of capitalism, to those written in order to demonstrate the superiority of the 'Aryan race' – all of which cases may be at the least dubious and, at the most, absurd.

The third question turns the tables, and has been begging for a long while. We have asked whether the practically motivated (and 'ideological') history 'book' is useless, and whether it is reprehensible. However, we now have to ask whether it is *avoidable*, because, as mentioned, there are those who insist that objectivity and truth are impossible ideals, or indeed philosophical chimera, in relation to the writing of history. Yet this exposition of the issues involved in 'what is history *for?*' began by distinguishing activity engaged in 'for its own sake' from that performed as a means to an end – and our ensuing discussion has been premised on the notion that this distinction applies as much to 'doing history', including the *communicating* of history, as to anything else. The clear implication is that the practically motivated (and 'ideological') history 'book' *is* avoidable, because history can be produced 'for its own sake'. But this needs to be established and further explored.

History written 'for its own sake'

History 'written for its own sake' is a particular example of a more general category – namely, that of communicating something for the sake of it. One can communicate in numerous ways – facial expressions, ideographs, etc. – but in the case of history we are limited to writing, speaking, and film-making, all of which I have referred to generically as the history 'book', and is what I mean here by 'written' history – i.e., its communication in whichever of these forms.

To understand what history 'written for its own sake' involves, then, we first need to examine the more *general* phenomenon of 'communication for the sake of it' to see the basic principles involved. Following our framework, the latter is simply an unexceptional example of doing something for the sake of it, where one does it for the experience of doing it – i.e., one 'enjoys oneself' doing it.

This implies that it is possible to (e.g.) say or write something without having any (extrinsic) practical motivation vis-a vis one's audience. Now, it is true that in saying things one wishes to be understood (except in some examples of practical motivation – e.g., deliberate obfuscation *in order* to deceive the audience or *in order* to conceal one's ignorance), but it would be misleading to claim that we say things

341

'in order to' be understood. Rather, 'being understood' is the *intrinsic rationale* of communication, not some objective for which communication is a *means*.

We have already discussed communicating things as a *means to an end* in our treatment of practically motivated history – as good an example of the principles of practically motivated communication as any other. When, however, we communicate something *for the sake of* communicating it, this is what I have called a 'final' action, undertaken for the experience of doing it – and a little reflection will show that saying (or writing) things 'for the sake of it' is a widespread phenomenon, from the trivial remark, 'what a lovely day it is!', to the abstract academic thesis on the mathematics of chaos theory, for all it means is that in saying something one is *sharing* a thought (or set of ideas) with the audience, without having any practical objective. For example, one might say 'what a lovely day it is!' *in order to* break the ice with a stranger, or *in order to* change the topic of conversation, or *in order to* persuade a friend to accompany one on a walk. These are all examples of practically motivated communication. But alternatively, one may simply say it for the sake of it, where, as a sharing of the thought, one intends *no more* than that – i.e., communicating *per se* is not undertaken *in order* to share thoughts; it *is* the sharing of thoughts, (i.e., it is the *intrinsic rationale* of communication) and can be undertaken simply as such. Indeed, so prevalent is this phenomenon that one might be puzzled at the ubiquity of literally 'pointless' conversation in human intercourse. However, on a positive note it can be seen as one manifestation of the essentially *social* nature of human beings (even where the effort to share thoughts 'for the sake of it' requires the apparently *anti*-social conditions of solitude demanded by writers).

Now it is difficult not to see that expressing a thought for the sake of doing so is, by that fact, to believe oneself to be saying something *true*. Argued in reverse, why should anyone deliberately say something *false* simply for the sake of saying it? Rather, one must have an objective in knowingly lying or misleading, which always means such utterances are practically inspired. What is said, because false, must be a means to achieve some (exterior) purpose. Arguing the same point directly, we can remind ourselves that when someone does something for its own sake, there is nothing prompting him to do less than justice to it – i.e., perform the action according to the criteria demanded by it. Applied to saying things (i.e., of a *propositional* nature rather than, e.g., issuing a command, or asking a question), what else could this mean other than intending to say something *true*? The very nature of statements is that they convey information, ideas, or observations, and it would be strange indeed if our constant expectation of them is that they are intended as untrue, on the grounds that falsity is an intrinsic feature of what it is to state something. It is in this sense, then, that in equating saying something 'for the sake of it' with '*doing justice*' to saying things, the intention to say something *true* is necessarily implied.

It also follows that, where one says (or writes) something for the sake of it, not only is one intending to say something true, but that there is something in human

342

beings which makes the *sharing* of 'truth' enjoyable in itself. What that 'something' is may be a mystery beyond the scope of this exposition, but it reinforces the suggestion that 'communication for the sake of it' is powerful evidence of an innate sociability in human-beings – i.e., it is an ubiquitous example of our doing things for others, with no self-serving motive.

Having suggested these general principles underlying *any* communication 'for the sake of it', let us relate them specifically to 'the history book' by first observing how they affect the *general* kind of communicating under which 'the history book' falls. As already observed, there are markedly different kinds and degrees of (propositional) 'communication', ranging from the trite remark at the bus-stop to the lengthy and complex mathematical dissertation, such that although 'truth' remains the criterion when things are 'said' for their own sake, the implications of this vary depending on the kind of communication. 'The history book' falls under the category of academic writing in general, and the principal points about such communications are threefold. First, they issue from more or less careful thinking, unlike the trite observation at the bus-stop. Second, as *products* they are carefully *constructed* communications rather than spontaneous outbursts or 'streams of consciousness' (the stuff of much that is said 'for its own sake'). Third, because they are *written*, they allow the communicator to *revisit* and *reflect* on what he has produced, to ensure that 'the book' is as he wishes it to be. This involves two things. First, 'doing justice' to what is an intrinsic feature of communication (irrespective of its motivation); namely, to *make clear* what he means – and second, better to ensure that 'the book' meets his motivation in producing it, i.e., whether intended as communicating ideas 'for their own sake', or as a means to achieving some external objective thereby, (hence the injunction that 'nothing is ever well written, only well *re*-written').

When applied to the writing of history, these features mean that when the historian produces a book 'for the sake of it', he is able to reflect on and revise what he says, better to fulfil the criteria involved. Those criteria, as we have seen, revolve around the special problems which 'truth' and 'objectivity' pose for historical work in particular – problems which some regard as impossible to surmount. Yet it is difficult to see why the historian who writes history 'for its own sake' is not precisely engaged in overcoming these problems as he carefully constructs and revises his work. He can double-check his facts to ensure the numerous statements he makes are, to the best of his knowledge and diligence, true – and where in doubt, he can say so, presenting them as provisional, (unlike in practically motivated history writings, and particularly those consciously inspired by an ideology, where to cast doubt on 'facts' especially important for one's readers to accept, if one is to achieve one's objective, is self-defeating). Part of this may involve his revisiting the assumptions he made in the process of inference, to check they were not extravagant or relying on some unconventional 'theory' of 'how the world works'.

In addition, he can constantly ask of what he has written, 'why did I include that?', to remove passages which, despite himself, might have been practically motivated, if only as expressions of some of his 'conceits'. Vice-versa, he can ask why he *excluded* certain things, again to check that his process of selection and omission did not stem from the extrinsic considerations imposed by some practical objective. Also, and crucially, he can review not only the numerous individual statements he makes but also 'the account as a whole', to ask whether the 'impression' it gives is impartially arrived at or has been influenced by some 'ideological' position. This is to say that historians are no less capable of thinking about their thinking, and of thinking about what they have written, than anyone else – and that, given their subject-matter, they are as aware of what 'ideological bias' is, if not more so.

We have noted that the latter can be perfectly explicit and consciously held – and here the only question is if the historian *wishes* his work to support this or that ideology. If he does, then he is quite entitled to write in that manner – but because he has that objective in mind, he cannot complain if his work is judged to be partial and, for the reasons outlined, to fall short of being 'true' history. On the other hand, we have noted that an ideological viewpoint may be 'unconsciously' at work in peoples' thinking and writing. But here, one of the explicit features of 'thinking about one's thinking' (which the activity of *writing* permits so well) is that, in making one *self-aware*, it allows one to bring what might have been in 'the unconscious' into consciousness. Values, assumptions, and prejudices which might 'unconsciously' have influenced what one writes, can on 'reflexion' be recognised – and, if one has a mind to, one can remove the bias, distortion, or partiality they have occasioned. Where, then, one is intending to write history 'for the sake of it', one would precisely have a mind to do this, since one intends to say things impartially and to give a 'true' account. To suggest, as some do, that this is difficult, is to overstate the problem for the historian. It is true there are numerous contexts in which saying things 'for the sake of it' can nonetheless fail to produce impartial and true statements because of the influence of unconscious 'ideology', and to that extent are self-delusory efforts. But in the context of academic work, and perhaps the writing of history in particular, the kind of communicating is so carefully and reflexively constructed that, if the historian wishes to avoid practical motivations and/or ideology, it is difficult to see why he should not be able to. And as for those who claim that impartiality and truth, rather than being difficult, are *impossible* – and no more so than in the case of *historians* because, in particular, of 'unconscious' ideology – one can only puzzle why those so sure of their capacity to uncover 'ideology' in others, by implication deny it in themselves, for their view seems to be that we can all recognise ideological influence in other peoples' writings, but not in those we produce ourselves. So curious is this view that one is tempted to suggest the irony that it must *itself* stem from some *ideological* position, such that what it purports to offer as an objective and true observation on the nature of historical writings is anything but.

Narrative history 'for its own sake'

Having shown it *is* possible to avoid the practically motivated and/ or ideologically inspired history 'book' by setting out the alternative principles involved in writing history 'for the sake of it', it behoves us to give some indication of how this works in actual practice. Here, given the previous chapter's emphasis, it is appropriate to restrict analysis to *narrative* history (leaving the reader to construe how those same principles can also be applied to descriptive and analytic history).

As analysed in the previous chapter, narrative is the form of discourse intrinsic to saying 'what happened' by linking occurrences into an intelligible sequence governed, not by causality, but via the formula 'this happened, *then* that happened', such that the 'subsequent' occurrence is conventionally understood to 'follow from' the 'prior' occurrence. In short, it is the form all *stories* take, although (like some of them) a narrative need not have a distinct *ending*. However, where the narrative explicates the nature of a particular 'event' (i.e., a parametered sequence of happenings as in e.g., a war), it will share that feature of the typical 'story'.

To see what an historical narrative 'for its own sake' involves we do not need to extend the previous chapter's analysis of how narrative works and what it achieves. Rather, the answers are already implicit, and simply involve considering in what way 'narrative for its own sake' differs from other narrative.

The first distinction is that between fictional and factual narrative. The archetypal fictional narrative is that found in the novel, short story, or (screen)play – and both common-sense and experience tell us that no one invents a (thereby) fictional story simply for the sake of it. Rather, one must always have an objective over and above that of simply making a sequence of happenings intelligible – i.e., the novelist exploits the narrative form always *in order to* achieve something *by* recounting a story, rather than inventing the story 'for the sake of it'. In short, the fictional story-teller is always *practically* motivated in our sense of the term. What his objectives may be – e.g., to excite, to highlight injustice – is a contingent matter, but objectives there must be if we are to make sense of the activity of *inventing* stories. (As for whether the notion of 'art for art's sake' contradicts this claim, this falls outside our remit, being a matter for the philosophy of aesthetics.)

The fictional story-teller, then, conjures his narrative from invented happenings – but this is not to say he can escape the basic logic of narrative, which at the minimum must make the sequence of events follow each other intelligibly (even if, as in the detective novel, only 'at the end'). He is, then, involved in that process of selection and omission of events necessitated by the narrative form, whereby he will on occasions need to invent an occurrence merely to link together *other* occurrences he particularly *wishes* to include in order to fulfil whatever objectives he has in writing the story. But it is these *other* occurrences which are his real concern, and however bizarre they might be, his ingenuity can steer the narrative towards their inclusion. Indeed, one might say that the ability to make a narrative *flow*, such that it is credible, is a fundamental skill of the fictional story-teller. But more important is the observation that, although he can of course choose to invent

345

any occurrences he likes, it is not that they are chosen/invented *per se* that matters – it is that they are chosen *in order to* fulfil his practical motivation. In short, he is constantly 'angling' his narrative to achieve his end – precisely the feature of all activity undertaken as a means to an end rather than 'for its own sake'.

Factual narrative, on the other hand, requires that the events recounted are 'true' or 'real', and this may suggest it is in principle different from fiction. But this is not necessarily so. It is true that the need to avoid imaginary happenings constrains the process of selection of 'facts', but this does not mean that the narrative cannot still be 'angled' towards a distorted, even false, account which serves some (external) objective. The historian can do this via the carefully devised (or possibly 'unconscious') exploitation of the selection and omission process intrinsic to the form of narrative. To use a legal analogy, is this woman in the dock so structuring her story (the individual facts of which are true) in order to incriminate the defendant? More directly, is this historian so selecting and omitting his facts, in e.g., his account of the English Civil War, in order to present himself as a radical, or e.g., in order to discredit a rival historian's account, or e.g., in order to support the Marxist school of historical interpretation? In each case the individual facts he selects are true, and their ordering constructs a narrative which makes sense as such. But here we can see even more clearly the difference between the 'truth' of individual statements, and the slightly different sense of the 'truth' of an account as whole. The vengeful woman in the dock has an objective beyond simply saying 'what happened', just as does the historian in our examples. Their narratives or 'stories' are not told 'for their own sake', but are 'distorted' by their practical motivation – and sooner or later this should become apparent to the reader. This is because, of the numerous things that *could* be selected as happening 'next' in any narrative, the practically motivated historian can choose that which contributes towards the 'message' he wishes to convey.

Thus, if all *fictional* narrative goes beyond the intrinsic rationale of the narrative form, *exploiting* it because the narrator *must* have some practical (hence 'extrinsic') objective in inventing 'what happened', so factual narrative (despite being restricted to 'true' events) *can* likewise be exploited. But it does not *have* to be. It can be engaged in 'for its own sake', and we see how this can be done by reverting to our analysis of its intrinsic structure.

What we are positing is the situation where the historian (as narrator) has no 'message' to deliver, no practical purpose to achieve, by constructing his account (or 'story'). But what, then, determines what he chooses to select and omit as he puts together his narrative?

Last chapter's analysis showed that selection and omission of occurrences is a necessary feature of narrative *per se*, and is thus as much a feature of narrative written for its own sake as of narrative written to serve a practical purpose. This is because, in the real world, any number of things can be said to happen 'next', and it is neither necessary nor even possible to construct a literally exhaustive sequence of 'every' thing that happened 'next'. Instead, since the function of the narrative form is to make occurrences intelligible by sequencing them into 'this happened *then* that', and (often) to make the sequence *as a whole* an intelligible phenomenon (i.e., explicating the nature of an overall 'event'), its intrinsic rationale is not exhaustiveness of detail, but the achievement of an economy of intelligibility. Thus (as we saw) narrative does not progress in the manner of a to b to c to d, etc., but *omits* those intervening occurrences until it reaches one which could *not* be (conventionally) understood as 'following' from its starting point – e.g., point k. It therefore inserts the point prior to k, such that the sequence would be 'a happened, then j happened, then k happened'. It is true that logic dictates that some other point between a and k could be chosen instead, but a, j, k seems the most basic and obvious manner in which narrative 'for its own sake' is structured, (point k being succeeded by the same process of selection and omission).

This model shows two things. First, it shows how to construct a narrative without any extrinsic practical purpose governing the selection and spacing of content. And second, it shows that such narratives do not therefore have to include 'every' occurrence to avoid being practically 'distorted'. In short, whereas the practically motivated narrative will display itself as such by progressing, for example, a, c, o, x, or whatever it chooses, so long as intelligibility is maintained (selecting things it need not include, but which specifically steer towards the intended 'message', and omitting things irrelevant to it or even counterproductive), narrative 'for its own sake' offers an 'objective' account of 'what happened'.

'Relevant' and 'significant' facts

Left at this, however, the model remains somewhat abstract, such that questions remain as to the actual practice of constructing such 'impartial' narratives. Where does one begin them? Can they go on forever (like the proverbial 'soaps')? Despite the model, are not some events more 'relevant' than others, and some more 'significant'? Such questions reflect the actual experience of 'doing history' (for its own sake), where we know, for example, that the 'origins' of something stretch back to earlier origins, and the 'consequences' of something stretch forward into manifold future aftermaths.

Most of these problems are mitigated by recognising that the historian, like the reporter, has a topic. He does not just dive into the mêlée of 'happenings' and begin giving an account. Not even our abstract model (a, j, k) could accommodate such arbitrariness. Rather, his topic configures the particular 'events' he is interested in exploring – for example, a war, a political struggle for reform, the emergence of a new art-form, a scientific discovery, and so on. Now, in giving an objective account of such events, some of the individual happenings they incorporate can be taken for granted and thus omitted. Others, however, are particular to that event and require mentioning. By analogy, if one were to give an account of a journey, at a minimum the reader wants to know who made the journey, when, for what reason, from where, to where, and by what means. Beyond that, if everything went smoothly according to conventional expectations regarding journeys, there is nothing more to be said about the event. In theory the same might be said of a war. Having established who the contenders were, and what was at issue, if its outcome was predictable there would be little else to say – 'It was a typical war, that's all'.

In reality, however, few events are so 'paradigmatic'. Particular things occur within them which, if not surprising, at least require explanation since their occurrence is not obvious. It is these occurrences which resemble our point k. They are 'relevant' to include in the narrative, because they are relevant to the *particular* nature of this or that event, (and history feeds on 'the particular', if not indeed on 'the unique'). For example, in addition to the particular aspects of a journey already singled out, in the real world things often do not 'go smoothly'. A flat tyre, a near accident, an interesting hitch-hiker, a speeding ticket – all these things make *this* journey particular.

What this shows, then, is that in *giving an account* of an event for its own sake, the historian's narrative is not only an 'explication' of the event, it is also in effect a 'description' of it (akin to describing *objects*). This is because, when we *describe* something, we do not say what is *essential* to it – that is to *define* something – but what is *particular* about it. For example, in describing *this* house we will omit that it has doors, windows, and rooms, and instead focus on what is *inessential* about it, which make it this particular house. This constitutes a description undertaken 'for the sake of it'. Just so, in narrating an event 'for the sake of it', the historian does not include everything that happened as part of it, nor the obviously essential. Rather, his narrative focuses on those occurrences which, in *not* obviously following 'next', require to be included and made intelligible. In short, because narrating an event for its own sake is analogous to describing an object for its own sake, then to narrate an event in this manner is to nullify the problem of 'relevance', because all that one includes will be 'relevant'. (The reader can work out how a description undertaken *to serve some practical objective* would differ in what it includes and omits – i.e., have *goal-orientated* criteria for what is 'relevant'.)

In addition to the need to include occurrences which are 'relevant', the other factor which *can* play a part in the process of selection, even when writing history for its own sake, is the inclusion of occurrences which are 'significant'. Now it might be argued that to regard an occurrence, or an entire event, as 'significant' is to engage in a *subjective* judgement, and thus should play no part in the construction of (impartial) history for its own sake. This can be true, but it is not *necessarily* the case. This is because something which occurs in an account (or 'story') is 'significant' only in the light of some *other* event(s), where what occurs in the former is a 'relevant' part of the latter. For example, an historian could give an account (for its own sake) of a military campaign, incorporating what is *relevant* to include in the manner outlined above. Much that happened would therefore be omitted, amongst which we might suppose the conduct of this or that individual. However, if our historian also happened to be interested in giving an account of that individual's subsequent career, and if a relevant moment in it was e.g., promotion because of his earlier conduct in the military campaign, then that conduct (otherwise ignored in the account of the campaign) becomes 'significant' in the light of those later events the historian also happens to be interested in. Thus, numerous occurrences in one overall event (some included because 'relevant', and others excluded) can be 'significant' because relevant to some other sequence of events. As such, whether an occurrence (or even an entire event) is 'significant' is an arbitrary matter, dependent upon what other 'stories' interest one. But it is not a *subjective* matter. The individual's earlier conduct either did or did not make for his promotion, such that the singling out of an occurrence as 'significant' in one story because 'relevant' to another story, need not imply that one makes that judgement out of bias or partiality. In short, the notion of an occurrence being judged as *significant* need not conflict with (narrative) history written for its own sake.

Summary

Many more questions relate to the actual practice of constructing historical narrative 'for its own sake' – for instance, can the 'blockbuster' history of e.g., the USA, come under this category? But their exploration would take us into the narrower concerns of historical methodology. Rather, the rationale of this section has been to argue that history *can* be written for its own sake; to explain the principles involved; and to demonstrate how (at least in the most important respects) these work out in the actual practice of constructing (narrative) history. And it has been essential to *argue* this, rather than merely assert it, to substantiate the larger point which looms when we ask what 'history' is *for*.

Empirically, we have seen that history *can* be written for many reasons, but that the most fundamental distinction is that between history written to serve a purpose (whatever that might be) and history written for its own sake. Just as examples of the former abound, so do examples of the latter. The latter, in other words, is not some misguided ideal conjured up by some philosophers (and most historians) who suffer the 'delusion' that it is possible to write history which meets the criteria of 'objectivity' and 'truth'. This is not to say history written in that frame of mind will always succeed in those criteria, (just as the enthusiast who gardens for the sake of it may produce a poor garden). In the real world, lapses of attention, lack of adequate knowledge, 'blind spots' which escape reflexive self-awareness, pressures of time, and the display of an author's 'conceits' are all factors which may mar work otherwise done for its own sake. But this does not mean such work is impossible; rather, whatever defects it may have can soon enough be pointed out by like-minded historians and others.

But the other dimension to the question of what history 'is' written *for*, is where we really mean, 'what *should* it be written for?'. We have seen it can serve many a practical purpose (e.g., political persuasion), and have suggested there is no need to 'morally' disapprove of such work. From the same perspective, then, there is no 'moral' superiority attached to writing history for the sake of it. Although it might be tempting to claim such history is 'superior', all we can reasonably mean by this is that such history is more likely to offer true and impartial accounts. But this only makes it 'better' history if we *idealise* the activity of writing 'history' such that, if we do not write it in that way, we have failed to live up to some impersonal paradigm of what it 'is'. Rather, all that needs to be said is that such history is *different* from that written to serve a practical end, and that if one 'prefers' one's understanding of the past to be derived from accounts whose rationale guards 'truth' and 'impartiality', one will in that sense regard such history as 'better'. But to go further than this, to argue that everyone *ought* to prefer such history, one would have to make the case that truth and objectivity *ought* to be valued above all else – not an easy case to argue and, more to the point, not one that *needs* arguing if, as I have suggested, there is something in us which, in impelling us so frequently to communicate 'for the sake of it', already implies a natural propensity to share knowledge we take to be straight and true.

Why *read* history?

So far, we have restricted consideration of 'what is history *for?*' to the work of the practising historian, both in the manner in which he *pursues* knowledge of the past and how he *communicates* that knowledge. But, as argued in the Introduction, in exploring what history is *for* we can validly include amongst those who 'do history', those members of the public and students who *read* and study what historians write – for although studying history as it is communicated *to* them does not make them into practising historians, their intimate connection as 'consumers' of the practice of history warrants their consideration when exploring what the point of the discipline of history is. In addition, to the extent that readers of history can be *critical* of what they read (e.g., by comparing different accounts of the same events and reflecting on alternative 'interpretations'), they can be more than 'mere' consumers, such that *their* expectations of what they read as 'history' may be regarded as playing a role in debating what it is (and/or should be) 'for'. Why do (and/or should) people read history?

Here, we do not need to change the general approach already adopted regarding what history is 'for'. The broad distinction is between reading history 'for its own sake' and reading it in order to achieve some (extrinsic) objective thereby. And since the last sections were devoted to the notion of history for its own sake (including *writing* it), let us continue that theme by first seeing how that notion applies to *reading* history.

Reading history 'for the sake of it'

Where we read history for the sake of reading it, we do not do so to achieve any extrinsic objective, but solely to experience the intrinsic rationale of that activity – i.e., as with any conduct undertaken for its own sake we must assume that, in seeking the experience, it is 'enjoyed' as such. Now, 'the history book' is the kind of book which *imparts information* – in this case, about some aspect of the past. As argued earlier, it would thus be misleading to say one reads such a book *in order to* acquire information. Rather, the reading of the book *is* the receiving of information, and this experience *can* be sought for its own sake, rather than one always wanting to achieve some *objective*, for which the acquiring of the information is a *means* (as we would normally expect when one reads, e.g., a car repair manual).

It is possible, then, to read a book whose rationale is the imparting of knowledge 'for the sake of' the information it contains (i.e., without wishing to *do* anything with the information). Because it is reasonable to claim that one 'enjoys' the information or knowledge, what is this but to suggest that the satisfying of *curiosity* and/or the gaining of *understanding* is what is involved? For example, one can read a geography book purely for the interest of the information it contains, rather than, e.g., in order to prepare for travelling in a strange country. Likewise with a history book, where one is simply interested to discover 'what it was like' (descriptive history), or to understand the factors involved in how things were (analytic history), or perhaps above all to discover 'what happened and why', (narrative history). As with this Part's emphasis, it is this last – narrative history – which is the more interesting and complex case.

As claimed earlier, a narrative is essentially a story, even if (unlike the archetypal story) it has no ending. I mention this because our proclivity to enjoy stories is universal. Throughout history it seems people have been avid consumers of 'stories', and the enjoyment they generate might thus be thought to stand as an exemplar of receiving information 'for the sake of it'. However, this is to overlook the difference between factual ('historical') stories and fiction, and thus to neglect some important distinctions. When we read a fictional story it is difficult to see why the information the narrative feeds on should interest us in its own right, since it is, after all, fiction. Facts, however, *can* be interesting in their own right precisely because they are *facts*. In the case of history, 'what happened' is interesting (i.e., to those who enjoy history for its own sake) partly *because* it *actually* happened. It does not have to be particularly strange or dramatic (although it is well known that truth is often stranger than fiction, because whereas fiction must exploit conventional understandings of 'what happened *next*', factual events can defy conventional expectations in most unusual and sometimes shocking ways, beyond the temerity of any dramatist). On the other hand, as already suggested, fiction is always *designed* by the writer to achieve some effect in the reader, through freely inventing events to recount and merge into a story, also usually with a 'satisfying' ending. The desired effects may be emotional states of melancholy, expectation, titillation, and the like – or perhaps in the loftier kind of fiction a presumed heightened *understanding* of human nature through displaying its workings (albeit via fiction). Plato, in his *Republic*, is famously controversial for thus voicing his disapproval of fiction ('poetry') as exploitative, exaggerative, and careless of truth.

The historian, on the other hand, cannot invent the events he recounts, although we have seen that where he, like the novelist, has a *practical* purpose in writing, he can to an extent choose which to mention and can, in part, direct the course of his narrative. But we have denied such *designed* selectivity to the historian who simply relates 'what happened' for the sake of it, claiming he can rely on the inherent logic of the narrative form. In this case, we have to expect that the writer anticipates readers who will simply find the narrative 'interesting' principally because it actually happened – and vice-versa, this will be the expectation of many a *reader* of history. They do not want to be preached at, converted to a political stance, or be emotionally 'entertained'. They find it sufficient to be informed of 'what happened' – but as argued earlier, this is far from a naive, simplistic absorbing of information. On the contrary, an historical narrative not only conveys an *explanation* of the various happenings within it, but also transmits an *understanding* of large 'events' or 'story-objects' (such as wars, revolutions, cultural movements) through its explicatory power, and it can do both these to varying degrees of sophistication, depending on the quality of the writer.

Now it is true that some 'exterior' motivations might also accompany reading (narrative) history for the sake of it, which may be viewed as bonus by-products even where not deliberately concocted by the writer. Often, as with fiction, where the events are dramatic the reader is gripped by the 'story' so that he becomes intensely interested to find out what happened *next*. This is a form of 'entertainment' which we should not complain about if historical material happens to generate it! Another bonus is where a history (usually concerning recent times) is regarded by the reader to offer an understanding of some aspect of the *present*, so that he feels he can now better see where a certain situation has 'come from'. Again, this is a by-product not to be dismissed, although if the history is *written* with this intention it is clearly an 'angled' narrative, constructed in order to serve as a means, and this should be taken into account when assessing its 'truth' and 'objectivity'.

A third 'bonus' is where the reader feels he can extract relevant contemporary *lessons* from the past – i.e., that history can *teach* us useful things such as the the correctness of certain political stategies (e.g., to appease or not to appease), the efficacy of certain social measures (e.g., regarding the treatment of crime), and even 'universal truths' about human nature. Machiavelli, for example, read classical history avidly, and although he 'enjoyed' it for its own sake he also extracted from it what he took to be numerous lessons of practical relevance to the exercise of statecraft. Moreover, he claimed it is for the *latter* reason that people should read history – i.e., that this is what history is 'for', at least from the reader's point of view. However, (himself a writer of some histories), he does not say history should be *written* to serve this practical end, and if it were we would have to repeat those reservations voiced above about its status as objective and 'true'.

In all these cases where the enjoyment inherent in reading history 'for its own sake' can be enhanced by bonus 'by-products', we can offer no complaint but rather rejoice where they occur. However, in enjoying history for its own sake they should neither be sought for by the readers (because they might be disappointed), nor engineered by the writers (i.e., if they aspire to research into and write about the past for the sake of it).

There might be little more to say about reading history 'for the sake of it' as *one* answer to 'why read history?', except to remark that for many who *teach* history at university level this is *the* answer – i.e., it is the ideal motivation they look for in their students, despite a degree of pressure on the educational establishment to ensure that university courses are in some sense 'useful' to society at large. Amidst such pressure, reading history for its own sake sits uneasily, and the profession variously responds by claiming such history can be seen as part of 'civic training', or (relatedly) as integral to the 'liberal arts' which carry forward the high ideals of culture and tolerance ensconsed in the old *studia humanitatis* beloved by figures such as Erasmus, of whose 'civilising' effects he had such high hopes in his troubled early sixteenth-century Europe. Others, where they can, point to the 'relevance' of history to 'the community', whilst less vaguely some point up the *occupational* skills which history students acquire, such as the ability to understand complex scenarios, arbitrate between alternative points of view, argue an interpretation, comprehend what it is to be 'objective', and manifest a confident articulacy both in writing and speaking. The hope is such claims can stave off any further scrutiny by those who might ask the same we are asking in this chapter – namely, what is history *for?* – but do so not out of academic interest but out of concern for the public purse. In short, there are those who might recognise that history can be read for its own sake, and even that this may be the 'best' motivation – but claim that if this is the case, why should public finance be involved in an activity undertaken for the enjoyment of it? The most the honest historian can do, perhaps, is either to hope the above range of arguments are convincing enough to maintain a still widespread desire that history be studied, or that any such scrutiny be engulfed in the wider issue of 'education for its own sake' as distinct from 'education for life' or education for vocational or other practical benefits. The alternative, it would seem, is to keep quiet about reading history for its own sake – or at least not to elevate that as the 'best' motivation – and instead to look at the other answers to 'why read history?', all of which can be subsumed under the notion of reading history *in order to* achieve some extrinsic objective, and to which we now turn.

Reading history as a means to an end

To bear in mind that people can often combine doing something for its own sake with also doing it as a means to an end makes the first example of this more palatable – namely, where in the context of school and university education students read history in order to gain academic qualifications, themselves sought for career purposes. Fortunately they are not *forced* to study history, and thus we can assume an element of 'enjoying' it accompanies their practical motivation – and perhaps more so in the case of history because, with the obvious exception of becoming a history teacher, it appears a subject peculiarly divorced from occupational needs compared to others (even in the humanities/arts). However, we have already noted the 'skills bonus' associated with studying history (i.e., for the reader), and they are rightly recounted by many an admissions tutor to reassure attracted but hesitant students as they make their subject-choices. If we also recognise that most professions nowadays put their graduates through their own training programmes, the apparent irrelevance of history becomes that much less important compared to the sound springboard its disciplined reading provides for just such training (e.g., high standards of literacy, perspicacity, objectivity, articulation, and the capacity to make sense of complex events and arguments).

A second example of a practical motivation for reading history again relates to occupation, but in this case more directly to one in particular – namely, the profession of politics. Ever since the days of the classical Athenian *polis*, the crucial role played by rhetoric in political activity has been recognised – i.e., the ability to acquire authority, to get people to follow you, by the persuasive power of speech alone. A knowledge and *appreciation* of history has always been an essential component of political rhetoric, and in many a persons' mind surpasses the study of 'political science' or 'political theory' as a preparation for engaging in politics, including government itself. The ability to put a problem into historical perspective, to explain to sometimes confused and worried fellow-citizens why a certain situation has emerged, to cite previous such situations and say whether they were dealt with well or badly – such abilities can raise an individual in the eyes of many an audience to the point where they will accede to his political proposals on the grounds that he 'knows what he's talking about'. The only problem with this powerful tool provided by the reading of history is that, for the art of rhetoric, it matters not whether the 'history' appealed to is 'true' or not – the point is, can historical knowledge be used persuasively? Because of this, many would doubtless balk at someone who only read history in order to use it as a rhetorical resource for a political career, and regard this as an exploitative manipulation of their discipline. Fortunately, however, these same individuals who read history for its own sake have the opportunity, despite themselves, to put their knowledge to practical use – namely, to expose errors, misinformation, bias, and contorted interpretations appearing in the history politicians expound as part of their rhetoric (unless, of course, they support the political aims, in which case they may choose to keep quiet, entitled as they are to place their own politics above their love of history).

A third example of reading history as a means to an end is worth revisiting to distinguish it from using history as a rhetorical tool – namely, where one only reads it in order to search for the supposed lessons it can teach. Some argue this will always be a flawed exercise because in human affairs every situation is unique – paradoxically, itself a lesson history *does* teach, and a salutary one at that! Others, however, believe that even if history never repeats itself in every detail, its study shows that situations can be sufficiently similar to warrant drawing lessons from. Machiavelli used a simple philosophical idea to support this notion – namely, that human nature never changes, and thus similar contexts will generate the same human responses with outcomes sufficiently predictable to permit (a degree of) controlled manipulation by intelligent legislation and governance. Others look to history with similar hopes, but without any philosophical underpinning. Rather, they read it with a view to discovering instructive parallels between past and present events. Such a motivation can best be seen as the urge to learn by *experience*, although because more elaborate a case than where we commonly do so in our *personal* affairs, it is that much more ambitious and uncertain an enterprise.

I take the above to be the more usual reasons people have for reading history from a practical motivation. There are others, such as reading history to confirms one's political ideology (in which case the 'history' needs to be carefully chosen!), or to bolster one's sense of identity (i.e., by concentrating on 'national' or 'ethnic' histories) – but it would be remiss of us, lastly, not to mention one in particular; namely that special case where individuals read history in order to discover some overall pattern and/or meaning in it – i.e., read it in order to construe a speculative *philosophy* of history. Here, the audacity of the motivation is apparent in those who have actually gone on to *write* such books (of which we have given important examples in Part I), and is only matched by the scepticism afforded such efforts from *analytic* philosophers of history. Variously disapproving, or diffident, as the latter might be towards some of the reasons we have identified for reading history – including (as we will see in the last chapter) reading history for its own sake – we have to assume that they would *all* condemn this particular motivation, since they appear unanimous in *rejecting* speculative philosophy of history altogether.

This may seem an ungenerous, even inconsistent, stance from a group of thinkers who are, after all, 'philosophers' themselves, but it is symptomatic of that 'turn' taken by Anglo-American philosophy towards the end of the nineteenth century, away from philosophy as the grand speculative project of total explanation towards linguistic and analytic investigation into the meaning of statements. This tended to make 'philosophy' esoteric, and less accessible to the intelligent layman. Additionally, as the twentieth century progressed and Europe underwent vast political and military struggles involving ideologies which explicitly appealed to their own theories of history (e.g., Nazism and Marxism-Leninism), the idea of speculative philosophy of history *per se* became increasingly regarded as 'politically incorrect' among the liberal intelligentsia. And if we add to these two factors the growing secularism, indeed atheism, of the later twentieth century, to which any notion of an overall meaning or direction to history seemed to imply a mindful agent behind it, simply beggaring belief, it is reasonable to suppose that few today read history as a means to finding 'the meaning of life'.

To the extent this latter supposition is correct, some might find it regrettable, because although there may be good reasons for suggesting history 'should' be studied for its own sake rather than in order to achieve some (exterior) objective, nevertheless the urge to read history in order to discover some overall meaning, although an example of the latter kind of motivation, is surely a noble motivation in a class of its own, reflective of that same kind of ambition which, before people had much 'history' at all to survey, prompted them instead to look out at the stars, not 'for the sake of it', but to divine some overall meaning to the scheme of things.

Conclusion

The theme of this chapter has been to ask 'what is history *for?*, and the answers (whether about researching into and writing history, or about 'merely' reading history) have throughout been organised into two overall categories of human motivation – doing something 'for its own sake', and doing something in order to achieve some (external) objective. We have explored what the former means and involves when applied to 'doing history', and also the latter, suggesting a variety of the more usual *practical* motives individuals may have. Although I have indicated where qualitative distinctions are wont be made – e.g., the purist's adherence to 'doing history' for its own sake, or perhaps the 'superiority' of one *practical* motivation as distinct from another – we should probably leave the question of 'what is the *point* of studying history?' open. After all, it is just one more human activity – and although whether people do it for its own sake or in order to achieve some (outside) objective do make differences to that activity, it is difficult to see how anyone has the right to decree what the point of studying history 'should' be.

But in any event, if we are to believe some current strands of thought, the question does not matter, since from two different angles they posit that 'history' is finished anyway! From one angle it is argued that the discipline we know as 'history' simply falls apart when its claims are scrutinised, whereas from another angle altogether it is argued that, viable as the *discipline* is, 'history' itself (i.e., 'history' as the march of change over the ages) has come to an end. The former argument comes from *analytic* philosophy of history, the latter from *speculative* philosophy of history, and it is fitting that in devoting our final part to these interesting claims we shall be visiting both these branches of philosophy of history, so far kept in separate Parts of this book.

Part III

THE END OF HISTORY?

14

THE END OF HISTORY?

The postmodernist challenge

Introduction

It is appropriate that this 'guide' should conclude by exploring the cutting edges of present debates within 'philosophy of history', both as speculative and analytic. But it also means concluding on a note of supreme irony. It so happens that in both manifestations we are confronted with something like the notion that 'history' has come to an end – i.e., from the speculative approach, 'history' as the huge story of changing eras, and from the analytic approach, 'history' as a viable discipline able to deliver concrete knowledge of the past. I say 'it so happens' because the two viewpoints are not obviously connected. On the contrary, we shall see how it could be argued that, coming from markedly different perspectives, they are in flat contradiction to each other. But, despite this, we shall also see how it may be no coincidence that both announcements of 'the end of history' appeared roughly contemporaneously – i.e., in the last two decades.

The exploration of these two versions involves markedly different exercises, not only because one comes from analytic, the other from speculative, philosophy of history, but because the former stems from an entire 'movement' in latter day twentieth-century theory – namely, postmodernism – thereby requiring its distillation for purposes of exposition, whilst the latter stems from the speculative thoughts of one individual, Francis Fukuyama.

This Part is thus divided into two chapters, and because the preceding Part focused on analytic philosophy of history, we will continue that momentum by beginning with the postmodernist challenge to history as a discipline.

The nature of postmodernist theory

The basic postmodernist perspective

For those unfamiliar with 'postmodernism', let us first characterise its principal thrust. Essentially, those who subscribe to 'postmodernism' do not believe that language faithfully 'represents' reality – and that not only is it unlikely that anything else can 'represent' it, but that the very concept of 'reality', understood as given, objective, is fallacious. This means there can be no (single) truth about the world, but that our knowledge of 'reality' is always a construct, mediated by the multifarious contexts we inhabit (race, gender, economy, culture, and so on). 'Truth' – e.g., about justice, beauty, morality, progress, events – is therefore radically relative, there being no 'essential' meaning to things which the subject can, godlike, apprehend as 'object' of his knowledge. Rather, the very notion of 'the subject' as the detached understander of 'the object' has no meaning, just as the notion of 'the subject' as an autonomous agent in a world of known and manipulable objects has no meaning. Instead, both in our knowing and in our doing we are differing manifestations of an immense complex of ultimately groundless 'positions' occupied and lived out by diverse millions of individuals and groupings. There is no ultimate or fixed 'reality', there are no transcendental truths, there is no authoritative projection into the future, nor an 'objective' history from which to derive it. Whereas modern philosophy and science, from the seventeenth century onwards, spawned the Enlightenment belief in the rational instrumentality of mankind to increasingly understand and master its world so as to fulfil 'the nature of man', the game is up – the myth is exposed. Man's own reflective insight into his consciousness (itself an Enlightenment project) has revealed the fallacy of a world which can be 'represented' in objective, universalist terms.

Also, this 'crisis in representation' is not merely a theoretical perspective on 'reality'. Since at least the 1970s 'reality' itself has increasingly reflected its inherent relativity, both in the output of the Western intellectual avant-garde (literature, film, fine art, architecture) and in the groundless culture of mass consumer society where values and life-styles are radically eclectic. This is linked to the twin phenomena of decolonisation and global capitalism, creating a world where 'differences' are unamenable to homogenisation by any universalistic ideals, and where economic production is 'post-industrial', increasingly devoted to information technology, and focused precisely on the commodification of 'differences' via its reproduction and marketing of any and every 'life-style' as exemplified in their various status-signs.

Before proceeding, two points are worth making. First, it should already be apparent that, from this 'anti-representationalist' postmodernist perspective, the discipline of history is going to be in trouble! And as we shall see, this is indeed an implication which postmodernists draw, even to the extent that it implodes as a viable 'discipline' and becomes just one more kind of 'discourse' sharing the same ultimate groundlessness as any other.

Second, it is proper to forestall the error of representing postmodernist theorists as forming one united 'school of thought' who draw the same political, philosophical, and moral implications. On the contrary, diverse positions emerge amongst them. For example, politically some draw left-wing implications, others liberal, others even conservative – whilst others again draw none and retreat into either pessimism or irony. This *eclecticism* regarding the implications of postmodernism is not, however, to be seen as emblematic of the postmodernist perspective, nicely logical as that might be. Rather, it is a feature of *all* those cultural/ intellectual phenomena which, in lacking the cohesiveness and purpose of a *school* of thought (e.g., Marxism), are better called 'movements'[1] – and it is in this light that we can best develop our account of postmodernism to the point where it impinges on the status of history in particular.

Postmodernism as a 'movement'

By treating postmodernism as a 'movement' I mean it is best understood as originating as a few key ideas, which were however of such a nature that, when combined with 'the times' they were proposed in, influenced many other areas of thought. Here, the example of Renaissance humanism[2] is an instructive parallel. That movement began, it seems, in the field of the literary arts, where many were influenced by the new sensibilities which Petrarch introduced into his poetry and literary criticism. Just so, it seems, postmodernism began (in the 1950s) 'primarily as a response to artistic innovation',[3] first in poetry and fiction. Just as the Renaissance humanists' inspiration flowed from rejecting their preceding intellectual heritage (medieval scholasticism), so were the first 'postmodernists' inspired by a rejection of the principles underlying what they took to be their preceding cultural heritage, 'modernism'. They identified 'modernism' (in the arts) with the intellectualism of the 'rationalistic liberal humanism' characterising Western culture since the Renaissance (itself harking back to Classical culture) and which dominated the scene since the 1789 French Revolution. Underlying this Western 'modernism' is the fundamental supposition of the individual as a thinking 'subject' which confronts Nature as a world of 'objects', a world that can be understood from the distance of 'rationality', and increasingly rearranged to meet recognised universal humanistic goals (freedom, justice, beauty, social consensus, economic efficiency). Again, just as we saw the Renaissance humanists did have *predecessors* for aspects of their ideas, so can many 'postmodernist' ideas be traced back as developments from philosophies integral to *modernism* – for example, the ideas of Nietzsche, Wittgenstein's notion of 'language games', and the existentialist school of thought. (This merely exemplifies how difficult it is, particularly in the case of historical 'movements', to locate authentic *origins*.)

To pursue our parallel, just as the literary origins of Renaissance humanism spread out to influence painting, sculpture, and architecture, so the literary origins of postmodernism developed into painting, dance, architecture, and other areas of the arts, as well as deepening its impact upon literary criticism itself. It is just this 'spreading' effect which typifies the emergence of 'a movement', and one would be tempted to use the analogy of dropping a stone into a pond and witnessing the ripples spreading out to affect much else further out in the water, were it not that ripples weaken as they get further from their source, whereas historical 'movements' *gain* in momentum, incorporating increasingly distant areas. The latter was the case with Renaissance humanism, which spread its influence beyond the arts to philosophy, political thought, religion, social attitudes, and economic activity. In short, the influence of Renaissance humanism, as a cultural/intellectual movement, can be construed as an integral factor in *forming* those wider features which characterise the period of the Renaissance itself, although many would say this is to claim too much instrumentality to what was, after all, 'only' a cultural movement. Be this as it may (and the truth about the dialectic between Renaissance *culture* and Renaissance *society* probably lies in the middle), a similar outspreading of postmodernist influence occurred, such that by the 1980s it impacted upon (some) contemporary philosophy, political theory, and sociology. Again, the parallel between Renaissance humanism and postmodernism as 'movements' prevails (albeit necessarily provisionally, since the latter has only begun so recently), because 'postmodernism' has extended into so many facets of contemporary society that it becomes difficult to maintain a separation between it as 'influencer' and the (allegedly) 'postmodern' society we inhabit.

Another (related) parallel between our 'movements' is that although Renaissance humanism originated amongst high intellectuals, its general ethos became *fashionable*, both in the literal sense of affecting modes of dress and styles of consumer consumption, and in being regarded as valuable for *practical* purposes of employment and 'getting on' in the world as an up-to-date person. A similar phenomenon has accompanied postmodernism. It began amongst the avant-garde literary circles, but spread not only to other arts and disciplines but also into *popular* culture, including dress and music, patterns of consumption, life-styles, and employment (the latter becoming increasingly 'post-industrial', eclectically and happily short-term contractual, and broadly focused around information technology). However, disagreement exists amongst postmodernists as to whether 'the masses' display genuine 'postmodern' sensibilities, or whether this is limited to the new 'bourgeoisie' of Western societies, the former merely being mute captives of consumer culture.

But such a disagreement is only one amongst many in the postmodernist movement, and this is yet another parallel with Renaissance humanism, for the latter encompassed a variety of often conflicting views on e.g., philosophy and politics. The same characterises postmodern theorists, such that no singular philosophy, political message, nor social prescription can be identified with them. In short, if Renaissance humanists were agreed on the attraction of the individualistic, secular culture of classical Antiquity, but developed diverse views from that starting point, so postmodernists agree on their 'anti-representationalist' alternative suppositions to the liberal-universalist grounding of 'modernism', yet develop divergent political and social views therefrom.

The final parallel is that, with any 'movement', numerous people remain unaffected by it for generations. It neither affects their thinking nor their life-styles, and this can be because they are simply ignorant of it, or because they reject it as simply 'wrong-headed', or because, given their circumstances (location, occupation), it simply does not impinge on them. This was the case with Renaissance humanism, where millions in early-modern Europe continued their rural, medieval ways of life and thinking for at least two centuries, and where even the intellectual elites by no means unanimously adopted its ethos in, for example, education and secular values. The same applies to postmodernism. Seen either as a new intellectual outlook, or as referring to the actual outlines of a new kind of society – a new period in history – it passes numerous people by. But it has not passed the field of historical criticism by, occupying a niche whose potentially destructive influence may yet turn to good, or prove to be a merely passing threat.

Some key postmodernist ideas

Derrida

There is an abundance of literature manifesting and exploring the diverse contributions of postmodernists. Our task now, preparatory to addressing their specific implications for history, is to extract from that abundance some of its key underlying ideas. (In addition, I will indicate some of the differing *political* perspectives advanced by postmodernist theorists, since these also offer intimations relevant to *speculative* philosophy of history.)

From the 1960s onwards the Algerian-French thinker, Jacques Derrida, has been one those 'deconstructionists' concerned to show that language is not neutral, but is inextricably bound up with the culture in which it is used. In itself, this is hardly a novel proposition. But Derrida and others take their analyses far beyond the point where anyone can recognise language as 'value-laden' or 'ideological'. Rather, Derrida can be understood as claiming that insofar as language is expressive of consciousness, and consciousness is that of specific human beings' experience within a definite spatial/temporal context, then language is not denotive of 'reality' as some 'objective' phenomenon. And yet the very function of language, on the surface, *is* to translate our experience of 'reality' into consciousness – i.e., to make it *known*. But language is itself *part of* that reality, and thus one is caught in an infinite regression where the medium via which we are supposed to understand reality needs itself to be understood – and how is this to be done other than through the same medium, language? Thus, the apparent project of consciousness – to know reality – is self-contradictory. The apparent simplicity of language, as the fixed signifier of a signified reality, is shown to be an illusion. When it is 'deconstructed' we find it feeds on suppositions derived from Western logic, and expressed in the structure of grammar, which have no ultimate or 'true' grounding (e.g., the metaphysical distinction between 'subject' and 'object', the notion that a thing either is or is not).

Such 'deconstructionism' has been seen either as a continuation of *modern* philosophy, or as part of *post*modernism. Whichever, it has contributed significantly to that basic attack upon what postmodernists take to be the grand illusion underlying the Western metaphysical framework of thought – namely, that reality can be faithfully 'represented' through language (and other media of 'signification' such as photography, fine art, and drama).

Foucault

Another seminal influence on postmodernism is the French thinker, Foucault (1926–1984). Although proposing similar ideas to Derrida's about language, Foucault's focus was initially more on the *historical* contextuality of thought. He tried to show that the manner in which we order the world in our consciousness, including our own identities, emerges from that 'being in the world' rather than from any prior logic which our experience has to be fitted into. Language, however, can give the impression via its meanings and rules that just such a pre-set structuring does characterise experience, lending it some fixed, metaphysical grounding, and thus fostering the illusion that there is some essential meaning to things, including the identities we attach to ourselves as 'subjects' and 'agents'. Yet for Foucault it would seem that all we can talk about are the different modes of practices from and within which the meanings and rules of language emerge, such that at its most radical he has been understood as saying that 'all we have are material effects and material acts; there is no essential meaning to things – no essential subject behind action'. Further, and of special interest to us, it follows that 'there is no essential order to history',[4] since (whether we realise it or not) not only is history always written from the point of view of the present, both in the mundane sense that historians choose topics of interest to them *now* (often involving their rewriting history because applying their contemporary meanings to things), but also in the more radical sense that the discipline of history can lapse into the illusion that some causal efficacy and continuity must always underlie the past, thus giving it an order. But, as above, this is merely a feature (usually) of historical *discourse*, which (like any discourse) has no prior grounding or ultimate veracity behind it.

Much of the above arose from Foucault's (1961) study of the historicity of the concepts of 'reason' and 'madness', and of the changing institutions and practices adopted respecting the latter. Later (in the 1970s) Foucault developed this to argue that the 'knowledge' which is expressed in various discourses is a form of power. Institutionalised power (e.g., the treatment of crime and punishment) is not the application of some a-historical rationality, but is co-extensive with the manner in which it construes that which it deals with. The 'knowledge' contained in a mode of discourse and its referents has an authoritative instrumentality, and thus the workings of power can be understood through studying the social practices which have given rise to particular forms of discourse. Thus in itself 'power' has no grounded, independent source, and Foucault claimed that nowadays in particular it is located in numerous parts of society, not only in official institutions and large organisations. Wherever a recognisable mode of living develops its own linguistic discourse, this becomes a form of 'knowledge' which empowers those groups who practise that mode. For this reason, Foucault can approve of the positive effects such empowerment can have for groups otherwise excluded from consideration in the social field. The idea that 'knowledge' is never objective, but an intrinsic part of particular social practices and relations, and the idea that 'knowledge' is 'power', means that 'power' is never objectively grounded or defensible in universalistic terms, and is potentially dispersable throughout society – and these notions became an important feature of postmodernist political and social thought, as well as having obvious implications (if true) for the subject of history.

Lyotard

If these ideas of Foucault and Derrida might be seen as avant-garde examples of *modern* philosophy, their further extension underlies the theoretical writings of the *post*modernist movement, one of whose leading figures is the Frenchman Jean-François Lyotard (born in 1924), influential amongst USA intellectuals from the 1980s onwards. Emerging from a Marxist background in the 1960s, Lyotard came to reject Marxism because he saw it as just another version of the attempt to impose a universalistic set of ideas and values upon the world. Lyotard called such attempts 'metanarratives', and the essence of his 'postmodernism' revolves around exposing and challenging them. By a 'metanarrative' he is referring to the suppositions he sees as interwoven in entire ways of thinking. The latter are articulated via their own kinds of discourse, and manifested in corresponding practices and institutions. For example, Marxism proposes that societies are fundamentally orientated around the productive process, are divided into different classes, are therefore unjust, and that progress demands the restructuring of the economic base in order not only to redress injustice but also to achieve universal rationality and fulfilment for people. This set of ideas, replete with its key words, assumptions about the nature of 'society', and values, served to legitimate a particular outlook which pervaded the approach to life shared by millions. Another 'metanarrative' is the liberal-rational-humanist perspective endemic to modern Western culture, whereby it is assumed that the basis for the progress of societies is the accumulation of 'scientific' knowledge, not only for the sake of 'enlightenment' regarding 'truth' but also for its application to efficient economic production, 'just' government and administration, and harmonious social engineering.[5]

These are examples – religions are others – of great overriding 'stories' or (for Lyotard) 'narratives' which are so embedded in a culture's consciousness (via its institutions and its language – i.e., its 'discourse of representations') that they insidiously justify norms and practices to the point where they are regarded as universally 'true' because 'natural' and 'obvious'. However, part of the point of calling them 'metanarratives' is that they are 'stories' which have no external grounding in *fact*. Moreover, 'narratives' are always constructed and handed down through the telling. Just so, 'metanarratives' underlie the supposed coherence of a society – although they are not told explicitly, but are implicit in the very mode(s) of articulation employed by the society. Lyotard draws from this the notion that 'knowledge' is indistinguishable from the form it takes, and is, if not the determinant of a society, extremely influential on its characteristics. Yet it does not objectively 'represent' reality. Such a 'knowledge' or 'representation' is impossible, since it can only be legitimised by some *other* alleged 'knowledge' or form of discourse, equally groundless. Neither is 'science' exempt, since it can only validate the 'truth' of the knowledge it produces either by reference to some grand metanarrative outside its own terms of reference, or by accepting that the 'truths' it uncovers are only expressions *within* the 'language game' which constitutes the 'rules' of scientific discourse.

Indeed, Lyotard uses the example of science to typify what he means by the *post*modern condition in general. If there is still a 'modern' science confident of the objectivity and universality of the propositions it produces concerning the world, there is also now a *post*modern science which feeds on uncovering the chaotic, unpredictable, and undecidable in the world, and which rejects the modern notion of 'science' as *instrumental* knowledge for ordering the world. This state of affairs is mirrored throughout postmodern society at large, however, for now we are confronted by a multiplicity of different contexts and identities, each sustained through their own terms of reference or 'language games', and whose legitimation cannot be subsumed under some (old) 'metanarrative'. Now we have to recognise that differences (e.g., gender, sexual orientation, work styles, family structures, ethnic practices and values) 'legitimate' *themselves* through the 'regimes of discourse' in which they are respectively expressed. The 'knowledges' which such diverse contexts represent cannot and should not be reconciled under some overarching, universal notion of the 'proper' norms for living. Rather, they are *expressive* of the plurality of ways of living, none of which can be privileged as 'better' or more 'right' than others. Dissensus, rather than consensus, characterises the postmodern world, and this is something Lyotard (followed by many 'mere' liberals) applauds. It is true that this generates *conflicting* ideas, and sometimes the gulf between them is such that no common ground can be found (e.g., on what is just, beautiful, worthwhile). Lyotard refers to this as the emergence of a 'differend', and insists that its unknowability must be respected rather than some consensus being forced upon the parties, or one or other party being silenced. Indeed, exploration of a 'differend' may generate yet new insights into as yet unknowable modes of experiencing the world – in particular, perhaps, opening up the more 'sublime' aspects of life which have been repressed by the universalising, instrumentality-orientated 'knowledge' of modernity.

However, this latter possibility assumes our ability to choose for ourselves (albeit in a radically existentialist manner) which 'language games' to immerse ourselves in. Latterly, Lyotard appears to move from the potentially emancipatory implication of a pluralistic, relativistic world to a more sinister one where we are not self-determining *subjects*, but simply manifestations of (different) praxes exemplified in what he now called the 'regimes of discourses' which sustain them. As with Foucault, the subject (understood as a thinking and acting agent confronting and managing an exterior, objectively knowable world) ceases to have any real meaning. Rather, the 'subject-object' dichotomy is itelf but part of the many metanarratives characteristic of (especially Western) experience, expressive of the multiplicity of identities and praxes into and out of which we toss, as corks in a vast ocean.

Baudrillard

If Lyotard's thought centres on the impossibility of 'representing' reality, so does that of the French thinker, Jean Baudrillard, born in 1929 – but from a different perspective. Like a latterday Rousseau, Baudrillard is a man radically at odds with his times. Rightly, he sees himself living in a world increasingly dominated by an economy geared towards consumerism – but his analysis of this fact has generated considerable controversy. For Baudrillard we have reached a new stage in history – (in fact, a kind of 'end of history' in terms of its ability to generate any future real meaning) – because societies are no longer based on the production of objects to satisfy 'objective' economic needs and desires (if they ever were). Rather, what the postmodern capitalist system produces are objects as '*signs*' of particular life-styles. Here, advertising, information technology, marketing, the media, and computer-simulation play a crucial role in creating a world where what we consume is related to status and (alleged) identity. We do not so much buy a suit, a drink, or a car for the 'real' needs these 'real' objects satisfy, as *buy into* this or that life-style and the values which these objects signify. Because these 'signs' are 'simulations' of some allegedly 'real' object, they can not only be ceaselessly *reproduced* by modern technology, but their variety is also virtually infinite. Postmodern capitalism is thus devoted to the eclectic reproduction of 'sign-objects' representing whatever life-style, values, or identities will sell – the latter being in the control of the media rather than determined by any objectively grounded utilitarian needs and rational aspirations. The world in which we increasingly live out our social lives is a complex of simulated contexts which have no real meaning in terms of being our experience of 'being in the world', for the 'real' world is superseded by a world of 'simulations' which we inhabit and subscribe to as its consumers.

But this is not only the changed character of society in terms of its *productive* system and the logic of work, consumption, and social life which attends this. It is also the changed character of society in terms of what Marxists call its 'superstructure', particularly the state, politics, and their ideological underpinnings. For Baudrillard these spheres are equally 'simulations' which have lost any reference to grounded reality. The combined ability of communication technology and the media to reproduce and manipulate 'simulations' and flood the masses with 'information' means that 'power' can sustain itself through incessant self-referencing devoid of any objective grounding. For example, much media coverage of 'the news' functions through polling, just as elections are themselves giant polls. But these exercises establish no real information because devised through the 'question-and-answer' form, which in addition to depending on what questions are asked, is an empty tautology because a self-answering system of 'information' – a product of its own 'rules' of ordering and evaluating facts, ideas, and responses. 'The public' is not real; 'public affairs' are not real. Dialogue, criticism, opposition, are not real. They may be concocted, or even recognised for what they are, but only if they can be *reincorporated* into the self-sustaining logic of the simulation of 'reality' generated in the media.

The upshot of this is that, for Baudrillard, we no longer live in a real world where we produce to meet our needs and fulfil our desires, guided by values rationally generated by our confrontation with the restraints and possibilities the objective world of nature provides, and struggling to organise better social structures through the management of real political processes. Rather, in most respects we live in 'hyperreality', a world of groundless, endlessly reproducible 'significations', which reproduce an 'unreal' world. For Baudrillard, the USA is archetypal. In actuality, the USA is not 'real' but 'hyperreal', and the function of Disneyland (as an *explicitly* simulated world of fantasy) is to make Americans believe that their world *is* 'real', because they can contrast it with Disneyland. Yet, for Baudrillard, Disneyland *is* the 'reality' of the USA, because it *reveals* the self-referencing simulation which the USA has actually become; i.e., the USA as simulacrum generates the simulacrum, Disneyland, precisely to sustain its groundless identity. At a more sinister level Baudrillard suggests that the self-referencing logic of the hyperreal world leads to collusion between different simulations within it. If, at one level, the USA needs Disneyland, at another level all societies in the postmodern, hyperreal world need to self-reference themselves as, and through, 'simulations', whereby (for example) an act of cruelty in a hostile society can be *welcomed* in its opposing society because it is used to confirm the latter's values, just as the retaliation it provokes against the hostile society (bombing, economic sanctions) can be *welcomed* by the latter in turn, because fostering patriotic support from its own citizens. This does not mean that such events as massacres and retaliatory bombings are not 'real' enough for those involved – but it does mean that the 'reality' of events referred to as 'wars', or, indeed, 'peace-processes', is brought into question. For Baudrillard there is a sense in which many of these 'events' are 'unreal' – not so much because they are constructs of 'spin', but in the sense that they are manifestations of a 'hyperreality' which functions through the logic of simulacra rather than what we take to be the logic of the real world. The (ostensible), 'war against terrorism' since the events of 11 September, 2001 in New York and Washington may offer a rich example for those who regard Baudrillard's perspective as profound. Others, however, have argued that his analysis is trite because he is in fact merely dressing up the well-recognised machinations of 'realpolitik', where the participants deliberately practise collusion and media-spin. Baudrillard's point, however, (rightly or wrongly) is that the participants are *not* engaged in 'realpolitik' but are simply unwitting agents of the postmodern world – i.e., are prisoners of hyperreality.

Finally, as for how it might be possible to escape this vacuous world of simulations and return to one ordered according to some grasp of 'the real', Baudrillard suggests a catastrophic strategy whereby the consumerist masses take the system to its logical extremes in an orgy of eclectic 'buying into' any and everything that's going, such that the hyperreal may implode under the weight of its own meaninglessness – akin to going along with a plan one knows to be absurd, in order for it to reveal itself as such in practice.

Jameson

Partly influenced by Baudrillard, the US theorist Fredric Jameson is also a well-known figure in the postmodernist movement, although as much a critical exponent of postmodernism as a practitioner of its perspectives. Once again, his thinking emanates from the claim that we live in a 'postmodern' world whose principal feature is the loss of 'representation' in its culture. Although his writings include analyses of art, architecture, philosophy, and politics, we can more easily grasp Jameson's approach by his analysis of consumer society and its TV and film culture. Like many, Jameson claims that at some (disputed) time after the Second World War, Western capitalism entered a new stage where it became multi-national, post-industrial, and consumerist, this having profound effects upon social life and culture. Coupled with the new electronic technology, TV and the media generally have become the dominant form in which knowledge, information, or 'culture' in general have been disseminated to the consumerist populace. But the electronic image (e.g., TV) is not just the *form* of communication – as in McLuhan's famous dictum that 'the medium is the message', it profoundly influences the content. For Jameson, electronically reproduced images, adverts, and texts ceaselessly bombard the populace, but are devoid of any depth of content. Rather, under the relentless pressure of consumerist capitalism, TV programmes must be produced 24 hours around-the-clock, the press (both popular and high-brow) has to churn out something every day, and advertising needs to find novel, attention-catching images and slogans to replace their short shelf-life. The effect on peoples' consciousness, Jameson suggests, is that we lose our bearings amidst this mêlée of 'representations' which in fact 'represent' nothing but themselves – i.e., the technology of electronic reproduction. The culture it produces does not centre on representing reality – rather, it centres on the uninterrupted flow of simulated images, whose effect is to distort even our sense of time and place, since both these otherwise fundamental bases to our lives are constantly simulated by the media bombarding us with eclectic, quasi-'historical' references, and architecture, products, and life-styles which bear no intrinsic relation to the place where they happen to appear. The danger, for Jameson, is that in this post-industrial, global capitalist world – as 'unreal' in a sense as Baudrillard's 'hyperreality' – we are unable to distance ourselves from the groundless 'reality' spawned by its culture, and our sense of *identity* is swallowed up, such that we lose the capacity to 'represent' the world to ourselves as independent, responding, challenging subjects.

Here again, then, we encounter the notion that 'the subject' is fast disappearing, and thus with it the possibility of 'understanding' the world around us – for that world offers us no depth of grounding in reality from which to perceive and challenge it. And, for Jameson, it seems it will not be challenged in its overall fundamentals until (or unless) it generates some class akin to the disaffected proletariat of classical industrial capitalism, whose very position and consciousness confronts the totality of the system from the viewpoint of a genuine alienation. Meanwhile, only temporary, local social struggles take place in the sphere of micro-politics (e.g., feminism, sexual orientation, Green issues) – relatively easily absorbed by today's economy and culture.

Postmodernism and the discipline of history

The issues

Hopefully the above selection of postmodern critiques has sufficiently conveyed something of their force and range. Although much of this may have struck some readers as bizarre, rather than offer *critical* remarks, what is important for us now is to extract the principal points which impinge on analytic philosophy of history (i.e., those issues discussed in the previous two chapters) – after which we will examine two examples of such postmodern thinking on the discipline of history.

The principal general points relevant to the discipline of history are clear enough. They derive from postmodernists' central notion of what Bertens has called 'the end of', or at least the 'crisis of' *representation*,[6] particularly in the humanities. And narrowed to *history*, the same applies. As Munslow puts it: overriding the various methodological problems involved in uncovering and interpreting evidence, 'the issue is the nature of representation, not the empirical research process as such'. This is because 'the past is not discovered or found. It is created and represented by the historian as a text',[7] and for Munslow and others this means that the overall anti-representational thrust of postmodernist theory comes home to roost emphatically in the historian's terrain. If we have lost our ability to 'represent' reality – or more to the point, that ability *never* existed, but has only *now* been fully exposed as an illusion – then inasmuch as the discipline of history is traditionally understood as the endeavour to represent *past* reality for what it actually *was* and what actually *happened*, its day is over. For those, then, who subscribe to this traditional view, it is the end of history, or at least, of *their* history – for if we accept the postmodernist perspective, a number of issues conspire to consign it to the dustbin of history.

First, if we cannot objectively 'represent' (know, understand) 'reality' which is present to us, presumably those same epistemological barriers apply to 'reality' which is *past* (and may even be compounded by its pastness). In short, how can we objectively (faithfully, truthfully) represent the past? Again, if the traditional dichotomy between 'subject' and 'object' (whereby the subject, as a kind of transcendental intellect, is *distanced* from the thus knowable object) is unsustainable, then how can the historian assume the role of detached subject confronting the past as 'object'? Rather, it raises the issue of what 'language game' or 'genre of discourse' (invariably subjective and relativistic) characterises history – and, to the extent that it is central to history, *narrative* in particular. Is the form of narrative no more than an *imposition* upon an essentially unstructurable past, constructing/inventing intelligibility where it has never in fact existed? Relatedly, is the discipline of history, however practised at different times, always simply some kind of 'simulation' which, far from being disengaged from the present, is inevitably *part* of the multifarious contexts of meanings which constitute *present* 'reality', none of which can claim privilege over others? In other words, is historical knowledge not real knowledge of the past, but simply one of the (necessarily ungrounded) experiences *in* present 'hyperreality'? If this is so (as the postmodernists confirm), then not only does 'history' lose the respect and authority it had, it loses its associated socio-political role of anchoring peoples' sense of *identity* in terms of where they have come from, what their achievements have been, and what values are worth holding on to. Whether this is what history is/should be *for* has been discussed in the previous chapter, but to the extent this role evaporates altogether under the postmodernist onslaught, it raises the question of what the socio-political function of 'history' might be instead? But the answer to this depends not only on what postmodernists think 'history' *is*, but whether they think anything at least resembling it is worthwhile pursuing, and what that might be. In short, (and brought full-circle), does postmodernism imply not only the end of history as traditionally conceived, but the end of history in *any* meaningful sense? Or do the two come to the same thing?

Postmodern history: two contemporary examples

We have just asked whether the postmodernist perspective means the end of history *per se*. Views vary. Some 'traditional' historians say it does indeed imply this, and is deeply and deplorably erroneous. Other traditionalists take the view that the discipline always has changed over time, and accept that their present notion of history will, quite properly, also change in the future. In other words, they leave room for some other kind of defensible 'history' to emerge, such that the demise of history as presently grounded does not mean the end of history *per se*. However, they may take the view that the *postmodernist* assumptions (revolving around 'anti-representationalism') are of such a radical nature that they cannot conceive of *any* kind of history informed by *that* perspective. As for postmodernists themselves, doubtless some think history is dead. But not all. Just as literature and architecture, for example, did not cease because of postmodern critiques, but instead became (some of it) 'postmodern', so the same possibility exists for history according to some. To see what they say it is instructive to take two examples, the first more measured in tone than the second.

Munslow – the problem with 'mainstream' history

One of the most active and knowledgeable exponents of the postmodernist perspective on the discipline of history is the contemporary British historical theorist, Alun Munslow. In his book, *Deconstructing History*,[8] Munslow gives a thorough survey of what he calls 'deconstructionism' in contemporary history (which equates with 'postmodernism' as applied to history), and the extensive variety of references to recent and contemporary writers he cites should be enough to convince readers of the vitality of the phenomenon, amongst which it is clear he includes himself. Indeed, he begins by insisting that:

> in our contemporary or postmodern world, history conceived of as an empirical research method based upon the belief in some reasonably accurate correspondence between the past, its interpretation and its narrative representation, is no longer a tenable conception of the task of the historian. Instead of beginning with the past we should start with its representation, because it is only by doing this that we can challenge the belief that there is a discoverable and accurately representable truthfulness in the reality of the past.[9]

Munslow organises his reasons for this under four general arguments, of which the most important is the familiar postmodernist rejection of 'empiricism' as the way of acquiring 'true' and/or 'objective' knowledge of the world (past or present). For Munslow, the traditional or 'mainstream' (i.e., non postmodernist) historian 'is an empiricist who believes in a knowable historical reality independent of the mind of the historian – subject and object are separated just as mind and knowledge are presumed to be'.[10] This belief, however, is mistaken, since it ignores the fact that all knowledge is mediated, not only through the various ideological assumptions of the knower whose ideas cannot but stem from his present culture, but also by the very terminology and linguistic forms in which it is expressed.

In the case of history in particular, the former sort of mediation arises where historians use (different) models or explanatory frameworks to organise their 'facts' into historical accounts (e.g., a Marxist approach, or the use of some 'covering law'). Whether they know it or not, they are thereby *imposing* some 'theory' of history on to the facts – and although some 'theories' may be better than others, they are all ultimately groundless. This 'impositionalism' goes deeper, however, since the establishment of 'the facts' themselves is equally mediated via the process of selecting and construing 'sources' as 'evidence', followed by the process of 'inference' (from that 'evidence') of what it means, what it tells us, and how significant it is. In short, '"facts" are never innocent because only when used by the historian is factual evidence invested with meaning as it is . . . placed within a context', and it is in just this process of 'contextualisng' 'where the historian's own views and cultural situation usually emerge', making it 'impossible to divorce the historian from the constitution of meaning through the creation of a context, even though this is seemingly and innocently derived from the facts'.[11]

Indeed, so much is this the case for Munslow that he expresses with approval Foucault's notion that 'evidence, rather than being the point of departure, is history's point of arrival. Metaphor is the point of departure'.[12]

This mention of 'metaphor' brings us to that *deeper* form whereby all historical knowledge is mediated – namely, the very terminology and linguistic forms in which it is expressed. In general this refers to those who accept something like

Derrida's overall position on language – namely, that language is not denotive of 'reality' as some 'objective' phenomenon but is suffused, both in its vocabulary and its structure, with the intermixedness of the language *user* and his/her experience of the world – i.e., it can (if 'deconstructed') only ever signify the cultural contextuality of the *knower*, rather than 'representing' the *known* 'real' world. Munslow accepts this, but is particularly interested in exploring its implications for *narrative*. This is because he believes that 'history's primary cognitive device . . . resides in its power of narration'.[13] What this means is that the historian has to 'emplot' the past with a story or narrative structure, and Munslow recognises that this is to employ 'a highly complex form of explanation of historical change'. However, precisely because narrative is an *emplotment* of the past, 'it is not history as it actually happened'.[14] Rather, narrative as a literary form must, it seems for Munslow, always be a *figurative* expression of the past rather than a direct representation of it, and he therefore draws attention to the ideas of the historical theorist Hayden White (as they appeared through the 1970s and 1980s). For White also, 'to understand what the past was about we must impose a narrative upon it', and this implies that therefore 'our knowledge of the past is through a poetic act. This is the element of fiction in all historical accounts'.[15] This notion prompted White to expore the different styles or modes which characterise all narratives ('fact' or fiction), and resulted in his formal and complex model which, at its simplest, claims that any narrative must be 'emplotted' as either romantic, tragic, comic, or satiric, and that each of these styles involves different kinds of interpretation and nuances of historical explanation. Although White did not intend his model to be rigidly deterministic, it is sufficiently detailed and suggestive for Munslow to recommend that scholars should take it seriously when they read what other historians have written, and *themselves* bear it in mind 'self-reflexively' when they write their *own* historical accounts.[16]

In addition, as the medium for expressing historical knowledge, this (allegedly) figurative nature of narrative, with its corresponding fictional elements, cuts even deeper for Munslow, for it prompts him to ask whether 'in reality' the past is a narrative (or collection of narratives) at *all*. In other words, if (because of narrative's literary character) we are always introducing some kind of metaphorical interpretation of the past when we 'emplot' it narratively, then, even aside from this, is narrative *per se* (irrespective of its literary nuances) the form in which the past occurs? Munslow seems hesitant about this, unlike White who claims that 'No one *lives* a story', and who may therefore be saying that there is no correspondence in reality between a narrative (as form) and the actual 'content' of people's (past) experience – a notably radical position. Rather, Munslow argues that even though (narrative) history is emphatically a *literary* endeavour, this does not necessarily mean that people living in the past did not indeed 'explain their lives to themselves as narratives', and that therefore 'there may be some kind of narrative correspondence possible between past events as *lived* and their *history* as emplotted later by historians'. But even if this is the case, Munslow asks us to consider whether such lived narratives were themselves 'emplotted' by their

373

experiencers according to some dominant cultural metaphor (which must therefore be taken into account by the historian if he uses their stories as evidence) – and further (and most speculatively, but also most interestingly), whether their changing literary modes have therefore played any determining role in 'the fundamental cultural transitions in Western society since the Renaissance'.[17]

These, then, are Munslow's principal reasons for complaining that mainstream historians 'refuse to slip the anchor of empiricism',[18] and that 'the real poverty of empiricism resides in its strenuous refusal to acknowledge the power of figuration in the narrativisation of the past . . .'.[19] Thus, 'Empiricism necessarily sells history short'.[20] It does this, not so much because mainstream historians fail to recognise that history is always open to different interpretations – (on the contrary, Munslow rightly points out that 'mainstreamers' of course recognise this) – but because at base it is still premised on the notion that there is an objective reality which can be known, instead of accepting the postmodernists' 'insistence that objectivity is impossible to achieve'.[21]

Munslow's alternative 'history'

But this does not mean the end of history for Munslow. On the contrary, he asserts 'that history, while it can no more depend on undisputed notions of truth, objectivity and factualism, can speak to new and even more challenging questions about how we gain knowledge of the past'.[22] What does this mean in practice? Here, when trying to explain what history *should* be instead, Munslow is less specific than when attacking its 'mainstream' version. The key to it seems to revolve around 'self-reflexivity', as will appear from the following cull of passages where Munslow attempts to explain the alternative kind of 'history' championed by postmodernists:

> . . . good history . . . is that which is self-reflexive enough to acknowledge its limits, especially aware that the writing of history is far more precarious and speculative than empiricists usually admit[23] . . . we may grasp more of the richness of historical analysis by incorporating into the study of the past the intertextual nature of history as a discourse[24] . . . the deconstructionist [i.e., postmodern] consciousness accepts history as what it might have been rather than what it actually was. . . . None of this precludes the deconstructively aware historian from believing that a past once existed. What it does mean is that he/she will write about a past within a self-conscious framework. It means accepting . . . the historian's dialogue with sources that do not necessarily correspond to the past and acknowledge that they are not projections of what actually happened because they are non-referential.[25]

And here, in line with his regret at many historians' 'wilful disregard of Foucault's work', Munslow approvingly summarises what he takes to be that writer's view – namely, that history should be 'self-reflexively engaged with its own philosophy', since 'the past construed as history is an endless process of interpretation by the historian as an act of imagination, and our categories of analysis, assumptions, models and figurative style all themselves become a part of the history we are trying to unravel'.[26] Again, 'while mainstream historians study evidence in order to wring out its true meaning, to deconstruct means to seek out its multiple messages and through the exercise of our imagination create possible ranges of meanings about referents'.[27] And finally (now following the other thinker Munslow believes mainstream historians wrongly disregard, Hayden White) '[t]he input of the historian . . . is his/her ability to develop the figurative or metaphorical nature of the narrative as a form of explanation – to expand the nature of his/her historical imagination'.[28]

If, as seems from above, the postmodern alternative history does not aspire to know the past 'as it actually happened', Munslow nevertheless insists: 'This is not anti-history, but is a conception of history as what it palpably is: a self-conscious narrative composition written in the here and now that recognises its literary form as its essential cognitive medium, and not merely its mode of report'.[29] Because of this, there is a sense in which for Munslow and others *the past* is not the same as *history* – indeed, he cites the historian Elizabeth Tonks' preferred use of 'representations of pastness' rather than 'history' – because 'the deconstructive consciousness makes us . . . aware that the way in which we metaphorically prefigure, organise, emplot, explain, and make moral judgements about the past is our only access to it'.[30]

In sum, then, for Munslow 'the overarching implication is that history can be no more, nor less, than a representation of pastness', and the key to writing *acceptable* (i.e., postmodern) history is the exercise of a deep self-reflexivity on the part of the historian (preferably informed, if not guided, by the ideas of Foucault, White, and such-like), such that 'by exploring how we represent the relationship between ourselves and the past we may see ourselves not as detached observers of the past but . . . [as] participants in its creation'.[31]

Critique

Although I will offer a general critique of the overall postmodern perspective later, some specific points about Munslow's ideas in particular are worth making. First, apart from his clear acceptance of the intimate relationship between history and narrative, and its derivation from evidence, Munslow's appeal to self-awareness or 'self-reflexivity' rings through these attempts to substantiate what 'kind' of history should dislodge its mainstream character, but little else. Yet hopefully historians *are* self-aware in any event, and to the extent they are it influences their preparatory ideas and their self-editing of what they initially wrote. But it is difficult to see how Munslow's 'self-reflexivity' adds so much to this that it requires 'history must be reassessed at its most basic level'.[32] Second, it would appear that under the postmodern dispensation much of the discipline of history would resolve into talking *about* historians' writings rather than producing them – a concern expressed by practising historians,[33] and unlikely to be allayed by Munslow's urging that 'history is the study not of change over time *per se*, but the study of the information produced by historians as they go about their task'.[34]

However, this criticism may be unfair, or at least premature, on two counts. On the one hand, few have been more energetic than Munslow himself, as editor of the journal *Rethinking History*, in encouraging and publishing examples of the kind of 'history' he is recommending – bolstered by his USA co-editor, Robert Rosenstone, who, for instance, cites a number of other examples in his article 'Experiments in Narrative'.[35] On the other hand, it could be argued that, because they reject their immediate past, many 'movements' begin more on a negative note than on a positive alternative, and thus that as postmodernism spreads to the subject of history its initial impact will concentrate on criticising 'traditional' history rather than on producing mature examples of its proposed alternative. (For example, the Renaissance humanist movement scorned its preceding culture, but unlike postmodern historians had the advantage of a ready-made positive alternative in the world of Classical Antiquity.)

Third, however, (and more damagingly) is the question of 'narrative', which Munslow rightly raises as central to any discussion of the logic of historical discourse. Although seeming hesitant to go as far as saying that 'stories' (i.e., narratives) are never 'real', but are always imposed upon past events, the broad thrust of his outlook points to that position. From our viewpoint the only way to partly salvage him from a fundamental mistake is to suggest a distinction (alluded to in our Chapter 12) between what we might call 'blockbuster' or 'mega' histories, and those that simply purport to discover 'what happened' in more obviously manageable contexts. In the former case (which might happily coincide with the postmodern notion of '*meta*-narrative'), where one attempts to uncover such vast and amorphous 'stories' as 'the history of the USA', 'the history of Western philosophy', or 'the history of European art', Munslow's claim that such narratives are *constructs* (or literary artefacts) will usually be true. This is because it is highly unlikely that such topics can be treated in such a manner that any *genuine* narrative continuity can be *sustained*. If, then, such 'histories' are nevertheless presented as narratives, the principles underlying the breathtaking selectivity necessarily involved cannot emerge from the diverse events themselves, but will indeed be the result of some kind of imaginative 'emplotment' carried out by the historian, (at its most obvious in TV blockbuster documentaries, where music and visual effects accompany the dialogue). To this extent Munslow is right, and it is reasonable to thus pursue the kind of explorations about 'emplotment' urged, for example, by Hayden White.

However, not all history is 'mega' (or 'meta') history, and as we descend from those dizzy 'heights' we can reach planes where the narrative form is not *imposed* upon history as if from without, but where the material *is*, of itself, narratively structured, and thus requires narrative *logic* for its apprehension, and the *form* of narrative for its communication. At its simplest, this directs us to an individual's actions, where he/she does 'this then that', the logic of which we examined in

Chapters 12 and 13. Although it is true that we must always leave room for *dis*continuity in an individual's behaviour (whereby he stops doing one thing and starts doing another), nevertheless where a genuine sequentiality of actions can be found, such that one thing 'follows from' another in the manner we earlier explained, we are confronted by what I have called a 'story-object' or 'narrative identity'. These range in complexity, from 'following' an individual's conduct to 'following' (or 'perceiving') an *event*, a term worth distinguishing from an individual's *actions* because I mean it to encompass the *interplay* between different individuals as they respond to each other. Clearly, 'events' themselves vary in 'size' and complexity, from a motor-car accident to a war (and I have tried elsewhere to distinguish different classes of 'story-objects' – in this case, within the history of *thought* – from the simplest to the most complex and threateningly amorphous[36]) – but in each case we are hoping to find *real* sequences, where 'this happened because of that happening', rather than *invent* continuities where they do not exist.

In short, actions and events are narratively structured. We perceive 'events', and (as argued earlier) 'events' and 'happenings' are as 'real' or 'objective' as the physical objects we perceive, (hence my term, 'story-*objects*'). But as also argued, whether objects and events in some further sense 'truly' exist is a non-question, spawned from the fallacy of the metaphysical enquirer. The *general* point is, does their apprehension and identification (via the meaning of words – e.g., a 'dog', a 'war') work in practice? But the *particular* point is that events are as 'real' as physical objects, emotions, relationships, colours, and other phenomena we abstract from the world around us. We do not invent them, and the discourse in which we communicate them (narrative) therefore does not have to be figurative. It can be factual.

This returns us to the distinction between fact and fiction in narrative, and here it could be argued that where Munslow (who is not alone in this) follows White's insistence that *any* narrative must be 'emplotted' in such a manner as to convey romance, comedy, tragedy, or satire (and is therefore a literary artefact rather than an objective account), he has got the matter upside-down.

First, we should recall that, whereas factual narrative *can* be employed in order to achieve some extrinsic objective (i.e., rather than simply explicating what happened), fictional narrative *must* be so employed, since it is inconceivable that anyone would *invent* a story merely 'for the sake of it'. It is only *because* of this that fictional narrative must indeed be explored for what it is trying to achieve by constructing a story – e.g., dramatic or comic effects, or many others. But to claim that all *factual* narrative must also be figuratively slanted along the same lines is to beg the question, for it precludes the possibility of narrative told for its own sake. In short, it implies that all narrative, whether fictional or factual, is *as if* it were fiction, whereas we have shown that *factual* narrative can be simply that, bearing none of fiction's necessary hallmarks.

Second, there can indeed be occasions where factual narrative written 'for the sake of it' nevertheless produces a 'story' which is indeed e.g., tragic, or ironic. But this does not *have* to be because the historian has imaginatively *made* it so (as must be the case in fiction). This again begs the question, for it assumes that, for example, 'the dramatic' is some invention imposed upon events from 'outside'. It may be, but it does not *have* to be. Some events are 'by their nature' dramatic, comic, and so on, which is why we *have* the terms 'dramatic', 'comic' and so forth. These terms have been construed by human beings to denote relevant aspects of their experience of the world, including the nature of the events within it. Thus it is that, without any figurative or literary invention, the story which the historian uncovers 'for its own sake' may be, for example, 'dramatic'. It does not mean the narrative is therefore necessarily not objective, or in some other sense 'untrue'. It simply means some dramas are 'real'. (For example, it is in this sense I choose to interpret the claim that the destruction of the World Trade Center towers was 'a work of art' – i.e., as an apt inversion of that faulty logic which claims that artistic/ aesthetic criteria are always imposed upon reality rather than being derived from real responses to real situations.)

Indeed, this insistence on the (allegedly inevitable) figurative, metaphoric nature of historical discourse may prompt one to speculate that postmodern historical theorists have been grievously flawed from the outset. The origins of the postmodern movement, we should recall, were in the field of literary criticism and the fine arts, areas which Plato famously distinguished from the world of *fact*. For him, the application of aesthetic criteria to factual reality (especially concerning human affairs) runs the risk of distortion, exaggeration, and dramatisation, trans- forming them into *fiction*, since the very purpose of *art* is to engage the emotions. Now, given the artistic origins of postmodernism we might say it never *was* concerned with factual reality, and quite properly so – such that those who nevertheless employ its insights to analyse discourse about factual reality have, from the outset, and in a profound manner, detached themselves from a sense of reality. In short, postmodernism never was about factual reality, and this runs like a corrupting core throughout postmodernist theorising about the discipline of history, however seductive it might otherwise be.

Jenkins on 'own-sakism'

Although sharing much of Munslow's perspective, it is instructive to look at the writings of another contemporary British theorist, Keith Jenkins, particularly his (1995) *On 'What is History?'*, as a second example of the attempt to apply post- modernist ideas to the discipline of history. More strident in tone, Jenkins makes some aspects of postmodern 'history' clearer in places where Munslow is hesitant or merely indicative. What does Jenkins add? Essentially, he explicitly *politicises* both the postmodern critique of 'traditional' history and its putative replacement.

In his critique of mainstream history, like Munslow and others Jenkins approves of the 'anti-essentialist, anti-teleological, anti-foundationalist, anti- representationalist and anti-realist implications' of the postmodern perspective for history.[37] Accordingly, he makes it clear in particular that:

today we know of no such things as neutral/objective 'interpretations', as 'innocent surveys', as 'unpositioned positions'. Rather, we should all know by now that the best we can do is to alert . . . 'readers' to the position we are interpreting from, rather than imagining . . . that some interpretations are not interpretive at all but 'the truth'.[38]

The logic of these unequivocal assertions rules out the possibility (urged in our preceding two chapters) of engaging in historical narrative 'for its own sake' – and Jenkins does just that. First, he tells us that, living in our postmodern times, it is no longer credible to subscribe to any overarching 'ideology' or philosophy of history which purports to give meaning to history, and in this connection he singles out the 'meta-historical' frameworks employed by 'bourgeois' and 'proletarian' modernist history – i.e., history as construed along Marxist or 'liberal-democratic' lines. This is 'upper-case History' (akin, we might note, to speculative philosophy of history, if only implicitly), and because the respective hopes behind History with a capital H (either of a consummated class-war or of a liberal utopia of rational optimism) have been dashed by the uncertainties of the postmodern world, 'nobody really believes in that particular fantasy any more'. Instead, according to Jenkins, as more of the bourgeoisie 'made it' in society, their conservative elements developed an approach to history which, in not being threatening, served the function of sustaining their position – namely, the abandonment of any 'metanarrative claims' to history and its replacement by the study of the past 'for its own sake'. This kind of history – 'lower-case' history, denoted dismissively by Jenkins as 'own-sakism' – has come to dominate the universities and is regarded as 'almost natural'. It purports to study the past 'objectively' and 'disinterestedly', and yet, for Jenkins, it is 'just as ideological as any upper case history ever was', because 'the idea that the proper study of history is actually "own-sakism" is recognised as just the mystifying way in which a bourgeoisie conveniently articulates its own interests as if they belonged to the past itself'.[39]

In further explanation, Jenkins singles out the ideas of Geoffrey Elton, whom he identifies as a 'conservative (Tory) historian', because in his influential book, *The Practice of History*, Elton, following the nineteenth-century historian Ranke, argued in effect 'that, once upon a time and especially in Europe, earlier fumbling attempts to understand the past had been made, but that only in the nineteenth century was the bulk of previous mystical, religious, and metaphysical approaches sloughed-off, allowing proper history to emerge'. What was this 'proper history'? Jenkins quotes Elton directly: 'the principles of respectable historiography [can] be reduced to one main precept: to study history for its own sake'. This account, according to Jenkins, is in fact 'Whiggish', even 'Hegelian', in seeing the 'Rankean-type . . . lower case (bourgeois) . . . professional own-sakist "academic" study' of the past as the culmination of the progress of historiography. But for Jenkins, this is to fail 'to see lower case history in "real" historical terms (i.e., in terms to do with power, with class and ethnic and gender location, with material exigencies and ideological positions and so on)'.

Jenkins is clear, then. History which emerges as the effort to study the past 'for its own sake' is not impartial and objective (and to that extent aspiring to 'truth'), but is 'bourgeois' because serving conservative-liberal interests. What is not so clear, however, is whether its 'bourgeois' character is an historical accident, such that 'own-sakism' could be associated with some *other* ideological position. Be this as it may, it seems that, given Jenkins' denial of the possibility of 'neutral' positions, 'own-sakism' must for him *always* reflect the very feature which it aspires to avoid – namely, bias, partiality, 'ideology'. For Jenkins, then, those who see themselves as understanding something solely for the sake of understanding it are under an illusion, since such activity is impossible. Quite why it is impossible is not made clear, however. We, on the other hand, have striven not only to demonstrate that it *is* possible, but also to analyse its implications by distinguishing it from (intellectual) activities undertaken to serve some practical objective – and it is hardly necessary to elaborate here upon how those arguments serve to refute Jenkins' attack upon 'own-sakism'.

What is worth noting, however, is that when Jenkins claims to identify the 'bourgeois' and 'Whiggish' character of 'own-sakism' he offers us an historical account of its emergence – presumably as a 'true' account? If so, then, does his understanding of its historical roots emerge from his trying to understand what happened (in historiography) 'for its own sake', thereby laying claim to being 'true' because done in the objective spirit? Presumably not, since he has denied the validity of such understanding. In which case, what he says about the origins and nature of 'own-sakism' is not objective, but is deliberately 'biased', and its 'truth' is to that extent suspect – in short, why should we 'believe' what he says? But Jenkins clearly does want us to believe what he says. Yet nevertheless, and tellingly, he evidences his own uneasiness at his position because, when complaining of Elton's (allegedly) naive belief in objectivity, he says that Elton did not understand 'lower case history in "real" historical terms', putting the word 'real' in inverted commas.[40] Whether this device is expressive of embarassment on Jenkins' part, or an example of 'ironic self-reflexivity', it is certainly disingenuous in trying to have matters both ways round – a syndrome found quite commonly in postmodernist theorising, where they justify their critique of 'modernism' by placing it within an historical perspective which they present as 'true'.

This, in fact, merely highlights a paradox faced by postmodernists (and anyone else) who share Jenkins' notion that 'neutral', 'objective' knowledge is impossible; namely, is the statement that 'all knowledge is ideological' *itself* an 'ideological' statement, and therefore (possibly) untrue? In other words, is not such a statement logically impossible, as in the old conundrum, 'Everything I say is a lie'? One way out of this conundrum is to amend the statement to the following: 'With the exception of what I am saying now, everything I say is a lie'. And such, it seems, is the only way to make sense of Jenkins *et al.* when they, for example, give an historical account of 'modernism' and its (alleged) demise, or advance theoretical/ philosophical arguments in support of their viewpoint. An unkind critic might say that their position amounts to the following: that anything anyone else might say is ideologically distorted, and that even what they themselves say is ideologically distorted, except when they make precisely this proposition – in other words, the only 'truth' to be found in discourse is that where postmodernists explain and defend themselves! But the gaping question must be, '*why?*' – i.e., returning to the conundrum, 'if everything I say is a lie except what I am saying now', on what *grounds* is this exception made? No explanation is forthcoming.

Kinder critics, however, will recognise that many postmodernists are aware of this threatening conundrum, and commend (where apparent) their attempts to confront it. Jenkins is amongst these when he defends the North American postmodern theorist, Richard Rorty, against accusations that his pragmatic stance on 'truth' is so relativistic that its very possibility evaporates, everything proposed inevitably coming from some 'position' or other. Rorty has been interpreted as claiming that 'truth' should therefore be seen as those statements which it is *good to believe in* (for Rorty, the use of 'language-games' which, for example, entail respect for and tolerance of others' opinions, the avoidance of force in disputes, and, from an ironic perspective, accommodate the liberal life-styles and systems of bourgeois North-Atlantic societies). Jenkins (clearly aware that such a position on 'truth' is indeed weak, if not foolish) urges readers that this is to misrepresent Rorty, since Rorty's notion of 'truth' is not solely dependent on what it is good to believe in. Rather, Jenkins quotes Rorty as saying 'that truth is "the name of whatever proves itself to be good in the way of belief, *and good, too, for definite, assignable reasons*"'. What are these reasons? They are, according to Jenkins, 'the usual sorts of definite, assignable reasons generally available', which are to be found in the 'thousands of words' Rorty has written explaining his views.[41] Readers must pursue for themselves how convincing is this attempt to confront the conundrum of truth as it appears for Jenkins and other postmodernists. But since 'truth' does not present itself as a conundrum for those who accept the possibility and distinctness of understanding something *for the sake of* understanding it, and its linkage to 'truth', we may move on from the *critical* thrust of Jenkins's ideas (especially against 'own-sakism' in historical study) to the *constructive* side of his thought – namely, if mainstream history is no longer valid, then what should replace it?

Jenkins on the postmodern alternative 'history'

Whereas I have suggested that Munslow's *Deconstructing History* remains vague about this, Jenkins is somewhat clearer due to his more explicitly *political* approach to historiography. Having identified 'own-sakism' (which he equates with professional, mainstream, academic history) as 'bourgeois', then its abandonment (along with claims that the past can be objectively 'represented' by historians) 'usher[s] in new possibilities; new opportunities'.[42] It does this because, once it is recognised that the structure and intelligibility which conventional history imposes upon the past is a fallacy, the way is cleared to accept the 'openness and meaninglessness' of the past. Whereas the authoritative narratives of conventional history served as 'ideological closures' on the meaning and significance of past events, restricting visions for the future, Jenkins approvingly quotes White's notion that it is precisely only the recognition of history's meaning*lessness* 'that can "alone goad living human beings to make their lives different for themselves and their children"'. Indeed, Jenkins tells us that White has even queried whether historical narrative *per se* is not 'a general ideological instrument of anti-utopian closure', such that historians might move forward 'by refusing to attempt a narrativist mode for the representation of . . . "truth"'. Instead, history based on the recognition of rupture and discontinuity within the past would be a discourse far better able to accommodate the needs, viewpoints, and aspirations of 'subordinate, emergent, or resisting social groups'.[43] Although Jenkins claims that White 'has not gone on to explain how . . . his history of discontinuity would actually work in practice',[44] it is clear that whatever approach to history it might imply (e.g., descriptive vignettes, the dramatisation of alternative reminiscences, and other such forms found in the journal *Rethinking History*), for Jenkins and others it should be 'a study of the past that fully recognises the openness and uncontrollable nature of it *in order to* encourage an open and different emancipatory future'.[45]

In short, it seems that for those of Jenkins' mind, since no history can escape being politically ideological, then let it be openly such, and be directed towards the objective of 'emancipation' – and of whom? The answer (echoing Foucault) lies in the equation of information with power. Mainstream 'metanarrative' and 'own-sakist' history legitimises the dominant social orders, political structures, and economic systems, ignoring the disadvantaged positions of 'the other', and in its 'rationality' turns attention away from the ever-present possibility, throughout history, of reaching for something 'sublime', outside the mentality of those comfortably entrenched in the instrumental routines of society. Thus it is that Jenkins approvingly quotes the postmodern historian, Brenda Marshall's, description of postmodern history: '"It asks: Whose history gets told? In whose name? For what purpose? Postmodernism is about histories not told, retold, untold. History as it never was. Histories forgotten, hidden, invisible, considered unimportant, changed, eradicated". . .'.[46] In thus giving a voice to 'the other', the postmodern study of history can empower and help emancipate not only 'the other' but all of us.

Critique

Such, then, is the approach to 'history' Jenkins and some other postmodernists think should replace its current nature as a discipline – although others draw different, and often less robust, *political* implications. For example, in *Deconstructing History* Munslow also claims that historians should 'seek out' that which mainstream history texts omit; namely, 'the other', meaning the repressed and marginalised, of which (in 1997) he gives the following examples – 'Jews, Serbs, Croats, women, the poor, lesbians, immigrants, aboriginals, gays'[47] – but he does not highlight an explicitly emancipatory *objective* for the discipline of history. Jenkins does, and although in doing so he can claim the virtue of consistency – (i.e., if history is invariably ideological, then let us not pretend to be otherwise in our own prescriptions for how the discipline should be 'rethought') – many will see the openly ideological nature of his approach, if adopted, as one amongst other factors indeed harbingering 'the end of history'; that is, 'history' understood as the endeavour to establish what pertained, what happened, and why, in the human past – an activity whose validity and importance is otherwise accepted without question.

This judgement on Jenkins' position, let it be clear, does not derive from any *political* considerations, and particularly not from any bias against 'the other'. On that issue, although much mischief surrounds the concept such that it positively invites 'ideological' discriminations *within* it – (e.g., note the above mention of Jews, but not of Palestinians) – the reason 'the other's' history has been less explored is that although it is of legitimate interest to those groups who fall under this rubric, they may not have played any significant role in the dominant themes which historians and others (economists, political scientists, sociological theorists) perceive as having shaped the changing nature of societies and the international scene. Earlier (Chapter 12) we argued, by analogy, that just as the architect will focus on the principal features of a building in order to understand/explain it, so do (most) historians' instincts lead them to study the principal events associated with the changing nature of societies – and where a grouping we might call part of 'the other' has played a role, then its history *is* likely to be explored – otherwise not. This has long been a feature of historical practice, from the study of medieval heretical sects which, coming out of obscurity, impacted their surrounding society (e.g., the Cathars), to the Diggers' and True Levellers' influence in the English Civil War; and in contemporary times the influence of 'the gay community' upon social change and legislation.

Rather, Jenkins' explicitly ideological approach can be seen as harbingering 'the end of history' simply because, whatever the ideology, it means that the past is not studied 'for its own sake' but quite consciously as a practical activity – in this case, to reiterate Jenkins, 'in order to encourage an open and different emancipatory future'. From our viewpoint it does not matter *what* practical (extrinsic) objective might motivate the study of the past. The problem is when *any* external motivation is in play, thereby threatening the impartiality, all-roundedness, objectivity, and 'truthfulness' of historical accounts – particularly where its practical purpose is not, for example, to gain a professional qualification or write a lucrative book, but *to persuade readers to a political end*. Insofar as we have earlier laboured to distinguish between things done 'for their own sake' and things done in order to achieve some extrinsic objective, and drawn out the implications both in general and specifically for the activity of history, we can leave to readers' deliberations how far this aspect of Jenkins' approach implies 'the end of history'.

There is, however, a second respect in which those who endorse Jenkins' postmodernist approach may be accused, despite their protestations, of signalling 'the end of history'. This returns us to the unease we expressed over the apparent implication in Munslow that postmodern history is more 'the study of the information produced by historians' than 'the study of . . . change over time *per se*'.[48] Characteristically, Jenkins is bolder on this crucial issue, but arguably to the point of recklessness. He concludes *What is History?* by telling us that 'history is . . . a narrative prose discourse of which . . . the content is as much invented as found', and that 'understood . . . as a rhetorical, metaphorical, textual practice, . . . the cogency of historical work can be admitted without the past *per se* ever entering into it – except rhetorically'.[49] In other words, and at face-value, the discipline of history either does and/or (?) *should* proceed without the reality of past events constituting its foundation!

So extraordinary is this claim that it is worth exploring whether this is what Jenkins means – but other parts of his text suggest he indeed does. Earlier he claims that conventional history has been revealed as 'an ideological-interpretive discourse without any "real" access to the past as such; unable to engage in any dialogue with "reality". In fact, "history" now appears to be just one more "expression" in a world of postmodern expressions: which of course is what it is'.[50] However, to forestall readers' potential alarm that the past has somehow disappeared, Jenkins later makes it clear that 'it is no part of any postmodernist argument . . . to deny the material existence of the past . . . [T]here is indeed an actual world "out there" . . . which has a past'. However, the postmodernist 'strong insistence' is 'that that once actual past is . . . only accessible to us through texts and thus as a "reading"'.[51] (Whether he means 'texts' as history books, i.e., secondary source material, or as primary source-material such as archives, letters, and State papers – or as both – is not clear.) Because of this, then although postmodernists do not deny the objective existence of things in the past, the fact that they existed/ happened 'does not in the slightest way tell you how to go about making the historical representation of [them] true and/or objective'. Rather, because 'objectivity and truth are not derived in any way from the mere existence of an object of enquiry', these features of knowledge can only derive from 'the internal mechanisms and coherences of methods of explanation that are applied to it'. Thus, to achieve objective and true statements about (i.e., 'representations of') the past, what is needed is 'an epistemology and a method'.[52]

Correct as this is, many historians and theorists, however, think we already have them. The postmodernists, on the other hand, deny the viability of mainstream historical method and epistemology for the reasons we have expounded – or do they? It is more accurate to say they deny *the claims to truth and objectivity* made for mainstream history. It is far from clear they deny its *method*, based on finding evidence, inferring from it, and (if the case) constructing narrative accounts premised on the notion that 'truth' is that property of discourse where what one proposes to be the case is indeed the case – for what other approach do they propose? Rather, they seem to have none, but are stuck with one which according to them cannot achieve objective knowledge of the actual past. Rather than look for a real alternative, there is no point in their doing so since, for them, *no* form of discourse can *ever* faithfully 'represent' reality (past or present) anyway.

In short, we return to that corrosive core, not of postmodernism itself as an approach to aesthetics, but of postmodernism when applied to the world of factual reality. For Jenkins *et al.* 'the past' was real, actual, objective, but precisely these features cannot be recaptured either in today's mainstream historical discourse *or any other*.

Thus we may indeed interpret Jenkins at face value as saying that history already is, and also *should* be, a discourse or discipline 'without the past *per se* entering into it'. The difference, however, is that the postmodern *awareness* of this should not only, as in Munslow, stimulate a greater 'self-reflexivity' on historians' part. Also (since 'history' is for postmodernists virtually a species of *fiction* anyway) it should give them a license to *use* 'history' as an instrument for promoting the 'emancipation' of 'the other'; (indeed, the two might amount to the same thing, since Munslow's 'self-reflexivity' is, arguably, but a surreptitious ideology of 'the other').

To the extent that all the above is a fair rendering of Jenkins principal points and, as importantly, a fair drawing out of their implications, the reader may appreciate just why many historians and theorists regard the postmodern analytic philosophy of history (at least, when expounded so robustly as in Jenkins) as representing 'the end of history' were it to become the cornerstone of the discipline. The past *per se* does not enter into it; it is impossible to make either objective or 'true' statements about the past – 'history' cannot be studied 'for its own sake'; 'history' should settle for being a (now self-conscious) exercise in ideological persuasion. As mentioned initially, some postmodernists *do* accept the logic that this indeed means 'the end of history', and presumably have no more to do with it – a perfectly respectable and consistent (if flawed) position. Curiously, however, others not only see this as *not* 'the end of history', but as its *beginning*, at last stripped of previous errors and illusions – to many, a dawn as strange as it is false.

Conclusion: the foundations of postmodernism revisited

Despite differences of emphasis and political viewpoint amongst them, the fact that postmodernist history theorists are deeply embedded in the *fundamental* premises of postmodern thought make it worth revisiting the latter before leaving this version of (arguably) 'the end of history'.

Essentially, postmodernism is a movement based on challenging the current foundations of epistemology – i.e., the manner in which we think we achieve knowledge of reality. This, in its turn, centres on the forms in which we purport to 'represent' reality – e.g., film, painting – but particularly *language* as a 'representer' of reality. Postmodernist theorists insist on the inability of language to correspond to reality, such that although some (e.g., Munslow and Jenkins) accept that there is such a thing as an 'objective', 'true' reality 'out there' but deny its accessibility via linguistic representation, others discard the notion of 'reality' altogether.

We have suggested that, since postmodernism began as a critique of art and literature, it was already at one remove from 'reality', such that its application to the world of 'fact' (the distinctive, but not unique, domain of history) was bound to be problematic. This observation, I suggest, can stand, and is borne out in the two writers we have examined. More precisely, however, in their case it is the notion that suppositions are embedded in language, and underlie the way we *use* language, which informs their perspective on how far, if at all, anything true or objective can be advanced in historical discourse. Most explicitly in Jenkins' case (but at the base of most postmodernist theory) these suppositions are presented as 'ideological', meaning 'political', bias in the broad sense of moral, political, social, and economic 'positionings'. This is not to neglect that for postmodernists (and others) such bias also operates in the very *choice* of what one talks about – e.g., the editing process of choosing 'the news', historians' choices of topics. But it is the notion that 'discourse' *itself* (i.e., the use of language) is *inherently* 'ideological', such that 'reality' is inaccessible via language as a medium of knowledge, which is the more *philosophical* point, and invites scrutiny.

'Ideology': shallow and deep

The correspondence (or lack of it) between language and 'reality' in our efforts to 'know' the latter is not a new problematic. Indeed, earlier in this book we encountered examples of thinkers who grappled with this aspect of epistemology – Hobbes in the seventeenth century, Vico in the eighteenth, and Marx in the nineteenth; and the 'linguistic turn' taken by much twentieth-century philosophy is well-known. In this respect, then, the postmodernists' focus is hardly novel. What, however, particularly characterises *their* approach is their emphasis upon the role of 'ideology' (in the broad sense just denoted), and it is thus to this topic that our critical attention should be restricted, rather than wander far and wide over centuries of different contributions to the problem of 'language and reality'.

Here, I suggest a distinction between what might be called 'shallow' and 'deep' ideology. By the former I mean those instances where language is *overtly* ideological; that is, where both the vocabulary employed (e.g., various derogatory terms denoting different races/ethnicities), and the import of *statements* constructed in the *use* of language (e.g., 'we hold these truths to be self-evident, that all men are created equal, that they are endowed by their Creator with certain unalienable Rights, that among these are Life, liberty and the pursuit of happiness') are manifest expressions of value-assumptions, whether those who utter them realise this or not. It is true that there are *degrees* of overtness in such discourse, such that on occasions its 'ideological' nature needs revealing through analysis. However, I suggest these are degrees *within* a general level of 'ideological' influence that either hits us straight in the face or is at least recognisable after a little thought – and we have already analysed the manner in which such discourse, in reflecting partiality and bias, imparts 'false' knowledge (or at least not 'the whole truth') of what it addresses.

Likewise, however, we have also claimed that, precisely *because* such 'shallow' ideology is recognisable, then reflective writers can expunge it from their own writings – that is, if it is there, and if they wish to. Indeed, from the other side of the same coin we have argued that it is both a *necessary* and a *possible* feature of any discourse which purports to convey knowledge 'for its own sake' that its author avoids being 'ideological'.

Our postmodernist historians, however, appear to subscribe to the general postmodernist fallacy that *any* discourse must be 'ideological' at this 'shallow' level, simply dismissing the notion that it is possible to avoid being so. Whatever *they* mean by 'self-reflexivity', it does not mean the ability to reflect on one's thinking and writing to flush out any overt ideological 'positioning'. But it does mean this for those historians and fellow-intellectuals who are concerned to uncover and communicate 'true', 'objective' knowledge about reality. In doing so, they use language. But far from this automatically making knowledge of reality inaccessible, we might instead point to the spectacular success of language in 'representing' reality, particularly in the numerous disciplines which emerged as part of that 'modern' history which postmodernists castigate.

We can conclude from this that whilst postmodern historical theorists' critique of 'mainline' history (largely) centres on its (alleged) overtly ideological character, that critique is unsustainable as a philosophical premise – for although it is true that there *are* examples of overtly 'ideological' history (long ago analysed by, e.g., Tudor, who called it 'political myth' rather than 'history'),[53] it is far from true that this *must*, and therefore *does*, characterise all historical discourse.

However, I suggest there is another level of 'ideology', namely, 'deep' ideology – and where other postmodernists appear occasionally to touch on this, they might have a point, albeit one different to that advanced by postmodernist *historical* theorists.

By 'deep' ideology I mean to point not to where language is overtly value-laden or politically biased, but to what is, indeed, a *genuinely* inherent restriction on the capacity of language to denote reality. Here, I revert to my brief discussion in Chapter 12 on the meaning of words, where I argued: that words are contrived by human-beings to denote or 'single out' something in 'the world out there' worth noticing and distinguishing from other things; that the reason we have for noticing things is that they are relevant to us; that things are relevant to us in terms of the myriad of our 'interests' (material, aesthetic, sexual, etc.); that other beings with different bodies and/or different mentalities would 'single out' and denote different 'things' to those we identify; that when we therefore single out something and call it 'a tree', the meaning of the word derives from the reason we have for noticing it; that whether there are 'truly' such things as, e.g., 'trees', 'holidays', or 'teenagers' is a non-question since none of these 'things' pre-exist us as already objectively meaningful 'trees' etc.; that instead, the point is not, are 'trees' etc., 'true' or 'real'?, but does the use of the term, given what we mean by it, work *in practice*? Is it relevant, workable, and reliable to use that word when understanding 'the world out there'?

This approach to language and its relation to 'reality' extends beyond the meaning of words, to how they are put together in grammatical constructs – e.g., 'this is a tree', 'he ran down the street and then went in the house', 'why did she leave?'. Here the same may apply; namely, that the manner in which reality is apprehended through the logic of linguistic constructions (including narrative) does not accord with some prior, pre-existent logical objective in 'the world out there', but that they are simply ways which human beings have found to make relevant, workable, and reliable sense of that world *for them*.

Along these lines, then, we could indeed concede that *any* discourse is 'ideological', including that specifically devoted to saying 'true' things about reality for the sake of it (unlike 'shallow' ideology). This is because we cannot but experience, 'perceive', or 'know' reality as *human beings* rather than as disembodied 'spirits' or as differently embodied (e.g., as ants). At this level, for example, we could ask why we commonly identify people via gender pronouns – '*he* went for a walk', '*she* left the room'. Here, following the above analysis, it could be argued we are not being 'objective', but instead being partial because singling out a specific feature of individuals. (Trans-sexuals have indeed complained of this 'ideological' feature of language). Likewise, it could be argued that where language is structured around the use of transitive verbs – 'he posts the letter' – this assumes the fact of human agency/will; or that when we narrate a sequence (such as, above, 'he ran down the street and then went in the house'), it assumes the 'reality' of 'stories'. In each case – gender pronouns, transitive verbs, narrative, (and we could add, for example, the different tenses) – the question is not whether such terminology and linguistic constructs correlate with 'objective reality', thereby making language afford 'true' knowledge (or 'representations') of reality, but do they work, and if so, why?

Such an exploratory approach to the 'logos' of our consciousness or ideas – (hence 'ideo-logy') – seems eminently worthwhile, and could even apply to what (if any) linguistic forms are essential to *historical* discourse. Yet such forays into 'deep' ideology are qualitatively different from that perspective on the relation between language and reality which suffuses postmodernist critiques. They – and no more so than when applied to the discipline of history – revolve around 'shallow' ideology; that is, the manner in which value-presuppositions *about* 'reality' affect our knowledge of it, whereas 'deep' ideology concerns the way we see reality *in the first place*. Whereas the former *can* be avoided – and '*should*' be when we try to understand things for the sake of it – the latter seems inescapably linked to our fundamental human condition, irrespective of the temporary situations people find themselves in and which generate different 'positionings'.

The upshot of this is, then, that our knowledge of reality is always limited by being human knowledge, (if 'limit' is the appropriate term) – but need not be *further* limited because it stems from *this* or *that* human being, placed in such and such a position. Knowledge of the past ('history') is no exception. It cannot exceed the boundaries of originating in human beings, escaping from there into some metaphysical fairy-land of ultimate, transcendental 'objectivity' and 'truth'. But *within* its boundaries it can, like other 'discourses', discover and communicate knowledge 'for the sake of it', unimpaired by 'shallow' ideology. This, after all, is all we can sensibly *mean* by the words 'objectivity' and 'truth', and I suggest they have served us well over the ages as, indeed, *themselves* workable, relevant, and reliable distinctions worth singling out amongst the otherwise random torrent of human conversation. If, in some confused sense, we failed to recognise the difference between 'shallow' and 'deep' ideology, we would fall into the trap which appears to have been set by postmodern history theorists – namely, of affording the former the same status as 'deep' ideology, thereby signalling not only 'the end of history' as a viable discipline, but (following postmodern philosophers) 'the end of knowledge' *per se*, (i.e., understood as the ability of language to 'represent reality' rather than distort it).

15

THE END OF HISTORY?

Fukuyama's speculative philosophy of history

Introduction

'The times we live in'

In the previous chapter we saw the emergence of a contemporary school of *analytic* philosophy of history interpreted by many – particularly irate historians – as heralding 'the end of history' as a viable discipline, were it to be taken seriously. Deriving from the postmodernist movement in general, its proponents relate their perceptions to the times we live in. The troubled twentieth century, combined with novel features of contemporary capitalism, convinces them of the need to rethink the very basis upon which we approach 'knowing' reality.

Such efforts, of course, are not new in the history of thought, and it is tempting to suggest they always correlate with what their proponents perceived as particularly 'troubled', or at least 'interesting', times. For example, battling to defend Christianity at a crucial period under the Roman Empire, Augustine urged people to stop relying on the power of reason, and instead ground their understanding on an act of faith – 'believe in order to understand'. Or, as we saw, Renaissance humanists proposed a fresh start to how people understood the world and themselves, whilst we noted Hegel's awe at seeing Napoleon in Jena. Or, finally, moving to what he regarded as revolutionary times, we might cite the epistemological radicalism behind Marx's 'historical materialism'.

But counter-examples cast doubt on the *necessity* behind such correlations. For instance, it would be difficult to claim that originators of 'the Scientific Revolution' (e.g., Galileo, Bacon) or of modern philosophy (e.g., Descartes, Spinoza) were responding to any feelings they might have harboured about the special propitiousness of their times. Perhaps above all, this applies to Vico (in the early eighteenth century), whose passion to revolutionise the basis of knowledge prompted his proclamation that 'we must reckon as if there were no books in the world' which have been any use up to now – and yet nothing suggests he regarded his own times as exceptional.

Attempts to 'rethink' how we approach understanding the world are, then, neither uncommon nor necessarily related (in their proponents' minds) to 'exceptional' times. However, we have seen that postmodernists *do* draw such a correlation (when expounding their epistemological notion of a 'crisis in representation'). The same, although for markedly different reasons, applies with Francis Fukuyama's philosophy of history.

Essentially, we will find Fukuyama arguing that 'History, . . . understood as a single, coherent, evolutionary process,'[1] has reached its end-goal, such that we can expect no new developments in the basic structure already characterising the majority of the world's states – namely, the combination of free-market (i.e., capitalist) economies and liberal-democratic political constitutions. Countries presently lacking these features will sooner or later catch up, thereby completing the demise of 'the historical world' and the full arrival of 'the post-historical world'.[2]

Fukuyama thus presents a thesis stemming from *speculative* philosophy of history – and he is suggesting there is something distinctive about our times which should prompt us to rethink modern assumptions underlying our approach to knowledge of *history* in particular.

For Fukuyama, writing in the early 1990s, and having worked in the US State Department's Policy Planning Staff (although now a professional academic), what is special about today's world is that, having undergone a century of 'troubled times' including two world wars, the Holocaust, the Cold War, and barbarous experiments in government from both Communist and fascist regimes, the ideals of liberal democracy have not only survived but have palpably triumphed, such that the prospect of a 'world-wide liberal revolution' is now evident. Apart from the defeat of Nazism, many right-wing authoritarian regimes around the world have since become democracies, whilst communism has collapsed in Russia and Eastern Europe.

Although there is much to elaborate upon here, sufficient has been said to explain why Fukuyama believes our times are indeed special. But even if we accept that we are on the brink of a world-wide liberal revolution (backed up by the globalisation of capitalism), why should this prompt us to rethink the very manner in which we approach understanding history?

The revival of speculative philosophy of history

The answer is as simple as it is bold. Fukuyama believes there should be a revival of *speculative* philosophy of history. This would help inform our historical understanding (and, it would seem, future *policy* both domestically and internationally). He suggests that discussion of whether there is some overall meaning to human history was 'more or less abandoned'[3] in the twentieth century because events increasingly made people into 'deep historical pessimists'; 'our deepest thinkers have concluded that there is no such thing as History – i.e., a meaningful order to the broad sweep of human events'.[4]

Previously, various attempts had been made to construct overall theories of history, and Fukuyama includes examples omitted from our Part I, such as Kant's sketchy ideas (in the 1780s) and the dubious notions of Spengler and Toynbee in the early twentieth century. (Surprisingly, he neglects to mention Vico.) But he principally centres on Hegel and Marx, whose writings constitute 'the most serious efforts at writing Universal Histories',[5] continuing the legacy of those earlier thinkers who 'saw the central issue in history as the development of Freedom', believing that 'History was not a blind concatenation of events, but a meaningful whole in which human ideas concerning the nature of a just political and social order developed and played themselves out'.[6] But, apart from minor exceptions, Fukuyama correctly implies that after Marx great speculative philosophy of history disappeared.

Yet he believes this rejection of speculative philosophy of history is misguided. Rather, he believes we should rethink – not, however, rethink the actual *content* of history, but our *approach* to that history. Later, he urges that '"history" is not a given, nor merely a catalogue of everything that happened in the past, but a deliberate effort of abstraction in which we separate out important from unimportant events' – and that 'this is all the more true of a Universal History, which raises the level of abstraction to an even higher degree'. In short, he implies the *discipline* of history could benefit from a shift in *focus* regarding those factors deemed to be 'important' in understanding the past, by affording consideration to the speculative framework of the 'Universal History' he is to unfold.

This is worth noting, if only to mark the clear distinction between his thinking and that of the postmodernists. Both he and they relate their ideas to 'the times we live in', but there the similarity ends. The postmodernists interpret our times as generating the need for a revolution (however ill-defined) in the very methodology and suppositions brought to the discipline of history, whereas the implications of Fukuyama's ideas for *analytic* philosophy of history are that, apart from the question of *focus*, the discipline as presently practised is perfectly valid. Indeed, the difference goes further. The postmodernists could be seen as a radical example of that *pessimism* about the twentieth century which Fukuyama thinks is misguided, for they have abandoned all hope whatsoever in the ability to say anything objective or true about the past, let alone construct some overall *meaning* to it. Such a project would strike postmodernists as an absurd and exaggerated example of 'metanarrative'.

Fukuyama, however, insists that it is just this 'reference to a standard that exists somewhere "outside" of history (and, incidentally, outside of the sphere of competence of professional historians *qua* historians)' that always does operate in the choices historians make between what is 'important and unimportant'.[7] Hence the need to accept this openly, and allow the reappearance of speculative philosophy of history into our understanding of the past, particularly since the events of the twentieth century can indeed be shown to validate the notion of an overall logic to historical development.

The logic of historical development

The 'Mechanism' of modern natural science

Having outlined Fukuyama's overall thesis (including his reasoning in reviving speculative philosophy of history), let us now explore its arguments. He begins by asking: 'Is history directional, and is there reason to think that there will be a universal evolution in the direction of liberal democracy?' His answer to the first part is that history is not repetitive, but is indeed directional. Thus, 'a constant and uniform Mechanism or set of historical first causes . . . dictates evolution in a single direction',[8] and he identifies just such a mechanism – namely, within 'the entire range of human social endeavour, the only one that is by common consensus unequivocally cumulative' is scientific knowledge. Although its effect on societies' historical development may be difficult to perceive in earlier history, it was always present – but 'a qualitative change occurred in the relationship of scientific knowledge to the historical process with the rise of *modern* natural science'.[9]

Initially its effects were felt in military competition. Not only did lesser scientifically developed countries have to catch up with the latest military technology emerging from the seventeenth century Scientific Revolution, this also involved modernising their societies by unifying their countries, centralising taxation, and improving education. Fukuyama gives many historical examples, from the emergence of the early-modern state in Europe (e.g., Spain, France), the Ottoman Empire after Napoleon's invasion, the Japanese in the mid-nineteenth century, and suggests the most recent example 'was the initial phase of Mikhail Gorbachev's own *perestroika*'.[10] The message is clear, though Fukuyama spares making it. Once the scientific knowledge behind nuclear and other weapons of mass destruction (biological, chemical) is uncovered, there is no going back, just as the rifle rendered the spear forever outdated.

The second irreversible impact of modern scientific knowledge on societies' historical evolution is, for Fukuyama, even more important, for it concerns nothing less than how it directs 'the progressive conquest of nature for the purpose of satisfying human desires'. Understood in that broad sense, he is content to refer to it as 'economic development'. Here, Fukuyama points not only to the spectacular successes of industrialisation in vastly increasing per capita income, but also to 'the bringing to bear of human reason to the problem of social organisation and the creation of a rational division of labour'.[11] Just as military competition involved certain common 'modernising' processes, so 'economic growth produced certain uniform social transformations in all societies, regardless of their prior social structure',[12] and he cites among other examples the extreme case of the necessary breakdown of apartheid in South Africa as a precondition of the 'rational bureaucratic organisation' that economic development nowadays requires.

The effect of scientific knowledge, particularly *modern* science, thus provides a mechanism which impacts cumulatively upon the evolution of societies through military competition and economic development. But *is* it irreversible? His answer is yes. Aware that 'the deliberate rejection of technology and a rationalised society has been suggested by any number of groups in modern times'[13] – e.g., the hippies, Islamic fundamentalism, and the environmentalists – he finds their origins in the 'back to nature' ideas of Jean-Jacques Rousseau. But for Fukuyama it is simply unrealistic to expect people, 'once they have experienced the consumerism of a technological society', to turn back the clock of economic development. It would mean becoming 'reacquainted with the life of a poor peasant tied to the land in an unending cycle of back-breaking labour'.[14]

Alternatively, some nuclear holocaust might push many countries 'back to nature' against their will. But, whatever the effects on the world as a whole, Fukuyama does not believe that 'modern natural science . . . can ever be forgotten or "un-invented"', short of 'the physical annihilation of the human race'.[15]

Thus, the 'Mechanism' provided by scientific knowledge produces an irreversible directionality to human history – and Fukuyama's next point is that *economically* this leads to, and *culminates* in, modern capitalism (i.e., the principles of economic liberalism). Here again the twentieth century has been a testing-bed for competing economic systems, and it is clear to Fukuyama that the free-market economy has emerged victorious. The centralised, state-planned economies of the communist bloc ultimately failed to keep up with the productive power of Western capitalist economies once the latter moved from the age of heavy manufacture into the 'information age'. Today's 'post-industrial' world thrives on innovation, which requires freedom of thought and individual initiative. Also, 'the complexity of modern economies proved to be simply beyond the capacities of centralised bureaucracies to manage',[16] whilst control over prices and the allocation of goods prohibited communist economies 'from participating in the international division of labour'.[17] Finally, central planning undermined people's incentive to work.

Taken together, Fukuyama suggests that 'it was in the highly complex and dynamic "post-industrial" economic world that Marxism-Leninism as an economic system met its Waterloo',[18] and he observes that 'by the end of the 1980s . . . China, the Soviet Union, and the countries of Eastern Europe can be seen as having succumbed to the economic logic of advanced industrialisation'.[19]

He argues the same applies to Third World countries. Although, ever since Lenin's thesis about imperialism (1916), there have been theorists claiming that 'the global capitalist economic order' kept undeveloped countries in 'a state of perpetual dependent development', such that many regarded socialism as a more promising economic strategy for Third World countries, this theory 'has by now been exploded . . . by one large phenomenon it cannot possibly explain: that is, the economic development of East Asia in the postwar period'.[20] Countries such as South Korea, Singapore, and Malaysia 'demonstrated that late modernisers were actually *advantaged* relative to more established industrial powers', and where regions such as Latin-America have not grown so fast, this is because of complex *cultural* factors (including the nature of the work-ethic), combined with the fact that 'capitalism has never worked in Latin America and other parts of the Third World because it has never been seriously tried'.[21]

Fukuyama admits that 'the logic of a progressive modern natural science predisposes human societies towards capitalism only to the extent that men can see their own economic self-interest clearly', but he claims that the empirical experience of regions such as Asia and Eastern Europe should contribute towards 'a very strong *predisposition* for all human societies' to participate in the economic liberalism of globalisation.[22] Cultures which appear less favourable to this development *can* change.

But not only is the 'mechanism' of modern science *irreversible* in its economic effects, progressively bringing countries towards a capitalist economic system. For Fukuyama it also *culminates* in capitalism. Conceding that 'the Mechanism is . . . a kind of Marxist interpretation of history' because based on 'the desire of "man the species-being" to produce and consume' – 'a highly elastic desire' not limited to so-called 'natural needs', but 'whose own horizon of possibilities is constantly being pushed back' – nevertheless 'the kind of society that permits people to produce and consume the largest quantity of products on the most equal basis is not a communist one, but a capitalist society'.[23] And it would appear that Fukuyama, having rejected the historical alternatives to capitalism, cannot conceive of any other economic system which could better fulfil man's *economic* drives. As such, then, capitalism is the end-story of the irreversible directionality which the progress of science produces in terms of *economic* systems.

The 'Mechanism' behind liberal democracy

Fukuyama then asks whether this same 'mechanism' also determines that, *politically*, societies should culminate as *liberal democracies*. His answer is no. Although many have argued a necessary correlation between liberal democracy and the high degree of economic development afforded by capitalism, he disputes this. Whilst agreeing that there are many *empirical* examples of such correlations both today and from history, he does not find the *generalities* derived from these cases convincing – for example, that 'only democracy is capable of mediating the complex web of conflicting interests that are created by a modern economy';[24] or that dictatorial regimes (of either the right or left) 'naturally' evolve into democracies because unable to hold in check the struggles between the elite groups they spawn; or that 'successful industrialisation produces middle-class societies, and that middle-class societies demand political participation and equality of rights'.[25]

None of these arguments explain 'why there should be a *universal* evolution in the direction of liberal democracy',[26] and look even more unconvincing when one recognises that 'there is considerable evidence to indicate that market-oriented *authoritarian* modernisers do better economically than their democratic counterparts'[27] – e.g., Meiji Japan, Chile under Pinochet, and particularly the newly industrialised economies in Asia (e.g., Taiwan, South Korea, Thailand). These typically conservative, authoritarian regimes are, according to Fukuyama, 'on principle better able to follow truly liberal economic policies undistorted by redistributive goals that constrain growth', whereas not only do democratic states attempt the latter, they are also reluctant to restrain competition. Yet, 'state intervention in the market, competently executed and remaining within the broad parameters of a competitive market, has quite evidently been fully compatible with very high levels of growth'.

For these reasons Fukuyama concludes that 'the Mechanism underlying our directional history', although leading to capitalist economies, does not necessarily lead to political democracy, but 'leads equally well to a bureaucratic-authoritarian future as to a liberal one'.[28] Thus he asks, what has driven the evolution to *democracy* if it has not been the product of capitalism, itself the product of the 'Mechanism' of modern natural science? His answer brings us to the *philosophical heart* of Fukuyama's thesis.

We have just seen Fukuyama rejecting any *necessary* connection between capitalist economics and liberal-democratic politics. He goes further, saying that in historical development 'there are other aspects of human motivation that have nothing to do with economics', and that 'democracy is almost never chosen for economic reasons'.[29] Not only this, but even if the 'mechanism' of modern natural science and its necessary link to capitalism *were* proposed as the sole motor of historical change, this would only apply since the seventeenth-century Scientific Revolution. Also, there have been 'discontinuities' apparently contradicting, or at least interrupting, the meaningful flow of history (he cites the Holocaust in that light) which any satisfactory universal theory of history should also be able to accommodate.

Fukuyama thus declares the need to find a second and deeper 'Mechanism' on which to ground a truly Universal History, and claims to find it in Hegel. 'For Hegel, the primary motor of human history is not modern natural science or the ever expanding horizon of desire that powers it, but rather a totally non-economic drive, the *struggle for recognition*'.[30] This 'motor' not only allows us to account for the apparent 'discontinuities' in history occasioned by wars of e.g., religion and nationalism, but its Hegelian derivation also encourages us to view historical development as emerging from *contradictions* which are resolved by successively higher socio-political structures – i.e., what both Hegel and Marx called 'dialectics'. This is important for Fukuyama, since if history reaches a point where there are *no longer* any fundamental 'contradictions', then History is ended. In this light, Fukuyama asks, 'Are there any "contradictions" in our contemporary liberal democratic social order that would lead us to expect that the historical process will continue, and produce a new, higher order?'.[31] His answer is going to be 'no'.

Some preparatory reservations

In explaining why not, Fukuyama cites his enormous respect for the ideas of the mid-twentieth-century French-Russian philosopher, Alexandre Kojève, who built upon Hegel's ideas about 'the struggle for recognition', and concluded that 'the modern liberal democratic world . . . is free of contradictions', and that therefore 'we have reached the end of history because life in the universal and homogenous state is *completely satisfying* to its citizens'.[32] From this, it is fair to say that Fukuyama's book is both an update and an elaboration of Kojève's thesis, itself derived from the latter's reading of Hegel.

To further complicate the provenance of Fukuyama's central philosophical theme, he also claims to find the same essential idea about 'the struggle for recognition' in Plato's characterisation of that 'spirited' part of the soul, different from both its reasoning and its desiring part, which he termed '*thymos*' – the feature Plato thought should dominate the Guardian class of his *Republic*, since their function was to employ their public-spiritedness in fighting for the honour of the state.

In another context this somewhat complex sourcing of Fukuyama's key philosophical idea could occasion sustained critical comment, for it is by no means certain he has understood Hegel correctly, and his appeal to Plato could be seen as a forced argument. But because we should deal with Fukuyama's arguments as they stand (their origins strictly speaking being irrelevant to his thesis), let us straight away suggest where he might have misinterpreted and/or misused both Hegel and Plato, and then leave the matter at that.

Fukuyama makes much of Hegel's analysis of 'the bloody battle for recognition' by which the first men distinguished themselves from animals (see below). For Fukuyama this is quintessentially an example of 'spirit' in operation, and as Gourevitch rightly notes in a critical essay, Fukuyama simply treats Hegel's notion of 'Spirit' or '*Geist*' as 'collective human consciousness', thereby appearing 'fully to accept Kojève's utterly anthropologised Hegel' by neglecting any *transcendental* (or 'metaphysical') dimension to the latter's philosophy. This is so tendentious as to be seriously misleading to those unfamiliar with Hegel, and thus needs pointing out. We might add that in the same context it is curious that Fukuyama, having extracted what Hegel says about 'the struggle for recognition' from his *Phenomenology of Mind*, virtually ignores those two later works where Hegel himself directly addresses philosophy of history – namely, *The Philosophy of Right* and *The Philosophy of History*!

Similar concerns apply to Fukuyama's appeal to Plato's notion of *thymos* or 'spiritedness'. Gourevitch notes Fukuyama's 'apparent dismissal of the decisive difference between Socrates-Plato's "spiritedness" and Hegel-Kojève's "recognition"'.[33] To this serious complaint we might add that, whatever Plato meant by 'thymos', it never occurred to him that it was the key to understanding the motor of historical change! (A like complaint can be made of Fukuyama's reading of Hobbes's notion of 'glory', which with similar tendentiousness he again equates with a non-materialistic desire for 'recognition',[34] despite Hobbes' theory that men seek power for security, and that 'reputation' is merely one kind of 'power' amongst others.)

This said, we should acknowledge that Fukuyama himself recognises that the Hegel he takes from Kojève's interpretation might not be 'really Hegel as he understood himself', and has the candour to confess that in his appeal to Hegel (to which he could have added e.g., Plato and Hobbes) 'we will be more interested in the ideas themselves than in the philosophers who originally articulated them'.[35] Still somewhat disingenuous – (for *did* they articulate them?) – we should proceed by accepting the spirit of Fukuyama's remarks and focus on the idea of 'recognition' which *he* intuits.

'Spirit', thymos, the desire for recognition

After this necessary interlude, let us briefly re-locate our exposition. Because the 'mechanism' of modern science, although explaining capitalism, cannot explain liberal democracy, some other factor has been in play throughout history. Fukuyama claims to find this in that permanent, 'trans-historical', feature of human nature which he calls *the desire for recognition*.

To explain what he means he first refers to what he takes to be Hegel's account of 'the state of nature', where, from the beginning, man not only desired the physical objects necessary for survival and comfort, 'but also objects that are totally non-material'. Of the latter, and 'above all, he desires the desire of other men, that is, to be wanted by others or to be *recognised*'.[36] This is the very condition of man being *self*-conscious – i.e., that he is recognised by others, such that 'his own sense of self-worth and identity is intimately connected with the value that other people place on him'.

But this impulse goes deeper, for man is (allegedly) different from animals not only in seeking recognition from others, but this recognition must revolve around what makes him *human* – and what makes man *human* is his preparedness to risk his life in defence of his sense of worth. 'In the beginning' there thus ensues a 'bloody battle' between men where 'each contestant seeks to make the other "recognise" him by risking his own life'. Either both die, one dies, or 'the battle can terminate in the relationship of lordship and bondage, in which one of the contestants decides to submit to a life of slavery rather than face the risk of violent death'.[37] The master has thus achieved recognition of his willingness to risk his life 'for pure prestige', and this struggle of 'self-creation' is 'the first authentically human act'. But, says Fukuyama, 'it is far from the last', for it clearly 'leaves us still a very long way from modern liberal democracy'. Rather, 'the problem of human history can be seen . . . as the search for a way to satisfy the desire of *both* masters and slaves for recognition on a mutual and equal basis; history ends with the victory of a social order that accomplishes this goal'.[38]

Fukuyama thus puts an enormous weight upon 'the desire for recognition' as a motor behind the socio-political evolution of human history – and partly because he is aware that, as a foundation for political order, this feature is alien to the thinking behind the Western liberal-democratic tradition as it emerged from the 'social contract' theories of, particularly, Hobbes and Locke, he devotes an interesting chapter to explaining the difference. Uncontroversially, Fukuyama points out that the 'social contract' theory centres on a one-dimensional view of man which sees him as a rational being pursuing his own self-interest – the latter, in addition, being construed (narrowly) in terms of self-preservation and material welfare. But for Fukuyama this results in liberal society's 'most typical product', the *bourgeois* individual, who does 'not need to be public-spirited, patriotic, or concerned for the welfare of those around him',[39] and he asks whether there is 'not something deeply contemptible about a man who cannot raise his sights' to the 'noble passions of patriotism, courage, generosity, and public-spiritedness?'. There is, then, something higher in human nature – namely, that *moral* dimension whereby throughout history man has repeatedly shown himself capable of risking his life 'for an objective or principle that lies beyond the body'. Hegel called it 'Freedom', Fukuyama derives it from 'the desire for recognition', and he repeats that 'it is this moral dimension, and the struggle to have it recognised, that is the motor driving the dialectical process of history'.[40]

Given its importance, Fukuyama elaborates further upon this aspect of human nature, claiming it is a notion 'as old as Western political philosophy itself', Plato having first analysed it as *thymos*.[41] In Plato's tripartite division of the soul, to appetite and reason is added the sense of *self-esteem*, which, when trampled upon, generates anger. As Fukuyama sees it, in explaining the powerful relationship between self-esteem, the sense of indignation, and the self-disregarding anger which follows, '*thymos* is something like an innate human sense of justice', the desire that we should be recognised 'according to our own estimate of our worth'. As such, 'Plato's thymos is therefore nothing other than the psychological seat of Hegel's desire for recognition',[42] and Fukuyama goes on to give what (for him) is a telling example of it at work in recent times. Under the communist regimes of Eastern Europe people were daily faced with having to make moral compromises – e.g., saying things they did not believe in, remaining silent while colleagues were persecuted – in order to carry on their lives. This affront to the 'thymotic' part of their nature caused them a sense of humiliation and indignation, and it was this, according to Havel, who became president of Czechoslovakia in 1989, which was the chief factor in the failure of communism to satisfy its citizens: not a failure to satisfy 'economic' man, but the failure to satisfy man's moral longing for justice and esteem. Thus, for Fukuyama, 'the desire for recognition has . . . played a critical role in bringing about the anti-communist earthquake in the Soviet Union, Eastern Europe, and China'.[43]

Pursuing this, Fukuyama not only attacks communist states for suppressing *thymos* in their citizens, but claims this defect 'pervades many aspects of day-to-day life that we commonly think of as economic', including in liberal democratic states.

Again criticising the (utilitarian) 'social contract' theory, he says that 'the good political order needs to be something more than a mutual non-aggression pact'. Rather, 'it must also satisfy man's just desire for recognition of his dignity and worth',[44] and thus provide outlets for the nobler virtues of courage, moral integrity, and public-spiritedness. Indeed, so accustomed have we become to overlooking these human instincts derived from *thymos*, and instead concentrating on the combination of desire and reason which delineate *economic* man, we risk neglecting the immense role the former plays in history. For example, wage struggles are not only about material wealth, but also about status; revolutions are not so much caused by poverty but by the rising expectations generated as people compare their already developing societies with wealthy countries, 'and grow angry as a result'. Fukuyama applies this to the 1789 French Revolution, and observes that 'in the contemporary world, only the poorest and richest countries tend to be stable'.[45] Likewise, the American Civil War cannot be interpreted on economic grounds. The goals of the opposing sides concerned their respective senses of *identity*, partly related to the slavery issue and their respective ways of life. In the same vein Fukuyama points to many issues of contemporary American politics – e.g., abortion, racism, civil rights in general – which have little real economic content, instead being 'thymotic contests over recognition of competing understandings of justice and human dignity'.[46]

For Fukuyama, all such scenarios demonstrate a crucial feature of *thymos* – namely, that it can extend from individuals seeking recognition for their *own* worth to seeking recognition for *other* peoples' worth, often of one's own grouping (e.g., ethnicity), but also of those to which one does not belong (e.g., the international anti-apartheid movement). Indeed, we should recognise the complex psychology by which the essentially self-assertive character of *thymos* leads to the struggle to indeed *impose* one's own moral values on others, and not confuse such situations with the simple pursuit of self-interest.

The graphically archetypal exemplar of all these aspects of *thymos* are represented, for Fukuyama, by the pictures of the lone man confronting a tank in Tiananmen Square during the 1989 student protests in Beijing. Since then, however, others might point more ominously to the relentless series of suicide bombings by Palestinians on Israeli 'targets' or, of course, the suicide plane attacks on New York and Washington on 11 September 2001, as confirmation of the notion that in their 'struggle for recognition' some are prepared not only to risk their lives, but to give them.

Megalothymia

If the last remarks point to an alarming aspect to *thymos*, (unless one construed such acts as its *perversion*), Fukuyama himself now introduces a qualification to his concept of *thymos* which is to play a crucial role in his philosophy of history. Having so far presented *thymos* 'as the source of . . . noble virtues', he urges that 'there is a dark side to the desire for recognition as well, . . . that has led many philosophers to believe that *thymos* is the fundamental source of human evil'.[47] This is the desire in some people not to be regarded as *equal* to others, but as *superior*. This passion (for it can become such) exhibits itself as much 'in the concert pianist who wants to be recognised as the foremost interpreter of Beethoven' as it does 'in the tyrant who invades and enslaves a neighbouring people so that they will recognise his authority',[48] and Fukuyama terms it '*megalothymia*'. (He thus finds a new term for the *benign* form of thymos, where one simply demands *equal* respect – namely, '*isothymia*'). But it is indeed in *political* life 'that *megalothymia* is a highly problematic passion', for it has spawned 'the tyrannical ambition of a Caesar or a Stalin', and Fukuyama interprets much Western political thought as trying to address the dangers it poses to societies (e.g., concerns about imperialism in the Middle Ages, Machiavelli's concept of 'glory', and early-modern liberal thinkers who saw in the development of *commercial* societies a way of curbing the warlike passion of princes and the aristocratic class).[49]

As the desire for greatness, *megalothymia* has thus played a crucial role in historical political life. Indeed, Fukuyama goes so far as to claim that if we paid proper attention to the twin sides of 'the desire for recognition', *megalothymia* and *isothymia*, it would suggest 'a very different way of reading the historical process, not as the story of the unfolding of modern natural science or of the logic of economic development, but rather as the emergence, growth, and eventual decline of *megalothymia*'.[50]

But, for Fukuyama, regrettably we do not pay attention to it. Why not? Precisely because 'in terms of what we say about ourselves, [*megalothymia*] has been ethically vanquished in the modern world'. He suggests two reasons for this. First, he refers to the 'thorough-going *economisation* of life', through which the desiring part of the soul has ousted *megalothymia* in our materialist, consumer cultures. Second, it has been eclipsed in modern times by the *other* side to *thymos*, namely, *isothymia*. If the language of glory and superiority has become politically incorrect, 'words like "dignity", "respect", "self-respect", and "self-esteem" . . . permeate our political life and are indispensable to an understanding of the democratic transformation that has occurred around the world in the late twentieth century'.

Isothymia

Fukuyuma suggests that this contemporary dominance of *isothymia* might, in fact, be seen as representing a *failure* on behalf of 'the founders of the Anglo-Saxon tradition of modern liberalism', because they had 'sought to banish *thymos* from political life' altogether. But this would be to equate that utilitarian 'social contract' basis to liberalism with more contemporary liberalism. The latter, according to Fukuyama, does not suppress *thymos* altogether, but 'tries to preserve the thymotic side of the human personality rather than exiling it from the realm of politics'.[51] It does this by fulfilling *isothymia*, and this achievement offers us a higher understanding of the nature of modern liberal democracy – i.e., the 'universal and homogenous state' with its universal citizenship and equality of rights.

The exploration of this logic reverts Fukuyama to Hegel. If, 'in the beginning', the 'bloody battle for recognition' led to lordship and bondage, that situation could not hold. In winning the prestige battle, the master is recognised by the slave. But the slave failed to achieve his *own* humanity 'due to his having given in to his natural fear of death', and thus 'the master's worth is therefore recognised by someone not quite human'.[52] The master's desire for recognition as human is to that extent unsatisfied, although in pre-modern history he often tried to satisfy it by warring with other masters.

However, Fukuyama is more interested in the slave's mentality. The slave is also unsatisfied, but in his case this leads to 'creative and enriching change'. The reasons for this centre on what the slave does – namely, *work*. Although forced to work, his motive eventually changes from one of fear of punishment to one of 'a sense of duty and self-discipline' – i.e., a work-ethic. This involves suppressing his animal desires, and is thus a humanising factor in his experience. The latter develops as the slave realises he can transform the materials of nature into 'something else based on a pre-existing idea or concept',[53] and it is this freedom to create, outside the constraints of natural need, which confirms man's *human* nature. Thus, the slave conceives of the idea of freedom from, and mastery over, nature, and its connection with what it is to be human.

Not yet *actually* free from his master, however, the slave is thus limited to 'philosophising' about freedom and being truly human, this resulting in various slave ideologies such as Stoicism and Scepticism – but the most important of them was Christianity, because it 'was the first to establish the principle of the universal equality of all men in the sight of God, on the basis of their faculty for moral choice'. As Fukuyama puts it, 'the thymotic sense of self-worth . . . has something in common with the inner dignity and freedom of the Christian believer', whilst 'the Kingdom of Heaven . . . presents the prospect of a world in which the *isothymia* of every man – though not the *megalothymia* of the vainglorious – will be satisfied'. As in Hegel, then, for Fukuyama, Christianity's contribution to the development of history was immense because of its humanising effect on people's consciousness – particularly, of course, the lower orders' longing for equal recognition.

But the other side to Christianity, as a 'slave' ideology, is to *reconcile* 'real-world slaves to their lack of freedom by telling them not to expect liberation in this life'.[54] What Christianity proffered as a hope it took away in reality, and what was required was the final recognition that God was *man's* creation, and that man was merely subjecting himself to a new form of slavery insofar as he bowed down in self-abnegation before 'God'. Extraordinarily, Fukuyama offers the latter ideas as Hegel's, whereas most commentators would identify them as distinctive to Hegel's severe *critic*, Feuerbach, who argued that man's idea of God was in fact man's idea of the potential of his *own* species (an idea taken up by the young Marx). Be this as it may, what was required for the 'completion of the historical process' whereby 'the free and autonomous individual . . . is recognised universally and reciprocally by all men', was 'a secularisation of Christianity, that is, a translation of the

Christian idea of freedom into the here-and-now'. But this fulfilment (as Marx would have pointed out) could not come about simply by a revolution in *thought* (that is, although Fukuyama does not *expressly* say so, by the abandoning of the Christian *religion*), but also 'required one more bloody battle, the battle in which the slave liberates himself from the master'.[55] And, as in Hegel, for Fukuyama this was the significance of the 1789 French Revolution, which, if it did not complete the process all at once, heralded its fulfilment.

The point for Fukuyama of the above analysis of *thymos* and its two constituents, *megalothymia* and *isothymia*, is fourfold. First, he has identified a second 'mechanism' in addition to the irreversible progress of modern natural science. The latter culminates *economically* in capitalist societies, and he concedes it only really applies to roughly the last four hundred years, whereas the motor of *thymos* applies to history from the earliest times. Second, the latter drives the *political* development of societies, thus explaining factors and 'discontinuities' in history which cannot be explained on a purely utilitarian or economic basis. Third, it provides 'the missing link between liberal economics and liberal politics', such that we can better understand why the two have (eventually) come to operate in tandem in the modern world. And fourth, analysis of the logic underlying *thymos* vindicates the notion that, if capitalism is the *final* form of *economic* evolution, so liberal democracy is the *final* form of its *political* evolution, thus completing his 'end of history' thesis.

Fukuyama, however, recognises this *last* assertion as particularly controversial, and thus proceeds to defend it. Rightly, the issue for him is not so much whether, *empirically*, liberal democracies abound and are still gaining ground in today's world, but whether on *philosophical* grounds their form, 'the universal and homogenous state', is indeed 'the last stage in human history because it [is] *completely satisfying* to man',[56] thereby not only resolving earlier 'contradictions' but ensuring no *new* ones emerge to change history *further*. This leads him to elaborate on the (*thymotic*) logic behind liberal democracy, and to explore 'both the prospects and limitations of the current worldwide liberal revolution'[57] to see whether that logic is indeed working in practice.

Because his exploration of this involves him in a sustained analysis of the *current* world and, indeed, its future prospects, we might almost say that the remainder of his book is more devoted to contemporary political philosophy, his speculative philosophy of history having been completed by this point. This is partly true, but because his exploration is so intimately informed by his preceding philosophy (in fact, constituting his vindication of it) then, in shedding further light on it, it is worthwhile following the principal points he makes.

The contemporary world

Thymos *and liberal democracy*

First, Fukuyama defends his equation of liberal democracy with what he has called 'the universal and homogenous state'. Whereas 'Hobbesian or Lockean liberalism can be interpreted as the pursuit of rational self-interest', contemporary liberalism (following Hegel) 'can be seen as the pursuit of *rational recognition*, that is, recognition on a universal basis in which the dignity of each person as a free and autonomous person is recognised by all'.[58] The properly liberal state does just this. It is *universal* because it 'grant[s] recognition to all its citizens because they are human beings, and not because they are members of some particular national, ethnic, or racial group'. And it is *homogenous* because 'it creates a classless society based on the abolition of the distinction between master and slaves'. Lastly it is *rational* insofar as 'the authority of the state does not arise out of age-old tradition or from the murky depths of religious faith', but from citizens' explicit agreement on the terms by which they live together.[59] These key features of liberal democracy are exemplified in the *equal rights* such societies attribute to citizens, amongst which Fukuyama cites the right to life, property, freedom of expression, and political participation (voting, standing for office, etc.) although it is perhaps significant that he does not refer to that clarion call represented by *The Universal Declaration of Human Rights* (1948), nor the *European Convention on Human Rights* (1950), possibly because the former is a United Nations document (and he has his doubts about the UN) and the latter, similarly sourced, also contains extra 'rights' which some argue cannot be truly 'universal'.[60]

Second, however, Fukuyama recognises that liberal democracy has not yet become universal around the world despite his claim that, apart from the Islamic world, there is 'a general consensus' on the superiority of liberal democratic *ideology*. Moreover, even where states *are* liberal-democratic, they are not always stable as such. The reason for these obstacles 'lies ultimately in the incomplete correspondence between peoples and states'.[61] 'Peoples' are *cultural* phenomena, with their own distinctive customs, religions, family structures, and the like – and, as such, they are 'sub-political', whilst 'states impose themselves on top of peoples' and 'in many cases sit in uneasy tension' with them.

In short, however 'rational' the liberal-democratic state is, it 'requires a degree of conformity' between its ideals and the pre-existing cultural and moral characteristics of its people.[62] The latter are features coming from the *thymotic* part of human nature, and Fukuyama thus suggests existing liberal democracies should take care to inculcate in their citizens 'a certain irrational thymotic pride in their political system and way of life',[63] rather than relying for stability on their capacity to deliver economic prosperity and equal rights. As for countries not yet democratic, cultural factors such as highly developed nationalism, illiberal religions, or long-standing severe class hierarchies, constitute sources of resistance to their full democratisation. However, Fukuyama disagrees with the view that liberal democracy depends *necessarily* on certain cultural prerequisites, for a people's culture *can* change over time – and in any event he believes it can in fact be advantageous to *preserve* facets of 'sub-political' culture within liberal democracies as a way of enriching the *thymotic* basis to their otherwise somewhat coldly liberal-rationalistic states.

Thymos *and economics*

If the influence of the *thymotic* phenomenon of 'culture' is crucial in assessing the stability and future prospects of liberal democracy, so it is in considering *capitalism's* stability as an *economic* system, and its prospects for world-wide adoption. This is important because not only is capitalism the effect of one of Fukuyama's two 'mechanisms' of historical development – i.e., modern natural science. Also, 'the strong correlation between advanced industrialisation and democracy' suggests that if capitalism is not stable then liberal democracy is also at risk.

Here, Fukuyama's prime concern is again to challenge the purely utilitarian-based understanding of societies – but in this case applied to their economies. Centred on *work* as the source of production and consumption, the economic world can be construed solely in terms of 'reason satisfying desire' – and granted the universal desire for wealth, it might seem that differing government policies are therefore the sole factor determining economic development. But for Fukuyama this would be to ignore the crucial role *thymos* plays in economic life.

He observes that 'most successful modern economies may be capitalist', but 'not all capitalist economies are successful – or, at any rate, as successful as others'.[64] The reason for this implicates *thymos*, for he argues that 'culture affects economic behaviour in certain critical ways just as it affects the ability of a people to sustain liberal democracy', citing such examples as 'the superior economic performance . . . of the Jews in Europe, the Chinese on Southeast Asia', and, in the USA, the contrast between 'the descendants of blacks who voluntarily immigrated from the West Indies, and those who were brought directly to the country from Africa as slaves'.[65] These differences are not explicable via simple economic motivation, but 'are determined by culture and custom, and are therefore related in some way to *thymos*'.[66]

One such way is the relation between different religions and their respective 'work-ethics'. For instance, the 'Protestant work-ethic', whereby work was seen as 'a "calling" which the believer hoped would reflect his status as either saved or damned', can be contrasted with the *discouraging* ethos of the Hindu religion's sanctification of poverty for the lower castes, which Fukuyama suggests 'induces . . . a certain kind of "this-wordly" torpor and inertia which is in many respects the opposite of the spirit of capitalism'.[67] Interestingly, he speculates whether, as countries such as USA and Japan become increasingly secularised, and thus divorced from their respective cultural roots, their work-ethics might be undermined by the 'consumer society', leading to 'an undermining of capitalism itself'.[68] On the other hand, *thymotic* motives other than religious belief, such as working for the good of one's family, or (as in many parts of Asia) in the interests of group loyalty, may counteract this potential threat to economic stability in capitalist economies, and Fukuyama concludes the theme by suggesting the most obvious fact is the comparative failure of many *Third* World countries to make capitalism work. Correct policies would help, but '"irrational" forms of *thymos* – religion, nationalism, the ability . . . to maintain standards and pride in work – continue to influence economic behaviour in countless ways that contribute to the wealth or poverty of nations'.[69] Because of this, he claims substantial international differences between countries' economic performance will remain a feature in the world-scene – but no longer because of *ideological* differences (the ideology of capitalism having triumphed): rather, because of *cultural* factors relating to *thymos*.

Now, Fukuyama argues, *because* the differing cultures of countries affect their economic performance, this impinges upon that crucial link between capitalism and liberal democracy which underpins his notion of 'the end of history'. Where economic progress towards capitalism is impeded by cultural factors, so therefore are the prospects of a country's becoming liberal-democratic in its politics. Instead, 'some new authoritarian alternatives, perhaps never before seen in history, may assert themselves in the future'. He claims this has already happened in the case of the revival of Islamic fundamentalism in countries such as Iran, where 'illiberal doctrines' have emerged 'out of economic failure'. He interprets this in *thymotic* terms, viewing it 'as a response to the failure of Muslim societies generally to maintain their dignity vis-a-vis the non-Muslim West',[70] (although he claims that the ideological 'revival' is more an invention of some *alleged* past rather than a reassertion of authentic 'traditional' Muslim values).

But, he adds, the same lack of correspondence between capitalism and liberal democracy (involving *cultural* factors) can occur because of economic success rather than failure – e.g., those many Asian countries whose retention of aspects of their non-democratic political culture worked to their advantage as they embarked on economic modernisation and capitalism. Their 'tremendous economic success' stemmed from their combining 'liberal economics with a kind of paternalistic authoritarianism',[71] and Fukuyama warns that a number of factors, especially the manner in which the West treats Asian societies *attitudinally*, may conspire to encourage 'a systematic illiberal and non-democratic alternative combining technical economic rationalism with paternalistic authoritarianism . . . in the Far East'.[72]

Overall, from these analyses of the linkages between capitalism, liberal-democracy, and the thymotic phenomenon of 'culture', Fukuyama concludes that, in principle, 'important differences between states will remain' because, although the current world has witnessed 'the victory of the universal and homogenous state', leaving behind earlier politico-economic forms, in practice 'the possible interpretations of the surviving forms, capitalism and liberal democracy, continue to be varied'.[73] In short, although 'the end of history' may point in theory to the eventual *literal* emergence of a one-world 'universal and homogenous' state, Fukuyama recognises that the present reality of a world comprising numerous different states will continue into the future.

Because of this, the realm of *international relations* will continue into 'the end of history', and Fukuyama is thus rightly prompted into considering whether their prognosis could indeed *contradict* his thesis by provoking some *new* stage of historical development (either of a higher order, or some kind of *reverse* of history, as in cyclical theories). I say 'rightly prompted' because, although historians rarely think in the manner and scope of Fukuyama – i.e., speculative philosophy of history – nevertheless, of the few 'general rules' most *would* admit to accepting is this: that *war* is the greatest harbinger of historical change. This lends extra urgency to how successfully Fukuyama incorporates the problem of international relations into 'the end of history'.

International relations and war

He begins by saying that, if history is indeed uni-directional, then what 'the universal and homogenous state' means for individuals *within* states – equal recognition and the abolition of lordship and bondage – should apply to relationships *between* states; namely, the end of imperialism and the wars associated with it. (Fukuyama often uses 'imperialism' to encompass *any* warlike activities.) However, he is aware of the many *realpolitik* theories about international relations which claim 'that insecurity is a universal and permanent feature of the international order, due to the latter's abidingly anarchic character'.[74] Such 'realist' assumptions dictate the necessity of states' preparedness for war, as well as strategies to avoid it – including alliances and the maintenance of a 'balance of power', exemplified in the Cold War. Such is the grip of 'realpolitik' upon international strategists that Fukuyama ruefully observes that, even after the circumstances provoking the Cold War were over (with the collapse of the Soviet Union), many regretted the disappearance of bipolar Europe and feared a period of great instability.

Fukuyama rejects this perspective on international relations because, for him, it is based on the *unrealistic* and simplistic notion that neither human nature nor societies' motivations ever change. In a (contentious) interpretation of Hobbes' 'state of nature', he suggests instead that 'in an anarchic international order' there is 'absolutely no reason to assume that any state should feel threatened by another state',[75] unless one were to believe that people, and states, are inherently aggressive. According to Fukuyama, they are not. Rather, what provokes war *within* societies, and *between* them, is not the instinct for self-preservation but more the *desire for recognition* taking the form of wishing to impose one's, or a society's, views upon another – i.e., *megaloythmia*. In history, he claims, war has been such a prevalent feature because some states have been 'like giant thymotic individuals' who 'seek acknowledgement of their value or dignity on dynastic, religious, nationalist, or ideological grounds, and in the process force other states either to fight or to submit'. This, then, 'is the original source of imperialism' and 'the ultimate ground of war among states . . ., [i.e.] *thymos* rather than self-preservation'.[76]

But not all states behave in such ways. Although it might be true that all states seek 'power' (to achieve their national objectives), this is to employ a notion of 'power' so elastic – incorporating economic expansion, colonisation *and* decolonisation, prestige – as to rob it of any analytic value. What is clear, rather, is that the *maximising* of their 'power', particularly in its *military* form, is by no means a universal feature of states' behaviour – and Fukuyama cites contemporary Canada, Spain, Holland, and Mexico as examples.

Thus, rather than interpret international relations and the history of war as simply an endemic 'power-game', Fukuyama points instead to the influence of the concept of *legitimacy* and its connection to *thymos*. The notion of 'self-respect' and the desire to be esteemed by others has always played a crucial role in states' behaviour – either, as in some modern examples of decolonisation, to reduce aggression and domination, or, as in earlier times, to legitimate imperialistic ventures whose logic extends to the achievement of a world-empire. In the latter case, 'the striving of princes for universal but *unequal* recognition was widely regarded as legitimate', and for Fukuyama exemplifies the *megalothymia* which characterised *aristocracy*-based societies which dominated history for so long. The wars that ensued were not only, nor solely, about *territorial* conquest. Some were about imposing religious beliefs, e.g., as late as in the sixteenth and seventeenth centuries in Europe. In their case, they were finally ended, as were the attitudes legitimising them, by 'the bourgeois revolution' which,

> sought to morally elevate the slave's fear of death over the aristocratic virtue of the master, and thereby to sublimate irrational manifestations of *thymos* like princely ambition and religious fanaticism into the unlimited accumulation of property.[77]

In short, the civil peace which accompanied the eventual emergence of liberal, commercial societies 'should logically have its counterpart in relations between states', because 'imperialism and war were historically the product of aristocratic societies',[78] and Fukuyama notes 'the fundamentally un-warlike character of liberal societies . . . evident in the extraordinarily peaceful relations they maintain among one another', citing studies which claim 'few, if any, instances of one liberal democracy going to war with another'. This, he suggests, is because 'in such states *megalothymia* has found other outlets besides war, or else has atrophied'.[79] Indeed, such is the 'thoroughly bourgeois character of life in present-day Europe' that it is unthinkable that its states will return to 'the competitive great power behaviour of the nineteenth century'.

This, however, does not rule out liberal democracies fighting wars against *non-liberal* regimes, and this of course occurred precisely in the twentieth century, which showed that 'history's most destructive wars have in fact occurred *since* the bourgeois revolution'. One explanation is that, at least earlier in the century, despite the liberal-bourgeois revolution which Europe had mainly achieved, its ruling classes were still drawn from the aristocracy, 'for whom concepts of national greatness and glory had not been displaced by commerce'. But Fukuyama suggests a deeper reason 'drawn directly from the history of *thymos*'; namely, that 'between the older forms of recognition represented by dynastic and religious ambition, and the fully modern resolution it finds in the universal and homogenous state, *thymos* can take the form of nationalism'.[80] The latter not only 'had much to do with the wars' of the twentieth century but, writing in the early 1990s, Fukuyama claims that nationalism's resurgence continues to threaten the peace of post-communist Europe. This powerful force thus needs to be understood. In particular, the above implication that it is only a *transitional* phenomenon which will eventually disappear at 'the end of history' is one he sets about considering.

Nationalism

Fukuyama begins by claiming that nationalism 'is a specifically modern phenomenon' because *within* a country it involves 'mutual and equal recognition' between citizens. Yet nationalism is not fully 'rational' because 'the dignity nationalists seeks to have recognised is not universal human dignity, but dignity for their group'.[81] Thus, it remains a source of war because representing the incomplete sublimation of 'the master's *megalothymia*'. Although he had said earlier that '*megalothymia* – the desire to be recognised as superior – has been ethically vanquished in the modern world',[82] it would appear that this is not entirely the case. Some states still act 'like giant thymotic individuals', and they do so under the influence of nationalism.

But this need not continue as some ineradicable feature of human nature and international relations. Rather, nationalism is a specifically *historical* phenomenon related to those circumstances in modern history when a society, 'having gone through the first phases of economic modernisation, is denied both national identity and political freedom'[83] – and just as, in Fukuyama's judgement, the 'combination of liberalism and economic self-interest . . . *vanquished religion in Europe*', such that religion has been ousted from politics and instead 'relegated to the sphere of private life', so the same combination can 'defang' and 'modernise' nationalism. In short, *political* nationalism can become *cultural* nationalism, where 'national groups can retain their separate languages and senses of identity',[84] but express no political intolerance whatever towards other nationalities and countries. Again, the very *historicity* (and thus transitoriness) of nationalism is demonstrated by the circumstances in which it resurfaced to disturb the peace in the 1990s in Eastern Europe, where 'national and ethnic groups long denied a voice express[ed] themselves in favour of sovereignty and independent existence', and Fukuyama concedes that 'the breakup of long-standing multi-ethnic states promises to be a violent and bloody affair',[85] just as was the 'almost virtually triumphant' rise of Third World nationalism which drove the French 'out of Vietnam and Algeria, the

USA out of Vietnam, the Soviets out of Afghanistan, the Libyans out of Chad, the Vietnamese out of Cambodia, and so forth'.

Fukuyama recognises the understandable intensity of nationalism in such contexts, but again complains of the shortsightedness of those who thus believe it will continue as a permanent feature in world affairs. Rather, those same forces which originally fostered it – democratisation breaking down class barriers and economic modernisation creating 'centralised, linguistically homogenous' societies – are leaving nationalism behind them in many parts of the world, as they now encourage 'the creation of a single, integrated world market', such that sooner or later history will see 'the final political neutralisation of nationalism' altogether.[86]

In the meantime, however, where industrialisation and nationalism are late arrivals – principally the Third World – nationalism will still provoke wars. Indeed, Fukuyama suggests that in these regions there will not only be nationalist conflicts, but also religious and ideological ones. And this prompts him to introduce a bold vocabulary, albeit one perfectly in line with his overall thesis – namely, the notion that at present the world is divided into a *post-historical* part and an *historical* part, the latter being 'still stuck in history'.[87] The post-historical world (of liberal-democratic states with capitalist economies) will still be divided into nation-states, but they will remain at peace because nationalism's political fangs have been drawn.

Indeed, such is the difference between the post-historical and historical worlds that, although 'the boundary line . . . is changing rapidly and is therefore hard to draw',[88] Fukuyama suggests they will have comparatively little to do with each other – except, that is, where they collide. And this is likely to happen over oil, immigration, and 'world-order' issues such as the proliferation of weapons of mass destruction and environmental threats. To the extent such collisions involve the historical world using the 'realist' strategy of power-politics, the post-historical world must be prepared to use the same methods in defence. However, Fukuyama is quite clear that the latter should not go on the military *offensive* in order to spread itself further around the planet. Rather, he urges that peace is best procured by the post-historical states relying on the principles of democratic legitimacy and the manner in which they 'satisfy the human longing for recognition'.[89] Writing in the early 1990s it is interesting to note his assertion: 'No one, of course, would advocate a policy of military challenge to non-democratic states armed with powerful weapons, especially nuclear ones';[90] and his urging that human rights issues should not be shelved to 'accommodate' states in the historical world, nor if having to engage militarily with them.

Rather, liberal-democratic states should keep banging the *ideological* drum, by which means they can better hope both to keep international peace and promote liberal democracy elsewhere – a mutually enhancing strategy.

The end of history?

The preceding section has explored Fukuyama's estimation of how far a *factual* analysis of the *present* world vindicates his theory of history. But just as it has not been strictly to our purpose to follow exhaustively all the examples his impressive survey embraces, neither has it been to challenge his judgements. Rather, the section has been germane because it has revealed further insights into his overall philosophy of history. First, his survey involved him in many *historical* examples of his concrete application, in particular, of *thymos* to actual societies, bringing this otherwise 'philosophical' concept to life. But also he has quite properly raised and considered many possible objections to his theory which that survey might suggest. For example, he concedes that 'cultural' factors can interfere with the link that otherwise operates between economic modernisation and liberal democracy, such that new authoritarian types of regime might emerge – and, for example, his view that political nationalism is by no means a spent force. To that extent he is prepared to be self-critical about his notion of 'the end of history', reserving that status at present to the 'post-historical' world. However, this self-criticism does not extend to his having to concede that the 'historical' world is *not* subject to the same irreversible 'mechanisms' of development in the long run. On the contrary, he uses his notion of '*thymos*' precisely to *explain* why certain states lag behind in that recalcitrant world – but also why the vast majority of the world *will* indeed arrive at liberal democracy and free-market capitalism.

What doubts Fukuyama expresses, then, are not about the efficacy of his two 'mechanisms'. Rather, they concern his claim that the (presently dominant) 'post-historical' world will remain for evermore essentially *unchanged*. It is *this* aspect of his overall theory which has attracted most controversy, particularly since Fukuyama has been simplistically portrayed as promoting its unassailable truth. But this is a misrepresentation. The matter is less than certain in his mind. There are strong elements in his theory to sustain that thesis, but in his view these same elements could also point to its being a fallacy. In short, he thinks he has got the *mechanisms* of history right, but is it 'the *end* of history'?

Fukuyama devotes the last part of his book to considering this in terms of two interrelated questions. Is liberal democracy desirable *in itself* as fully satisfying? And, are there 'contradictions' still inherent in liberal democracy which would leave history unfinished?

The challenge from the Left

He first reminds us of that other 'mechanism' driving history in addition to *thymos*, – namely, modern science fulfilling *economic* desire, and asks whether these two mechanisms may not *collide* rather than collude. The Left, he maintains, can be interpreted as implying they do, because the *economic* inequalities endemic to capitalism leave 'the promise of universal, reciprocal recognition . . . essentially unfulfilled in liberal societies'. Fukuyama concedes that problems of inequality are indeed 'in a certain sense, unresolvable within the context of liberalism',[91] but he does not regard them as sufficiently serious as to constitute the kind of *fundamental* 'contradiction' liable to foster historical change. He argues that some inequalities are the result of 'convention' – e.g., legal barriers such as apartheid, and cultural barriers such as racism. Difficult in particular as are the latter kind, nevertheless 'all truly liberal societies are in principle dedicated to the elimination of conventional sources of inequality',[92] and he cites the extent to which racism, sexism, and homophobia are now high profile issues being addressed – so much so, indeed, that the passion shown in 'democratic America' to completely eliminate 'any vestiges of inequality' are in fact a tribute to 'the smallness of its actual remaining inequalities'.[93]

The other source of inequality is nature itself – i.e., 'the unequal distribution of natural abilities and attributes'. Some of these are simply ineradicable, such as differences in artistic ability, whilst others are exploited by the rational division of labour demanded by capitalist economics, which cannot function 'without creating winners and losers' because capital must be free to shift its location. Fukuyama views this as simply a *necessity* of capitalism – and in any event, he insists that capitalist societies are in fact 'far more egalitarian in their social effects than the agricultural societies they replaced'.[94]

These factors, then, mitigate the inequalities in liberal democratic, capitalist societies. However, says Fukuyama, there is one kind of inequality which cannot be mitigated, and remains serious – namely, that deriving from the occupational division of labour. The inequality of wealth associated with different jobs under capitalism 'will continue to fail to satisfy the human desire for equal recognition, or *isothymia*'. But for Fukuyama this is not so much a matter of income as of *dignity*. Basic social welfare provisions feature in all liberal societies, even the USA, such that 'the problem of poverty has been transformed from one of natural need, into one of recognition. The real injury . . . done to poor or homeless people is less to their physical well-being than to their dignity', as is also the case with the differing degrees of respect accorded to, e.g., garbage men and brain surgeons. Because of this, Fukuyama concludes that 'major social inequalities will remain even in the most perfect of liberal societies', such that 'there will be a continuing tension between the twin principles of liberty and equality'.

He believes we should accept this as simply 'necessary and inevitable',[95] but is aware that others do not. Rather than encourage such dissenters, however, Fukuyama identifies them as exemplifying what he sees as the Left-wing urge to get rid of *all* inequality – and he warns this is a *threat* to liberal democracy itself.

His argument centres on the notion of 'equal rights', concerning which he bemoans 'the incoherence in our current discourse'. Echoing debates about the concept of universal human rights, Fukuyama complains of the 'massive proliferation of new "rights"', which extend far beyond their traditional compass of the right to life, liberty, and property, into such areas as privacy, abortion, and travel, where they become 'ambiguous in their social content and mutually contradictory'.[96] In pushing for such proliferation, the Left is in danger of *obscuring* that which vindicates human rights, namely, their function in protecting what it is to be *human*. For Fukuyama, this is man's *dignity*, inseparable from his capacity to make moral choices. But not only, according to him, is this fundamental perception or 'philosophy' neglected by most people, there is no current consensus on what *makes* man human. The danger is that not only is it claimed there are not, or should not be, *any* differences between human beings, neither should there be between human beings and animals, for whence comes human superiority? The animal rights movement, for example, argues cases where they believe animals have as much right to exist and prosper as human beings have, because they too can suffer *pain*. But, as Fukuyama puts it, why stop the argument there? In perfectly respectable philosophical fashion, he pushes the point *ad absurdum* to reveal its weakness. Perhaps the HIV virus can suffer, and should therefore be accorded 'equal rights' to human beings? In short, unless we can say why man has 'more dignity than any [other] part of the natural world', then 'the liberal concept of an equal and universal humanity with a specifically human dignity'[97] will in effect be under attack – the implication being, who knows what kind of society would then replace liberal democracy?

The challenge from the Right

Although the Left may be correct in complaining of 'the more intractable forms of inequality'[98] in liberal society (whereby, Fukuyama's concedes, *isothymia* remains unfulfilled because it still affords the unequal recognition of equal people), the obfuscation introduced by the Left's confusedly extravagant proliferation of alleged 'equal rights' suggests to him that the threat it poses to liberal democracy need not be taken too seriously. Rather, he argues, 'the greater and ultimately more serious threat comes from the Right'. This is because there is another side to the *isothymia* coin in liberal-democratic societies – namely, their 'tendency to grant *equal* recognition to *unequal* people'.[99]

Here, Fukuyama turns to the ideas of the Prussian philosopher, Friedrich Nietzsche (1844–1900), who influenced many by claiming that 'God is dead', and that the Christian values of humility and kindness led to a mediocrity which needed to be overcome by the courage of the 'overman' to instil new values based on affirming the creativity of the will, the true 'life-force'. Because of this, Nietzsche voiced his contempt for 'bourgeois' society and its rationalistic liberal-democratic ideals, and this prompts Fukuyama to interpret him as, in effect, raising the question: 'Is recognition that can be universalised worth having in the first place?'. Going back to Hegel's 'bloody battle for recognition', initially won by the master, history has evolved to where the slave is now victorious, the ideology of equality forming the heart of 'the slave ideology'. But from Nietzsche's perspective, 'is not the *quality* of recognition far more important than its universality? And does not the goal of universalising recognition inevitably trivialise and de-value it?'.[100]

Fukuyama recognises the resonance of this viewpoint for today, complaining that the dominance of *isothymia* has gone so far as to become corrupted into the empty belief that everyone should be equally esteemed, whatever they do. In short, we live in a radically *relativist* ('postmodern'?) morality which refuses to make qualitative judgements where they *should*, in fact, be made. For Fukuyama, 'to truly esteem oneself means that one must be capable of feeling shame or self-disgust when one does not live up to a certain standard', and the same preparedness to face up to moral decisions applies when esteeming *others*. For example, 'in the end, the mother will know if she has neglected her child, the father will know if he has gone back to drinking'. Relatedly, if the dominant ethic of *isothymia* involves the urge to be recognised as equal *to* everyone else *by* everyone else, then is such purely formal recognition worth having? Rather, it matters *who* is esteeming one, because 'the satisfaction one derives from recognition depend[s], in large measure, on the quality of the person doing the esteeming'.[101] But in liberal democracy, one is esteemed simply in virtue of one's citizenship rather than for particular, concrete qualities which proffer the opportunity for meaningful moral evaluation. In short, it is to a degree a phony 'recognition' of being human, (exactly the point made by Marx, albeit seemingly unbeknownst to Fukuyama, in his critique of 'the universal rights of man and citizen', where he criticised the liberal state for its phony, because entirely abstract, universality).[102]

Instead, (glossing Nietzsche), the more authentic fulfilment of man's basic *thymos* is in fact secured though the desire to be recognised as *superior* to others – *megaloythmia* – and this is best satisfied in aristocratic rather than democratic societies. Here, the free reign given to *megalothymia* encourages the creative freedom of individuals to excel, for the desire to be superior to others requires that one desires to surpass *oneself* – that is, to overcome the fear of physical discomfort or, if the case, to disdain material security, and strive towards great achievements in the higher aspects of life (art, science, politics). The problem with democratic societies, Fukuyama suggests, is that, being based on the equality of all, they are dedicated to the principle of *toleration*, 'unable to affirm that any particular way of life is superior to another'. Hence the only value they can focus around is the lowest common denominator, material welfare. Thus, claims Fukuyama, 'it is not an accident that people in democratic societies are preoccupied with material gain'[103] and do not want to be tormented by *moral* questions. Indeed, he goes further by suggesting that the torpor and mediocrity of ambition that characterises modern materialistic man is exacerbated by the manner in which modern *education* consciously instils the historical awareness that 'all horizons and value systems are relative to their time and place', and none are more nor less inherently valuable than others. Modern, aware, man thus has an *ironic* sense of relativism, for he '*knows* better than to risk his life for a cause'.[104] But for the same reason he can feel alienated because lacking firm beliefs and attachments. Rather than satiated by 'the victory of the slave over the master', he does not *feel* 'like his own master at all, but weak and impotent in the face of events he cannot control'.[105]

Fukuyama recognises that the overall gist of these defects in liberal democracy has been agreed by many since Nietzsche, and he himself shares their concern that this 'last man', (at the end of history because he has achieved both recognition of his humanity and the material welfare secured through science), will cease to exist as '"Man properly so-called" . . . because he will have ceased to work and struggle'. No longer needing to fight wars of recognition or combat injustice, and materially secure, 'the last men' will return to 'become animals again, as they were before the bloody battle that began history'.[106] 'Happy' they might be, but would they be *satisfied?*, Fukuyama asks. If *not*, would these 'last men' be 'hence ready to drag the world back into history with all its wars, injustices, and revolution?'. And of obvious importance to Fukuyama, for whom these 'last men' are not hypothetical future beings but already populate the 'post-historical' world, is this flaw in liberal democracy – i.e., the threat of the reassertion of *megolythmia* – sufficient of a 'contradiction' to render null and void that part of his philosophy which claims we are at 'the *end* of history'?

Thymos *and the future: Fukuyama's doubts*

Fukuyama takes this potentially fatal flaw to his theory seriously because, even if we should reject Nietzsche's openly intolerant, aristocratic, and cruel morality, 'we can readily accept many of Nietzsche's acute psychological observations'. Above all, if *megalothymia* is altogether purged from life, 'human beings will rebel', because, apart from anything else, they will become *bored*. 'They will want to have ideals by which to live and die'; they will want to risk their lives in war despite the universal peace promised by the world-wide triumph of liberal democracy. And for Fukuyama, 'This is the "contradiction" that liberal democracy has not yet solved'.[107] In short, although 'the end of history' is conceivably threatened by an excess of *isothymia* (from the Left), this is most unlikely. Rather, Fukuyama 'intuits' it is far more at risk from an excess of *megaloythmia*, precisely because of liberal democracy's tendency to wish to suppress it. It follows that unless liberal democracy can achieve a balance satisfying *both* aspects of *thymos* (i.e., *isothymia* and *megalothymia*), it will disappear under the strain – and with it, 'the end of history' as an intelligible theory. Thus, Fukuyama urges that 'liberal democracy *needs megalothymia* and will never survive on the basis of universal and equal recognition alone'.[108]

Fortunately many outlets for *megalothymia* already exist (although Fukuyama is also being prescriptive here). Most important is the scope in a capitalist economy for entrepreneurship, where those truly driven by *megalothymia* 'stake their fortunes, status, and reputations for the sake of a certain kind of glory'.[109] Not only does their innovativeness and energy create wealth, it keeps them out of politics and the military, where such *megalothymotic* qualities could create severe problems. This is not to say that politics itself is not a useful outlet, but given the restrictions put upon the role of individuals in domestic affairs, 'it is primarily in the realm of foreign policy that *democratic* politicians can still achieve a degree of recognition unavailable in virtually any other walk of life',[110] so weighty are the decisions involved. A third outlet is provided by sporting activities, and (relatedly) in an interesting reference to California as 'the most post-historical part of the United States', he notes Californians' 'obsession' with 'high-risk leisure activities' which

415

'shake' them 'out of the comfort of a bourgeois existence'. In addition to these notable outlets, there are numerous others – e.g., academic and scientific achievement (and, we might add, nowadays it is difficult not to think of media celebrity status). So varied are they that Fukuyama reckons 'virtually the only forms of *megalothymia* . . . not permitted in contemporary democracies are those leading to political tyranny', despite the fact that they 'exist in a certain tension with the publicly stated ideals of society' – i.e., equality.[111]

Somewhat as an exception, there is one further outlet Fukuyama identifies – different, because less dramatic than full-blown *megalothymia*, and also because, according to Fukuyama, it is *diminishing* in liberal societies. This is the recognition one can gain by involvement in the *community*. In practice, given the sheer size of most modern states, active citizenship 'is best exercised through so-called "mediating institutions"' such as school boards, trade unions, interest groups, and local associations. Here, 'one can take daily pride' in being a member of an *actual* little community which has concrete aims and values, and by which one can be esteemed for specifically relevant qualities (rather than for the abstract universality of simply being a person like any other, as the state 'esteems' one). Even the family is such a 'community', and Fukuyama cites it as an example of a general tendency in liberal democracies towards the weakening of community ties. The family is now nuclear rather than extended; and, like other forms of communal affiliation, it is not only undermined by the increased social mobility within capitalist economies but also by the principle of equality. (Indeed, in 1999 Fukuyama published *The Great Disruption*[112] in which he pursued the theme of the disintegration of 'the family', particularly under threat from women's control over their fertility and their access to the workplace.)

As Fukuyama puts it, 'the strongest communities are bound together by certain moral laws that define wrong and right for its members',[113] thereby excluding those who do not share these loyalties. But rather than tolerate such different standards, the tendency in modern democracy is to assert 'their essential equality . . . and therefore oppose the kind of exclusivity engendered by strong and cohesive communities'.[114] Here, again, Fukuyama notes the stronger sense of community found in Asian countries, derived not from mere self-interest (as in liberal theory) but from religion or some other 'irrational' (*thymotic*) cultural feature. And such is the importance he attaches to community involvement as an outlet for the *megalothymotic* instincts of man, he goes so far as to suggest that individuals in modern liberal societies should be prepared to 'give back certain of their rights to communities, and accept the return of certain historical forms of intolerance', otherwise 'no fundamental strengthening of community life will be possible'.[115]

But if the diminution of community involvement is a *tendency*, we should recall Fukuyama's claim that *war* between liberal democracies is virtually *outlawed* – and yet war is the clearest context in which human beings can demonstrate (for good or evil) those sterling qualities of honour and self-sacrifice called forth by their *thymotic* natures. Bolder spirits than Fukuyama have thus glorified war as providing 'the ultimate crucible of citizenship' in which people are prepared to risk their very lives to assert the values of their society, and he clearly has some (theoretical) sympathy with this view. Indeed, he interprets Hegel as suggesting that 'a liberal democracy that could fight a short and decisive war every generation or so to defend its own liberty and independence would be far healthier and more satisfied than one that experienced nothing but continuous peace'.[116]

Leaving aside the tempting observation that this is precisely what *does* seem to have happened in certain 'liberal democracies' since the Cold War, and seems likely to *continue* to – and also leaving aside Fukuyama's *own* earlier implication that many opportunities remain for ('post-historical') liberal democracies to go to war so long as the 'historical' world still exists – his focus here is on that hypothetical 'end of history' prefigured by his theory. Here, 'the world has become "filled up" . . . with liberal democracies, such that there exist no tyranny and oppression worthy of the name against which to struggle'. And in such a context Fukuyama claims that 'if men cannot struggle on behalf of a just cause . . ., they will struggle for the sake of struggle', and this would mean 'they will struggle *against* [the] peace and prosperity, and . . . democracy' of the 'post-historical' world. They will do so 'out of a certain boredom', and he claims that 'experience suggests' this has happened before, citing it as an 'intangible but crucial factor' leading to the First World War, when 'many European publics simply wanted war because they were fed up with the dullness and lack of community in civilian life'[117] – hence the war-euphoria of 1914.

But what of the *relativism* that characterises our tolerant liberal societies today? Has not Fukuyama earlier said that we 'know' too much to value one culture above another, and thus fight for it? He had, after all, offered this notion in support of his projected 'end of history'. But now he reveals the other side to relativism, for he warns that it 'is not a weapon that can be aimed selectively at the enemies one chooses', but 'fires indiscriminately', such that that very tolerance apparently wedded to it becomes *itself* regarded as a purely 'relativistic' value. Then, 'cherished principles like human equality have to go by the wayside as well',[118] threatening instead the kind of war-like nihilistic psychology lauded by Nietzsche, and practised by Nazism.

Fukuyama's doubts resolved?

Such, then, are the many objections that Fukuyama, in good academic fashion, has raised against his own theory that history is in the process of 'ending'. Above all, his concern is that to the extent liberal democracies rely entirely on the rational principle of universal recognition afforded by the homogenous state, then their ability 'to establish and sustain themselves on a rational basis over the long term is open to some doubt'. And, in casting doubt on his notion of 'the end of history', this brings to his mind those various *cyclical* theories of history which see it as an endless repetition of different phases, even going back to the 'bestial first' men.

But it is this very reflection which persuades Fukuyama of the likely *success* of 'the end of history'. Precisely because the twentieth century 'has taught us the horrendous consequences of the effort to resurrect unbridled *megalothymia*', and because, worse, we now 'have nuclear and other weapons of mass destruction, which will allow millions to be killed instantly and anonymously', the presumption must be that 'we who live in the old age of mankind' would not countenance turning back the clock as a way of satisfying *megalothymia*. Also 'standing as a bulwark against the revival of history and the return of the first man is the imposing Mechanism of modern natural science'. Its economic benefits are so great, and war so disruptive, that although some countries may (as in the past) sacrifice economic security in pursuit of other aims, 'it is questionable whether the world as a whole can make such a rupture for any extended length of time'.[119] That human feature of 'unlimited desire guided by reason', which drives science, will not disappear.

For these reasons, Fukuyama suggests that his theory of 'the end of history' is indeed plausible. Although he does not believe that the 'host of problems such as unemployment, pollution, drugs, crime',[120] which 'plague' liberal democracies are so fundamental as to destroy them, yet like *any* form of society, liberal democracy has to grapple with the absolutely *elemental* force of *thymos* in human nature which has previously driven historical change. In this, it might not succeed *perfectly*, but in practice it does achieve a sufficient balance between *isothymia* and *megalothymia*, and between them and economic progress, to make 'liberal democracy in reality [constitute] the best possible solution to the human problem'. And in a parting shot (which, incidentally, could be perfectly aimed at 'post-modernism' – a target he singled out, however, in a later defence of his theory[121]) he concludes that 'the chief threat to democracy [is] our own confusion about what is really at stake'. This arises from the failure of 'relativists' both 'to come to a consensus on what constitutes man and his specific dignity, and consequently [on] the rights of man', as well as to recognise 'that history is being driven in a coherent direction'.[122]

However, even this obstacle might, logically, be expected to disappear, because that which provoked relativism – twentieth-century Europe's confrontation with different cultures – should cease to be a factor as the politics and economics of the world as a whole become increasingly homogenised.

Fukuyama concludes by likening the historical process to a wagon train whose wagons are stretched out along the journey, some getting stuck for while, others temporarily losing direction, but where the great majority will eventually arrive 'in town' – i.e., in that 'post-historical' world heralded by 'the recent worldwide liberal revolution'. If enough do so arrive, then 'any reasonable person . . . would be forced to agree that there had been only one journey and one destination', and for all the reasons he has given this is clearly what Fukuyama believes will be the case. However, as befits any theory, until the evidence is clear it 'must remain provisionally inconclusive', and he therefore (somewhat perfunctorily) concedes that 'it is doubtful if we are at that point' where sufficient have arrived – nor, even if we *do* get to that point, whether our 'last men', 'having looked around a bit at their new surroundings, will not find them inadequate and set their eyes on a new and more distant journey'.[123]

Critique

The above survey of Fukuyama's estimation of the present world's propensity for becoming fully 'the end of the history' concludes our exposition of his overall speculative philosophy of history, during which I have mostly refrained from criticism. This task now beckons, but because Fukuyama's book has occasioned critical interest from so many angles, I will restrict attention to those points relating more specifically to the grand theme of speculative philosophy of history, and how Fukuyama has approached it.

There are three perspectives from which to comment on his philosophy – the strictly academic, his empirical judgements, and his philosophical basis – and although it is the last which should principally concern us, the former two invite some brief comments.

On strictly academic grounds we have already queried the provenance of some of Fukuyama's appeals to previous philosophers' ideas, and our exposition has revealed further respects in which his book can be criticised for involving both misreadings and non-readings of previous thinkers who had much to say, often of an alternative if not contrary nature, on the very themes he deals with. Yet two things can be said in his defence. First, as urged earlier, what is ultimately important are the ideas he advances rather than their academic backing. That they might be improved, or changed, by such backing is open to question – yet that they deserve respect as they stand is amply evidenced by the interest they have generated. And second, it is clear that Fukuyama's thinking has not stood still since *The End of History and the Last Man*. On the contrary, in his *Our Post-human Future*,[124] he has turned his attention to the implications of bio-engineering for 'human nature', in which he speculates upon its potential for producing a 'recommencement of history'. So recent is this book that your 'guide' cannot incorporate it here, but it will clearly be interesting to see whether it evidences changes in Fukuyama's fundamental 'end of history' theory.

Empirical judgements

As for the numerous practical judgements embracing perceptions both on the histories of different countries and on their present circumstances, Fukuyama incorporates a refreshingly multi-disciplinary mixture of political, economic, sociological, and 'cultural' observations. Such matters are of course integral to his thesis because any philosophy of history which did not appeal to the 'empirical facts' (albeit necessarily selectively) would be a grotesquely pointless exercise. Not surprisingly, however, many of his perceptions and/or judgements have been challenged – and no more so than when he surveys the *present* as presaging 'the end of history'. Put simply, even were his theory of what *drives* history correct – and, from that, also his logical extrapolation of an '*end* of history' – the notion that the *present* correlates with that impending 'end' strikes many as bizarre.

These, then, are matters of empirical judgement, not philosophy. For example, one critic summarises a widespread disagreement with Fukuyama's perception of today's Asian world by claiming that, 'In the foreseeable future, establishing liberal democracy in the Eurasian space is a utopian dream'. The same critic, echoing a view widely held (and passionately so by Western 'anti-capitalist' protest movements), claims that globalisation overwhelms people and makes them feel powerless, tearing them from the traditions of their communities and endangering the environment, to the extent that far from the present heralding Fukuyama's harmonious 'end of history', we should 'ready our minds for a New History'.[125] Alternatively, we might recall Paul Kennedy's thinly veiled prophecy (in 1988) about China's potential to become the new world power – namely, 'It is only a matter of time'.[126]

Some readers may be surprised by other judgements Fukuyama makes – for example (and despite his own reservations) the capacity for liberal democracies to command a loyalty from their citizens sufficient to sustain indefinitely a political system ('democracy') flawed by apathy and the power of money. We noted his reference to Hegel's idea that fighting a war every generation is helpful – (a recent survey discovered that many of the older UK generation today relate 'what it means to be British' to the Second World War) – and this is reminiscent of Machiavelli's notion that to maintain the public-spiritedness on which republics depend, a purge might be necessary every ten years or so. Fukuyama himself suggests that liberal democracy needs some 'irrational' (*thymotic*) source of enthusiasm,[127] but fails to say convincingly (other than war and/or the need to accept more *intolerance* between 'communities') where this might come from and *how it may be maintained*. In short, he is somewhat hoisted on his own petard, for having set out the case for the crucial role *thymos* plays in historical change, one suspects he himself senses he perceives today's 'democracies' through somewhat rose-tinted spectacles.

The Islamic world

It is in pursuit of this theme that we might suggest where Fukuyama's practical judgements are most challenging – namely, his assessment of the *Islamic* world. This, of course, is just *one* of those world-historical religio-cultural groups, all of which are supposed by his theory to eventually succumb to 'the worldwide liberal revolution'. But not only did the Islamic world appear to pose a problem for Fukuyama when he wrote his book (1992), its relevance has been heightened by the ramifications of the attack of 11 September 2001 on the USA, such that it is worth looking more closely at how he perceives it.

One reason the Islamic world poses a problem for Fukuyama is his claim that, unlike other great religions, it shares with Christianity an ideology which 'is potentially universal, reaching out to all men as men, and not just to members of

a particular ethnic or national group'. It is 'a systematic and coherent ideology
... with its own code of morality and doctrine of political and social justice', and
incorporates 'one-fifth of the world's population'.[128] And yet, despite its universalist
principles, it is the exception to what Fukuyama claims is otherwise a world-wide
'general consensus that accepts liberal democracy's claims to be the most rational
form of government'.[129] (It is important to note, here, that Fukuyama is not
referring to Islamic *fundamentalism*, which he sees as a temporary phenomenon
responding to economic failure and a sense of indignity towards the West.)
Although it may accommodate some form of 'democracy' because it does believe
in 'universal human equality', it is nonetheless 'very hard to reconcile with
liberalism and the recognition of universal rights, particularly freedom of
conscience or religion'.[130] In short, although previous systems have either been
consigned to history or are on their way there (ultimately because of their failure
to recognise human equality), the Islamic world is different in that it could, theoretically, contradict Fukuyama's 'end of history' theory, either by persisting
indefinitely, or indeed by offering an alternative 'ending'.

Fukuyama's judgement on this (in 1990) was that despite its power, 'it remains
the case that this religion has virtually no appeal outside those areas that were
culturally Islamic to begin with. The days of Islam's cultural conquests, it would
seem, are over: it can win back lapsed adherents, but has no resonance for young
people in Berlin, Tokyo, or Moscow'.[131] An *empirical* observation on his part, this
estimation of Islam's potential future impact (or lack of it) on world history has
no *theoretical* backing in Fukuyama's philosophy of historical evolution – and it
may even be suspect as an observation, since a case could be made for claiming
that 'Western' youth *can* see an attraction in Islam because of some of those
same drawbacks to 'liberal' culture which Fukuyama himself concedes, e.g., the
aimlessness of 'relativism', decline of community, the urge towards 'a cause' to
live for.

At present, however, the waters have been too muddied by 'Sept. 11, '01' and
its aftermath to pursue such considerations, since a regrettable confusion exists in
some peoples' minds between mainstream Islam and its extremist fundamentalist
offshoots – the latter clearly unattractive to Western women in particular. The
same events have also reinforced the doubts of those already sceptical of Fukuyama's
'end of history' thesis. Rather, they wonder whether a growing scenario of cross-
global confrontation between Islam and Western culture might not assume such
proportions, with such unforeseen consequences, as to constitute nothing less than
a new *phase* to history, (i.e., rather than merely involve a temporary series of 'anti-
terrorist' campaigns and minor wars). Such an eventuality would indeed render
untenable at least the 'end of history' part of Fukuyama's philosophy.

Aware of this, however, Fukuyama responded within a month after the
September 11 attack with an article for the *Wall Street Journal*[132] in which he
reiterated his view – now some twelve years on – that 'modernity is a very powerful
freight train that will not be derailed by recent events, however painful. Democracy
and free markets will continue to expand as the dominant organising principles for

much of the world'. He notes that 'there does seem to be something about Islam, or at least the fundamentalist versions . . . , that makes Muslim societies particularly resistant to modernity', and wonders whether 'this rejection is somehow inherent in Islam, or indeed no more than "a lunatic fringe"'. Somewhat undecided on this (given the breadth and depth of anti-Americanism the event revealed), he perhaps unwittingly altered his earlier notion that Islam has no appeal to other cultures by now saying '*Radical* Islam has virtually no appeal in the contemporary world apart from those who are culturally Islamic to begin with'[133], and that 'for Muslims themselves', in practice, 'political Islam [e.g., the Taliban regime] has proved much more appealing in the abstract than in reality'. This shift of emphasis towards now talking of 'radical' Islam, however, can surely be seen as Fukuyama evading the issue of Islam 'proper'. Nonetheless, from this he concludes that 'We remain at the end of history because there is only one system that will continue to dominate world politics, that of the liberal-democratic west'. The latter does confront 'a series of rearguard actions from societies whose traditional existence is . . . threatened by modernisation' – but his very terminology puts them firmly back in that old 'historical' world whose days are numbered, and during which wars might need to be fought, but in no sense challenges the now heralded 'end of history'.

Philosophy and ideology

The final and, for us, most important perspective for critical assessment of Fukuyama's philosophy of history comes from 'philosophy' itself – and by way of a conclusion to this 'guide' it is fitting to take the opportunity to pursue this task within the broader context of themes our book has encountered and considered.

We may start with an overview of Fukuyama's theory. For him, history is *meaningful*; it is *progressive*; it is *cumulative*; it is *irreversible*; it *culminates*; and its motor is *imminent*, rather than the product of any transcendental 'force', 'God', 'Spirit', or 'Intelligence' – i.e., his philosophy is entirely *secular*.

As such, then, Fukuyama's book not only falls squarely within that corpus of works we have referred to as 'speculative philosophy of history', it represents a *revival* of it – and, it would seem, a resounding one insofar as it 'has apparently struck a nerve'.[134] (That it is also distinctly political simply confirms what our study of earlier speculative philosophies of history revealed – namely, that as we approach modern times they become increasingly *politically* orientated. Indeed, some have dismissed Fukuyama's book as being pure ideology, a matter we will shortly address.)

We noted the demise of speculative philosophy of history as a 'respectable' intellectual endeavour as, turning into the twentieth century, huge historical theories became *academically* out of fashion, whilst crude, bastardised versions were employed by warring twentieth-century ideologies (fascism and communism), inviting further opprobrium from alarmed liberal circles. In short, the project of trying to make sense of, and find meaning in, the scope of human history threatened to become entirely obsolete – and correspondingly (amongst other things) a piece-meal approach to the *discipline* of history grew apace with its increasing professionalisation. In this light alone, Fukuyama's book is an unusual occurrence; but also, I suggest, a welcome one because, in reintroducing *ideas* into the study of history, it reintroduces historians and others to ideas of what history is *about*. One could be forgiven for thinking that all we can say about 'history' is that it is 'about the past', and probably add 'the *human* past', but that beyond that we have been left uncharted and overwhelmingly at sea. The project of speculative philosophy of history (however executed) challenges this by daring, at the least, to *pose* the question of whether history is *about* anything in particular, and if so, what? Here, historians who might otherwise see themselves as at loggerheads with their postmodernist critics could nevertheless be accused of *colluding* with them on this issue. This is because for postmodernists the vaguest whiff of the notion that history is 'about' anything is anathema, for how can history be *about* anything if 'history' itself is a 'discourse' which, in imagining it can 'represent' past reality, is futile to begin with? Although most historians disagree with the latter, there is a sense in which their practice – stubbornly resistant to 'theorising' about the past – accords perfectly with the nihilistic urgings of their postmodernist critics. If Fukuyama, or anyone else prepared to engage in speculative philosophy of history, can bounce historians (and, in that sense, 'history') out of this torpor, this alone might be reason for praising his book.

As for the philosophical *content* of his book, we have noted it has been attacked as blatantly 'ideological'. For us, the potential seriousness of this criticism extends beyond what many mean by it – i.e., they merely *disagree* with the political implications and prescriptions within it. In short, (since it is evident enough), Fukuyama clearly supports the values and ideals embraced by 'liberal-democratic' ideology, sees them as *superior* to other systems and cultures, and looks forward to their world-wide and enduring triumph – i.e., to when 'the West has won', as put crudely in the headline *The Guardian* used in its reproduction of Fukuyama's *Wall Street Journal* article mentioned above. If this were to mean his book was no more than ideology dressed up as philosophy, we might be as suspicious of it as proper speculative *philosophy* of history as we were concerning Augustine's *City of God*,[135] seeing it instead as resting on unexamined assumptions and partial 'facts' in order to persuade readers towards a political commitment.

Although such a judgement can only properly emerge from the close scrutiny *historians of thought* bring to such texts, at face value this would nonetheless seem an inaccurate description of Fukuyama's book. Not only does he make amply clear the conceptual framework he employs rather than rely on unexamined assumptions, he also raises potential objections to many of his ideas – and not as a mere rhetorical device, but with sufficient seriousness that he retains (and openly conveys) a degree of scepticism about some of his conclusions. This is no more evident than when he explains his concept of 'the last men', for as the consummation of the historical process he is by no means sure their situation equates with some kind of millennialist bliss.

For these reasons I suggest his book supersedes 'mere political ideology' and should be seen as the product of genuinely philosophical reflection – i.e., from the attempt, first and foremost, to reach an impartial understanding of its topic. But this is not to say that such books must not contain a 'message', political or otherwise. Were that the case, one would be hard-pressed to find, for example, a work of political or moral *philosophy* in the entire history of thought, since they all contain *prescriptive* implications. Are we, for example, to therefore deny Aristotle was a philosopher, and approach his writings as we should Hitler's *Mein Kampf*, i.e., as 'ideology'?

Thus, we can concede that Fukuyama's book does contain a prescriptive 'message' – but I suggest it is not that 'liberal democracy' is a good, or the best, thing. This is to diminish his attempt to philosophise about the meaning of history. Rather, his real message stems from, and should be assessed within, the context of previous speculative philosophy of history. In this light, it would appear to be the following: that (apart from natural catastrophes which might alter its evolution from 'outside') history can best be understood as a self-sustaining developmental process which continues cumulatively and irreversibly towards a consummation. Thus, history is not cyclical or reversible. Also, its development is unremittingly *progressive*, such that its consummation is not the final doom of a humanity whose history has represented the progressive *deterioration* of man from some Rousseau-istic pristine nature. On the contrary, the logic of Fukuyama's analysis points to a world in which human-beings have fashioned the best economic and political system to satisfy their unlimited capacity for material 'desire' as well as their deepest human urgings for 'recognition' – a world which will persist indefinitely because neither the politico-economic system (both domestically and internationally) nor the satisfactions it awards contain any negative or 'contradictory' factors of sufficient import to cause either a new phase of history or some kind of cyclical reverse. Such is the *logic* of history for Fukuyama. Yet his remarks on 'the last men' evince his own hesitations, and it is here, I suggest, that his real message can be found – a message, moreover, reminiscent of Vico (of whose ideas we have suggested Fukuyama was unaware when he wrote his book).

Fukuyama's message?

We may briefly recall Vico's graphic summary of the trajectory of man's development:

> Men first feel necessity, then look for utility, next attend to comfort: still later [they] amuse themselves with pleasure, then grow dissolute in luxury, and finally go mad and waste their substance.

Amongst other symptoms of decline 'at the end', there is a corresponding *intellectual* decline into *scepticism* whereby there 'arose a false eloquence, ready to uphold either of the opposed sides of a case indifferently', which, if unchecked, leads men 'into beasts made more inhuman by the barbarism of reflection than the first men had been made by the barbarism of sense'.[136] Vico, in short, feared that the cyclical element he had found in history would not stop at 'the last men', but begin some kind of re-enactment – and I urged that the most likely explanation for his extraordinary dedication in repeatedly reworking his *New Science* was that he wished to instruct people on how to prevent such a (human-made) catastrophe.

If, then, Vico's message was 'stop the cycle!', so, it could be argued, is Fukuyama's. Although he does not describe the 'last men' as in danger of 'going mad and wasting their substance', he does suggest the dangerous enervating effects of effortless material prosperity and security, including warnings about 'relativism' (= 'scepticism' = postmodernism?). Frequently he shows a wistful respect, if not admiration, for various cultural features of non-Western societies in the 'historical' world, and is aware (by proxy) that the kind of criticisms Vico makes about 'the last men' are precisely those made by Islam (and other cultures) against the 'decadent' West. Hence those many express and implicit prescriptions we find littered throughout Fukuyama's book, in effect warning of the *less* than certain 'end of history' *if* certain trends are 'left unchecked' – for instance, the decline of communities, the need for a restoration of some intolerance, the confused rush into 'equal rights' for everyone and everything. If we are correct in claiming that this is Fukuyama's real 'message', then its dimensions supersede mere shallow political ideology because originating from genuine speculative philosophy of history.

Thymos *revisited*

This said in defence of Fukuyama, however, it does not mean his philosophy is unproblematic in its foundations. But here I will restrict comment to two points – one specific, and one of a general nature which may permit me to complete this guide by bringing together certain points in the manner of a conclusion.

The specific problem relates to Fukuyama's concept of *thymos* and his use of it. The concept ('the desire for recognition') is completely fundamental to his philosophy of history. It is clear enough what he means by it, and many might find it both novel and persuasive. Yet complications emerge when he divides it into *isothymia* and *megalothymia*, not because each is difficult to comprehend (they are not), but because of their common root despite their differences – differences which are substantial in practice, yet sometimes glossed over by Fukuyama's resorting to the general terms '*thymos*' and '*thymotic*' when trying to explain something, (for example, the need for a certain 'irrational thymotic pride' in liberal democracy). And this, I suggest, is symptomatic of a deeper problem with '*thymos*' – namely, that too much is put upon it as an explanatory factor. Fukuyama himself tells us that it 'allows us to reinterpret [such phenomena] as culture, religion, work, nationalism, and war'.[137] It also provides the link between capitalism and democracy, as well as helping explain imperialism, revolutions, liberalism, and forms of tyranny. It is true that dividing it into two strands sometimes helps give it operative force, but overall can we not say of *thymos* what Fukuyama himself said about the vulnerability of the concept of 'power' for explaining things? The concept of '*power*' can be used so broadly that it encompasses markedly *different* things which would otherwise require their own specific explanations. Thus, although on a broad interpretation of it, 'the quest for power . . . is indeed universal, . . . its meaning becomes trivial'.[138] The same, ultimately, could be said for the concept which lies at the foundation of Fukuyama's philosophy – namely, *thymos*. In explaining so much, perhaps it *really* explains very little?

Concluding reflections

On a more general note we can perhaps best get an overall philosophical perspective on Fukuyama's theory by, initially, comparing his thinking on 'the meaning of history' with those ideas of the young Marx (i.e., before his 'historical materialist' conversion). Somewhat akin to Fukuyama, Marx put forward the notion that human history is driven, progressively and imminently by human activity, towards a consummation which is such because it finally satisfies 'human nature'. Man's work in the world throughout history has been to 'humanise' nature and to 'naturalise' man, such that he is released (as far as possible) from natural need, and from being 'alienated' from his true (free) nature. In both respects he becomes 'free', and 'pre-history' (cf. Fukuyama's 'historical world') ends, heralding the beginning of 'human' history (cf. Fukuyama's 'post-historical world'). We know that, unlike in Fukuyama, Marx's 'human' history would be based on the money-less communal ownership and control of economic resources, combined with an unspecified stateless radical 'democracy' – but beyond that not much more, partly because the whole point of 'human' history for Marx is that people, at last free from economic and political constraints, would be able to 'make' their own history – i.e., as social individuals, free to explore and fulfil their diverse potential. *What* human beings would do with their freedom is thus (with some logic) left open, and thus exactly what that 'human nature' *is*, which awaits to be realised, remains a problem (at least in reading the early Marx). In short, he does not tell us what 'the meaning of life' is – rather, he tells us the precondition of being able to realise it, namely, 'freedom'.

For Fukuyama also, history reaches a consummation where it at last satisfies 'human nature'. As Fukuyama argued in his text, it is therefore crucial to know what that essential 'human nature' is, or, put another way, what 'the meaning of life' is. He derives his answer to this from his reading of Plato, who (he suggests) divided the human 'soul' into three parts, each of which needs to be satisfied to fulfil human nature: desire, reason, and *thymos*. For Fukuyama 'desire' principally means man's economic needs, 'reason' means the capacity to understand and manipulate the environment (natural and social) to achieve one's ends, and *thymos* means the urge for respect both from oneself and from others as a *human* being rather than an animal. And the 'end of history' equates with the satisfaction of these three components of human nature.

Now, it could be argued that this neo-Platonic triad offers a clearer picture than does Marx of what that human nature *is* which history eventually fulfils – and in that sense, what the 'meaning of life' is (or should be) under the ideal circumstances of the 'post-historical world'. In short, it implies 'what we should be doing with our lives', or, put another way, what kind of world we should aspire to build or (if we think we have already built it) to maintain.

Such, then, is the grand stature of speculative philosophy of history, Fukuyama's book included. As claimed in our Introduction, it invites reflection on the loftiest themes, whose very intractability demands (if we are so-minded) that we resort to 'philosophy' to approach them.

But philosophy is open-ended, and thus I would like to conclude this guide by suggesting an alternative understanding of that 'human nature' which lies at the foundation of Fukuyama's philosophy of history. In his triad – desire, reason, respect – arguably this otherwise suggestive framework is diminished by the apparently purely *utilitarian* significance Fukuyama attaches to 'reason' (which for operative purposes he virtually equates with modern natural science). Some other philosophers (e.g., Aristotle, Spinoza, Hegel) see matters differently, for whilst they recognise the *instrumental* utility of 'reason' in helping us achieve objectives (i.e., its *practical* side), they also recognise the capacity to 'reason' about things solely to understand them. (Readers may recognise this from my earlier reference to its 'theoretical' side.) This is not to say that Fukuyama does not recognise this aspect of 'reason'. Yet (as he also does with the *arts*) he appears to treat intellectual activity 'for its own sake' not as self-sufficient but as emanating from *thymos* – i.e., as expressions of the desire to be esteemed, or even, as in *megalothymia*, the desire to excel.

The contrast I have in mind with Fukuyama's perspective can best be exemplified by a dictum penned by the sixteenth-century French thinker, Bodin, who wrote: 'those things least in order of dignity come first in order of necessity'. He went on to explain that (somewhat akin to Fukuyama) there are three aspects to life. First, we must secure our material well-being – i.e., the economic life. This accords with Fukuyama's 'desire'. But, said Bodin, the economic life is 'ordained to' the *moral* life, by which he meant there is a *higher* dimension to life than the merely economic (whose role is to enable and support it) – namely, that entire forum focused on human relations (e.g., family, politics, the administration of *justice*). This, I suggest, is fairly akin to Fukuyama's *thymotic* dimension to life. But then Bodin went on to say that the 'moral' life is in *its* turn 'ordained to' the 'intellectual' life, i.e., 'the contemplation of the noblest subjects . . . human, natural, and divine' – by which he meant that there is a *higher* dimension than the moral (*thymotic?*) life, namely, intellectual, 'contemplative', activity – what I have called 'understanding for the sake of it'. And the moral life is subservient to it, its role being to provide the conditions under which 'the intellective and contemplative virtues' can be exercised.

427

Perhaps characteristically for a philosopher, (and for true academics generally) Bodin claimed that this third dimension to life is the highest – the most in 'dignity'! But the point for us is that Bodin is far from alone in singling out that aspect of 'reason' – the effort to understand '*for the sake of it*' rather than in order to achieve some practical objective – as a human quality so distinctive and separate from other aspects of 'human nature' that it cannot be subsumed under them, nor be confused with them, but should stand proud as the ultimate *telos* or 'final end' of human society.[139]

As I have claimed, Fukuyama does not award such significance to 'the intellectual life', whereas others might prefer Bodin's version of what human life is ultimately about. But if so, then apart from the fact that history would clearly not have 'ended', how or even if such a philosophy might affect an attempt to 'make sense of' history is another story.

NOTES

INTRODUCTION

1   B. Mazlish, *The Riddle of History*, New York and London, Harper & Row, 1966, p. i.
2   R. Nisbet, *History of the Idea of Progress*, London, Heinemann, 1980, p. 327.
3   p. 328, ibid.
4   Mazlish, op. cit., p. 1.

1 SPECULATIVE PHILOSOPHY OF HISTORY

1   B. Mazlish, *The Riddle of History*, New York and London, Harper & Row, 1966, see pp. 59–69.
2   P. Gardiner, *The Philosophy of History*, Oxford, Oxford University Press, 1982, p. 2.
3   cf. p. 30, Mazlish, op. cit. for an example of such a use of the term.
4   See below, Chapter 13.

2 PRE-CLASSICAL IDEAS ON 'HISTORY'

1   M. C. Lemon, *The Discipline of History and the History of Thought*, London, Routledge, 1995, cf. pp. 245–50.
2   H. Frankfort *et al.*, *Before Philosophy*, Harmondsworth, Penguin, 1968, p. 12.
3   R. A. Nisbet, *History of the Idea of Progress*, London, Heinemann, 1980, p. 14.
4   p. 24, Frankfort, op. cit.
5   cf. pp. 37–41, Lemon, op. cit.
6   S. L. Jaki, *Science and Creation – From Eternal Cycles to an Oscillating Universe*, Edinburgh, Scottish Academic Press, 1974, p. 99.
7   p. 80. ibid.
8   See Chapter 14, below.

3 CLASSICAL GREEK AND ROMAN SPECULATIONS ON HISTORY

1   e.g., R. Nisbet, *History of the Idea of Progress*, London, Heinemann, 1980, e.g., p. 33.
2   H. Frankfort *et al.*, *Before Philosophy*, Harmondsworth, Penguin, 1968, p. 251.
3   e.g., Frankfort (op. cit.); E. Cassirer, *Essay on Man*, New Haven, Yale University Press, 1945.
4   See p. 250, Frankfort, op. cit.
5   p. 238, ibid.
6   pp. 248–249, ibid.
7   i.e., R. Nisbet, in his *Social Change and History*, Oxford: Oxford University Press, 1970.
8   As quoted by G. W. Trompf, *The Idea of Historical Recurrence in Western Thought*

     – *From Antiquity to the Reformation*, Berkeley, Los Angeles, London, University of California Press, 1979, p. 11.

9 As quoted by S. L. Jaki, *Science and Creation*, Edinburgh, Scottish Academic Press, 1974, p. 109.

10 As quoted by Jaki, p. 114, ibid.

11 cf. p. 112, ibid.

12 pp. 16–17, Nisbet, *Social Change and History*, (op. cit.).

13 quoted by Nisbet, p. 25, ibid.

14 p. 104, Jaki, op. cit.

15 p. 69 and p. 104, Trompf, op. cit.

16 Nisbet quoting Hesiod, p. 14, *History of the Idea of Progress*, (op. cit.).

17 pp. 15–17, ibid.

18 i.e., in his *Social Change and History*, op. cit.

19 p. 32, Nisbet, *History of the Idea of Progress*, (op. cit.).

20 p. 34, ibid.

21 p. 113, Jaki, op. cit.

22 p. 112, ibid.

23 p. 130, ibid.

24 p. 357, ibid.

25 p. 351, Nisbet, op. cit.

26 p. 357, ibid.

4 THE CHRISTIAN CHALLENGE TO GRAECO-ROMAN HISTORICAL PERSPECTIVES

1 G. W. Trompf, *The Idea of Historical Recurrence in Western Thought – From Antiquity to the Reformation*, Berkeley, Los Angeles, London, University of California Press, 1979, see p.186.

2 P. Kennedy, *The Rise and Fall of the Great Powers*, London, Fontana Press, 1989, p. 591.

3 F. Fukuyama, *The End of History and the Last Man*, London, Penguin, 1992.

4 p. 188, Trompf, op. cit.

5 p. 189, ibid.

6 p. 191, ibid.

7 Trompf quoting Ammianus, p. 192, ibid.

8 p. 202, ibid.

9 N. Cohn, *The Pursuit of the Millennium*, London, Mercury Books, 1962, pp. 2–3.

10 p. 4, ibid.

11 p. 5, ibid.

12 p. 8, ibid., quoting *Revelations*.

13 See pp. 8–13, ibid.

14 R. Nisbet, *History of the Idea of Progress*, London, Heinemann, 1980, p. 60.

15 S. Jaki, *Science and Creation*, Edinburgh, Scottish Academic Press, 1974, p. 177.

16 See p. 181, ibid.

17 See note 2 on p. 117 Trompf, op. cit., for a list (to which we can add Jaki).

18 p. 117, ibid.

19 p. 179, ibid.

20 p. 185, ibid.

21 p. 206, ibid.

22 p. 313, ibid.

23 ibid.

24 p. 315, ibid.

25 See note 17 above.

26 p. 48, Nisbet, op. cit.

27 p. 34, ibid.
28 p. 47, ibid.
29 p. 68, ibid.
30 p. 354, ibid.
31 p. 352, ibid.
32 p. 141, ibid.
33 p. 357, ibid.
34 p. 313, Trompf, op cit.
35 p. 120, D. R. Bultmann, *History and Eschatology*, Edinburgh, 1975.
36 p. 357, Jaki, op. cit.
37 p. 202, ibid. – see also p. 208.
38 p. 71, Nisbet, op. cit.
39 H. A. Deane, *The Political and Social Ideas of St. Augustine*, Columbia University Press, 1963, p. viii.
40 p. 317, ibid.
41 p. 223, Trompf, op. cit.
42 p. 238, ibid.
43 p. 71, Deane, op. cit.
44 E. L. Fortin, 'Augustine's City of God and the Modern Historical Consciousness', *The Review of Politics*, Vol., 41, No. 3, July, 1979, p. 328.
45 p. 336, ibid.
46 p. 339, ibid.
47 p. 343, ibid.
48 p. 177, Jaki, op. cit.
49 p. 178, ibid.
50 p. 183, ibid. – (my italics).
51 ibid.
52 p. 58, Nisbet, op. cit.
53 p. 61, ibid.
54 p. 67, ibid.
55 p. 75, ibid.
56 Spinoza, *Tractatus Theologico-Politicus*, in Vol.1, *The Chief Works of Benedict de Spinoza*, trans. R. H. M. Elwes, New York, Dover Publications, 1955, p. 86.
57 See p. 246, Trompf, op. cit., for discussion and references.
58 G. Sabine, *A History of Political Theory*, 3rd. edition, London, Harrap & Co., 1963, see p. 191 and note 13.
59 M. C. Lemon, *The Discipline of History and the History of Thought*, London, Routledge, 1995, pp. 184–225
60 V. J. Bourke's 'Introduction' to his edition of Augustine's *City of God*, New York, Image Books, 1958, p. 8.
61 *Hegel's Philosophy of Right* (Preface), trans. T. Knox, Oxford, Clarendon Press, 1962, p. 12.

5 A CHANGING CONSCIOUSNESS OF HISTORY

1 P. Heather, 'Late Antiquity and the Early Medieval West', in *Companion to Historiography*, ed. M. Bentley, London, Routledge, 1997, p. 74.
2 See Chapter 4, R. Southern, *Medieval Humanism and Other Studies*, Oxford, Blackwell, 1970.
3 J.M. Smith, 'Regarding Medievalists' in *Companion to Historiography*, op. cit., p. 106.
4 Aquinas, *De Regimine Principum*, in Aquinas, *Selected Political Writings*, ed. A. P. D'Entrèves, Oxford, Blackwell, 1965, p. 79.
5 p. 60, Southern, op. cit.

6 P. Kristeller, *Eight Philosophers of the Italian Renaissance*, California, Stanford University Press, 1964, p. 4.

7 E. Rice and A. Grafton, *The Foundations of Early Modern Europe, 1460–1559*, New York, W. W. Norton, 1994, p. 81.

8 e.g., see C. Nauert, *Humanism and the Culture of Renaissance Europe*, Cambridge University Press, 1995, pp. 30–3.

9 *Pace* Nauert's complaint against Burkhardt, p. 2, ibid.

10 e.g., *German Ideology*, in Vol. 5, *Karl Marx: Frederick Engels, Collected Works*, London, Lawrence & Wishart, 1976, pp. 63–74.

11 p. 214, Nauert, op. cit.

12 ibid.

13 p. 7 Rice and Grafton, op. cit.

14 p. 10, ibid.

15 ibid.

16 Julia Smith, 'Regarding Medievalists', in *Companion to Historiography*, op. cit., p. 107.

17 ibid.

18 M. C. Lemon, *The Discipline of History and the History of Thought*, London, Routledge, 1995, pp. 250–59.

19 e.g., see the section, 'Denials', *The Renaissance Debate*, ed. D. Hay, New York, Holt, Rinehart, & Winston, 1965, pp. 77–91.

20 e.g., Henri Saint-Simon.

21 p. 91, *The Renaissance Debate*, op. cit.

22 More, *Utopia*, Harmondsworth, Penguin, 1965, p. 76.

23 P. Kropotkin, in *The Essential Kropotkin*, (eds) E. Capouya and K. Thompkins, London, Macmillan, 1976, p. 109.

24 p. 63, More, op. cit.

25 *Command and Conquer*, Virgin Interactive Entertainment, 1996.

26 L. Strauss, *Thoughts on Machiavelli*, Seattle, University of Washington Press, 1969, p. 9.

27 Jean-Jacques Rousseau, *The Social Contract*, Everyman edition of *The Social Contract and Discourses*, trans. G. D. H. Cole, London, 1966, p. 59.

28 Sebastian de Grazia, *Machiavelli in Hell* – my references (below) are to the Picador edition, London, 1992.

29 See Hegel, *Philosophy of Right*, trans. and ed. by T. M. Knox, Oxford, Clarendon Press, 1962, paragraphs 137–40.

30 cf. pp. 295–96 De Grazia, op. cit.; also p. 252 Trompf, G.W., *The Idea of Historical Recurrence in Western Thought – From Antiquity to the Reformation*, Berkeley, Los Angeles, London, University of California Press, 1979.

31 p. 85, de Grazia, op. cit.

32 N. Machiavelli, *The Discourses*, in *The Prince and the Discourses*, ed. E. Vincent, New York, The Modern Library, 1950, p. 101.

33 p. 103, ibid.

34 p. 104, ibid.

35 ibid.

36 p. 105, ibid.

37 ibid.

38 pp. 117–18, ibid.

39 p. 208, ibid.

40 p. 474, ibid.

41 p. 182, ibid.

42 p. 66, *The Prince*, ibid.

43 ibid.

44 p. 272, *Discourses*, ibid.

45 p. 273, ibid.
46 p. 539, ibid.
47 p. 146, ibid.
48 p. 146, ibid.
49 p. 151, ibid.
50 p. 285, ibid.
51 e.g., see p. 101ff, de Grazia, op. cit.
52 p. 94, *The Prince*, op. cit.
53 p. 91, ibid.
54 Jaki, S. L. *Science and Creation*, Edinburgh, Scottish Academic Press, 1974, p. 256.
55 Nisbet, R. A. *History of the Idea of Progress*, London, Heinemann, 1980, p. 106.
56 p. 101, ibid.
57 Trompf, G. W. *The Idea of Historical Recurrence in Western Thought*, Berkeley, London, University of California Press, 1979, p. 249.
58 p. 258, ibid.
59 p. 200, de Grazia, op. cit.
60 p. 201, ibid.
61 p .202, ibid.
62 p. 91, *The Prince*, op. cit.
63 ibid.
64 p. 201, de Grazia, op. cit.
65 e.g., cf. D. Earl, *The Moral and Political Tradition of Rome*, London, Thames & Hudson, 1967, pp. 74–83.

6 AN INNOVATIVE INTERLUDE: FROM MACHIAVELLI TO VICO

1 See Chapter 4.
2 Vico, *The New Science of Giambattista Vico*, revised translation of the Third Edition (1744) by T.G. Bergin and M. H. Fisch, New York, Cornell University Press, 1968, paragraph 330.
3 See B. Cohen, 'The Eighteenth-century Origins of the Concept of Scientific Revolution', *Journal of the History of Ideas*, Vol. 37, No. 2, 1976.
4 H. Butterfield, *The Origins of Modern Science*, New York, 1952, p. viii, as cited in *The Western Intellectual Tradition*, J. Bronowski and B. Mazlish, London, Hutchinson,1960, p.107.
5 Quoted by L. Olschki, 'Galileo's Philosophy of Science' in *Intellectual Movements in Modern European History*, ed. F. L. Bauer, London, Macmillan, 1969, p. 51.
6 p. 47, ibid.
7 p. 195, Bronowski and Mazlish, op. cit.
8 p. 77, Hobbes, T. *Leviathan*, ed. J. Plamenatz, London, Fontana, 1962.
9 p. 111, ibid.
10 Spinoza, B., Introduction to Part 3, *The Ethics*, in *The Chief Works of Benedict de Spinoza*, trans. R. H. M. Elwes, New York, Dover Publications, 1955, Vol. 2, p. 129.
11 Spinoza, B., *On the Improvement of the Understanding*, in *The Chief Works of Benedict de Spinoza*, Vol. 2, op.cit., p. 7.
12 p. 111, Hobbes, op.cit.
13 p. 90, ibid.
14 e.g., cf. R. Tuck, *Philosophy and Government, 1572–1651*, Cambridge, Cambridge University Press, 1993, (especially Chapter 2).
15 p. 143, Hobbes, op. cit.
16 see J. H. Franklyn, *Jean Bodin and the Sixteenth-century Revolution in the Methodology of Law and History*, New York and London, Columbia University Press, 1966.
17 G. E. Aylmer, 'Introductory Survey: From the Renaissance to the Eighteenth

Century', in *Companion to Historiography*, ed. M. Bentley, London, Routledge, 1997, pp. 249–50.

18 B. Willey, 'The Touch of Cold Philosophy', in *Intellectual Movements in Modern European History*, op.cit., p. 60.

19 Hobbes, *Thomas White's 'De Mundo' Examined*, trans. H. W. Jones, London, Bradford University Press, 1976, p. 434.

20 p. 74, Spinoza, Appendix, *Ethics*, op. cit.

21 p. 61, Spinoza, Note to Proof to Prop. XVII, ibid.

22 see p.112–13, Hobbes, *Leviathan*, op. cit.

23 paragraph 330, Vico, op.cit.

24 paragraph 331, ibid.

25 paragraph 330, ibid.

7 VICO'S PHILOSOPHY OF HISTORY

1 P. Burke, *Vico*, Oxford, Oxford University Press, 1985, p. 12.

2 See e.g., J. M. Levine, 'Quarrel between the Ancients and the Moderns', in *Journal of the History of Ideas*, Vol. LII, No. 1, 1991.

3 p. 58 ibid.

4 Vico, *On the Heroic Mind*, trans. E. Sewell and A. Sirignano, in *Social Research*, No. 43, 1976, p. 901.

5 Vico, *Universal Right*, trans. and ed. G. Pinton and M. Diehl, Amsterdam Atlanta, Rodopi, 2000.

6 See e.g., J. C. Morrison, 'Vico's Principle of *Verum* is *Factum* and the Problem of Historicism', *Journal of the History of Ideas*, Vol. 39, Issue 2, 1978.

7 See above, Chapter 6.

8 Vico, *The New Science of Giambattista Vico*, revised translation of the Third Edition (1744) by T. G. Bergin and M. H. Fisch, New York, Cornell University Press, 1968, paragraph 164 – all subsequent references to this text are given by paragraph number only in this chapter.

9 119

10 120

11 125

12 127

13 349

14 138

15 359

16 140

17 139

18 137

19 138

20 331

21 349

22 140

23 163

24 349 (also 393)

25 1096

26 ibid.

27 211–212

28 215–216

29 240

30 298

31 369

32 374
33 377
34 380
35 379
36 504
37 504–505
38 12–13
39 333
40 564
41 944
42 372
43 553
44 179
45 338
46 555
47 18
48 555
49 556
50 926
51 555 (my emphasis)
52 582
53 926
54 923
55 916
56 553
57 816
58 708
59 401
60 228–229–230
61 814
62 221
63 814
64 221
65 918
66 935
67 460
68 32
69 29
70 925
71 926
72 559
73 20
74 927
75 1038
76 326–327
77 1040
78 See below, Chapter 10.
79 1008
80 951
81 29
82 951
83 1008 (my emphasis)
84 951

85 1008
86 918
87 1102
88 1101
89 1102
90 241
91 242
92 1105
93 1102
94 1106
95 1047
96 1103
97 1102
98 1105
99 1106
100 1108
101 1108
102 348
103 349
104 1046
105 1056
106 1008
107 1084
108 1104
109 1104 – See also 1008.
110 243–244
111 1108
112 1008
113 1088 (my emphasis)
114 1047
115 1048
116 e.g., see L. Strauss, *Persecution and the Art of Writing*, University of Chicago Press, 1988.
117 13
118 372
119 9
120 167
121 313
122 9
123 329
124 9
125 54
126 165
127 125
128 68
129 396
130 365
131 948
132 1092
133 334 (my emphasis)
134 95
135 40
136 1094

137 136
138 141
139 381
140 365
141 132–133
142 1108
143 343
144 344
145 324
146 349
147 345
148 136
149 313
150 329
151 1047 (my emphasis)
152 310
153 See Chapter 5.
154 1109
155 334
156 1110
157 1106
158 1093
159 674
160 670
161 672
162 Vico, *On the Heroic Mind*, op. cit., p. 888.
163 p. 901 ibid.
164 p. 902 ibid.
165 See below, Chapter 10.
166 J. C. Morrison, op. cit., p. 589.
167 ibid.

8 SPECULATIVE PHILOSOPHY OF HISTORY DURING THE ENLIGHTENMENT

1 Rousseau, *The Confessions*, Harmondsworth, Penguin Books, 1965, p. 328.
2 Rousseau, *Discourse on the Arts and Sciences*, trans. G. D. H. Cole, London, Everyman, Dent, 1966, p. 140.
3 p. 121 ibid.
4 p. 122 ibid.
5 p. 138 ibid.
6 p. 122 ibid.
7 p. 136 ibid.
8 p. 131 ibid.
9 p.140 ibid.
10 p. 120 ibid.
11 p. 121 ibid.
12 p. 123 ibid.
13 p. 129 ibid.
14 p. 124 ibid.
15 pp. 124–8 ibid.
16 p. 124 ibid.
17 p. 122 ibid.

18 p. 123 ibid.
19 p. 362, *The Confessions*, op. cit.
20 Rousseau, *Discourse on the Origins of Inequality*, trans. G. D. H. Cole, London, Everyman, Dent, 1966 p. 161.
21 p. 162 ibid.
22 p. 169 ibid.
23 p. 170 ibid.
24 p. 185 ibid.
25 p. 167 ibid.
26 p. 190 ibid.
27 pp. 192 and 193 ibid.
28 pp. 194–6 ibid.
29 p. 197 ibid.
30 p. 198 ibid.
31 p. 199 Rousseau, op. cit
32 p. 202 ibid.
33 p. 205 ibid.
34 p. 192 ibid.
35 p. 207 ibid.
36 pp. 214–15
37 p. 219 ibid.
38 p. 220 ibid.
39 p. 228–9 ibid.
40 Rousseau, *The Social Contract*, trans. G. D. H. Cole, London, Everyman, London, 1966, p. 6.
41 p. 8 ibid.
42 p. 12 ibid.
43 p. 16 ibid.
44 ibid.
45 p. 32 ibid.
46 p. 219, *Discourse on Inequality*, op. cit.
47 p. 17–18, *Social Contract*, op. cit.
48 B. Mazlish, *The Riddle of History*, New York and London, Harper & Row, 1966, p. 75.
49 F. Manuel, *The Prophets of Paris*, New York, Harper and Row, 1965, p. 61.
50 p. 15 ibid.
51 p. 13 ibid.
52 See note 49 above.
53 p. 36 ibid.
54 p. 18 ibid.
55 p. 32 ibid. (my emphasis).
56 p. 38 ibid.
57 p. 40 ibid.
58 p. 44 ibid.
59 p. 14 ibid.
60 p. 73, Mazlish, op. cit.
61 Quoted by Mazlish, p. 80, ibid.
62 p. 70, Manuel, op. cit.
63 pp. 77–78, Mazlish, op. cit.
64 Quoted by Mazlish, p. 86 ibid.
65 pp. 89 and 99 ibid.
66 Quoted by Mazlish, p. 81 ibid.
67 Quoted by Mazlish, p. 89 ibid.
68 p. 20, Manuel, op. cit.

69 p. 100 ibid.
70 p. 87ff, Manuel, op. cit.
71 pp. 93–5, Mazlish, op. cit.
72 Quoted by Mazlish, p. 90 ibid.
73 p. 36, Manuel, op. cit.
74 p. 91, Mazlish, op. cit
75 pp. 72–3, Manuel, op. cit.
76 Quoted by Conor Cruise O'Brien on p. 35 of his 'Introduction' to the Pelican edition of *Reflections on the Revolution in France*, which he edited. Harmondsworth, Penguin Books, 1969 – all subsequent quotations are from this edition.
77 For a recent and celebrated account of this 'conservative disposition', see M. Oakeshott's essay, 'On Being Conservative', in his *Rationalism in Politics*, London, Methuen, 1962.
78 p. 194, Burke, *Reflections on the Revolution in France*, op. cit.
79 Bentham, *An Introduction to the Principles of Morals and Legislation*, Oxford, Blackwell, 1967, p. 126.
80 p. 152, Burke, op. cit.
81 p. 153 ibid.
82 p. 118 ibid.
83 p. 153 ibid.
84 G. Sabine, *A History of Political Theory*, (third edition), London, Harrap, 1963, pp. 618–19.
85 p. 105, Burke, op. cit.

9 HEGEL'S PHILOSOPHY OF HISTORY

1 This is the title as translated by J. B. Baillie in his edition first published in London by Allen & Unwin, and in New York by Humanities Press, in 1910. The title was differently translated by A. V. Miller, in the Oxford University Press edition of 1977, as *Phenomenology of Spirit*.
2 For the Rankean historical school, see M. Bentley, 'Approaches to Modernity', in *Companion to Historiography*, (ed.) M. Bentley, London, Routledge, 1997, pp. 420–23.
3 P. H. Reill, *The German Enlightenment and the Rise of Historicism*, Berkley, University of California Press, 1975.
4 pp. 2–4, ibid.
5 Philosophers will recognise here something like Spinoza's distinction between *Natura naturata* and *Natura naturans*.
6 K. Leidecker, Preface to W. Orynski, *Hegel – Highlights: an annotated selection*, New York, Philosophical Library, 1960, p. vii.
7 Hegel, *The Philosophy of History*, p. 25, see note 26.
8 pp. 30–3 ibid.
9 e.g., Hegel, (Preface) *Philosophy of Right*, trans. T. M. Knox, Oxford, Clarendon Press, 1962, p. 10.
10 Hegel, *Philosophy of Right*, op. cit., p. 305 (translator's notes).
11 Hegel, p. 21 ibid.
12 See *Hegel's Philosophy of Mind*, trans. W. Wallace and A. Miller, Oxford, Clarendon Press, 1971, pp. 158–68 (i.e., sections from the *Encyclopaedia*).
13 pp. 20–3, Hegel, *Philosophy of Right*, op. cit.
14 p. 57 ibid.
15 p. 67 ibid.
16 p. 73 ibid.
17 See pp. 256–58 ibid.

18 p. 92 ibid.
19 p. 105 ibid.
20 p. 110 ibid. (my emphasis)
21 p. 118 ibid.
22 pp. 130–31 ibid.
23 p. 154 ibid.
24 p. 155 ibid.
25 p. 156 ibid.
26 p. 160 ibid.
27 Subsequent editions and translations appeared. All references below are to the 1840 edition, translated by J. Sibree, *Hegel G., The Philosophy of History*, New York, Dover Publications, 1956.
28 p. 17 ibid.
29 p. 19 ibid.
30 p. 17 ibid.
31 *Philosophy of Right*, op. cit., p. 227.
32 *Philosophy of History*, op. cit., p. iv.
33 pp. 17–18 ibid.
34 pp. 19–20 ibid.
35 p. 63 ibid.
36 p. 9 ibid.
37 p. 10 ibid.
38 pp. 64–5 ibid.
39 p. 38 ibid.
40 p. 46 ibid.
41 p. 49 ibid.
42 p. 63 ibid.
43 pp. 61–2 ibid.
44 p. 80 ibid.
45 pp. 52–3
46 *Philosophy of Right*, op. cit., pp. 218–19.
47 See *Philosophy of History*, op. cit., pp. 80–1.
48 pp. 84–7 ibid.
49 pp. 91–6 ibid.
50 pp. 98–9 ibid.
51 p. 99 ibid.
52 p. 104 ibid.
53 pp. 104–5 ibid.
54 p. 222 ibid.
55 p. 106 ibid.
56 p. 223 ibid.
57 pp. 105–6 ibid.
58 *Philosophy of Right*, op. cit. p. 288.
59 p. 221 ibid.
60 *Philosophy of History*, op. cit., p. 223.
61 p. 107 ibid.
62 p. 279 ibid.
63 p.108 ibid.
64 p. 284 ibid.
65 *Philosophy of Right*, op. cit., p. 222.
66 *Philosophy of History*, op. cit., p. 108.
67 *Philosophy of Right*, op. cit., p. 222.
68 *Philosophy of History*, op. cit., p. 342.

69 p. 109 ibid.
70 p. 344 ibid.
71 p. 109 ibid.
72 p. 344 ibid.
73 pp. 408–11 ibid.
74 pp. 412–15 ibid.
75 pp. 416–17 ibid.
76 pp. 109–10 ibid.
77 p. 419 ibid.
78 pp. 424–27 ibid.
79 pp. 439–40 ibid.
80 pp. 442–43 ibid.
81 p. 449 ibid.
82 p. 452 ibid.
83 p. 449 ibid.
84 But see p. 376, note by Knox (translator) to Hegel's *Philosophy of Right*, op. cit., for a contrary view.
85 *Philosophy of History*, op. cit., p. 452.
86 *Philosophy of Right*, op. cit., p. 278: see also pp. 148–50 ibid.
87 *Philosophy of History*, op. cit, p. 452.
88 p. 449, 453 ibid.
89 pp. 454–55 ibid.
90 pp. 108–9 ibid.
91 pp. 86–7 ibid.
92 pp. 456–57 ibid.
93 *Philosophy of Right*, op. cit., p. 10.
94 Philosophers may recognise here something akin to Spinoza's notion that Thought and Extension are but attributes of (the same) Substance.
95 Hegel, *Phenomenology of Mind*, (trans. J. B. Baillie), London, Allen & Unwin, 1966, p. 276.

10 MARX ON HISTORY

1 F. Engels, *Schelling and Revelation* (written late 1841, early 1842), in Vol. 2, *Karl Marx/Frederick Engels, Collected Works*, London, Lawrence & Wishart, 1975, pp. 239–40.
2 ibid.
3 Marx, *Contribution to the Critique of Hegel's Philosophy of Law*, in Vol. 3, *Collected Works*, London, Lawrence & Wishart, 1976, p. 77.
4 Marx, *On the Jewish Question*, in Vol. 3, *Collected Works*, op. cit., p. 153.
5 p. 167, ibid.
6 p. 166 ibid.
7 Marx, *Contribution to the Critique of Hegel's Philosophy of Law*, op. cit., pp. 30–1.
8 p. 50 ibid.
9 p. 162–3, ibid.
10 p. 168, ibid.
11 Marx, *Contribution to the Critique of Hegel's Philosophy of Law – Introduction*, Vol. 3, *Collected Works*, op. cit., p. 179.
12 pp. 184, 185, 186, ibid.
13 p. 182 ibid.
14 pp. 186, 187 ibid.
15 pp. 176, 181 ibid.
16 Marx, *Economic and Philosophic Manuscripts of 1844*, in Vol. 3, *Collected Works*, op. cit., pp. 271–2.

17 ibid.
18 p. 274 ibid.
19 p. 276 ibid.
20 pp. 302–4, ibid.
21 p. 277 ibid.
22 pp. 296–7 ibid.
23 p. 297 ibid.
24 L. Feuerbach, *Principles of the Philosophy of the Future*, New York, Bobbs-Merrill, 1966, p. 51.
25 p. 24 ibid.
26 p. 9 ibid.
27 p. 48 ibid.
28 pp. 30–1 ibid.
29 p. 73 ibid.
30 p. 67 ibid.
31 p. 71 ibid.
32 Marx, *Economic and Philosophic Manuscripts*, in Vol. 3, *Collected Works*, op. cit., p. 334.
33 p. 337 ibid.
34 p. 341 ibid.
35 Interestingly, it is to these very concerns that F. Fukuyama (see Chapter 15) has recently turned his attention.
36 pp. 275–6 ibid.
37 pp. 299–302 ibid.
38 'Forming', from the German 'Bildung', meaning 'education' in the broadest sense.
39 pp. 301–2 ibid.
40 p. 302 ibid.
41 p. 337 ibid.
42 p. 279 ibid.
43 Marx, *Theses on Feuerbach*, Vol. 5, *Collected Works*, op. cit., p. 3.
44 pp. 4–5 ibid.
45 Hegel, *Philosophy of Right*, (trans. T. Knox), Oxford, Clarendon Press, 1962, pp. 11–12.
46 e.g., see Marx, 'Communism and the Augsburg Allgemeine Zeitung' in Vol. 1, *Collected Works*, op. cit., p. 220.
47 Marx, *The German Ideology*, Vol. 5, *Collected Works*, op. cit., p. 41.
48 pp. 41–2 ibid.
49 p. 31 ibid.
50 p. 42 ibid.
51 p. 31 ibid.
52 pp. 42–4 ibid.
53 p. 45 ibid.
54 p. 46 ibid.
55 p. 32 ibid.
56 p. 46 ibid.
57 p. 32 ibid.
58 p. 47 ibid.
59 p. 90 ibid.
60 Engels, pp. 46–7 ibid.
61 Marx, pp. 50–1 ibid.
62 pp. 53–4 ibid.
63 p. 37 ibid.
64 p. 60 ibid.
65 pp. 61–2 ibid.
66 p. 82 ibid.

67 p. 74 ibid.
68 p. 82 ibid.
69 p. 74 ibid.
70 p. 33 ibid.
71 pp. 34–5 ibid.
72 pp. 66 to 9 ibid.
73 p. 72 ibid.
74 p. 72 ibid.
75 pp. 72–3 ibid.
76 p. 78 ibid.
77 p. 49 ibid.
78 pp. 51–2 ibid.
79 Marx, *A Contribution to the Critique of Political Economy*, Vol. 29, *Collected Works*, op. cit., p. 264.
80 Marx, *The German Ideology*, op. cit., p. 77.
81 p. 79 ibid.
82 pp. 87–8 ibid.
83 p. 52 ibid.
84 See Vol. 28 of *Karl Marx/Frederick Engels, Collected Works*, op. cit. – also known as *Grundrisse*, Harmondsworth, Penguin Books, 1973.
85 Marx and Engels, *Manifesto of the Communist Party*, Vol. 6, *Collected Works*, op. cit., p. 482.
86 Marx, *The German Ideology*, op. cit., p. 74.
87 pp. 52–3 ibid.
88 ibid.
89 e.g., see G. Lichtheim, *Marxism – An Historical and Critical Study*, London, Routledge & Kegan Paul, 1964, pp. 244–8.
90 Marx, *A Contribution to the Critique of Political Economy*, op. cit., pp. 264–5.
91 *Pace* Fukuyama, see Chapter 15.
92 Marx, *The German Ideology*, op. cit., pp. 48–9.
93 ibid., p. 37: 'real, positive science' translated from the original German, 'wirkliche, positive Wissenschaft', *Deutsche Ideologie*, Vol.3, *Karl Marx – Friedrich Engels: Werke*, Berlin, Dietz Verlag, 1969, p. 27.
94 Marx and Engels, *Manifesto of the Communist Party*, op. cit., p. 498.
95 Its original German title was *Die Entwicklung des Sozialismus von der Utopie zur Wissenschaft*, and its French title was *Socialisme Utopique et Socialisme Scientifique*, see Vol. 19, op. cit., pp. 177, 179.
96 In German, 'Wissenschaft'.
97 Marx, *Theses on Feuerbach*, Vol.5, *Collected Works*, op. cit., p. 3

11 ANALYTIC PHILOSOPHY OF HISTORY

1 The above quotes and account are taken from J. Franklyn's indispensable *Jean Bodin and the Sixteenth-Century Revolution in the Methodology of Law and History*, New York and London, Columbia University Press, 1966, pp. 152–4.

12 THE 'WHAT IS HISTORY?' DEBATE

1 See my *The Discipline of History and the History of Thought*, London, Routledge, 1995.

14 THE END OF HISTORY

1 cf. pp. 250–59, M. C. Lemon, *The Discipline of History and the History of Thought*, London, Routledge, 1995.
2 Described in Chapter 5.
3 H. Bertens, *The Idea of the Postmodern – a History*, London and New York, Routledge, 1995, p. 35.
4 J. Lechte, *Fifty Key Contemporary Thinkers – From Structuralism to Postmodernity*, London and New York, Routledge, 1994, p. 111.
5 cf. Condorcet, see Chapter 8 above.
6 pp. 239 and 240, Bertens, op. cit.
7 A. Munslow, *Deconstructing History*, London and New York, Routledge, 1997, p. 178.
8 Munslow, op. cit.
9 ibid. pp. 1–3
10 ibid. p.165
11 ibid. pp. 6 and 7
12 ibid. p. 127
13 ibid. pp. 5 and 164
14 ibid. p. 174
15 ibid. p. 143
16 ibid., p. 154
17 ibid. p. 144
18 ibid. p. 35
19 ibid. p. 162
20 ibid. p. 176
21 ibid. p. 177
22 ibid. p. 18
23 ibid. p. 70
24 ibid. p. 74
25 ibid. pp. 117–18
26 ibid. p. 138, p. 121
27 ibid. p. 130
28 ibid. p. 146
29 ibid. pp. 163–4
30 ibid. p. 166
31 ibid. p. 178
32 ibid. p. 1
33 e.g., Eric Evans, 'The Theory Man', in *History Today*, Vol. 47, June 1997.
34 Munslow, op. cit. p. 2.
35 See pp. 411–16, *Rethinking History*, Vol. 5, No. 3, 2001.
36 cf. pp. 225–59, M. C. Lemon, op. cit.
37 K. Jenkins, *On 'What is History?'*, London and New York, Routledge, 1995, p. 63.
38 p. 13 ibid.
39 pp. 8 and 9 ibid.
40 pp. 69–70 ibid.
41 p. 125 ibid.
42 p. 63 ibid.
43 pp. 142–3 ibid.
44 p. 145 ibid.
45 p. 138 ibid. (my italics)
46 p. 38 ibid.
47 p. 102, Munslow, op. cit.
48 p. 2 ibid.

49 p. 178–9, Jenkins, op. cit.
50 p. 9 ibid.
51 p. 29 ibid. (cf. also Munslow, p. 149 op. cit.).
52 p. 79 ibid.
53 H. Tudor, *Political Myth*, London, Pall Mall Press, 1972, see pp. 123–5.

15 THE END OF HISTORY? FUKUYAMA'S SPECULATIVE PHILOSOPHY OF HISTORY

1 Francis Fukuyama, *The End of History and the Last Man*, London, Penguin Books, 1992 edition, p. xii.
2 e.g., see p. 276 ibid. for these terms.
3 p. xiv ibid.
4 p. 3 ibid.
5 p. 57 ibid.
6 p. 51 ibid.
7 p. 138 and 139 ibid.
8 p. 71 ibid.
9 p. 72 ibid.
10 p. 75 ibid.
11 p. 76 ibid.
12 p. 77 ibid.
13 p. 83 ibid.
14 p. 85 ibid.
15 p. 88 ibid.
16 p. 93 ibid.
17 p. 94 ibid.
18 p. 93 ibid.
19 p. 96 ibid.
20 p. 100 ibid.
21 p. 103 ibid.
22 p. 108 ibid.
23 p. 131 ibid.
24 p. 112 ibid.
25 p. 115–16 ibid.
26 p. 121 ibid.
27 p. 123 ibid. (my emphasis)
28 p. 125 ibid.
29 p. 133–4 ibid.
30 p. 135 ibid.
31 p.136 ibid.
32 p. 139 ibid.
33 V. Gourevitch, 'The End of History?' in *After History? Francis Fukuyama and His Critics*, ed. T. Burns, Maryland, Towman & Littlefield, 1994, p. 129.
34 p. 154, Fukuyama, op. cit.
35 p. 144 ibid.
36 p. 146 ibid.
37 p. 147 ibid.
38 p. 152 ibid.
39 p. 160 ibid.
40 p. 161 ibid.
41 p. 162 ibid.
42 p. 165 ibid.

43 p. 177 ibid.
44 p. 170 ibid.
45 p. 175 ibid.
46 p. 176 ibid.
47 p. 181 ibid.
48 p. 182 ibid.
49 cf. A. Hirschman, *The Passions and the Interests*, New Jersey, Princeton University Press, 1997.
50 p. 189, Fukuyama, op. cit.
51 p. 190–1 ibid.
52 p. 193 ibid.
53 p. 194 ibid.
54 p. 196–7 ibid.
55 p. 198 ibid.
56 p. 206 ibid.
57 p. 208 ibid.
58 p. 200 ibid.
59 p. 202 ibid.
60 e.g., see M. Cranston, 'Human Rights, Real and Supposed', in *Political Theory and the Rights of Man*, ed. D. Raphael, London, Macmillan, 1967, pp. 43–53.
61 p. 212, Fukuyama, op. cit.
62 p. 213 ibid.
63 p. 215 ibid.
64 p. 223 ibid.
65 p. 224 ibid.
66 p. 225 ibid.
67 p. 228 ibid.
68 p. 230 ibid.
69 p. 234 ibid.
70 p. 235–6 ibid.
71 p. 238 ibid.
72 p. 243 ibid.
73 p. 244 ibid.
74 p. 247 ibid.
75 p. 254 ibid.
76 p. 255–6 ibid.
77 p. 259 ibid.
78 p. 260 ibid.
79 p. 262–3 ibid.
80 p. 265 ibid.
81 p. 266 ibid.
82 p. 190 ibid.
83 p. 270 ibid.
84 p. 271 ibid.
85 p. 272 ibid.
86 p. 275 ibid.
87 p. 276 ibid.
88 p. 277 ibid.
89 p. 279 ibid.
90 p. 280 ibid.
91 p. 289 ibid.
92 p. 290 ibid.
93 p. 295 ibid.

94 p. 290 ibid.
95 p. 292 ibid.
96 p. 296 ibid.
97 p. 298 ibid.
98 p. 293 ibid.
99 p. 299 (my emphasis)
100 p. 301 ibid.
101 p. 303 ibid.
102 See our Chapter 10.
103 p. 305 ibid.
104 p. 307 ibid.
105 p. 309 ibid.
106 pp. 310–11 ibid.
107 pp. 313–14 ibid.
108 p. 315 ibid. (my emphasis)
109 p. 316 ibid.
110 p. 318 ibid.
111 pp. 319–21 ibid.
112 F. Fukuyama, *The Great Disruption: Human Nature and the Reconstitution of Social Order*, Profile Books, 1999.
113 F. Fukuyama, *The End of History and the Last Man*, op. cit., p. 323.
114 p. 324 ibid.
115 p. 326 ibid.
116 p. 329 ibid.
117 pp. 330–1 ibid.
118 p. 332 ibid.
119 pp. 335–6 ibid.
120 p. 288 ibid.
121 F. Fukuyama, 'Reflections on *The End of History* – Five Years Later', in *After History? Francis Fukuyama and His Critics*, ed. T. Burns, Maryland, Littlefield Adams, 1994, see pp. 247–50.
122 F. Fukuyama, *The End of History and the Last Man*, op. cit., pp. 337–8.
123 p. 339 ibid.
124 F. Fukuyama, *Our Posthuman Future: Consequences of the Bio-technology Revolution*, Profile Books, 2002.
125 T. Von Laue, 'From Fukuyama to Reality: A Critical Essay', in *After History? Francis Fukuyama and His Critics*, op. cit., pp. 32 and 37.
126 See note 2 to our Chapter 4.
127 F. Fukuyama, *The End of History and the Last Man*, op. cit., pp. xix, xx and 222.
128 p. 45 and 46 ibid.
129 p. 211 ibid.
130 p. 217 ibid.
131 p. 46 ibid.
132 reprinted in *The Guardian* (UK), p. 21, 11 October, 2001.
133 My emphasis.
134 G. B. Smith, 'The "End of History" or a Portal to the Future: Does Anything Lie Beyond Late Modernity?', in *After History? Francis Fukuyama and His Critics*, op. cit., p. 1.
135 See our Chapter 4.
136 See the section, 'The potential demise of "the age of men"', in our Chapter 7.
137 p. xix, Fukuyama, op. cit.
138 p. 257 ibid.
139 J. Bodin, *Six Books of the Commonwealth*, ed. M. J. Tooley, Oxford, Blackwell, 1967, pp. 3–5.

BIBLIOGRAPHY

Aquinas, *De Regimine Principum*, in *Aquinas, Selected Political Writings*, ed. A. P. D'Entreves, Oxford, Blackwell, 1965.

Augustine, *City of God*, ed. V. J. Bourke, New York, Image Books, 1958.

Bauer, F. L. (ed.) *Intellectual Movements in Modern European History*, London, Macmillan, 1969.

Bentham, J. *An Introduction to the Principles of Morals and Legislation*, Oxford, Blackwell, 1967.

Bentley, M. (ed.) *Companion to Historiography*, London, Routledge, 1997.

Bertens, H. *The Idea of the Postmodern – a History*, London and New York, Routledge, 1995.

Bodin, J. *Six Books of the Commonwealth*, ed. M. J. Tooley, Oxford, Blackwell, 1967.

Bronowski, J. and Mazlish, B. *The Western Intellectual Tradition*, London, Hutchinson, 1960.

Bultmann, D. R. *History and Eschatology*, Edinburgh, 1975.

Burke, E. *Reflections on the Revolution in France*, ed. C. C. O'Brien, Harmondsworth, Penguin Books, 1969.

Burke, P. *Vico*, Oxford, Oxford University Press, 1985.

Burns, T. (ed.) *After History? Francis Fukuyama and His Critics*, Maryland, Towman & Littlefield, 1994.

Cassirer, E. *Essay on Man*, New Haven, Yale University Press, 1945.

Cohen, B. 'The Eighteenth-century Origins of the Concept of Scientific Revolution', *Journal of the History of Ideas*, Vol.37, No.2, 1976.

Cohn, N. *The Pursuit of the Millennium*, London, Mercury Books, 1962.

Deane, H. A. *The Political and Social Ideas of St. Augustine*, Columbia University Press, 1963.

De Grazia, S. *Machiavelli in Hell*, London, Picador, 1992.

D'Entrèves, A. P. (ed.) *Aquinas – Selected Political Writings*, Oxford, Blackwell, 1965.

Earl, D. *The Moral and Political Tradition of Rome*, London, Thames & Hudson, 1967.

Engels, F. *Schelling and Revelation*, in Vol. 2, *Karl Marx/Frederick Engels, Collected Works*, London, Lawrence & Wishart, 1975.

Evans, E. 'The Theory Man', *History Today*, Vol. 47, June 1997.

Feuerbach, L. *Principles of the Philosophy of the Future*, New York, Bobbs-Merrill, 1966.

Fortin, E. L. 'Augustine's City of God and the Modern Historical Consciousness', *The Review of Politics*, Vol. 41, No. 3, July, 1979.

Frankfort H., *et al.*, *Before Philosophy*, Harmondsworth, Penguin, 1968.

448

Franklyn, J. H. *Jean Bodin and the Sixteenth-Century Revolution in the Methodology of Law and History*, New York & London, Columbia University Press, 1966.

Fukuyama, F. *The End of History and the Last Man*, London, Penguin Books, 1992.

Fukuyama, F. *The Great Disruption: Human Nature and the Reconstitution of Social Order*, Profile Books, 1999.

Fukuyama, F. *Our Posthuman Future: Consequences of the Bio-technology Revolution*, Profile Books, 2002.

Gardiner, P. *The Philosophy of History*, Oxford, Oxford University Press, 1982.

Hay, D. (ed.) *The Renaissance Debate*, New York, Holt, Rinehart, & Winston, 1965.

Hegel. G. W. F. *The Philosophy of History*, trans. J. Sibree, New York, Dover Publications, 1956.

Hegel, G. W. F. *Philosophy of Right*, trans. T. M. Knox, Oxford, Clarendon Press, 1962.

Hegel, G. W. F. *Phenomenology of Mind*, trans. J. B. Baillie, London, Allen & Unwin, 1966.

Hegel, G. W. F. *Science of Logic*, trans. A. V. Miller, London, George Allen & Unwin, 1969.

Hegel, G. W. F. *Philosophy of Mind*, trans. W. Wallace and A. Miller, Oxford, Clarendon Press, 1971.

Hirschman, A. *The Passions and the Interests*, New Jersey, Princeton University Press, 1997.

Hobbes, T. *Leviathan*, ed. J. Plamenatz, London, Fontana, 1962.

Hobbes, T. *Thomas White's 'De Mundo' Examined*, trans. H. W. Jones, London, Bradford University Press, 1976.

Jaki, S. L. *Science and Creation – From Eternal Cycles to an Oscillating Universe*, Edinburgh, Scottish Academic Press, 1974.

Jenkins, K. *On 'What is History?'*, London and New York, Routledge, 1995.

Kennedy, P. *The Rise and Fall of the Great Powers*, London, Fontana Press, 1989.

Kristeller, P. *Eight Philosophers of the Italian Renaissance*, California, Stanford University Press, 1964.

Kropotkin, P. in *The Essential Kropotkin*, (eds E. Capouya and K. Thompkins), London, Macmillan, 1976.

Lechte, J. *Fifty Key Contemporary Thinkers – From Structuralism to Postmodernity*, London and New York, Routledge, 1994.

Lemon, M. C. *The Discipline of History and the History of Thought*, London, Routledge, 1995.

Levine, J. M. 'Quarrel between the Ancients and the Moderns', *Journal of the History of Ideas*, Vol. LII, No. 1, 1991.

Lichtheim, G. *Marxism – An Historical and Critical Study*, London, Routledge & Kegan Paul, 1964.

Machiavelli, N. *The Discourses*, in *The Prince and the Discourses*, New York, The Modern Library, 1950.

Machiavelli, N. *The Prince*, Harmondsworth, Penguin Books, 1961.

Manuel, F. *The Prophets of Paris*, New York, Harper & Row, 1965.

Marx, K. *Contribution to the Critique of Hegel's Philosophy of Law – Introduction*, in Vol. 3, *Karl Marx/Frederick Engels; Collected Works*, London, Lawrence & Wishart, 1976.

Marx, K. *Contribution to the Critique of Hegel's Philosophy of Law*, in Vol. 3, *Karl Marx/Frederick Engels; Collected Works*, London, Lawrence & Wishart, 1976.

Marx, K. *On the Jewish Question*, in Vol. 3, *Karl Marx/Frederick Engels; Collected Works*, London, Lawrence & Wishart, 1976.

Marx, K. *Economic and Philosophic Manuscripts of 1844*, in Vol. 3, *Karl Marx/Frederick Engels; Collected Works*, London, Lawrence & Wishart, 1976.

Marx, K. *Theses on Feuerbach, in Vol, 5, Karl Marx/Frederick Engels; Collected Works*, London, Lawrence & Wishart, 1976.

Marx, K. *A Contribution to the Critique of Political Economy, in Vol, 29, Karl Marx/Frederick Engels; Collected Works*, London, Lawrence & Wishart, 1976.

Marx, K. and Engels, F. 'Deutsche Ideologie', in Vol. 3, *Karl Marx/Friedrich Engels: Werke*, Berlin, Dietz Verlag, 1969.

Marx K. and Engels, F. 'German Ideology', in Vol. 5, *Karl Marx/Frederick Engels, Collected Works*; London, Lawrence & Wishart, 1976.

Marx, K. and Engels, F. Manifesto of the Communist Party, in Vol. 6, *Karl Marx: Frederick Engels; Collected Works*, London, Lawrence & Wishart, 1976.

Mazlish, B. *The Riddle of History*, New York and London, Harper & Row, 1966.

More, T. *Utopia*, Harmondsworth, Penguin, 1965.

Morrison, J. C. 'Vico's Principle of *Verum* is *Factum* and the Problem of Historicism', *Journal of the History of Ideas*, Vol. 39, Issue 2, 1978.

Munslow, A. *Deconstructing History*, London and New York, Routledge, 1997.

Nauert, C. *Humanism and the Culture of Renaissance Europe*, Cambridge University Press, 1995.

Nisbet, R. A. *History of the Idea of Progress*, London, Heinemann, 1980.

Nisbet, R. A. *Social Change and History*, Oxford, Oxford University Press, 1970.

Oakeshott, M. *Rationalism in Politics*, London, Methuen, 1962.

Orynski, W. *Hegel – Highlights: an annotated selection*, New York, Philosophical Library, 1960.

Raphael, D. (ed.) *Political Theory and the Rights of Man*, London, Macmillan, 1967.

Reill, P. H. *The German Enlightenment and the Rise of Historicism*, Berkeley, University of California Press, 1975.

Rice, E. and Grafton, A. *The Foundations of Early Modern Europe, 1460–1559*, New York, W. W. Norton, 1994.

Rosenstone, R. 'Experiments in Narrative', *Rethinking History*, Vol. 5, No. 3, 2001.

Rousseau, J-J. *The Confessions*, Harmondsworth, Penguin Books, 1965.

Rousseau, J-J. *Discourse on the Origins of Inequality*, trans. G. D. H. Cole, London, Everyman, 1966.

Rousseau, J-J. *Discourse on the Arts and Sciences*, London, Everyman, 1966.

Rousseau, J-J. *The Social Contract*, trans. G. D. H. Cole, London, Everyman edition of *The Social Contract and Discourses*, 1966.

Sabine, G. *A History of Political Theory*, 3rd Edition, London, Harrap & Co., 1963.

Southern, R. *Medieval Humanism and Other Studies*, Oxford, Blackwell, 1970.

Spinoza, B. *Tractatus Theologico-Politicus*, Vol. 1, The *Chief Works of Benedict de Spinoza*, trans. R. H. M. Elwes, New York, Dover Publications, 1955.

Spinoza, B., *The Ethics*, Vol. 2, The *Chief Works of Benedict de Spinoza*, trans. R. H. M. Elwes, New York, Dover Publications, 1955.

Spinoza, B. *On the Improvement of the Understanding*, Vol. 2, The *Chief Works of Benedict de Spinoza*, trans. R. H. M. Elwes, New York, Dover Publications, 1955.

Strauss, L. *Thoughts on Machiavelli*, Seattle, University of Washington Press, 1969.

Strauss, L. *Persecution and the Art of Writing*, University of Chicago Press, 1988.

Trompf, G. W. *The Idea of Historical Recurrence in Western Thought – From Antiquity to the Reformation*, Berkeley, Los Angeles, London, University of California Press, 1979.

Tuck, R. *Philosophy and Government, 1572–1651*, Cambridge, Cambridge University Press, 1993.

Tudor, H. *Political Myth*, London, Pall Mall Press, 1972.

Vico, G. *The New Science of Giambattista Vico*, revised translation of the third edition (1744) by T. G. Bergin and M. H. Fisch, New York, Cornell University Press, 1968.

Vico, G. *On the Heroic Mind*, trans. E. Sewell and A. Sirignano, in *Social Research*, no. 43, 1976.

Vico, G. *Universal Right*, trans. and ed. G. Pinton and M. Diehl, Amsterdam – Atlanta, Rodopi, 2000.

INDEX